TURBULENT

A GLOBAL HISTORY OF THE TWENTIETH CENTURY

PASSAGE

MICHAEL ADAS
RUTGERS UNIVERSITY

PETER N. STEARNS
CARNEGIE MELLON UNIVERSITY

STUART B. SCHWARTZ
UNIVERSITY OF MINNESOTA

HarperCollins*CollegePublishers*

Executive Editor: Bruce Borland

Developmental Editor: Carol Einhorn

Project Coordination and Cover Design: PC&F, Inc.

Cover Illustration: *Guernica* by Pablo Picasso, 1937. Museo del Prado,
    Madrid. © 1994 ARS, New York/SPADEM, Paris

Photo Researcher: Karen Koblik

Production Manager: Willie Lane

Compositor: Clarinda

Printer and Binder: Malloy Lithographing, Inc.

Cover Printer: Malloy Lithographing, Inc.

Turbulent Passage: A Global History of the Twentieth Century

Copyright © 1994 by HarperCollins College Publishers

Library of Congress Cataloging-in-Publication Data

Adas, Michael
    Turbulent passage : a global history of the twentieth century /
Michael Adas, Peter N. Stearns, Stuart B. Schwartz.
        p.   cm.
    Includes bibliographical references and index.
    ISBN 0-06-501039-6
    1. History, Modern—20th century.   I. Stearns, Peter N.
II. Schwartz, Stuart B.   III. Title.
D421.A33 1993
909.82—dc20   93-32762
                                                          CIP

94 95 96 9 8 7 6 5 4 3 2

TURBULENT

PASSAGE

Brief Contents

Detailed Contents

Preface

As the 20th century approaches its chronological end, it has increasingly become a subject of historical inquiry in its own right. With the breakup of the Soviet Union and the collapse of the Communist command economies there and in the rest of Eastern Europe, the human community around the globe has clearly moved into a new phase of history, a new century in the most meaningful sense of the term. Viewed from its final years, the 20th century has been a period of change and social upheaval; of political turmoil, war, and violence; of material advancement and environmental peril without precedent in the epoch in which the human species has dominated the earth.

In many ways the 20th century has been an era of painful transitions, a working out of the profound transformations set in motion by the industrial revolutions of the 18th and 19th centuries. By the start of the 20th century scientific and technological advances had given one civilization (Europe and its settlement outliers in North America) a degree of hegemony over the rest of the peoples and societies of the globe that had no parallel in history. Much of the century has been dominated by the responses of non-Western civilizations and cultures to this hegemony and the struggles for liberation from the colonial order that the industrial West imposed on most of the rest of the globe. As the viability of early patterns of industrialization come under scrutiny in the crowded, increasingly computerized, ecologically stressed decades at century's end, it becomes clear that the history of the 21st century will differ in fundamental ways from that of the 20th.

APPROACH

Turbulent Passage, which provides perhaps the most apt metaphor for global history in the 20th century, fills what we preceive as a gap in the literature on this critical era in human history. Though texts that aim to cover the history of the world in the 20th century exist, none give adequate attention to both the pre-1914 decades that led up to and vitally shaped the era of the First World War and to the post-1945 period in which the upheavals precipitated by the Second World War were played out across the globe. Parts I and III of *Turbulent Passage* are devoted to the pre-1914 and post-1945 eras, respectively. Part II covers the decades that are the focus of existing histories of the 20th century.

By happy accident, *Turbulent Passage* was written during one of those moments in world history (1989–1993) when many established patterns seem to change. Thus the text incorporates accounts of the recent upheavals in Russia, Eastern Europe, and the Middle East, not as completed events, to be sure, but as key points of transition from patterns established in earlier decades. The text is thus up to date not only in its presentation of facts but also in relating recent events to larger analytical patterns.

In dealing with each of these phases and the 20th century as a whole, we seek to maintain a genuinely global perspective. Developments in Europe and North America are treated in depth, but unlike the presentation in many existing texts, the West does not become the focal point in ways that would blur the distinction between a history of Western civilization and a real *world* history text. Civilizations and societies often slighted in world history texts—such as those of Latin America and the Pacific Rim—are discussed quite extensively. Decisions about coverage have been made in terms of global criteria, thus giving the West its respectful due but not pride of place.

Unlike several of the recent global histories of the 20th century that strive for comprehensive coverage and end up being little more than compendiums of facts and dates, we take a more selective approach. Building on comparisons between a number of key civilizations that have shaped the 20th-century experience in critical ways, we identify patterns and pivotal themes both within each civilization and in cross-cultural encounters at various points in the centry. We also tie these patterns and themes to larger global issues that have dominated 20th-century history to a greater extent than in any previous epoch of the human experience. Our goal throughout is to relate fact to interpretation while still allowing ample room for classroom exploration of key issues. Analytical emphasis is evident in the attention to periodization, which is closely tied to key shifts in global trends and cross-cultural interaction. Comparative issues are strongly emphasized, both as a means of raising the level of discussion above that of mere memorization and of bridging the gaps between sections devoted to individual civilizations.

A review of available 20th-century global history texts also convinced us that those that did make some attempt to discern larger patterns and global trends focused almost exclusively on political and diplomatic, and to a lesser extent military, history. Though these aspects of 20th-century history are vital and are treated in depth in *Turbulent Passage,* we also give the social, cultural, and economic dimensions of the global experience their full due. We place particular emphasis on changes in gender roles and relationships at the family, local, community, and state levels that have been such a prominent feature of the 20th century. Gender shifts are in turn set in larger contexts of social upheaval that have been played out in terms of widely varying mixes of class, ethnic, racial, and national identities. We devote considerable attention to ideas and intellectual currents that shaped social movements and political agendas in the 20th century. Where appropriate, we also go beyond broad patterns and global structures to show how remarkable individuals, such as Lenin, Indira Gandhi, and Martin Luther King, Jr., have helped shape the course of 20th-century history, and to demonstrate the impact of global processes on the lives of peasants in China or Russia, of workers in Pittsburgh or Singapore, and of the ascendant middle classes from France to Japan.

PEDAGOGICAL AIDS

Teachers (and students) of world history come from a wide range of personal and academic backgrounds. To support the thematic and analytical features of *Turbulent Passage* and to make all facets of world history as accessible as possible, a number of pedagogical features have been integrated into the book.

In addition to narrative part openers that set forth key themes in each unit, parts begin with an extensive but manageable timeline that establishes the period under consideration. The timeline includes events in all the societies involved.

Chapters open with an outline for a quick overview of major topics and with a detailed timeline specific to the topics to be discussed. Chapter introductions highlight key themes and analytical issues to consider in reading.

Each chapter contains one or more documents in a discrete section. The documents are preceded by a brief scene-setting narration and followed by probing questions. Each chapter also contains an analytical essay on a topic of broad application; the essay is followed by questions intended both to probe student appreciation of the topic and to suggest questions or interpretive issues for further thought.

The text is accompanied by photographs, line drawings, and a series of maps specially developed to enhance the global orientation. Maps in the part introductions and in the chapters highlight major developments during each period and familiarize students with many non-Western arenas.

Each chapter ends with a conclusion that goes beyond a mere summary of events. Conclusions reiterate the key themes and issues raised in the chapter and again suggest areas for reflection and anticipation. Each chapter also includes several paragraphs of annotated suggested readings, so that readers can pursue additional topics on their own.

✖ ACKNOWLEDGMENTS

Grateful acknowledgement is made to the following colleagues and reviewers, who made many useful suggestions during the development of this book:

Steward Doty, *University of Maine at Orono*

Joseph A. Jarvis, *East Stroudsburg University*

Gersham Nelson, *Frostburg State University*

Edward O'Day, *Southern Illinois University*

Jerry Surh, *North Carolina State University*

Larry Wilcox, *University of Toledo*

Michael Adas
Peter N. Stearns
Stuart B. Schwartz

Prologue

From our present perspective, it is difficult to determine the extent to which the 20th century represents the last phase of an era of global history, with its origins as far back as the 15th century, or a decisive break with the past and the beginning of a new epoch in the human experience. We are so close to the patterns involved that reasoned judgment is difficult. Previous periods, though they generate continued debate, at least constitute stories with known endings. We can easily see, for example, that the Industrial Revolution ushered in profound changes for the West and some other parts of the world by 1900. We can even more easily see that during the 19th century, Western nations gained unprecedented power in the world at large, building on earlier colonialism but also measurably surpassing it. It is not difficult, in other words, to define the 19th century in terms of its contrasts with the early modern period, to see what its new ingredients were and how many of them turned out.

We ourselves are engaged in the 20th century, which makes judgment far more tentative. In the 19th century, for example, many people were not explicitly aware of the Industrial Revolution, even when they were involved in it. They would be much more likely to point to some recent political event or cultural current in defining their era. Most historians, however, now take a different view and argue that what people thought was significant may have been somewhat less vital than the underlying processes of which contemporaries were only dimly aware. Knowing this, we must admit uncertainty in trying to place our age in the larger scheme of global history. How significant in world history, for example, was the surge of Nazism of the 1930s? Here was a fearsome new political movement that at the time seemed to threaten some permanent changes in political trends and that disrupted two decades and, through World War II, contributed to undeniably important shifts in many parts of the world. Almost any historian, at least in the Western world, writing in the 1950s would have seen the rise of Nazism as a major turning point. Yet from the vantage point of the 1990s, Nazism seems one of a number of developments that mark a key subperiod rather than a fundamental feature of the whole century, though some similar racist movements still survive. Many Americans in the 1990s would rate the rise of Japan to the status of industrial superpower far more important in creating a novel international context for our century than Nazism was. Nazism's decisive focus has diluted with the passage of time—which is another way of reminding us that our judgment of the 20th century in terms of world history periodization is highly conditioned by how we feel about world conditions now.

1

Given the problems of perspective, two contradictory impulses can affect historians' efforts to place their century as part of a larger scheme of periodization. One impulse is to emphasize the continuities, lest we be misled into exaggerating the novelty of our time and perhaps forget the importance of the past. At the end of the 1980s, amid a host of changes in Russia and Eastern Europe, nationalist sentiment revived in the Balkans and a number of other ethnic regions. Bulgaria tried to eliminate a Turkish minority (by expelling them or making them adopt Bulgarian names); Romanians clashed with Hungarians. Despite more than 50 years of war, revolution, and massive attendant political change in this region, passions dating from at least the 19th century remained lively. Which is more important: all the new developments or the fact that, in the minds of many, basic loyalties had changed so little?

At the other extreme, some historians and many other observers caught in a modern culture that emphasizes rapid and fundamental change as a condition of contemporary life are prone to see the 20th century as a decisive new stage in human history. They write of the 20th century as a "third revolution," comparable only to the Neolithic and Industrial Revolutions of the past in setting up basic new conditions for human existence. Or they see the 20th century defined by the final exhaustion of human frontiers (at least on this planet), as a result of massive population growth and new technologies. As the remaining tropical forests are being chopped down at an alarming rate and as human crowding reaches proportions never before imagined, these historians stress the extent to which the 20th century has altered the human condition in ways that have no clear precedent at all. We are moving, according to those thinkers who are captivated by the centrality of change, into uncharted waters.

Given the difficulties involved in assessing the long-term meanings of events in which we ourselves are participating and of predicting the outcomes of unfinished processes, it is perhaps wise to strike a balance between continuity and change in trying to place the 20th century in the larger scheme of global history. From this perspective, we can see the 20th century not as an epoch in itself but as a time of accelerated transition, as a turbulent era of passage from one epoch to the next. On the one hand, this time of transition represents the culmination of a broader watershed in global history that resulted from an extraordinary convergence of political, socioeconomic, and intellectual changes in western Europe from the 15th century onward. From another perspec-

tive, the 20th century marks a significant break from patterns characteristic of the 19th century and earlier epochs.

Building on earlier technological innovations and social shifts, the Europeans expanded overseas with increasing scale and intensity in the four centuries after the voyages of exploration in the 15th century. Despite much resistance and counterthrusts that slowed their advance, the great trading and military powers of Europe gradually forged a new world order oriented to the capitalist economies of the West and dominated politically by their colonial empires. Efforts to forge this global order were greatly advanced by two further processes that fundamentally transformed first western European and eventually all human history: the scientific revolution that spread across much of Europe in the 17th century and the Industrial Revolution that was clearly under way by the late 1700s. Taken together these transformations represented one of the pivotal watersheds in human history, comparable to that associated with the rise of agriculture and town life in the Neolithic era more than nine thousand years earlier.

Most of the other great civilizations and the multitude of local cultures spread over the rest of the globe were at first little affected by the great changes that were occurring in Europe and increasingly in its settlement outliers, particularly the United States. Excepting peoples, such as the Amerindians, whose long isolation made them disastrously vulnerable to the tactics, technology, and especially the diseases that the Europeans carried overseas, European domination was not pronounced in most areas of the world until well into the 18th century. At the end of the 18th century, however, and throughout the 19th, the expansive nations of industrial Europe and North America divided most of the known world into rival colonial empires, pulled all but the most isolated of peoples into the Europe-centered world market system, and linked the diverse cultures of the globe with industrial communications and transport systems.

Seen in the context of these global transformations, the 20th century has been an era in which the processes set in motion by Europe's scientific and industrial revolutions were accelerated, intensified, and diffused to much of the rest of the globe. But despite continuities, the pace and scale of innovation and diffusion increased to levels without precedent in human history. In addition, advances in communications and transportation associated with the scientific and industrial revolutions meant that contacts among civilizations and local cultures were vastly more numerous and more extensive in the 20th century than in perhaps all of the earlier periods of human history combined. In fact, cross-cultural interaction among the diverse peoples and societies that populate much of the earth has become so intense in the late 20th century that a genuinely global culture and community has begun to emerge for the first time. Earlier empires and trading networks linked large portions of the globe. But never before has such a large portion of humanity been represented in a single political organization (the United Nations), been so dependent on international commercial exchanges, and shared so many aspects of culture—from skyscrapers to rock music—that are central to everyday life.

In the chapters that follow, we seek to strike a balance between an examination of the ways in which the history of the 20th century represented a culmination of key transformations from preceding centuries and the ways in which it marked radical departures from earlier developments. Some of the key, common links to the past have been suggested above, but these connections have also varied widely from one civilization and culture to the next. Special attention is given to these variations in terms of the historical and cultural legacies that tempered the differing responses of Asian, African, and Latin American peoples to European expansion and the concomitant spread of aspects of the scientific and industrial revolutions.

In identifying both broad global patterns and regional variations, we also place great emphasis on the ways in which 20th-century history represented significant breaks from the past and pointed to a new era taking shape for the global community. These shifts can be grouped under three basic processes: fundamental alterations in the balance among civilizations that have occurred over the course of the 20th century, the intensification and multiplication of cross-cultural contacts, and major transformations in politics and culture that have spread throughout much of the world. Because an awareness of these underlying processes is vital to understanding the discussion of specific areas and events that follows, we need to consider each in some detail at the outset of our exploration of world history in the 20th century.

✸ THE REPOSITIONING OF THE WEST

The 20th-century shift in balance among civilizations has featured the relative decline of the West. This resulted in part from the two intensely destructive internal wars fought in the West between 1914 and 1945, which in each case expanded into global conflict. The West's relative decline also reflected the patterns of change and development in a number of other societies (including, of course, the two—Russia and Japan—that had begun an industrial revolution even before 1900). The rise of the United States to new international importance maintained Western influence to some extent, but this merely enhanced western Europe's relative decline and did not prevent the relative slippage of the West as a whole. Despite great Western strength, including European revival after 1945 and again in the 1990s, the pattern of the 19th century prevailed no more. The rise of the West to steadily more powerful international positions—militarily, commercially, and politically—stopped and then reversed during the 20th century, even with the United States added to the West's leadership ranks.

The West's relative decline showed in several areas. Western population (including that of the United States) began to decrease rapidly as a percentage of world totals, reversing a pattern that had begun to develop in the 12th century. Western birth control (matched, to be sure, in a few other areas, such as the Soviet Union and Japan) combined with rapid population growth rates elsewhere to produce this result. What the long-term outcome of the West's population slide will be remains unclear; many analysts argue that since the Industrial Revolution, rapid population growth has been a source of weakness, not a strength. At the very least, the West's population stagnation opened Europe and the United States to rapid immigration from other societies. Here was a new pattern that might either add to Western dynamism or lead to crippling new tensions.

More specific than population rebalancing was the decline and then virtual end of the great Western empires, a process clearly under way by the 1920s and then culminating after 1945. The West, which dominated most of the world directly or indirectly by 1920, ruled little beyond its own borders by 1980. Its influence remained very great—change in this area was complex—but literal political control unquestionably receded, again reversing a centuries-long trend. Monopoly over the most advanced weapons systems, a key Western advantage since the 16th century, also ended, though key Western nations—led after 1945 by the United States—retained a major share in leadership. Japan and then the Soviet Union joined the West as world military giants, while other societies, though not quite as advanced, gained ground. Further, alternative forms of warfare—particularly guerrilla tactics used in colonial struggles but to some extent terrorism as well—allowed certain technologically inferior regions to counter Western military supremacy. In terms of warfare, the world (from a Western standpoint) became more complicated, after centuries of a steadily advancing edge in raw power.

In 1991 the United States and various allies decisively defeated the nation of Iraq in the Persian Gulf War, using a variety of high-technology weaponry. Clearly, Western-dominated military advances were again demonstrated, as only a few hundred allied soldiers died in combat compared to possibly 100,000 Iraqis. But even this war showed how the 20th century had become more complex than the easy days of Western imperialism. It took months of military buildup, a force of over half a million men and women, and expenditures of over $50 billion to defeat (overwhelmingly, to be sure) a medium-sized Arab state.

The West also lost its unchallenged preeminence as world trader and manufacturer. Of course, much of the world economic system established beginning in the 16th century persisted. Important regions still sent cheap raw materials—based on low-paid labor—into international trade, which constrained not only their economic levels but also their political independence. Nations with heavy international debts faced substantial outside intervention in a 20th-century version of international inequality. Only a few societies won the bulk of the profits from international trade, because they ran the shipping and banking facilities and produced the most expensive processed products. In this basic sense there was substantial continuity from earlier periods in world history. But the actors changed, which is where the West's relative decline showed up. Although the West continued to be among the dominant economic agents, by the 1960s it was joined by Japan and an increasing number of other East Asian centers.

The rise of the West, one of the leading processes in world history since the 15th century, clearly leveled off on a number of fronts, with the 1920s and 1930s forming a key turning point. The results of this change were diffuse. No single civilization emerged by the 1990s to claim the kind of growing world leadership the West had long maintained. In part this was because the West itself still remained quite strong, with its influence pervasive on many international fronts. Parts of East Asia now matched the West economically, but other areas generated new international influence in military or cultural sectors. As with the decline of Arab civilization earlier in world history, a number of new centers of power emerged. Perhaps one center will ultimately take

primary leadership as the West had ultimately done after Arab recession, but this is not inevitable and is not likely to be speedy.

More obvious was the increased autonomy the West's relative decline made possible for a number of regional centers. Thus Brazil, India, and the Middle East could develop new combinations of tradition and change that had some relationship to Western models but were not dictated by them. The proliferation of new nations around the world in the decades after 1945 was a revealing index of opportunities for political innovation; a host of states had to establish political legitimacy and decide on appropriate state structures. Even in the economic area, where Western and Japanese prominence remained extremely influential, a number of world regions managed to generate substantial internal economic growth and win a role as exporters of manufactured goods. Brazil, for example, became the world's fourth largest computer exporter by the 1990s, behind only the high-tech leaders: Japan, the United States, and Western Europe. These patterns will be explored in the chapters that conclude this volume, on the last phase of the 20th century.

A TRANSCULTURAL AND GLOBAL AGE

No period of human history is better suited to a world or global perspective than the 20th century. The extent and intensity of cross-cultural interaction in this era are without precedent and continue to accelerate as the century draws to a close. Industrial communication technologies facilitate the multiplication of political, economic, and cultural links among peoples and societies in virtually every every area of the globe. These linkages mean that at the end of the 20th century, more than in any previous period in history, innovations, natural disasters, or social upheavals in one region are likely to have major repercussions throughout the world. Never before have political disruptions in even the most remote of regions, such as Ethiopia or Bosnia-Herzegovina, had such immediate and profound global ramifications. In earlier centuries calamities, such as civil war and famine in Somalia or floods in Bangladesh, would have been localized concerns. In the late 20th century such events quickly develop into international obsessions. The heads of multinational corporations make decisions about factory locations and commodity development aimed at enhancing the international standing of their firms rather than strengthening the nation-state in which they are headquartered. The decisions of ranchers or developers to burn the rain forest in the Amazon or on the island of Borneo contribute to the degradation of the overall global environment and the warming of the planet's atmosphere as a whole.

At a number of points in the 20th century, a few areas pulled back into relative isolation: the Soviet Union from the late 1920s through the 1970s, when a largely independent national economy was forged with little involvement in wider world trade, and China, especially after 1956. Nevertheless, even relative isolation was difficult, for the dominant trends urged increasing interaction. Technology was critical: Innovations included faster communication via wireless radio and, later, satellite and computer; faster transport, using the airplane; and larger capacity for both communication and movement of goods. World trade levels steadily increased, and more and more corporations (particularly from the West and Japan) operated on an international basis.

World wars and peacetime alliances demonstrated the new levels of international contact on other fronts. Great diversity of interests remained, but diplomatic contacts were internationalized as never before; thus the intensity and importance of United States–Chinese diplomacy, to choose one example, rivaled the relationships between Britain and Germany a century before. International cultural influences also increased in tandem with improved communications and the efforts of multinational corporations. Films, scientific research, and artistic styles all spread widely at both popular and elite levels. The result was not a single world culture, for extent of penetration and regional reactions varied widely. But most cultures had to come to terms with the impact of Hollywood movies, Parisian art, or British-American popular music. Interest in international sports constituted another unprecedented development across civilization lines: Soccer football won mass enthusiasm virtually everywhere; the Olympic Games, which were reestablished in the 1890s and gradually shifted from an initial Western dominance to global participation, both symbolized and promoted this facet of new cultural contacts.

INTERNATIONAL CHALLENGES IN POLITICS AND CULTURE

Parallelisms in patterns of change resulted partly from outright imitation, particularly of Western models and also from regional efforts to push back Western dominance. One result was a sweeping pattern of political change. Almost no society aside from some of the more stable Western nations (United States, Britain, and Scandinavia) had the same form of government by 1990 that it had maintained in 1900. Monarchies crumbled, replaced by democracies, totalitarian governments, or authoritarian regimes. The results were varied, but the fact of innovation was virtually universal, as major civilizations tried to come to terms with Western examples while also developing governments vigorous enough to gain or maintain independence. More concretely, revolutions and decolonization compelled political experiments almost everywhere outside the West, as well as in key areas within Western society. Moreover, along with new political forms came new functions. Governments generally took on new roles in trying to further economic growth. They also accepted new and unprecedented responsibilities in education and health care, and their contact with masses of citizens increased greatly as a result. Regardless of prior political traditions and ongoing diversity, the governments of the 20th-century world innovated in several common directions.

Changes or modifications in previous belief systems formed another current that swept over many national and civilizational boundaries. Most of the world's people in 1850 adhered to one of the great religions or philosophical systems created during the classical or postclassical eras: Confucianism, Christianity, Islam, and the like. These systems were still lively in 1950, and some were even winning new converts. In most parts of the world, however, they had been modified or challenged by new systems of beliefs that were more strictly secular in orientation, such as liberalism, nationalism, or communism. They were also quite widely challenged by growing interest in science, a staple of the burgeoning mass education systems. As with politics, belief changes took no single direction, but the encounter with fundamentally novel ideas was a genuinely international experience—and one of the key developments of 20th-century world history.

Changes in ideas and politics related to a third general international current: the displacement of long-standing beliefs in rigid social inequalities. All the great agricultural civilizations had developed highly structured systems of inequality, though some of the civilizations complicated these systems through religious beliefs in the spiritual equality of all souls. Western ideas, expressed in such great movements as the French Revolution of 1789, had attacked assumptions of structured inequality and legal privilege. Also, the abolition of slavery throughout most of the world in the 19th century signaled the end of another traditional institution of inequality. The further spread of Western ideas, together with new movements, such as Russian and Chinese communism and the nationalisms of Asia and Africa, brought a more widespread attack on rigid inequalities in the 20th century. Caste systems and aristocracies "officially" crumbled, with only rare exceptions. Societies turned to new efforts at equality or at least equality of opportunity, including widespread voting rights, though countercurrents of racist beliefs or gender inequalities complicated the picture. Inequality did not end, but older ideas that had sanctified it did yield to new beliefs.

Patterns of economic change were more diverse. Despite a general interest in improving production levels, some societies remained largely agricultural, whereas others began to move into industrial ranks. Nevertheless, efforts at change, as well as the influence of international corporations and trade, prompted some widespread social effects. Most societies witnessed new levels of social mobility, as earlier caste or class lines loosened. The social status of women was almost everywhere reconsidered, as a result of new levels of education and new involvement in work outside the home, though again specific results varied.

Two additional trends suggest ways in which the 20th century marks a decisive break from earlier historical epochs. The first is the staggering increase in human population, as well as in the numbers of domesticated animals that humans breed for a variety of uses. It had taken humankind tens of thousands of years to reach a population of around a billion and a half by the middle of the 19th century. By the year 2000, 150 years later, world population will have increased more than four times to well over six billion—and it will continue to increase, even with the most ambitious application of family-planning measures, well into the 21st century. This massive increase of humans and the numbers of domesticated animals dependent on them has obviously placed an increasing strain on the resources of the planet. It has also contributed greatly to a second trend that sets the 20th century off from all previous eras: an unprecedented level of human intervention in and exploitation of the natural environment. New technologies have been developed—in part to offset accelerating population increases—to permit ever more intensive farming, ever greater depletion of fresh water reservoirs, and ever higher yields of forest and mineral products. Both runaway population growth and the application of new technologies have combined to raise local and global pollution and ecological degradation to levels that for the first time in human history pose fundamental threats to the planetary environment on which all life depends.

STAGES IN A TURBULENT PASSAGE TO A NEW AGE

As with most centuries, the rather arbitrary chronological beginning and ending dates of the 20th century, 1900 and 2000, have little historical meaning. The year 1900 was by no stretch of the imagination a watershed year; and, as we argue in the final chapters of this study, events of the late 1980s brought the third and last phase of the 20th century to a close, a decade before its official stop point in the year 2000. Some historians have argued that 1914, the year World War I began, is the most meaningful place to start the 20th century. But beginning with the dramatic breaks with previous history that the 1914–1918 war set in motion distorts by obscuring important continuities with earlier centuries. If we start in 1914, we cannot understand the origins of the war; we also miss key episodes in the decades leading up to the war that permit us to assess the impact of that global conflagration on the period of turmoil that followed in the 1920s and 1930s.

In terms of the underlying themes and historical trends that make the 20th century a distinctive and coherent era, strong arguments can be made for beginning the century in the 1860s and 1870s. In those decades several new global powers, most notably Germany, Japan, and the United States, emerged to challenge Britain, France, China, and Russia, which had long dominated international politics. At the same time, a number of important literary works were published that brought to the forefront ideologies, such as Marxism, Darwinism, and liberalism, that would vitally shape social thinking and political movements during much of the 20th century. Those decades also saw the culminating phase of centuries of European overseas expansion and the colonization of much of the world by the Western powers, including the United States. In important ways this outburst of imperialism was prompted by major social and economic shifts that were also occurring in Europe and the United States in that era, and the forces of colonialism diffused those changes to much of the rest of the globe.

From this perspective, then, 1914 marks the end of the first phase of 20th-century history and the beginning of the second, which is dominated by a succession of global crises. Between 1914 and 1945, the second phase of 20th-century history, the world was shaken by a series of catastrophic events, most of which were directly linked to the two world wars and the massive global depression that define this period. In this phase state power and, in many countries, repressive capacity reached unprecedented levels. War, between industrial and scientifically advanced powers, was vastly more devastating than anything in the past, and all pretense at distinguishing between military and civilian sectors was discarded in the face of massed aerial bombardments and a number of state-organized campaigns of genocide. The 1914–1945 period also witnessed the emergence of a new international order that featured the relative decline of western Europe and the establishment of new power centers, particularly the Soviet Union, the United States, and Japan until its defeat in the Pacific War in the mid-1940s. Several major political revolutions occurred in this era of crisis, which ushered in new regimes in Mexico, China, Russia, and (if a top-down revolution is included) Turkey. Struggles for independence—some of them, like that in Vietnam, revolutionary; others, gradualist—also gained force in much of the colonized world.

The decades between 1945 and the late 1980s, which form the third and final phase of the 20th century, are dominated by the cold war struggles between the United States and Soviet Union superpowers and their allies; the decolonization of Africa, Asia, and parts of Latin America; and the remarkable efforts of Europe and Japan to recover from wartime devastation and to adjust to the postcolonial world order. This period also saw a new wave of revolutions, most notably in Vietnam, Cuba, and Iran, which had powerful global ramifications. During this third phase new patterns of social organization and mobility, changes in gender relations, and redefinitions of the roles of government were vital features of global history, although some of these developments had begun in the crisis decades between 1914 and 1945.

In our treatment of each of these phases of the 20th century and their relationship to dramatic new developments since 1989, we combine analysis of general global processes with accounts of specific events and divergent patterns of development in different civilizations and culture areas. In assessing the meaning of the history made and experienced at both levels, it is difficult to know which events and transformations will be the most critical in shaping the new epoch of history into which we appear to be moving. The history of the 20th century allows us to see the forces overturning the global order that had developed between the 15th and the 19th centuries, but it permits only glimpses of what the new world order might be. We know, for example, that the new period will not be dominated by the West to the same extent the previous age was, but we cannot be sure whether a successor will emerge or what that successor will be.

In addition, in the long term other kinds of shifts may prove to be much more important than the relative decline of the West that has so fascinated 20th-century observers or the recent breakup of the Soviet superpower and its satellite empire, which has seemed so central to the history made in the last few years. A much more influential factor in shaping the lives of future generations may be the radically new technological framework that has been built around computers in the last couple of decades. This framework has increasingly supplanted the steam-driven machinery and production techniques of the industrial age. It opens the possibility of a postindustrial age, at least for the more economically advanced portions of the globe. For less developed areas, the new computer technology may make it possible to bypass the industrial stage of development, with its high levels of pollution and resource depletion. These outcomes, which represent only a small portion of possible alternatives, suggest the difficulty of predicting future trends on the basis of our recent past or present experience. But grasping what has already occurred in the most recent phase of world history and what is now happening is the best basis for understanding what is yet to come.

1860–1868 Civil strife in Japan

1861–1865 American
Civil War

1870–1910 Acceleration
of "demographic transi-
tion" in western Europe
and the United States

1871–1912 High
point of European
imperialism

1853 Perry expedition
to Edo Bay in Japan

1863 Emancipation
of slaves in U.S.

1854–1856
Crimean War

1867 Union of central and eastern Canada

1867 Publication of Volume I of *Das Kapital* by Karl Marx

1850–1864 Taiping
rebellion in China

1864–1871 German
unification

1868–1912 Meiji (reform) era in Japan

1857–1858 Great Mutiny in India

1870–1910 Expansion of
commercial export econ-
omy in Latin America

1858 British Parliament assumes control over India

1859 Publication of *On Liberty* by J.S. Mill and
Origin of the Species by Charles Darwin

1861 Emancipation of serfs
in Russia; reform era begins

1870 Establishment of
Japanese Ministry of
Industry

Accelerating Change and the Transition to the 20th Century

1 WESTERN INDUSTRIALIZATION
AND THE FOUNDATIONS OF
THE 20TH CENTURY

2 EXTENDING THE CORE:
THE EMERGENCE OF
RUSSIA AND JAPAN AS
20TH-CENTURY POWERS

3 INDUSTRIALIZATION
AND IMPERIALISM:
THE MAKING OF THE
EUROPEAN GLOBAL ORDER

4 PRECARIOUS SOVEREIGNTY:
WESTERN EMPIRE AND
CONSTRICTED DEVELOPMENT
IN LATIN AMERICA,
THE MIDDLE EAST, AND CHINA

With the Eiffel tower as its centerpiece, the Paris exposition of 1889 not only
celebrated the scientific and technological triumphs of the industrial West but also
underscored the fact that France had joined the exclusive club of advanced,
industrial societies.

PART

I

The Birth of the 20th Century

ACCELERATING CHANGE AND THE TRANSITION TO THE 20TH CENTURY. Finding a specific date or precise starting point for the 20th century would prove a frustrating and fruitless exercise. Though chronologically correct, 1900 was not a year of significant transition in world history. It came only at the end of decades of transformations that had thoroughly remade the 19th-century world, which had been dominated by the French Revolution and Napoleonic Wars, as well as the first phase of industrialization and the vast expansion of a world economic system oriented to western Europe. Alternatively, the outbreak of World War I in August 1914 is frequently cited as the "real" beginning of the new century. Though the coming of the war was clearly a key point of transition, starting in 1914 leaves us not only ignorant of the causes of the "Great War" but also with little sense of the larger forces that had been building up throughout the world in decades before the war. These forces gave rise to a global order that differed fundamentally from that characteristic of the 19th century, and they proved to be the seedbed for the processes, struggles, and dilemmas that set the 20th century off as a distinct era in world history.

Though specific years are of little value in demarcating the transition from the 19th to the 20th century, the decades of the 1860s and 1870s were clearly a watershed period in which many of the dominant political, socio-economic, and intellectual currents of the 20th century emerged. Thus the last three or four decades of the

1800s, combined with the years between 1900 and 1914, can be seen as the first phase of the 20th-century world history.

✺ REDRAWING THE GLOBAL MAP

The most apparent shifts in the global order that came in the first phase of the 20th century, roughly from the 1860s to 1914, involved the emergence of several new powers and the decline of some that had been dominant throughout most of the 19th century. These shifts also included the partition of an already partly colonized world, with the lion's share going to the industrialized nations of western Europe and the United States. Thus although long-established powers, such as France, Great Britain, Austria-Hungary, and Russia, still played major roles in international politics in the pre–World War I era, their relative strength and ability to shape global history clearly slipped. The emergence of Germany, the United States, and Japan as first economic and later major military and political actors in the international arena was central to the decline of the older powers, which was in turn a major factor in the coming of World War I. The collapse of the Qing dynasty in China, combined with the simultaneous ex-

pansion of the European colonial empires and the beginnings of major challenges to them, also marked the last decades of the 1800s as a phase of critical transitions.

In western Europe, which overseas expansion and industrialization had established as the core of the global economy and paramount center of military and political power, the unification of Germany and Italy utterly transformed the geopolitical map. By the late 1860s, the traditional buffer zones (and battlegrounds, if the Napoleonic Wars are any guide) of Europe had been filled in by highly chauvinistic new states. In addition, two new competitors had entered into the incessant contests for land and influence that had been characteristic of the European state system for centuries. For both Italy and Germany the process of unification had taken decades and had involved both wars against external enemies and considerable, often very violent, internal strife. German unification in particular had disrupted the established power alignment. Not only was the German nation built on victorious wars against its neighbors, but also the populous, highly industrialized new state appeared destined to translate its economic and military might into the political domination of continental Europe.

Industrial Development in Key Regional Centers, about 1900

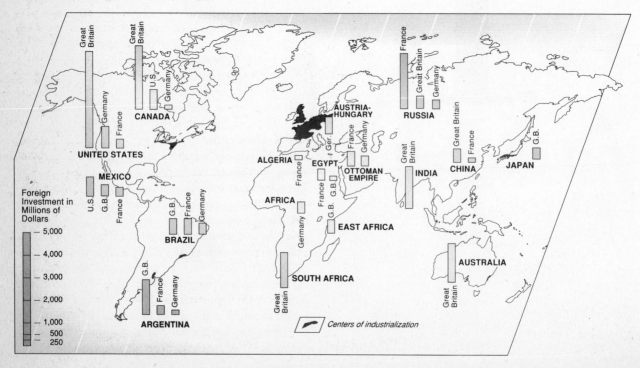

The wars that brought about German unification rather graphically illustrated the decline of the old order and the rise of the new. The first war in 1864, pitted Prussia (the core kingdom of the German nation in the making) against tiny Denmark. The British, who wished to assist the Danes, found that they could do little to affect the outcome of a land war in Europe. The rout of the Austrians in 1866 left the Prussians the paramount power in central Europe. In the third and final war of unification in 1870, the wily Prussian Chancellor, Otto von Bismarck, drew the French into a conflict that sealed German ascendancy on the continent as a whole. The Franco-Prussian War not only led to the formal unification of Germany in 1871 but also made obvious what many observers had suspected for decades, namely, that France's post-Napoleonic decline was irretrievable. The conduct of the war also demonstrated the awesome killing power of the new, mass-produced weapons, including machine guns and rifled artillery that were among the more dubious products of industrialization. Continuing French resistance, after most of their armies had been defeated in regular battle, also provided a preview of the guerrilla warfare and draconian reprisals that would become a prominent feature of many 20th-century military conflicts.

Although Bismarck cleverly sought to disguise the fact by renouncing further territorial claims and maintaining alliances with threatened older powers, such as Russia and Austria-Hungary, the German victory in the Franco-Prussian War irrevocably shattered the 19th-century balance of power. The growing strength of Germany, which the emperor Wilhelm II who dismissed Bismarck in 1890 did little to conceal, sent its neighbors scurrying for protective alliances. In the decades before 1914, war scares and unprecedented levels of military buildup hardened the divisions between the allied camps and engendered the atmosphere of paranoia that had much to do with the outbreak of World War I.

Tensions among the powers in this period were also fed by intensified economic competition and related quarrels over territorial expansion, both within Europe (especially the Balkans) and overseas. In the late 1800s, for the first time, a non-European Western nation, the United States, emerged as a significant player in these contests for global dominance. Forcibly reunited by the North's victory over the South in the Civil War of the

Perhaps no invention symbolized better than the machine gun the extent to which science and technology allowed Westerners to dominate the other peoples of the world in the last decades of the 19th century. Here the newspaper reporter and intrepid explorer Henry Morton Stanley employs his Maxim gun to overawe a party of African warriors deemed hostile to his expedition's intrusion.

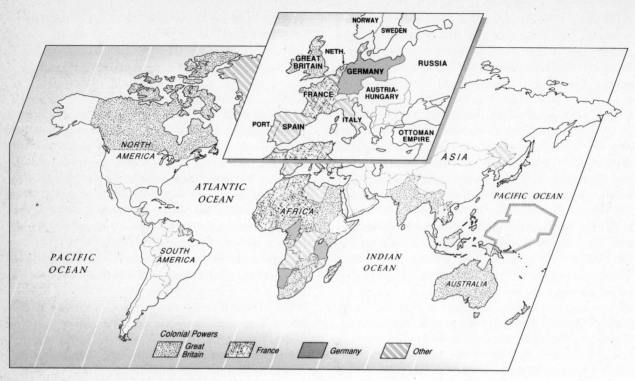

Main Colonial Holdings, about 1914

early 1860s, the industrializing and expansive U.S. republic sought increasingly to project its growing economic capacity and newfound political power across the Atlantic and Pacific oceans. Beginning in the 1870s competition inevitably spawned by the spread of the Industrial Revolution within western Europe and to the United States and Russia was exacerbated by the onset of a cycle of agricultural and industrial depressions that extended into the 1890s. The alternating phases of economic boom and bust in these decades fed social unrest among the working classes and prompted political leaders to seek economic outlets and political distractions in "little wars" overseas.

Thus tensions and rivalries in Europe and the United States were projected outward through a stunning burst of imperialist expansion that led to the formal colonization of most of Africa, Southeast Asia, and the South Pacific. Ironically, in the decades when Western global hegemony was at its zenith, movements were developing in colonized areas, especially India and the Philippines, that would provide major challenges to the colonial order by the early 1900s and eventually lead to its overthrow later in the 20th century.

In Latin America, China, and Persia the European powers, and increasingly the United States and Japan as well, vied for economic advantage and political influence without direct colonial control. In Latin America divisions within the political elites and an already established economic dependence on Europe left ample openings for manipulation by the industrial powers. The accelerating collapse of the Qing dynasty in China reduced the oldest continuous and largest civilization to a massive black hole sucking in missionaries, merchants, and the squabbling diplomats of the Great Powers. The leaders of other noncolonized states, most notably Siam and Persia, proved more adept at warding off European advances, mainly by playing off the rival European powers against one another. But only Japan was able to preserve its independence in the face of the Western intrusions, to borrow heavily from the West without violating its own social and cultural integrity, and to industrialize and become an expansive power in its own right in the first half of the 20th century.

Because of the unusual importance of western Europe in the later 19th century, it is easy to distort what the world framework was by 1900. Many Europeans made the mistake of dividing the world between the West and the rest, assuming that only Europe had achieved civilization and that all other groups, despite some varied idiosyncrasies, could be lumped into an "uncivilized" category. Observers in the late 20th century, looking back a hundred years, will not make this crude mistake of confusing Europe's undeniable power position with some sort of monopoly on civilization itself. A host of societies in Asia, Africa, and Latin America clearly had developed impressive civilization traditions before the 19th century and retained many of them even in the face of new levels of European interference. But it remains easy to make a more subtle mistake of assuming that Europe was now setting the agenda for the rest of the world, whether civilized or not. In this rendering the non-European world (presumably excepting the United States and a few other places) had become merely passive by 1900, not necessarily capable yet of imitating Europe fully but unable to generate alternative responses.

In fact in many parts of the world the 19th century saw important developments that were only partly dependent on reactions to Western industrialization and imperialism. The spread of nationalism, for example, allowed an initially European ideology to embrace a host of local ingredients in such places as India or the Middle East. Beginning early in the 19th century Islam began to win new masses of converts in sub-Saharan Africa because it offered allegiance to a major religion that was not Western, and this process has continued to the present day. Latin America, though inferior to western Europe and the United States economically, built new national governments and sketched elements of a distinctive culture that was linked to that of the West without being subsumed by it.

Clearly, though the 19th century offered growing worldwide Western influence as a dominant theme, a host of diverse trends was taking shape. The world was clearly not becoming homogenized, and although it was changing rapidly, the directions of change varied from place to place, depending on previous tradition as well as the nature of European interference. By 1900 the position of the West itself was anomalous, precisely because its grip on the world was in many ways tenuous. The unprecedented extent of Western power set the stage for the reassertion of other areas, building on their own traditions and on distinctive trends that had developed, often a bit beneath the surface or under apparently standard headings such as nationalism or reform, during the 19th century. Even before the more obvious international complexities of the 20th century, it is vital to grasp the underlying diversities of the 19th-century setting.

SOCIAL TRANSFORMATIONS AND THE COMING OF THE 20TH CENTURY

The dramatic political changes that signaled the beginning of the 20th century were paralleled by social transformations that departed less decisively from 19th-century patterns but that nonetheless suggested transition to a new era. In the industrialized West the numbers of the middle classes continued to grow, and their long-standing dominance in invention, commerce, and manufacturing was steadily extended to politics, diplomacy, education, and the arts. Throughout Europe the aristocracy remained a potent force in the military, in government, and especially in the diplomatic corps, trends that would be decisively reversed only as a result of the failed leadership that came to be associated with World War I.

In both Europe and the United States the proportion of the population living in cities continued to increase, as it had from the onset of the Industrial Revolution. The numbers of the urban working classes also continued to rise, but workers' organizations, particularly unions and socialist-leaning political parties, became major economic and social forces in the industrial nations for the first time. The increased voice of the working classes owed much to the introduction of compulsory education and the spread of mass literacy, which are hallmarks of the first phase of 20th-century social history. Also critical was the rise of the mass press, which heightened working-class consciousness while raising the aspirations of the lower middle class and drew larger and larger segments of both social strata into the political struggles of their respective nation-states. The burgeoning mass press also gave a major boost to the culture of consumption, which became a key attribute of increasingly affluent industrial societies in the 20th century. Department stores, carefully organized leisure activities—especially sporting events, popular entertainments, and family vacations—and a proliferation of mass-produced commodities for the home and personal use all served to separate the late 1800s from the earlier industrial era, to indicate the beginning of a new century.

Of all of the social movements in the West, perhaps none signaled the onset of a new era as dramatically as the campaigns for women's rights that emerged in most of the industrialized West and its settler offshoots in

The poor living and working conditions that accompanied the alternating boom and depression of late-19th-century industrialization in Europe and the United States spawned widespread labor unrest. In 1894 hundreds of unemployed workers, led by the radical businessman Jacob Coxey, marched on Washington, D.C. to demand government relief.

Canada and Australia in the decades before World War I. Though focused on winning the vote for women, feminist organizations were also engaged in causes that ranged from efforts to improve women's legal standing and educational opportunities to opposition to draconian measures to regulate prostitution. The struggle for women's rights and the myriad gender issues it subsequently raised for public debate have persisted as dominant themes, first in the West and then over much of the globe, throughout the 20th century.

Outside of the West, the decades that laid the foundations for the 20th century were marked more by continuity than change in terms of the social trends they exhibited. In directly colonized areas indigenous elite groups either perished resisting European conquest or—more often—vied with one another to win positions of influence under the new rulers. In Latin America and other areas that came under European or U.S. influence but not direct control, leaders and merchants collaborated with the agents of imperialism in the pursuit of greater wealth and political control within their own societies. The working classes in most of the formally and indirectly colonized world remained minuscule or nonexistent. The fate of the peasant classes was as varied and complex as these social groupings themselves. But the great majority were drawn more fully into the Western-dominated world market and thus rendered more dependent on fluctuations in the global economic system. As markets expanded, indigenous commercial groups—both long established and newly emerging—increased in numbers and wealth. As subsistence production declined and specialized production became more pronounced throughout much of the globe, the market became the arbiter of human livelihood to a degree that was unimaginable in earlier eras.

Although Africans and Asians had begun to acquire Western education and adopt aspects of Western culture as early as the first decades of the 19th century, substantial Western-educated middle classes emerged in such colonized areas as India, Senegal, and the Philippines only in the late 1800s. In fact, the great increase in the numbers and influence of those belonging to this social strata provides a key distinction between the 19th- and 20th-century social history of colonized peoples. The increasing politicization of these classes in the decades before World War I also marks a major difference between the two eras. At this elite level women among the colonized peoples sometimes shared in the educational opportunities enjoyed by larger numbers of their male counterparts. In some instances women were also the beneficiaries of major campaigns for social reform undertaken by the colonizers, often in alliance with members of the Western-educated, indigenous middle classes. But for the vast majority of women in nonindustrial societies political rights and social emancipation would come, if at all, only in the wake of the great revolutions that sought to remake the global order in last half of the 20th century.

❀ INTELLECTUAL FOUNDATIONS FOR A NEW CENTURY

The political and social transitions that began in the 1860s and 1870s were in most cases closely linked to the ascendancy in roughly the same time period of ideologies, such as Marxism and liberalism, that originated in the 19th century. In fact, with the exception of the formulation of Freudian theory and the revolution in scientific thinking that occurred just before and after 1900, the intellectual discourses that were to dominate much of the 20th century were under way in the decades after 1860.

In his tract *On Liberty*, which was first published in 1859, John Stuart Mill enunciated the principles of liberalism, which, in its 19th-century European variant, stressed individual rights, the sanctity of private property, laissez-faire economics, and minimal state intervention in the lives of its citizens. In his *Self-Help*, published in that same year, and his numerous biographies of enterprising English people that followed, Samuel

Charles Darwin's theory of evolution was subjected in many quarters to ridicule, as is readily apparent in this caricature, which wrongly implies that Darwin believed that humans had evolved directly from worms through the great apes.

MAN·IS·BVT·A·WORM.

Smiles extolled the virtues of hard work, competition, self-reliance, and inventiveness. Readers of Charles Darwin's *Origin of the Species*, also published in 1859, and his *Descent of Man*, which followed in 1870, were likely to see in his theory of evolution by natural selection historical confirmation of the centrality of competitiveness and necessity for inventiveness stressed by Smiles and other popular writers.

Though Darwin's vision of the evolutionary process was decidedly not progressive and much of his thinking was crudely and mistakenly appropriated by contemporary writers, his ideas deeply influenced the theories of prominent social thinkers in his day. The Social Darwinists, for example, who wrongly claimed that Darwin's findings supported their views, stressed the centrality of the "struggle for survival" within the human species (in contrast to Darwin, who emphasized interspecies competition). In the early decades of the 20th century their writings had a major impact on public opinion and government policy formation in areas as varied as decisions for imperialist expansion; the treatment of "primitive" or aboriginal peoples, such as the Amerindians, whom Social Darwinists concluded were doomed to extinction; and the eugenics movement, which advocated measures to improve the breeding stock of the dominant races and to limit population increase among "inferior" peoples.

Counterpoised to these celebrations of the virtues and aspirations of the capitalist middle and skilled working classes were the writings of Karl Marx and Frederich Engels. Though numerous works, including the *Communist Manifesto*, had appeared in earlier decades, the successive volumes of Marx's masterwork *On Capital* were published in the 1860s and 1870s. In these later works he mounted an extensive critique of industrial capitalism and set forth a vision of history grounded in shifts in technology and production techniques that periodically resulted in revolutionary social upheavals. On the basis of what he considered a thoroughly scientific analysis of capitalist, industrial societies, Marx predicted that exploited and alienated working classes would rise up and overthrow the capitalist system and its middle-class managers and rulers. The fall of the middle classes would open the way for the creation of socialist societies that would eventually bring an end to class divisions and social strife.

Marx's ideas have proved to be among the most influential of the 20th century. Leaders as disparate as Lenin, Mao Zedong, and Fidel Castro have launched major revolutions aimed at fulfilling Marx's analysis of the past and prognosis for the future of humanity. Revisionist socialists have struggled to provide convincing, reformist alternatives to Marx's path to utopia. The thinkers and politicians of the capitalist West have expended much effort to refute Marxist doctrines and frustrate Marxist-inspired social movements in both the industrial and developing nations.

Although the ideas of European thinkers have dominated international discourse in the 20th century, important intellectual transitions were also occurring in the colonized world in the decades before World War I. The collapse of the Confucian political and social systems in China in this period left a quarter of humanity without ideological bearings. For much of the 20th century Chinese intellectuals have debated alternatives drawn from both indigenous and Western precedents or a blending of the two. In neighboring Japan a small ruling clique drawn mainly from the military classes was the first in the non-Western world to tackle the challenge of remaking its political system and social order so as to withstand the intrusions of the West. Across the colonized world in the late 1800s and early 1900s, leaders of resistance movements sought to rework the teachings of Islam and Buddhism or local animist creeds to rally supporters in their struggle against the dominance of the West. In addition, the rising Western-educated elites in these areas produced both critics of industrial capitalism and colonialism and nationalist ideologues who formulated visions of national independence and development free of imperialist constraints.

PART OVERVIEW

In the four chapters that follow, we explore in greater detail these key developments that defined the first phase of the 20th century in different areas of the globe. Chapter 1 is devoted to the impact of industrialization on the nations of western Europe and the United States. The next chapter looks at the diffusion of this process to Russia and Japan. Chapter 3 focuses on the tensions in the industrial order that contributed to the great outburst of imperialist expansion by the European powers and the United States in the decades before the outbreak of World War I and the effects of colonization on the peoples of Africa, Asia, and the South Pacific. Chapter 4 explores key themes in the history of Latin America, the Middle East and China—areas that the industrial powers dominated economically and politically in the first decades of the 20th century but did not formally colonize.

Western Europe				
		1859–1870 Unification of Italy		**1871–1914** High point of European imperialism
				1864–1871 German unification
	1848 ff. Writings of Karl Marx; rise of socialism			**1870–1879** Institution of French Third Republic
		1859 Darwin's *Origin of Species*		**1870s ff.** Rapid birthrate decline
				1870s ff. Spread of compulsory education laws

Extensions of Western Civilization				
			1860–1870 Second Maori War	
	1852 New constitution in New Zealand; elected councils			**1867** British North America Act, unites eastern and central Canada
	1846–1848 Mexican-American War			
			1861–1865 American Civil War	
	1850 Australia's Colonies Government Act allows legislature and more autonomy		**1863** Emancipation of slaves	

Western Industrialization and the Foundations of the 20th Century

INTRODUCTION. The most dynamic force in 19th-century world history, and the most urgent backdrop to the history of the 20th-century world, was the process of industrialization. The Industrial Revolution, centered first in western Europe and the new United States, transformed the societies involved. It forced major political changes, including widespread voting rights and new government functions, such as mass education. It revolutionized the activities of families by moving work outside the family context. It challenged established artistic styles and elevated the importance of science and technology in Western intellectual life. The changes associated with the Industrial Revolution provided great challenge and opportunity, but they also imposed tremendous strain on any society involved.

The industrialization process of the 19th century had almost immediate repercussions in the world at large, enhancing the power of industrializing areas at the expense of other regions. The West, already a dynamic civilization before 1800, now became the international trend setter in many respects. Western technology, applied to weaponry, provided a massive military advantage over most other societies. Steamboats could sail the rivers of Africa or China; repeating rifles and machine guns could make mockery of valiant but traditional fighting forces in the Middle East or Japan. Growing industrial economies sought

---

1879–1907 Alliance system: Germany-Austria (1879); Germany-Austria-Russia (1881); Germany-Italy-Austria (1882); France-Russia (1891); Britain-France (1904); Britain-Russia (1907)

1912–1913 Balkan Wars

1880s ff. High point of impressionism in art

1881–1889 German social insurance laws enacted

1914 Beginning of World War I

1881–1914 Build Canadian Pacific Railway

1893 U.S. annexes Hawaii

1899 U.S. acquires part of Samoa

1891–1898 Australia and New Zealand restrict Asian immigration

1907 New Zealand dominion status in British Empire

1917 U.S. enters World War I

1901 Commonwealth of Australia, creates national federation

1882 U.S. excludes Chinese immigrants

1893 Women's suffrage in New Zealand

1898 Spanish-American War; U.S. acquires Puerto Rico, Guam, Philippines

new international markets and resources. The stress of Western industrialization also played a role in driving many adventurers, and governments, to seek secure markets and sources of raw materials by conquering new territories outside their own borders. Industrialization, in sum, revolutionized world power relationships and led to a century of growing Western dominance. This was the context, in turn, in which the 20th century began and against which a host of new trends, including anti-Western nationalism and diverse patterns of economic growth, would play out after 1900.

This chapter focuses on the nature of Western industrial society and related developments in Western diplomacy, culture, and society that were strongly influenced by industrialization. Creation of an industrial society was by no means an accomplished process by 1900, even in Great Britain, where the new economic and technological forms had first taken root. The West's 20th-century history would continue to show how the massive range of innovation compelled ongoing adjustments in institutional policies and personal lives. The later 1800s did, however, see something of an apogee in the position of world power that the Industrial Revolution had created for the West.

The critical influence of the Industrial Revolution on 20th-century world history thus took several forms. It created a new set of challenges and sweeping changes in industrial or industrializing societies in the West itself, and it posed new challenges to other, older centers of civilization as it realigned the international balance of power. The importance of industrial influences means that the context for contemporary world history began to take shape in the mid-18th century with the rise of industrialization itself; hence the need for a brief backward glance prior to taking up the events that most immediately preceded the new century.

THE INDUSTRIAL REVOLUTION IN EUROPE

The process of industrialization began to emerge more than a century before 1900, initially in Great Britain. Beginning about 1820, industrialization spread to parts of continental western Europe and to the United States. The essence of this industrial revolution was technological change, particularly the application of coal-powered engines (or, later, engines powered by other fossil fuels) to the production process. The new engines replaced people and animals as the key sources of energy in many aspects of production. They were joined by new production equipment that could apply power to manufacturing through more automatic

processes. Thus spindles now wrapped fiber automatically into thread, and looms mixed thread automatically without direct human intervention. Hammering and rolling devices allowed application of power machinery to metals. And although textile and metallurgical production received primary attention in early industrialization, engines were also used in sugar refining, printing, and other processes.

The British Industrial Revolution resulted from a host of factors, including favorable natural resources and strong capital reserves won from previous trade. Industrialization was also fed by new problems and new ideas. Population pressure, intense in Britain, forced innovations at all social levels. European population growth exploded in the late 18th and early 19th centuries, with growth rates of 150 percent or more. These rates could be sustained only by radical economic innovation. The conviction that economic innovation was a necessity was also reinforced by the writings of 18th-century social thinkers. Proclaiming faith in progress and the capacity of humans to dominate nature, these thinkers also sanctioned a devotion to improving material life. Here were motivations for inventing new processes of resource extraction and manufacture and applying them widely.

Europe's industrialization also resulted, somewhat ironically, from the advantages Britain and other Western nations had already gained in world trade. Well before the great economic transformations had begun, western Europe had become the dominant force in international commerce. This commercial dominance provided the capital without which industrialization could not have occurred as readily or as rapidly. It also created world markets for the increased manufacturing output that the new industry made possible. Many centuries earlier, the Europeans had realized that great profits could be earned by selling processed goods to other areas and importing cheaper raw materials. Industrialization further enhanced Europe's preeminence in world trade—not the first time, or the last, that the relatively rich got richer.

The key inventions of early industrialization developed in Britain during the 18th century. Automatic machinery in textiles was initially intended for manual use in the domestic system. Then in the 1770s the Scottish artisan James Watt devised a steam engine that could be used to concentrate production in ever larger units, called factories, and the Industrial Revolution was off and running. Within a decade in Britain the domestic manufacture of key materials, such as cotton thread, was converted to factory-housed machines, at the expense of thousands of home workers, mostly women. Changes of this sort spurred the creation of new industries to build machines and also the rapid expansion of coal mining to fuel the new productive engines.

Additional inventions followed on the heels of the original set, for a key feature of the Industrial Revolution was recurrent technological change. Early machine spindles were expanded, so that a given worker could supervise even vaster output. U.S. inventors devised a production system of interchangeable parts, initially for rifles, that helped standardize and so mechanize the production of machinery itself. Metallurgy advanced by use of coal and coke, instead of charcoal, for smelting and refining, allowing the creation of larger furnaces and greater output.

Technological change was quickly applied to transportation and communication, essential areas now that there were more goods to be moved to ever more distant markets. The development of the telegraph, steam shipping, and the railway, all early in the 19th century, provided new speed in the movement of information and goods. These inventions were vital in facilitating a new stage in Western penetration of world affairs; they also kept the Industrial Revolution going in the West, by promoting mass-marketing techniques and providing direct orders for rails and other industrial goods.

Although technological change lay at the heart of industrialization, several basic economic changes were inherent in the process as well. The Industrial Revolution depended on improvements in agriculture. Industrialization concentrated increasing amounts of manufacturing in cities, where power sources could be brought together with labor. City growth, dizzying during the first decades of industrialization, relied on better agricultural production, accomplished through improved equipment and seeds, and increasing use of fertilizers. Better agriculture freed up a growing percentage of the labor force for nonagricultural pursuits, and fairly soon in vigorous industrializing nations, such as Britain, manufacturing output surpassed that of farming in importance.

Industrialization also meant a factory system. Steam engines had to be concentrated, for their power could not be widely diffused until the later application of electricity. Factory labor separated work from the home— one of the basic human changes inherent in the Industrial Revolution. It also allowed manufacturers to introduce greater specialization of labor and more explicit rules and discipline, which along with the incessant demands of the noisy machines permanently changed the nature of human labor.

Once Britain launched industrialization, other Western nations quickly saw the need to imitate. Britain's industrial power helped the nation hold out against Napoleon and led to huge profits for successful businesspeople by the early 19th century. Hence in Belgium, Germany, and New England both governments and individual entrepreneurs soon rushed to copy. Since most

Railway bridges, such as this spectacular trestle at Frankenstein in Germany, were among the engineering wonders of the industrial age.

of the general factors that permitted industrialization were present in these areas as well, including population pressure and an ideology of material progress, industrialization spread relatively swiftly throughout much of the Western world.

Belgium and France began to industrialize in the 1820s; the United States and Germany followed soon thereafter. Industrialization did not immediately sweep all before it, even in Britain; artisan production expanded for a time as cities grew and rural labor remained vital. But the forms of the Industrial Revolution gained ground steadily once implanted in the West, and factory workers and their managers became increasingly important minorities in the general labor force.

THE DISRUPTIONS OF INDUSTRIAL LIFE

The Industrial Revolution involved huge movements of people from countryside to city. Families were disrupted in this process, as young adults proved to be the prime migrants. Cities themselves, poorly equipped to begin with and now crowded beyond all precedent, became hellholes for many new residents. Health conditions worsened in poor districts because of packed housing and inadequate sanitation. Crime increased for a time. New social divisions opened up, as middle-class families sought to move away from the center-city poor, beginning a pattern of suburbanization that continued into the later 20th century.

Work became more unpleasant for many people. Not only was it largely separated from family, but also the new machines and factory rules compelled a rapid pace and coordination that pulverized traditional values of leisurely, quality production. First in Britain and then elsewhere, groups of workers responded to the new machines by outright attack; for example, Luddite protests, named after a mythical British machine breaker called Ned Ludd, failed to stop industrialization, but they showed the stress involved. Many traditional business and farm families were also appalled by the noise, dirt, and sheer novelty involved in the Industrial Revolution.

The Industrial Revolution also forced new constraints on traditions of popular leisure. Factory owners, bent on getting as much work as possible from their labor force to help pay for expensive machines, deliberately reduced recreational aspects of work; they tried to ban singing, napping, drinking, and other customary frivolities on the job. Off the job, new business-led city governments, backed by expanding police forces, attacked popular festivals, animal contests, and gambling in the name of proper discipline and good order. Attempts were made to reduce social drinking as well, but they largely failed in light of workers' insistence on some recreational outlets. Nevertheless, the Industrial Revolution considerably reduced key leisure traditions and community ties, which made the early phases of the experience still more disorienting and grim for many people involved.

Changes in family life revealed some of the wider stresses of the industrialization process. Middle-class people quickly moved to enhance the redefinition of the family already begun in the early modern centuries: The family for them served as an image of affection and purity. Children and women were to be sheltered from the storms of the new work world. Women, traditionally active partners to merchants, now withdrew from formal jobs. They gained new roles in caring for children and the home, and their moral stature in many ways improved, but their sphere was more radically separate from that of men than had been true before. Children, too, were redefined. The middle class led in seeing education, not work and apprenticeship, as the logical role for children to prepare them for a complex future and, it was hoped, to maintain their innocence until they were prepared to cope with business or professional life.

The working-class family changed as well, though it could not afford all these indulgences. Young children, increasingly unnecessary on the job, were often sent to school. Women worked from adolescence until marriage, when they were often pulled away because of the demands of shopping, home care, and motherhood. Even when on the job, working-class women were more likely to be sent into domestic service in middle-class households than to factories, though there was an important minority of female factory hands. The working class, in sum, developed its own version of separate spheres, in part simply to compensate for the new distinction between job and home. Family life became more important than ever before, to provide homemaking services and to offer some hope of emotional satisfaction in a confusing world. Marriages encountered new stress, but the marriage rate went up fairly steadily.

These changes in family roles and values show how deeply the Industrial Revolution reached into personal life, particularly for factory workers but for other groups as well. The changes were not all bad, and many people found ways to use family satisfactions or community institutions, such as neighborhood taverns, to help compensate for a loss of power at work. Yet considerable confusion and anxiety remained. As a leading French industrialist lamented, "Progress is not necessarily progressive. If it were not inevitable, it might be better to stop it."

The West's Industrial Revolution changed the situation of women in many ways. Some of the changes have occurred more recently in other civilizations; others were particularly characteristic of the 19th-century West. Industrialization cut into women's traditional work and protest roles (for example, in spearheading bread riots as attention shifted to work-based strikes), but it tended to expand educational opportunities. Some new work roles and protest outlets, including feminism, developed by 1914. Important changes occurred in the home as well. New ideas and standards at once elevated women's position and set up more demanding tasks. Relations among women were also affected by the growing use of domestic servants (the most common urban job for working-class women) and new attitudes by middle- and lower-class women alike.

The first document that follows sketches the idealization of middle-class women; it comes from an American moral tract of 1837, anonymously authored, probably by a man. The second document, written by a woman in an English woman's magazine, shows new household standards of another sort, with a critical tone also common in middle-class literature. Finally, a British housewife discusses her servant problems, reflecting yet another facet of women's lives. How could women decide what their domestic roles were and whether they brought satisfaction or not?

WOMEN AS CIVILIZERS (1837)

As a sister, she soothes the troubled heart, chastens and tempers the wild daring of the hurt mind restless with disappointed pride or fired with ambition. As a mistress, she inspires the nobler sentiment of purer love, and the sober purpose of conquering himself for virtue's sake. As a wife, she consoles him in grief, animates him with hope in despair, restrains him in prosperity, cheers him in poverty and trouble, swells the pulsations of his throbbing breast that beats for honorable distinction, and rewards his toils with the undivided homage of a grateful heart. In the important and endearing character of mother, she watches and directs the various impulses of unfledged genius, instills into the tender and susceptible mind the quickening seeds of virtue, fits us to brave dangers in time of peril, and consecrates to truth and virtue the best affections of our nature.

MOTHERHOOD AS POWER AND BURDEN (1877)

Every woman who has charge of a household should have a practical knowledge of nursing, simple doctoring and physicianing. The professional doctor must be called in for real illness. But the Home Doctor may do so much to render professional visits very few and far between. And her knowledge will be of infinite value when it is necessary to carry out the doctor's orders. . . .

THE MOTHER BUILDER

It is a curious fact that architects who design and builders who carry out their plans must have a training for this work. But the Mother Builder is supposed to have to know by instinct how to put in each tiny brick which builds up the "human." The result of leaving it to "instinct" is that the child starts out with bad foundations and a jerry-built constitution. . . .

When one considers that one child in every three born dies before the age of five years, it is evident how wide-spread must be the ignorance as to the feeding and care of these little ones. It is a matter of surprise to those who understand the constitution and needs of infants that, considering the conditions under which the large number of them are reared, the mortality is not greater. . . .

THE RISKS BABIES RUN

To begin with, the popular superstition that a young baby must be "hungry" because it lives on milk, and is on this plea the recipient of scraps and bits of vegetables, potato and gravy, crusts, and other heterogeneous articles of diet, has much to answer for. Then, the artistic sense of the mother which leads her to display mottled necks, dimpled arms, and chubby legs, instead of warmly covering these charming portions of baby's anatomy, goes hugely to swell the death-rate. Mistakes in feeding and covering have much to answer for in the high mortality of infants.

THE SERVANT "PROBLEM" (1860)

So we lost Mary, and Peggy reigned in her stead for some six weeks. . . .

But Peggy differed greatly from her predecessor, Mary. She was not clean in her person, and my mother declared that her presence was not desirable within a few feet. Moreover she had no notion of putting things in their places, but always left all her working materials in the apartment where they were last used. It was not therefore pleasant, when one wanted a sweeping brush, to have to sit down and think which room Peggy had swept the last, and so on with all the paraphernalia for dusting and scrubbing. But this was not the worst. My mother, accustomed to receive almost reverential respect from her old servants, could not endure poor Peggy's familiar ways. . . .

Now, though I am quite willing to acknowledge the mutual obligation which exists between the employer and employed, I do *not* agree with my charwoman that she is the only person who ought to be considered as conferring a favor. I desire to treat her with all kindness, showing every possible regard to her comfort, and I expect from her no more work than I would cheerfully and easily perform in the same time. But when I scrupulously perform my part of the bargain, both as regards food and wages, not to mention much thought and care in order to make things easy for her and which were not in the agreement at all, I think she ought not only to keep faith with me if possible, but to abstain from hinting at the obligation she confers in coming.

It is not pleasant, as my mother says, to beg and pray for the help for which we also pay liberally. But it is worse for my kitchen helper to be continually reminding me that she need not go out unless she likes, and that it was only to oblige me she ever came at all. I do not relish this utter ignoring of her wages, etc., or her being quite deaf because I choose to offer a suggestion as to the propriety of dusting out the corners, or when I mildly hint that I should prefer her doing something in my way. . . .

But if I were to detail all my experiences, I should never have done. I have had many good and willing workers; but few on whose punctuality and regularity I could rely.

Questions: In what ways did industrialization increase differences between women and men in the 19th-century West? What were the main changes in women's roles and ideals? How did middle-class and working-class women differ?

REVOLUTIONARY POLITICS

The Industrial Revolution was paralleled by a far-reaching political upheaval in the West. Challenges to existing political regimes initially arose at the end of the 18th century, stemming from early stages of economic change, together with new ideas about liberty and democracy. By the mid-19th century political shifts began to combine with the forces of the Industrial Revolution to produce new constitutional structures and a realignment of the functions of the European state.

The era of political revolution began in 1775 with the rebellion of the American colonies against Britain. The new United States that emerged in the 1780s was remote from Europe but provided a model of a republican regime, instead of a monarchy, with a strong congressional system and constitutional guarantees of many citizen rights. This precedent played some role in inspiring the great French Revolution of 1789, which swept away France's monarchy and the principles of an aristocratic social structure, establishing religious freedom, equality under the law, and a variety of commercial liberties in place of the institutions of the old regime. The French Revolution, as it fought the armies of Europe's monarchies, also promoted a new form of nationalism, as French citizens were called on to rally their loyalties and abandon traditional allegiances to church or locality. A new citizens' army established a related principle of mass military conscription. The French Revolution and its conquests spread new political movements to other parts of western Europe. In France the revolution, after successive parliamentary and radical phases, failed to establish a durable new regime, and ultimately a reformed monarchy returned. But a total restoration of Europe's old politics proved impossible.

In the wake of the great revolution, new political movements spread throughout western Europe by the 1820s. Liberals advocated limits on state interference in individual life, along with constitutional, parliamentary rule. Radicals accepted most liberal premises but also sought wider voting rights, even full adult male suffrage. A small current of socialism urged the rejection of private property in the name of the worker, and nationalists argued for the importance of national unity and glory, winning particular audience amid the divided states of Italy and Germany. A host of revolutions followed from the clash among these various movements and the established monarchies supported by church leaders. Even aside from revolution, major reform measures brought

Centers of Revolutionary Insurgency in 19th- and early 20th-Century Europe

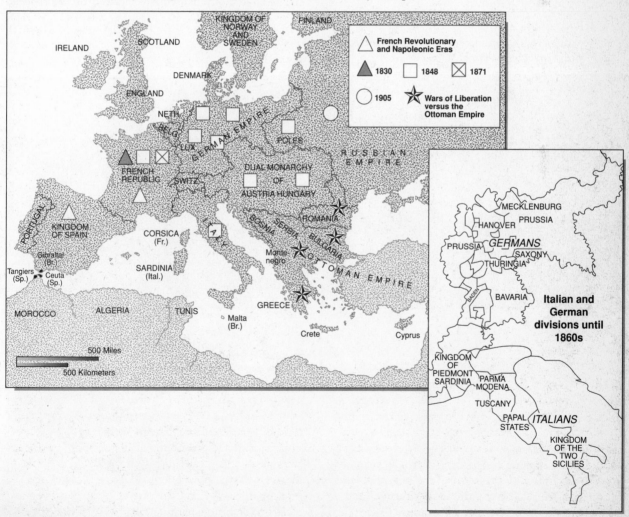

expanded voting rights in Britain (where the middle class gained the vote in 1823) and many northern states in the United States.

Ongoing political unrest stemmed from several factors. Rapid economic change required major adaptations in commercial laws and government functions. One of several goals of nationalists in Italy, for example, was to obtain enough national unity to provide a larger market for goods. At the same time, groups that were gaining ground on the basis of economic innovation sought new political voice. Yet groups being displaced, such as urban artisans, sought voice as well, in hopes that government would find ways to compensate for their growing insecurity. This was the revolutionary brew in the West during the first half of the 19th century, setting in motion new political currents that lasted well into the 20th century. This was a brew also that would ferment in other societies during the 20th century.

Partly in response to agitation, partly in an effort to promote economic growth, most western European governments began some accommodation to the process of industrialization. Laws were changed to facilitate the movement of labor and the introduction of new technologies; traditional craft groups were weakened or outlawed in favor of freer commercial expansion. By the 1830s most governments began promoting railroad development; they also promoted technical exhibits and scientific training.

In 1848 and 1849 a final round of European-wide revolution occurred, beginning in Paris. Revolution spread throughout central Europe, where nationalist demands joined democratic pressure and intense unrest from urban workers, particularly artisans. These revolutions failed in a formal sense, as conservative monarchies regained their hold in the states of Germany and Italy and as an authoritarian empire replaced the short-lived

In 1848 crowds, mainly urban artisans, stormed the military arsenal in Berlin during the last great revolution in the industrial West.

republic that had emerged in France. Yet the new or restored regimes quickly began to introduce some political changes and to give new elements of the middle class a limited political voice. They introduced some social legislation to appeal to working-class groups, and they uniformly abolished the manorial system (where it had not already been destroyed after 1789), which had burdened peasants with obligations to an aristocratic landlord class.

The ongoing social changes brought by industrialization also played a role in ending political revolution in the West. The artisan class, whose sense of organization and older values had been crucial to revolts through 1848, began to decline as factory industry continued to gain ground. Artisans did not disappear, but they lost some of their sense of mission. Many began to concentrate on personal advancement or a solid but moderate craft trade unionism that sought improvements within the system rather than a different system. While many grievances continued for new and old social groups, the belief that political upheaval could stem the tide of industrialization began to fade.

Finally, the experience of decades of recurrent revolution, together with industrialization itself, created new social divisions that made uprisings more difficult. The period of revolution had been predicated on old-style social divisions that pitted commoners against the privileges of the aristocracy and against other institutions, such as unreconstructed monarchies or established churches that did not give ordinary people a voice. Divisions of interest obviously existed among commoners, depending on wealth or on urban as opposed to rural residence, but they also shared interest in attacking the structures of the old regime. By 1850 an industrial class structure had come to predominate. Earlier revolutionary gains had reduced the legal privileges of the aristocracy, and the rise of business had eroded the aristocrats' economic dominance. With industrialization social structure came to rest less on privilege and birth and more on money. Key divisions by 1850 pitted middle-class property owners against workers of various sorts. The old alliances that had produced the revolutions were now dissolved. New social cleavages would produce important unrest, and those who sought to foment it would use ideologies inspired by liberalism and radicalism but not in the classic revolutionary mold. An era of transition had ended. Through intended and unanticipated results of earlier revolutions and the steady gains of an industrial economy, a new society had been created in western Europe and North America—an industrial world combined with political change in ways that reduced the revolutionary potential in the West—from 1850 until our own day.

THE CONSOLIDATION OF THE INDUSTRIAL ORDER, 1850–1914

In most respects the 65 years after 1850 seemed calmer than the frenzied period of political upheaval and initial industrialization. Many people became accustomed to change. City growth continued in the West, and indeed several countries, starting with Britain, neared the 50 percent mark in urbanization, the first time in human history that more than a minority of a population had lived in cities. But the rate of city growth slowed. Furthermore, city government began to gain ground on the pressing problems growth had created. Sanitation improved, and death rates fell below birthrates for the first time in urban history. Parks, museums, effective regulation of food and housing facilities, more efficient police forces—all added to the safety and the physical and cultural amenities of urban life. Hosts of problems remained, but the horror stories of early industrialization began to abate. Revealingly, crime rates began to stabilize or even drop in several industrial areas, a sign of more effective social control and also of a more disciplined population.

ADJUSTMENTS TO INDUSTRIAL LIFE

The theme of adjustment and stabilization applied to family life. Illegitimacy rates stopped rising—until 1960—which suggested that some earlier disruption in personal habits was easing. Within families, birthrates began to drop as Western society initiated a substantial *demographic transition* to a new system that promoted fairly stable population levels through a new combination of relatively low birthrates and death rates. Led initially by the middle classes, the low birthrate involved a reassessment of the purposes of children. Children were now seen as a source of emotional satisfaction and considerable parental responsibility, not as contributors to a family economy. This meant that individual children would be highly valued, but the total number would be reduced. Other social groups soon accepted this reassessment, which reflected the progressive disappearance of child labor and promoted the economic well-being of all family members. Family life might still prove difficult, as expectations for improvements in standards of living or

Middle- and working-class excursionists made trips to the seaside popular before costumes fully adjusted, as seen in this scene from Yarmouth, England.

for emotional rewards might outpace reality. Merely effecting lower birthrates could be challenging, for although birth control devices began to spread after 1850, they were still unfamiliar and not fully reliable, which meant that many families had to practice new levels of sexual restraint. Nevertheless, some of the starkest pressures began to yield in family life as a result of significant adjustments to new realities.

Material conditions generally improved after 1850. There were important fluctuations; the industrial economy was unstable, and frequent depressions caused falling wages and unemployment. Huge income gaps also continued to divide various social groups. Nevertheless, the general trend was upward. By 1900 probably two-thirds of the Western population enjoyed conditions above the subsistence level; people could afford a few amenities, such as newspapers or family outings, and their diet and housing improved. Health got better. The decades from 1880 to 1920 saw a revolution in children's health, thanks in part to better hygiene during childbirth and better parental care. Infancy and death separated for the first time in human history. Instead of one-third or more of all children dying by age ten, rates fell to under 10 percent and continued to plummet. Adult health also benefited from better nutrition and improved work safety. French researcher Louis Pasteur's discovery of germs led by the 1880s to more conscientious sanitary regulations and procedures by doctors and other health care specialists; this in turn reduced the deaths of women in childbirth. Women now

began to outlive men by a noticeable margin, but men's health also improved.

Although material life gained in several measurable respects, the workplace recurrently challenged established habits. Industrial jobs continued to involve a fast pace and severe limitations on worker autonomy. These characteristics worsened after 1850. New machines in textiles and metallurgy sped up work while reducing skill levels. The typical industrial worker was now semiskilled, trained in very limited areas that involved little sense of pride or creativity. New methods of supervision, often pioneered in the United States, involved detailed calculations by efficiency engineers designed to spur output and limit wasted motion. From this base, managers in such industries as automobile production introduced assembly-line procedures early in the 20th century, with workers deliberately reduced to machinelike repetitions.

Yet as workers suffered under these new conditions, there were new ways to compensate. Important labor movements took shape among industrial workers by the 1890s, with massive strike movements by miners, metalworkers, and others from the United States to Germany. The new trade union movement stressed the massed power of workers, and although often defeated by management-government coalitions, it won some important gains and gave workers some sense of voice and dignity. Furthermore, both within the labor movement and as individuals, many workers learned to react to the new systems of work instrumentally. The instrumentalist reaction urged workers to regard their jobs not as ends in themselves but as vehicles for other goals. Many workers, as instrumentalists, learned to bargain for better pay and shorter hours so that less of their lives would be invested in the work process.

POLITICAL TRENDS

The consolidation theme clearly applies to Western politics after the failures of the revolutions of 1848. Quite simply, issues that had dominated the Western political agenda for many decades were largely resolved within a generation. The great debates about fundamental constitutions and government structure, which had emerged first in the 17th century with the rise of absolutism and new political theory and then raged during the decades of revolution, at last grew quiet.

Many Western leaders worked to reduce the need for political revolution after 1850. Liberals decided that revolution was too risky and became more willing to compromise. Key conservatives strove to develop a new political consensus that would save elements of the old regime, including power for the landed aristocracy and the monarchy, but through reform would not engender resistance down the line. Conservatives realized that

they could allow parliaments with limited powers, appeal to workers through limited social reforms, and even extend the vote without necessarily losing power. Thus in 1867 a British conservative leader, Benjamin Disraeli, took the initiative of granting the vote to working-class males. In the Italian state of Piedmont Count Camillo di Cavour began even earlier to support industrial development and extend the powers of parliament in order to please liberal forces. In Prussia a new prime minister, Otto von Bismarck, similarly began to work with a parliament and extended the vote to all adult males (though grouping them in wealth categories that protected the country from full democracy). These developments fell short of full liberal demands; parliaments did not have basic control over the appointment of ministries, but many groups gained some effective political voice. Other Prussian reforms granted freedom to Jews, extended (without guaranteeing) rights to the press, and promoted mass education. The gap between liberal and conservative regimes narrowed in the West, though it remained significant.

The new conservatives also began to use the force of nationalism to win support for the existing social order. Previously nationalism had been a radical force, challenging established arrangements in the name of new

The Unifications of Italy and Germany

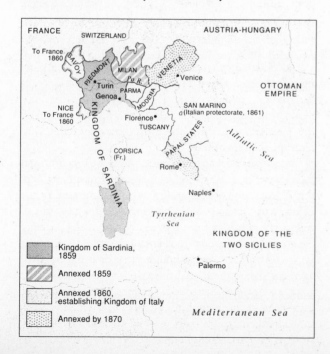

loyalties. Many liberals continued to defend nationalist causes. Now, however, conservative politicians learned how to wrap themselves in the flag, often promoting an active foreign policy in the interests of promoting domestic calm. Thus British conservatives became champions of expanding the empire, and in the United States by the 1890s the Republican party became increasingly identified with imperialist causes.

The most important new uses of nationalism within the West occurred in Italy and Germany. Cavour, after wooing liberal support, formed an alliance with France that enabled him to attack Austrian control of northern Italian provinces in 1858. The nationalist rebellion set in motion in other parts of the peninsula allowed Cavour to unite most of Italy under the Piedmontese king. This led to a reduction of the political power of the Catholic pope, already an opponent of liberal and nationalist ideas—an important part of the general reduction of Church power in Western politics.

Following Cavour's example, Bismarck in Prussia staged a series of wars in the 1860s that expanded Prussian power in Germany. A final war, against France, led to outright German unity in 1871. The new German Empire boasted a national parliament with a lower house based on universal male suffrage and an upper house that favored conservative state governments. This kind of compromise, combined with the dizzying joy of nationalist success, won support for the new regime from most liberals and many conservatives.

France, after its defeat by Germany in 1870, overthrew its short-lived echo of the Napoleonic Empire and established a conservative republic—with votes for all adult men, a reduction of Church power, and expansion of education, but no major social reform or tampering with existing property relationships. Just as a conservative Bismarck could be selectively radical, so France proved that liberals could be very cautious.

With these changes the war between conservatives and liberals yielded to petty skirmishes and sniper attacks. The big issues that divided the two groups were gone. Virtually the entire West now had a parliamentary system, usually a democracy of some sort, in which religious and other freedoms were widely protected. In this system liberal and conservative ministries could alternate without major changes of internal policy. Indeed, Italy developed a process called *transformismo*, or transformism, in which parliamentary deputies, no matter what platforms they professed, were transformed once in Rome to a single-minded pursuit of political office and support of the status quo.

THE SOCIAL QUESTION AND NEW GOVERNMENT FUNCTIONS

The decline of basic constitutional disputes by the 1870s opened the way for a new set of political issues in the West and promoted the fuller development of an industrial-style state. At the same time, the unifications of Italy and particularly of Germany had a major impact on the diplomacy of western Europe. Germany, once unified, was immediately a dominant European power, with a rapidly expanding industrial base. Its ascendancy, together with the sheer addition of novel diplomatic actors on the European stage, inevitably unsettled international relations among the Western states. Here, too, was an agenda item of growing importance after 1870, following many decades in which major diplomatic issues had been downplayed in favor of concentration on internal economic development and political challenge.

Government functions and personnel expanded rapidly throughout the Western world after 1870. All Western governments introduced civil service examinations to test applicants on the basis of talent rather than on connections or birth alone—thus unwittingly imitating Chinese innovations over a thousand years before. With a growing bureaucracy and improved recruitment, governments began to extend their regulatory apparatus—inspecting factory safety, the health of prostitutes, hospital conditions, and even (through the introduction of passports and border controls) personal travel.

Schooling expanded, becoming generally compulsory up to age 12. By 1900 many U.S. states also began to require high school education, and most Western nations expanded their public secondary school systems. Here was a huge addition to the ways governments and individuals interacted. The new school systems promoted literacy, long gaining ground in the West and now becoming virtually universal; by 1900, 90 to 95 percent of all adults in western Europe and the United States could read. They promoted numerical skills and other job-related aptitudes. They also encouraged certain social agendas. Girls were carefully taught about the importance of home and women's moral mission; domestic science programs were designed to promote better nutrition and hygiene. Boys and girls alike were taught the advantages of medical science over other health measures, and in general governments played a major role in promoting the use of doctors. Schools also carefully propounded nationalism, teaching the superiority of the nation's language and history, as well as attacking minority or immigrant cultures.

Governments also began to introduce wider welfare measures, again replacing or supplementing such traditional groups as churches and families. Bismarck was a pioneer in this area too in the 1880s, as he sought to wean German workers from their attraction to socialism. His tactic failed, as socialism steadily advanced, but his measures had lasting importance. German social insurance began to provide assistance in cases of accident, illness, and old age. Soon some measures to aid the unemployed were also added, initially in Britain. These early welfare programs were small and their utility limited, but they sketched a major extension of government power.

The growth of government obviously required new financing. Western governments benefited from the advancing prosperity brought by industrialization. They also introduced personal income taxes by 1900, here too starting small but gradually expanding the take.

Amid many individual variants, the industrial-style government widely introduced by Western nations at the end of the 19th century had considerably more contact with ordinary people than any Western government had ever before maintained. It also sought active loyalty, not mere calm. It began to take over many functions previously performed by families and communities, in part because these institutions had weakened or changed under the impact of industrialization.

Accompanying the quiet revolution in government functions during the later 19th century in the Western world was a realignment of the political spectrum that involved the replacement of constitutional issues by social issues—what people of the time called "the social question"—as the key criteria for political partisanship. Socialist and feminist movements surged to the political fore, placing liberals as well as conservatives in a new, though by no means unsuccessful, defensive posture.

The rise of socialism depended above all on the power of grievance of the working class, with allies from other groups. It also reflected a major redefinition of political theory accomplished, from 1848 through the 1860s, by one of the leading intellectuals of the century in the West, Karl Marx. Early socialist doctrine, from the Enlightenment through 1848, had focused on human perfectibility: Set up a few exemplary communities, where work and rewards would be shared, and the evils of capitalism would end as people exercised their rational judgment to choose the better way. Marx's socialism was tough-minded, and he blasted earlier theorists as giddy utopians. Marx saw socialism as the final phase of an inexorable march of history, which could be studied dispassionately and scientifically. History for

Marx was shaped by the available means of production and who controlled those means—an obvious reflection of the looming role of technology in the industrial world forming at that time. Class struggle always pitted a group out of power with the group controlling the means of production; hence, in the era just passed, the middle class had battled the feudal aristocracy. Now the middle class had won; it dominated production and, through this, the state and culture as well. But it had created a new class enemy, the propertyless worker proletariat, that would grow until revolution became inevitable. Then, after a transitional period in which proletarian dictatorship would clean up the remnants of the bourgeois social order, full freedom would be achieved. People would benefit justly from their work, as essential equality would prevail, and the state would wither away; the historic class struggle would at last end because classes themselves would be eliminated.

Marx's vision was a powerful one. It clearly identified capitalist evil. It told workers that their low wages were exploitive and unjust. It urged the need for violent action but also assured workers that revolution was part of the inexorable tides of history. Victory was certain, and the result would be heaven on earth—ultimately, an Enlightenment-like vision of progress.

Marx's message also came at a good time. Earlier socialist movements had withered in the collapse of the revolutions of 1848, partly because they seemed so impractical and partly because of government crackdowns on radical leaders. By the 1860s, when working-class activity began to revive, Marxist doctrine provided encouragement and structure. Marx himself continued to concentrate on ideological development and purity, but leaders in many countries translated his doctrine into practical political parties.

Germany led the way. As Bismarck extended the vote, socialist leaders in the 1860s and 1870s were the first to understand the implications of mass electioneering. Socialist movements were always strong in the provision of grassroots organization; available to constituents not only in election periods, they also provided fiery speakers who courted popular support instead of appealing, as many liberals and conservatives did, on the basis of their elevated social station and the respect it deserved. By the 1880s socialists in Germany were cutting into liberal support, and by 1900 the party was the largest single political force in the nation. Socialist parties in Austria, France, and elsewhere followed a roughly similar course, everywhere emerging as a strong minority force. Only in Britain and particularly the United States did socialism lag somewhat, in part because workers already had the habit of looking to liberal movements as their political expression. In Britain, too, socialism became a significant third force by 1914.

The rise of socialism terrified many people in Western society, who took the revolutionary message literally. In combination with major industrial strikes and unionization, it was possible to see social issues portending outright social war. But socialism itself was not unchanging. As socialist parties gained strength, they often allied with other groups to achieve more moderate reforms, and in the main they became firm supporters of parliamentary democracy. A movement called *revisionism* arose, which argued that Marx's revolutionary vision was wrong—it needed revising—because industrial workers were not becoming a full majority and because success could be achieved by peaceful, gradual means. Many socialist leaders denounced revisionism, but in fact most behaved in revisionist fashion, putting their energies into building electoral victories rather than plotting violent revolution. Western socialism, in other words, although it reflected bitter grievances and class divisions as against a mood of consolidation and adjustment, worked to a great extent within the democratic political system.

Socialism was not the only challenge to the existing order. Powerful feminist movements arose by 1900 seeking various legal and economic gains for women, such as equal access to professions and higher education, as well as the right to vote. Feminism won support particularly from middle-class women, who argued that the very moral superiority granted to women in the home should be translated into political voice. Many middle-class women also chafed against the confines of their domestic roles, particularly as family size declined. A small but important group of women entered the professions directly, challenging ideas of inherent male superiority; a larger number became teachers and nurses, increasingly dominating semiprofessions that gave women both a new work role, at least before marriage, and a new sense that their opportunities were unjustly limited. In several countries feminism combined with socialism, but in Britain, the United States, Australia, and Scandinavia a separate feminist current arose that petitioned widely and even conducted acts of violence in order to win the vote. Here, too, was a major threat to political adjustment, but it was one that might be managed. Several U.S. states and Scandinavian countries extended the vote to women by 1914, in a pattern that would spread to Britain, Germany, and the whole United States after 1918.

Agitating for the vote after 1900, militant "suffragettes" blocked public ways in England, provoking many confrontations with police.

The politics of Western society remained lively, with new forces jostling older interests and assumptions. Outside of formal policy—for example, in some new cultural currents—tensions were even more pronounced, as against the mood of complacency—of confidence in industrial and political progress—that remained widespread around 1900.

POPULAR CULTURE AND HIGH CULTURE

Key developments in popular culture reflected the maturation of industrial society in the West in the decades before 1900. Mass leisure culture began to emerge. Popular newspapers, with bold headlines and compelling human-interest stories, won millions of subscribers in the industrial West. Rather than appeals to reason or political principle, they featured shock and entertainment. Crime, imperialist exploits, sports, and even comics became the items of the day. Popular theater soared. Comedy routines and musical reviews drew thousands of patrons to music halls; after 1900 some of these entertainment themes dominated the new medium of motion pictures. Vacation trips became increasingly common, and seaside resorts grew to the level of big business.

Leisure outlets of these sorts were designed for fun. They appealed to impulse and escapism. Leisure was now a commodity to be enjoyed regularly, perhaps daily, rather than through periodic festivals as in traditional society. With work increasingly disciplined, many saw leisure not as a chance for restraint and self-improvement, as the middle class still sometimes tried to insist, but as recreation.

The rise of team sports readily expressed the complexities of the late-19th-century leisure revolution. Here was another Western-wide development, though one that soon had international impact. Soccer, football, and baseball all surged into new prominence, at both amateur and professional levels. These new sports reflected industrial life. Though based on traditional games, they were organized with rules and umpires. They taught the virtues of coordination and discipline and could be viewed as useful preparation for work or military life. They were suitably commercial; sports equipment, based on the ability to mass-produce rubber balls, and professional teams and stadia quickly became major businesses. But sports also expressed impulse and violence. They furthered irrational community loyalties and even, as Olympic Games were reintroduced in 1892, nationalist passions.

Overall, new leisure interests suggested a complex set of attitudes on the part of ordinary people in Western society. They demonstrated growing secularism. Religion still counted for something among some groups, but religious practice had declined markedly as people looked increasingly for worldly entertainments and gave allegiance to secular faiths such as nationalism or socialism or simply the growing prestige of science. Many people would have agreed that progress was possible on this earth through rational planning and individual self-control. Yet mass leisure and growing consumerism also suggested a more impulsive side to popular outlook, one bent on display of passion or at least, as spectators, vicarious participation in emotional release.

SCIENCE AND ART

A similar, though more formal, dualism developed in intellectual life in the West, with roots going back to the early 19th century. On the one hand, science continued to gain ground; on the other hand, a bewildering array

of intellectual movements attempted to provide alternative views of reality and a less structured approach to human understanding. There were some common basic themes. The size of the intellectual and artistic community in the West expanded steadily, with rising prosperity and advancing educational levels. A growing audience existed for various intellectual and artistic products, making it more possible than ever before for people to hope to earn a living through painting or writing or scientific research. The bulk of the new activity was resolutely secular. Though new churches were built as cities grew, and missionary activity reached new heights outside the Western world, the churches no longer served as centers for the most creative intellectual life.

A major portion of Western cultural activity built on the traditions of rationalism that had been firmed up by the 18th-century Enlightenment. Major political theories, such as liberalism, assumed that people were basically rational and improvable and that human society could be grasped through investigation of fundamental social laws. Thus liberals stressed the importance of education and freedom of inquiry, while also urging that economic activity, for example, could be grasped through basic operations of supply and demand. Karl Marx, though arguing that large historical forces dominated individual action, also urged rational investigation, claiming that his revolutionary society would place rational human nature and benevolence in full command at last.

Continuing advances in science kept alive the rationalist tradition. Universities and other research establishments increasingly applied science to practical affairs, linking science and technology in the popular mind under a general aura of progress. Improvements in medical pathology and the germ theory joined science and medicine, though no breakthrough therapies as yet resulted. Science was applied to agriculture, with Germany and then the United States in the lead, through studies of seed yields and chemical fertilizers.

The great advance in theoretical science came in biology, with publication of Charles Darwin's theory of evolution in 1859. On the basis of careful observation, Darwin argued that all living species had evolved into their present form through the ability to adapt in a struggle for survival. Biological development could be scientifically understood as a process taking place over time, with some animal and plant species disappearing and others evolving from earlier forms. Darwin's ideas clashed with traditional beliefs that God had fashioned humankind as part of initial creation, and the resultant debate further weakened the intellectual hold of religion. Darwin's advance also created a more complex picture of nature than Newton's simple physical laws had suggested. Nature now worked through random struggle, and people were seen as animals with large brains, not as supremely rational. The theory of evolution confirmed the link between science and advancement of knowledge, and Darwin's theory was in fact compatible with a continued belief in progress.

Developments in physics continued as well, with work on electromagnetic behavior and then, around 1900, increasing knowledge of the behavior of the atom and its major components. New theories arose, based on complex mathematics, to explain the behavior of planetary motion and the movement of electrical particles, where Newtonian laws seemed too simple. After 1900 Albert Einstein's theory of relativity formalized this new work by adding time as a factor in physical measurement. Again, science seemed to be steadily advancing in its grasp of the physical universe, though it was also important to note that its complexity now surpassed the grasp even of educated laypeople.

The social sciences also continued to advance, on the basis of observation, experiment, and rationalist theorizing. Great efforts went into compilations of statistical data concerning populations, economic patterns, and health conditions. Sheer empirical knowledge about human affairs had never been more extensive. At the level of theory, leading economists tried to explain business cycles and the causes of poverty, and social psychologists studied the behavior of crowds. Toward the end of the 19th century the Viennese physician Sigmund Freud began to develop his theories of the workings of the human unconscious, arguing that much behavior is determined by impulses but that emotional problems can be relieved if they are brought into the light of rational discussion. Social scientists were thus complicating the traditional Enlightenment view of human nature by studying the animal impulses and unconscious strivings of human beings. Still, they continued to rely on standard scientific methods in their work, believing that human behavior can be described in rational categories; most social scientists asserted that ultimately human reason would prevail. Social scientists claimed that personal

Impressionists sought to escape literal representation, favoring visual impressions of natural settings. This painting, *On the Seine at Bennecourt*, was completed by Claude Monet (1868) as the experimental style was getting under way.

and social problems alike could be reduced through knowledge and logical planning, and indeed the role of social science experts in advising governments and even individual families increased steadily.

The development of modern artistic styles brought continual innovation into literature and art. This linked art to other facets of Western society where change and novelty were the name of the game, but it distressed many people who hoped that art would confirm traditional values. Artists sought to portray passions and alternative versions of reality rather than to confirm established styles. Poetry did not have to rhyme; drama did not necessarily need plot; painting could be evocative, even abstract (for literal portrayals, painters could now argue, use a camera). Each generation of artists proved more defiant than the last. After 1900 the new styles began to have an international influence, but they also pulled into the Western experience stylistic lessons from African and East Asian art, newly accessible as a result of growing cultural links.

Within the West itself, a split between rationalists and most artists ensured continued debate about the nature of truth. The debate had institutional implications: Most scientists and social scientists by 1900 worked in or around growing research universities, whereas artists often had no set institutional apparatus. Scientists were viewed as bastions of progress, as an essential part of industrial society, whereas artists might be seen as dangerous experimenters or immoral vagabonds. Despite the imbalance, the modern art impulse continued to expand, which meant that many creative Westerners required a vision different from that of the established order and that elements of a wider public also wanted an outlet for expressing some of the confusion of modern life and the human personality.

INDUSTRIALIZATION AND THE RISE OF THE UNITED STATES TO GLOBAL POWER

Although it began as a settler society and colony of Great Britain, the United States shared many key patterns with the states of western Europe in the last half of the 19th century. This offshoot of Europe had coalesced as a nation at the end of the 1700s, nearly a century before Italy or Germany. But the United States, increasingly divided through the early decades of the 19th century, was torn asunder by the long and bloody Civil War that raged between 1861 and 1865. The forced unification that resulted from the North's victory and the great expansion of industrialization that was both fed by and followed the conflict established the foundations of U.S. global power. In contrast to the new nations of Latin America, which had won their independence in the early decades of the 19th century, the United States joined the small club of Western industrial nations. In the decades that led into the 20th century the United States also became an expansive imperial power in its own right—first within the North American continent and Western hemisphere and by the 1890s across the Pacific Ocean as well.

Despite important parallels with its western European counterparts, in the late 19th century the United States also shared key patterns with other settler societies, such as Canada and Australia. Though only the United States colonized overseas, the Americans, like the Australians, Canadians, Afrikaners, and New Zealanders, expanded steadily within the region they had originally settled. Like other settlement colonies, the United States received millions of immigrants from Europe, particularly in the last decades of the century. As the population of areas occupied in the 17th and 18th centuries increased due to immigration and natural increase, more and more settlers pushed into the fertile and vast interior of North America to farm, mine, and raise livestock. The Native American inhabitants of these areas were more numerous, better organized, and more able to wage wars of resistance to pioneer incursions than were their counterparts in Australia or Canada. But in the decades after the end of the Civil War, when westward expansion became the focus of growth in the industrializing U.S. republic, the Amerindian peoples were defeated and dispossessed, and the survivors were increasingly confined to enclaves, or reservations, clearly set off from the areas of white settlement.

Until World War I the great powers of western Europe rarely treated the United States as a major player in global diplomacy. The United States had a colonial empire, but in the eyes of most European statesmen its possessions were little more than clusters of islands that none of the other powers chose to claim. Despite its rather large and growing population, the United States had, except in the period of the Civil War, only a tiny standing army that, by European standards, appeared to be ill-trained and equipped and poorly led. Europeans tended to view Americans as unruly and excessively violence-prone country bumpkins—a vision that was enhanced by books and later photographs from the "Wild West." These stereotypes were also reinforced by U.S. writers and artists, such as Henry James and James McNeill Whistler, who sought inspiration in London, Paris, and other centers of European culture rather than

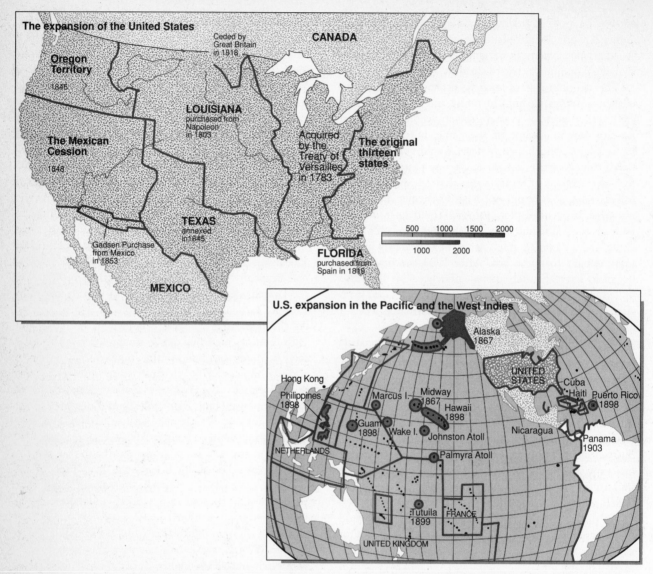

Continental and Overseas Expansion of the U.S. Republic in the 19th and Early 20th Centuries

in New York or Boston and sometimes elected to become expatriate citizens of European countries. But the remarkable inventiveness of the U.S. people, industrialization, mass education, and population growth, combined with the seemingly inexhaustible resources of the North American continent, led to a stunning increase in the wealth and potential power of the United States during the last decades of the 19th century. Thus decades before the United States was widely acknowledged as a great power in the World War I era, it had generated the potential to become one of the dominant forces in 20th-century global history.

ANALYSIS

THE UNITED STATES IN WORLD HISTORY

World history surveys often have some problems in integrating the United States, after some coverage of colonial origins as part of Western explorations and trade. World history already offers a full menu. U.S. students always take some separate U.S. history courses. So why not simplify life and leave the United States out of world surveys?

This approach gains added support from the fact that until the late 19th century the United States, relatively isolated save for the arrival of immigrants, was not particularly important in the larger stream of world history. American preoccupation lay in internal development, including westward expansion. This brought clashes with Mexico, an important foretaste of the rebalancing in power between the United States and Latin America. Westward expansion also brought some posturing against European nations tempted to interfere in the Western hemisphere. The Monroe Doctrine (1820) warned against meddling in Latin America. In fact it was British policy and naval power that kept the hemisphere largely free from new colonialism.

The United States counted for little in world diplomacy. The nation's population, though growing, was small. Its economy, though developing, exported little until the great surge of agricultural exports followed by an industrial outflow in the 1870s and 1880s. The United States was a debtor nation, depending on loans from European banks for much of its development until 1914. The nation did play an important role in receiving European immigrants, just as it earlier had affected African history through its role in the slave trade. And the nation symbolized, especially to some Europeans, a land of freedom and prosperity; revolutionaries in 1848, for example, invoked American institutions, just as Latin American independence fighters had done around 1820. But although the United States depended on world currents of immigration, loans, and culture, it had yet to contribute much in detail.

By the end of the 19th century the tentativeness and isolation of the United States in world affairs, though they still affected U.S. perceptions in promoting a belief that the nation could be shielded from international involvements, had really passed. U.S. agriculture poured goods into the markets of Europe. U.S. industry was rising, along with that of Germany, to the top of world output rankings. The United States had clearly become, along with western Europe, part of the dominant economic core in world trade. U.S. naval power led to the acquisition of important colonies in Asia and the West Indies. As it gained in international impact, the United States, while retaining some of its earlier image as a revolutionary new nation, became increasingly similar to major western European powers in defending existing world power alignments.

Since the international importance of the United States did grow, leaving the nation out of world history until the late 19th century risks missing significant early patterns. But building U.S. history in, even after 1870, raises some conceptual as well as practical problems.

There is a legitimate historical question about whether to treat the United States as a separate civilization (along, perhaps, with Canada and other places that mixed dominant Western settlement with frontier conditions). Latin America, because of the peculiarities of its colonial experience, its ongoing position in the world economy, and above all its blending of European, Indian, and African influences, cannot be subsumed as part of an expanding Western civilization. Does the same hold true for the United States?

Because the United States is so often treated separately in history courses, there is a ready assumption of American uniqueness. The United States had purer diplomatic motives than did western Europe—look at the idealism of Woodrow Wilson. It had its own cultural movements, such as the religious "great awakening" of the 18th century or transcendentalism in the 19th. The United States had the unique experience of wave after wave of immigrants reaching its shores, contributing great cultural diversity but also promoting considerable cultural and social integration under the banners of "Americanization." Many of these assumptions of uniqueness are mere reflexes, not supported by serious comparative study. There is, however, a more careful school of historians who argue for American *exceptionalism*—that is, the United States as its own civilization, not part of larger Western patterns. American exceptionalism need not contend that the United States was immune from contact with western Europe, which would be ridiculous, but it argues that this contact was incidental to the larger development of the United States on its own terms.

American exceptionalists can point to a number of factors that caused the development of a separate U.S. civilization. The Atlantic colonies gained political and cultural characteristics in relative isolation—they were, among other things, unusually democratic (among white males) compared to Europe at the time. Though colonial immigrants often intended to duplicate European styles of life, the vastness and wealth of the new land quickly forced changes. As a result U.S. families gave greater voice to women and children, and abundant land created a class of independent farmers rather than a traditionalist peasantry with its tight-knit villages. Even after the colonial era, distinctive institutions, created by the successful revolution and its federal Constitution, continued to shape a political life different from that of western Europe. The frontier, which lasted until the 1890s and had cultural impact even beyond that date, continued to make Americans unusually mobile and restless, while draining off some of the social grievances that arose in western Europe.

Distinctive causes, furthermore, produced distinctive results. There is no question that the United States, into the 20th century, had a different agricultural setup from that of western Europe. American politics—with the huge exception of the Civil War—emphasized relatively small disagreements between two major political parties, with third-party movements typically pulled into the mainstream rather quickly. There was less political fragmentation and extremism than in western Europe and more stability (some would add boredom). No strong socialist movement took shape. Religion was more important in U.S. than in European life by the later 19th century. Religion served immigrants as a badge of identity and helped all Americans a retain some sense of moorings as they built new society. The absence of established churches in the United States kept religion out of politics, in contrast to Europe, where churches got caught up in more general attacks on the political establishment.

The American exceptionalist argument often appeals particularly to things Americans like to believe about themselves—more religious, less socialistic, full of the competence that came from taming a frontier—but it must embrace some less savory distinctiveness as well. The existence of slavery, and then the racist attitudes and institutions that arose following its abolition, created ongoing issues in American life that had no direct counterpart in western Europe. Europe, correspondingly, had less direct contact with African culture; jazz was one of the key products of this aspect of U.S. life.

The exceptionalist argument is powerful, particularly because Americans (and Europeans) are normally schooled to think of the U.S. history as a largely separate line of development. Yet from a world history standpoint, the United States must be seen also, and perhaps primarily, as an offshoot of Western civilization. The colonial experience showed the powerful impact of Western political ideas, culture, and even family styles. U.S. history in the 19th century followed patterns common in western Europe. The development of parliamentary life and the spread of democracy, though unusually early in the United States, fits a larger Western trajectory. U.S. industrialization was a direct offshoot of Europe and followed a basically common dynamic. U.S. intellectuals kept in close contact with European developments, and there were few purely American styles. Conditions for women and wider patterns of family life, in areas

such as birth control or disciplining children, were similar on both sides of the North Atlantic, which shows that the United States not only imitated western Europe but also paralleled it.

Because the United States was freer from peasant and aristocratic traditions, in some important cases it pioneered developments that would soon surface in western Europe. This was true to an extent in politics; it was true in the development of mass consumer culture and mass media (for example, the popular press and popular films). In these areas the United States can be seen not as distinctive to the point of forming a separate civilization but as anticipating some developments that would become common in Western civilization in part because of American example.

American exceptions remain—the Civil War and racial issues, the absence of serious socialism (but not of trade unionism and bitter labor strife, quite similar to western European patterns), and the importance of religion. American distinctiveness remains in another respect: The United States was rising to world power just as key European nations, notably Britain, began to decline. The trajectory of U.S. history is somewhat different from that of western Europe, and the 20th century revealed growing U.S. ability to play power politics in western Europe itself. Just as American exceptionalists must admit special Western influences, so those who argue the United States as part of the West must work in special features and dynamics.

Although the shared Western experience provides the most accurate framework, given not only mutual influence but also so many common impulses, the main point is to analyze American history in careful, comparative terms as part of removing the nation's history from the isolation in which it is so often taught and viewed.

There is, finally, one other vantage point, not definitive but suggestive, that uses the world history framework in the form of analogy. The United States here is Rome compared to western Europe's Greece. Like classical Greece, western Europe produced the basic cultural creativity of the civilization and its first expansion (the Atlantic, of course, replaced the Mediterranean). Like Greece, western Europe could never really unite, and its empires were fragile as a result. Like Rome, the United States went through a republican period in considerable isolation, full of stern virtue and the strengths of a solid farming community. It initially feared Western culture as corrupting. But as the United States gained power, like Rome, its initial political and social institutions gave way to a more powerful state, larger armies, and huge corporations (the equivalent of Rome's great estates). American power, like Roman, soon eclipsed the power of the civilization's source. Yet the United States never matched Europe's cultural creativity; its strength lay in highways, stadia, organizational ability, and brash self-confidence. Here, then, in analogy, is a restatement of American participation in Western history, as well as of a distinctive American role. Is the analogy useful? Does it suggest the same last chapter: an American collapse that will affect the whole of Western civilization save, perhaps, for a "third Rome" somewhere else?

Questions: Which argument has the greater strength in describing 19th-century history: the United States as a separate civilization or the United States as part of the West? Have the United States and western Europe become more or less similar in the 20th century? Why? 🟤

THE FIRST NON-EUROPEAN INDUSTRIAL REVOLUTION

Along with Germany, U.S. industrialization formed the great economic success story in world history in the last half of the 19th century. U.S. industrial growth began in the 1820s, with the imports of technological systems from Britain. U.S. inventors contributed significantly to the industrialization process through such achievements at the mechanical gin for removing seeds from cotton fiber and the major strides in devising the system of interchangeable parts. But the United States remained dependent on European technological advances throughout the 19th century—British and French at first, then German and Swedish in such industries as chemicals. U.S. business was quick to imitate; U.S. locomotive construction began just a year after the first British model reached the United States. Although only local lines were laid before 1830, 3000 miles of track were set out in the following decade, mainly in the Northeast, and major interregional lines were launched by the 1840s, with the usual result of directly increasing demand in heavy industry while facilitating other industrial operations. Extensive canal building also contributed to the burgeoning process.

Textile factories formed the core of initial U.S. factory industry, as factory towns spread out in New England, using both water and steam power. But there were also advances in machine building, printing, and other manufacturing sectors. The invention of the sewing machine in the 1840s began a transformation of clothing manufacture from handwork to faster-paced mechanized output, not only in New England but also in midwestern factory centers such as Cincinnati, which by 1840 was the nation's third largest industrial city.

The first phase of U.S. industrialization increased the amount of manufactured goods in circulation and encouraged the further development of market specialization in other areas, such as agriculture, even as the bulk of the nation's economy remained nonindustrial. The process was also marked by relatively favorable labor

Skyscrapers, the giant buildings that have dominated the urban skylines of the 20th century, were pioneered in the U.S. midwestern metropolis of Chicago, not in London, Paris, or New York. This photo of the Carson, Pirie, Scott building under construction gives a sense of the dramatic increase in scale that the skyscraper represented.

conditions. Workers were in short supply, and recruitment required paying relatively high wages. Many women were drawn into the factories, expecting to put in a few years of work before returning, with a nest egg, to a farm family. Skilled male workers were also relatively well treated. They also, unlike their counterparts in Europe, had the vote, which encouraged their sense of connection to the larger society. Conditions began to worsen in the 1830s, provoking a number of labor strikes; then in the 1840s growing numbers of immigrants, particularly Irish, fed the urban labor force, and standards of living deteriorated in many factory centers.

The second phase of U.S. industrialization took off with the expansion of war industries during the Civil War. American arms manufacturers extended their operations, beginning a tradition of extensive arms sales abroad, when the domestic market shrank after 1865. Development of intercontinental rail links spurred industrial growth on another front. Railroad companies were in private hands and pioneered in a number of aspects of big business in the American context: huge capital investments, a large labor force, and attempts to ensure regional monopolies over service.

Industrialization in the United States obviously displayed much the same big-business surge that characterized Germany in the same decades. Investment banks helped coordinate the growth of multifaceted companies. As in Germany also, the sheer speed of the U.S. industrial explosion altered the world's economic context with dizzying rapidity. Indeed, it was through industrial expansion that the United States began to make an independent mark in world history by the 1870s. Several U.S. companies began establishing branches abroad; two American firms, in sewing machines and agricultural equipment, respectively, were the largest industrial enterprises in Russia by 1900. More than in Germany, much U.S. public opinion remained committed to a rhetoric of free enterprise, even as big business grew and the government actively contributed to industrial expansion through not only grants of land but also high protective tariffs.

Larger and more sophisticated organization meant, finally, the spread of giant corporations—again a trend already intrinsic to industrial economies by the 1880s but extended steadily thereafter. Hundreds of new corporations formed each year in France, the United States, and other countries. Some of the companies were small, but they had, through the sales of shares to the public, considerable resources for expansion. Huge firms strengthened their hold in heavy industry and chemicals.

Newer industrial sectors, such as the burgeoning automobile industry, initially opened the way for newer, small-scale industrialists.

INDUSTRIALIZATION AND THE TRANSFORMATION OF U.S. SOCIETY

As in western Europe, the process of industrialization left its mark on virtually all aspects of U.S. life. New classes emerged; others increased in numbers and status or declined, some virtually disappearing. Gender roles and the composition of the household were altered, particularly in urban areas, and the balance between the proportion of the population engaged in agriculture and industry shifted dramatically in favor of the latter. In addition, the degree to which different geographical areas within the United States were industrialized had vital bearing on the resolution of long-standing interstate disputes, most critically the impasse between North and South over free versus slave labor, which was broken only by nearly a half decade of bloody civil war. Through much of the last half of the 19th century, industrialization also fueled U.S. expansion westward and eventually overseas across the Pacific Ocean.

The growth of the factory labor force during the Industrial Revolution provided the most dynamic change in social composition. The numbers of urban workers and miners expanded more quickly than those of any other social group. This situation began to change as the industrial economy matured after the 1880s. The factory labor force continued to expand, but its rate of growth was surpassed by an essentially new service sector.

The service sector emerged from the expansion of commerce and the growth of business and government bureaucracy—a handmaiden to expanding levels of organization. Accelerating industrial output necessitated new sales outlets, and the department store, already introduced during the Industrial Revolution, was an obvious response. With the advent of the typewriter, the female secretary began to come into her own. Growing banks needed tellers. Hotels for business travelers or vacationers needed staff. A growing white-collar work force serviced a variety of commercial establishments and leisure facilities.

Large organizations needed secretaries, file clerks, and low-level managers. Technology also spurred new opportunities; the occupation of telephone operator was added to the list of available jobs by the later 19th century. The steady growth of government functions led to increased numbers of not only clerks but also teachers, factory inspectors, and police officers. These workers varied in status somewhat, but they shared with other lower-middle-class workers a dependence on wage earnings, avoidance of outright manual labor, and a lack of high, professional standing. The growth in hospitals, whether public or private, produced another set of employees, in addition to professional doctors, as nurses and medical technicians formed a growing service sector of their own.

These developments set the stage for the redefinition of the relationship between leisure and industrial life. Leisure opportunities, fiercely reduced during the Industrial Revolution, began to explode. Popular theater emerged—called music hall in Britain and vaudeville in the United States—and the mixture of song and comedy helped lead directly to the new motion picture industry after 1900. Professional sports teams drew huge crowds to football and baseball, rather than rugby or soccer, games in the maverick United States. The new leisure activities organized masses of people for rather standardized commercial fare. They provided escape from the daily routine, but in some versions (notably sports) they also replicated features of industrial work, such as rules, speed consciousness, and specialization. Much of the

new leisure also depended on industrial technology, from the tram lines that took the urban masses to huge concrete and metal stadia to the vulcanized rubber balls that could be mass produced from the 1840s onward. Clearly, an industrial revolution in leisure was occurring but a bit later than the Industrial Revolution itself.

Wider consumer values were not new; they had surfaced in the 18th century, around the new interests in stylish clothing that had helped trigger the Industrial Revolution in the first place. By the late 19th century, however, consumerism could be more widely indulged, particularly in the urban areas of the United States. New products, such as bicycles—an 1880s fad—and then automobiles, created more expensive consumer items than had ever before sold widely. Interests in soaps and cosmetics reflected new interest in personal hygiene and appearance. For some people consumerism involved more than money to spend. It came to express deep personal impulses and identities, in a society where work conveyed less meaning than was traditionally the case. A growing advertising industry—another service sector outcropping—worked to encourage and channel impulse, to make people care deeply about the things they could acquire or aspire to acquire.

In the decades leading up to 1900 men and women at every class level were enthusiastic about spectator sports, as this 1887 engraving of a baseball game in progress at the Polo Grounds in New York illustrates.

U.S. workers showed less interest than their European counterparts in socialism, especially its revolutionary variants, such as Marxism. Nonetheless, in the late 19th century Americans participated actively in industrial campaigns and protest movements similar to those in Europe. These were peak decades of factory conflict. Strike rates rose steadily, with strikes focusing on improving wages and hours. Workers also showed an increasing ability to articulate progressive demands, asking for a shorter working day and other conditions they were convinced they deserved but that had not existed before. Workers were increasingly represented by labor unions, such as the American Federation of Labor, in their struggles with factory, mine, and railway owners. In the decades that shaped U.S. entry into the 20th century, workers also derived great benefit from the spread of elementary education among both the urban and rural laboring classes and the extension of the vote to virtually the entire male population.

REGIONAL CONFLICT AND U.S. TERRITORIAL EXPANSION

Because industrialization was concentrated largely in New England and the Northeast, the transformations associated with this process exacerbated long-standing contrasts between these areas and the states to the south, where slave-plantation agriculture continued as the backbone of the economy and social order. The North eclipsed the South in wealth and productive capacity, and its intellectuals and political leaders came to see the slave labor system, which had never taken hold outside of the South, as both economically unproductive and morally repugnant. These issues in turn became entangled in yet another enduring dispute between the northern and southern states over states' rights versus the power of the national government. By the late 1850s these quarrels had thoroughly polarized opinion in all sections of the country along proslavery and abolitionist lines. The passionate advocacy of the champions of each position led to sporadic violence and then in early 1861 to the secession of the states of the slave-holding South. President Lincoln's determination to resist the breakup of the republic by force of arms made a long and costly Civil War inevitable.

The armies of the South were exceedingly well led, and their soldiers fought with great courage and tenacity. But the North's advantages of a much larger population and especially its much higher level of industrialization proved decisive in a war that dragged on for nearly five years and left much of the South devastated. The North's victory sealed the triumph of free, wage labor over slave, but the punitive reconstruction policies followed by Lincoln's successors left the forced union still far from united. The economic plight of the freed slaves, most of whom remained in the South, continued. Racism persisted both in the South, where it was institutionalized through a system of segregation, and in the North, were slaves were free but clearly second-class citizens.

The end of the war also ushered in a new surge of growth and territorial expansion. War production fed industrial growth and laid the basis for the rise of giant corporations, the scarcely regulated fortune seeking of the "robber barons," and the ongoing struggles of the laboring classes for fair wages and decent working conditions. The enhanced energies of the nation, fed by a literal flood of immigrants from Europe, were also directed to settling and developing the interior of the vast North American continent. The greatly heightened influx of settlers into the Great Plains led to an intensification of the violent resistance of the Amerindian peoples who had earlier spread into these areas. Indian wars were a prominent feature of the last decades of the late 19th century. Though mobile and skilled at war, the Plains peoples were ultimately no match for the far more numerous advancing pioneers, backed by the repeating rifles and Gatling guns of the U.S. military. With the catastrophic slaughter of the buffalo herds, on which the Plains Indians' material culture depended, their capacity and will to resist were undermined. By the first years of the 20th century, most of the Amerindians had been confined to reservations. They appeared to be doomed to follow other "aboriginal" peoples into the state of extinction that contemporary social Darwinist thinkers judged inevitable for such "primitive" peoples throughout the globe.

U.S. westward expansion was complemented by the increasing role that the reunified republic was playing in the outside world. Before the Civil War, the United States had frequently intervened in the affairs of its neighbors in North and South America and had occasionally—most dramatically in Perry's "opening" of Japan in the 1850s—effected major changes in the international arena. In the last decades of the 19th century, however, U.S. leaders strove to win the nation's entrance into the small club of world powers. Projecting its power mainly through naval strength, the United States vied

Custer's last stand at the Battle of the Little Bighorn is graphically depicted in this remarkable painting of the engagement by a Native American artist, Amos Badheart Bull.

The slaughter of the massive buffalo herds of the North American Great Plains was at times systematically pursued to undermine the basis of the societies of Native Americans that lived in this contested area. Here a hapless buffalo herd is massacred from the comfort of railway cars.

with Great Britain to dominate both the economic and political life of the Latin American republics; joined the colonial powers with the seizure of island possessions, such as Hawaii, Puerto Rico, and the Philippines; and strove to play the role of honest broker in hotly disputed areas, such as China. Along with the emergence of Germany and Japan, America's rise to Great Power status proved to be one of the major forces in shaping global history throughout the 20th century.

DIPLOMATIC TENSIONS AMONG THE WESTERN POWERS

Western expansion had its limits, however, and these limits were beginning to tell on the Western heartland by 1900. The rise of new parts of the Western world, particularly the growing strength and assertiveness of the United States, added to the sense of national competition. Along with Germany's new-found muscle, the U.S.

presence on the world diplomatic scene made rivalries for empire and trade more intense.

More important still at this point was the fact that by 1900 there were few parts of the world available for Western seizure. Latin America was independent but under extensive U.S. influence, so that a new intrusion of colonialism was impossible. Africa was almost entirely carved up. The few final colonies taken after 1900—Morocco by France and Tripoli (Libya) by Italy—caused great diplomatic furor on the part of other colonial powers worried about the balance of force on that continent. China and the Middle East were technically independent but were in fact crisscrossed by rivalries among the Western powers and Russia (and in China's case, Japan). No agreement was possible on further takeovers.

Yet for several decades the growth of empire had served as a vital outlet for Western diplomatic and military energies. The tensions among the Western nation-states had escalated dangerously after the unifications of Italy and Germany. Bismarck, the architect of German unity, cleverly devised an alliance system during the 1870s and 1880s that neutralized France, a "natural enemy" that feared the growing power of the German neighbor and resented the loss of territories after the war in 1870–1871. Germany allied directly with Austria and Italy and had had a separate understanding with Russia. This intricate alliance system was in fact preserved by the interest key nations took in overseas expansion. France worried less about the rivalry with Germany than about gaining new colonies in Africa and Indochina, and Germany entered the imperialist game by seizures in Africa and East Asia. Britain remained preoccupied with colonial expansion.

Imperialist expansion, however, fed the sense of rivalry among key nation-states. Britain, in particular, grew worried about Germany's overseas drive, supplemented after 1890 by the construction of a large navy. Economic competition between a surging Germany and a lagging Britain added fuel to the fire. France, eager to escape the Bismarck-engineered isolation, was willing to play down traditional rivalries with Britain. The French also took the opportunity to ally with Russia, when after 1890 Germany dropped this particular alliance because of Russian-Austrian enmity.

By 1907 most major European nations were paired off in two alliance systems: Germany, Austria-Hungary, and Italy formed the Triple Alliance, while Britain, Russia, and France constituted the newer Triple Entente.

Three against three seemed fair, but in fact Germany grew increasingly concerned about facing potential enemies to both the east (Russia) and west (France). All the powers steadily built up their military arsenals in what turned out to be the first of several arms races in the 20th century. All powers save Britain had instituted peacetime military conscription to provide large armies and even larger trained reserves. Artillery levels and naval forces built steadily—the addition of a new kind of battleship, the Dreadnought, to naval arsenals was a key escalation—while discussions about reducing armament levels got nowhere.

Furthermore, each alliance system was dependent on an unstable partner. Russia suffered a revolution in 1905, and its allies worried that any further diplomatic setbacks might paralyze the eastern giant. Austria-Hungary was plagued by nationalities disputes, particularly by minority Slavic groups; German leaders fretted that a diplomatic setback might bring chaos. Both Austria and Russia were heavily involved, finally, in maneuverings in the Balkans—the final piece in what became a nightmare puzzle.

Small Balkan nations had won independence from the Ottoman Empire during the 19th century; as Turkish power declined, local nationalism rose, and Russian support for its Slavic neighbors paid off. But the nations were intensely hostile to each other. Furthermore, Balkan nationalism threatened Austria, which had a large southern Slav population. Russia and Austria nearly came to blows on several occasions over Balkan issues, for Austria felt that it must keep the Slavs in line, whereas Russia looked to the Balkans as a place where it might pick up needed diplomatic prestige. Then in 1912 and 1913 the Balkan nations engaged in two internal wars, which led to territorial gains for several states but satisfied no one. Serbia, particularly, which bordered Austria to the south, had hoped for greater gains. At the same time, Austria grew nervous over the gains Serbia had achieved. In 1914 a Serbian nationalist assassinated an Austrian archduke on behalf of Serbian claims. Austria vowed to punish Serbia. Russia rushed to the defense of Serbia and mobilized its troops against Austria. Germany, worried about Austria and also eager to be able to strike against France before Russia's cumbersome mobilization was complete, called up its reserves and then declared war on August I. Britain hesitated briefly, then joined its allies. World War I had begun, and with it came a host of new problems for Western society.

The arms race began in earnest in the late 1890s. The massive "Dreadnought" class of battleship, first launched in 1906, was developed in Britain but provoked a rapid German buildup in response.

CONCLUSION

DIPLOMACY AND SOCIETY

The tensions that spiraled into major war are not easy to explain. Diplomatic maneuverings can seem quite remote from the central concerns of most people, if only because key decisions—for example, with whom to ally—are made by a specialist elite. Even as the West became more democratic, few ordinary people placed foreign affairs high on their election agendas.

The West had long been characterized by political divisions and rivalries. By comparison with some other civilizations, this was an endemic weakness of the Western political system. In a sense what happened in the first phase of the 20th century was that the nation-state system got out of hand, encouraged by the absence of serious challenge from any other civilizations. The details of this development, involving the rise of Germany and the new tensions in the Balkans, are obviously important, but the link with a longer-term Western problem area should not be forgotten.

At the same time, the diplomatic escalation also had some links with the strains of Western society under the impact of industrialization. Obviously the fact that modern war proved so horrible, as had already been suggested in the U.S. Civil War, stemmed directly from the destructive power of modern factory-produced weaponry, from massive new guns and ships to steady improvements in the explosive power of chemical combinations. The causes of war, also, related to industrial patterns.

Most obviously, established leadership in the West continued to worry about social protest and the growing visibility of the masses. Leaders tended as a result to seek diplomatic successes in order to distract. This procedure worked nicely for a few decades when imperialist gains came easily. But then it proved a straitjacket. German officials around 1914, fearful of the power of the socialists, wondered if war would not aid national unity; British leaders, beset by feminist as well as labor unrest, failed to think through their own diplomatic options. Leaders also depended on military buildups for economic purposes. Modern industry, pressed to sell the soaring output of its factories, found naval purchases and army equipment a vital supplement.

The masses themselves had some role to play. Though some groups, particularly in the socialist camp, were hostile to the alliance system and to imperialism, many workers and clerks found the diplomatic successes of their nations exciting. In an increasingly disciplined and organized society, with work frequently routine if not downright boring, the idea of violence and energy, even of war, could find appeal. Mass newspapers that fanned nationalist pride with stories of conquest and tales of the evils of rival nations helped shape this belligerent popular culture.

The consolidation of industrial society in the West, in other words, had continued to generate strain at various levels. Consolidation meant more powerful armies and governments, a more potent industrial machine. It also meant continued social frictions and an ongoing tug of war between rational restraint and a desire to break out, to dare something wild.

Thus, just a few years after celebrating a century of material progress and relative peace, ordinary Europeans went to war almost gaily in 1914. Troops departed for the front, convinced that war would be exciting with quick victories, their departure hailed by enthusiastic civilians who draped their trains with flowers. Four years later almost everyone agreed that war had been unmitigated hell. The complexities of industrial society were such, however, that war's advent seemed almost a welcome breath of the unexpected, a chance to get away from the disciplined stability of everyday life.

FURTHER READINGS

Two excellent studies survey Europe's industrial revolution: Sidney Pollard's *Peaceful Conquest: The Industrialization of Europe* (1981) and David Landes's *The Unbound Prometheus: Technological Change and Industrial Development in Western Europe from 1700 to the Present* (1969). See also Phyllis Dean's *The First Industrial Revolution* (1980), on Britain. On the demographic experience, see Thomas McKeown's *The Modern Rise of Population* (1977).

Major developments concerning women and the family are covered in Louise Tilly and Joan Scott's *Women, Work and Family* (1978) and Steven Mintz and Susan Kellogg's *Domestic Revolutions: A Social History of American Family Life* (1989). See also R. Evans's *The Feminists: Women's Emancipation in Europe, America and Australia* (1979). An important age group is treated in John Gillis's *Youth and History* (1981).

For an overview on social change, see Peter Stearns and Herrick Chapman's *European Society in Upheaval* (1991). On labor history, see Michael Hanagan's *The Logic of Solidarity* (1981) and Albert Lindemann's *History of European Socialism* (1983). Eugen Weber's *Peasants into Frenchmen: The Modernization of Rural France* (1976) and Harvey Graff, ed., *Literacy and Social Development in the West* (1982) deal with important special topics.

On political and cultural history, see Gordon Wright's *France in Modern Times* (1981), Gordon Craig's *Germany, 1866–1945* (1978), and Louis Snyder's *Roots of German Nationalism* (1978). J. H. Randall's *The Making of the Modern Mind* (1976) is a useful survey; see also O. Chadwick's *The Secularization of the European Mind in the Nineteenth Century* (1976). On major diplomatic developments, see D. K. Fieldhouse's *Economics and Empire, 1830–1914* (1970) and David Kaiser's *Politics and War: European Conflict from Philip II to Hitler* (1990).

Russia

1860s–1870s Alexander II reforms

1861 Russian eman-
cipation of serfs

1854–1856 Crimean War

1856 Romania gains virtual independence

1867 Russia sells Alaska to U.S.

1865–1876 Russian conquests in central Asia

Japan

1860–1868 Civil strife

1870–1940 Population growth

1870 Ministry of Industry established

1853 Perry expedition to Edo Bay

1868–1912 Meiji period

1872 Universal military service
established

1854 Follow-up American
and British fleet visits

1867 Mutsuhito, emperor of Japan

Extending the Industrial Core: The Emergence of Russia and Japan as 20th-Century Powers

INTRODUCTION.   For most areas of the world in the 19th century, including the most populous societies, Western industrialization meant increasing Western economic and military pressure in the form of heightened imperialism. But in two significant exceptions to this pattern Western pressure resulted in substantial reform programs, including early industrialization. These responses, in Russia and Japan, did not produce new versions of Western society—in this the two nations differed markedly from the United States or Australia, for they already had well-established prior cultures. Their responses did, however, trigger new dynamism, bringing Russia and Japan into the network of expanding, aggressive nations by the end of the 19th century.

Russia and Japan had very little in common prior to the late 19th century. Japan had spent several centuries in virtual isolation from the rest of the world. It had an ongoing feudal tradition, though a centralized government, the Tokugawa shogunate, had imposed considerable order during the 17th and 18th centuries by pacifying the samurai warrior class. Russia featured a much more strongly centralized regime under the tsar, or emperor. It had been expanding territorially into Siberia, Central Asia, and eastern Europe for several centuries. It had a tightly constructed system of serfdom, with forced peasant labor

---

1881–1905 Growing repression, attacks on minorities

1898 Formation of Marxist Social Democratic Party

1884–1887 New gains in central Asia

1875–1877 Russian-Ottoman war, Russia wins new territory

1904–1905 Loss in Russo-Japanese War

1884–1914 Beginnings of Russian industrialization; near-completion of trans-Siberian railway (full linkage 1916)

1914 World War I

1917 Revolution and Bolshevik victory

1878 Bulgaria gains independence

1905–1906 Revolution results in peasant reforms and duma

1892–1903 Sergey Witte, minister of finance

1881 Anarchist assassination of Alexander II

1912–1913 Balkan Wars

1889–1890 New constitution and legal code

1904–1905 Russo-Japanese War

1902 Loose alliance with Britain

1916–1918 Seizure of former German holdings in Pacific and China

1910 Annexation of Korea

1877 Final samurai rising

1894–1895 Sino-Japanese war

1912 Growing party strife in Parliament

1914 Entry to World War I

sustaining much of its agricultural production. Though less urbanized and commercial than Japan, Russia had established more extensive contacts with western Europe and by the 19th century was contributing literature and music to a common European elite culture.

Both Russia and Japan maintained reasonably vigorous governments prior to 1850, which gave them an advantage in meeting the new challenge of Western industrialization. Also, both had a tradition of successful imitation—Japan from China from the first centuries A.D., Russia from the West since the 17th century—that provided object lessons in how to borrow without losing identity. This, too, served as an important basis for response, differentiating these countries from China or the Middle East, for example, where assumptions of cultural superiority limited openness to the possibility of imitation.

Neither Russia nor Japan generated significant change during the first half of the 19th century. Russia responded to the tide of political revolution in the West by tightening tsarist controls, expanding the secret police, and imprisoning or exiling intellectuals eager to copy Western political ideas. The system of serfdom remained rigorous, with work service increased to spur grain production for export in a highly agricultural economy. The early 1800s were relatively uneventful in Japan, though the shogunate had recurrent difficulties in raising sufficient tax revenue. Most intellectual activity centered on various schools of Confucianism, urging attention to traditional values and obedience to authority. Only the so-called Dutch school, formed around translators who dealt with Dutch merchants in the port of Nagasaki (Japan's only contact with the outside world), pushed for a cultural reorientation, calling for attention to the scientific and medical advances that were occurring in the West.

Both Japan and Russia received a rude reminder of the cost of their stand-pat policies during the 1850s, when the imperialistic West drove home its growing superiority in power over all societies that were not industrializing—that is, over literally all the other civilizations in the world. Russia, continuing its policy of territorial expansion in central Asia, had won a war with the Turkish Ottoman Empire in 1853 and claimed a big chunk of territory in the Crimea, north of the Black Sea. Britain and France objected to these gains, wanting to advance their own interests in the Middle East and, in Britain's case, to prevent any Great Power from getting too close to its holdings in India. The ensuing Crimean War, 1854–1856, was fought literally in Russia's backyard, yet the Western nations won, forcing Russia to return most of its Crimean gains to the Turks. The Western edge was industrial: With the factories to produce modern equipment and the ships to send them expeditiously, Britain and France were able to beat back the tsarist forces. Russian leadership reluctantly concluded that the time had come for major reforms that would open the possibility for economic change.

Japan's rather rude awakening began when a U.S. fleet sailed into Tokyo Harbor in 1853 and demanded that the nation open its markets to Western goods. Other fleets followed, from Britain as well as the United States, and some violence occurred as Westerners began to enter Japan. The crisis triggered internal unrest in Japan, with some aristocrats urging that Japan do its best to keep Westerners out and other samurai arguing for major reforms that would allow Japan to retain independence through change. Fighting between the two groups broke out in 1866, with reform-minded samurai arming themselves with surplus weapons from the U.S. Civil War. The conservatives around the shogun were finally defeated, and with a restored emperor (long a symbol of legitimacy but now emerging as a political actor) Japan embarked on a major period of reform in 1868—the onset of the Meiji era, from the formal title for the new emperor, "enlightened one."

REFORMS IN RUSSIA, 1861–1914

The cornerstone of Russia's reform structure involved freeing the masses of serfs, a process necessary to make Russia's social structure more like that of the West (where a lighter manorial system had been removed some centuries before) and, above all, to increase the mobility of labor.

The final decision to emancipate the serfs, in 1861, came at roughly the same time that the United States decided to free slaves. Neither slavery nor rigorous serfdom suited the economic needs of a society seeking an independent position in Western-dominated world trade.

In some ways the emancipation of the serfs was more generous than the liberation of slaves in the Americas. Although aristocrats retained part of the land, including the most fertile holdings, the serfs got most of it—in contrast to slaves, who received their freedom but nothing else. Russian emancipation, however, was careful to preserve essential aristocratic power; the tsar was not interested in destroying the nobility, who remained his most reliable political ally and the source of most bureaucrats. Even more, emancipation was designed to retain the tight grip of the tsarist state. The serfs obtained no new political rights at a national level. They were still tied to their villages until they could pay for the land they were given—the redemption money going to the aristocrats to help preserve this class. Redemption payments added greatly to peasants' material hardship and were infuriating, for peasants thought that the land belonged to them, with no need to pay for its return. Enforcement of redemption obligations meant that many peasants could still not move freely or even sell their land, though some became more mobile. High redemption payments, in addition to state taxes that increased as Russia sought funds to build railroads and factories, kept most Russian peasants miserably poor.

Emancipation did bring change; it helped create a larger urban labor force. But it did not spur a revolution in agricultural productivity, as most peasants continued to use traditional methods on their small plots. And it did not bring contentment. Indeed, peasant uprisings became more common as hopes for a brighter future now seemed dashed by the limits of change.

To be sure, the reform movement did not end with emancipation. Alexander II introduced a host of further measures in the 1860s and early 1870s. New law codes reduced traditional punishments now that serfs were legally free in the eyes of the law (though subject to important transitional restrictions). The tsar created local political councils, the *zemstvoes*, that had a voice in regulating roads, schools, and other regional policies. Some form of local government was essential now that the nobles no longer directly ruled the peasantry. The zemstvoes gave some Russians, particularly middle-class people such as doctors and lawyers, new political experience, and they undertook important inquiries into local problems. The councils, however, had no influence on national policy; the tsar resolutely maintained his own authority and that of his extensive bureaucracy. Another important area of change was the army, where the Crimean War had shown the need for reform. The officer corps was improved through promotion by merit and a new organization of essential services. Recruitment was extended, and many peasants learned new skills, including literacy, through their military service. Some strides were made also in providing state-sponsored basic education, though schools spread unevenly.

This roadside scene depicts the poverty of a Russian peasant village in the late 19th century.

These adjustments, like emancipation itself, were important. They imitated some Western principles; the new law codes, for example, included a more humanitarian approach to punishment for crime as well as technical equality before the law. The reforms were sufficient to spur the beginnings of Russian industrialization but not to provide a stable social base for this inherently traumatic economic upheaval.

The move toward industrialization was part of the wider process of change. The tsar's government was not always in agreement over industrialization goals, with some conservatives rightly fearing the impact of economic change on the existing social and political structure. On the whole, however, state support for industrialization continued even after the reform era ended in the late 1870s. And state support was vital, for Russia lacked a preexisting middle class and substantial capital; state enterprises had to make up part of the gap, in the tradition of economic activity that went back to Peter the Great.

The first step toward industrialization came with railroads, a clear necessity for military and political coordination as well as economic development in the vast land. Russia began to create an extensive railroad network in the 1870s. The establishment of the trans-Siberian railroad, which connected European Russia with the Pacific, was the crowning achievement of this drive when it was substantially completed by the end of the 1880s. The railroad boom directly stimulated expansion of Russia's iron and coal sectors. Rails also allowed fuller utilization of Russia's rich holdings in both resources, for in contrast to England and Germany (and to an extent the United States) Russia lacked waterways that could do the job, as the north-south flow of rivers did not link up coal and iron deposits. Railroad development also stimulated the export of grain to the West, which now became essential to earn foreign currency needed in payment for advanced Western machinery. The railroads also opened Siberia up to new development, which in turn brought Russia into a more active and contested Asian role.

By the 1880s, when Russia's railroad network had almost quintupled compared to 1860, modern factories were beginning to spring up in Moscow, St. Petersburg, and several Polish cities, and an urban working class was growing apace. Printing factories and metalworking shops greatly expanded the skilled artisanry in the cities, while huge new works in metallurgy and textiles created a still newer, semiskilled industrial labor force recruited from the troubled countryside.

Under Count Witte, minister of finance from 1892 to 1903 and an ardent economic modernizer, the government enacted high tariffs to protect new Russian industry, improved its banking system, and encouraged Western investors to build great factories with advanced technology. Witte and others were confident that strong government controls could keep the foreigners in line rather than converting Russia into a new imperialist playground, and certainly foreign influence over basic government policy was not extensive. Although the foreign presence and foreign profit taking created resentments from workers and conservatives alike, there was some clear payoff. By 1900 Russia had surged to fourth rank in the world in steel production and was second to the United States in the newer area of petroleum production and refining. Russian textile output was also impressive. Longstanding Russian economic lags were beginning to yield though Russia's industrial revolution remained in its early stages.

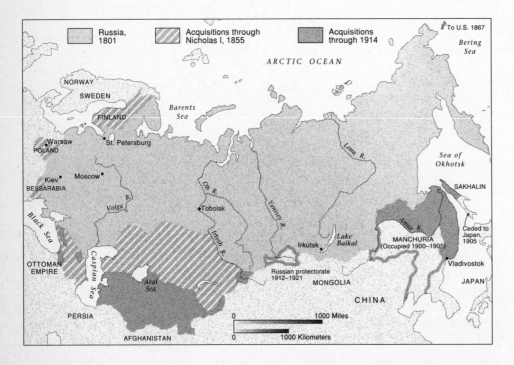

Russian Expansion, 1815–1914

Russian conservatives continued to define a special Russian tradition in contrast to Westernizing initiatives up to the 1917 revolution. Their arguments help explain why Russia avoided basic political change; their assumptions about popular support seem somewhat fanciful in light of ultimate revolution. Yet the attempt to argue for an alternative to Western forms was important not only in explaining Russian policies for several decades but also in suggesting reasons that people in various societies—including Russia itself even after 1917—might seek to avoid a strict Western model. The statement that follows, written in the shock of Alexander II's assassination in 1881, comes from a speech by a leading Slavophile, Ivan Aksakov.

DOCUMENT: RUSSIAN CONSERVATISM AND THE WEST

The Emperor is murdered; the same Emperor who was the greatest benefactor to his country, who emancipated, bestowing upon them human and civil rights, tens of millions of Russian peasants. He is murdered; not from personal vengeance, not for booty, but precisely because he is the Emperor, the crowned head, the representative, the first man of his country, that vital, single man, who personified the very essence, the whole image, the whole strength and power, of Russia. From time immemorial that power constituted the strength of the country. The attempt directed against the person of the Tsar is always directed against the whole people; but in this case the whole historical principle of the national life has been attacked, the autocratic power bestowed upon the Emperor by the country itself. Who are those who dared to bring that awful shame upon the people, and, as if by mockery, in the name of the people? . . .

Can it be anything else but the logical, extreme expression of that Westernism which, since the time of Peter the Great, demoralized both our government and our society, and has already marred all the spiritual manifestations of our national life? Not content to profit by all the riches of European thought and knowledge, we borrowed her spirit, developed by a foreign history and foreign religion. We began idolizing Europe, worshiping her gods and her idols! Who is to be blamed? Some forty years ago has not Khomiakov warned us, threatening us with Divine punishment for 'deserting all that is sacred to our hearts'? But really, what are these 'Anarchists,' 'Social Democrats,' and Revolutionists, as they call themselves? Have they the smallest particle of Russian spirit in all their aspirations and aims? Is there the slightest shade in their teachings of a protest against the real shortcomings of which Russia is suffering? Just the opposite; what they despise most is precisely the Russian people. . . .

Our peasantry, forming almost eighty percent of the whole realm, now possess land, organization, and the most complete self-government. To this very day, that fourth class is the keeper of our historical instinct, of our religion, and of the whole element of our political organism. They, and not the so-called 'Intelligentsia,' are the real supporters of our country. . . .

Who accepts the causes has also to accept their logical consequences. Who accepts the Western Constitution has also to bear the last expression of Western political life, viz., social revolution with all its manifestations.

But can such be the result of the historical thousand years' harvest of the Russian people? Its patience conquered all, every kind of misfortune, and remained, in spite of all, faithful to its civil and moral principles. Worse than all the external calamities was the moral treason of its leading class, powerful through knowledge and development. The reforms of Peter the Great weakened our memory and disabled us from understanding our own history—so very different from that of the West. Conquest is not at the bottom of our historical life, as is the case in all the Western countries. Our history begins with quite a voluntary and rational appeal to power. The same appeal was repeated much later, in 1612, and gave the foundation to the present reigning dynasty, empowered with autocracy, and nothing and nobody could induce the country to alter that shape of government. Such was the will, such was the inspiration of the national spirit.

Our history does not possess, therefore, that fundamental fact, which characterizes the political life of the Western powers of Europe, the antagonism between the people and a power imposed by conquest. That antagonism, however, is the very foundation of Western constitutionalism. It is a mere agreement; a compromise between two camps hostile to each other, mistrusting each other; a kind of treaty, surrounded with all sorts of conditions. To evade those conditions *without contradicting the letter of the agreement,* constitutes the great talent of the rulers as well as of those who are ruled. Struggle for power—that is the real sense of the political life of European countries. The foundation of their administration is a kind of mechanical apparatus; the center of power and mind, or an *unlimited power,* belongs to the majority of voices based upon the numbers of the representatives. Thus some ten voices—often bribed and bought—automatically decide the destinies of the people, forming the actual majority, in comparison of which the parliamentary majority is a few grains of sand compared to the sandy wilderness of Sahara. But that autocrat, composed of several numerical units, bears no moral responsibility before its conscience and the country, responsibility which falls heavily on the one personal representative of the supreme power.

During the First Republic the French Representative Assembly declared—quite legally as far as the form was concerned, and in the name of the people—that worship addressed to God was null, and replaced by adoration of the `Goddess of Reason'; and all that in the face of tens of millions of true believers, but of men deprived of any legal voice, and thus unable to protest at all. The same thing happened in France the other day. It is ordered now to put in all the primary schools, instead of the word God, the word *Nature*. Is this not a study illustrative of popular Western representation? What is the use of political rights which allow, in the name of liberty and law, such a revolting infraction of freedom and truth?

Such are the kinds of freedom promised to Russia by worshipers of European liberal institutions. But the instincts and the notions of freedom in the Russian people are higher and broader than in any part of the world, because they are free from the conventional and formal element, and are based on *moral truth*. They are easily traced in our self-government, the broadest of Europe, and in the largest application of the *elective element*. There was no antagonism between our Emperor and the people, as our superior power has been voluntarily recognized by the whole country.

The Russian people has not entrusted full power to a heartless, soulless, mechanical apparatus, but to the `holiest of beings'—to a man with a human soul, with a Russian heart, and a Christian conscience. The people know, and know well, the drawbacks of every human institution, but feel at the same time the power to overcome and improve them. And our former Tsars have not deceived their hopes and confidence; they held majestically and rigorously their imperial tide. . . . There was no mentioning any political rights, or supporting any kind of political doctrine. It was the regular, the natural manifestation of national life itself. Neither the people nor the autocratic Tsar ever thought themselves otherwise than in a constant moral and intellectual alliance of unity.

Questions: In what ways does Aksakov define the special Russian spirit? Why, in this judgment, are Western values inferior to Russian traditions? What kind of political system, according to this view, works best in Russia?

🕮 PROTEST AND REVOLUTION

A rising tide of unrest accompanied Russia's period of transformation. Alexander II's reforms, as well as economic change with the greater population mobility it involved, helped encourage demands by minority nationalities in the great empire. Intellectuals explored the cultural traditions of Ukrainians and other groups. This cultural nationalism could lead to political demands, particularly when state power, through military recruitment and school expansion, was beginning to increase. Nationalist beliefs were initially imported from western

Europe, but here, and elsewhere in eastern Europe, they encouraged divisive minority agitation of a sort that multinational states, such as Russia or Austria-Hungary, found very difficult to handle. Nationalist pressures were not the main problem in Russia, but in combination with other kinds of protest and given Russia's mainstream nationalist insistence on the distinctive superiorities of a Russian tradition, they did cause problems.

Social protest was more vigorous still, heightened by not only the limitations of reform but also industrialization itself. Peasant discontent was not a constant force, but it continued to burst forth. Recurrent famines regularly provoked uprising. Peasants deeply resented redemption payments and taxes and frequently attacked and burned the records that indicated what they "owed" for the land. Peasants' sense of natural justice, heightened by population pressure, also turned them against aristocratic estates.

Many educated Russians, including some aristocrats, also clamored for revolutionary change. Two strands developed. Although not extremely aggressive, many business and professional people began to seek a fuller political voice and new rights, such as greater freedom in the schools and press; they thus argued for liberal reforms. At the same time, a group of radical *intelligentsia*—a Russian term denoting articulate intellectuals as a class—became increasingly active, building on earlier intellectual discontent. This kind of intellectual alienation utilized some of the principles that had earlier disturbed intellectuals in the West, but it went deeper in the Russian case. It was the first example of a kind of intellectual radicalism, capable of motivating outright terrorism, that would characterize other societies caught in uncompleted change during the 20th century. The goals and motives of the Russian intelligentsia varied, but in general they wanted political freedom and deep social reform while maintaining a Russian culture different from that of the West, which they saw as hopelessly plutocratic and materialist. Their radicalism may have stemmed from the demanding task they set themselves: simultaneously to attack key Russian institutions while building a new society that would not reproduce the injustices and crippling limitations of the Western world.

Not surprisingly, the recurrent waves of violent protest sponsored by radical intellectuals and students merely strengthened the tsarist regime's resolve to avoid further political change, in what became a vicious circle in 19th-century Russian politics. By the late 1870s Alexander II was retreating from his reform interest,

fearing that change was getting out of hand. Censorship of newspapers and political meetings tightened; many dissidents were arrested and sent to Siberia. Alexander II was assassinated by a terrorist bomb in 1881, after a series of botched attempts. His successors, while escalating the effort to industrialize, continued to oppose further political reform. New measures of repression were also directed against minority nationalities, partly to dampen their unrest and partly to gain the support of upper-class conservatives who were wary of the industrialization process and could be satisfied only by vigorous backing for Russian dominance in language and culture. The Poles and other nationalities were carefully supervised. Russian-language instruction was forced on other people, such as the Ukrainians. Persecution of the large Jewish minority was stepped up, resulting in many executions—called *pogroms*—and seizures of property; as a consequence, many Russian Jews emigrated.

By the 1890s the protest currents were complemented by two other developments. In the first place Marxist doctrines spread from the Western socialist movement to a segment of the Russian intelligentsia. One of the most active Marxist leaders was Vladimir Ilyich Ulyanov. Lenin, as he was known, came from a bureaucratic family; his brother had been killed by the political police. Lenin introduced important innovations in Marxist theory to make it more appropriate for the Russian scene. He argued that the spread of international capitalism was leading to the development of a

Early Russian industrialization is depicted in this 1888 photo of the commercial department of the Abrikosova and Son factory.

proletariat worldwide in advance of industrialization. Russia, then, could have a proletarian revolution without going through a distinct middle-class phase. Lenin also insisted on the importance of disciplined revolutionary cells that could maintain doctrinal purity and effective action even amid severe police repression. Small but dedicated revolutionary cadres, not the mass electioneering of the Western socialist parties whose revisionism Lenin detested, would be the path to the future. Lenin's approach animated the group of Russian Marxists known as *Bolsheviks,* or majority party; ironically, however, they were a minority in the Russian Marxist movement as a whole, much of which remained more wedded to the idea of an initial middle-class revolution. The Leninist approach proved ideal for Russian conditions.

Working-class unrest in the cities developed apace with the new currents among the intelligentsia. Russian workers became far more radical than their Western counterparts. They formed unions and conducted strikes—all illegal—but many of them also had firm political goals in mind. Their radicalism stemmed partly from the absence of legal political outlets and partly from rural unrest, for these new workers pulled in peasant grievances against the existing order. They stemmed partly from the severe conditions of early industrialization, exacerbated by large factories and frequent foreign ownership. Although many workers were not linked to any particular doctrine, some became interested in one of the revolutionary agendas—including bolshevism—and they were urged on by passionate organizers.

THE REVOLUTION OF 1905

Military defeats in 1904 and 1905 finally lit this tinderbox. Russia had maintained its expansionist foreign policy through the later 19th century, in part because of tradition and in part because diplomatic success might draw the venom from some internal unrest. Russia also wanted to match the imperialist strides of the Western powers. A war with the Ottoman Empire in the 1870s brought substantial gains, which were then pushed back at the insistence of France and Britain. Russia also successfully aided the creation of new Slavic nations in the Balkans, such as Serbia and Bulgaria, the "little Slavic brothers" that filled nationalist hearts with pride. Some conservative writers even talked in terms of a Pan-Slavic movement that would unite the Slavic people, under Russian leadership of course. Russia participated vigor-

ously in other Middle Eastern and central Asia areas. Russia and Britain both increased their influence in Persia and Afghanistan, reaching some uneasy truces that divided spheres of activity early in the 20th century. Russia was also active in China. The development of the trans-Siberian railroad encouraged Russia to incorporate some northern portions of Manchuria, violating the 18th-century Amur River agreement. Russia also joined Western powers in obtaining long-term leases to Chinese territory during the 1890s.

These were important gains, but they did not satisfy growing Russian ambitions, and they also brought trouble. Russia now risked an overextension, as its diplomatic aspirations were not backed by increases in military power. The problem first came to a head in 1904. Japan, increasingly powerful in its own right, became worried about further Russian expansion in northern China and efforts to extend influence into Korea. War broke out in 1904. Against all expectation save Japan's, the Japanese won. Russia could not move its fleet quickly to the Pacific, and the Russian military organization in general proved too cumbersome to oppose more effective Japanese maneuvers. Japan gained the opportunity to move into Korea, as the balance of power in the Far East began to shift.

Unexpected defeat in war unleashed massive protests on the home front in the Revolution of 1905. Urban workers mounted well-organized general strikes designed above all for political gains. Peasants produced a tumultuous series of insurrections, while liberal groups also agitated. After first trying brutal police repression—which only infuriated the urban crowds—and worried about the reliability of the peasant-based army, the tsarist regime had to change course. It granted little to the workers, for new rights for unions and Marxist political parties were almost immediately stripped away—though not before worker organizations gained further ground. But liberals were wooed through the creation of a national parliament, the *duma.* And the minister Stolypin introduced an important series of reforms for the peasantry. The emancipation system was greatly loosened. Peasants gained greater freedom from redemption payments and village controls. They could buy and sell land quite liberally. The goal here was to create a stratified, market-oriented peasantry in which successful farmers would move away from the peasant masses, becoming rural capitalists. Indeed, peasant unrest did die down, and a minority of aggressive entrepreneurs, called *kulaks,* began to increase agricultural production and buy additional land. Yet the reform package overall quickly came unglued. Not only were workers' rights withdrawn, triggering a new series of strikes and underground activities, but also the duma was progressively stripped of power. Nicholas II, a weak man who was badly advised, simply could not surrender the tradition of autocratic rule, and the duma became a hollow institution, representing and satisfying no one. Police repression also resumed, creating new opponents for the regime.

Pressed in the diplomatic arena by the closing of the Far Eastern theater through Japanese advance yet eager to counter paralyzing internal pressures by some foreign policy success, the Russian government turned once again to the Ottoman Empire and the Balkans. Various stratagems to acquire new rights of access to the Mediterranean and to back Slavic allies in the Balkans yielded no concrete results, but they did stir the pot in this vulnerable area and helped lead to World War I. And this war, in which Russia participated in order to maintain her diplomatic standing and live up to the billing of Slavic protector while hoping for new territorial gains, led to one of the great revolutions of modern times.

JAPAN: REFORM, INDUSTRIALIZATION, AND RISE TO GLOBAL POWER

Like Russia, Japan faced new pressures from the West during the 1850s, in the form of demands for more open trade and admission of foreigners rather than outright military conflict. Japan's response was more direct than Russia's and, on the whole, more immediately successful. Despite its long history of isolation, Japanese society was better adapted than Russia's to the challenge of industrial change. Market forms were more extensive, reaching into peasant agriculture; levels of literacy were higher. Nevertheless, Japan had to rework many of its institutions during the final decades of the 19th century, and the process produced significant strain. The result, by 1900, was different both from purely Western patterns and from the more obvious tensions of Russian society.

The Meiji government, which had been established in 1868 mainly in response to the threats posed by Western intrusion, promptly set about abolishing feudalism. In 1871 it replaced the domains of the feudal lords with a system of nationally appointed prefects (carefully chosen from different regions). Political power was effectively centralized and, from this base in turn, the Meiji rulers—the emperor and his close advisors drawn from loyal segments of the upper *samurai,* or military classes—began to expand the power of the state to effect economic and social change.

Soon after these reforms were initiated the Japanese government sent samurai officials to western Europe and the United States to study economics, political institutions, and technology. These samurai, deeply impressed by what they saw, pulled back from their earlier antiforeign mood and gained increasing voice over domestic development, accompanied by a diplomatic policy that carefully avoided antagonizing the Western powers.

POLITICAL CHANGE

The restructuring of the state and its new policy commitments were accompanied by a fundamental improvement in government finance. Between 1873 and 1876 the Meiji ministers introduced a true social revolution, abolishing the samurai class and the stipends this group had received. The samurai were compensated with government-backed bonds, but these decreased in value, and most samurai became impoverished. The tax on agriculture was converted to a wider tax, payable in money. The government also introduced an army based on national conscription, and by 1878 the nation was militarily secure.

The final capping of the process of political reconstruction came in the 1890s, when Meiji leaders traveled abroad to gather suggestions about appropriate modern political forms. In 1884 they created a new conservative nobility, stocked by former aristocrats and Meiji leaders, that would operate a British-style House of Peers. Next the bureaucracy was reorganized, insulated from political pressures, and opened to talent on the basis of civil service examinations. The bureaucracy simultaneously began rapidly to expand; it grew from 29,000 officials in 1890 to 72,000 in 1908. Finally, the constitution, issued in 1889, ensured major prerogatives for the emperor along with limited powers for the lower house of the Diet (as the new Parliament was called), which was elected by the wealthiest 5 percent of the male population.

Japan's political structure thus came to involve centralized imperial rule, wielded by a handful of Meiji advisors, combined with limited representative institutions copied from the West. This combination gave great power to an oligarchy of wealthy business leaders and former nobles, who influenced the emperor and also pulled strings within Parliament. Political parties arose, but a coherent oligarchy overrode their divisions into the 20th century. Japan thus followed its new policy of imitating the West, but it retained its own identity. It devised a structure that appeased many former samurai by giving them a voice in Parliament, while also creating the effective central government necessary to reorganize military and economic affairs. Finally, the Japanese political solution compared interestingly to Russian institutions after Alexander II's reforms. Both states were centralized and authoritarian, but Japan had incorporated business leaders into its governing structure, whereas Russia defended a more traditional social elite.

JAPAN'S INDUSTRIAL REVOLUTION

As Japan shaped its new political system, it also focused attention on creating the conditions necessary for industrialization. The government established new banks to fund growing trade and to provide capital for industry. State-built railroads spread across the country, and the islands were connected by rapid steamers. The market emphasis in agriculture increased, as new methods were introduced to raise output to feed the people of the growing cities.

Government initiative dominated manufacturing not only in the creation of transportation networks but also in state operation of mines, shipyards, and metallurgical plants. Scarce capital and the unfamiliarity of new technology seemed to compel state direction—as occurred in Russia at the same time. Government control also helped check the many foreign advisors early Japanese industry required, and here Japan maintained closer supervision than its Russian neighbor. Japan established the Ministry of Industry in 1870, and it quickly became one of the key government agencies, setting overall economic policy and operating specific sectors. By the 1880s, model shipyards, arsenals, and factories, though not yet capable of substantial output, provided many Japanese with experience in new technology and disciplined work systems. Finally, by expanding technical training and education, setting up banks and post offices, and regularizing commercial laws, the government provided a structure within which Japan could develop on many fronts. Measures in this area largely copied established practices in the West but with adaptation suitable for Japanese conditions; thus, well before any European university, Tokyo Imperial University had a faculty of agriculture.

Private enterprise quickly played a role in Japan's growing economy, particularly in the vital textiles sector. Some business leaders came from older merchant families, though some of the great houses had been ruined along with the financial destruction of the samurai class. There were also newcomers, some rising from peasant ranks. Shuibuzawa Eiichi, for example, born a peasant, became a merchant and then an official of the Finance Ministry. He turned to banking in 1873, using other people's money to set up cotton-spinning mills and other textile operations. Chemicals, construction material, and food products (including beer) were other areas dominated by private entrepreneurs, many of whom, however, had government experience. By the 1890s huge new industrial combines, later known as *zaibatsu,* were being formed as the result of accumulations of capital and far-flung merchant and industrial operations.

By 1900 the Japanese economy was fully launched in an industrial revolution. It rested on a political and social structure different from that of Russia, one that had in most respects changed more substantially. Japan's success in organizing industrialization, including its careful management of foreign advice and models, proved to be one of the great developments of later 19th-century history. Toward the end of the 20th century many Americans, pressed by Japanese competition, would fondly imagine that Japan's economic success was due to U.S. guidance and generosity after 1945. The fact was that industrialization came about through largely Japanese efforts, as indeed must be the case given the fundamental transformation involved.

It is important to keep these early phases of Japanese industrialization in perspective. Pre–World War I Japan was far from the West's equal. It depended on substantial imports of Western equipment and also of raw materials such as coal—for Japan was, for industrial purposes, a resource-poor nation. Although economic growth and careful government policy allowed Japan to avoid Western domination, Japan was newly dependent on world economic conditions and often at a disadvantage in the process. Exports were vital to pay for machine and resource imports, and these in turn required hordes of inexpensive labor. Silk production grew rapidly, the bulk of it destined for Western markets. Much of this production was based on poorly paid workers laboring at home or in sweatshops, not in mechanized factories. Correspondingly the Japanese economy, in this fragile transition period, had little leeway for expansive social measures. A few big companies provided social organizations and other benefits for their employees, which helped maintain low-wage

This silk factory, based on imported technology and designed mainly for the burgeoning export
trade to the West, is representative of early Japanese industrialization.

policies but also translated group-loyalty traditions from
the feudal past. Most workers, however, were given a
poor salary and nothing more. Efforts at labor organization or other means of protest were greeted by vigorous
repression. This exploitive mood was not a permanent
feature of Japanese industrialization, but it was widely
characteristic of this first period, which meant that the
social impact of Japan's industrial revolution had much in
common with its earlier counterpart in the West or in
contemporary Russia.

In some respects Japan's early industrialization was
distinctive, compared to either the West or Russia. The
need to rely on low-paid labor to produce manufacturing
exports had some similarity to Western practice during
the 18th century, but the fact that Japan had no prior
capital built up from earlier foreign trade sharpened this
characteristic. The export momentum also differed from
the Russian case, for Russia's industrialization could utilize earnings from grain exports. Japan's industry was not
geared in this direction. The Russian focus rested on
heavy industry and production for domestic use, including government purchases for rails and military expansion. Japan produced ships and heavy industrial goods
and built up its military forces, but because of its lack of
domestic energy sources, it was inevitably more involved
in a vigorous drive to sell manufactured goods abroad,
even though this was a very new enterprise for the

Japanese. These differences between Japanese and Russian industrial patterns would have ongoing implications
in the 20th century, affecting relationships with the
wider world as well.

ANALYSIS:

THE SEPARATE PATHS OF JAPAN AND CHINA

Japan's ability to change in response to new Western
pressure contrasted strikingly with the sluggishness of
Chinese reactions into the 20th century. The contrast
draws particular attention because China and Japan had
been part of the same civilization orbit for so long,
which means that some of the assets Japan possessed in
dealing with change were present in China as well. Indeed by the mid-19th century Japan turned out to benefit from having become more like China in key respects
during the Tokugawa period. The link between Chinese
and Japanese traditions should not be overdrawn, of
course, and earlier differences help explain the diver-
gence that opened so clearly in the later 19th century. A
problem of interpretation remains, however, as the East
Asian world now split apart, with Japan seizing eagerly
on Chinese weakness to target a series of attacks from

the 1890s to 1945—which of course merely made China's troubles worse.

Japan and China had both chosen isolation from larger world currents from about 1600 until the West forced new openings between 1830 and 1860. Japan's isolation was the more complete. Both countries lagged behind the West because of their self-containment, which was why Western industrialization caught them unprepared. China's power and wealth roused Western greed and interference first, which gave Japan some relative leeway.

China, however, surpassed Japan in some areas that should have aided it in reacting to the Western challenge. Its leadership, devoted to Confucianism, was more thoroughly secular and bureaucratic in outlook. There was no need to brush aside otherworldly commitments or feudal distractions in order to deal with the West's material and organizational power. Government centralization, still an issue in Japan, had a long tradition in China. With a rich history of technological innovation and scientific discovery in its past as well, China might appear to be a natural to lead the Asian world in responding to the West.

That role, however, fell to Japan. Several aspects of Japanese tradition turned out to give it a flexibility that China lacked. It already knew the benefits of imitation, which China, save for a period of attraction to Buddhism, had never acknowledged. Japan's slower government growth had allowed a stronger, more autonomous merchant tradition, even as both societies became more commercial in the 17th and early 18th centuries. Feudal traditions, though declining under the Tokugawa shogunate, also limited the heavy hand of government controls while stimulating some sense of competitiveness—as in the West. China's government, in contrast, probably tried to control too much by the 18th century and squashed initiative in the process.

China was also oppressed by massive population growth from the 17th century onward. This population pressure consumed great energy, leaving scant capital for more fundamental economic initiatives. Japan's population stability into the 19th century, though a sign of economic sluggishness, was more manageable and pressed resources less severely. Japan's island status made the nation more sensitive to Western naval pressures.

Finally, China and Japan were enmeshed in somewhat different trajectories when the Western challenge intruded in the mid-19th century. China was suffering one of its recurrent dynastic declines. Government became less efficient, intellectual life stagnated, and popular unrest surged. Quite possibly a cycle of renewal would have followed, with a new dynasty seizing more vigorous reins. But Western interference distorted this process, complicating reform and creating various new discontents that ultimately overturned the imperial office. China's sluggish leadership, convinced of the nation's superiority, finally provoked reformers to radical action as they saw their country torn apart by foreign imperialists.

Japan, in contrast, maintained considerable political and economic vigor into the 19th century. There were some new political challenges and an increase of peasant revolt. Whereas by the late 19th century China ironically needed Western guidance simply to handle such bureaucratic affairs as tariff collection or repression of peasant rebellion, Japan suffered no such breakdown of authority, using foreign advisors far more selectively.

Once a different pattern of response was established, every decade increased the gap. Western exploitation of Chinese assets as well as dilution of government power made conditions more chaotic, while Japanese strength steadily grew after a very brief period of uncertainty. By the 20th century the two nations were not only enemies—with Japan, for the first time, the stronger—but seemed to be in different orbits. Japan was an increasing industrial success, with a conservative state that would yield after World War II to a more fully parliamentary form. China, after decades of revolution, finally won its 20th-century political solution, in communism.

Yet today, near the arrival of the 21st century, it becomes possible to wonder if East Asia was split as permanently as 19th- and early 20th-century developments had suggested. Japan's industrial lead remains, but China's economy begins perhaps to stir, along with other innovations along Asia's Pacific coast. Common cultural habits of group cooperation and decision making remind us that beneath different political systems, a fruitful shared heritage continues to operate—a heritage quite different from that of the West but seemingly fully adaptable to the demands of economic change. And so Westerners begin to wonder if a Pacific century is about to dawn.

Questions: What civilization features had Japan and China shared before the 19th century? In what ways were Japanese political institutions more adaptable than Chinese institutions? Why was Russia able to change earlier and more fundamentally than 19th-century China? 🌐

SOCIAL AND ECONOMIC EFFECTS OF INDUSTRIALIZATION

The Industrial Revolution and the wider extensions of manufacturing and commercial agriculture, along with political change, had significant ramifications within Japanese culture and society. The government introduced a universal education system, providing primary schools for all. This education stressed science and technical subjects along with political loyalty to the nation and emperor. Elite students at the university level also emphasized science, many of them studying technical subjects abroad. The rapid assimilation of a scientific outlook built on the earlier secularization of Japanese elite culture, but it was a major new ingredient.

As in the West earlier, industrialization altered social structure. Although an important group of aristocrats and people from the samurai warrior class entered the ranks of successful business leaders and officials, a new elite was formed that embraced leading entrepreneurs for the first time. Among the masses, the rise of a huge, propertyless class of urban workers was a new development. Both peasants and workers endured low wages and high taxes, as Japanese leaders required profits and tax revenue to amass the capital needed for further investment. Japan's industrial success did not come easily as far as the lower classes were concerned. And although the new elite did not cultivate the luxurious life-style of Western business magnates, being content with lower profit rates, it did insist on retaining power. Unions and lower-class political parties began to emerge by 1900 but made only slow headway, and a militant socialist movement was outlawed. Periodic strike movements were brutally repressed, though a legacy of serious class bitterness remained.

Japanese society was also disrupted by massive population growth. Better nutrition and new medical provisions reduced death rates, and the upheaval of the rural masses cut into traditional restraints on births. The result was a steady population surge that strained Japanese resources and stability, though it also ensured an ongoing supply of low-cost labor.

Many Japanese copied Western fashions as part of the effort to become modern. Western-style haircuts replaced the samurai shaved head with a topknot—another example of the fascinating pattern of the Westernization of hair in world history. Western standards of hygiene spread, and the Japanese became enthusiastic toothbrushers and consumers of patent medicines. Japan

In the Meiji era in the late 19th century, Japanese women learned Western musical forms and how to play Western instruments. Note the Western impact on Japanese fashions.

also adopted the Western calendar and the metric system. Few Japanese converted to Christianity, however, and despite fads for Western popular culture, the Japanese managed to preserve an emphasis on their own values. Nevertheless, many conservatives lamented the changes that had occurred, setting up tensions that would long persist in Japan. Emphasis on nationalism and loyalty to the emperor helped preserve unity and motivation amid change, as Japanese virtues of obedience and harmony were touted over Western individualism.

Japanese family life retained many traditional emphases. The birthrate dropped as rapid population growth forced increasing numbers of people off the land. Meanwhile the rise of factory industry, separating work from home, made the labor of children less useful.

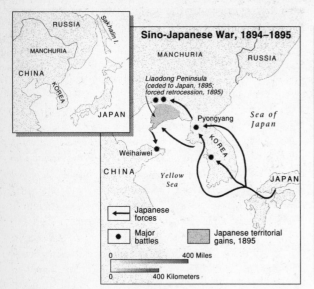

Japanese Colonial Expansion to 1914

Here was a trend, developed earlier in the West, that seems inseparable from successful industrialization. There were new signs of family instability as well. Many men moved to cities, leaving wives behind in rural manufacturing. The result in 1900, until legal changes made procedures more difficult, was the highest divorce rate in the world. On the more traditional side, however, the Japanese were eager to maintain the inferiority of women in the home. The position of Western women repelled them. Japanese government visitors to the United States were appalled by what they saw as the bossy ways of women: "The way women are treated here is like the way parents are respected in our country." Standards of Japanese courtesy also contrasted with the more open and boisterous behavior of Westerners—particularly Americans. "Obscenity is inherent in the customs of this country," noted another samurai visitor to the United States. Other basic features of Japanese life, including diet, were maintained in the face of Western influence. Certain Japanese religious values were also preserved. Buddhism lost some ground, though it remained important, but Shintoism, which appealed to the new nationalist concern with Japan's distinctive mission and the religious functions of the emperor, won new interest.

Japan's transformation had not brought the country to Western levels, and the Japanese remained intensely fearful for their independence. Economic change and the tensions as well as the power it generated did,

however, produce a shift in Japanese foreign policy. With only one previous exception, the Japanese had never before been interested in territorial expansion, but by the 1890s they joined the ranks of imperialist powers. Partly this shift was an imitation of Western models and at the same time an effort to prevent Western encroachment. Imperialism also relieved some strains within Japanese society, giving displaced samurai a chance to exercise their military talents elsewhere and providing symbols of nationalist achievement for the populace as a whole. The Japanese economy also required access to markets and raw materials. Because Japan was poor in many basic materials, including coal and oil for energy, the pressure for expansion was particularly great.

In the quarrel for influence over Korea in 1894 and 1895, Japan's quick victory over China was a first step toward expansion. Japan convincingly demonstrated its new superiority over all other purely Asian powers. Humiliated by Western insistence that it abandon the Liaotung peninsula it had just won, the Japanese planned a war with Russia as a means of striking out against the nearest European power. A 1902 alliance with Britain was an important sign of Japan's arrival as an equal nation in the Western-dominated world diplomatic system. The Japanese were also eager to dent Russia's growing strength in East Asia, after the development of the trans-Siberian railroad. Disputes over Russian influence in Manchuria and Japanese influence in Korea led to the Russo-Japanese War in 1904, which Japan won handily on the basis of its superior navy. Japan annexed Korea in 1910; it was now not only a modern industrial power but a new imperialist power as well.

CONCLUSION

JAPAN, RUSSIA, AND WORLD WAR I

The beginnings of serious industrialization in Russia and Japan and the unprecedented entry of Japan into world affairs contributed important new ingredients to the world diplomatic picture by the early 20th century. Developments in both countries, along with the rise of the United States, added to the growing sense of rivalry among the established Western powers. Japan's surge, and particularly its surprising military victories, promoted a fear in the West of a new "yellow peril" that should be opposed through greater imperialist efforts. Outright colonial acquisitions by the new powers added directly to the competitive atmosphere, particularly in the Far East. Japan, to be sure, was not yet a major world player, but it was beginning to make its muscle felt.

Furthermore, the strains of early industrialization, including the need to appease embittered conservative aristocrats as well as aggrieved masses, made both Russia and Japan increasingly dependent on diplomatic success. After 1912, for example, Japan faced growing political party competition in Parliament, with frequent if futile parliamentary defiance of the emperor's ministers. Massive popular protest added fuel to the fire as Japanese workers and peasants developed new political expectations and allegiances. It was in this setting that Japan joined the Allied side in World War I, hoping not for a significant military role but for the chance to seize German colonies in the Pacific—which it quickly gobbled up. Russia, of course, launched into the war from the outset as a central actor, as its narrowing diplomatic options combined with internal pressures to preclude any alternative. Japan and Russia were not unique in finding diplomacy affected by new domestic rifts—the Western industrial leaders faced some similar tensions—but they were unquestionably caught up in a new spiral.

FURTHER READINGS

Several studies deal with Russian industrialization. W. Blackwell's *The Industrialization of Russia* (1982) provides a useful overview. An older collection deals with Russian change in terms of modernization theory: C. Black, ed., *The Transformation of Russian Society* (1960). Economic backwardness and latecomer reactions are taken up in A. Gerschenkron's *Economic Backwardness in Historical Perspective* (1962).

A number of historians have advanced understanding of Russia's workers. See R. Zelnik's *Labor and Society in Tsarist Russia, 1855–1870* (1971) and Victoria Bonnell, ed., *The Russian Worker: Life and Labor under the Tsarist Regime* (1983). On rural conditions, see T. Emmons's *The Russian Landed Gentry and the Peasant Emancipation of 1861* (1968). Political agitation is discussed in A. B. Ulam's *Russia's Failed Revolutionaries* (1981). Army service and protest form the subject of John Bushnell's *Mutiny and Repression: Russian Soldiers in the Revolution of 1905–1906* (1983). Barbara Engel's *Mothers and Daughters: Women of the Intelligentsia in Nineteenth Century Russia* (1983) takes up another vital topic. Finally, on popular culture, see Jeffrey Brooks's *When Russia Learned to Read: Literacy and Popular Culture* (1987) and Ben Eklof's *Russian Peasant Schools: Officialdom, Village Culture, and Popular Pedagogy, 1864–1914* (1986).

For general coverage of Japan in the period, consult G. Akita's *Foundations of Constitutional Government in Modern Japan, 1868–1900* (1967) and W. G. Beasley's *The Meiji Restoration* (1973). Several books cover economic trends: G. C. Allen's *A Short Economic History of Modern Japan* (1958), W. W. Lockwood's *The Economic Development of Japan* (1954), and R. Dore, ed., *Aspects of Social Change in Modern Japan* (1967).

Japanese industrial structure has received much recent attention from worried Americans. See J. C. Abegglen's *The Japanese Factory: Aspects of Its Social Organization* (1985), Hugh Patrick, ed., *Japanese Industrialization and Its Social Consequences* (1973), and the careful study by Andrew Gordon, *The Evolution of Labor Relations in Japan* (1985). On culture, E. O. Reischauer's *Japan, the Story of a Nation* (1981) is unusually readable, and M. Miyoshi's *Accomplices of Silence: The Modern Japanese Novel* (1974) is good. See also R. H. Myers and M. R. Beattie, eds., *The Japanese Colonial Empire 1895–1945* (1984).

1835 Decision to give state support for
English education in India; English adopted
as the language of Indian law courts

1853 First railway line constructed in India

1815 British annex Cape
Town and surrounding area

1857 Calcutta, Madras, and
Bombay universities founded

1858 British Parliament
assumes control over India
from the East India
Company

1850s Boer republics established in
the Orange Free State in Transvaal

1850s–1870s Maori wars
in New Zealand

1830 Start of the Boers'
Great Trek in South Africa

1857–1858 "Mutiny" or Great
Rebellion in north India

Industrialization and Imperialism: The Making of the European Global Order

3

INTRODUCTION. The process of industrialization that began to transform western European societies in the last half of the 18th century fundamentally altered the nature and impact of European overseas expansion. In the centuries of expansion before the industrial era, the Europeans went overseas because they sought material things they could not produce themselves and because they were threatened by powerful external enemies.

They initially sought precious metals, for which they traded in Africa and waged wars of conquest to control in the Americas. In the Americas they also seized land on which to grow high-priced commercial crops, such as sugar and coffee. In Asia, European traders and adventurers sought either manufactured goods, such as cotton and silk textiles (produced mainly in India, China, and the Middle East), or luxury items, such as spices, that would improve the living standards of the aristocracy and rising middle classes.

In the Americas, Africa, and Asia missionaries from Roman Catholic areas, such as Spain and Portugal, sought to convert what were regarded as "heathen" peoples to Christianity. Both the wealth gained from products brought home from overseas and the souls won for Christ were viewed as ways of strengthening Christian Europe in its long struggle with Muslim empires that threatened Europe from the south and east.

1879–1890s Partition of Africa

1914 Outbreak of World War I

1867 Diamonds discovered in the Orange Free State

1899–1902 Anglo-Boer War in South Africa

1879 Zulu victory over British at Isandhlwana; defeat at Rourke's Drift

1885 Indian National Congress Party founded in India; gold discovered in the Transvaal

1898 British-French crisis over Fashoda in the Sudan

1882 British invasion of Egypt

1890s Partition of East Africa

1869 Opening of the Suez Canal

1898 U.S. annexation of Hawaiian Islands Spanish-American War

Only on the eve of Columbus's voyage in 1492 were the Muslims driven from Spain into North Africa; the Ottoman Empire remained a formidable foe of the European powers throughout the first two centuries of overseas expansion.

In the industrial era, from roughly 1800 onward, the things that Europeans sought in the outside world changed dramatically, as did the source of the insecurities that drove them there. The main products the Europeans sought overseas were raw materials—metals, vegetable oils, dyes, cotton, and hemp—needed to feed the machines of Europe, not spices or manufactured goods. Industrialization made Europe for the first time the manufacturing center of the world, and overseas markets for machine-made European products became a key concern of those who pushed for colonial expansion. Christian missionaries, by then as likely to be Protestant as Roman Catholic, still sought to win converts overseas. But unlike the rulers of Portugal and Spain in the early centuries of expansion, European leaders in the industrial age rarely took initiatives overseas to promote Christian proselytization. In part this reflected the fact that western Europe itself was no longer seriously threatened by the Muslims or any other non-European people. The fears that fueled European imperialist expansion in the industrial age arose from internal rivalries among the European powers. Overseas peoples might resist the European advance, but the Europeans feared one another far more than even the largest non-European empires.

The contrast between European expansion in the preindustrial era and in the age of industrialization was also reflected in the extent to which the Europeans were able to sail to overseas areas, go ashore, and move inland. In the early centuries of overseas expansion European conquests were concentrated in the Americas, whose long isolation left their peoples particularly vulnerable to the technology and diseases of the expansive Europeans. In much of the rest of the world, European traders and conquistadores were confined largely to the sea-lanes, islands, and coastal enclaves. Now industrial technology and techniques of organization and discipline associated with the increasing mechanization of the West gave the Europeans the capacity to reach and infiltrate any foreign land. From the populous, highly centralized, and technologically sophisticated Chinese Empire to small bands of hunters and gatherers struggling to survive in the harsh environment of Tierra del Fuego on the southern coast of South America, few peoples were remote enough to be out of reach of the steamships and railways that carried the Europeans to and across all continents of the globe. No culture was strong enough to remain untouched by the European drive for global dominance in this era, and none could long resist the profound changes unleashed by European conquest and colonization.

The shift from the preindustrial to the industrial phase of European overseas expansion was gradual and cumulative, extending roughly from 1750 to 1850. By the middle decades of the 19th century, few who were attuned to international events could doubt that a watershed had been crossed. The early sections of this chapter focus on the forces in Europe, the United States, and areas undergoing colonization that led to the great burst of imperialist expansion in the last decades of the 19th century. Despite major changes beginning in the post–World War I era, European and U.S. conquest and colonization shaped the character of the international order that has persisted through much of the 20th century. The bulk of this chapter is devoted to an exploration of some of the key consequences of Western imperialism for the societies and cultures of the colonized peoples of Africa, Asia, and Oceania.

INDUSTRIAL RIVALRIES AND THE PARTITION OF THE WORLD, C. 1870–1914

The spread of the Industrial Revolution from the British Isles to continental Europe and North America greatly increased the already considerable advantages the Western powers possessed in manufacturing capacity and the ability to wage war on other peoples and civilizations. These advantages resulted in increasing levels of European—and U.S.—involvement in the outside world and culminated in the virtually unchallenged domination of the globe by the western powers by the last decades of the 19th century. Beginning in the 1870s the Europeans indulged in an orgy of overseas conquests that reduced most of Africa, Asia, and the Pacific Ocean region to colonial possessions by the time of the outbreak of the First World War in 1914. During each year of that time period, the Western powers added an area larger than France to their empires. By 1914 Europe and its colonial possessions occupied more than 80 percent of the inhabitable lands of the earth. Areas not annexed directly, such as China and Persia, were forcibly "opened" to European trade and investment and divided into informal "spheres of influence" of the various Western nations. The remaking of the world economic order to industrial Europe's specifications was completed. According to the new global division of labor, Europe and increasingly North America provided finance and machine capital, entrepreneurial and managerial talent, and manufactured goods. The rest of the world provided raw materials for Europe's factories, cheap labor, and abundant, if not always fertile, land. Thus it was not without reason that the Europeans came to regard themselves as the "lords of humankind."

Though science and industry gave the Europeans the capacity to run roughshod over the rest of the world, they also heightened economic competition and political rivalries among the European powers. In the first half of the 19th century industrial Britain, with its seemingly insurmountable naval superiority, was left alone to dominate overseas trade and empire building. By the last decades of the century Belgium, France, and especially Germany and the United States were challenging Britain's industrial supremacy and actively building (or in the case of France, adding to) colonial empires of their own. Many of the political leaders of these expansive nations viewed the possession of colonies as an essential attribute of states that aspired to Great Power

status. Colonies were also seen as insurance against shortages of raw materials and the loss of overseas market outlets to European or North American rivals.

Quarrels over the division of the colonial spoils were cited by those who sought to justify the arms buildup and general militarism of the age. Colonial rivalries greatly intensified the growing tension and paranoia that dominated Great Power interaction in the decades before World War I. As Europe divided into armed camps, successive crises over control of the Sudan, Morocco, and the Balkans (which the Great Powers treated very much like colonies) had much to do with the alliances that formed and the crisis mentality that contributed so much to the outbreak of the conflict in August 1914.

MOTIVES BEHIND THE GLOBAL SCRAMBLE FOR COLONIES

During much of the 20th century, historians have argued about the reasons for the unprecedented drive for colonial expansion that seized Europe and, to a lesser

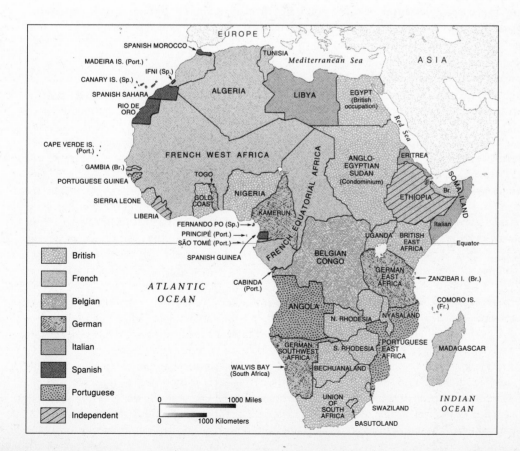

The Partition of Africa to 1914

extent, the United States in the last decades of the 19th century. The majority of those engaged in this often heated debate have tended to join one of two camps: one favoring a political explanation for the outburst of territorial aggrandizement and the other arguing that it was fundamentally economic in origin. The truth may well be found by combining the two views—by recognizing that political leaders, not just business leaders, had to take into account economic concerns when deciding to intervene in disputes or to annex territories in Africa, Asia, or the South Pacific. The British obsession with protecting strategic overseas naval stations, such as those in Malaya and in South Africa, for example, was linked to an underlying perception of growing threats to their empire in India. That empire was in turn more than just their "garrison in the east" and largest colonial possession. It was a major source of raw materials for British industries and a key outlet for both British manufactured goods and British overseas investment. Thus political and economic motives were often impossible to separate; doing so unnecessarily oversimplifies and distorts our understanding of the forces behind the scramble for empire in the late 19th century.

It would also be a mistake to see a complete break between the pattern of European colonial expansion before and after 1870. Though a good deal more territory was annexed per year after that date, there were numerous colonial wars and additions to both the British and French empires all through the middle decades of the 19th century. One of the key differences between the two periods was that before 1870, Britain had only a weak France with which to compete in the outside world. This meant that the British were less likely than at the end of the century to be pushed into full-scale invasions and annexations out of fear that another European power was about to seize potentially valuable colonies. It also allowed the British to rely heavily on threats and gunboat raids rather than outright conquest to bring African kings or Asian emperors into line. With its "white" settler colonies (Canada, Australia, and New Zealand), India, and enclaves in Africa and Southeast Asia, the British already had all the empire they could handle. Most British politicians were cautious about or firmly opposed to adding more colonies. The British were wary of French advances in various parts of the globe, which were usually made to restore France's standing as a Great Power following setbacks in Europe. But the French were far too weak economically and too politically divided to contest Britain's naval mastery or its standing as the greatest colonial power.

The Partition of Southeast Asia and the Pacific Islands to 1914

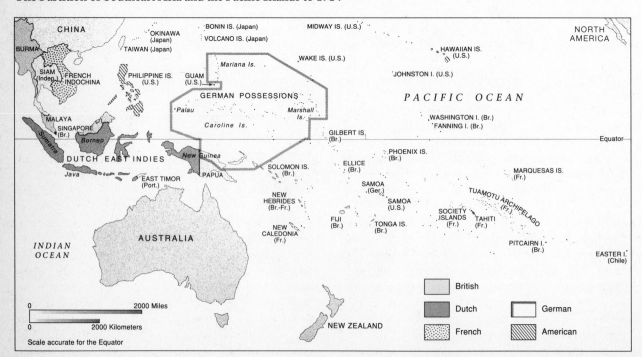

Once Germany was united in 1870 and the German Empire and the United States began to pass Britain as industrial powers, the situation changed significantly. India and the rest of the empire were now seen as essential to Britain's maintenance of its Great Power standing. British politicians worried that if Britain stood still while the rest of the powers built up overseas empires, it would soon be supplanted as the primary naval and colonial power. The concern here was both economic and strategic. The last decades of the 19th century were a period of recurring economic depressions in Europe and the United States. The leaders of the newly industrialized nations had little experience in handling the overproduction and unemployment that came with each of these economic crises. They were understandably deeply concerned about the social unrest and in some cases what appeared to them to be stirrings of revolution that each phase of depression engendered. Some political theorists argued that as destinations to which unemployed workers might migrate and as potential markets for surplus goods, colonial possessions could serve as safety valves to release the pressure built up in times of industrial slumps.

Thus although a colony seemed to be of little economic value when it was annexed, it could prove a valuable asset later on. Industrial Europe's growing need for raw materials gave added credence to this line of reasoning. Each power felt compelled to conquer and annex vast territories—which often consisted of lightly populated, arid lands—because it feared that otherwise a rival would take them. In letting a competitor grab what might prove to be a mineral-rich colony, Britain or Germany might be foreclosing on its future chances to remain a global power.

Competition among the Great Powers had much to do with another major cause of the late-19th-century scramble for colonial possessions. Britain's successful application of gunboat diplomacy and indirect control over African and Asian kingdoms in the early 19th century depended heavily on the existence of reasonably strong African and Asian leaders who could enforce the demands made by the Europeans. With the intensification of European rivalries in the late 19th century, these leaders attempted to play the powers off one another. This reduced the value of their cooperation and often prompted one of the powers to invade their lands, remove them from power, and find less troublesome collaborators. In addition, decades and even centuries of European economic penetration and political interference had resulted in the disintegration of indigenous governments and societies as a whole in many areas, particularly in Africa. Lacking a local center of power through which to exert control and fearing the growing social dislocations in areas where one or more of the powers had a strong strategic or economic stake, European policymakers concluded that military intervention and formal annexation were their only option.

As these motives suggest, in the era of the scramble for colonial possessions, political leaders in Europe played a much more prominent role in decisions to annex overseas territories than they had earlier, even in the first half of the 19th century. In part this was due to improved communications. Telegraphs and railways not only made it possible to transmit orders from the capitals of Europe to the tropics much more rapidly but also allowed ministers in Europe to play a much more active role in the ongoing governance of the colonies.

Politicians were not the only ones involved in late-19th-century decisions to add to the colonial empires. The jingoistic "penny" press and the extension of the vote to the lower middle and working classes throughout much of industrial Europe and in the United States made public opinion a major factor in foreign policy. Though stalwart explorers might on their own initiative make treaties with local African or Asian potentates who assigned their lands to France or Germany, these annexations had to be ratified by the home government. In most cases ratification meant fierce parliamentary debates that often spilled over into press wars and popular demonstrations. Empires were no longer the personal projects of private trading concerns and ambitious individuals; they were the property and pride of the nations of Europe and North America.

UNEQUAL COMBAT: COLONIAL WARS AND THE APEX OF IMPERIALISM

Industrial change both justified the Europeans' grab for colonial possessions and made them much easier to acquire. By the last decades of the 19th century scientific discoveries and technological innovations had catapulted the Europeans far ahead of all other peoples in the capacity to wage war. The Europeans could tap mineral resources that most peoples did not even know existed, and European chemists mixed ever more deadly explosives. Advances in metallurgy made possible the mass production of light and mobile artillery pieces that rendered suicidal the massed cavalry or infantry charges that were the mainstay of Asian and African armies. Advances in artillery were matched by great improvements in hand arms. Much more accurate and faster-firing, breech-loading rifles replaced the clumsy muzzle-loading muskets of the first phase of empire building. Decades of experimentation had made the machine gun an effective battlefield weapon by the 1880s. Railroads gave the Europeans the mobility of the swiftest African or Asian horsemen, as well as the ability to supply large armies in the field for extended periods of time. On the sea, Europe's already formidable advantages were awesomely increased by industrial transformations. After the opening of the Suez canal in 1869, steam power supplanted the sail, iron hulls replaced wood, and massive guns, capable of hitting enemy vessels miles away, were introduced into the Great Powers' fleets.

The dazzling array of new weaponry with which the Europeans set out on their expeditions to the Indian frontiers or the African "bush" made the wars of colonial conquest very lopsided affairs. This was particularly true when the Europeans encountered resistance from peoples, such as those in the interior of Africa or the Pacific islands, who had been cut off from most preindustrial advances in technology and thus fought the European machine guns with spears, arrows, and leather shields. One African leader, whose people struggled with little hope to halt the German advance into East Africa, resorted to natural imagery to account for the power of the invaders' weapons:

On Monday we heard a shuddering like Leviathan, the voice of many cannon; we heard the roar like waves on the rocks and rumble like thunder in the rains. We heard a crashing like elephants or monsters and our hearts melted at the number of shells. We knew that we were hearing the battle of Pangani; the guns were like a hurricane in our ears.

Not even peoples with advanced preindustrial technology and sophisticated military organization, such as the Chinese and Vietnamese, could stand against or really comprehend the Europeans' fearful killing devices. In advising the Vietnamese emperor to give in to European demands, one of his officials, who had led the fight against the French invaders, warned:

Nobody can resist them. They go where they choose. . . . Under heaven, everything is feasible to them, save only the matter of life and death.

Despite the odds against them, African and Asian peoples often fiercely resisted the imposition of colonial rule. West African leaders, such as Samory and Ahmadou Sekou, held back the European advance for decades, and when rulers, such as the Vietnamese emperors, refused to fight, local officials organized guerrilla resistance in defense of the traditional regime. Martial

An engraving from the popular *Illustrated London News* shows British warships and gunboats bombarding the East African port of Mombasa in 1874. As in the early centuries of European expansion, sea power remained a critical way for the British and other colonizers to project their power overseas throughout the 19th century.

peoples, such as the Zulus in South Africa, had the courage and discipline to face and defeat sizable British forces in set piece (or conventional and critical) battles, such as that at Isandhlwana in 1879. But conventional resistance eventually ended in defeat. The guerrilla bands in Vietnam were eventually run to the ground; even at Isandhlwana, 3000 Zulus lost their lives in the victory over 800 British and 500 African troops. In addition, within days of the Zulu victory, a tiny force of 120 British troops held off an army of three or four thousand Zulus. Given the European advantages in conventional battles, guerrilla resistance, sabotage, and in some cases banditry proved the most effective means of fighting the Europeans' attempts to assert political control. Religious leaders were often in the forefront of these struggles. The magic potions and divine assistance they offered for the protection of their followers seemed to be the only way to offset the demoralizing killing power of the Europeans' weapons.

However admirable the courage of those who resisted the European advance and despite temporary setbacks, by the eve of World War I in 1914 little of the earth was left for the Europeans to conquer. Excepting Ethiopia, all of Africa had been divided among the European powers. Maps of Africa became a patchwork of the colors representing the colonizers—red for Great Britain, green for France, blue for Germany, and so on. In Southeast Asia only Siam remained independent, in part because Britain and France could not decide which of them should have it. The Americans had replaced the Spanish as the colonial overlords of the Philippines, and the Dutch were completing the conquest of the "outer islands" of the Indonesian archipelago. Even the island clusters of the Pacific had been divided among the hungry industrial powers. China, Persia, and the Middle East had not yet been occupied, but many believed that the "informal" political and economic influences the European powers exerted in these areas were the prelude to formal annexation.

What was perhaps most striking was how easy this division of the world had been. There had been prolonged resistance in desolate places, such as the Sudan and the rain forests of Vietnam, but overall the Europeans had conquered most of the earth in a matter of decades with a remarkably low level of expense and loss of *European* lives. They had divided the world with little thought for the reactions of the peoples who came under their rule. European leaders quarreled and bargained at green, felt-topped tables in Paris or Berlin over lands they scarcely knew anything about. It was like a colossal

This rather romantic depiction of the 1879 battle of Isandhlwana in the Natal province of South Africa shows that, despite their superior firepower, the Europeans could be defeated, if only temporarily, by well-organized and determined African or Asian resistance forces.

game of *Diplomacy* or *Risk,* with armies and fleets moved and colonies won, lost, and traded at the gaming tables of the European diplomats. To expand on an image offered by the archimperialist King Leopold of the Belgians, industrial technology had turned the world into a giant *gateau,* or cake, to be sliced up and divided among the European powers.

PATTERNS OF DOMINANCE: CONTINUITY AND CHANGE

By the end of the 19th century the European colonial order was made up of two quite different kinds of colonies. The greater portion of the European empires consisted of tropical dependencies in Africa, Asia, and the South Pacific in which small numbers of Europeans ruled large numbers of non-Western peoples. The tropical dependencies represented a vast extension of the pattern of dominance the British, Dutch, and French had worked out earlier in India, Java, and African enclaves such as Senegal. Most of these had been brought, often quite suddenly, under European rule in the last decades of the 19th century and the first years of the 20th century. The following sections devoted to this form of colonization focus on the new forms of colonial rule and changing patterns of social interaction between colonizer and colonized that emerged in the decades of imperialist expansion before World War I.

Settlement colonies made up the second major type of European overseas possession, but within this type there were two different patterns of European settlement and indigenous response. The first pattern was exhibited by colonies such as Canada and Australia, which the British labeled the "White Dominions." The White Dominions accounted for a good portion of the land area but only a tiny minority of the population of Britain's global empire. The descendants of European settlers made up the overwhelming majority of the population in these colonies, in which small numbers of native inhabitants had been decimated by diseases and wars of conquest. These patterns of substantial European settlement and the precipitous decline of the indigenous population were also found in those portions of North America that came to form the United States. Though Canada and Australia remained within the British Empire, each moved steadily toward self-government and parliamentary rule in the late 19th century.

In some areas where large numbers of Europeans had migrated, a second major variation on the settlement type of colony developed. Both in regions that had been colonized as early as North America, such as South Africa, and in those the Europeans and Americans had begun to occupy only in the mid- or late 19th century, such as Algeria, Kenya, New Zealand, and Hawaii, the key demographic characteristics of both the settler colonies and tropical dependencies were combined. Temperate climates and relatively mild disease environments in these areas made it possible for tens or hundreds of thousands of Europeans to settle on a permanent basis. Despite the Europeans' arrival, large indigenous populations survived and then began to increase rapidly. As a result, in these areas for which the label *contested settler colonies* seems most apt, Europeans and indigenous peoples increasingly clashed over land rights, resource control, social status, and cultural differences. From the 19th century onward, the history of contested settler societies has been dominated by the interaction between European settlers and indigenous peoples. The last sections of this chapter are devoted to case studies of three of the most important and representative examples of the contested settler variation on the settlement colony pattern: South Africa, New Zealand, and Hawaii.

COLONIAL RULE IN THE TROPICAL DEPENDENCIES

As the Europeans imposed their rule over tens of millions of additional Africans and Asians in the late 19th century, they drew heavily on precedents set in older colonies, particularly India, in establishing administrative, legal, and educational systems. As in India (or in Java and Senegal), the Europeans exploited long-standing ethnic and cultural divisions among the peoples of their new African or Asian colonies to put down resistance and maintain control. In West and East Africa in particular, they used the peoples who followed animistic religions (those that focused on the propitiation of nature or ancestral spirits) or those who had converted to Christianity against the Muslim communities that existed in most colonies. In official reports and censuses, colonial administrators rigidified and enhanced existing ethnic differences by dividing the peoples in each colony into "tribes." The label itself, with its connotations of primitiveness and backwardness, says a great deal about general European attitudes toward the peoples of sub-Saharan Africa. In Southeast Asia the colonizers sought to use hill-dwelling "tribal" minorities against the majority populations that lived in the lowlands and cultivated wet rice. In each colonial area favored minorities, often Christians, were recruited into the civil service and police. Their collaboration not only resulted in a sense of loyalty to the colonizers but also antagonized less-favored ethnic and religious groups, thus bolstering the Europeans' divide-and-rule strategy.

As had been the case in India, Java, and Senegal small numbers of Europeans, who lived mainly in the capital city and major provincial towns, oversaw the administration of the African and Asian colonies, which was actually carried out at the local level mainly by hundreds or thousands of African and Asian subordinates. Some—normally those in positions of the greatest authority—were Western educated, but the majority were recruited from indigenous elite groups, including village heads, local notables, and regional lords. In Burma, Malaya, and East Africa numerous Indian administra-

A pointedly dramatized engraving of the submission in 1896 of King Prempeh of the powerful Asante kingdom in present-day Ghana underscores the importance European colonizers placed on alliances with or the forced submission of indigenous African rulers and local leaders.

tors and soldiers assisted the British in ruling new additions to their empire. The Europeans also recruited promising male youths in the newly colonized areas for Western schooling that would make them fit for jobs as government clerks or railway mechanics.

In contrast to Java and India, where schools were heavily state-supported, Western-language education in Africa was left largely to Protestant and Catholic missionaries. As a result of deep-seated racial prejudices held by virtually all the colonizers, higher education was not promoted in Africa, and college graduates there were rare compared to India, the Dutch East Indies, or even smaller Asian colonies such as Burma and Vietnam. Of course, this policy stunted the growth of a middle class in black Africa, a consequence that European colonial officials increasingly intended. As nationalist agitation spread among the Western-educated classes in India and other Asian colonies, colonial policymakers

warned against the dangers posed by college graduates. Those with advanced educations among the colonized, according to this argument, aspired to jobs that were beyond their capacity and were understandably disgruntled when they could not find employment.

ANALYSIS:
WESTERN EDUCATION AND THE RISE OF AN AFRICAN AND ASIAN MIDDLE CLASS

To varying degrees and for many of the same reasons as the British in India, all European colonizers sought to educate the children of African and Asian elite groups in Western-language schools. An early 19th-century debate over education in India was paralleled, for example, by an equally hard-fought controversy among French officials and missionaries regarding the proper schooling for the peoples of Senegal in West Africa. The Dutch did not develop European-language schools for the sons of the Javanese elite until the mid-19th century, and until the end of the century many young Japanese males continued to be educated in the homes of the Dutch residing in the colonies. Like the British, the French and Dutch needed administrative assistants and postal clerks, and also like the British they could neither recruit enough Europeans to fill these posts nor afford the wages European employees would have demanded.

One of the chief advantages of having Western-educated African and Asian subordinates—for they were always below European officials or managers in the office or on the parade ground—was that their salaries were considerably lower than what Europeans would have been paid for doing the same work. The Europeans had no trouble rationalizing this inequity. Africans and Asians served in their own lands and were thus accustomed to life in the hot, humid, insect- and disease-ridden tropics. For the Europeans who worked in the colonies, life in these environments was deemed difficult, even dangerous. Higher pay was thought to compensate them for the "sacrifices" involved in colonial service. The Europeans also had a higher standard of living than Africans or Asians, and colonial officials assumed that European employees would be more hardworking and efficient.

Beyond the need for government functionaries and business assistants, each European colonizer stressed different objectives in designing Western-language schools for the children of upper-class families. The transmission of Western scientific learning and production techniques was a high priority for the British in India. Educational policymakers also sought to teach the Indians Western literature and manners and to instill in them a Western sense of morality. As Thomas Macaulay put it, they hoped that English-language schools would turn out brown "English gentlemen" who would in turn teach other Indians the ways of the West.

The French, at least until the end of the 19th century, went even further. They stressed the importance of Africans and other colonial students mastering the French language and the subtleties of French culture. When the lessons had been fully absorbed and the students fully assimilated to French culture, they could become full citizens of France, no matter what their family origins or the color of their skin. Though only a tiny minority of the population of any French colony had the op-

portunity for the sort of schooling that would qualify them for French citizenship, thousands of Senegalese and hundreds of Vietnamese or Tunisians could carry French passports, vote in French elections, and even run for seats in the French Parliament. Other European colonial powers adopted either the British or the French approach to education and its aims. The Dutch and Germans, for example, followed the British pattern, whereas the Portuguese pushed assimilation for even smaller numbers of the elite classes among the peoples they colonized.

Western education in the colonies succeeded in producing clerks and railway conductors, brown Indian gentlemen and black French citizens. It also had effects not intended by those who shaped colonial educational policy, effects that a generation or two after the European conquest produced major challenges to the continuation of European colonial dominance. The population of most colonized areas was divided into many ethnic, religious, and language groups with separate histories and identities. Western-language schools gave the sons (and in limited instances, the daughters) of the leading families a common language in which to communicate. The schools also inculcated common attitudes and ideas and imparted to the members of diverse groups a common body of knowledge. In all European colonial societies Western education led to similar occupational opportunities—in government service, with Western business firms, or as professionals (lawyers, doctors, journalists, etc.). Thus within a generation after their introduction, Western-language schools had in effect created a new middle class in the colonies that had no counterpart in precolonial African or Asian societies.

Occupying social strata and economic niches in the middle range between the European colonizers and the old aristocracy on the one hand, and the peasantry and urban laborers on the other, Western-educated Africans and Asians within each colony became increasingly aware of their shared interests and grievances. They often found themselves at odds with the traditional rulers or the landed gentry, who ironically were often their parents or grandparents. Members of the new middle class also felt alienated from the peasantry, whose beliefs and way of life were so different from those they had learned in Western-language schools. For over a generation they clung to their European tutors and employers. Eventually, however, they grew increasingly resentful of their lower salaries, of European competition for scarce jobs, and of their social segregation from the Europeans, who often made little effort to disguise their contempt for even the most accomplished of the African or Asian students of Western ways. Thus members of the new middle class in the colonies were caught between two worlds: the traditional ways and teachings of their parents and the "modern" world of their European masters. Finding that they would be fully admitted to neither world, they rejected the first and set about supplanting the Europeans and building their own modern world.

Questions: Why did the Europeans continue to provide Western-language education for Africans and Asians once it was clear they were creating a class that might challenge their position of dominance? Why were challenges from this new class much more effective than resistance on the part of the peasantry or movements led by the traditional religious and political elites? Do you think the European colonial order would have lasted longer if Western-language education had been denied to colonized peoples?

CHANGING SOCIAL RELATIONS BETWEEN COLONIZER AND COLONIZED

In both long-held and newly acquired colonies the growing tensions between the colonizers and the rising African and Asian middle classes reflected a larger shift in European social interaction with the colonized peoples. This shift had actually begun long before the scramble for colonies in the late 19th century. Its causes are complex, but the growing size and changing makeup of European communities in the colonies were critical factors. As more and more Europeans went to the colonies, they tended to keep to themselves on social occasions rather than mixing with the "natives." New medicines and increasingly segregated living quarters enabled government officials and European military officers (but not the rank and file until well into the 20th century) to bring out to the colonies their wives and families. Wives and family further closed the social circle of the colonized, and European women looked disapprovingly on liaisons between European men and Asian or African women. Brothels were put off limits for upper-class officials and officers, and mixed marriages or living arrangements met with more and more vocal disapproval both within the constricted world of the colonial communities and back home in Europe. The growing numbers of missionaries and pastors for European congregations in the colonies obviously served to strengthen these taboos.

European women were once held to be the chief culprits in the growing social gap between colonizer and colonized, but male officials may well have been mainly responsible. They established laws restricting or prohibiting miscegenation and other sorts of interracial liaisons, and they pushed for housing arrangements and police practices designed specifically to keep social contacts between European women and the colonized at a minimum. These measures locked European women in the colonies into an almost exclusively European world. They still had numerous "native" servants and "native" nannies for their children, but they rarely came into contact with men or women of their own social standing from the colonized peoples. Occasions when they did were highly public and strictly formal.

The trend toward social exclusivism on the part of Europeans in the colonies and their open disdain for the culture of colonized peoples were reinforced by notions of white racial supremacy, which peaked in acceptance in the decades before World War I. It was widely believed that the mental and moral superiority of whites over the rest of humankind, which was usually divided into racial types according to the crude criterion of skin color, had been demonstrated by scientific experiments. Because the inferior intelligence and weak sense of morality of non-Europeans were believed to be inherent and permanent, there seemed little motivation for Europeans to socialize with the colonized and many good reasons for fighting the earlier tendency to adopt elements of the culture and life-style of subject peoples. As photos from the late 19th century reveal, stiff collars and ties for men, and corsets and long skirts for women became obligatory for the respectable colonial functionaries and their wives. The colonizers' houses were filled with the overstuffed furniture and bric-a-brac that the late Victorians loved so dearly. European social life in the colonies revolved around the infamous clubs, where the only "natives" allowed were the servants. In the heat of the summer months most of the administrators and virtually all of the colonizers' families retreated to the hill stations, where the cool air and the quaint architecture made it seem almost as if they were home again—or at least in a Swiss mountain resort.

SHIFTS IN METHODS OF ECONOMIC EXTRACTION

The relationship between the colonizers and the mass of the colonized remained much as it had been in the centuries of European overseas expansion before the

Industrial Revolution. District officers, with the help of many "native" subordinates, continued to do their paternal duty to settle disputes between peasant villagers, punish criminals, and collect taxes. European planters and merchants still relied on African or Asian overseers and brokers to manage laborers and purchase crops and handicraft manufactures. But late-19th-century colonial bureaucrats and managers sought to instruct African and Asian peasants in "scientific" farming techniques and to compel the colonized peoples more generally to work harder and more efficiently. Here was an important extension of dependent status in the Western-dominated world economy, as pressure for new work habits supported the drive for cheap raw materials (exports) and drew in a growing segment of the colonial labor force.

A wide range of incentives was devised in response to the expansion of production for export and also the abolition of prior forms of slavery. Some of these incentives benefited the colonized peoples, such as the cheap consumer goods that could be purchased with cash earned producing marketable crops or laboring on European plantations. In many instances, however, colonized peoples were simply forced to produce, for little or no remuneration, crops or raw materials that the Europeans desired. Head and hut taxes were imposed that could be paid only in ivory, palm nuts, or wages earned working on European estates. Villagers were forced to grow market produce on lands they normally devoted to food crops. Under the worst of these forced-labor schemes, such as those inflicted on the peoples of the Belgian Congo in the final decades of the 19th century, villagers were flogged and killed if they failed to meet production quotas, and women and children were held hostage to ensure that their menfolk would deliver the products demanded on time. Whether out of self-interest or fear, the colonial overlords were determined to draw their subjects into fuller participation in the European-dominated global market economy.

As increasing numbers of the colonized peoples were drawn into the production of crops or minerals intended for export to Europe, colonized areas in Africa, India, and Southeast Asia were reduced to dependence on the industrializing European economies. Roads and railways were built primarily to facilitate the movement of farm produce and raw materials from the interior of colonized areas to port areas for shipment to Europe. Benefiting from Europe's technological advances, mining sectors grew dramatically in most of the colonies. Vast areas that had been previously uncultivated or (more commonly) planted in food crops were converted to the production of commodities—such as cocoa, palm oil, rubber, and hemp—in great demand in the markets of Europe and, increasingly, the United States.

The profits from the precious metals and minerals extracted from Africa's mines or the rubber grown in Malaya went mainly to European merchants and industrialists. The raw materials themselves were shipped to Europe to be processed and sold or used in the manufacture of industrial products. The finished products were intended mainly for European consumers, whether these be members of middle- and working-class families or government contractors. The African and Asian laborers who produced these products were generally poorly paid—if indeed they were paid at all. The laborers and colonial economies as a whole were steadily reduced to dependence on the European-dominated global market. Thus economic dependence complemented the political subjugation and social subordination of colonized African and Asian peoples in a world order overwhelmingly loaded in favor of the expansionist nations of western Europe.

WHITE DOMINIONS AND CONTESTED SETTLER COLONIES

The contested settler colonies that developed in Africa and the Pacific in the 19th century were in important ways similar to the White Dominions. In fact, the early history of South Africa, one of the largest of the contested settler colonies, exhibited interesting comparisons and contrasts with Canada and Australia, the largest of the White Dominions. European settlers began to move into the southwest corner of South Africa and eastern Canada in the middle decades of the 17th century, long before the settlement of Australia got under way in the 1840s. The initial Dutch colony at Cape Town was established to provide a way station where Dutch merchant ships could take on water and fresh foods in the middle of their long journey from Europe to the East Indies. In contrast to Canada, where French fur trappers and missionaries quickly moved into the interior, the small community of Dutch settlers stayed near the coast for decades after their arrival. But like the settlers in Australia, the Boers (or farmers), as the Dutch in South Africa came to be called, eventually began to move into the vast interior regions of the continent. Though the settlers in each of the three areas were confronted by wild, uncharted, and in some ways

DOCUMENT:
CONTRARY IMAGES: THE COLONIZER VS. THE COLONIZED ON THE "CIVILIZING MISSION"

Each of the following passages from novels written in the colonial era expresses a different view of the reasons behind and the consequences of European colonization in Africa and Asia. The first is taken from an adventure story written by John Buchan entitled *Prestor John*, a favorite in the pre–World War I decades among English schoolboys—many of whom would go out as young men to administer in the colonies. Davie, the protagonist in the story, is a "tall, square-set lad . . . renown [for his] prowess at Rugby football." He summarizes key elements of the "civilizing mission" credo by which so many European thinkers and political leaders attempted to justify their colonization of most of the rest of the world.

I knew then [after Davie's struggle to thwart a "native" rising in South Africa] the meaning of the white man's duty. He has to take all the risks, reck[on]ing nothing of his life or his fortunes and well content to find his reward in the fulfillment of his task. That is the difference between white and black, the gift of responsibility, the power of being in a little way a king; and so long as we know this and practise it, we will rule not in Africa alone but wherever there are dark men who live only for the day and their own bellies. Moreover the work made me pitiful and kindly. I learned much of the untold grievances of the natives and saw something of their strange, twisted reasoning.

The second passage is taken from René Maran's *Batouala*, which was first published in 1921 just after the First World War. Though a French colonial official in West Africa, Maran was an Afro-American, born in Martinique, who was highly sensitive to the plight of the colonized in Africa. Here his protagonist, a local African leader named Batouala, complains of the burdens rather than the benefits of colonial rule and mocks the self-important European agents of the vaunted civilizing mission.

But what good does it do to talk about it? It's nothing new to us that men of white skin are more delicate than men of black skin.

One example of a thousand possible. Everyone knows that the whites, saying that they are "collecting taxes," force all blacks of a marriageable age to carry voluminous packages from when the sun rises to when it sets.

These trips last two, three, five days. Little matter to them the weight of these packages which are called "sandoukous." They don't sink under the burden. Rain, sun, cold? They don't suffer. So they pay no attention. And long live the worst weather, provided the whites are sheltered.

Whites fret about mosquito bites. . . . They fear mason bees. They are also afraid of the "prakongo," the scorpion who lives, black and venomous, among decaying roofs, under rubble, or in the midst of debris.

In a word, everything worries them. As if a man worthy of the name would worry about everything which lives, crawls, or moves around him.

The whites, aha! The whites . . . didn't everyone know that their feet were just a stinking mass? And what a ridiculous idea to encase feet in black, white, or banana-colored skins! And if it were only their feet which stank! *Lalala*—their whole body smelled like a corpse.

Questions: What sorts of roles does Davie assume that the Europeans must play in the colonies? What benefits accrue to colonized peoples from their rule? What impression does he convey of the thinking and behavior of the colonized peoples? In what ways do Batouala's views of the Europeans conflict with Davie's assumptions about himself and other colonizers? Does Batouala agree with Davie's conviction that colonial rule is beneficial for the Africans? What sorts of burdens does Batouala believe it imposes? According to Batouala, what advantages do Africans have over Europeans?

inhospitable frontier regions, they also found a temperate climate in which they could grow the crops and raise the livestock they were accustomed to in Europe. Equally important, they encountered a disease environment they could withstand.

The Boers and Australians found the areas into which they moved sparsely populated. In this respect their experience was somewhat different from that of the settlers in Canada, where the Amerindian population, though far from dense, was organized into powerful tribal confederations. The Boers and Australians faced much less resistance as they took possession of the lands once occupied by hunting-and-gathering peoples. The Boer farmers and cattle ranchers enslaved these peoples, the Khoikhoi, while at the same time integrating them into their large frontier homesteads. Extensive miscegenation between the Boers and Khoikhoi in these early centuries of European colonization produced the sizable "colored" population that exists in South Africa today, which is regarded as quite distinct from the black, or African, majority. The Australian and Canadian settlers drove the "aborigines" they encountered before them into the interior, eventually leaving those who survived their invasions the uneasy occupants of remote tracts of waste, which did not seem to be worth settling. In both cases, but particularly in Canada, the indigenous population was also decimated by many of the same diseases that had turned contacts with the Europeans into a demographic disaster for the rest of the Americas in the early centuries of European overseas expansion.

Thus until the first decades of the 19th century, the process of colonization in South Africa paralleled that in Canada and Australia quite closely. Small numbers of Europeans had migrated into lands they considered "empty" or undeveloped. After driving away or subjugating the indigenous peoples, the Europeans farmed, mined, and grazed their herds on these lands, which they claimed as their own. But whereas the settler societies in Canada and Australia went on to develop, rather peacefully, into loyal and largely self-governing dominions of the British Empire, the arrival of the same British overlords in South Africa in the early 19th century sent the Boers reeling onto a very different historical path.

LAYING THE FOUNDATIONS FOR NATIONHOOD IN THE WHITE DOMINIONS

Canada, won by Britain in wars with France in the 18th century, had been preserved from the contagion of the American Revolution. Religious differences between French Catholic settlers and British rulers and settlers troubled the area recurrently, and a number of uprisings occurred early in the 19th century. Determined not to lose this colony as it had lost the United States, the British began in 1839 to grant increasing self-rule. Canada set up its own parliament and laws, while remaining attached to the larger empire. Initially this system applied primarily to the province of Ontario, but other provinces were included, creating a federal system that describes Canada to this day. French hostilities were eased somewhat by the creation of a separate province, Quebec, where the majority of French speakers were located. Massive railroad building, beginning in the 1850s, brought settlement to western territories and a great expansion of mining and commercial agriculture in the vast plains. As in the United States, immigrants from southern and particularly eastern Europe poured in during the last decades of the century, attracted by Canada's growing commercial development and spurring further gains.

Britain's Australian colonies originated in 1788 when a ship deposited convicts to establish a penal settlement at Sydney. By 1840 Australia had 140,000 European inhabitants, based mainly on a prosperous sheep-growing agriculture that provided needed wool for British industries. Exportation of convicts ceased in 1853, by which time most settlers were free immigrants. Discovery of gold in 1851 spurred further pioneering, leading to a population of over a million by 1861. As in Canada, major provinces were granted self-government with a multiparty parliamentary system. A unified federal nation was proclaimed on the first day of the 20th century, by which time considerable industrialization, a growing Socialist party, and significant welfare legislation had occurred.

Like the United States, Canada and Australia each had distinct national flavors and national issues. But the white Dominions were far more dependent on the European, particularly the British, economy than was the United States. Industrialization did not overshadow commercial agriculture and mining, even in Australia, so that exchanges with Europe remained unusually important. Nevertheless, despite their distinctive features, these countries followed basic patterns of Western civilization from this point onward, from political forms to key leisure activities. Currents of liberalism, socialism, modern art, and scientific education that described Western civilization to 1900 and beyond thus largely characterized these important new extensions. These

As this engraving of a cattle roundup in Queensland, Australia, suggests, cattle herding played as pivotal a role in the settlement of the Australian outback frontier as it did in the United States.

nations in the making also looked primarily to Europe for cultural styles and intellectual leadership. They followed common Western patterns in such areas as family life, the valuation of women, and the extension of mass education and culture. Unlike the United States, however, Canada and Australia remained part of the British Empire, though with growing autonomy.

It was these areas, finally, along with the United States and part of Latin America, particularly Brazil and Argentina, that received new waves of European emigrants during the 19th century. Though Europe's population growth rate slowed after 1800, it still advanced rapidly on the basis of previous gains—that is, as more children reached adulthood and had children of their own. Europe's expansion was in fact greater than Asia's in percentage terms, with both continents relying heavily on the use of foodstuffs initially discovered in the New World, and Europe's export of people helped explain how Western societies could take shape in such distant areas.

BOER VERSUS BRITISH IN SOUTH AFRICA

Canada and Australia moved steadily and peacefully toward nationhood in the last decades of the 19th century, but the Boer farmers who had settled the Cape Colony region in South Africa clashed repeatedly with their British overlords. The British had captured Cape Town during the wars precipitated by the French Revolution in the 1790s, when Holland was overrun by France, thus making Dutch colonies targets of British assaults. The British held the area during the Napoleonic wars that followed and annexed it permanently in 1815 as a vital link with their premier colony in India.

Made up mainly of people of Dutch and French Protestant descent, the Boer community at the Cape differed from the British newcomers in almost every way possible. The Boers spoke a different language and lived mostly in isolated rural homesteads that had missed the scientific, industrial, and urban revolutions that had transformed British society and attitudes. Most critically, the Evangelical missionaries who entered South Africa under the protection of the new British overlords were deeply committed to eradicating slavery. They made no exception for the domestic pattern of enslavement that had developed in Boer homesteads and communities. By the 1830s missionary pressure and increasing British interference in their lives drove a handful of Boers to open but futile rebellion, and many of the remaining Boers fled the Cape Colony.

In the decades of the Great Trek that followed, tens of thousands of Boer farmers migrated in covered wagons pulled by oxen, first east across the Great Fish River and then over the mountains into the *veld,* the rolling grassy plains that make up much of the South African interior. In these areas the Boers collided head-on with populous, militarily powerful, and well-organized African states built by Bantu peoples such as the Zulus and the Xhosa. Throughout the middle decades of the 19th century, the migrating Boers clashed again and again with the Bantu peoples, who were determined to resist the seizure of the lands where they pastured their great herds of cattle and grew subsistence foods. The British in effect followed the Boer pioneers along the southern and eastern coast, eventually establishing a second major outpost at Durban in Natal. Tensions between Boers and Britain remained high, but the British were often drawn into the frontier wars against the Bantu peoples, even though they were not always formally allied to the Boers.

In the early 1850s Boer hard-liners established two republics in the interior, the Orange Free State and the Transvaal, which they sought to keep free of British influence. For over a decade they managed to keep the British out of their affairs. But when diamonds were discovered in the Orange Free State in 1867, British entrepreneurs, such as Cecil Rhodes, and prospectors began to move in, and tensions between Boers and British

began to build anew. In 1880 and 1881, these tensions led to a brief war in which the Boers were victorious. The tide of British immigration into the republics, however, rose even higher after gold was discovered in the Transvaal in 1885.

Though the British had pretty much left the Boers to deal with the African peoples who lived in the republics as they pleased, British migrants and financiers grew more and more resentful of Boer efforts to limit their numbers and curb their civil rights. British efforts to protect the settlers and bring the feisty and independent Boers into line led to the republics' declaration of war against the British in late 1899, and Boer attacks on British bases in Natal, the Cape Colony, and elsewhere. The Anglo-Boer War that resulted raged until 1902 and began the process of decolonization for the European settlers of South Africa, while at the same time it opened the way for their dominance over the African majority.

PACIFIC TRAGEDIES

The territories the Europeans, Americans, and Japanese claimed throughout the South Pacific in the 19th century were in some cases outposts of true empire, in others contested settler colonies. In both situations,

Well-to-do Afrikaner homes near Cape Town in South Africa are the focal point of this 1864 engraving. The abundance of mulatto servants, shown in the foreground, was typical of Boer homesteads, where color lines were quite permeable and miscegenation was not uncommon until well into the 19th century.

however, the coming of colonial rule resulted in demographic disasters and social disruptions of a magnitude that had not been seen since the first century of European expansion into the Americas. Like the Amerindian peoples of the New World, the peoples of the South Pacific had long lived in isolation. This meant that like the Amerindians they had no immunities to many of the diseases European explorers and later merchants, missionaries, and settlers carried to their island homes from the 1760s onward. In addition, their cultures were extremely vulnerable to the corrosive effects of outside influences, such as new religions, different sexual mores, more lethal weapons, and sudden influxes of cheap consumer goods. Thus whatever the intentions of the incoming Europeans and Americans—and they were by no means always benevolent—their contacts with the peoples of the Pacific islands almost invariably ushered in periods of social disintegration and widespread human suffering.

Of the many cases of contact between the expansive peoples of the West and the long isolated island cultures of the South Pacific, the confrontations in New Zealand and Hawaii are among the most informative. Quite sophisticated cultures and fairly complex societies had developed in each of these areas. In addition, the two island groups contained, at the time of the European explorers' arrivals, some of the largest concentrations of population in the entire Pacific region. Both areas were subjected to European influences carried by a variety of agents—from whalers and merchants to missionaries and colonial administrators. After the first decades of contact, the peoples of both New Zealand and Hawaii experienced a period of crisis so severe that their continued survival was in doubt. In both cases, however, the threatened peoples and cultures rebounded and found enduring solutions to the challenges from overseas that combined accommodation to outside influences and revivals of traditional beliefs and practices.

NEW ZEALAND. The Maoris of New Zealand went through two periods of profound disruption and danger. The first began in the 1790s when timber merchants and whalers established small settlements on the New Zealand coast. Maoris living near these settlements were afflicted with alcoholism and the spread of prostitution. In addition, they traded wood and food for European firearms that soon revolutionized Maori warfare—in part by rendering it much more deadly—and upset the existing balance among different tribal groups. Even more devastating was the impact of diseases, such as smallpox, tuberculosis, and even the common cold, that ravaged Maori communities throughout the north island. By the 1840s only eighty to ninety thousand Maoris remained of a population that had been as high as 130,000 less than a century earlier. But the Maoris survived these calamities and began to adjust to the imports of the foreigners. They took up farming with European implements and grazed cattle purchased from European traders. They cut timber, built windmills, and traded extensively with the merchants who frequented their shores. Many even converted to Christianity, which the missionaries began to proselytize after their first station was established in 1814, though observers noted the Maoris' continuing adherence to their old beliefs and rituals.

The arrival of British farmers and herders in search of land in the early 1850s and the British decision to claim the islands as part of their global empire again plunged the Maoris into misery and despair. Backed by the military clout of the colonial government, the settlers occupied some of the most fertile areas of the north island. The warlike Maori fought back, sometimes with temporary successes, but they were steadily driven back into the interior of the island. In desperation in the 1860s and 1870s, they flocked to religious prophets who promised them magical charms and supernatural assistance in their efforts to drive out the invaders. When the prophets also failed them, the Maoris seemed for a time to face extinction. In fact, some British writers, heavily influenced by the work of "social Darwinists," such as Herbert Spencer, predicted that within generations the Maoris, like the Arawaks and Tasmanians before them, would die out.

The Maoris displayed surprising resilience. As they built up immunities to new diseases, they also learned to use European laws and political institutions to defend themselves and preserve what was left of their ancestral lands. Because the British had in effect turned the internal administration of the islands over to the settlers' representatives, the Maoris' main struggle was with the invaders who had come to stay. Western schooling and a growing ability to win British colonial officials over to their point of view eventually enabled the Maoris to hold their own in their ongoing legal contests and daily exchanges with the settlers. A multiracial society has now evolved in which there is a reasonable level of European and Maori accommodation and interaction and that has allowed the Maori to preserve much of value in their traditional culture.

HAWAII.   The conversion of Hawaii to settler colony status followed familiar basic imperialist patterns but with a number of specific twists. Hawaii did not become a colony until the United States proclaimed annexation in 1898, though an overzealous British official had briefly declared the islands for his nation in 1843. Hawaii came under increasing Western influence, however, from the late 18th century onward—politically at the hands of the British, culturally and economically from the United States, whose westward surge quickly spilled into the Pacific Ocean.

Although very occasional contact with Spanish ships during the 16th and 17th centuries is probable, Hawaii was effectively opened to the West through the voyages of Captain James Cook from 1777 to 1779. Cook was first welcomed as a god, partly because he had the good luck to land during a sacred period when war was forbidden. A later and less well-timed visit brought Cook's death, as Hawaiian warriors sought to take over his ship with its metal nails, much prized by a people whose elaborate culture rested on a Neolithic technology. Cook and later British expeditions convinced a young Hawaiian prince, Kamehameha, that some imitation of Western ways could produce a unified kingdom under his leadership, replacing the small and warring regional units that had previously prevailed. A series of vigorous wars, backed by British weapons and advisors, won Kamehameha his kingdom between 1794 and 1810. The new king and his successors promoted economic change, encouraging Western merchants to establish export trade in Hawaiian goods in return for increasing revenues to the royal treasury.

Hawaiian royalty began to imitate Western habits, in some cases traveling to Britain and often building Western-style palaces. Two powerful queens advanced the process of change by insisting that traditional taboos subordinating women be abandoned. In this context vigorous missionary efforts from Protestant New England, beginning in 1819, brought extensive conversions to Christianity. As with other conversion processes, religious change had wide implications. Missionaries railed against traditional Hawaiian costumes, insisting that women cover their breasts, and a new garment, the muumuu, was fashioned from homespun American nightgowns with the sleeves cut off. Backed by the Hawaiian monarchy, missionaries also quickly established an extensive school system, by 1831 serving 50,000 students from a culture that had not previously developed writing.

The combination of Hawaiian interest and Western intrusion produced creative political and cultural changes, though inevitably at the expense of previous values. Demographic and economic trends had more insidious effects. Western-imported disease, particularly venereal disease and tuberculosis, had the usual tragic consequences for a previously isolated people: By 1850 only about eighty thousand Hawaiians remained of a population of about half a million. Westerners more consciously exploited the Hawaiian economy. Whalers helped create raucous seaport towns. Western settlers (called *haoles* by the Hawaiians) from various countries experimented with potential commercial crops, soon concentrating on sugar. Many missionary families turned to leasing land or buying it outright, impatient with the subsistence habits of Hawaiian commoners. They did not entirely forget their religious motives—among other things, many American missionaries had a strong antislavery background and shunned the most intense forms of exploitation—but it remained true that many families who came to Hawaii to do good ended by doing well.

Western businesses were mainly encouraged by the Hawaiian monarchy, eager for revenues and impressed by the West's military power. In 1848 an edict called the Great Mahele imposed Western concepts of property on Hawaiian land that had previously been shared by commoners and aristocrats. Most of the newly defined private property went to the king and the nobles, who gradually sold most of it to investors from the West. As sugar estates spread, increasing numbers of Americans moved in to take up other commercial and professional positions—hence an increasingly "settler" pattern even in a technically independent state. Given Hawaiian population decline, it was also necessary to import Asian workers to staff the estates. The first Chinese contract workers were brought in before 1800, and after 1868 a larger current of Japanese swelled the immigrant throng.

Literal imperialism came as an anticlimax. The abilities of Hawaiian kings declined after 1872, in one case because of problems of disease and alcoholism. Under a weakened state, powerful planter interests pressed for special treaties with the United States that would promote their sugar exports, and the American government claimed naval rights at the Pearl Harbor base by

The extent to which Hawaii had come under Western influence by the late 19th century is dramatically illustrated by the dress of the female attendants at a feast given for U.S. and British naval officers by the ruler of the islands.

1887. As the last Hawaiian monarchs turned increasingly to the promotion of culture, writing a number of lasting Hawaiian songs but also spending considerable money on luxurious appointments, American planters concluded that their economic interests required outright U.S. control. An "annexation committee" persuaded American naval officers to "protect American lives and property" by posting troops around Honolulu in 1893, and the monarchy was disbanded. An imperial-minded U.S. Congress obligingly took over the islands in 1898.

As in New Zealand, Western control combined with considerable respect for Polynesian culture. Americans in Hawaii did not apply the same degree of racism that had described earlier relations with North American Indians or with African slaves. Hawaii's status as a settler colony was further complicated by the arrival of so many Asian immigrants. Nevertheless, Western cultural and particularly economic influence extended steadily, and the ultimate political seizure merely ratified the colonization of the islands.

CONCLUSION:

THE PATTERN OF THE AGE OF IMPERIALISM

Though the basic patterns of domination in European colonial empires remained similar to those worked out in Java and India in the early industrial period, the style of colonial rule and patterns of social interaction between colonizer and colonized changed considerably in the late 19th century. Racism and social snobbery became pervasive in contacts between the colonizers and their African and Asian subordinates. The Europeans consciously renounced the ways of dressing, eating habits, and pastimes that had earlier been borrowed from or shared with the peoples of the colonies. The colonizers no longer saw themselves simply as the most successful competitors in a many-sided struggle for political power. They were convinced that they were inherently superior beings, citizens of the most powerful, civilized, and advanced societies on earth. Colonial officials in the age of "high imperialism" were much more concerned than earlier administrators to pull the peasants, who made up the overwhelming majority of the population of all colonized societies, into the market economy and teach them the value of hard work and discipline. Colonial educators were determined to impress on the children of the colonized elite classes the superiority of Western learning and of everything from political organization to fashions in clothing.

In striving for these objectives the European colonizers started with the assumption that it was their duty to impose their own views and ways of doing things, rather than learn from others—to remake the world, insofar as the abilities of the "natives" would allow, in the image of industrial Europe. But in pushing for change within colonized societies that had ancient, deeply rooted cultures and patterns of civilized life, the Europeans frequently aroused resistance to specific policies and to colonial rule more generally. Though the colonizers were able to put down protest movements led by displaced princes and religious prophets, much more enduring and successful challenges to their rule came, ironically, from the leaders their social reforms and Western-language schools had done much to nurture. These nationalists reworked European ideas and resurrected those of their own cultures, borrowed European organizational techniques, and used the communications systems and common language the Europeans had introduced into the colonies to contest European dominance. The overwhelming dependence of the Europeans on the collaboration of colonized peoples to govern and police their empires rendered the Europeans particularly vulnerable to these challenges from within.

FURTHER READINGS

There is a vast literature on various aspects of European imperialism. Useful general histories on the different empires include Bernard Porter's *The Lion's Share: A Short History of British Imperialism 1850–1970* (1975), Raymond Betts's *Tricouleur* (1978), James J. Cooke's *The New French Imperialism, 1881–1910* (1973), and Woodruff D. Smith's *The German Colonial Empire* (1978).

Of the many contributions to the debate over late-19th-century imperialism, some of the most essential are those by D. C. M. Platt, Hans-Ulrich Wehler, William Appleman Williams, Jean Stengers, D. K. Fieldhouse, and Henri Brunschwig, as well as the earlier works by Lenin and J. A. Hobson. Winfried Baumgart's *Imperialism* (1982) provides a good overview of the literature and conflicting arguments. Very different perspectives on the partition of Africa can be found in Jean Suret-Canale's *French Colonialism in Tropical Africa, 1900–1945* (1971) and Ronald Robinson and John Gallagher's *Africa and the Victorians* (1961).

Most of the better studies on the impact of imperialism and social life in the colonies are specialized monographs, but Percival Spear's *The Nabobs* (1963) is a superb place to start on the latter from the European viewpoint. The works of Frantz Fanon, Albert Memmi, and O. Mannoni provide much information on the plight of the colonized. The impact of industrialization and other changes in Europe on European attitudes toward the colonized are treated in a number of works, including Philip Curtin's *The Image of Africa* (1964), William B. Cohen's *The French Encounter with Africans* (1980), and Michael Adas's *Machines as the Measure of Men* (1989). Important correctives relating to gender issues in the colonies as interpreted by early writers such as Spear are provided in a number of recent monographs, including Margaret Strobel's *European Women and the Second British Empire* (1991) and Helen Callaway's *Gender, Culture, and Empire* (1987). Though now somewhat dated, a good overview of the impact of imperialism on African and Asian women can be found in Ester Boserup's *Women's Role in Economic Development* (1970).

Latin America

1808–1825 Spanish-American wars of independence

1810 In Mexico, Father Hidalgo initiates rebellion against Spain

1792 Slave rebellion in St. Domingue (Haiti)

1808 Portuguese court flees Napoleon, arrives in Brazil; French armies invade Spain

1804 Haiti declares independence

1829–1852 Juan Manuel de Rosas rules Rio de la Plata

1822 Brazil declares independence; empire established under Dom Pedro I

1823 Monroe Doctrine indicates U.S. opposition to European ambitions in the Americas

1830 Bolívar dies; Gran Colombia dissolves into separate countries of Venezuela, Colombia, and Equador

1821 Mexico declares independence; empire under Iturbide lasts to 1823

1854 Benito Juárez leads reform in Mexico

1846–1848 Mexican-American War

1847–1855 Caste War in Yucatan

1850s Beginnings of railroad construction in Cuba, Chile, and Brazil

China and the Ottoman Empire

1789–1807 Reign of Ottoman Sultan Selim III

1805–1849 Reign of Muhammad Ali in Egypt

1736–1799 Reign of the Qianlong emperor in China

1768–1774 Disastrous Ottoman war with Russia

1772 Safavid dynasty falls in Persia

1807–1839 Reign of Ottoman Sultan Mahmud II

1780s Early efforts at reform in the Ottoman Empire

1798 British embassy to Qianlong emperor in China; French invasion of Egypt; Napoleon defeats Egypt's Mameluk rulers

1727 First printing press set up in the Ottoman Empire

1834 Postal system established in Ottoman Empire

1826 Ottoman Janissary corps destroyed

1838 Ottoman treaty with British removing trade restrictions in the empire

1839–1841 Opium War in China

1839–1876 Tanzimat reforms in the Ottoman Empire

1839–1897 Life of Islamic thinker Al-Afghani

A.D. 1800   A.D. 1820   A.D. 1840

Precarious Sovereignty: Western Informal Empire and Constricted Development in Latin America, the Middle East, and China

INTRODUCTION. The spread of Western imperialism resulted in the division of much of the world between the European powers and the United States during the 19th century. Africa, both north and south of the Sahara, was almost entirely swallowed up. Australia, New Zealand, and all the clusters of smaller Pacific islands, including Hawaii, were seized. Southeast Asia was carved up by the Western imperialist powers. In combination with earlier acquisitions the result was nearly a solid bloc of colonies (Siam excepted) from India in the west to the Philippines in the east.

For varying reasons, a number of non-Western societies managed to escape conquest and formal colonization by the industrialized powers of Europe and North America. In both Siam and Persia, for example, European rivals chose to leave indigenous rulers in power in order to provide buffer states between their respective colonies. As we have seen, Russia and Japan were able to "Westernize" sufficiently to ward off the threat of direct colonization by any of the industrial powers. Russia was, in any case, too large and had too long been a major player in European Great Power rivalries to be a serious candidate for conquest. By

---

1862–1867 French intervention in Mexico

1876–1911 Porfirio Díaz rules Mexico

1903 Panamanian independence; beginning of Panama Canal (opens in 1914)

1889 Fall of Brazilian Empire; republic established

1868–1878 Ten year war against Spain in Cuba

1865–1870 War of the Triple Alliance (Argentina, Brazil, and Uruguay against Paraguay)

1895–1898 Cuban Spanish-American War; U.S. acquires Puerto Rico and Philippines

1886–1888 Cuba and Brazil finally abolish slavery

1869 First school for girls in Mexico

1849–1905 Life of Muhammad Abduh

1870 Ottoman legal code reformed

1908 Young Turks seize power in Istanbul

1898–1901 Boxer Rebellion in China; 100 Days of Reform in China

1883 Mahdist victory over British-led Egyptian expeditionary force at Shakyan

1882 British invasion and occupation of Egypt; failed revolt led by Orabi in Egypt

1850–1864 Taiping rebellion in China

1876 Constitution promulgated for Ottoman Empire

1869 Opening of the Suez Canal

1877 Treaty of San Stefano; Ottomans driven from most of the Balkans

1905 Fatherland Party established in Egypt

1856–1860 Anglo-French war against China

1866 First railway begun in Ottoman Empire

1889 Young Turks established in Paris

1898 British-Egyptian army defeats the Mahdist army at Omdurman

1854–1856 Crimean War

1876–1908 Reign of Ottoman Sultan Abdul Hamid

contrast, Japan was too isolated from the European state system and was considered by imperial strategists to be too poor in market and natural-resource potential to justify the heavy costs of colonizing such a martial society. For rather different reasons, the imperial powers found it much easier to manipulate politically and exploit economically the new states of Latin America and the vast Qing Empire of China through sporadic applications of gunboat diplomacy rather than outright colonization. As a result, each area was divided into informal spheres of influence for each of the interested industrial powers. Within these spheres the designated power (or powers) enjoyed special preferences in trade and investment and periodically applied diplomatic pressure or military force to bring recalcitrant indigenous leaders into line.

As these examples suggest, even the areas that were not colonized directly were strongly affected by the economic penetration and political machinations of the Western industrial powers. Informal empire is perhaps the most apt label for the indirect control that resulted. Though challenged by the advance of Western imperialism, Japan managed to ward off Western control, while virtually all of the rest of the globe that was not formally colonized came within the economic and political spheres of influence of one or more of the Western powers. The new nations of Latin America were dominated economically by Great Britain and, increasingly, the United States, and interventions by both powers repeatedly violated their sovereignty. Western manufacturers and investment capital made ever greater inroads into the ancient civilizations of the Middle East and China. In each of these regions informal empire in the guise of Western military superiority and economic involvement led to major crises, not just for the dynasties in power but also for each of the long-standing civilizations.

In this chapter we explore the ways in which informal imperialism skewed and often constricted the social, economic, and political development of three key areas that were subject to this mode of Western dominance: Latin America, the Turkic- and Arab-speaking regions of the Middle East, and China. Though attention must be paid to the internal dynamics of developments within each of these areas, foreign influences and often direct Western intervention played decisive roles in shaping the circumstances under which the societies of each entered the 20th century.

THE CONSOLIDATION OF NEW NATIONS IN LATIN AMERICA

By 1830 the former Spanish and Portuguese colonies had become independent nations. The roughly twenty million inhabitants of these nations looked hopefully to the future. Born in the crisis of the old regime and Iberian colonialism, many of the leaders of independence shared the ideals of representative government, careers open to talent, freedom of commerce and trade, the right to private property, and a belief in the individual as the basis of society. They believed generally that the new nations should be sovereign and independent states, large enough to be economically viable and integrated by a common set of laws.

On the issue of freedom of religion and the position of the Church, however, there was less agreement among the leadership. Roman Catholicism had been the state religion and the only one allowed by the Spanish crown. Although most leaders sought to maintain Catholicism as the official religion of the new states, some sought to end the exclusion of other faiths. The defense of the Church became a rallying cry for the conservative forces.

The ideals of the early leaders of independence were often egalitarian. Bolívar had received aid from Haiti and had promised in return to abolish slavery in the areas he liberated. By 1854 slavery had been abolished everywhere except Spain's remaining colonies of Cuba and Puerto Rico and in Brazil (all places where the economy was profoundly based on it). Early promises to end Indian tribute and taxes on people of mixed origin came much slower because the new nations still needed the revenue such policies produced. Egalitarian sentiments were often tempered by fears that the mass of the population was unprepared for self-rule and democracy. Early constitutions sought to balance order and popular representation by imposing property or literacy restrictions. Invariably, voting rights were reserved for males. Women were still disenfranchised and usually unable to hold public office. The lack of trust of the Creole (American-born descendants of Europeans) elite was based on the fact that in many places the masses had not demonstrated a clear preference for the new regimes and had sometimes fought in royalist armies mobilized by traditional loyalties and regional interests. Although some mestizos had risen to leadership roles in the wars of independence, the old casta, or color distinctions, did not disappear easily. In Mexico, Guatemala, and the Andean nations the large Indian population remained mostly outside of national political life. The mass of the Latin American population—Indians and people of mixed origins—waited to see what was to come, and they were suspicious of the new political elite, whose members were often drawn from the old colonial aristocracy but were now also joined by a new commercial and urban bourgeoisie.

POLITICAL FRAGMENTATION

The new nations can be grouped into a number of regional blocs. Some of the early leaders for independence had dreamed of creating a unified nation in some form, but regional rivalries, economic competition, and political divisions soon made that hope, and even more modest versions of it, impossible. Mexico emerged as a short-lived monarchy until a republic was proclaimed in

1823, but its government remained unstable until the 1860s because of military coups, financial failures, foreign intervention, and political turmoil. Central America broke away from the Mexican monarchy and did form a union, but regional antagonisms and resentment of Guatemala, the largest nation in the region, eventually led to dissolution of the union in 1838. Spain's Caribbean colonies, Cuba and Puerto Rico, suppressed early movements for independence and remained outwardly loyal. The Dominican Republic was occupied by its neighbor; after resisting Haiti, as well as France and Spain, it finally gained independence in 1844. The Dominican example and the fear of a Haitian-style slave revolt tended to keep the Creole leaders of Cuba and Puerto Rico quiet.

In South America the old colonial viceroyalty of New Granada became the basis for Gran Colombia—the large new state Bolívar created that included modern

Latin America in the 19th Century

Ecuador, Colombia, Panama, and Venezuela. The union, made possible to some extent by Bolívar's personal reputation and leadership, disintegrated as his own standing declined, and it ended in 1830, the year of his death. In the south the viceroyalty of the Rio de la Plata served as the basis for a desired state that the peoples of Argentina hoped to lead. Other parts of the region resisted these hopes. Paraguay declared and maintained its autonomy under Dr. José Rodríguez de Francia, who ruled his isolated and landlocked country as a dictator until 1840. Modern Uruguay, formed by a revolution for independence against the dominant power of its large neighbors Argentina and Brazil, became an independent buffer between those two nations in 1828. The Andean nations of Peru and Bolivia, with their large Indian populations and conservative colonial aristocracies, flirted with union from 1829 to 1839 under the mestizo general Andrés Santa Cruz, but once again regional rivalries and the fears of their neighbors undermined the effort. Finally, Chile, somewhat isolated and blessed by the opening of trade in the Pacific, followed its own political course in a relatively stable fashion.

Most attempts at consolidation and union failed. Enormous geographical barriers and great distances separated nations and even regions within nations. Roads were poor and transportation rudimentary. To move goods 200 miles from Guayaquil on the coast to Quito in the Andes was an enormous task, and to send a message from Mexico City to Monterrey, California, took weeks. Geography, regional interests, and political divisions were too strong to overcome. Then, too, the colonial heritage, in which the Spanish crown had protected some interests and regions at the expense of others and had left the mass of the population outside the political process, carried over into the new regimes. The problems of national integration were daunting. What is striking is not that Spanish America became 18 separate nations but that it did not separate into even more.

"CAUDILLOS," POLITICS, AND THE CHURCH

Many problems confronted the new nations. Over a decade of warfare had disrupted the economies and devastated wide areas of Venezuela, Colombia, and Mexico. The mobilization of large armies whose loyalty to regional commanders was often based on their personal qualities rather than their rank or politics led to the rise of *caudillos,* independent leaders who dominated local areas by force in defiance of national policies and who sometimes seized the national government itself to im-

pose their concept of rule. In situations of intense division among civilian politicians, a powerful regional commander of the army became the arbiter of power, leading sometimes to a situation of "praetorian politics" in which the army made and unmade governments. Keeping the army in the barracks became a preoccupation of governments, and the amount of money spent on the military in national budgets far exceeded needs.

Military commanders and regional or national caudillos were usually interested in power for their own sake, but they could represent or mobilize different groups in society. Many often defended the interests of regional elites, usually landowners, but others were populists who mobilized and claimed to speak for Indians, peasants, and the poor and sometimes received their unquestioning support. A few, such as the conservative Rafael Carrera, who ruled Guatemala from 1839 to 1865, sincerely took the interest of the Indian majority to heart, but in other matters there was a disregard for the normal workings of an open political system and the rule of law among these personalist leaders.

Other common issues confronted many of the new nations. With the exception of Brazil and briefly Mexico, the political leaders were agreed on the republic as the basic form of government, but what kind of republic? A struggle often developed between centralists—who wished to create strong, centralized national governments with broad powers—and federalists—who wanted policies, especially fiscal and commercial ones, to be set by regional governments. Other tensions developed between liberals and conservatives. Liberals stressed the rights of the individual and attacked the corporate (membership in a group or organization) structure of colonial society. They dreamed of a secular society and looked to the models of the United States or France. Often they wanted a decentralized or federalist form of government. Conservatives usually believed in a strong centralized state, and they often wished to maintain aspects of colonial society. They believed that a structure in which corporate groups (such as the Indians), artisan guilds, or institutions (such as the Church) provided the most equitable basis of social action should be recognized in law. Rather than a society based on open competition and individualism, society for the conservatives was organic—each group was linked to the other like parts of a body whose health depended on the proper functioning of each part. Not all conservatives resisted change, and some—such as the Mexican intellectual and politician Lucas Alamán—were among the most "enlightened" leaders in terms of economic and commercial reforms, but as a group the conservatives were skeptical of secularism and individualism and strove to keep the Catholic Iberian heritage alive.

The role of the Church became a crucial issue in politics. The secularization of society and the role of the Church was a key matter that divided proclerical conservatives from the more secular liberals. In Mexico, for example, the Church had played a major role in education, the economy, and politics. Few questioned its dogma, but liberals sought to limit its role in civil life. The Church fought back with the aid of its proclerical supporters and with the power of the papacy, which until the 1840s refused to fill vacant positions in the hierarchy or to cooperate with the new governments.

Political parties, often calling themselves Liberal or Conservative, sprang up throughout Latin America. They struggled for power and sought to impose their vision of the future on society. Their leadership, however, was usually drawn from the same social class of landowners and urban bourgeoisie with little to differentiate them except their position in the Church or on the question of federalism versus centralization. The general population might be mobilized by the force and personality of a particular leader, such as Juan Manuel de Rosas in Argentina or Antonio López de Santa Anna in Mexico, but political ideology was rarely an issue for most of the population.

The result was political turmoil and insecurity in much of Latin America in the first 50 years following independence. Presidents came and went with sad rapidity. Written constitutions, which both Liberal and Conservative parties thought were a positive thing, were often short-lived and overturned with a change in government because the margin for interpretation of the constitution was slight. To some extent this was due to the Roman legal heritage that pervaded Hispanic law and emphasized written laws rather than the more interpretative common-law tradition. Great efforts were made to make constitutions precise, specific, and definitive, but this resulted in an attempt to change or at least modify the constitution each time the government changed. Some nations avoided the worst aspects of instability. Chile, after enacting a constitution in 1833 that gave the president broad powers, established a functioning political system that allowed for compromise. Brazil with its monarchical rule, despite a period of turmoil from 1832 to 1850, was able to maintain a political system of compromise, although it was dominated by the Conservatives, who were favored by the emperor. Its 1824 constitution remained in force until 1889.

It is fair to say that in much of Latin America the basic questions of government and society remained unresolved after independence. Some observers attributed these problems to personalism, a lack of civic responsibility, and other defects in the "Latin" character. Nevertheless, the parallel experience of later emerging nations in the 20th century suggests that these problems were typical of former colonial dependencies searching for order and economic security in a world in which their options were constrained by their own potential and by external conditions.

ECONOMIC RESURGENCE AND LIBERAL POLITICS

By the last quarter of the century, as the world economy entered into a phase of rapid expansion, there was a shift in attitude and possibilities in Latin America. Liberals returned to power in many places in Latin America and initiated a series of changes that began to transform their nations. The ideological basis of the new liberal surge was also changing. Based on the ideas of *positivism* of the French philosopher Auguste Comte, who stressed observation and a scientific approach to the problems of society, Latin American politicians and intellectuals found a guiding set of principles and a justification of their quest for political stability and economic growth.

This shift was due in large part to the general economic expansion of the "second" Industrial Revolution and the age of imperialism. The application of science to industry created new demands for Latin American products, such as copper and rubber, to accompany the increasing demand for its consumer products, such as wheat, sugar, and coffee. The population of Latin America doubled to over 43 million inhabitants in the 60 years between 1820 and 1880. After 1850 economies grew rapidly. Timing, of course, varied greatly, but the expansion of exports in Colombia, Argentina, and Brazil stimulated prosperity for some and a general belief in the advantages of the Liberal programs. The desire to participate in the capitalist expansion of the Western economy dominated the thinking of Latin American leaders. Foreign entrepreneurs and bankers joined hands with philosophical liberals, landowners, and urban merchants in Latin America to back Liberal party programs, which now became possible because of the increased revenues generated by exports.

The leaders of the post-1860 governments were of a new generation, politicians who had matured not in the age of independence but during the chaotic years of

The drive for progress made Latin American nations eager to accept foreign investment. Railroads were important for economic growth in that they often linked key exports to the ports and were designed principally to serve the needs of foreign capital.

postindependence politics. Their inspiration came from England, France, and the United States. They were firm believers in progress, education, and free competition within a secular society, but they were sometimes distrustful of the mass of their own people, who seemed to represent an ancient "barbarism" in contrast to the "civilization" of progress. That distrust and their sometimes insensitive application of foreign models to a very different reality in their own countries—what one Brazilian author has called "ideas out of place"—prevented many from achieving the progress they so ardently desired.

Economic growth and "progress" were costly. Responding to international demand, landowners increased their holdings, often aided by the governments they controlled or influenced. Peasant lands were expropriated in Chile, Peru, and Bolivia; small farmers were displaced in Brazil and Costa Rica; and Church lands were seized in Mexico. Labor was needed. Emigrants from Europe flooded into Argentina and Brazil, and new

forms of tenancy, peonage, and disguised servitude developed in other countries.

CULTURAL LIFE AND POLITICS

In Latin America little separated intellectual life and politics. The *pensador*, or thinker, who might write poetry, history, essays, and novels and combine that activity with political action, public office, and military command, was a common and highly respected figure.

The end of colonial rule opened up Latin America to direct influences from the rest of Europe. Scientific observers, travelers, and the just plain curious, often accompanied by artists, came to see and record and while doing so introduced new ideas and fashions. Artistic and cultural missions were sometimes brought directly from Europe by Latin American governments.

The elite in the new nations adopted the tastes and fashions of Europe. The battles and triumphs of independence were celebrated in paintings, hymns, odes, and theatrical pieces in the neoclassical style in an attempt to use Greece and Rome as a model for the present. In this Latin Americans followed the lead of Europe, especially France. The same neoclassical tradition was also apparent in the architecture of the early 19th century.

In the 1830s the generation that came of age after independence turned to romanticism and found the basis of a new nationality in historical images, the Indian, and local customs. This generation often had a romantic view of "liberty" and emphasized the exotic as well as the distinctive aspects of American society. In Brazil, for example, the poet Antônio Gonçalves Dias (1823–1864) used the Indian as a symbol of Brazil and America. In Cuba novels sympathetic to slaves began to appear by midcentury. In Argentina writers celebrated the pampas and its lonely open spaces. Sarmiento's critical account of the caudillos in *Facundo* described in depth the life of the gauchos, but it was José Hernández who wrote *Martin Fierro* in 1872, a romantic epic poem about the end of the way of the gaucho. Historical themes and the writing of history itself became a political act, because the analysis of the past became a way of setting out a proper program for the present. Many of Latin America's leading politicians were also excellent historians— Mitre in Argentina, Alamán in Mexico, and a remarkable group of liberal Chilean historians deeply influenced by positivism.

By the 1870s a new realism emerged in the arts and literature more in line with the scientific approach of positivism and the modernization of the new nations. As the economies of Latin America surged forward, novelists appeared who were unafraid to deal with such human frailties as corruption, prejudice, and greed. The Chilean Alberto Blest Gana and the Brazilian mulatto J. Machado de Assis (1839–1908) wrote critically about the social mores of their countries during this era.

Throughout the century the culture of the mass of the population had been little affected by the trends and taste of the elite. Popular arts, folk music, and dance flourished in traditional settings, demonstrating a vitality and adaptability to new situations that was often lacking in the more imitative fine arts. Sometimes authors in the romantic tradition or poets like Hernández turned to traditional themes for their subject and inspiration and in that way increasingly brought these traditions to the attention of their class and of the world. For the most part, however, popular artistic expressions were not ap-

Machado de Assis (1839–1908) was a gifted African-Brazilian author of humble origins whose psychological short stories and novels won him acclaim as Brazil's greatest novelist of the 19th century.

preciated or valued by the traditional elites, by the modernizing urban bourgeoisie, or by the newly arrived immigrants.

GENDER, CLASS, AND RACE

Although significant political changes make it appealing to deal with the 19th century as an era of great change and transformation in Latin America, it is necessary to recognize the persistence of old patterns and sometimes their reinforcement. To be sure, changes took place, but their effects were not felt equally by all classes or groups in society, and not all groups were attracted by the promises of the new political regimes and their views of progress.

Women, for example, gained little ground during most of the century. They had participated actively in the independence movements. Some had taken up arms or aided the insurgent forces, and some—such as the Colombian Policarpa (La Pola) Salvatierra, whose final words were "Do not forget my example"—had paid for their activities on the gallows. Following independence, there was virtually no change in the predominant attitudes toward women's proper role. Women were expected to be wives and mothers; they could not vote, hold public office, become lawyers, or, in some places, testify in a court of law. Despite a few exceptions, unmarried women under 25 remained subject to the power and authority of their fathers. Once married, women could not work, enter into contracts, or control their own estates without their husbands' permission. As in the colonial era, marriage, politics, and the creation of kinship links were essential elements in elite control of land and political power, and thus women remained a crucial resource in family strategies.

Lower-class women had more economic freedom—often controlling local marketing—and also more personal freedom than elite women under the constraints of powerful families. In legal terms, however, their situation was no better—and in material terms, much worse—than that of their elite sisters. Still, women were by the 1870s an important part of the work force.

Only in public education did women's situation begin to change significantly. There had already been a movement in this direction in the colonial era; at first the idea behind it was that since women were responsible for the education of their children, they should be educated so that the proper values could be passed to the next generation. By 1842 Mexico City required girls and boys of ages 7 to 15 to attend school, and in 1869 the first girls' school was created in Mexico. Liberals in Mexico wanted secular public education to prepare women for an enlightened role within the home, and similar sentiments were expressed by liberal regimes elsewhere. Public schools appeared throughout Latin America, although their impact was limited. Brazil, for example, had a population of 10 million in 1873 but only about one million men and half that number of women were literate.

The rise of secular public education created new opportunities for women. The demand for teachers at the primary level created the need for schools in which to train teachers. Since most teachers were women, these teacher training schools gave women access to advanced education; although the curriculum often emphasized traditional female roles, an increasing number of educated women began to be dissatisfied with the legal and social constraints on their lives. By the end of the 19th century these women were becoming increasingly active in advocating womens' rights and other political issues.

In most cases the new nations legally ended the old "society of castes" in which legal status and definition depended on color and ethnicity, but in reality much of that system continued. The stigma of skin color and former slave status created barriers to advancement. Indians in Mexico, Bolivia, and Peru often continued to labor under poor conditions and to suffer the effects of government failures. There was conflict. In Yucatán, a great rebellion, pitting the Maya against the central government and the whites, broke out in 1839 and then again in 1847, smoldering for ten years. Despite the intentions of governments, Indians proved resistant to changes imposed from outside their communities and willing to defend their traditional ways. The word "Indian" was still an insult in most places in Latin America. For some mestizos and others of mixed origin, the century presented opportunities for advancement in the army, professions, and commerce, but these cases were exceptions.

In many places expansion of the export economy resulted in a continuation and intensification of old patterns. Liberalism itself changed during the century, and once its program of secularization, rationalism, and rights of property were implanted as law, it displayed a more restrictive nature. Positivists of the end of the century still hoped for economic growth, but some were willing to gain it at the expense of individual freedoms. "Order and Progress," the motto chosen for the flag of the Brazilian republic, reflected that willingness. The positivists were generally convinced of the benefits of international trade for Latin America, and large landholdings increased in many areas at the expense of small farms or Indian communal lands as a result. A small landed, white Creole upper class controlled the economies and politics in most places and was sometimes joined in the political and economic functions by a strata of urban middle-class merchants, bureaucrats, and other bourgeois types. The landed and mercantile elite tended to merge over time to create one group that, in most places, controlled the government. Meanwhile, there were new social forces at work. The flood of immigration, beginning in earnest in the 1870s, to Argentina, Brazil, and a few other nations began to alter the social composition of those places. Increasingly, rapid urbanization also changed the nature of these societies. Still, Latin America, though politically independent, began the 1880s as a group of predominantly agrarian nations with rigid social structures and a continuing dependency on the world market.

ANALYSIS

EXPLAINING UNDERDEVELOPMENT

Whether we use the word *underdeveloped*, the more benign *developing*, or the old-fashioned *backward*, it is usually clear that the term describes a large number of nations in the world that seem to be beset by a series of economic and social problems. Because Latin America was the first part of what we now call the Third World to establish its independence and begin to compete within the world economy, it had to confront the reasons for its relative position and problems quite early and without many alternative models to follow.

At the time of Latin American independence the adoption of European models of economy, government, and law seemed to offer great hope. But as "progress," republican forms of government, free trade, and liberalism failed to bring about general prosperity and social harmony, Latin Americans and others began to search for alternative explanations of their continuing problems as a first step in resolving them. Some critics condemned the Hispanic cultural legacy; others saw the materialism of the modern world as the major problem and called for a return to religion and idealism. By the 20th century Marxism provided a powerful analysis of Latin America's history and present reality—though Marxists themselves could not decide if Latin American societies were essentially feudal and needed first to become capitalist or if they were already capitalist and ready for socialist revolution.

Throughout these discussions and debates Latin Americans often implicitly compared their situation to that of the United States and tried to explain the different economic positions of the two regions. At the beginning of the 19th century both regions were still primarily agricultural, and although a few places in North America were starting small industries, the mining sector in Latin America was far stronger than that of its northern neighbor. In 1850 Latin America had a population of 33 million in comparison to 23 million in the United States, and the per capita income in both regions was roughly equal; by 1940, however, Latin America's population was much larger, and its economic situation far worse than in the United States. Why and how this disparity arose preoccupied observers. Was there some flaw in the Latin American character, or were the explanations to be found in the economic and political differences of the two areas and how could these differences be explained? The answers to these questions were not easy to obtain, but increasingly they were sought not in the history of individual countries but in analyses of a world economic and political system.

Although there had long been a Marxist critique of colonialism and imperialism, the modern Latin American analysis of underdevelopment grew from different origins. During the 1950s a number of European and North American scholars developed the concept of "modernization," or "Westernization." Basing their ideas on the historical experience of western Europe, they believed that development was a matter of increasing per capita production in any society and that as development took place, various kinds of social changes would follow. The more industrialized, urban, and modern a society became, the more social change and improvement were possible as traditional patterns and attitudes were abandoned or transformed. Technology, communications, and the diffusion of material goods were the means by which the transformation would take place. Some scholars also believed that as this process occurred, there would be a natural movement toward more democratic forms of government and popular participation.

Modernization theory held out the promise that any society could move toward a brighter future by essentially following the path taken earlier by western Europe. Its message was one of improvement through gradual rather than radical or revolutionary change, and thus it tended to be politically conservative. It also tended to disregard cultural differences, internal class conflicts, and struggles for power within nations. Moreover, it was sometimes adopted by military regimes that believed that by imposing order, they could best promote the economic changes necessary for modernization.

The proponents of modernization theory had a difficult time convincing many people in the "underdeveloped" world, where the historical experience had been considerably different from that of western Europe. In 19th-century Latin America, for example, early attempts to develop industry had been faced with competition from the cheaper and better products of already industrialized nations, such as England and France, and so a similar path to development was impossible. Critics argued that each nation did not operate individually but was part of a world system that operated to keep some areas "developed" at the expense of others.

These ideas were first and most cogently expressed in Latin America. After World War II the United Nations established the Economic Commission for Latin America (ECLA). Under the leadership of the Argentine economist Raul Prebisch, the ECLA began to analyze the Latin American economies. Prebisch argued that "unequal exchange" between the developed nations at the center of the world economy and those like Latin America created structural blocks to economic growth. The ECLA suggested various policies to overcome the problems, especially the development of industries that would overcome the region's dependence on foreign imports.

From the structural analysis of the ECLA and from more traditional Marxist critiques, a new kind of explanation, usually called *dependency theory,* began to emerge in the 1960s. Rather than seeing underdevelopment or the lack of economic growth as the result of failed modernization, some scholars in Latin America began to argue that development and underdevelopment were not stages but rather part of the same process. They believed that the development and growth of some areas, such as western Europe and the United States, had been achieved at the expense of, or because of, the underdevelopment of dependent regions, such as Latin America. Agricultural economies at the periphery of the world economic system were always at a disadvantage in dealing with the industrial nations of the center and would thus become relatively poorer as the industrial nations got richer. The industrial nations would continually draw products, profits, and cheap labor from the periphery. This basic economic relationship of dependency meant that production, capital accumulation, and class relations in a dependent country were all essentially determined by external forces. Some theorists went even further and argued that Latin America and other nations of the Third World were also culturally dependent in their consumption of ideas and concepts. Both modernization theory and Mickey Mouse were seen as the agents of a cultural domination that was simply an extension of economic reality. These theorists usually argued that socialism was the only hope to break out of the dependency relationship.

These ideas dominated Latin American intellectual life and were broadly appealing to other areas of Asia and Africa that had recently emerged from colonial control. Forms of dependency analysis became popular in many areas of the world in the 1960s and 1970s. By the 1980s, however, dependency theory was losing its appeal. As an explanation of what had happened histori-cally in Latin America, it was useful, but as a theory that could predict what might happen elsewhere and what to do, it provided little help. Marxists argued that it overemphasized the circulation of goods (trade) rather than how things were produced and that it ignored the class conflicts they felt were the motor force of history. Moreover, with the rise of multinational corporations the nature of capitalism itself was changing, and thus an analysis based on trade relationships between countries became somewhat outdated.

Whether development can be widely diffused, as modernization theory argued, or whether the underdevelopment of some countries is inherent in the nature of the capitalist world economy, as the dependency theorists believe, is still a matter of dispute, but recent events in Eastern Europe have thrown the socialist alternative into question as well. A search for new explanations and new solutions to the problems of development will characterize the decade of the 1990s as peoples throughout the world seek to improve their lives.

Questions: In what sense was 19th-century Latin America a dependent economy? Which explanation or prediction about dependency best fits world economic trends today?

THE GREAT BOOM, 1880–1920

Between 1880 and 1920 Latin America, like certain areas of Asia and Africa, experienced a tremendous spurt of economic growth, stimulated by the increasing demand in industrializing Europe and the United States for raw materials, foodstuffs, and specialized tropical crops. Latin America was well prepared for this export-led economic expansion. The Liberal ideology of individual freedoms, an open market, and limited government intervention in the operation of the economy had triumphed in many places. Whereas this ideology had been the expression of the middle class in Europe, in Latin America it was adopted not only by the small urban middle sectors of lawyers, retailers, bureaucrats, and professionals but also by the large landowners, miners, and export merchants linked to the rural economy and the traditional patterns of wealth and landowning. In a number of countries the traditional aristocracy of wealth forged a political alliance with the new urban elements. Together they controlled the presidential offices and the congresses and imposed a business-as-usual approach to government at the expense of peasants and a newly emerging working class.

The expansion of Latin American economies was led by exports: bananas and coffee from Central America; tobacco and sugar from Cuba; rubber and coffee from Brazil; henequen (a fiber for making rope), copper, and silver from Mexico; wool, wheat, and beef from Argentina; and copper from Chile. In this era of strong demand and good prices these nations experienced high profits, which allowed for the import of large quantities of foreign manufactures and provided funds for the beautification of cities and other government projects. But export-led expansion was always risky because the world-market prices of Latin American commodities were ultimately determined by conditions outside the region. In that sense these economies were particularly vulnerable and in some ways dependent.

The expansion of Latin American trade was remarkable, increasing by about 50 percent between 1870 and 1890. Argentina's trade was increasing at about 5 percent a year in this period, one of the highest rates of growth ever recorded for a national economy. "As wealthy as an Argentine" became an expression in Paris, reflecting the fortunes that wool, beef, and grain were earning for some in Argentina. In Mexico an "oligarchic dictatorship," which maintained all the outward attributes of democracy but imposed "law and order" under the dictator Porfirio Díaz, created the conditions for unrestrained profits. Mexican exports doubled between 1877 and 1900, with similar gains in Chile, Costa Rica, and Bolivia.

This rapidly expanding commerce attracted the interest of foreign investors eager for high returns on their capital. British, French, German, and North Americans invested in mining, railroads, public utilities, and banking. Over half the foreign investments in Latin America were British, which alone increased to over £750 million by 1913, or to ten times as much as had been invested in 1870. But British leadership was no longer uncontested; Germany and increasingly the United States provided competition. The United States was particularly active in the Caribbean region and Mexico, but not until after World War I would U.S. capital predominate in the region.

Foreign investments provided Latin America with needed capital and services but tended to place key industries, transportation facilities, and services in foreign hands. These were thus vulnerable to external influences and decisions. Foreign investments also constrained Latin American governments in the social, commercial, and diplomatic policies that they could follow.

MEXICO AND ARGENTINA. We can use these two large Latin American nations as examples of different responses within the same general pattern. In Mexico the Liberal triumph of Juárez had set the stage for economic growth and constitutional government. In 1876 Porfirio Díaz, one of Juárez's generals, was elected president, and for the next 35 years he dominated politics either as president or as the power behind the scenes. Díaz suppressed regional rebellions and imposed a strong centralized government. Using foreign capital, the railroad system grew rapidly, providing a new way of integrating Mexican regional economies, moving goods to the ports for export, and allowing the movement of government troops to keep order. Industrialization began to take place. Foreign investment was encouraged in mining, transportation, and other sectors of the economy, and financial policies were changed to promote investments. U.S. investments, for example, expanded from about 30 million pesos in 1883 to over 1 billion by 1911.

The forms of Liberal democracy were maintained but were subverted in order to keep Díaz in power and to give his development plans an open track. Behind these policies were a number of Díaz's advisors, who were strongly influenced by positivist ideas and who wished to impose a scientific approach on the national economy. These *cientificos* set the tone for Mexico while the government suppressed any political opposition to these policies. Díaz's Mexico projected an image of modernization led by a Europeanized elite that greatly profited from the economic growth and the imposition of order under Don Porfirio.

Growth was often brought at the expense of Mexico's large rural peasantry and its growing urban and working classes. This population was essentially native, since unlike in Argentina and Brazil few emigrants came to Mexico. They participated very little in the prosperity of export-led growth. The expansion of henequen production in Yucatán displaced peasants, and their attempts at resistance led to arrests and deportation as convict laborers to Cuba. Indian rebellions in the north were similarly crushed. In Morelos in central Mexico, modernization of sugar production with the use of steam-powered mills increased the capacity of the haciendas. Their expansion at the expense of peasants and Indian communal lands created a volatile situation.

Strikes and labor unrest increased, particularly among railroad workers, miners, and textile workers. An especially violent strike took place at the U.S.-

owned Cananea Copper mines from 1906 to 1908. In the countryside a national police force, the *Rurales*, maintained order and the army was mobilized when needed. At the regional level political bosses linked to the Díaz regime in Mexico City delivered the votes in rigged elections.

For 35 years Díaz reigned supreme and oversaw the transformation of the Mexican economy. His opponents were arrested or driven into exile, whereas the small middle class, the landowners, miners, and foreign investors celebrated the progress of Mexico. In 1910, however, a middle-class movement with limited political goals seeking electoral reform began to mushroom into a more general uprising in which the frustrations of the poor, the workers, the peasants, and nationalist intellectuals of various political persuasions erupted in a bloody ten-year civil war, the Mexican Revolution.

At the other end of the hemisphere, Argentina followed an alternative path of economic expansion. By 1880 the Indians on the southern pampa had finally been conquered and vast new tracts of land opened to ranching. The strange relationship between Buenos Aires and the rest of the nation had finally been resolved when Buenos Aires had been made a federal district. With a rapidly expanding economy it became "the Paris

of the Americas," an expression that reflected the drive by wealthy Argentines to establish their credentials as a modern nation. By 1914 Buenos Aires had over two million inhabitants, or about one-fourth of the national population. Its political leaders, the "Generation of 1880," were the inheritors of the Liberal program of Sarmiento and Mitre, and they were able to enact their programs because of the high levels of income generated by the expanding economy.

Technological changes contributed to Argentine prosperity. Refrigerated ships allowed fresh beef to be sent directly to Europe, and this, along with wool and wheat, provided the basis of expansion. Labor was provided by a flood of immigrants. Some were *golondrinas*, which literally means swallows, who were able to work one harvest in Italy and then a second in Argentina because of the differences in seasons in the two hemispheres, but many immigrants elected to stay. Almost 3.5 million immigrants stayed in Argentina between 1857 and 1930, and unlike in Mexico by 1914, about one-third of the Argentine population was foreign-born. Italians, Germans, Russians, and Jews came to "hacer America"—that is, "to make America"—and remained. In a way, quite unlike those in Mexico, they really did Europeanize Argentina, introducing the folkways and

The tremendous boom in the Argentine economy was reflected in the growth of Buenos Aires, the so-called Paris of South America, as a cosmopolitan urban center.

ideologies of the European rural and working classes. The result was a fusion of cultures that produced not only a radical workers' movement but also the distinctive music of the "tango," which combined Spanish, African, and other musical elements in the cafés and red-light districts of Buenos Aires. The tango became the music of the Argentine urban working class.

As the immigrant flood increased, workers began to seek political expression. A Socialist party was formed in the 1890s, seeking to elect representatives to office. Anarchists hoped to smash the political system and called for strikes and walkouts. Moved to some extent by European ideological battles, the struggle spilled into the streets. Violent strikes and government repression characterized the decade after 1910, culminating in a series of strikes in 1918 that led to extreme repression. Development had its social costs.

The Argentine oligarchy was capable of some internal reform, however. Critics of corruption emerged within the political system, and a new party representing the emerging middle class began to organize. It was aided by an electoral law in 1912 that called for secret ballots, universal male suffrage, and compulsory voting. With this change the Radical party, promising political reform and more liberal policies for workers, came to power in 1916, but faced with labor unrest it acted as repressively as its predecessors. The oligarchy made room for middle-class politicians and interests, but the problems of Argentina's expanding labor force remained unresolved, and Argentina's economy remained closely tied to the international market for its exports.

With considerable variations, similar patterns of economic growth, political domination by oligarchies formed by traditional aristocracies and "progressive" middle classes, and a rising tide of labor unrest or rural rebellion can be noted elsewhere in Latin America. Modernization and "progress" were not welcomed by all sectors of society. Messianic religious movements in Brazil, Indian resistance to the loss of lands in Colombia, and banditry in Mexico were all to some extent reactions to the changes being forced on the societies by national governments tied to the ideology of progress and often insensitive to its effects.

UNCLE SAM GOES SOUTH

After its Civil War, the United States began to take a more direct and active interest in the politics and economic situation of Latin America. Commerce and investments began to expand rapidly in this period, espe-cially in Mexico and Central America. American industry was seeking new markets and raw materials, and the growing population of the United States created a demand for Latin American products. Attempts were made to create inter-American cooperation, but a major turning point came in 1898 with the outbreak of war between Spain and the United States, which now began to join the nations of western Europe in the age of imperialism.

The war centered on Cuba and Puerto Rico, Spain's last colonies in the Americas. The Cuban economy had boomed in the 19th century, based on its exports of sugar and tobacco grown with slave labor. A ten-year civil war for independence beginning in 1868 had failed in its main objective but had won the island some autonomy. A number of ardent Cuban nationalists, such as the journalist and poet José Marti, had gone into exile to continue the struggle. Fighting erupted again in 1895 and the United States joined in 1898, declaring war on Spain and occupying Cuba, Puerto Rico, and the Philippines.

In fact, U.S. investments in Cuba had been rapidly increasing prior to the war, and the United States had become a major market for Cuban sugar. The Cuban Spanish-American War now opened the door to direct U.S. involvement in the Caribbean. The Cuban army was treated poorly by its American allies, and a U.S. government of occupation was imposed on Cuba and Puerto Rico. When the occupation ended in 1902, the series of onerous conditions imposed on independent Cuba made it a virtual American dependency, a status that was, in fact, legally imposed in Puerto Rico.

For strategic, commercial, and economic reasons Latin America, particularly the Caribbean and Mexico, began to attract American interest at the turn of the century. These considerations lay behind the drive to construct a canal across Central America to shorten the route between the Atlantic and Pacific. When Colombia proved reluctant to meet American proposals, the United States backed a Panamanian movement for independence and then signed a treaty with its representative that granted the United States extensive rights over a transisthmus canal. President Theodore Roosevelt was a major force behind the canal, which opened to traffic in 1908.

The Panama Canal was a remarkable engineering feat and a fitting symbol of the technological and industrial strength of the United States. North Americans were proud of these achievements and hoped to demonstrate the superiority of the "American way," a feeling fed to some extent by racist ideas and a sense of cultural superiority. Latin Americans were now wary of American power and intentions in the area. A number of intellectuals cautioned against the expansionist designs of the United States and against what they viewed as the materialism of American culture. The Uruguayan José Enrique Rodó, in his essay *Ariel* (1900), compared the spirituality of Hispanic culture to the materialism of the United States. Elsewhere in Latin America, others offered similar critiques.

Latin American criticism had a variety of origins: nationalism, a Catholic defense of traditional values, and also some socialist attacks on expansive capitalism. In a way Latin America, which had achieved its political independence in the 19th century and had been part of European developments, was able to articulate clearly the fears and the reactions of the areas that had become the colonies and semicolonies of western Europe and the United States in the age of empire.

✽ CIVILIZATIONS IN CRISIS: THE MIDDLE EAST AND CHINA

Conditions in those parts of Asia that were not outright European colonies differed in many ways from those in Latin America during the 19th century. Problems of political decline and reactions of highly successful traditional cultures to new challenges predominated, particularly in the great empires of China and the Middle East. The threat of Western imperialism was more menacing, though larger problems of dealing with the West's industrial lead and the intensified world economy overlapped with issues in Latin America.

By the early decades of the 18th century the Middle Eastern Islamic and Chinese civilizations were still capable of contesting the European drive for global dominance but headed in very different directions. Under its Manchu rulers China was enjoying yet another early dynastic period of growth and general prosperity. The territory controlled by the Manchus was greater than that claimed by any Chinese dynasty since the Tang in the 7th century. China's population was growing steadily, and its trade and agricultural production were keeping pace. China's border defenses were strong; its huge armies, led by the elite "banner" units made up of ethnic Manchu soldiers, appeared capable of defending the empire against any outside threat. The functionaries of the ruling Qing dynasty closely controlled the Europeans and other "barbarian" peoples. European traders were confined to the ports of Macao and Canton on China's south coast. In the early 18th century the Qing emperor had severely curtailed missionary activities in China without fear of foreign reprisals. Thus despite signs of growing poverty and social unrest in some districts, the Manchus appeared not only to have restored good government and the well-being of the general populace but also to have carried China to a new level of political and cultural dominance in East Asia.

At the other end of Asia, the fate of the Ottomans appeared to be exactly the reverse. After centuries of able rule and expansion at the expense of their Christian and Muslim neighbors, the Ottomans were in full retreat by the first decades of the 18th century. From the west the Austrian Habsburgs chipped away at the Ottomans' European possessions, while a revived Russia closed in from the north. Muslim kingdoms in North Africa broke away from the empire, and imperial governors and local notables throughout the Arab portions of the Middle East grew more and more independent of the ruling Sultan in Istanbul. Political decline was accompanied by rising economic and social disruption. Inflation was rampant throughout much of the empire, and European imports were rapidly destroying what was left of the already battered Ottoman handicraft industries. The empire was wracked by social tensions, crime, and rebellion in some areas. The divided Ottoman elite could not agree on a strategy to reinvigorate state and society or to drive back the Christian infidels whose advance was undoing centuries of hard-won conquests. With its

The Ottoman Empire in the 19th Century

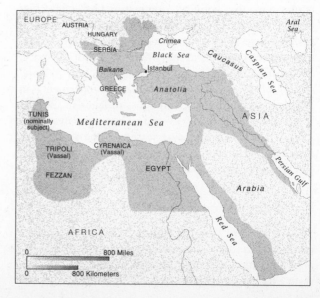

Ottoman defenders reduced, the very heartlands of the Islamic world were increasingly at risk.

In a little over a century the very different paths these two civilizations appeared to be following suddenly converged, and then the Ottomans gained strength as China fell apart. A combination of internal weaknesses and growing pressure from the industrializing European powers threw China into a period of prolonged crisis in the early 19th century. If anything, Chinese civilization was revealed as even more exposed and vulnerable than the Islamic world the Ottomans sought to defend in the face of internal decay and European inroads. The Ottomans began to find new sources of leadership and to introduce reforms on the basis of Western precedents, but the Manchus were paralyzed by the shock of devastating defeats at the hands of the European "barbarians." Overpopulation, drug addiction—particularly that afflicting members of the scholar-gentry elite—and massive rebellions sapped China's strength from within, and European gunboats and armies broke down its outer defenses. By the first years of the 20th century, internal disruptions and external pressures had literally demolished the foundations of Chinese civilization, which had flourished for nearly four millennia.

As old China died, its leaders struggled to find a new and viable system to put in its place. That struggle would be carried on throughout a half century (roughly from 1898 to 1949) of foreign invasion, revolution, and social and economic breakdown that produced suffering on a scale unmatched in all human history. In sharp contrast, by the end of the 19th century the new leaders who emerged in the Ottoman Empire were able to overthrow the sultanate with a minimum of bloodshed and to begin the process of nation making in the Turkic-speaking portions of the empire (largely the present-day nation of Turkey). Unfortunately, Ottoman weaknesses in earlier decades left the rest of the Middle East exposed to European inroads, and a larger Islamic crisis proved impervious to Turkish solutions.

REFORM AND SURVIVAL IN THE OTTOMAN EMPIRE

Despite almost two centuries of unrelieved defeats on the battlefield and steady losses of territory, the Ottoman Empire somehow managed to survive into the 20th century. In part this was due to divisions among the European powers, each of which feared that the others would gain more from the total dismemberment of the empire. In fact the British concern to prevent the

Russians from controlling Istanbul—thus gaining direct access to and threatening British naval dominance in the Mediterranean—led them to prop up the tottering Ottoman regime repeatedly in the last half of the 19th century. Ultimately, the Ottomans' survival depended on reforms from within—reforms initiated by the sultans and their advisors at the top of the imperial system and carried out in stages over most of the 19th century. At each stage, reform initiatives intensified tensions within the ruling elite. Some advocated far-reaching change along European lines; others argued for reforms based on precedents from the early Ottoman period; and still others had a vested interest in blocking change of any sort.

These deep divisions within the Ottoman elite rendered reform a dangerous enterprise. Though modest innovations, including the introduction of the first printing press in 1727, had been enacted in the 18th century, Sultan Selim III (1789–1807) believed that bolder initiatives were required if the dynasty and empire were to survive. But his reform efforts, which were aimed at improving administrative efficiency and building a new army and navy capable of reversing a century of defeats at the hands of the European powers, angered powerful factions within the bureaucracy. They were also viewed by the Janissary corps (special troops originally recruited by enslaving Christian youths from the Balkans), which had long been the dominant force within the Ottoman military, as a direct and vital threat. Selim's rather modest initiatives cost him his throne—he was toppled by a Janissary revolt in 1807—and ultimately his life.

Two decades later, a more skillful sultan, Mahmud II, succeeded where Selim III had failed. After secretly building a small professional army with the help of European advisors, in 1826 Mahmud II ordered his agents to incite a mutiny of the Janissaries. This began when the angry Janissaries overturned the huge soup kettles in their mess area. With little thought or preparation, the Janissaries, more a mob than a military force, poured into the streets of Istanbul, where they were shocked to be confronted by the sultan's well-trained new army. The confrontation ended in the slaughter of the Janissaries, their families, and the Janissaries' religious allies.

After cowing the ayan, or provincial notables, into at least formal submission to the throne, Mahmud II launched a program of much more far-reaching reforms than Selim III had attempted. Though the ulama, or religious experts, and some of Mahmud's advisors argued for self-strengthening through a return to the Ottoman and Islamic past, Mahmud II patterned his reform program on Western precedents. After all, the Western

The European view of the Ottoman Empire as an exotic and bizarrely antique land is captured in this late-18th-century engraving of the Ottoman sultan entertaining the French ambassador and his entourage.

empire, extensive legal reforms were enacted, and in 1876 a constitution, based heavily on European prototypes, was promulgated. These legal reforms greatly improved the position of minority religious groups, whose role in the Ottoman economy increased steadily.

Some groups were adversely affected by these changes that opened the empire more and more to Western influences. This was especially true of the artisans, whose position was gravely weakened by an 1838 treaty with the British, which removed import taxes and other barriers to foreign trade that had protected indigenous producers from competition from the West. Other social groups, particularly women, gained little from the Tanzimat reforms. Though proposals for women's education and the end to seclusion, polygamy, and veiling were debated in Ottoman intellectual circles from the 1860s onward, few improvements in the position of women—even among the elite classes—were won until after the fall of the dynasty in 1908.

REPRESSION AND REVOLT

Though the reforms initiated by the sultans and their advisors did improve somewhat the Ottomans' ability to fend off, or at least deflect, the assaults of foreign aggressors, they increasingly threatened the dynasty responsible for them. Western-educated bureaucrats, military officers, and professionals came increasingly to view the sultanate as a major barrier to even more radical reforms—some of which involved proposals for constitutional checks on the rulers' authority—and the full transformation of society. The new elites also clashed with conservative but powerful groups, such as the ulama and ayan, that had a vested interest in preserving as much as possible of the old order. The new elite was also divided between those who had derived great benefit from the early reforms and were wary of further changes and those who saw the reforms already enacted as the entering wedge for a much more radical restructuring of Ottoman institutions and society.

The Ottoman Sultan Abdul Hamid responded to the growing threat from Westernized officers and civilians by attempting to return to despotic absolutism during his long reign from 1878 to 1908. He nullified the constitution, restricted civil liberties, particularly the freedom of the press, and deprived Westernized elite groups of the considerable initiative they had gained in the formulation of imperial policies. Legal safeguards were flouted as dissidents or even suspected troublemakers were summarily imprisoned and sometimes tortured and

powers had made a shambles of his empire. He established a diplomatic corps on Western lines and exchanged ambassadors with the European powers. The Westernization of the army was expanded from Mahmud's secret force to the whole military establishment. European military advisors, both army and navy, were imported to supervise the overhaul of Ottoman training, armament, and officers' education.

In the following decades Western influences were pervasive at the upper levels of Ottoman society, particularly during the period of the Tanzimat reforms between 1839 and 1876. University education was reorganized on Western lines, including the introduction of training in the European sciences and mathematics. State-run postal and telegraph systems were introduced in the 1830s, and railways were begun in the 1860s. Newspapers were established in the major towns of the

killed. But the deep impact that decades of reform had made on the empire was demonstrated by the fact that even Abdul Hamid continued to push for Westernization in certain areas. The military continued to adopt European arms and techniques, increasingly under the instruction of German advisors. In addition, railways, including the famed line that linked Berlin to Baghdad, and telegraph lines were constructed between the main population centers, more often than not under the aegis of German investors and supervisors. Western-style educational institutions continued to grow, and judicial reforms continued. Under Abdul Hamid the old bureaucratic apparatus remained largely in place and social reforms were minimal, but the military and communications infrastructure for a modern state was established.

The despotism of Abdul Hamid came to an abrupt end in the nearly bloodless coup of 1908. Resistance to his authoritarian rule had led exiled Turkish intellectuals and political agitators to found an organization, the Ottoman Society for Union and Progress, in Paris in 1889. Though professing their loyalty to the Ottoman regime, the Young Turks, as members of the society came to be known, were determined to restore the 1876 constitution and resume far-reaching reforms within the empire. The Young Turks' clandestine printing presses turned out tracts denouncing the regime and outlining the further steps to be taken to modernize and thus save the empire. Assassinations were attempted and coups plotted, but until 1908 all were undone by a combination of divisions within the ranks of the Westernized dissidents and police countermeasures.

Widespread sympathy within the military for the 1908 coup had much to do with its success, as did the fact that only a handful of the sultan's supporters were willing to die defending the regime. Though a group of officers came to power, they restored the constitution and press freedoms and promised reforms in education, administration, and even the status of women. The sultan was retained as a political figurehead and the highest religious authority in Islam.

Unfortunately, the officers soon became embroiled in factional fights that took up much of the limited time remaining before the outbreak of World War I. In addition, their hold on power was shaken as they lost a new round of wars in the Balkans and against Italy over the Ottomans' last remaining possession in North Africa, Libya. Just as the sultans had before them, however, the Young Turk officers managed to stave off the collapse of the empire with last-gasp military victories and by playing the hostile European powers against one another.

The fascination of European intellectuals with the Young Turks and what appeared to be their revolutionary movement is reflected in the cover drawing and story of a 1909 edition of the popular French periodical *Le Petit Parisien*. It is also suggested by the continuing radical or avant-garde connotations of the label "Young Turk."

Though it is difficult to know how the Young Turks would have fared if it had not been for the outbreak of the First World War, their failure to resolve a number of critical issues did not bode well for the future. They had overthrown the sultan, but they could not bring themselves to give up the empire ruled by Turks for over 600 years. The peoples most affected by their decision to salvage what was left of the empire were the Arabs of the Fertile Crescent and coastal Arabia, who still remained under Ottoman control. Arab leaders in Beirut and Damascus had initially favored the 1908 coup because they believed it would bring about the end of their long domination by the Turks. To their dismay, the Arabs discovered that the Young Turks not only meant to continue their subjugation but also were determined to enforce state control to a degree unthinkable to the later Ottoman sultans. The quarrels between the leaders of the Young Turk coalition and the growing resistance in the Arab portions of what was left of the Ottoman Empire were quite suddenly cut short by a much larger global crisis brought on by the outbreak of general war in Europe in August 1914. Turkish entry into and defeat in the First World War brought about the dissolution of the Ottoman Empire. This also gave rise to the leader Mustafa Kemal, or Ataturk, and some of the forces that proved critical in the emergence of the modern nation of Turkey from the ruins of the empire. However able a military commander he might have been, Ataturk's successes would not have been possible without the struggles and reforms of the last century and a half of the Ottoman Empire.

WESTERN INTRUSIONS AND THE CRISIS IN THE ARAB ISLAMIC HEARTLANDS

By the early 1800s the Arab peoples of the Fertile Crescent, Egypt, coastal Arabia, and North Africa had lived for centuries under Ottoman-Turkish rule. Though most Arabs resented Turkish domination, they could identify with the Ottomans as fellow Muslims, who were both ardent defenders of the faith and patrons of Islamic culture. Still, the steadily diminishing capacity of the Ottomans to defend the Arab Islamic heartlands left them exposed to the danger of conquest by the aggressive European powers. The European capture of outlying but highly developed Islamic states in the Indonesian archipelago and India to Algeria in North Africa engendered a sense of crisis among the Islamic faithful in the Middle Eastern heartlands. From the terror of Christendom and the encirclers of its European bastion, the Muslims had become the besieged. Islam had been displaced by Europe as the leading civilization in a wide range of endeavors from scientific inquiry to monumental architecture. Much of the Muslim community was forced to live under infidel European overlords; what remained was threatened by European conquest.

The profound crisis of Islamic confidence brought on by successive reverses and the increasing strength of their old European rivals gave rise to a wide variety of responses in the Islamic world. Islamic thinkers debated the best way of reversing the decline and driving back the Europeans. Some argued for a return to the Islamic past; others favored a large-scale adoption of Western ways; still others sought to find ways to combine the two approaches. Reformist leaders, such as those in 19th-century Turkey, tried to graft on elements of Western culture while preserving the old state and society pretty much intact. Religious leaders, sometimes proclaiming themselves divinely appointed prophets, rose up to lead their followers in *jihads*, or holy wars, against the advancing Europeans. Though we cannot examine all of these responses in each of the Islamic lands, we will focus on key responses on the part of Arab peoples in Egypt and the Sudan in the 19th century. In these areas European involvement was intense, and the growing challenges posed by the West generated important attempts to find ways of reversing the decline of Islamic civilization and restoring it to its former glory.

EGYPTIAN BANKRUPTCY, EUROPEAN INTERVENTION, AND STRATEGIES OF RESISTANCE

Egypt provided the entering wedge for the advance of European imperialism in the Arab heartlands of the Middle East. The region was first conquered by Napoleon's armies in 1798, but the British navy and growing internal resistance soon ousted the French forces. In the chaos that followed the French withdrawal in 1801, a military adventurer from Albania, Muhammad Ali, founded a new dynasty, subject to the nominal authority of the Ottoman overlords at Istanbul. For most of the first half of the 19th century Muhammad Ali struggled to introduce largely European-inspired economic and military reforms into Egyptian society and to expand his domains at the expense of the Ottoman sultans. A combination of Western and Ottoman opposition to Muhammad Ali's grand schemes and internal resistance to his sometimes draconian methods of introducing his innovations frustrated most of his ambitious plans to transform Egypt along Western lines.

Muhammad Ali's successors, called Khedives, made a muddle of his efforts to reform and revitalize Egyptian society. Although cotton production increased and the landlord class profited, the great majority of the peasants went hungry or starved. The long-term consequences of these developments were equally troubling. The great expansion of cotton production at the expense of food grains and alternative market crops rendered Egypt dependent on a single export and vulnerable to fluctuations in demand on the European markets to which most of it was exported. Some educational advances were made, mainly at elite schools where French was the language of instruction. But the advances were too limited to benefit the populace by making government more efficient or stimulating public works projects and improved health care.

Much of the revenue the khedives managed to collect was wasted on extravagant pastimes and fruitless military campaigns to assert Egyptian authority over the Sudanic peoples along the Upper Nile. The increasing inability of the khedives to balance their books led in the middle decades of the 19th century to their growing indebtedness to European financiers. The latter lent money to the profligate khedives and members of the Turkish elite because the financiers desired both continued access to Egypt's cheap cotton and, by the 1850s, a share in the potentially lucrative schemes to build a canal across the Isthmus of Suez to connect the Mediterranean and Red seas. The completion of the Suez Canal in 1869 shortened the distance by sea between Europe and Asia and allowed steamboats to replace sailing vessels, which had earlier proved better able to weather the rough passage around Africa.

The ineptitude of the khedival regime and the Ottoman sultans, their nominal overlords, prompted a good deal of discussion among Muslim intellectuals and political activists as to how they might find the leadership and means to ward off the growing European menace. Egypt, and particularly Cairo's ancient Muslim University of al-Azhar, became in the middle decades of the 19th century one of the key meeting places of these thinkers from throughout the Islamic world. Some prominent Islamic scholars called for a jihad (holy war) to drive the infidels from Muslim lands. They also argued that the Muslim world could be saved only by a return to the patterns of religious observance and social interaction that they believed had existed in the "golden age" of the Prophet.

Other thinkers, such as al-Afghani (1839–1897) and his disciple Muhammad Abduh (1849–1905), stressed the need for Muslims to borrow scientific learning and technology from the West and to revive their earlier capacity to innovate. They argued that Islamic civilization had once taught the Europeans much in the sciences and mathematics, including such critical concepts as the Indian ("Arabic" in the West) numerals. Thus it was fitting that Muslims learn from the advances the Europeans had made with the help of Islamic borrowings. Those

The construction of a canal over the desert wastes of the Isthmus of Suez was a remarkable engineering feat. As this contemporary photo illustrates, a massive investment in up-to-date technology was essential to the success of the venture.

who advocated this approach also stressed the importance of the tradition of rational inquiry in Islamic history. They strongly disputed the views of fundamentalist theorists who contended that the Quran was the source of all truth and should be interpreted literally.

Though both fundamentalists and those who stressed the need for imports from the West agreed on the need for Muslim unity in the face of the growing European threat, they could not reconcile their very different approaches to Islamic revival. Their differences and the uncertainties they have injected into Islamic efforts to cope with the challenges of the West remain central problems in the Muslim world today.

The mounting debts of the khedival regime and the strategic importance of the canal gave the European powers, particularly Britain and France, a growing stake in the stability and accessibility of Egypt. French and

One of the oldest universities in the world, al-Azhar in Cairo has been one of the main centers of Muslim intellectual ferment in the modern era.

British bankers, who had bought up a good portion of the khedive's shares in the canal, urged their governments to intervene militarily when the khedives proved unable to meet their loan payments. At the same time, French and British diplomats quarreled over how much influence their nations should exercise within Egypt. In the early 1880s a genuinely nationalist challenge to both the puppet khedival regime and the European powers prompted the British to intervene militarily to the chagrin of the French, who at that point were in no position to do likewise.

The challenge was mounted by the supporters of a charismatic young Egyptian officer named Achmad Orabi. The son of a small farmer in lower Egypt, Orabi had attended Quranic school and studied under the reform-minded Muhammad Abduh at al-Azhar. Though a native Egyptian, Orabi had risen in the ranks of the khedival army and had become increasingly critical of the fact that the officer corps was dominated by Turks with strong ties to the khedival regime. An attempt by the khedive to save money by disbanding Egyptian regiments and dismissing Egyptian officers sparked a revolt led by Orabi in the summer of 1882. Riots in the city of Alexandria, associated with mutinies in the Egyptian armies, drove the frightened khedive to seek British assistance. After bombarding coastal batteries set up by Orabi's troops, the British sent ashore an expeditionary force that crushed Orabi's rebellion and secured the position of the khedive. Though Egypt was not formally colonized, the British intervention began decades of dominance by both British consuls, who ruled through the puppet khedives, and British advisors to all high-ranking Egyptian administrators. British officials controlled Egypt's finances and foreign affairs, and British troops ensured that their directives were heeded by Egyptian administrators. Direct European control over the Islamic heartlands had begun.

JIHAD: THE MAHDIST REVOLT IN THE SUDAN

As Egypt fell under British control, the invaders were inevitably drawn into the turmoil and conflict that gripped the Sudanic region to the south in the last decades of the 19th century. Egyptian efforts to conquer and rule the Sudan, beginning in the 1820s, were fiercely resisted, particularly by the camel- and cattle-herding nomads who occupied the vast, arid plains that stretched west and east from the Upper Nile. The sedentary peoples who worked the narrow strip of fertile land along the river were more easily dominated. Thus Egyptian authority, insofar as it existed at all, was concentrated in these areas and in river towns, such as Khartoum, the center of Egyptian administration.

Even in the riverine areas Egyptian overlordship was greatly resented. The Egyptian regime was notoriously corrupt, and its taxes placed a heavy burden on the peasants compelled to pay them. The Egyptians were clearly carpet-bagging outsiders, and the favoritism they showed some of the Sudanic tribes was guaranteed to alienate the others. In addition, virtually all groups in the Muslim areas in the north Sudan were angered by Egyptian attempts in the 1870s to eradicate the slave trade. The trade had long been a great source of profit for both the merchants of the Nile towns and the nomads, who attacked non-Muslim peoples, such as the Dinka in the south, in order to capture slaves. British advisors at the khedive's court had strongly pushed for the antislavery effort, and an English commander, George Gordon, had taken charge of the campaign and on occasion employed very heavy-handed methods to suppress the trade.

By the late 1870s Egyptian oppression and British intervention had aroused deep resentment and hostility, particularly among the Muslim peoples of the northern Sudan. But a leader was needed to unite the diverse and often divided peoples of the region and to provide an ideology that would give focus and meaning to rebellion. The son of a boat builder named Muhammad Achmad, who had been educated by the head of a local Sufi (mystical) brotherhood, proved to be that leader. The fact that his family claimed descent from the Prophet and that he had the physical signs—a cleft in his teeth and a mole on his right cheek—that the local people associated with the promised deliverer did much to advance his reputation. The visions he began to experience after he had broken with his Sufi master and established his own sectarian following also suggested that a remarkable future was in store. What was seen to be a miraculous escape from a bungled Egyptian effort to capture and imprison Muhammad Achmad soon led to his widespread acceptance as a divinely appointed leader of revolt against the foreign intruders.

The jihad that Muhammad Achmad, known to his followers as the Mahdi (the promised deliverer), proclaimed against both the Egyptian heretics and the British infidels was one of a number of such movements that had swept sub-Saharan Africa since the 18th century. It represented the most extreme and violent Islamic response to what was perceived as the dilution of Islam in the African environment and the growing threat of

Europe. Muhammad Achmad promised to purge Islam of what he viewed as superstitious beliefs and degrading practices that had built up over the centuries, and to return Islam to what he claimed was its original purity. He led his followers in a violent assault on the Egyptians, who he believed professed this corrupt version of the faith, and on the European infidels. At one point his successors dreamed of toppling the Ottoman sultans and invading Europe itself.

The Mahdi's skillful use of guerrilla tactics and the confidence his followers placed in his blessings and magical charms earned his forces a number of stunning victories over the Egyptians. In 1883 the Mahdi's commanders drew a force of 8000 Egyptians, led by British officers, deep into the desert wilderness and ambushed and destroyed it in a desolate valley called Shaykan. By the end of 1883 the Mahdi's forces controlled most of the northern Sudan and were besieging the Egyptians' last major stronghold, at Khartoum. In both ignorance and arrogance the British sent just a single officer, General Gordon, who had earlier overseen the suppression of the slave trade, up the Nile to Khartoum to command the Egyptian garrison and put down the Mahdist rebellion. Less than a year after Gordon's arrival, the city was taken and he was killed by the Mahdi's followers. The Mahdists had driven off the Egyptians, slaughtered their British commanders, and were now the masters of the Sudan.

At the peak of his power, the Mahdi fell ill from typhus and died just months after the capture of Khartoum. In contrast to many movements of this type, which have collapsed rapidly after the death of their prophetic leaders, the Mahdists found a capable successor to Muhammad Achmad in the Khalifa Abdallahi, one of his most skillful military commanders. Under Abdallahi, the Mahdists built a strong, expansive state and a closely controlled society in which smoking, dancing, and alcoholic drink were forbidden and theft, prostitution, and adultery were severely punished. For nearly a decade Mahdist armies attacked or threatened neighboring states on all sides, including the Egyptians to the north, whose territories the Mahdists planned to invade. But in the fall of 1896 the famed British General Kitchener was sent with an expeditionary force to put an end to what was one of the most serious threats to European domination in Africa. The spears and magical garments of the Mahdist forces proved no match for the machine guns and artillery of Kitchener's columns, and at the battle of Omdurman in 1898 the bulk of the Mahdist cavalry and Abdallahi himself were slaughtered. The

Mahdist state collapsed, and British power advanced still farther into the interior of Africa.

RETREAT AND ANXIETY: ISLAM IMPERILED

The 19th century was a time of severe reverses for the peoples of the Islamic world. Outflanked and outfought by their old European rivals, Islamic leaders either became puppets of European overlords or saw their lands pass under the rule of infidel colonial rulers. Diverse forms of resistance, from the reformist path taken by the Ottoman sultans to the prophetic rebellions of leaders such as Muhammad Achmad, slowed but could not halt the European advance. European products and demands steadily eroded the economic fabric and heightened social tensions in Islamic lands. The stunning military and economic successes of the Christian Europeans cast doubts on Muslim claims to possession of the one true faith. By the first years of the 20th century, it was clear that neither the fundamentalists, who called for a return to a purified Islam free of Western influences, nor the reformers, who argued that some borrowing from the West was essential for survival, had come up with a successful formula for dealing with the powerful challenges posed by the industrial West. Failing to find adequate responses and deeply divided within, the Islamic community grew increasingly anxious over the dangers that lay ahead. Islamic civilization was by no means defeated, but its continued viability was clearly threatened by the powerful neighbor that had become master of the world.

✵ THE LAST DYNASTY: THE FALL OF THE QING EMPIRE IN CHINA

By the early decades of the 19th century a major collision between the aggressive, expanding European industrial powers and China, the largest and most enduring of preindustrial civilizations, was unavoidable. For centuries the rulers of China had superciliously resisted European attempts to "open up" their rich lands and vast population to Christian missionary campaigns or the market economy the Europeans had extended over much of the globe. European traders were confined to two ports—Macao, which had been established by the Portuguese in the 16th century, and Canton, where their activities were strictly supervised by Chinese officials. The Chinese refused to accept European ambassadors or even to recognize European nations, such as Britain and France, as their equals. Chinese officials treated European merchants and emissaries with the contempt they

felt the "southern (because they came by sea from the south) barbarians" deserved. Because they believed that the Europeans had little to offer in the way of civilized attainments, the rulers of China made little effort to learn about the nation-states they represented. The Chinese knew next to nothing about the Renaissance and Reformation and very little about Europe's scientific and industrial revolutions. As a result, when the Chinese were confronted by the armed intervention of the European powers in the first decades of the 19th century, they struck out blindly against adversaries whose motives they could not understand and whose power they were not at all prepared to reckon with.

Though China had been strong enough to get away with its policies of isolation and attitudes of disdain in the early centuries of expansion, by the early 19th century these were outmoded and dangerous. Not only had the Europeans grown incomparably stronger than they had been in the early centuries of expansion, but also Chinese society was crumbling from within. Over a century of strong rule by the Manchus and a high degree of social stability, if not prosperity, for the Chinese people gave way to rampant official corruption, severe economic dislocations, and social unrest by the last decades of the 18th century. The remaining portions of this chapter will explore the consequences of Europe's forcible entry into China and the slow demise of the last Chinese dynasty.

ROT FROM WITHIN: BUREAUCRATIC BREAKDOWN AND SOCIAL DISINTEGRATION

As early as the late 18th century it was clear that, like so many Chinese dynasties of the past, the Qing was in decline. The signs of decline were pervasive and familiar. The bureaucratic foundations of the Chinese Empire were rotting from within. The exam system, which had done well in selecting able and honest bureaucrats in the early decades of the dynasty, had become riddled with cheating and favoritism. Despite formal restrictions, places in the ever-growing bureaucracy were often ensured for sons of high officials. Even more disturbing was the fact that virtually anyone with enough money could buy posts for sons or brothers. Impoverished scholars could be paid to take the exams for poorly educated or poorly qualified relatives, and examiners could be bribed to approve their credentials or look the other way when candidates consulted cheat sheets while taking their exams. In one of the most notorious cases of cheating, a merchant's son won high honors, despite the fact

This 19th-century engraving shows the cubicles in which Chinese students and bureaucrats took the imperial civil service examinations that were given in the capital at Beijing. Examinees were confined to the cubicles for days and completed their exams under the constant surveillance of official proctors.

that he had spent the days of testing in a brothel hundreds of miles from the examination.

Cheating had become so blatant as early as the first decades of the 18th century that in 1711 students who had failed the exams at Yangzhou held a public demonstration to protest bribes given to the exam officials by wealthy salt merchants. The growing influx of merchant and poorly educated landlords' sons into the bureaucracy was particularly troubling because few of them had received the classical Confucian education that stressed the responsibilities of the educated ruling classes and their obligation to serve the people. Increasingly, positions in the bureaucracy were regarded by the wealthy as a means of exerting influence over local officials and judges, as well as a way of enhancing family fortunes without regard for the effects of bureaucratic decisions on the peasantry and urban laborers.

Over a period of decades, the diversion of revenue from state projects to the enrichment of individual families had a devastating impact on Chinese society. For example, funds needed to maintain the armies and fleets that defended the huge empire fell off sharply, resulting in a noticeable drop in the training and armament of the military. Even more critical for the mass of the people were reductions in spending on public works projects. Of these, the most vital were the great dikes that confined the Yellow River in northern China. Over the millennia, the silting of the river bottom and the continual repair of and additions to the dikes created a situation

where river and dikes were raised high above the densely populated farmlands through which they passed. Thus when neglected for lack of funds and proper official supervision of repairs, leaking dikes and rampaging waters of the great river meant catastrophe for much of northeastern China.

Nowhere was this disaster more apparent than in the region of the Shandong peninsula. Before the mid-19th century, the Yellow River emptied into the sea south of the peninsula. By the 1850s, however, the neglected dikes had broken down over much of the area, and the river had flooded hundreds of square miles of heavily cultivated farmland. By the 1860s the main channel of the river flowed north of the peninsula. The lands in between had been flooded and the farms wiped out. Millions of peasants were left without livestock or land to cultivate; tens, perhaps hundreds, of thousands of peasants died of famine and disease.

As the condition of the peasantry deteriorated in many parts of the empire, further signs of dynastic decline appeared. Food shortages and landlord exactions prompted mass migrations; vagabond bands clogged the roads and beggars crowded the city streets. Banditry, long seen by the Chinese as one of the surest gauges of the extent of dynastic decline, became a major problem in many districts. As the following verse from a popular ditty of the 1860s illustrates, the government's inability to deal with the bandits was seen as a further sign of Qing weakness:

When the bandits arrive, where are the troops?
When the troops come, the bandits have vanished.
Alas, when will the bandits and troops meet?

The assumption then widely held by Chinese thinkers—that the dynastic cycle would again run its course, with the Manchus being replaced by a new and vigorous dynasty—was belied by the magnitude of the problems confronting the leaders of China. The belief that China's future could be predicted by the patterns of its past history ignored the fact that in a number of ways, there were no precedents for the critical changes that had occurred in China under Manchu rule. Some of these changes had their roots in the preceding Ming era, in which, for example, food crops from the New World had set in motion a population explosion. An already large population had nearly doubled to more than 200 million in the first century (c. 1650–1750) of Manchu rule; in the following century it doubled again to 410 to 415 million. However successful they had been in the past, Chinese social and economic systems were simply not capable of carrying a population of this magnitude. China desperately needed innovations, breakthroughs in technology and organization that would increase its productivity to the point where its exploding population could be supported at a reasonable level. The corrupt and highly conservative late-Manchu regime was in-

creasingly an obstacle to, rather than a source of, these desperately needed changes.

BARBARIANS AT THE SOUTHERN GATES

A second major difference between the forces sapping the strength of the Manchus and those that had brought down earlier dynasties was the nature of the so-called barbarians who threatened the empire from outside. Nomadic incursions had traditionally played a large role in the dynastic cycle. Their bolder and more frequent incursions into the agrarian regions protected by the Great Wall was one of the surest signs of the impending end of a dynasty. But in the past the nomads, even when, like the Manchus, they had established themselves as the new rulers of China, had soon been assimilated to China's more sophisticated culture and society and absorbed into the much larger Chinese population.

Though the Chinese, out of ignorance, treated the Europeans much like the nomads and other peoples whom they regarded as barbarians, the Europeans presented a very different sort of challenge. They came from a civilization that was China's equal in sophistication and complexity. In fact, though European nation-states such as Great Britain were much smaller in population (in the early 19th century England had 7 million people to China's 400 million), they could, thanks to the

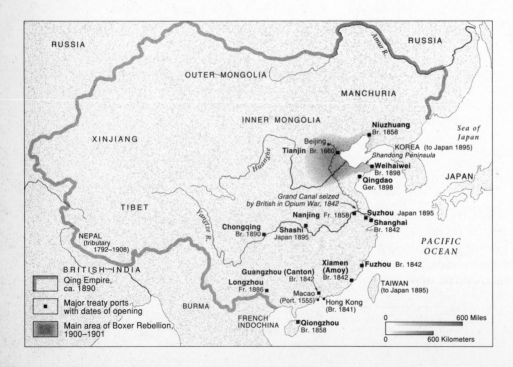

China during the Qing Era

scientific advances and industrial revolutions, compensate for their smaller numbers with better organization and superior technology. As tensions built up between the Europeans—who demanded that restrictions on their trading and religious proselytization in China be removed—and the Chinese—who were determined to limit foreigners' activities within the empire—the Europeans' advantages in technology and knowledge of the wider world became increasingly decisive. When violent clashes between the two led to wars between 1839 and 1842 as well as between 1856 and 1860, the underlying vulnerabilities of Chinese civilization were brutally exposed.

Stunning victories in these wars made it possible for the European powers to force China to open trade and diplomatic exchanges. After the first war, Hong Kong was established as an additional center of British commerce, and European trade was permitted at five other ports, where the Europeans were given land to build more warehouses and living quarters. By the 1890s, 90 ports of call were available to over 300,000 European and American traders, missionaries, and diplomats. Britain, France, Germany, and Russia had won long-term leases over several ports and surrounding territory, as imperialist expansion pressed China directly.

By the middle of the century China's foreign trade and customs were overseen by British officials. They were careful to ensure that European nationals had favored access to China's markets and that no protective tariffs, such as those the Americans were using at the time to protect their young industries, were established by the Chinese. Most humiliating of all for the Chinese was the fact that they were forced to accept European ambassadors at the Qing court. Not only were ambassadors traditionally (and usually quite rightly) regarded as spies, but also the exchange of diplomatic missions was a concession that European nations were equal in stature to China. Given the deeply entrenched Chinese conviction that their Middle Kingdom was the civilized center of the earth and that all other peoples were barbarians, this was indeed a very difficult concession to make. European battleships and firepower gave them little choice.

A CIVILIZATION AT RISK: REBELLION, FAILED REFORMS, AND THE FALL OF THE QING

Though it was not immediately apparent, China's defeats greatly contributed to a building crisis that threatened not just the Qing dynasty but Chinese civilization

as a whole. Defeat and the dislocations in south China brought on by the growing commercial encroachments of the West spawned a massive rebellion that convulsed much of south China in the 1850s and early 1860s and at one point threatened to overthrow the Qing dynasty. Led by a mentally unstable, semi-Christianized prophet named Hong Xiuquan, the Taiping rebellion exacerbated the already considerable stresses within Chinese society and further drained the diminishing resources of the ruling dynasty. Though widespread peasant risings, incited by the members of secret societies such as the White Lotus, had erupted as early as the 1770s, the Taiping movement was the first to pose a serious alternative both to the Qing dynasty and to Confucian civilization as a whole. In contrast to a number of contemporary rebellions in the west of China, the Taipings offered sweeping programs for social reform, land redistribution, and the liberation of women. They also attacked the traditional Confucian elite and the learning on which its claims to authority rested. Taiping rebels smashed ancestral tablets and shrines and proposed a simplified script and mass literacy that would have undermined one of the scholar-gentry's chief sources of power.

Their attack on the scholar-gentry, in fact, was one of the main causes of the Taipings' ultimate defeat. Left no option but to rally to the Manchu regime, the provincial gentry became the focus of resistance to the Taipings. Honest and able Qing officials, such as Zeng Guofan, raised more effective, provincially based military forces just in time to beat off the Taiping assault on northern China. Zeng and his allies in the government also sought to carry out needed reforms to root out corruption in the bureaucracy and to revive the stagnating Chinese economy.

In the last decades of the 19th century these dynamic provincial leaders were the most responsible for China's self-strengthening movement, which was aimed at countering the challenge from the West. They encouraged Western investment in railways and even factories in the areas they governed and sought to modernize their armies. Combined with the breakdown of Taiping leadership and the declining appeal of a movement that could not deliver on the promises it made to its followers, the efforts of the gentry brought about the eventual but very bloody suppression of the Taiping rebellion. Other movements were also crushed and banditry was brought under control for a time. But like the Ottoman sultans and their advisors, the Chinese gentry introduced changes that they viewed as limited, aimed

Faced with mounting intrusions by the Western powers into China, which the ruling Manchu dynasty appeared powerless to resist, Chinese political leaders and intellectuals debated the ways by which China could renew itself and thus survive the challenges from the industrialized West. As the following passages from his journal *A People Made New* (published from 1902–1905) illustrate, Liang Qichao, one of the main advocates of major reforms in Chinese society, recognized the need for significant borrowing from Europe and the United States. At the same time, late-19th- and early-20th-century champions of renewal like Liang sought to preserve the basic features of Chinese society as they had developed over two millennia of history.

DOCUMENT: BUILDING A NEW CHINA

Since the appearance of mankind on earth, thousands of countries have existed on the earth. Of these, however, only about a hundred still occupy a place on the map of the five continents. And among these hundred-odd countries there are only four or five great powers that are strong enough to dominate the world and to conquer nature. All countries have the same sun and moon, all have mountains and rivers, and all consist of people with feet and skulls; but some countries rise while others fall, and some become strong while others are weak. Why? Some attribute it to geographical advantages. But geographically, America today is the same as America in ancient times; why then do only the Anglo-Saxons enjoy the glory? Similarly, ancient Rome was the same as Rome today; why then have the Latin people declined in fame? Some attribute it to certain heroes. But Macedonia once had Alexander, and yet today it is no longer seen; Mongolia once had Chingis Khan, and yet today it can hardly maintain its existence. Ah! I know the reason. A state is formed by the assembling of people. The relationship of a nation to its people resembles that of the body to its four limbs, five viscera, muscles, veins, and corpuscles. It has never happened that the four limbs could be cut off, the five viscera wasted away, the muscles and veins injured, the corpuscles dried up, and yet the body still live. Similarly, it has never happened that a people could be foolish, timid, disorganized, and confused and yet the nation still stand. Therefore, if we wish the body to live for a long time, we must understand the methods of hygiene. If we wish the nation to be secure, rich, and honored, we must discuss the way for the people's being "made new."

The Meaning of "A People Made New." The term "people made new" does not mean that our people must give up entirely what is old in order to follow others. There are two meanings of "made new." One is to improve what is original in the people and so renew it; the other is to adopt what is originally lacking in the people and so make a new people. Without one of the two, there will be no success. . . .

A nation which can maintain itself in the world must have some peculiar characteristics on the part of its nationals. From morals and laws down to customs, habits, literature, and fine arts, all share an independent spirit which has been handed down from the forefathers to their descendants. Thus the group is formed and the nation develops. This is really the fundamental basis of nationalism. Our people have been established as a nation on the Asian continent for several thousand years, and we must have some special characteristics which are grand, noble, and perfect, and distinctly different from those of other races. We should preserve these characteristics and not let them be lost. What is called preserving, however, is not simply to let them exist and grow by themselves and then blithely say: "I am preserving them, I am preserving them." It is like a tree: unless some new buds come out every year, its withering away may soon be expected. Or like a well: unless there is always some new spring bubbling, its exhaustion is not far away.

If we wish to make our nation strong, we must investigate extensively the methods followed by other nations in becoming independent. We should select their superior points and appropriate them to make up our own shortcomings. Now with regard to politics, academic learning, and techniques, our critics know how to take the superior points of others to make up for our own weakness; but they do not know that the people's virtue, the people's wisdom, and the people's vitality are the great basis of politics, academic learning, and techniques. If they do not take the former but adopt the latter, neglect the roots but tend the branches, it will be no different from seeing the luxuriant growth of another tree and wishing to graft its branches onto our withered trunk, or seeing the bubbling flow of another well and wishing to draw its water to fill our dry well. Thus, how to adopt and make up for what we originally lacked so that our people may be made new, should be deeply and carefully considered.

Generally, those who talk about a "renovation" may be divided into two groups. The lower group consists of those who pick up others' trite expressions and assume a bold look in order to climb up the official hierarchy. Their Western learning is stale stuff, their diplomacy relies on bribes, and their travels are moving in the dark. These people, of course, are not worth mentioning. The higher group consists of those who are worried about the situation and try hard to develop the nation and to promote well-being. But when asked about their methods, they would begin with diplomacy, training of troops, purchase of arms and manufacture of instruments; then they would proceed to commerce, mining and railways; and finally they would come, as they did recently, to officers' training, police, and education. Are these not the most important and necessary things for modern civilized nations? Yes. But can we attain the level of modern civilization and place our nation in an invincible position by adopting a little of this and that, or taking a small step now and then? I know we cannot.

Let me illustrate this by commerce. Economic competition is one of the big problems of the world today. It is the method whereby the powers attempt to conquer us. It is also the method whereby we should fight for our existence. The importance of improving our foreign trade has been recognized by all. But in order to promote foreign trade, it is necessary to protect the rights of our domestic trade and industry; and in order to protect these rights, it is necessary to issue a set of commercial laws. Commercial laws, however, cannot stand by themselves, and so it is necessary to complement them with other laws. A law which is not carried out is tantamount to no law; it is therefore necessary to define the powers of the judiciary. Bad legislation is worse than no legislation, and so it is necessary to decide where the legislative power should belong. If those who violate the law are not punished, laws will become void as soon as they are proclaimed; therefore, the duties of the judiciary must be defined. When all these are carried to the logical conclusion, it will be seen that foreign trade cannot be promoted without a constitution, a parliament, and a responsible government. Those who talk about foreign trade today blithely say, "I am promoting it, I am promoting it," and nothing more. I do not know how they are going to promote it. The above is one illustration, but it is true with all other cases. Thus I know why the so-called new methods nowadays are ineffectual. Why? Because without destruction there can be no construction. . . . What, then, is the way to effect our salvation and to achieve progress? The answer is that we must shatter at a blow the despotic and confused governmental system of some thousands of years; we must sweep away the corrupt and sycophantic learning of these thousands of years.

Questions: What does Liang see as the key sources of Western strength? What does he believe China needs most to borrow from Europe and the United States? Do his recommendations strike you as specific enough to rescue China from its many crises?

at preserving the existing order, not fundamentally transforming it. They continued to profess loyalty to the gravely weakened Manchu regime because they saw it as a defender of the traditional order. At the same time, their own power grew to the point that the Manchus could control them only with great difficulty.

Resources were increasingly drained from the court center to the provincial governors, whose growing military and political power posed a potential threat to the Qing court. The basis of China's political fragmentation was building behind the crumbling facade of Manchu rule.

The archconservative empress Cixi, here shown strolling in the snow-clad gardens of the imperial palace, dominated Chinese politics throughout the critical years at the turn of the 20th century.

Despite their clearly desperate situation by the last decades of the 19th century, including a shocking loss in a war with Japan in 1894 and 1895, the Manchu rulers stubbornly resisted the far-reaching reforms that were the only hope of saving the regime, and, as it turned out, Chinese civilization. Manchu rulers on occasion moved to back those officials who pushed for extensive political and social reforms, some of which were inspired by the example of the West. But their efforts were repeatedly frustrated by the backlash of members of the imperial household who allied themselves with the great majority of the scholar-gentry, who were determined to preserve the old order with only minor changes and to make no concessions to the West.

The last decades of the dynasty were dominated by the ultraconservative dowager empress Cixi, who became the power behind the throne. In 1898 she and her faction crushed the most serious move toward reform from the top. Her nephew, the emperor, was imprisoned in the Forbidden City, and leading advocates for reform were executed or driven from China. On one occasion Cixi taunted the Westernizers by rechanneling funds that had been raised to build modern warships to defend China into the building of a huge marble boat in one of the lakes in the imperial gardens. With genuine reform blocked by Cixi and her faction, the Manchus relied on divisions among the provincial officials as well as among the European powers to maintain their position. The involvement of members of the Qing household in popular outbursts aimed at forcibly expelling the foreigners from China—such as the Boxer Rebellion that broke out in 1898 and was put down only through the intervention of the imperialist powers in 1901—resulted in further military setbacks and enhanced the control of the Europeans and the power of the provincial officials.

By the first years of the 20th century the days of the Manchus were clearly numbered. With the defeat of the Taipings, resistance to the Qing came to be centered in rival secret-society organizations, such as the Triads and the Society of Elders and Brothers. These underground organizations inspired numerous local risings against the dynasty but failed for lack of coordination and sufficient resources. But some of the secret-society cells became a valuable training ground that prepared the way for a new sort of resistance to the Manchus. By the end of the 19th century the sons of some of the scholar-gentry and especially of the comprador merchants in the port cities were becoming more and more involved in secret-society operations and other activities aimed at the overthrow of the regime. Because many of these young men had received European-style educations, their resistance was aimed at more than just getting rid of the Manchus. They envisioned power passing to Western-educated, reformist leaders who would build a new and strong nation-state in China patterned after those of the West, rather than simply establishing yet another imperial dynasty. For aspiring revolutionaries such as Sun Yat-sen, who emerged as one of their most articulate spokesmen, their seizure of power was also seen as a way of enacting desperately needed social programs to relieve the misery of the peasantry and urban workers.

Though they drew heavily on the West for ideas and organizational models, the revolutionaries from the rising middle classes were deeply hostile to the involvement of the imperialist powers in Chinese affairs and condemned the Manchus for their failure to control the foreigners. The young rebels cut off their queues in defiance of Manchu order that all ethnic Chinese wear their hair in this fashion and joined in uprisings fomented by the secret societies or plotted assassinations and acts of sabotage on their own. Attempts to coordinate an all-China rising floundered on a number of occasions due to personal animosities or amateurish incompetence. But in late 1911 opposition to the government's reliance on the Western powers for railway loans led to secret-society uprisings, student demonstrations, and mutinies on the part of imperial troops. When a number of key provincial officials refused to put down the spreading rebellion, the Manchus had no choice but to abdicate. In February 1912 the last emperor of China, a small boy named Puyi, was deposed, and one of the more powerful of the provincial lords was asked to establish a republican government in China.

THE END OF A CIVILIZATION?

The revolution of 1911 toppled the Qing dynasty, but in many ways a more important watershed for Chinese civilization had been crossed in 1905, when the civil service exams were given for the last time. Reluctantly, even the ultraconservative advisors of the empress Cixi had concluded that solutions to China's predicament could no longer be found in the Confucian learning the exams tested. The abandonment of the exams in effect signaled the end of a pattern of civilized life the Chinese had nurtured, improved, and held to for nearly 2500 years. The mix of philosophies and values that had come to be known as the Confucian system, the massive civil bureaucracy, rule by an educated and cultivated scholar-gentry elite, and even the artistic accomplishments of the old order were to come under increasing criticism in the early years of the 20th century. Many of these hallmarks of the most enduring civilization that had ever existed would be vehemently discarded, violently destroyed. But even though Confucian civilization, like so many before it, passed into history, many of its ideas, attitudes, and ways of approaching the world survived. Some of these played critical roles in the violent and painful struggle of the Chinese people to build a new civilization to replace the one that had failed them. The challenge of blending and balancing the two remains to the present day.

CONCLUSION

DIVERGENT APPROACHES TO THE CHALLENGE OF THE WEST

The peoples of Latin America, the Middle East, and China, informally colonized but not conquered outright in the 19th century, all faced major challenges from the expansive and powerful industrialized nations of western Europe and the United States. More than any other factor, these challenges linked the history of regions as diverse as China and Latin America with a larger global experience. At the same time, each of these threatened societies responded to Western influences somewhat differently, because each came to the encounter from its own historical givens and with its own cultural circumstances. In every case the confrontation with the West was but one of many developments that shaped the entry of these societies into the 20th century. Thus it is important to set the impact of the West in the context of broader internal trends that give each area a distinct history and in turn explain the different outcomes of each encounter with the West.

For China the influx of Western economic and political influences came suddenly and brutally. Within decades the Chinese had to revise their estimate of their empire as the center of the earth and the source of all civilized life to take into account severe defeats at the hands of peoples they once dismissed as barbarians. By contrast, the peoples of the Middle East had been warring and trading with the Europeans since the Middle Ages. What was new for the Muslim peoples was the much greater strength that the Europeans had gained from their global expansion and their scientific and industrial revolutions.

The Muslims could take comfort from the fact that in the Judeo-Christian and Greek traditions, they shared much with the ascendant Europeans and that elements of their own civilization had played critical roles in the rise of the West. This made it easier to justify Muslim borrowing from the West, which in any case could be set in a long tradition of exchanges with other civilizations. Though some Chinese technology had passed to the West, Chinese and Western leaders were largely unaware of early exchanges but deeply impressed by the profound differences between their societies. For the Chinese, borrowing from the barbarians required a painful reassessment of their place in the world—a reassessment many were unwilling to make.

In countering the thrusts from the West, the Muslims gained from the fact that they had many centers to defend—the fall of a single dynasty or regime did not mean the end of Islamic independence. The Muslims also gained from the more gradual nature of the Western advance. They had time to learn from earlier mistakes and try out different responses to the Western challenges. For the Chinese, the defense of their civilization came to be equated with the survival of the Qing dynasty—a line of thinking that the Manchus did all they could to promote. When the dynasty collapsed in the early 20th century, the Chinese lost faith in the formula for civilization they had successfully followed for more than two millennia. Again timing was critical. The crisis in China seemed to come without warning. Within decades the Qing went from the arrogant controller of the barbarians to a defeated and humbled pawn of the European powers.

FURTHER READINGS

Stanley J. and Barbara Stein's *The Colonial Heritage of Latin America* (1970) is a hard-hitting interpretation of colonial and 19th-century Latin America that emphasizes its continued dependency and its neocolonial status after independence. David Bushnell and Neil Macauley's *The Emergence of Latin America in the Nineteenth Century* (1988) provides an excellent overview that is critical of the dependency thesis. The classic study from the dependency perspective is Fernando Henrique Cardoso and Enzo Faletto's *Dependency and Development in Latin America* (1979). Roberto Cortés Conde's *The First Stages of Modernization in Spanish America* (1974) provides a good economic analysis. E. Bradford Burns's *Poverty or Progress: Latin America in the Nineteenth Century* (1973) provides challenging attack on the liberal programs and a defense of a "folk" political tradition.

Jean Franco's *The Modern Culture of Latin America: Society and the Artist* (1967) is a lively discussion of literature and the arts. Volumes 3 to 5 of the *Cambridge History of Latin America* (1985–1986) contain up-to-date essays on major themes and individual countries. A good essay from the collection is Robert Freeman Smith's "Latin America, the United States, and the European Powers, 1830–1930," vol. IV, 83–120. Silvia Arrom's *The Women of Mexico City* (1985) is a fine example of the growing literature in women's history, some of which is also seen in June Nash and Helen Safa, eds., *Sex and Class in Latin America* (1980). Hobart Spalding, Jr.'s *Organized Labor in Latin America* (1977) surveys urban labor, and Charles Berquist's *Labor in Latin America* (1986) is a comparative interpretive essay.

The best general introductions to the Ottoman decline and the origins of the nation of Turkey remain Bernard Lewis's *The Emergence of Modern Turkey* (1961) and the chapter "The Later Ottoman Empire" by Halil Inalcik in the *Cambridge History of Islam*, vol. I (1973). More narrowly focused studies of this process include the monographs of C. V. Findley, Ernest Ramsaur's *The Young Turks* (1957), Stanford Shaw's *Between Old and New* (1971), and David Kusher's essay *The Rise of Turkish Nationalism* (1977). On Egypt and the Islamic heartlands in this period, see P. M. Holt's *Egypt and the Fertile Crescent, 1516–1922* (1965) or P. J. Vatikiotis's *The History of Egypt* (1985). On women and changes in the family in the Ottoman realm, see Nermin Abadan-Unat's *Women in Turkish Society* (1981); in the Arab world, Nawal el Saadawi's *The Hidden Face of Eve* (1980).

On Qing rule in China among the most readable and useful works are Spence's *Emperor of China: Portrait of K'ang-hsi* (1974) and the relevant sections in his recent study in *The Search for Modern China* (1990); Susan Naquin and Evelyn Rawski's *Chinese Society in 18th Century China* (1987); and the essays in John Fairbank, ed., *Cambridge History of China: Late Ch'ing 1800–1911* (1978). A good survey of the causes and course of the Opium War is provided by Chang Hsin-pao's *Commissioner Lin and the Opium War* (1964). The Taiping rebellion is covered in Jen Yu-wen's *The Taiping Revolutionary Movement* (1973), and the first stages of the Chinese nationalist movement are examined in the essays in Mary Wright, ed., *China in Revolution: The First Phase* (1968). The early sections of Elisabeth Croll's *Feminism and Socialism in China* (1980) provide an excellent overview of the status and condition of women in the Qing era.

1910–1920 Mexican Revolution

1914–1918 World War I

1917 Russian Revolution

1919 Versailles peace settlement; League of Nations

1912 African National Congress party formed in South Africa

1912 Fall of Qing dynasty in China; beginning of Chinese revolution

1917 United States' entry to World War I

1919 Revolt in Egypt; first Pan-African Nationalist Congress

1917 Balfour Declaration promises Jews a homeland in Palestine

1916 Arab revolts against Ottomans

1920s "Jazz Age" in U.S. & Western Europe; Dadaism, Surrealism, Expressionism dominate art world

1921 Einstein wins the Nobel Prize for Physics

1922 First commercial radio station in Pittsburgh, PA

1921 Foundation of Chinese Communist party

1920 Treaty of Sèvres reorganizes Middle East

1927 Charles Lindberg's solo flight across Atlantic Ocean

First talking movie, *The Jazz Singer*

1927–1928 Stalin heads Soviet Union; five-year plans and collectivization begin

Decades of Turmoil

The depths of despair to which Europe had sunk after two world wars and a global depression is captured in Max Ernst's surrealist painting *Europe After the Rain, II, 1940–1942*, which depicts the barbaric condition into which the 20th century's once preeminent civilization had fallen under the Nazi reign of terror.

1930–1945
Vargas
regime in   **1933–1939** New Deal   **1939–1945** World War II
Brazil   in United States
1930s Great age of Mexican mural painting
            1933 Nazis rise to power in Germany   **1942–1945** Holocaust

1931–1947
Gandhi-led   **1934–1940** Cárdenas   **1943–1945** Manhattan Project
resistance in   reform period in Mexico   to develop atomic bomb
India
                                        1939 Nazi-Soviet pact
                              1937 Army officers
1929–1933 Height of Great Depression   in power in Japan;   **1941** United
                              invasion of China   States enters war

        1931 Japan invades Manchuria
                1935 German rearmament;
                Italy conquers Ethiopia

PART II

A Half-Century of Crisis, 1914–1945

DECADES OF TURMOIL. Two world wars of unprecedented extent and ferocity and a prolonged global depression set the context for the second major phase of 20th-century history. Beginning with the outbreak of what contemporaries called the Great War in August 1914 and ending with the surrender in August 1945 of Japan, the last of the Axis powers to be defeated by the Allies in World War II, this period is rightly seen as an era of intensifying global crisis. Because of the strong linkages between the First World War (1914–1918) and the Second (1939–1945), historians have often referred to these decades as the era of the "30 years' war." This allusion to an earlier, 17th-century conflict that ravaged much of Europe is apt because the 1914–1945 period witnessed armed conflicts, revolutions, civil wars, and state repression that produced destruction and human death and suffering on a scale inconceivable in any earlier century. But unlike the earlier Thirty Years' War, which was confined to Europe, the three decades of crisis that mark the middle period of the 20th century affected much of the globe, though direct involvement in the world wars and the impact of the Great Depression varied considerably in different regions.

Historians of these decades have, not surprisingly, tended to be preoccupied with the suffering and destruction that marred the second phase of 20th-century history. But an exclusive emphasis on disasters or their causes can result in dangerous oversimplification, including an excessive preoccupation with the woes and excesses of Western nations. Global wars and depressions led to important and enduring political, social, and economic innovations in many regions of the world and opened up opportunities for advancement by some nations and social groups, albeit usually at the expense of others. In World War I, for example, both the United States and Japan emerged as global economic powers, and the United States was suddenly, if temporarily, catapulted to the status of the world's most powerful military nation. As a result of the 1914–1918 war, regions in Africa and Asia that had been colonized by the Western powers in the 18th and 19th centuries found new openings for intellectual and political resistance to European domination, and movements for independence gathered strength in many colonial areas. The weakness of China's new military leadership in the face of Japan's demands during the war and at the Paris Peace Conference led to the student and worker protest that sent the ongoing process of revolution in China into new and more radical directions. The collapse of the autocratic regimes of central and eastern Europe as a result of defeat in World War I led to revolutions—both successful and frustrated—that opened up new possibilities for the liberation of formerly oppressed or disadvantaged ethnic minorities and social groups, such as workers, peasants, and women.

These revolutionary gains were largely reversed by the totalitarian dictatorships of the 1930s and early 1940s (and the 1920s as well in the case of Italy and much of eastern Europe), but lasting improvements remained in mass health care and education. In addition, the legitimacy of governments was increasingly judged according to the novel standard of how well they provided for the welfare of the citizens they ruled. Though the Great Depression proved devastating to the United States, Japan, and much of western Europe, its shocks were less harmful to the relatively isolated Soviet Union and some colonized areas not fully tied into the global market system. In addition, in some European countries and particularly the United States the depression led to necessary state regulation of banking and securities; long overdue welfare measures, such as social security; and massive public works projects, such as dams, bridges, and highways, that brought lasting improvements to the infrastructure. In Latin America, which was profoundly shaken by the worldwide economic downturn, new and constructive political forces and government policies emerged to meet the crisis. These not only made for major shifts in Latin American politics and society but also resulted in some amelioration of the long-standing handicaps that had skewed the participation of Latin American nations in international trade.

The Second World War saw great gains for the United States in global economic and military power. Despite enormous human suffering, it also enlarged the Soviet Union's sphere of direct control and influence, particularly in eastern Europe and Asia. And even in western Europe, the region most devastated by the succession of war, revolution, depression, and war, recovery from the decades of crisis was in many ways stunningly successful. The second phase of the 20th century did result in a significant diminution of western Europe's dominance over the rest of the globe and a complex rebalancing among civilizations after 1945. But Western society rebounded in many ways, creating a political, cultural, and economic vitality that contrasted markedly with the agonies of the 1914–1945 era. Thus although some Europeans who lived through the decades of crisis thought that civilization was coming to an end, their pessimism was countered by the rebirth of Europe from the late 1940s, which defied the seemingly intractable problems that had plagued earlier generations.

✻ FOUNDATIONS OF AN ERA OF REVOLUTIONS AND TOTALITARIAN STATES

The global ramifications of wars begun in Europe and an economic downturn triggered by the 1929 stock market collapse in the United States illustrate the extent to which the world network had intensified as a result of industrialization and Western imperialism. There had been previous wars with theaters of combat spread across the globe. The Seven Years' War (1756–1763), for example, had been fought in Europe, North America, the Caribbean, and India, and the same was true for the Napoleonic Wars of the early 19th century. But the two world wars of the 20th century were more genuinely international conflicts because in addition to spreading over a larger portion of the globe, they directly involved as both combatants and victims the peoples of Europe's vast colonial empires, as well as the citizens of rising powers, such as Japan and the United States.

Though different regions of the globe had long been tied to the expanding world market system centered on Europe and increasingly the United States, the intensity and extent of the shock waves set off by the Great Depression were unprecedented. A complex meshing of import-export exchanges, international monetary linkages, and loan agreements had bound the industrialized West to its African and Asian colonies, Japan, China, and Latin America. Thus a severe financial crisis in one part of the global economic system eventually threatened the entire international order. In fact, the tariff wars and sharp decrease in lending that marked the years of depression fragmented the global economy into increasingly closed economic blocs that corresponded ominously with the political adversaries that fought the Second World War.

The technological and organizational transformations that had linked the peoples of the globe together were also critical to key transformations within specific regions and nations in the decades of crisis. The quantum leap in killing power that accompanied the mass production of the new weaponry developed in the 19th and early 20th centuries made possible the slaughter or maiming of millions of soldiers in the First World War. The prevailing ineptitude of Europe's political and military leaders, most of whom had little idea of how to employ the new weapons, rendered the slaughter tragically senseless, since neither side could decisively defeat the other despite the appalling casualties. But the intensification of national rivalries and patriotic sentiments in the decades before 1914 had done much to bring on the conflict and made it possible for the hostile powers to mobilize tens of millions of conscripts and to keep most of them fighting, despite the futility of the conflict, for four long years. Industrial transportation (particularly the railway) and communications systems were essential to supplying and deploying these massive armies, and the mobilization of the combatants' civilian populations proved necessary to the continuation of the war effort. Military and civilian mobilization efforts led in turn to a dramatic increase in the power and functions of the state—a trend that would prove to be one of the central themes of global history in the 20th century.

The relentless demands of the war effort also produced severe dislocations that provided opportunities for some social groups while proving deeply detrimental to others. Women, for example, in European societies, the British Dominions, and the United States found their occupational prospects greatly enhanced, even in heavy industry and other spheres that had been all but closed to them in the 19th century. Also, the new latitude of social and sexual freedom provided openings for personal expression that would have been unthinkable in the Victorian era. By contrast, the power and reputation of Europe's aristocratic classes, which had played leading roles in the diplomatic corps that had been unable to control the crisis that led to war and in the failed military leadership that had rendered the conflict so costly, fell precipitously in the interwar era.

Although the war brought a sharp decline in the numbers and importance of the household servant classes in western Europe and the United States, it greatly strengthened the position of the working classes in most of the combatant societies. In wartime and in the postwar decades, socialist and labor parties shared power in most of western Europe. In the United States the legitimacy of workers' organizations, such as the American Federation of Labor, was greatly enhanced. In Russia and Germany the urban working classes provided the bulk of support for Marxist-Leninist revolutionary movements

that sought to seize power from defeated regimes in 1917 and 1918–1919, respectively. The disconnected risings in Germany failed, as did a postwar revolution in Hungary, but the more disciplined and centralized Bolshevik party managed to seize power in Russia in October 1917. Its ascendancy and survival in the bloody civil war that followed created a major division that persisted through much of the rest of the 20th century in the international community between a revolution-minded communist camp and the bourgeois democracies, whose leaders were often preoccupied with containing and ultimately crushing the radical menace. From the early 1920s onward the Russian Revolution also provided inspiration and material support for leftist revolutionaries in societies as diverse as China, British India, and the nations of Latin America and the Caribbean.

The Bolshevik victory also marked another great leap in state power and control over its subjects. Bolshevik efforts to survive the assaults of both domestic and external enemies and a party philosophy that espoused state-directed programs for social and economic transformation led to the growth of a massive bureaucracy, military establishment, and secret-police apparatus. After Stalin's consolidation of power over the Soviet state in the late 1920s, these trends toward centralization and bureaucratic control were accelerated in all spheres, marking a turn toward totalitarianism that distinguished the 1930s and early 1940s in Europe, eastern Asia, and parts of Latin America. The rise of Stalin's despotism had particularly tragic consequences for the peoples of the Soviet Union in the 1930s, as the artificial "famines" in the Ukraine and elsewhere, succession of party purges, and spread of concentration camps, or *gulags*, in Siberia amply testify. Partly in response to the perceived threat of the industrializing Soviet Union and the spread of communism, and taking full advantage of the dislocations and human suffering brought on by the Great Depression, fascist parties seized or shared power in Germany, Spain, and Argentina. Like Mussolini, who had used the threat of revolution from the left to gain power in Italy in the early 1920s, the Nazis in Germany and Falangists in Spain moved to destroy all political opposition and to establish party control over all aspects of economic and cultural life.

The external aggressiveness of the fascist regimes in Germany and Italy, as well as that of their uncertain ally in Japan, led to the Second World War, which pitted the Axis powers against the unlikely alliance of the Soviet Union and the Western democracies. The war demonstrated the daunting capacity of 20th-century states to regiment and mobilize their subject populations and underscored the awesome productive capacity of advanced

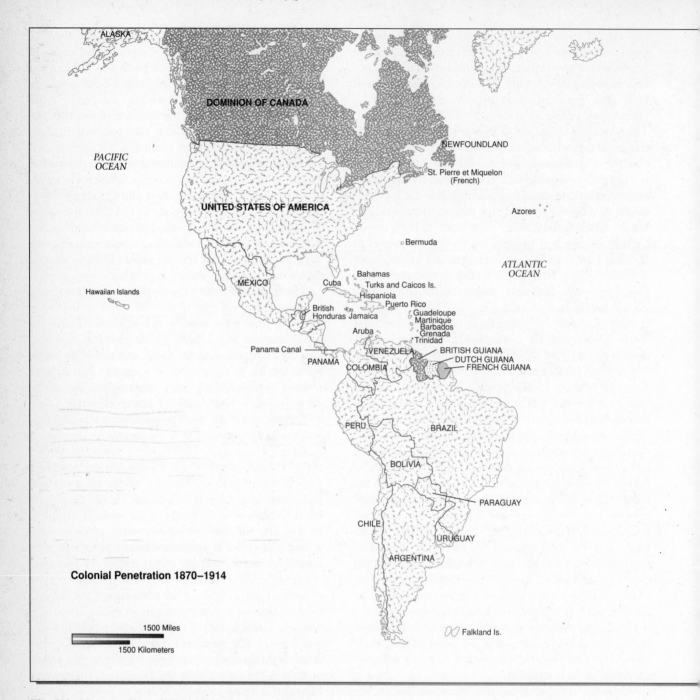

Colonial Penetration 1870–1914

1500 Miles
1500 Kilometers

The World on the Eve of World War I

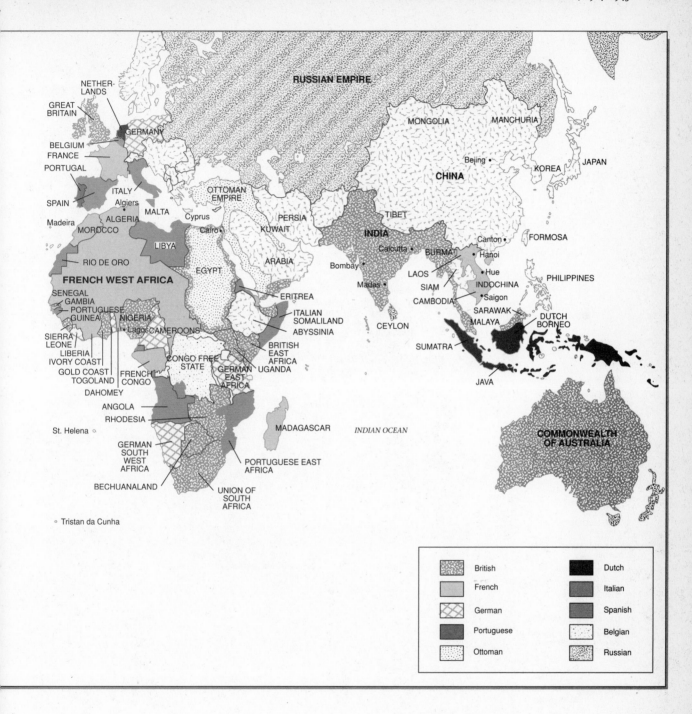

RUSSIAN EMPIRE

NETHER-
LANDS
GREAT
BRITAIN
GERMANY
BELGIUM
FRANCE
PORTUGAL
ITALY
SPAIN
Algiers
MALTA
Madeira
ALGERIA
MOROCCO
LIBYA
RIO DE ORO
FRENCH WEST AFRICA
SENEGAL
GAMBIA
PORTUGUESE
GUINEA
NIGERIA
SIERRA
LEONE
LIBERIA
IVORY COAST
Lagos
CAMEROONS
GOLD COAST
TOGOLAND
FRENCH
CONGO
DAHOMEY
CONGO FREE
STATE
GERMAN
EAST
AFRICA
UGANDA
ANGOLA
RHODESIA
St. Helena
GERMAN
SOUTH
WEST
AFRICA
BECHUANALAND
UNION OF
SOUTH
AFRICA
PORTUGUESE EAST
AFRICA
MADAGASCAR
INDIAN OCEAN

OTTOMAN
EMPIRE
Cyprus
PERSIA
KUWAIT
Cairo
ARABIA
EGYPT
ERITREA
ITALIAN
SOMALILAND
ABYSSINIA
BRITISH
EAST
AFRICA

MONGOLIA
MANCHURIA
Bejing •
CHINA
KOREA
JAPAN
TIBET
FORMOSA
Canton •
INDIA
Calcutta •
BURMA
Hanoi •
Bombay •
LAOS
• Hue
Madas •
SIAM
INDOCHINA
CAMBODIA
• Saigon
CEYLON
PHILIPPINES
SARAWAK
MALAYA
DUTCH
BORNEO
SUMATRA
JAVA
**COMMONWEALTH
OF AUSTRALIA**

◦ Tristan da Cunha

	British		Dutch
	French		Italian
	German		Spanish
	Portuguese		Belgian
	Ottoman		Russian

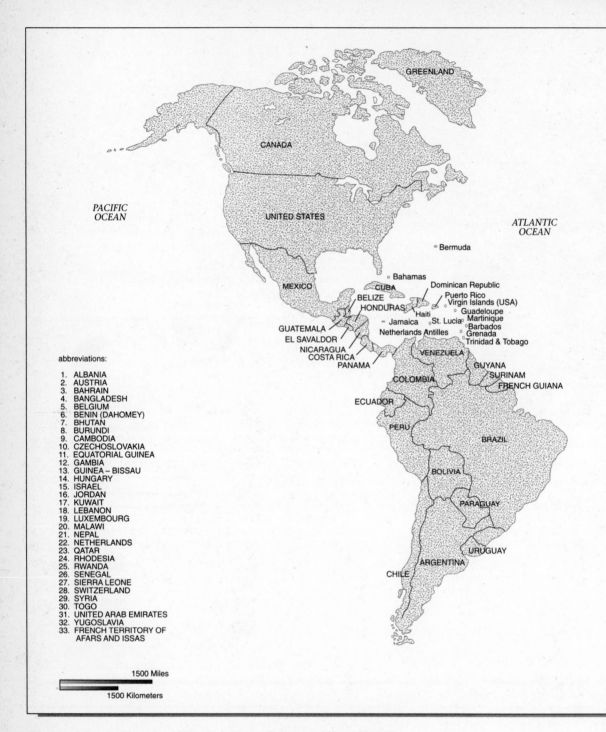

PACIFIC OCEAN

ATLANTIC OCEAN

GREENLAND

CANADA

UNITED STATES

MEXICO

Bermuda

Bahamas

CUBA

BELIZE
HONDURAS

Dominican Republic
Puerto Rico
Virgin Islands (USA)
Guadeloupe
Martinique
Haiti
Jamaica   St. Lucia
Netherlands Antilles   Barbados
Grenada
Trinidad & Tobago

GUATEMALA
EL SAVALDOR
NICARAGUA
COSTA RICA
PANAMA

VENEZUELA

GUYANA
SURINAM
FRENCH GUIANA

COLOMBIA

ECUADOR

PERU

BRAZIL

BOLIVIA

PARAGUAY

URUGUAY

ARGENTINA

CHILE

abbreviations:

1. ALBANIA
2. AUSTRIA
3. BAHRAIN
4. BANGLADESH
5. BELGIUM
6. BENIN (DAHOMEY)
7. BHUTAN
8. BURUNDI
9. CAMBODIA
10. CZECHOSLOVAKIA
11. EQUATORIAL GUINEA
12. GAMBIA
13. GUINEA – BISSAU
14. HUNGARY
15. ISRAEL
16. JORDAN
17. KUWAIT
18. LEBANON
19. LUXEMBOURG
20. MALAWI
21. NEPAL
22. NETHERLANDS
23. QATAR
24. RHODESIA
25. RWANDA
26. SENEGAL
27. SIERRA LEONE
28. SWITZERLAND
29. SYRIA
30. TOGO
31. UNITED ARAB EMIRATES
32. YUGOSLAVIA
33. FRENCH TERRITORY OF
    AFARS AND ISSAS

1500 Miles

1500 Kilometers

The World in the Decades of Decolonization Following World War II

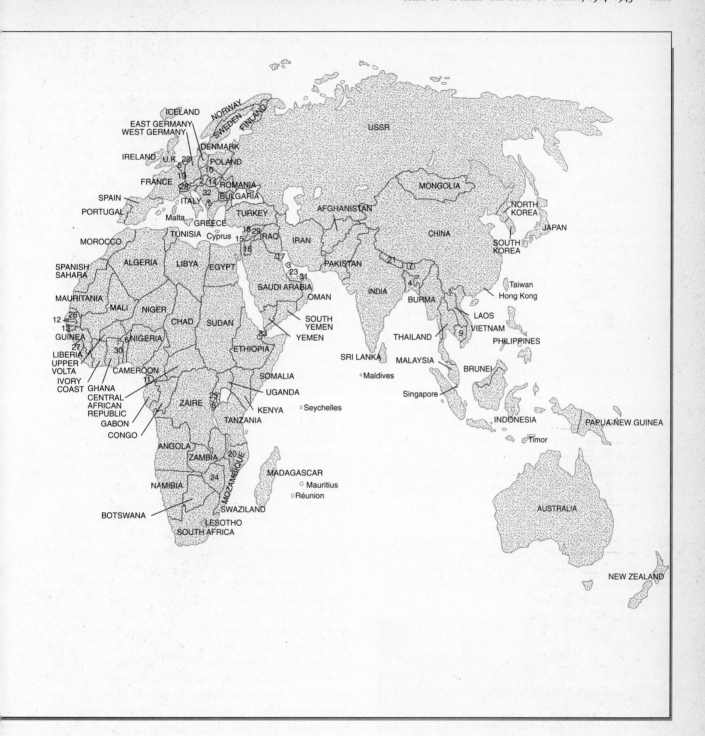

ICELAND
NORWAY
SWEDEN
FINLAND
EAST GERMANY
WEST GERMANY
DENMARK
IRELAND
U.K. 22
POLAND
5
19
10
FRANCE
2 14 ROMANIA
28
32 BULGARIA
SPAIN
ITALY
PORTUGAL
Malta
GREECE
TURKEY
MOROCCO
TUNISIA
Cyprus
18 29
15
IRAQ
18
IRAN
1 17
SPANISH
SAHARA
ALGERIA
LIBYA
EGYPT
3
23 31
4
MAURITANIA
MALI
NIGER
SAUDI ARABIA
OMAN
12 26
CHAD
SUDAN
SOUTH
YEMEN
13
GUINEA
27
33
YEMEN
LIBERIA
6 NIGERIA
UPPER
30
VOLTA
IVORY
COAST
GHANA
CENTRAL
AFRICAN
REPUBLIC
CAMEROON
11
ETHIOPIA
SOMALIA
GABON
ZAIRE
25
UGANDA
CONGO
8
KENYA
TANZANIA
USSR
MONGOLIA
NORTH
KOREA
JAPAN
AFGHANISTAN
SOUTH
KOREA
CHINA
PAKISTAN
21
7
Taiwan
INDIA
BURMA
Hong Kong
LAOS
THAILAND
VIETNAM
9
PHILIPPINES
SRI LANKA
MALAYSIA
Maldives
BRUNEI
Singapore
Seychelles
INDONESIA
PAPUA-NEW GUINEA
Timor
ANGOLA
20
ZAMBIA
MADAGASCAR
24
Mauritius
NAMIBIA
MOZAMBIQUE
Réunion
BOTSWANA
SWAZILAND
AUSTRALIA
LESOTHO
SOUTH AFRICA
NEW ZEALAND

industrialized societies. Nowhere was this combination more brutally apparent than in the assembly-line approach to genocide adopted by the Nazi bureaucracy that resulted in the imprisonment and then the systematic murder of millions of Jews, gypsies, ethnic minorities, political dissidents, and other "undesirables," such as homosexuals. As Walter Frankel so movingly relates in his account of the struggle to survive in the Nazi death camps, by the mid-20th century the state had the power to deprive individual subjects of their jobs, their rights as citizens, their homes and families, their clothing and the very hairs on their heads and bodies. Never before in history had the power of handfuls of leaders been so great; never before had the suffering of humanity been so massive.

The unprecedented growth of state power in these decades of crisis did not take place without resistance. Somewhat predictably, the most powerful and enduring forces that countered trends toward centralization and bureaucratic interference in the everyday lives of ordinary people emerged in areas where industrial technology was less established and appeals to patriotism and ideologies of racial supremacy rang hollow. In the colonized areas of Africa and Asia and the economically dominated informal colonies of China and Latin America, resistance to European and increasingly U.S. global dominance surged in the second phase of the 20th century. In all of these areas this resistance was built primarily on the support of peasants, or subsistence-oriented

Emiliano Zapata and his Indian peasant supporters played a major role during the early years of the Mexican Revolution. Under Zapata's charismatic leadership, his followers won back their lands and injected a genuinely populist element into the ongoing revolution.

farmers, the largest of all social groups in most societies for much of human history. Long exploited Amerindian communities and landless agricultural laborers played critical roles in the complex combination of regional upheavals that converged to produce the Mexican Revolution. Begun four years before the outbreak of the First World War, the Mexican conflict raged into the late 1920s and continued to produce aftershocks for decades thereafter. The first of the great revolutions of the 20th century, and much more than the Russian upheavals of 1917, the revolution in Mexico gave voice—however fleetingly—to the peasant masses. Though Marxist ideology would play a much greater role in most of the revolutions that followed later in the 20th century than it had in Mexico, the central role of the peasantry was reflected in revolutionary upheavals from China and Vietnam to Angola and Bolivia.

In the decades of crisis peasant struggles over much of Africa and Asia became caught up in broader movements of resistance to Western colonial dominance. Led mainly by Western-educated individuals from well-to-do families, these movements of liberation and nation building gave rise to the two most powerful approaches to resistance to state power in the 20th century. Guerrilla tactics had been very effectively used by the white Afrikaner farmers of South Africa to counter the superior numbers and firepower of the British colonizers as early as the Anglo-Boer war from 1899 to 1902. They had also been employed by regional leaders, such as Emiliano Zapata in the Mexican Revolution. But Chinese revolutionaries, especially Mao Zedong, crafted tactics employed rather haphazardly for millennia by the weak and poorly armed into comprehensive strategies for waging guerrilla warfare.

The violent thrust of the guerrilla response to Western political dominance and weapons superiority contrasted sharply with the techniques of civil disobedience and nonviolent resistance developed by Mahatma Gandhi and his followers. In their struggles against racial discrimination and colonial rule in South Africa and India from the early 1900s, Indian nationalists forged the second major option developed in the 20th century for those who wished to challenge the unprecedented power of the state. Though associated mainly with anticolonial movements in the decades of crisis, civil disobedience in the Gandhian mode was to play a major role in struggles against discrimination and injustice in the United States and Western Europe in the post–World War II era.

Growing resistance to European global dominance underscores one of the key trends of the decades of crisis after 1914—the growing number of significant actors in world affairs after an era in which western European na-

One of several remarkable photos taken immediately after the atomic explosion that destroyed Hiroshima on August 6, 1945, this picture shows stunned survivors at a first aid station in the south of the devastated city.

tions had monopolized center stage. This trend was sometimes masked by the continuing prominence of British, French, and German leaders in world councils and their ability to shore up European colonial regimes in most areas. Nonetheless, the shift in economic power and political influence was very real. The Europeans were increasingly under siege in their colonial bastions, and new rivals were rising to challenge their global leadership. As we have seen, the Soviet Union and the social revolutions it sought to foment abroad provided the most obvious and threatening of these rivals. But in the decades after World War I the most potent contender for world power was the United States, which came to dominate the international economy in many sectors and experimented cautiously and often inconsistently with global political leadership as well.

Many Americans, to be sure, vacillated between serious commitments to highly profitable international commercial exchanges and an inclination to retreat into political and military isolation. Americans also shifted between conventional Great Power maneuvers and a desire to inject idealism, which some leaders argued was peculiarly American, into the diplomatic process. Other peoples could not always easily adjust to the U.S. style, and particularly in the 1930s deep disagreements developed between the United States and other rivals for international influence, such as Japan and a revitalized Germany. Whatever the quarrels and powers involved, it was apparent that the decades of crisis of the mid-20th century marked the end of over a century of European global dominance. From the 1920s onward, world dramas involved a more and more varied cast, and western European actors—for all of their pretensions to imperial grandeur—were steadily pushed from center stage to the wings and often relegated to what amounted to bit parts.

PART OVERVIEW

The opening chapter of this unit on the middle period of 20th-century history provides an overview of the two global wars and the worldwide depression that set the context for this period of recurring crises in both international and domestic affairs. Chapter 6 focuses on the impact of these events and processes on the industrialized nations of the world, concentrating on western Europe, the United States, Japan, and the British Dominions. Chapter 7 explores the forces of revolution and repression generated by World War I and the Great Depression. The chapter begins with the Mexican upheavals that presaged the 1914–1918 catastrophe and the Russian revolutions that were among the major consequences of the war. After considering the ways in which Stalin turned revolutionary aspirations into a repressive police state, we examine the course of key revolutionary struggles in China and Vietnam. Chapter 8 is devoted to the struggle of colonized peoples in Asia and Africa to put an end to European rule and to establish independent states in the decades before and after the Second World War.

1914–1918 World War I   **1919–1939** Period of United States political isolation

1917 British Balfour Declaration
promises Jews a homeland in Palestine

1923 Treaty of Lausanne recognizes independence of Turkey

1918 German emperor abdicates

1916 Beginning of Arab revolt
against Ottoman Empire

1920 Treaty of Sèvres dissolves Ottoman Empire;
French and British mandates set up in Middle East

1915-1916 British promise Arabs postwar independence to win support

1917 Russian Revolution

1918 Treaty of Brest-Litovsk; Russia withdraws from war

1919 Versailles conference and treaty; League of Nations established

1915 Italy enters war

1919 Gandhi leads first non-violent protest movements in India

Treaty of St. Germain recognizes Czechoslovakia, Yugoslavia, Poland, and Hungary

1917 United States enters war

Descent into the Abyss: Global Wars and the Great Depression

5

INTRODUCTION. To many Western observers shortly before 1914, the main trends in world history seemed both clear and benign. During the previous century or more, Western society had become unquestionably richer and by many measurements more open and just. Mass education had become a fact of life. Health had improved, and the death of infants, long a constant in human history, was becoming increasingly rare. New political rights gave most adult men a direct voice in government and protected freedoms of religion and press. Knowledge advanced steadily, with increasing understanding of the physical universe. Dark corners of the physical and social environments existed still, but it was reasonable to assume that scientific planning, leavened by humanitarian concern, could reduce them steadily. Certainly, catastrophic war had no place in this vision—people and governments should be too enlightened to allow more than minor discord.

The optimism of many Westerners focused mainly on what they saw as progress in their own civilization, but there was also an international dimension to their belief in progress. Imperialists believed that Western leadership was bringing new enlightenment to the inferior peoples of the rest of the world, though they did not make it clear whether these peoples might someday learn enough to take care of themselves according to Western standards. Beyond outright imperialism, during the later 19th century there had been some interesting first steps at international organization, which might foreshadow a more smoothly and peacefully functioning world.

1942–1945 Allied conferences in Teheran, Yalta, Potsdam

1929–1939 Great Depression

1940 Axis agreement (Germany, Italy, Japan)

1946 United States grants Philippines independence

1947 Cold war begins between United States and Soviet Union

1936–1939 Spanish Civil War

1941 Japanese attack Pearl Harbor; United States enters war

1941 German invasion of Soviet Union

1939 Nazi-Soviet Pact

1944 Invasion of France by Allies

1933 Nazis to power in Germany

1939 World War II begins; Germany and Soviet Union invade Poland

1947 Wider decolonization begins with independence of India and Pakistan

1940 Fall of France

1945 End of World War II

1937 New Japanese attack on China; beginning of war in Asia

1942 Tide begins to turn in both war theaters; Soviet Union repulses attack on Stalingrad; Allies invade North Africa

1931 Japan invades Manchuria

1938 Germany's union (Anschluss) with Austria; Germany invades Czechoslovakia; Munich conference

1945 Atomic bomb dropped on Japan; United Nations established

1935 Germany rearms; Italy invades Ethiopia

In 1851, for example, the International Statistical Congress began meeting to standardize the practices of statistical services of the European governments. A more informal committee met in 1863 to prepare policies on the rights of neutral parties to aid the wounded during wars, and an official diplomatic conference redrafted these policies in 1864 at the Geneva Convention, establishing the Red Cross, an international agency for humanitarian service in wartime. The Telegraphic Union of 1865 blazed a new trail, followed ten years later by the Postal Union; both unions established international procedures for regular exchanges of letters and messages. Some of these steps constituted serious modifications of the idea that an individual national government could do as it pleased, and the practical agreements certainly facilitated the further development of international business arrangements. The habit of thinking internationally seemed to spread increasingly. Scientists met often in international conferences; industrialists showed their wares at international fairs and exhibitions, starting with London's great Crystal Palace display in 1851 and continuing through regular world's fairs in various parts of Europe and the United States. Western socialists formed an international movement, based on the idea that working peoples should unite across national boundaries. The establishment of the modern Olympic Games in the 1890s provided a new forum for international athletic competition.

These various moves toward internationalization constituted an important development in world history, both recognizing and furthering the intensification of world contacts. Many of the international systems and habits established in the decades before 1900 still facilitate world exchanges today—some, like easy international mailing, are so routine that they barely merit thought.

Despite genuine significance, however, the international movement had two related weaknesses. First, it was heavily based on Western dominance and control of empires. A few other governments fit in—from North America, Latin America, and Asia—but most of the initial arrangements were set primarily by and for Europeans. The process of weaning internationalism from Western control would be a long and painful one, focused particularly on the decades after 1945. Internationalization, furthermore, gained ground at the same time that European nationalism was at a height, as well as at a time when the idea of national independence and pride was spreading to new areas, such as India. Here was another limit on internationalist thinking, quickly visible in the Olympic Games, which turned into an international forum for fierce athletic competition among

rival nations rather than a format for international harmony.

The limits of internationalism showed clearly when the movement turned away from economic and goodwill areas to more directly political matters. In 1898 the Russian tsar urged the calling of a peace conference to seek agreement on reducing armaments levels among the world's powers. The move was prompted in part by Russia's economic problems as a nation just beginning to industrialize and its difficulty in keeping up with the arms costs escalating among the Western nations. Nevertheless, the discussions, held in The Hague in 1899, amplified international agreements on the treatment of war prisoners, temporarily prohibited weapons thrown from balloons, and banned gas warfare and some other new technologies (these latter measures were ignored in the world war that broke out 15 years later). Disarmament and the idea of compulsory arbitration of international disputes were shunted aside. But a permanent court of arbitration was established that nations could use to settle disputes. This court, now called the World Court, still sits in The Hague and has ruled on economic rights and minor boundary questions. Obviously, however, the promising move toward more genuine international discussion of the issues that might cause war did not proceed very far, given intense national rivalries then and now.

An optimistic observer before 1914 could legitimately believe that a more rational approach toward international problems was in the works. The strides that had occurred in setting up international mechanisms were limited but not entirely illusory. Obviously, the international movement did not prevent massive 20th-century war. It also did not die but rather was reinvoked, indeed, as part of the effort to settle World War I and again after World War II.

Still, the main point is the gap between confident assumptions in the West about internal and international progress alike and the disaster that beckoned in 1914. How did the West collapse into war, dragging much of the world along with it? The advent of an unprecedented kind of war seemed to make a mockery of widely held optimism, causing all the more havoc because so many people had fervently believed that such humanly created catastrophes were impossible.

THE FIRST WORLD WAR AND ITS AFTERMATH

By 1914 the fires of war in Europe burned far brighter than the sparks of internationalism. Diplomatic tensions had escalated fairly steadily among the major European powers—Britain, France, Russia, Germany, and Austria-Hungary—since the 1890s. Two rival alliances had formed, theoretically pitting the first three nations against the last two plus Italy. Germany had built its alliance system from the late 1870s, seeking to protect itself against revenge by France, which had lost both war and territory in 1870–1871. The Germans formed a firm bond with Austria-Hungary, which sought German protection against possible Russian expansionism. Italy joined in when Germany promised support for imperialism, for Italy's main rival in this field was France. The French alliance system formed more slowly, starting with a vital link with Russia in the 1890s. Britain, frightened by Germany's economic and imperial buildup, swallowed its colonial competition with France to join the grouping in 1904. Britain also had an understanding with Japan, though this focused primarily on policies in eastern Asia. The major alliances—Germany's Triple Alliance against France's newer Triple Entente—featured agreements to come to the allies' aid if they were attacked and some formal arrangements for military coordination in case of war.

The alliance system, menacing in itself, was embittered by the atmosphere generated by European imperialism. For two decades at the end of the 19th century, all the major European nations had become accustomed to rapid territorial expansion and easily won military and diplomatic prestige. Nationalist excitement built up in every country. Briefly, this process distracted from tensions back home. By 1900, however, most of the world's available territory had already been carved up. The final imperialist gains prompted much greater strains in Europe's diplomatic system. France thus pressed to acquire Morocco, partly because Moroccan raids were disrupting its older colony of Algeria. Germany deeply resented this French gain, and only British pressure, plus some territory for Germany drawn from the French Congo, prevented war in 1911. Italy, not to be outdone by France, seized the occasion to take Tripoli (present-day Libya) from the Ottoman Empire, also in 1911. Italian victory prompted the small states in the Balkans to sharpen their own knives against the Ottoman Empire, leading to two bitter Balkan wars in 1912–1913, which resulted in gains for Bulgaria and Serbia but left none of the combatants satisfied.

The point is obvious, at least in retrospect. With the available colonies fully taken, any further imperialist moves threatened direct confrontation among countries within Europe. Yet the passions imperialism had stirred

THE BOILING POINT.

The obvious fear displayed by an assortment of European leaders in this 1912 *Punch* cartoon is eerily prescient of the bafflement and concern that has seized European and world leaders in the midst of the Balkan wars of the 1990s.

persisted. Most European nations, large and small, were eager to press for new gains and fearful that some other country might advance at their expense.

Imperialism and the alliance system were both linked to steady military buildups. Naval rivalry was particularly intense. Germany's decision to build a competitive navy was one of the principal reasons that Britain had consented to alliance with France. Huge new warships, such as the Dreadnought battleship, kept the naval rivalry going full tilt, as all efforts at arms-reduction agreements failed. Army arsenals and training procedures were also steadily updated. In 1914, for example, Germany proved relatively eager for war in part because it feared that army changes being prepared in both Russia and France would place it at disadvantage.

Diplomatic and military competition tied foreign policy to spiraling domestic tensions. All the major industrial nations faced growing labor unrest, as strikes, trade unions, and socialist voting mounted steadily after 1900. The business classes and the political elites were alarmed at this challenge to their power. They sought diplomatic successes as distractions from social conflict. British ministers appealed for labor peace in the name of national unity against the German threat. German military and political leaders were tempted into war in 1914 in part because of their confusion and anxiety amidst the steady advance of the Social Democratic (socialist) party. Leadership groups also supported military buildups because they gave jobs to aristocratic generals and orders to metallurgical factories. Diplomacy, in sum, had become tied to the ongoing process of industrialization and to the anxieties this process spawned.

Finally, the alliance system linked France, Britain, Germany, and Italy to two nations with unusually great internal pressures. The dual monarchy of Austria-Hungary was beset by bitter national struggles among a number of Slavic minorities against the dominance of German and Hungarian leadership. Russia faced a revolutionary mood among workers and peasants—revolution had burst out directly in 1905—producing a belief that diplomatic success was essential. More stable nations, such as France, were so burdened by fears of their rivals that they refused to pull back from their less stable allies. The two alliance systems focused increasingly on the leading European trouble spot, the Balkans in the southeast, even before the two wars of 1912 and 1913. Russia was directly interested in the bitter competition among the Balkan nations because of its vaunted kinship with other Slavic peoples; Serbia and Bulgaria particularly, fell into this category. Austria-Hungary was interested because it feared the same south-Slavic nationalism. Austrian annexation of Slavic territory in Bosnia-Herzegovina in 1908, designed to provide a buffer against Serbian efforts to arouse Slavs within the dual monarchy, infuriated Serbia and made Russia judge that any further Slavic setbacks were intolerable.

The stage for war, in other words, was set by a combination of explicit diplomatic rivalries and an unusually inflexible, though theoretically defensive, alliance system. It was also fed by the social tensions among Western industrial powers, which had become accustomed to big armaments expenses as one means of supporting heavy industry, and among several eastern European nations caught in the stresses of an earlier phase of industrialization. The menu for war was fed finally by ethnic tensions in eastern Europe, where a variety of Slavic groups and small nations, particularly in the Balkans, competed for influence and tried to undermine multinational empires, such as Austria-Hungary.

The trigger for war occurred, not surprisingly, in the troubled Balkans. In July 1914 a Serbian nationalist shot the Austrian archduke Ferdinand, the emperor's nephew, hoping to strike a blow for Serbian acquisition of Slavic territories controlled by Austria. After years of tension, this was the last straw for Austria-Hungary: Serbia had to be attacked. Germany supported Austria, partly out of loyalty to a weak ally and partly because key leaders believed, for social and military reasons, that world war was inevitable and sooner was better than later. Russia refused to let Austria bully Serbia, lest it lose all influence in the Balkans, and France vowed to support Russia come what might. When Austria declared war on Serbia on July 28, Russia declared a general mobilization against both Austria-Hungary and Germany. Russia believed it had to prepare for war on both fronts because its procedures were slow. Mobilization frightened Germany, whose strategy called for a quick defeat of France before turning to Russia, so Germany declared war on both Russia and France on August 1. Britain hesitated, hoping for peace, but in fact the nation was heavily committed to France, and then was frightened and offended by Germany's invasion of Belgium, which was part of the German plan to knock France out quickly by attacking from both the north and the east. Britain entered the fray on August 4. After a century of considerable peace in Europe, the nation-states had once again launched a general war. But this one, fed by the new powers of the state, by new nationalist passions, and by the devastating armaments produced by industrialization, would have consequences much more awesome than any previous struggle.

PATTERNS OF WAR IN EUROPE

Two major fronts were quickly established as hostilities opened. One, mainly in France, pitted attacking German troops against French and British defenders. The second developed in eastern Europe, particularly in Russian Poland, where German armies battled Russian forces while trying also to support the weaker Austrian-Hungarian army to the south. After Italy entered the war on the side of France and Britain in 1915, wooed by promises of colonial territory to be seized from Austria and in the Middle East, a third front developed between Italians and Austrians. In addition to the war for land, there was an important contest for the seas. The large German surface fleet was bottled up by the British for most of the war, but German submarines played havoc with Atlantic sea-lanes, particularly through 1916. German attacks on U.S. ships bringing people and supplies

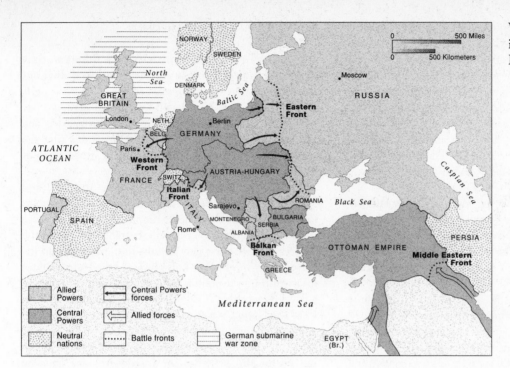

World War I Fronts
in Europe and the
Middle East

to Britain were the most important single cause of American entry into the war in 1917.

France thrust briefly into Germany in the late summer of 1914, but on the western front the German conquest of Belgium and advance through northern France constituted the big news. For a brief moment, as French forces pulled back in panic from their own offensive, it looked as though German hopes for a quick Western settlement might be met. But France rallied, aided by British reinforcements and by heroic civilian support, including a famous troop convoy organized by Parisian cabdrivers. Soon northern France was crisscrossed with trenches from which little advance was possible. The awesome technology of modern war was revealed in all its power, as devastating artillery, the withering fire of machine guns, barbed-wire fences, and the use of poison gas defined the deadening stalemate. By 1916 stagnation on the western front had turned into a nightmare as the Germans lost 850,000 men, the French 700,000, and the British 410,000 in the one year alone—without any appreciable change in the lines of battle. A German novelist later described life in the rat-infested trenches:

> The front is a cage in which we must await fearfully whatever may happen. We lie under the network of arching shells and live in a suspense of uncertainty. Over us Chance hovers.

Other fronts were slightly more mobile, although they too took huge tolls in lives. The Italian front also produced trench warfare, though it moved back and forth in northeastern Italy. In eastern Europe, Germany fought off a Russian offensive but had to aid Austria-Hungary, which was outclassed by Russian troops. Most of the fighting on the eastern front took place in the western portions of Russia, with some momentous battles. Fighting also spread to the Balkans, where Austria crushed Serbia and the other small states aligned variously in hopes of local advantage.

Along both the western and eastern fronts, the intensity of involvement among the combatants ran high. The conscripted and professional soldiers of the mass armies were most heavily engaged, of course, and even those who survived would long be marked by physical and psychological scars, often including a resentment against civilian authorities, especially politicians, who could not have known what the horror of war was. Yet civilian commitment was considerable, as each nation-state showed its power of mobilization to the fullest. Governments increasingly organized the major sectors of the economy to ration resources and production and to prevent crippling labor disputes. Whole industrial sectors, such as railroads, were administered outright by the state. Executive branches increasingly took over from parliaments—particularly in Germany, where by 1917 a top general virtually ran the country. Governments also leaned heavily on public opinion. Dissent was censored, and dissenters were arrested. Newspapers and other media were manipulated to create the most favorable public opinion possible. Thus the British (and through them, the Americans) were bombarded with exaggerated stories of German violence, and the Germans were so carefully shielded from news of their military setbacks after 1917 that many did not know they were losing until the end came. The power of governments to command resources and also beliefs and passions made this truly the first total war.

The war in essence sped up many developments already visible in industrial society. The power of organization increased, particularly through the new interventions of governments. To keep the social peace, socialists and trade union chiefs were given new recognition, serving on governing boards for industry and the like. By the same token, however, many labor leaders also became more involved in the existing system, which heightened revolutionary discontent among a minority of workers and others. Women's participation in the labor force increased greatly, although this proved to be a fragile trend as men recaptured many jobs at the war's end. At the same time, the war brought material shortages, even famine, to many people in the belligerent nations and imposed great psychological tensions on soldiers and civilians alike. These hardships, together with feverish hopes for a better world after war had ended, brought a revolutionary mood to many European nations after four years of struggle.

THE WAR OUTSIDE EUROPE

World War I was in many respects a European conflict, a particularly cruel result of the political divisions and rivalries that had long marked the Western experience and had been exacerbated by nationalism and other new forces during the 19th century. Nevertheless, given the West's world dominance, it was inevitable that the war spilled over into other areas and that it had some of its most important effects outside Europe.

British dominions, notably Canada, Australia, and New Zealand, were drawn into the war effort early on as loyal members of the British Empire. Forces from these countries played critical roles on several fronts and in the process brought their new nations into greater world involvements. World War I also brought the United States into world power politics as a major player, culminating a development that had been brewing for some time. By 1914 the United States was turning decisively away from a largely regional diplomatic role, with its Asian empire, centering on Hawaii and the Philippines, complementing its forceful activities in Central America and the West Indies. The advent of world war, however, caught the United States in a mood of considerable ambivalence. Distant from the battlefields, Americans disagreed over which side, if either, was in the right. American business, in the meantime, profited greatly from the war by selling goods to the various combatants and taking advantage of European distraction to gain new ground in other world markets. Rapidly rising exports, com-

The drastic shortage of farm and factory workers caused by the insatiable military manpower needs of World War I generals provided abundant (but often dangerous, as the munitions work shown here suggests) job outlets for young women.

bined with loans to European governments that needed credit in order to buy war materials and food, converted the United States from an international debtor to a creditor nation, essentially for the first time in the nation's history.

Despite all the gains resulting from noninvolvement, American leadership was on balance decidedly pro-British. Clumsy German attempts to influence American opinion, as well as the submarine warfare that affected American ships, including passenger vessels, moved the country toward a more interventionist mood. In 1917 the United States entered the war, soon sending fresh troops and needed supplies to the western front and unquestionably helping to turn the tide against the Germans. American leaders also brought into the war a new current of idealism, choosing to see their unaccustomed role as a battle for international justice and democracy; this input, too, would play an important role in the war's results.

The involvement of the United States and the British Commonwealth was only part of the war's international story. Minor skirmishes in the war were fought around the German colonies in Africa, but the major African involvement came in the use by France, and to a much lesser extent Britain, of many African troops in their armies on the European front. Britain also used military contingents from India throughout the war, especially in Africa and the Middle East. Indian nationalists backed the war effort, hoping that a British victory would promote India's freedom. Allied wartime declarations about national liberation inspired hope in India, as in Africa and elsewhere, again promoting new issues for the future. Experience in fighting in a European war gave the Africans and Asians involved increased awareness of European standards and of the contradiction between fierce nationalist pride in Europe and the subjugation of their own peoples. It was no accident that the first Pan-African Nationalist Congress occurred in 1919, as emerging African leaders pursued nationalist goals similar to those they had seen in Europe though without the internal divisiveness.

The war also spread to East Asia, where it fit into a new pattern of conflict. Japan entered the war on the side of Britain and France, honoring its previous alliance with Britain. The main Japanese purpose was to seize Germany's Pacific island colonies and holdings in China in an effort to advance its imperialist role and strengthen itself in relation to China. Australia and New Zealand seized German Samoa to forestall Japanese advance to the south. China declared war on Germany in 1917, hoping not to be ignored by the European powers. But Japan was the big gainer in the region, moving into German holdings in China's Shantung province and presenting additional demands for Chinese concessions. World War I in the Far East then, advanced already aggressive Japanese policy, setting the stage for later conflicts.

World War I had even wider ramifications in the Middle East. The Ottoman Empire, long attached to German military advisors, joined Germany in the war effort in late 1914. The Germans even hoped that the Turks would sponsor a Muslim uprising against British and French colonizers in North Africa, though this did not materialize. Rather, the war weakened the already feeble Ottoman state. Britain sponsored an attack on the Dardanelles, near Constantinople, hoping to open an additional front to rescue the smaller Balkan states and open a southern supply route to Russia. The campaign was a failure, yet it cost 150,000 British and colonial troops. Nevertheless, the British did back Arab nationalists in return for their support against their Ottoman overlords, winning important allies along the eastern Mediterranean. The British also promised support to Jewish settlers in Israel, through the Balfour Declaration of 1917. Allied actions, in sum, set in motion various forces hostile to Ottoman rule and eager for some kind of independence. They also encouraged contradictory goals in the Middle East itself, particularly between Arab and Jewish claimants to territory in Palestine.

Overall, the war's international ramifications constituted a substantial diminution of Europe's world power. Two new players, the United States and Japan, gained ground, winning new prestige or new territory. Europe's need for colonial support and its devotion to belligerent nationalism encouraged many other people in India, Africa, and the Middle East to a higher level of awareness of their own national rights and merits.

THE WAR'S END

The international context, save for the entry of the United States, did not play a large role in the central theaters of war, where attention riveted once more on the two major fronts by 1917. In February 1917 the pressures of war, added to the earlier massive strains in Russian society, caused a major revolution that toppled the tsarist government. The new government, strongly committed to Western-style liberalism, vowed to live up to Russian obligations under the prewar alliance, but in fact the Russian war effort began to falter even further.

Moreover, popular hostility to the impositions of war helped produce more radical agitation, aided by the activities of Communist leaders such as Lenin, who had been transported to Russia from a Swiss exile by the German government precisely in hopes of fomenting trouble. The result was a new revolt, in October 1917, that brought Lenin and the Communists to power. This leadership, bent on restructuring Russian society, wanted to escape the pressures of war. In March 1918 it reluctantly signed the Brest-Litovsk treaty with the Germans, giving the Germans substantial territories in western Russia in return for peace.

This proved to be the peak of German success, however, and indeed the treaty was a partial mistake. The Germans had to commit more troops to occupying its new territory than was sensible, reducing the abilities of a thoroughly war-torn nation to push new energy into the crucial western front. Heavy fighting there during 1917 caused massive losses on both sides, prior to the arrival of fresh American troops. A series of last-ditch German offensives in 1918 failed, leaving the nation with no reserves. Then a French, British, and American counteroffensive pressed forward, aided by the collapse of Austrian forces in Italy and the Balkans. The German generals, by now running the country, installed a new civilian government so that blame for defeat would not fall directly on their forces. This government, led ultimately by moderate socialists when the German emperor abdicated, had no choice but to sue for peace in November 1918.

THE PEACE AND THE AFTERMATH

Settlement of the war was difficult, even with Germany's military apparatus temporarily dismantled or underground. Diplomats of the victorious nations convened at Versailles, near Paris, where they debated the fate of much of the world, albeit with Russia, Germany, and indeed most of the world unrepresented. Not surprisingly, Versailles produced a world settlement on largely European terms.

In Europe itself France was bent on revenge against Germany and wanted assurance that Germany would be so weakened that it could not attack a third time. France got back the provinces surrendered after its 1871 war loss but not the security it yearned for. Italy wanted new territory in abundance; it received some but not enough and emerged unsatisfied as well. Germany lost territory to both France and the revived nation of Poland; Germany was also saddled with "war guilt"—responsibility

for causing the war—and heavy reparation payments to France and Belgium. Russian losses were confirmed through the creation of several new nations—of the Baltic states as well as Poland—carved out of the western portion of the empire. Here too was a festering sore, even though the nations had existed in earlier centuries.

In the wider world Japan hoped for a Great Power role but was largely ignored, which heightened Japanese discontent, despite the acquisition of former German colonies in China and the Pacific. President Woodrow Wilson of the United States espoused great ideals, hoping for just settlement of all nationalist issues—particularly in eastern Europe, where many nationalities struggled for recognition—and a new League of Nations to deal with future disputes and to make war unnecessary. But ideals were difficult to put into practice amid the welter of conflicting interests, and opinion back home prevented the United States from taking a consistently active role. The nation did not even join the League of Nations its representatives had devised. U.S. military isolationism contributed to French and British fears for the future, in a peacetime that was badly born.

The big losers at Versailles were, of course, Germany and Austria-Hungary in Europe. In Asia, China suffered particularly because of its losses to a surging Japan and internal unrest that followed the war, as China refused to sign away formally the Shantung province to Japan but was powerless to resist its occupation. The Austro-Hungarian Empire collapsed entirely, as nationalist groups carved out the new nations of Czechoslovakia, Hungary and an enlarged south Slavic state, Yugoslavia. This left a somewhat fragile Germanic Austria, cut off from its traditional markets as one of many small countries in a weakened region of Europe. Germany lost more than territory and reparations funds. The level of its military forces was limited, and the region west of the Rhine was supposed to remain demilitarized. These impositions created huge discontent in Germany, with many leaders vowing revenge on France as the leader of punitive peacemakers. The treatment of Communist Russia, now called the Soviet Union, as a pariah not even invited to Versailles provided additional potential for further disputes.

LARGER DISLOCATIONS

The legacy of World War I involved more than a complex and difficult diplomatic heritage. The war had devastated Europe's economy and society. More than ten million people had died, meaning that almost

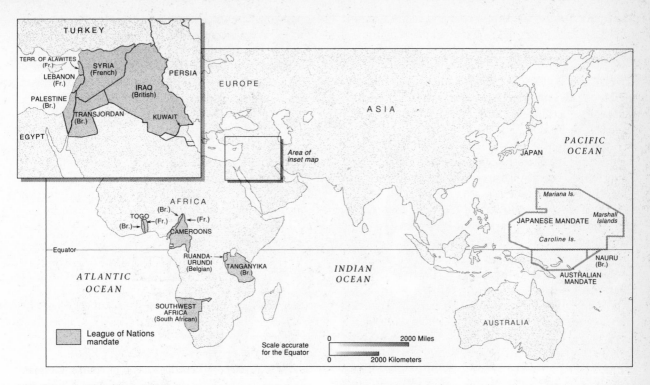

The Postwar World in 1920

every European family had a death to mourn. Never before had a war approached this level of devastation. France and Serbia were particularly hard hit; each lost more than one-tenth of its total population. Truly, this war was "the blood-red dawn of the 20th century." The loss of young men was an economic as well as a psychological blow, for these men were the potential cream of the upcoming labor force and leadership groups. Loss of men also hampered the European birthrate. Massive destruction of industrial property and agricultural land temporarily dislocated many economies, leading to a period of postwar instability that ended only in 1923. More serious than these largely temporary setbacks was an imbalance produced by the methods of financing the war. Most combatant regimes had borrowed heavily, unwilling to raise taxes too much lest civilian morale be destroyed. Despite government restrictions during the last years of war, prices began to rise because of the inflationary impact of increased government spending and money supplies. And after the war inflation soared in many countries. Although some groups could profit from rapidly rising prices, many people with fixed savings were nearly wiped out, whereas others, such as many farmers, were

encouraged to borrow unwisely, which would later leave them strapped for funds. In various ways, then, the war introduced basic dislocations that promised, and later produced, further trouble.

WORLDWIDE CHANGE

The peace settlement also set in motion the forces that hastened western Europe's decline in the wider world. To be sure, there was little outright loss of colonies, and indeed the 1920s constituted (on paper) the apogee of Western imperialism. Germany's African colonies were taken over by Britain and France, and much of the Middle East was divided among the victors. However, the new "colonies" were formally held as mandates of the League of Nations, not as outright possessions. The implication was that although colonial administrations might in fact be established, they were only temporary, and were obliged under international scrutiny to prepare their mandates for independence. In the Middle East and elsewhere, nationalist leaders seized on Wilsonian principles of self-determination, asking why they were applied only within Europe and not to the whole world.

At the Paris Peace Conference of 1919, the Arabs sought a new voice. The Arab representatives included Prince Feisel of Jordan and an Iraqi general. The Arabs did not win full application of the principles of national self-determination to their homelands.

Leadership in world diplomacy passed from strictly European hands. The U.S. role, though ultimately confused by potential isolationism, was vital. Japan gained international status as a wartime ally of Britain and France, though Japanese leaders emerged dissatisfied with their rewards, infuriated at exclusion from the European-U.S. Great Power conclaves at Versailles, and eager to resume their quest for expansion.

A crucial area of change involved the Middle East. The Ottoman Empire collapsed. Italy and Greece led an initial effort to carve up even those areas around Constantinople where Turks were in the majority, but a vigorous new Turkish republic by 1923 repulsed these efforts through war and negotiation. An independent Turkey emerged, expelling many ethnic Greeks in the aftermath of the nation's birth. The rest of the Ottoman holdings, however, were divided up as mandates of the League of Nations, with Britain taking Palestine and Iraq and France gaining Syria and Lebanon. A few new monarchies, notably the kingdom of Saudi Arabia, sprang up on the edge of the old Ottoman domains. The Middle East was recreated not only as a cauldron of un-satisfied Arab and Jewish nationalist demands but also as a series of separate fragments—a legacy that would burn through world affairs later in the 20th century. Here, as in Central Europe, the settlement simply asked for further trouble. New divisions replaced old multinational empires, with stability clearly jeopardized in the process.

The international economic results of the war continued to reverberate. American and Japanese businesses had captured many European export markets, which complicated Europe's immediate postwar recovery. Even when the Continent had regained greater health, America and Japan forced an unprecedented amount of international competition. Britain, particularly, never recovered the export position on which its eminence had so long depended. Debts to impatient U.S. creditors further complicated the international economic mix.

The war had less immediate economic impact on the nonindustrial economies of the world. Several agricultural exporters, however, including the United States and Argentina, boosted their production as European food supplies declined. This promised increased competition in these goods when more normal times returned in the 1920s. The war certainly produced little encouragement to more diverse economic development in Europe's colonies, as investment capital dried up in favor of the war effort.

Overall, the results of the war and its settlement provoked a host of new tensions within Europe and set the stage for further change in the larger world balance. The European nations remained major actors, their role exaggerated by Russian preoccupation with its internal revolution and American refusal to attend consistently to international affairs. Nationalist agitation in the colonies, new economic imbalances, and the heightened power of Japan and the United States all portended a new world structure that was not, however, clearly defined.

The war also gave rise to a new international organization, the League of Nations. The League established a number of subsidiary groups for dealing with such issues as setting standards for working conditions; these groups gathered information and focused international social concerns. The League itself, however, proved to be little more than a discussion forum, as real diplomacy continued on a nation-to-nation basis. Several disarmament conferences held in the 1920s, designed particularly to reduce naval competition, were ultimately ineffective. The international idea advanced, in sum, but it lacked muscle.

The peace settlement after World War I is routinely and correctly criticized for its failure to handle European tensions well. Too many small countries were created near dissatisfied Great Powers, notably the Soviet Union and Germany. Further conflict was inevitable. The peace settlement took insufficient account of Europe's reduced position in the world, blithely assuming in fact that imperialism was at most slightly modified. In fact, the war had roused nationalist ambitions virtually worldwide, and this was perhaps its most lasting legacy. The war taught Africans, Arabs, Jews, and Asians that nationalism was legitimate; by creating new European weakness, it also held out the hope that non-European nationalisms might also be feasible.

THE GREAT DEPRESSION

The next step in the mounting spiral of international crisis came with the onset of a global economic depression. The crash of the New York stock market hit the headlines in 1929, but in fact the depression had begun, sullenly, in many parts of the world economy even earlier. The depression resulted from new problems in the industrial economy of Europe and the United States, combined with the long-term weakness in economies, like those of Latin America, that depended on sales of cheap exports in the international market. The result was a worldwide collapse that spared only a few economies and brought political as well as economic pressures on virtually every society.

CAUSATION

The impact of the First World War on the European economy had led to several rocky years into the early 1920s. War-induced inflation was a particular problem in Germany, as prices soared daily and ordinary purchases required huge quantities of currency. Forceful government action finally resolved this crisis in 1923 but only by a massive devaluation of the mark, which did nothing to restore lost savings. More generally, a sharp, brief recession in 1920 and 1921 had reflected other postwar dislocations, though by 1923 production levels had regained or surpassed prewar levels. Great Britain, an industrial pioneer that was already victim of a loss of dynamism before the war, recovered more slowly, in part because of its unusually great dependence on an export market now open to wider competition.

Structural problems affected other areas of Europe besides Britain and lasted well beyond the predictable readjustments to peacetime. Farmers throughout much of the Western world, including the United States, faced almost chronic overproduction of food and resulting low prices. Food production had soared in response to wartime needs; during the postwar inflation many farmers, both in western Europe and in North America, borrowed heavily to buy new equipment, overconfident that their good markets would be sustained. But rising European production combined with large imports from the Americas and New Zealand sent prices down, which made debts harder to repay. One response was continued population flight from the countryside, as urbanization continued. Remaining farmers were hard pressed and unable to sustain high demand for manufactured goods.

Thus although economies in France and Germany seemed to have recovered by 1925, problems continued: the fears inflation had generated, which in turn limited the capacity of governments to respond to other problems, as well as the weaknesses in the buying power of key groups. In this situation, much of the middecade prosperity rested on exceedingly fragile grounds. Loans from U.S. banks to various European enterprises helped sustain demand for goods but on condition that additional loans pour in to help pay off the resultant debts.

Furthermore, most of the dependent areas in the world economy, colonies and noncolonies alike, were suffering badly. Pronounced tendencies toward overproduction developed in the smaller nations of eastern Europe, which sent agricultural goods to western Europe, as well as among tropical producers in Africa and Latin America. Here, continued efforts to win export revenue pressed local estate owners to drive up output in coffee, sugar, and rubber. As European governments and businesses organized their African colonies for more profitable exploitation, they set up large estates devoted to goods of this type. Again, production frequently exceeded demand, which drove prices and earnings down in both Africa and Latin America. This meant, in turn, that many colonies and dependent economies were unable to buy many industrial exports, which weakened demand for Western products precisely when output tended to rise amid growing U.S. and Japanese competition. Several food-exporting regions, including many of the new eastern European nations, fell into a depression, in terms of earnings and employment, by the mid-1920s, well before the full industrial catastrophe.

Governments of the leading industrial nations provided scant leadership during the emerging crisis of the 1920s. Knowledge of economics was often feeble within a Western leadership group not noteworthy for its quality even in more conventional areas. Nationalistic selfishness predominated. Western nations were more concerned about insisting on repayment of any debts owed to them or about constructing tariffs barriers to protect their own industries than about facilitating balanced world economic growth. Protectionism, in particular, as practiced even by traditionally free-trade Great Britain and by the many new nations in eastern Europe simply reduced market opportunities and made a bad situation worse. By the later 1920s employment in key Western industrial sectors—coal (also beset by new competition from imported oil), iron, and textiles—began to decline, the foretaste of more general collapse.

THE DEBACLE

The formal advent of depression occurred in October 1929, when the New York stock market collapsed. Stock values tumbled, as investors quickly lost confidence in issues that had been pushed ridiculously high. Banks, which had depended heavily on their stock investments, rapidly echoed the financial crisis, and many institutions failed, dragging their depositors along with them. Even before this crash, Americans had begun to call back earlier loans to Europe. Yet the European credit structure depended extensively on U.S. loans, which had fueled some industrial expansion but also less productive investments, such as German reparations payments and the construction of fancy town halls and other amenities. In Europe, as in the United States, many commercial enterprises existed on the basis not of real production power but of continued speculation. When one piece of the speculative spiral was withdrawn, the whole edifice quickly collapsed. Key bank failures in Austria and Germany followed the U.S. crisis. Throughout most of the industrial West, investment funds dried up as creditors went bankrupt or tried to pull in their horns.

With investment receding, industrial production quickly began to fall, beginning with the industries that produced capital goods and extending quickly to consumer products fields. Falling production—levels dropped by as much as one-third by 1932—meant falling employment and lower wages, which in turn withdrew still more demand from the economy and led to further hardship. The existing weakness of some markets, such as the farm sector or the nonindustrial world, was exacerbated as demand for foods and minerals plummeted. New and appalling problems developed among workers, now out of jobs or suffering from reduced hours and reduced pay, as well as among the middle classes. The depression, in sum, fed on itself, growing steadily worse from 1929 to 1933. Even countries initially less hard hit, such as France and Italy, saw themselves drawn into the vortex by 1931.

In itself the Great Depression was not entirely unprecedented. Previous periods had seen slumps triggered by bank failures and overspeculation, yielding several years of falling production, unemployment, and hardship. But the intensity of the Great Depression had no precedent in the brief history of industrial societies. Its duration was also unprecedented; in many countries full recovery came only after a decade and only with the forced production schedules provoked by World War II. Unlike earlier depressions, this one came on the heels of so much other distress—the economic hardships of war, for example, and the catastrophic inflation of the 1920s—and caught most governments totally unprepared.

The depression was more, of course, than an economic event. It reached into countless lives, creating hardship and tension that would be recalled even as the crisis itself eased. Loss of earnings, loss of work, or simply fears that loss would come devastated people at all social levels. The suicides of ruined investors in New

York were paralleled by the vagrants' camps and begging that spread among displaced workers. The statistics were grim; up to one-third of all blue-collar workers in the West lost their jobs for prolonged periods. White-collar unemployment, though not quite as severe, was also unparalleled. In Germany 600,000 of four million white-collar workers had lost their jobs by 1931. Graduating students could not find work or had to resort to jobs they regarded as insecure or demeaning. Six million overall unemployed in Germany and 22 percent of the labor force unemployed in Britain were statistics of stark misery and despair. Families were disrupted, as men felt emasculated at their inability to provide and women and children were disgusted at authority figures whose authority was now hollow. In some cases wives and mothers found it easier to gain jobs in a low-wage economy than their husbands did, and although this development had some promise in terms of new opportunities for women, it could also be confusing for standard family roles. For many the agony and personal disruption of the depression were desperately prolonged, with renewed re-

The hardships resulting from the widespread unemployment and poverty in the United States during the Great Depression are reflected in the face of this woman.

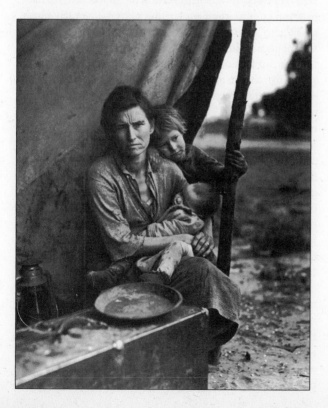

cession around 1937 and with unemployment still averaging ten percent or more in many countries as late as 1939.

The depression, like World War I, was an event that blatantly contradicted the optimistic assumptions of the later 19th century. To many it showed the fragility of any idea of progress, any belief that Western civilization was becoming more humane. To still more it challenged the notion that the parliamentary democracies of the West were able to control their own destinies. And because it was a second catastrophic event within a generation, the depression led to even more extreme results than the war itself had done—more bizarre experiments, more paralysis in the face of deepening despair. Just as the depression had been caused by a combination of specifically Western problems and wider weaknesses in the world economy, so its effects had both Western twists and international repercussions.

A few economies were buffered from the depression. The Soviet Union, busy building an industrial society under Communist control and under the heading "socialism in one country," had cut off all but the most insignificant economic ties with other nations. The result placed great hardships on many Russian people, called to sustain rapid industrial development without outside capital, but it did prevent anything like a depression during the 1930s. Soviet leaders pointed with pride to the steadily rising production rates and lack of serious unemployment, in a telling contrast with the miseries of Western capitalism at the time.

For most of the rest of the world, however, the depression worsened an already bleak economic picture. Western markets could absorb fewer commodity imports as production fell and incomes dwindled. Hence the nations that produced foods and raw materials saw prices and earnings drop even more than before. Unemployment rose rapidly in the export sectors of the Latin American economy, creating a major political challenge not unlike that faced by the Western nations. Japan, a new industrial country, still heavily depended on export earnings for financing its imports of essential fuel and raw materials. The Japanese silk industry, an export staple, was already suffering from the advent of artificial silklike fibers produced by Western chemical giants. Now Western luxury purchases collapsed, leading to severe unemployment in Japan and a crucial political crisis. Between 1929 and 1931, the value of Japanese exports plummeted by 50 percent. Workers' real income dropped by almost one-third, and more than three million people were unemployed. Depression was compounded by poor harvests in several regions, leading to rural begging and near starvation.

The Great Depression, though most familiar in its Western dimensions, was a truly international collapse, a sign of the tight bonds and serious imbalances that had developed in world trading patterns. The results of the collapse, and particularly the varied responses to it, are best traced in individual cases. For Latin America the depression stimulated new kinds of effective political action, particularly greater state involvement in economic planning and direction. New government vigor did not cure the economic effects of the depression, which escaped the control of most individual states, but it did set an important new phase in this civilization's political evolution. For Japan the depression increased suspicions of the West and helped promote new expansionism designed, among other things, to win more assured markets in Asia. In the West the depression led to new welfare programs that stimulated demand and helped restore confidence, but it also led to radical social and political experiments, such as German Nazism. What was common in this welter of reactions was the intractable global quality of the depression itself, which made it impossible for any purely national policy to restore full prosperity. Even Nazi Germany, which boasted of regaining full employment, continued to suffer from low wages and other dislocations aside from its obvious and growing dependence on military production. The reactions to the depression, including a sense of weakness and confusion in many quarters inside and outside policy circles, helped to bring the final great crisis of the first half of the 20th century: a second, and more fully international, world war.

WORLD WAR II AND THE POSTWAR SETTLEMENT

World War II, which broke out formally in 1939, but was preceded by a series of wars and clashes through the 1930s, was fed by two active agents and an excessively passive one. Deliberate strides toward military expansion on the part of new regimes in Japan and Germany formed the active causes, bringing the clouds of war to Asia and the Pacific as well as to Europe and the Mediterranean quite directly. The passivity centered on the most logical opponents to the new aggressors—the other powerful states in Europe and North America. Here nationalistic and ideological divisions, including widespread Western suspicion of the Communist regime in the Soviet Union, limited an ability to act. So did

weak leadership and paralyzing internal political disputes, which made positive response difficult until a late hour. The League of Nations' inability to take more than rhetorical action was a foregone conclusion, and it progressively withered as a policy instrument during the prewar decade.

Underlying all the factors contributing to war was the prior experience of war and economic depression. The aggressive regimes resulted from the tensions in Germany and Japan caused by economic collapse, supplemented in Germany's case by the wounds of prior defeat and a harsh peace. Western passivity followed also from the confusions engendered by prior crises. The imperialist legacy also played a role. Dissatisfied Western nations and Japan looked to expansion in Asia and Africa as a legitimate safety valve, and although non-Western nationalism was gaining strength, the military and economic advantages of the industrial regions remained overwhelming. World history, or at least those facets dominated by the Great Powers, seemed locked in a spiral of growing tragedy.

THE NEW REGIMES

The first scenes of this new tragedy involved the advent of new, militaristic governments in key national actors and an important supporting player. The early phases of the depression had triggered growing political fragmentation in Japan, particularly through the rise of various ultranationalist groups. Some opposed Western values in the name of Shintoism and Confucianism; others urged a Nazi-style authoritarian government free from parliamentary restraint and undue tradition. A military group, backed by many younger officers, urged a "defense state" under their control. In 1932 this group attacked key government and business offices and killed the prime minister. The result, satisfactory to no major group, was four years of moderate military rule under an older admiral, followed in 1936 and 1937 by a tougher military regime after another officer rebellion failed. Japanese voters continued to prefer more moderate parties, but effective leadership fell increasingly into militaristic hands.

The advent of military rule developed in a context of regional diplomatic crisis. During the later 1920s, Chinese nationalist forces seemed to be gaining ground in their effort to unify their chaotic nation after the 1911 revolution. Their success worried Japan's army leaders, who wanted to be able to influence the Manchurian province of China as a buffer between their colony of

DOCUMENT:
THE LEADER OF THE SOVIET UNION EVALUATES THE DEPRESSION

In March 1939 Joseph Stalin, uncontested leader of the Soviet state, spoke to the 18th Communist Party Congress on the state of the world and the implications for the Soviet Union. His evaluation of the nature of the depression and its implications were central to his overall policy statement.

NEW ECONOMIC CRISIS IN THE CAPITALIST COUNTRIES, INTENSIFICATION OF THE STRUGGLE FOR MARKETS AND SOURCES OF RAW MATERIAL, AND FOR A NEW REDIVISION OF THE WORLD

The economic crisis which broke out in the capitalist countries in the latter half of 1929 lasted until the end of 1933. After that the crisis passed into a depression, and was then followed by a certain revival, a certain upward trend of industry. But this upward trend of industry did not develop into a boom, as is usually the case in a period of revival. On the contrary, in the latter half of 1937 a new economic crisis began which seized the United States first of all and then England, France and a number of other countries.

The capitalist countries thus found themselves faced with a new economic crisis before they had even recovered from the ravages of the recent one.

This circumstance naturally led to an increase of unemployment. The number of unemployed in capitalist countries, which had fallen from 30,000,000 in 1933 to 14,000,000 in 1937, has now again risen to 18,000,000 as a result of the new crisis.

A distinguishing feature of the new crisis is that it differs in many respects from the preceding one, and, moreover, differs for the worse and not for the better.

Firstly, the new crisis did not begin after an industrial boom, as was the case in 1929, but after a depression and a certain revival, which, however, did not develop into a boom. This means that the present crisis will be more severe and more difficult to cope with than the previous crisis.

Further, the present crisis has broken out not in time of peace, but at a time when a second imperialist war has already begun; when Japan, already in the second year of her war with China, is disorganizing the immense Chinese market and rendering it almost inaccessible to the goods of other countries; when Italy and Germany have already placed their national economies on a war footing, squandering their reserves of raw material and foreign currency for this purpose; and when all the other big capitalist powers are beginning to reorganize themselves on a war footing. This means that capitalism will have far less resources at its disposal for a normal way out of the present crisis than during the preceding crisis.

Lastly, as distinct from the preceding crisis, the present crisis is not universal, but as yet involves chiefly the economically powerful countries which have not yet placed themselves on a war economy basis. As regards the aggressive countries such as Japan, Germany and Italy, who have already reorganized their economies on a war footing, they because of the intense development of their war industry, are not yet experiencing a crisis of overproduction, although they are approaching it. This means that by the time the economically powerful, nonaggressive countries begin to emerge from the phase of crisis the aggressive countries, having exhausted their reserves of gold and raw material in the course of the war fever, are bound to enter a phase of very severe crisis. . . .

The Soviet Union is the only country in the world where crises are unknown and where industry is continuously on the upgrade. Naturally, such an unfavorable turn of economic affairs could not but aggravate relations among the powers. The preceding crisis had already mixed the cards and sharpened the struggle for markets and sources of raw materials. The seizure of Manchuria and North China by Japan, the seizure of Abyssinia by Italy—all this reflected the acuteness of the struggle among the powers. The new economic crisis was bound to lead, and is actually leading, to a further sharpening of the imperialist struggle. It is no longer a question of competition in the markets, of a commercial war, of dumping. These methods of struggle have long been recognized as inadequate. It is now a question of a new redivision of the world, of spheres of influence and colonies, by military action. It is a distinguishing feature of the new imperialist war that it has not yet become universal, a world war. The war is being waged by aggressor states, who in every way infringe upon the interests of the nonaggressive states, primarily Britain, France and the U.S.A., while the latter draw back and retreat, making concession after concession to the aggressors.

Thus we are witnessing an open redivision of the world and spheres of influence at the expense of the nonaggressive states, without the least attempt at resistance, and even with a certain connivance, on their part.

Incredible, but true.

To what are we to attribute this one-sided and strange character of the new imperialist war?

How is it that the nonaggressive countries, which possess such vast opportunities, have so easily and without resistance abandoned their positions and their obligations to please the aggressors?

Is it to be attributed to the weakness of the nonaggressive states? Of course not! Combined, the nonaggressive, democratic states are unquestionably stronger than the fascist states, both economically and militarily.

To what then are we to attribute the systematic concession made by these states to the aggressors?

It might be attributed, for example, to the fear that a revolution might break out if the nonaggressive states were to go to war and the war were to assume world-wide proportions. The bourgeois politicians know, of course, that the first imperialist world war led to the victory of the revolution in one of the largest countries. They are afraid that the second imperialist world war may also lead to the victory of the revolution in one or several countries.

Questions: How did Stalin compare his nation's economy to that of the capitalist leaders? How did he relate the depression to the diplomatic crisis? Was his judgment accurate, or was it unduly biased by Communist theory? What would be the implications of this kind of analysis for Soviet foreign policy by 1939?

Korea and the Soviet Union. Japan had, in fact, dominated the Manchurian warlord since its victory over Russia in 1905. Fearful of losing ground and unimpeded by the weak civilian government in Tokyo, the Japanese army marched into Manchuria in 1931, proclaiming it an independent state. Japan's acts were condemned by the League of Nations—which, however, was unable to take effective action—and consequently Japan simply withdrew from the League. The resulting atmosphere of crisis aided the military's advance in domestic politics, for other leaders were reluctant to damage national military strength. This advance in turn set the scene for the next round of crisis—the outbreak of World War II in the Far East—in 1937.

In the meantime, however, a more decisive change of regime had occurred in Germany. Here, too, a trend toward growing conservatism and suspicion of parliamentary government had developed by the late 1920s. Then the advent of full depression triggered political chaos. The National Socialist (Nazi) party, led by Adolph Hitler, began to pick up strength after nearly fading from existence during the mid-1920s. Among the Nazis' leading goals were an authoritarian state under a single leader and an aggressive foreign policy that would reverse the humiliation of the Versailles treaty and gain Germany military glory and new territory for expansion. German parliamentary leaders bickered among themselves and failed to provide decisive policies to address the depression; as Communist strength grew on the left, Nazis won a growing minority of votes in general elections. They were also able to disrupt normal political meetings and win quiet support from many business and military leaders. Sponsored by conservatives, who erroneously thought they could control him, Hitler took power legally in 1933. He soon abolished the parliamentary regime and constructed a totalitarian state with himself at the helm.

The Nazi state was a radically new kind of regime. Hitler attacked competing sources of power within Germany, abolishing free trade unions and opposition political parties. Many political opponents were put in brutal concentration camps, and new political police added to the terror. Attacks on Jews and other "non-Aryans," the so-called enemies of "true" Germans,

The adulation that the German masses felt for Adolph Hitler in the mid-1930s is evident in this rally photo. Hitler's popularity rested primarily on his promises to rebuild Germany's deeply depressed economy and restore its world power status by reversing the 1919 Treaty of Paris ending World War I.

mounted steadily as part of Hitler's racist ideology. During World War II these attacks escalated into what Hitler called his "final solution," as six million Jews were forced into concentration camps and then murdered in gas chambers. Nazism also meant construction of a war machine. Hitler expanded armaments production, creating new jobs in the process, and also built up the army and separate Nazi military forces. In Hitler's view the essence of the state was authority, and the function of the state was war.

Hitler's advent galvanized the authoritarian regime of a nearby power, Italy, where a Fascist state had been formed in the 1920s, led by Benito Mussolini. Like Hitler, Mussolini had promised an aggressive foreign policy and new nationalist glories, but in fact his first decade had been rather moderate diplomatically. With Hitler in power, however, Mussolini began to experiment more boldly, if only to avoid being overshadowed completely. Here, then, was another destabilizing element in world politics.

THE STEPS TOWARD WAR

Hitler moved first. He suspended German reparation payments, thus renouncing this part of the Versailles settlement; he walked out of a disarmament conference and withdrew from the League of Nations. In 1935 he announced German rearmament and in 1936 brought military forces into the Rhineland—both moves in further violation of the Versailles treaty. When France and Britain loudly protested but did nothing more, and the

isolationist United States said even less, Hitler was poised for the further buildup of German strength and further diplomatic adventures that would ultimately lead to World War II.

In 1935 Mussolini attacked Ethiopia, planning to avenge Italy's failure to conquer this ancient land during the imperialist surge of the 1890s. The League of Nations condemned the action, but neither it nor the democratic powers in Europe and North America took action. Consequently, after some hard fighting, the Italians won their new colony.

In 1936 a civil war engulfed Spain, pitting authoritarian and military leaders against republicans and leftists. Germany and Italy quickly moved to support the Spanish right, sending in supplies and troops, gaining not only a measure of new glory but also precious military training in such specialties as bombing civilian targets. France, Britain, and the United States, in contrast, though vaguely supporting the Spanish republic, could agree on no concrete action. Only the Soviet Union sent effective government support, and by 1939 the republican forces had been defeated.

In 1938 Hitler proclaimed a long-sought union, or *Anschluss*, with Austria as a fellow German nation. Western powers complained and denounced but did nothing. That year Hitler marched into a German-speaking part of Czechoslovakia. War threatened, but a conference at Munich convinced French and British leaders that Hitler might be satisfied with acquiescence. Czechoslovakia was dismembered, and the western (Sudeten) region turned over to Germany. The British prime minister, Neville Chamberlain, duped by Hitler's apparent eagerness to compromise, proclaimed that his appeasement had won "peace in our time." ("Our time" turned out to be slightly more than a year.) Emboldened by Western weakness, in March 1939 Hitler took over all of Czechoslovakia and began to press Poland for territorial concessions. He also concluded an agreement with the Soviet Union, which was not ready for war with Germany and had despaired of Western resolve. The Soviets also coveted parts of Poland, the Baltic states, and Finland for their own, and when Hitler invaded Poland, Russia launched its own war to undo the Versailles settlement. Hitler attacked Poland on September 1, 1939, not necessarily expecting general war but clearly prepared to risk it; Britain and France, now convinced that nothing short of war would stop the Nazis, made their own declaration in response.

War had already broken out in China. Japan, continuing to press the ruling Chinese government lest it gain sufficient strength to threaten Japanese gains, became involved in a skirmish with Chinese forces in the Beijing area in 1937. Fighting spread, initially quite unplanned. Most Japanese military leaders opposed more general war, arguing that the nation's only interest was to defend Manchuria and Korea. However, influential figures on the General Staff held that China's armies should be de-

cisively defeated to prevent trouble in the future. This view prevailed, and Japanese forces quickly occupied the cities and railroads of eastern China. Several devastating bombing raids accompanied this invasion. The Chinese army refused to give in, however, and held the main rural areas. The resulting stalemate lasted until 1945, with neither side capable of major new advance.

The two main areas of conflict, Europe and the Pacific, were joined in 1940, when Germany and Italy (already uneasy allies) signed an agreement with Japan. Japanese leaders had long admired Germany and welcomed Hitler's basic hostility to the Soviet Union and communism. Full alliance was prevented by the Nazi-Soviet agreement, which briefly drove Japan to try to resolve disputes with the United States. But the United States insisted that the Japanese evacuate China, so full reconciliation was impossible. Meanwhile, early German successes in the European war and Japanese realization that expansion in the Pacific would pit Japan against the United States combined to argue for a more formal alliance. A Tripartite Pact was signed by Germany, Japan, and Italy—the Axis Powers—in September 1940. In fact, Japan and Germany never collaborated closely; Japan refused to participate in Germany's ultimate war with the Soviet Union, despite long-standing opposition to Russian strength. Nevertheless, the union of the

The Main Theaters of World War II

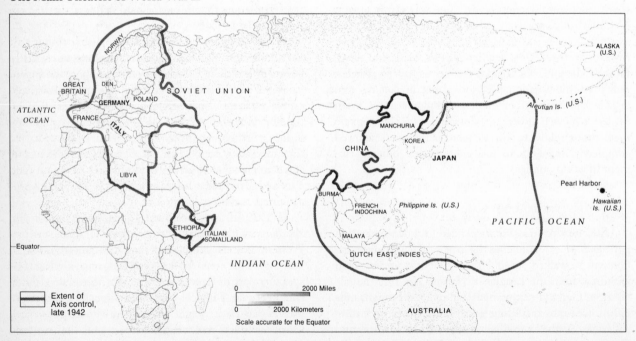

aggressor states, however hollow in practice, seemed to align the powers of the world between those on the attack and those legitimately on the defense—a symbolism particularly influential for the United States.

As war broke out from 1937 to 1939, the powers most interested in preserving the status quo remained unprepared, hopeful that war could be deflected by talk and concessions. France and Britain continued to feel the debilitating effects of World War I and were not eager for another conflict. Depression-induced tensions made it difficult to agree on any active policy, and political leftists and conservatives even disagreed over which was the greater enemy, Germany or the Soviet Union. The United States was less polarized but eager to maintain its policy of isolationism in order not to complicate the delicate process of constructing a new set of government programs to fight the depression. Only by late 1938 did Western leaders begin to admit that war was likely, launching some measures of military preparedness, including army expansion and aircraft production. Britain took the lead here, and its efforts proved vital in allowing successful defense of the nation in the first stages of the war with Germany. But the Western effort was too little and too late to stop war itself.

THE COURSE OF THE WAR: JAPAN'S ADVANCE AND RETREAT

The background to World War II made it obvious that war would be fought in two major centers—the Pacific and the European regions, the latter spilling over into North Africa and the Middle East. The background also made it inevitable that the first years of the war would feature almost unremitting German and Japanese success against ill-prepared opponents. Only in 1942 and 1943 did the tide begin to turn, based on the fact that the powers that had been drawn into war were more powerful, economically and in population size, than their ambitious taunters.

The bitter war in Asia, pitting Japan against the United States with Britain and China in important supporting roles, followed a fairly simple course of thrust and counterthrust. Stalemated in China, Japan used the outbreak of war in Europe as an occasion to turn its attention to other parts of Asia. It seized Indochina from France's troops. The alliance with Germany and Italy, along with continued war in China, put the Japanese on a collision course with the United States, which as a Pacific power was unwilling to allow Japan to become a predominant force in the Far East. U.S. holdings in

Japan's military buildup included marine machine gun squads, such as this one in occupied Shanghai, China.

Hawaii and the Philippines, together with attempts to withhold materials necessary to Japan's war economy, convinced Japanese leaders that a clash was inevitable. Negotiations with the United States broke down when Americans insisted that Japan renounce all gains acquired since 1931. It was in this setting that the Japanese attacked Pearl Harbor on December 7, 1941, and then in the following months seized U.S. possessions in the eastern Pacific, including the Philippine Islands.

In these same months the Japanese also struck at the British colonies in Malaya and Burma and overran the Dutch East Indies. Along with their conquests in the Pacific, the Japanese had with stunning speed put together a far-flung empire from which they could draw the oil, tin, rice, and other raw materials that would be essential to waging a sustained war with the United States and Great Britain. Though the attack on Pearl Harbor greatly facilitated this empire building, it had failed in one of its main objectives: the destruction of the U.S. aircraft carrier fleet. With its carriers intact, the United States was able first to check the Japanese forward tide at the Battle of the Coral Sea in May 1942 and then decisively to defeat the main Japanese air forces and battle fleet at the Battle of Midway in the following month. By the end of 1942 the United States had begun to gain the upper hand in the Pacific war, using its greater numbers and superior level of industrialization to good effect. The Allies reconquered scattered islands in 1943, with appalling losses on both sides and regained the Philippines in 1944; while massive air raids began an onslaught on Japan itself. Meanwhile, American, British, and Chinese forces continued to tie down a considerable Japanese army on the Asian mainland.

GERMANY OVERREACHES

In Europe the early years of World War II carried key trends of the 1930s toward even deeper tragedy. Germany seemed unstoppable, and the Western democracies suffered accordingly. German strategy focused on the *Blitzkrieg*, or "lightning war," involving rapid movement of troops, tanks, and mechanized carriers. With this the Germans crushed Poland and, after a brief lull, pushed early in 1940 into Denmark and Norway. The next targets were Holland, Belgium, and France, with invasion prepared by massive bombardments of civilian targets. Rotterdam, for example, was flattened at the cost of 40,000 lives.

As in the 1930s, German dynamism was matched by Allied weakness. France fell surprisingly quickly, partly because the French were unprepared for war and relied on an outdated defensive strategy, partly because French troops were quickly demoralized due to the deep tensions within their own society. By the summer of 1940 most of France lay in German hands, and a semi-Fascist collaborative regime, based in the city of Vichy, ruled the remainder. Only Britain stood apart, able to withstand Hitler's air offensive and win the contest for its skies in what became known as the Battle of Britain. Imaginative air tactics, combined with solid new leadership under a coalition government headed by Winston Churchill and the iron resolve on the part of British citizens were effective in resisting the devastating air raids. Hitler's hopes for a British collapse were dashed.

In 1940 Germany controlled the bulk of the European continent. It aided its ally, Italy, in a conquest of Yugoslavia and Greece. It moved into North Africa to press British and French holdings. Conquered territories were forced to supply materials, troops, and compulsory slave labor to the German war machine. Hitler also stepped up his campaign against the Jews, aiming at a "final solution" that meant mass slaughter in Germany as well as its tribute territories. Even as Germany ground out its war effort, it forced Jews from all parts of Europe into concentration camps and gas chambers. This Holocaust was the most shocking aspect of the war, an act of genocide on an unprecedented scale.

The balance in the war began to shift slightly in 1941. Blocked from invasion of Britain, Hitler turned east toward the tempting target of Russia, viewed as an inferior Slavic state in Nazi racial ideology. Germany's attack began in June, all pretense of alliance was abandoned, and the Germans easily penetrated into central Russia. Yet the Soviet forces, while giving ground amid massive loss of life, did not collapse. They moved back, relocating Soviet industry eastward. As with Napoleon's invasion attempt more than a century before, weather also came to the Russians' aid, as a harsh winter caught the Germans, who were counting on another quick victory, off guard. As in Britain, civilian morale in Russia greatly aided the war effort, and although German forces continued to advance through 1942, the knockout blow eluded them. The invasion attempt also stretched German resources very thin, revealing how ill-prepared Hitler's economy was for a long-haul effort and how inefficient the economy was in many aspects of war production.

Late 1941 also brought the United States into the war, spurred initially by the Japanese attack on Pearl Harbor, which in fact took place against German wishes. The U.S. government had already supported Britain with loans and supplies and now eagerly used the bombing of Pearl Harbor to enter the war in Europe and Asia against what seemed a clear threat to Western democracy, perhaps even to Western civilization. U.S. involvement, delayed because of lack of full prior preparation, began to make itself felt in 1942, when U.S. and British forces challenged the Germans in North Africa. In the same year, the Soviet Union pushed back an intensive German siege of the city of Stalingrad, which if successful might have opened the way to the Ural Mountains and the nation's new industrial heartland. More than one-third of the German force surrendered, and the Red armies began a gradual push westward that would take them past their own borders, through eastern Europe, and by 1945 deep into Germany.

In the meantime, British and U.S. forces moved into the Italian peninsula from North Africa, ousting Mussolini, while also bombing German industrial and civilian targets. Then in 1944 the Allies invaded France, pushing the Germans back with the aid of French "resistance" forces hostile to fascism. Amid bitter fighting—Hitler decided to battle as fiercely as possible—and goaded in part by Allied insistence that Germany surrender without conditions, the Anglo-American forces gradually surged into western Germany. In late April 1945 Russian and U.S. troops met on the Elbe River. On April 30 Hitler committed suicide in his Berlin bunker, and in the following month German military commanders surrendered their country to the victorious invaders.

Within months the war in the Pacific also ended. This conflict had become primarily a duel between Japan and the United States, but British and Chinese forces

These Japanese soldiers were captured by Chinese forces in the interior of China after a bitter battle in 1942.

were also engaged; after the European theater of operations closed, the Soviet Union turned its attention eastward as well. Japan's surrender was precipitated by U.S. use of atomic bombs on two cities, Hiroshima and Nagasaki, which forced a full Japanese surrender and a period of U.S. occupation.

HUMAN COSTS

World War II had been a huge killer, with wanton cruelty adding to the effect of unprecedented weapons. Japanese troops in China had killed countless civilians, often after torturing them, when they captured cities that had tried to hold out; in Nanking, for example, as many as 300,000 were killed after the city had fallen. Hitler's decision to eliminate Jews throughout Europe led to six million dead in the gas chambers of the Holocaust. Hitler's forces also deliberately attacked civilian centers through bombing raids, in the usually mistaken belief that such destruction would destroy morale. Allied forces, as they became more powerful, paid back in kind. The British air force firebombed the German city of Dresden in retaliation for earlier German raids. Firebombing of Japanese cities led to as many as 80,000 dead in a single raid. The U.S. decision to drop its newly developed atomic bomb on Japan was taken in this atmosphere. U.S. officials wanted to force Japan to surrender without a needlessly costly invasion, and they also hurried to prevent Soviet advance in Asia. The bombing of Hiroshima killed more than 78,000 civilians, and the raid on Nagasaki two days later also killed tens of thou-

sands. Radiation fallout ultimately killed thousands more, as the new U.S. President, Harry Truman, termed the bombing "the greatest thing in history." Overall, at least 35 million people were killed in the war—20 million in the Soviet Union alone.

ANALYSIS:
TOTAL WAR

In the earlier history of civilization the nature of war changed, losing its ritual characteristics and becoming more commonly an all-out battle in which any tactics and weapons that would aid in victory were now countenanced. War, in other words, became less restrained than it had been among more "primitive" peoples who often enjoyed bluff and scare more than all-out violence. All sorts of wars were fought between the early period of civilization and the 20th century, as weapons and military organization changed and varied. Particularly bloody episodes often involved peoples from different cultures, including Westerners battling what they conveniently regarded as "savages"; this was a key feature of the imperialist expansion. Sometimes, at the other extreme, a ritual element might return, as in the carefully uniformed parades of troops who fought Europe's battles in the 18th century, recognizing the importance of stylized maneuvers over random bloodshed.

It was the 20th century, however, that most clearly saw the introduction of a fundamentally new kind of war—total war, in which vast resources and emotional commitments of the belligerent nations were marshaled to support military effort. The two world wars were thus novel not only in their geographical sweep but also in their mobilization of the major combatants. The features of total war also fed some regional conflicts later in the 20th century, such as the long Iran-Iraq War in the Middle East in the 1980s. They colored other forms of struggle, helping to explain brutal guerrilla and terrorist acts among groups not powerful enough to mount total wars but nonetheless affected by their methods and passions.

Total war can be seen as resulting from the impact of industrialization on military effort, reflecting both the technological innovation and the organizational capacity that accompanied the industrial economy from its early stages. Key steps in the development of total war thus emerged in the West from the end of the 18th century onward. The French Revolution, building new power for the state in contact with ordinary citizens, introduced mass conscription of men, forming larger armies than had ever before been possible. New citizen involvement was reflected in incitements to nationalism and stirring military songs, including—a new idea itself—aggressive national anthems. Industrial technology was first applied to war on a large scale in the U.S. Civil War. Railroads allowed wider movement of mass armies, and mass-produced guns and artillery made a mockery of earlier cavalry charges and might redefine the kind of personal bravery needed to fight in war.

It was World War I, however, that fully revealed the nature of total war. Steadily more destructive technology included battleships, submarines, tanks, airplanes, poison gas (theoretically banned by international agree-

ment prior to the war), machine guns, and long-range artillery. Organization for war included not only massive, compulsory recruitment—the draft—but also government control of economic activity through obligatory planning and rationing, which altered management policy, labor relations, and personal consumption options. It included unprecedented control of media through effective censorship and the jailing of dissidents, as well as through powerful propaganda designed to incite passionate, all-out commitment to the national cause and deep, unreasoned hatred of the enemy. Vivid posters, flaming speeches, and outright falsehood combined in the emotional mobilization effort. All of these features returned with a vengeance, of course, in World War II, from the new technology of bombing, rocketry, and ultimately the atomic bomb to the enhanced eco-

This World War I British government cartoon appealing for loans from the public shows a simple, almost sportive and jocular war, with a British Tommy confronting a ridiculous German emperor.

nomic mobilization effort organized by government planners.

The people most affected by the character of total war were the troops, who endured—bled and died from—the new technology. But one measure of total war was a blurring of the distinction between military and civilians, a distinction that had often restrained war's impact earlier in world history. Entire civilian populations, not just those unfortunate enough to be near front lines, were now forced into certain types of work, urged to certain types of beliefs. The bombing raids, including the German rockets directed against British cities late in World War II, subjected civilians to some of the most lethal weapons available, as many belligerents deliberately focused attacks on densely populated cities. Correspondingly psychological suffering, though less common among civilians than among front-line soldiers, could occur quite widely in the populations involved in war.

Total war, like any major historical development, had mixed results. Greater government economic direction often included new measures to protect workers and give them a voice on management boards. Labor force mobilization often produced at least temporary breakthroughs for women. And intense efforts to organize technological research often produced side results of more general economic benefit, as in the invention of new materials, such as synthetic rubber.

Still, total war was notable especially for its devastation. The idea of throwing all possible resources into a military effort and having the organizational ability and transportation capacity to do so made war much more disruptive economically than had been the case before, at least in terms of short-term impact. The passions unleashed in total war produced embittered veterans who might vent their anger by attacking established political values. It certainly made postwar diplomacy more difficult. One result of total war was a tendency to be inflexible in negotiations at war's end: People who fought so hard found it difficult to treat enemies generously, and the results of a quest for vengeance often produced new tensions that led directly, and quickly, to further conflict. War-induced passions and disruptions could also spark new violence at home, as crime rates often soared right after the war ended (a traditional result), and for longer time periods. Trying to determine how much the passions sparked by total war altered basic processes, such as diplomacy, crime, or even family life, yields a set of key questions about wider aspects of 20th-century history. How much of the nature of life even today has been determined by the consequences of total war?

Questions: How did being a soldier in a total war differ from being a soldier in a more traditional war? How did the experience of total war affect social and political patterns after the war's end? Why do many historians believe that total war made rational peacetime settlements more difficult than earlier in history? ☙

THE SETTLEMENT OF WORLD WAR II

World War II did not produce the sweeping peace settlement, untidy as it was, that had officially ended World War I. The major Allies opposed to Germany and Japan did meet on several occasions, earnestly trying to construct a peace that would avoid the mistakes of Versailles. The Allies agreed that a new international organization, the United Nations, should be set up, with better international representation than had characterized the League of Nations. The United States pledged to join and indeed ultimately housed the UN headquarters in New York. The Soviet Union was included, and China (represented by the Nationalist government) attained Great Power status for the first time in modern history. Britain and France were the other nations that would have a permanent seat on the Security Council—the steering committee for the new organization. Internationalism now moved beyond the conventional Western orbit, though the Western leaders sought to retain dominance. Like the League, the United Nations had as its primary mission provision of a forum for negotiating disputes, but it also took over the apparatus of more specialized international agencies that addressed world problems in agriculture, labor, and the like.

Beyond agreeing on a new, if ultimately fairly modest, international apparatus, the wartime Allies found it increasingly difficult to reach accord on the shape of the postwar world. Some leaders wanted virtually to destroy Germany's industrial structure, to prevent any recurrence of threat from this quarter, but others held out for milder measures—though all agreed that Hitler's regime must go and that Germany must surrender unconditionally, a stance that may have discouraged some peace movements within the German military. The key problem that emerged involved growing tension between the Soviet Union and the United States, along with British representatives who feared Soviet ambitions.

Initial discussions among U.S., British, and Soviet governments began in 1942, focusing at first on purely military issues. Heads of the three states met in 1943, in

Teheran, Iran, where the Soviet government pressed the Western powers to open a new front in France, which was of course done with the invasion of Normandy in 1944. The decision to focus on France rather than moving up from the Mediterranean in effect gave the Soviet forces a free hand to move through the smaller nations of eastern Europe as they pushed the Nazi armies back. Britain negotiated separately with the Soviets to ensure Western preponderance in postwar Greece as well as equality in Hungary and Yugoslavia, with Soviet control of Rumania and Bulgaria, but the United States resisted this kind of un-Wilsonian scorn for the rights of small nations.

With the war nearly over, the next settlement meeting took place in Yalta in the Soviet Crimea early in 1945. President Franklin Roosevelt of the United States was eager to press the Soviet Union for assistance against Japan and to this end promised the Soviets important territorial gains in Manchuria and the northern Japanese islands. The organization of the United Nations was confirmed. As to Europe, however, agreement was more difficult. The three powers easily arranged to divide Germany into four occupation zones (liberated

France getting a chunk), which would be disarmed and purged of Nazi influence. Britain, however, resisted Soviet zeal to eliminate German industrial power, seeing a viable Germany as a potential ally in a subsequent Western-Soviet contest. Bitter disagreement also raged over the smaller nations of Eastern Europe. No one disagreed that they should be friendly to their Soviet neighbor, but the Western leaders also wanted them to be free and democratic. Stalin, the Soviet leader, had to make some concessions by including non-Communist leaders in what was already a Soviet-controlled government in liberated Poland—concessions that he soon violated.

The final postwar conference occurred in the Berlin suburb of Potsdam in July 1945. Russian forces now occupied not only most of Eastern Europe but eastern Germany as well. This de facto situation prompted agreement that the Soviet Union could take over much of what had been eastern Poland, with the Poles gaining part of eastern Germany in compensation. Germany was divided pending a final peace treaty (which was not to come for more than 40 years). Austria was also divided and occupied, gaining unity and independence only in 1956 on condition of neutrality between the United States and the Soviet Union. Amid great difficulty, treaties were worked out for Germany's other allies, including Italy, but the United States and, later, the Soviet Union signed separate treaties with Japan.

All these maneuvers had several results. Japan was occupied by the United States and its wartime gains stripped away; even Korea, taken earlier, was freed but was divided between U.S. and Soviet zones of occupation (the basis for the North–South Korea division still in effect today). Former Asian colonies were returned to their old "masters," though often quite briefly, as new independence movements quickly challenged the control of the weakened imperialist powers. China regained most of its former territory, though here too stability was promptly challenged by renewed fighting between Communist and nationalist forces within the nation, aided by the Soviet Union and the United States, respectively.

The effort to confirm old colonial regimes applied also to the Middle East, India, and Africa. Indian and African troops had fought for Britain during the war, as in World War I, though Britain imprisoned key nationalist leaders and put independence plans on hold. African leaders had participated constructively in the French resistance to its authoritarian wartime government. The Middle East and North Africa had been shaken by German invasions and Allied counterattacks. Irritability increased, and so did expectations for change.

Central Europe after World War II

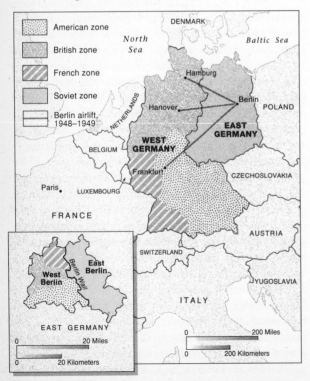

With Europe's imperial powers further weakened by their war effort, adjustments seemed inevitable, as in those parts of Asia invaded by the Japanese.

In Europe the boundaries of the Soviet Union pushed westward, with virtually all the losses after World War I erased. Independent nations created in 1918 were for the most part restored (though the former Baltic states of Latvia, Lithuania, and Estonia became Soviet provinces because they had been Russian provinces before World War I). Except for Greece and Yugoslavia, the new nations quickly fell under Soviet domination, with Communist governments forced on them and Soviet troops in occupation. The nations of Western Europe were free to set up or confirm democratic regimes, but most of them lived under the shadow of growing U.S. influence, manifested in continued occupation by U.S. troops, substantial economic aid and coordination, and no small amount of outright policy manipulation.

The stage was set, in other words, for two of the great movements that would shape the ensuing decades in world history. The first comprised challenges by subject peoples to the tired vestiges of control by the great European empires—the movement known as decolonization that in a few decades would create scores of new nations in Asia, Africa, and the West Indies. The second great theme was the confrontation between the two superpowers that emerged from the war—the United States and the Soviet Union, each with new international influence and new military might. This confrontation was quickly dubbed the "cold war," and many believed it would soon become a war in a more literal and devastating sense. That these trends constituted a peace settlement was difficult to imagine in 1945 or 1947, yet they seemed the best that could be done.

CONCLUSION

A BRUTAL TRANSITION, 1914–1945

The framework for world history established through the two world wars and the Great Depression was only that—a framework. It must be explored by more detailed consideration of developments in key individual areas during the first half of the 20th century. Understanding of the framework itself requires more detailed probing. War and depression, for example, did not inevitably produce the horrors of nazism in Germany; other factors must be explored even in the connections among war, depression, and renewed war.

The consequences of the war-torn international framework must also be explored by probing the major trends of the century's third phase, trends that were by no means all anticipated by the tense war settlement that emerged after 1945. The overarching global context that has taken shape in the past forty years has proved far freer from the ascending spiral of disaster that seemed to engulf the world between 1914 and 1945.

The best way to capture the essential results of the many events that marked the second phase of the 20th century is to view them as part of an exceedingly painful transition from Western world dominance to a different kind of world order. Whether this transition would have occurred had the major powers of Europe not tried twice to destroy one another, oblivious to the impact on their wider world role, cannot be determined. Certainly the transition would not have occurred so quickly.

The world wars weakened and distracted the nations that had long formed the core of Western civilization. They allowed new powers—the United States and the Soviet Union, as well as Japan despite the crushing defeat in 1945—to gain new roles. They allowed new independence movements and revolutionary uprisings. The Japanese forces that invaded Vietnam, the Philippines, and the Netherlands Indies (later Indonesia) during the early 1940s were often cordially detested by their new subjects, but they did teach that the Western overlords could be defeated and that a nonwhite people could put the West on the run. The lessons were important in supporting nationalist demands that had already been voiced by Asian leaders. World wars and depression broke the political framework western Europe had established during the preceding century, and they dented, though less simply and decisively, the older Western-dominated world economic framework as well. The major events of the decades after 1914 constituted the death throes of one world order and the bloody birth pains of a new one. Thus for each individual society during the 20th century, a set of common questions can be asked. How did world wars and resultant international rebalancing affect the society? What was the impact of depression in shaping new political and social responses?

Yet the world wars, particularly, had one further long-range result beyond stirring new expectations and resentments and reducing Europe's world role. They also raised the specter of war itself to a new level. Two world wars in a single generation had to haunt the world's people in 1945, particularly those in Europe, China, Japan,

Southeast Asia, the Soviet Union, and even the United States (spared direct combat on its own soil) who had lived through one or both wars so directly. The lack of complete settlement after World War II was profoundly troubling as well, because it resulted from the almost immediate crescendo of a new conflict between the United States and the Soviet Union. Finally, war had become increasingly terrible, its destructive power mounting with every passing year. Again, the end of World War II, with the inauguration of the two atomic bombs dropped on Japan, could only stir a feeling of dread. Even optimistic Americans went through at least six years of pressing anxiety as they tried to come to terms with the nuclear monster they had created.

Yet the end of World War II brought new leadership to almost every part of the globe as a result of new elections, the toppling of colonial regimes, the discrediting of defeated governments, and a new revolutionary surge in China. Many new leaders vowed to undo some of the mistakes of the past, though they disagreed profoundly over what the mistakes had been and how they should be remedied. How new leadership confronted the issues that had brought depression and war to world dominance during the first half of the 20th century raises another set of questions that must be addressed with regard to almost every major society in exploring its most recent history.

FURTHER READINGS

A number of important books have dealt with the origins of World War I. L. Lafore's *The Long Fuse* (1965) is a very readable introduction; see also James Joll's *Origins of World War I* (1984), which is slightly more up to date. A controversial interpretation is F. Fischer's *Germany's Aims in the First World War* (1967); see also P. Kennedy's *The Rise of the Anglo-German Antago-*

nism 1860–1914 (1980). I. Geiss's *July 1914* (1967) is a collection of documents on the subject.

For a wider perspective, G. Barraclough's *An Introduction to Contemporary History* (1968) is extremely interesting. On the war's cultural impact, P. Fussell's *The Great War and Modern Memory* (1975) is a brilliant treatment. See also R. J. Sontag's *A Broken World, 1919–1939* (1971) for a survey of the period, dealing mainly with Europe. On the war itself, see K. Robbins's *The First World War* (1984); see also J. Williams's *The Other Battleground: The Home Fronts, Britain, France, and Germany, 1911–1918* (1972) and R. Wohl's *The Generation of 1914* (1979). On the peace settlement, see A. J. Mayer's *The Politics and Diplomacy of Peacemaking* (1968).

On the depression, C. Kindleberger's *The World in Depression, 1929–1939* (1973), is a solid introduction. See also J. Galbraith's *The Great Crash of 1929* (1980) and, for a useful collection of articles, W. Laqueur and G. L. Mosse, eds., *The Great Depression* (1970). Japan's experience is covered in I. Morris, ed., *Japan, 1931–1945: Militarism, Fascism, Japanism?* (1963).

A good introduction to World War II is Gordon Wright's *The Ordeal of Total War, 1939–1945* (1968); see also W. Murray's *The Change in the European Balance of Power* (1984). On the war itself, see B. H. Liddell Hart's *History of the Second World War*, vol. 2 (1971). The U.S. role is the subject of R. A. Divine's *The Reluctant Belligerent: American Entry into World War II* (1979). On the Asian front, see J. H. Boyle's *China and Japan at War, 1937–1945* (1972) and R. Butow's *Japan's Decision to Surrender* (1954). See also S. Ienaga's *The Pacific War* (1978) and Chi Hsi-sheng's *Nationalist China at War* (1982).

On the war's immediate aftermath, see H. Feis's *From Trust to Terror: The Onset of the Cold War, 1945–1950* (1970) and Martin Sherwin's *A World Destroyed: The Atomic Bomb and the Grand Alliance* (1975). For a more general assessment of war's role in the 20th century, see Raymond Aron's *Century of Total War* (1985).

North America and Western Europe		
	1918 November armistice ends World War I	
	1919 Treaty of Paris signed at Versailles; Leftist revolution put down in Germany	
	1918–1923 Postwar adjustments; new republic in Germany; economic recession and recovery; emergence of communist movement	
	mid–1920s Period of hyperinflation in Germany	**1929** New York Stock Market crash precipitates a global depression
		1928 Introduction of penicillin
		1925 Locarno agreements regularize Germany's diplomatic relations
	1922 Mussolini takes power in Italy	**1928** Kellogg-Briand Pact

Japan	
	1923 Tokyo earthquake
	1923 Defeat of Japanese bill for universal suffrage

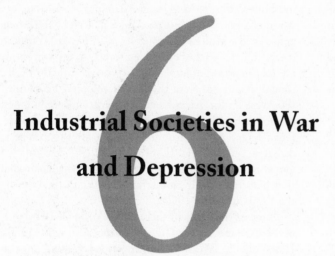

Industrial Societies in War and Depression

6

INTRODUCTION.   The theme of Western history during the decades before World War I was a new consolidation of political and social forms as the industrialization process matured. Tensions among social classes worked in part within the existing system, and the state took on new functions that met some pressing needs and also allowed new kinds of discipline through schools and military recruitment.

Much of western Europe's consolidation was also paralleled in the United States, where the sheer novelty of industrialization and urbanization began to wear off. Although masses of new immigrants encountered great stress, the settled middle classes had some confidence that reform and efficient management could combine to reduce the worst social problems. This "search for order" was a major goal of changes in city government and regulatory law backed by the Progressive political movement.

Japan in 1914 was a less advanced industrial society than those in western Europe or the United States. Stresses of initial industrialization and unaccustomed imitation of Western forms showed in many ways, from an extremely high divorce rate to the grinding poverty of many peasants and workers. Nevertheless, Japan had built a successful modern state, complete with

1933–1937 New Deal in United States

1931 Statute of Westminster, full autonomy for the British Dominions of Canada, Australia, New Zealand, South Africa and the Irish Free State

1936 Popular Front government in France

1945 End of World War II

1933 Hitler becomes chancellor of Germany

1938 Munich agreement allows Hitler to begin the destruction of Czechoslovakia

1935 Nuremberg laws deprive German Jews of citizenship

1930 Rapid rise of Nazi party

1932 Franklin Roosevelt begins a four-term tenure as U.S. President

1939 German invasion of Poland ignites Second World War

1938 Attacks on German Jews increase

1942 Hitler decides on extermination of European Jews

1931 Rebellion in Korea; Japanese repression; rise of nationalism, new hostility to West; height of depression, impact on Japan; bad harvests

1936 Assassination of several Japanese political leaders; young army officer rebellion

1945 Japan defeated; American occupation

1938 Japan's war budget; state control of economic life

1937 Full-scale invasion of China; increasingly open rule by military officers; arrest of opposition politicians

a parliament and a new, adaptable upper class that combined older aristocrats with big-business leaders. Social protest was kept under control with forceful police measures and appeals to loyalty to the emperor.

Both Japan and the United States emerged from World War I in relatively good shape, despite frustrated ambitions and a new wariness about European diplomacy. The 1920s saw important new developments in both societies; the United States pioneered a new mass-consumption society, with Hollywood an entertainment symbol well beyond the nation's borders. Japan undertook a fuller commitment to political democracy and showed renewed creativity in literature and the arts as it confirmed its identity amid powerful Western influences.

Yet dislocation and challenge, not continuity of adjustment to industrial society, form the dominant themes of the interwar decades, particularly in western Europe, the United States, and Japan. All these societies exhibited the distorting effects of total war and then catastrophic depression. The three decades after 1914 were among the most troubled in Western and Japanese history alike. Political forms that had seemed so successful, revolving around some kind of representative institutions, either were cast aside in favor of new radical regimes or threatened to stop functioning with any efficacy. Cultural emphases grounded in beliefs in human rationality were challenged by new movements that deliberately appealed to the vicious and impulsive traits in human nature.

The contortions of Western societies and Japan, particularly during the 1930s, left important scars—nazism, Japanese militarism, and sheer impotence in the face of mounting economic problems—that form part of the world's memory even today. The same contortions had direct impact on most other parts of the world, drawn into military conflict and economic dislocation. In the thrashings of leading industrial societies further elements of the framework of modern world history can be traced.

Yet the interwar years were complex. If social polarization and military conflict predominated in the West and Japan, more constructive innovations took shape as well. Science and modern art forms advanced. Institutions of the welfare state were established in some nations. New leadership groups challenged traditional elites even amid the hardships of depression or the horrors of nazism or fascism.

Innovation, in turn, helps explain why some of the setbacks of the interwar years proved temporary in both

Japan and the West. The seemingly endless string of catastrophes did finally end. For both the West and Japan, then, post-1914 history divides into two periods: one marked by deterioration and distortion; the other by considerable resurgence. Between 1914 and 1945 the history of the world's industrialized societies was dominated by the impact of war and depression. But somewhat surprisingly they shook off much of this crisis atmosphere after 1945. Despite Europe's decline in the world at large—a decline partially balanced by the emergence of the United States as a world power—Western ideals and approaches continued to play a disproportionate role in world affairs. Western revival after 1945, although it did not stem the loss of colonies, maintained the West as the pacesetter in international economics, culture, technology, and to a degree in political style. Japan surged to new economic heights after its complete defeat in World War II. From the 1950s onward, the global influence of the Japanese easily outstripped what they had tried to win through military aggression during the 1930s and early 1940s.

Some of the seeds of these post–World War II developments were planted during the 1920s and 1930s. Japan and the West, in sum, provided graphic illustrations of the vulnerabilities of industrial societies during the troubled decades between the world wars, but they also exhibited varied and often creative responses to the successive crises of that era.

THE DISARRAY OF WESTERN EUROPE, 1914–1945

World War I quickly shattered the confidence many Europeans had maintained around the turn of the century. The war also caused serious structural damage to the European economy, diplomatic relations among Western states, and political systems in many countries.

Although the ultimate effects of World War I involved Europe's world position, the war also brought tremendous dislocation within Europe. Though some of the damage was quickly repaired, much persisted for the subsequent two decades. The key battlegrounds for four bloody years had been in Europe. The sheer rate of death and maiming, as well as the frustration of nearly four years of virtual stalemate, had had a devastating material and psychological impact on the European combatants. More than ten million Europeans had died. In Britain, France, and Germany the percentage killed had severely reduced the number of young men available. Vast amounts of property had been destroyed.

Most governments had failed to tax their populations enough to pay for the war effort—lest they weaken domestic support—so huge debts accumulated, leading to inflationary pressure even before the war was over. Key prewar regimes were toppled when the German emperor abdicated and the Habsburg Empire collapsed.

Germany, indeed, was close to revolution in 1918–1919, as worker soviets were proclaimed in some cities and a separate Socialist government briefly emerged in Bavaria. The extreme left was put down, and the moderate Socialists ushered in Germany's new Weimar republic, but the atmosphere of political extremes, far right as well as far left, would continue to complicate German development.

A significant new political movement also emerged in Italy in the wake of the war. In 1919 a former Socialist and former solider, Benito Mussolini, formed the *fascio di combattimento,* or union for struggle. Italian Fascists vaguely advocated a corporate state that would replace both capitalism and socialism with a new national unity. They pointed to the need for an aggressive, nationalistic foreign policy. Above all, however, Fascists worked to seize power by any means and to build a strong state under a strong leader. They violently attacked rival political groups, seeking to promote an atmosphere of chaos.

Amid growing political divisions and a rising threat from the working-class left, in 1922 the Italian king called on Mussolini to form a new government. Though the Fascists themselves had only limited popular support, they seemed the only hope to stem left-wing agitation and parliamentary ineptitude.

Once in power, Mussolini eliminated most opposition, suspending elections outright in 1926, while seeking greater state direction of the economy and issuing strident propaganda about the glories of military conquest. This first Fascist regime moved with some caution, fitting into the briefly hopeful negotiations among European states in the 1920s, but the principles it espoused suggested how far European politics had been unseated from the widespread prewar agreements on parliamentary rule.

THE ROARING TWENTIES

Despite all the disruptions, a brief period of stability, even optimism, emerged in the mid-1920s. Diplomatic tensions eased somewhat within Europe, as Germany made some moves to accommodate its reduced position in return for partial relief from the reparations payments. Although Germany refused definitively to accept its new eastern boundaries, it did promise friendship all around. Hopes that the Versailles settlement could be permanent ran so high that an American and a French leader coauthored a treaty outlawing war forever (the Kellogg-Briand Pact of 1928, which a number of nations dutifully ratified)—a sign of the shallow hopes of the decade.

Internal politics also seemed to calm. The war's end and immediate economic dislocations, as well as the impact of the Russian Revolution, had inspired a new political polarization in many western European countries. Many veterans joined groups on the far right that wanted an authoritarian government and recovery of national honor; the labor movement on the left split, with a minority wing becoming Communist, taking cues from the revolutionary regime in the Soviet Union. Both radical factions scared each other, further complicating parliamentary life. Germany produced an admirable constitution for its new democratic republic, but many groups did not accept it and there were understandable fears for its life. Even Britain, long known for its political stability, saw a major shift as the Labour party replaced the Liberals as the second major political force. Generally, the liberal middle sector of European politics was weakened. Nevertheless, the middle years of the 1920s brought a brief respite, as the extremist groups declined in force.

Economic prosperity buoyed hopes in the middle of the decade. The worst inflationary pressures were resolved at the cost of wiping out the value of savings for many propertied groups. Industrial production boomed, though more markedly in the United States than in western Europe. Mass-consumption standards rose for several years. New products, such as the artificial fiber rayon and radios, spread widely. Household appliances proliferated, as technology's impact on daily life reached a new height.

Finally, the 1920s saw a burst of cultural creativity in many parts of the West. Filmmakers experimented with this genre for both artistic expression and mass entertainment. Modern artists developed geometrical cubist styles and other innovations. Writers and playwrights pioneered new forms, reducing plot lines and often seeking audience involvement in dramas. In retrospect the mood of the 1920s, in terms of high culture and popular culture alike, seemed somewhat frenzied. The defiance of traditional styles—the growing abstraction of modern art and novelists' efforts to capture unconscious impulses over structured plots—attempted to convey some of the menacing tensions beneath the surface of modern life.

This magazine cover by John Held, Jr., depicts the coed of 1926 as a combination of sweetness and sophistication.

Women, particularly in the middle class, registered important gains. Women's involvement in the labor force during the war was short-lived, as men pushed them out at war's end. However, postwar legislation granted women suffrage in Britain, Germany, and the United States. Further, prosperity and the declining birthrate gave many women the chance to develop new leisure habits and less restrictive fashions. Young women in the United States began to date more freely, as a preliminary to courtship. Wives in Britain wrote of new interests in sexual pleasure, while maintaining commitment to marriage. Here were developments, like the more general rise of consumerism, that would gain momentum later on.

THE DEPRESSION'S IMPACT

All the hopeful signs seemed to vanish with the onset of depression in 1929; the Great Depression revealed that neither the economic nor the political achievements of the mid-1920s had been as solidly based as had been hoped. Political consequences were inevitable with so many people out of work or threatened with unemployment. The relatively weak Western governments responded to the onset of the catastrophe counterproductively. National tariffs were raised to keep out the goods of other countries, but this merely worsened the international economy and curbed sales for everyone. Most governments tried to cut spending, reflecting the decline in revenues that accompanied falling production. They were concerned about avoiding renewed inflation, but in fact their measures further reduced economic stimulus and pushed additional workers—government employees—out of jobs. Confidence in the normal political process deteriorated. In many countries the depression heightened political polarization. People sought solutions from radical parties or movements, both on the left and on the right. Support for Communist parties increased in many countries, and in important cases the authoritarian movement on the radical right gained increased attention. Even in relatively stable countries, such as Britain, battles between conservative and labor movements made decisive policy difficult. Class conflict rose to new levels, in and out of politics.

There were a few cases of constructive political response. Scandinavian states, most of them directed by moderate Socialist movements, increased government spending, providing new levels of social insurance against illness and unemployment and foreshadowing the modern welfare state. In key cases, however, the Great Depression led to one of two effects: either a parliamentary system that became increasingly incapacitated, unable to come to grips with the new economic dilemma and too divided to take vigorous action, even in foreign policy, or the outright overturning of the parliamentary system.

France was a prime example of the first pattern. The French government reacted sluggishly to the depression. Voters responded by moving toward the political extremes. Socialist and then Communist parties expanded. Rightist movements calling for a strong leader and fervent nationalism grew, their adherents often disrupting political meetings in order to discredit the parliamentary system. In response Liberal, Socialist, and Communist parties formed the Popular Front in 1936 to win the election. The Popular Front government, however, was unable to take strong measures of social reform because of the ongoing strength of conservative republicans and the authoritarian right. The same paralysis crept into foreign policy, as Popular Front leaders, initially eager to support the new liberal regime in Spain that was attacked by conservative army leaders in the Spanish Civil War, found themselves forced to pull back. The Popular Front fell in 1938, but even before this France was close to a standstill.

FASCISM

In Germany the impact of the depression led directly to a new fascist regime. Germany had suffered the shock of loss in World War I, enhanced by treaty arrangements that cast primary blame for the war on the German nation, which had only recent and shaky parliamentary traditions. A number of factors, in sum, combined to make Germany a fertile breeding ground for fascism, though it took the depression to bring this current to the fore.

Fascism was a product of the war. The movement's advocates, many of them former veterans, attacked the weakness of parliamentary democracy and the corruption and class conflict of Western capitalism. They proposed a strong state ruled by a powerful leader who would revive the nation's forces through vigorous foreign and military policy. Fascists vaguely promised social reforms to alleviate class antagonisms, and their attacks on trade unions as well as Socialist and Communist parties pleased landlords and business groups. Although fascism won outright control only in Italy in the movement's early years, Fascist parties complicated the political process in a number of other nations during the 1920s and beyond. But it was the advent of the National Socialist, or Nazi, regime in Germany under Adolf Hitler that made this new political movement a major force in world history. Here, a modern Western commitment to liberal, democratic political forms was challenged and reversed.

In his vote-gathering campaigns Hitler repeated standard Fascist arguments about the need for unity and the hopeless weakness of parliamentary politics. The state should provide guidance, for it was greater than the sum of individual interests, and the leader should guide the state. Hitler promised many groups a return to more traditional ways; thus many artisans voted for him in the belief that preindustrial economic institutions, such as the guilds, would be revived. Middle-class elements, including big-business leaders, were attracted to Hitler's commitment to a firm stance against socialism and communism. Hitler also focused grievances against various currents in modern life, from big department stores to feminism, by attacking what he claimed were Jewish influences in Germany. And he promised a glorious foreign policy to undo the wrongs of the Versailles treaty. Finally, Hitler represented a hope for effective action against the depression. Although the Nazis never won a majority vote in a free election, his party did win the largest single slice in 1932, and this enabled Hitler to make arrangements with other political leaders for his rise to power legally in 1933.

Once in power, Hitler quickly set about constructing a *totalitarian* state—a new kind of government that would exercise massive, direct control over virtually all the activities of its subjects. Hitler eliminated all opposition parties; he purged the bureaucracy and military, installing loyal Nazis in many posts. His secret police, the *Gestapo*, arrested hundreds of thousands of political opponents. Trade unions were replaced by government-sponsored bodies that tried to appease low-paid workers by offering full employment and various welfare benefits. Government economic planning helped restore production levels, with particular emphasis on armaments construction. Hitler cemented his regime by continual well-staged propaganda bombardments, strident nationalism, and an incessant attack on Germany's large Jewish minority.

Hitler's hatred of Jews ran deep; he blamed them for various personal misfortunes and also for socialism and excessive capitalism—movements that in his view had weakened the German spirit. Obviously, anti-Semitism served as a catchall for a host of diverse dissatisfactions, and as such it appealed to many Germans. Anti-Semitism also played into Hitler's hands by providing a scapegoat that could rouse national passions and distract the population from other problems. Measures against Jews became more and more severe; they were forced to wear special emblems, their property was attacked and seized, and increasing numbers were sent to concentration camps. After 1940 Hitler's policy insanely turned to the literal elimination of European Jewry, as the Holocaust raged in the concentration camps of Germany and conquered territories.

Hitler's foreign and military policies were based on preparation for war. He wanted to not only recoup Germany's World War I losses but also create a land empire that would extend across much of Europe, particularly toward the east against what he saw as the inferior Slavic peoples. Progressively Hitler violated the limits on German armaments and annexed neighboring territories, provoking only weak response from the Western democracies. When war finally began in 1939, Hitler's forces pressed forward for three years before his opponents

German Nazis moved the orchestrated mass rally to a high art form, profoundly influencing those who participated and those who could feel its power and solidarity through the radio or the movie screen.

were able to regroup. By late 1942 Soviet armies had recovered from German invasion, with some assistance in the form of armaments from the United States, and pressed inexorably toward Germany's eastern borders. Germany was driven first from North Africa and then gradually from Italy by U.S. and British forces, aided by resistance movements against Nazi occupation.

As U.S.-Anglo armies in 1944 met Soviet forces along the Elbe River—Germany's new divide—Hitler committed suicide, and the war in Europe drew to a close. Only with defeat in war could the Nazi regime be dislodged in Germany itself. The years from one world war through the next read like a tragic drama in Western history. One dire event led almost inexorably to the next, with none of the major participants able to tamper with fate.

PATTERNS IN EUROPEAN HISTORY, 1914–1945

Some key patterns can be discerned amid this sequence of events. In the first place the relentless unfolding of the Western tragedy had three key sources. The escalation of national conflicts, visible already in the later 19th century, was one such source. World War I, creating new grievances and imbalances, simply enhanced this nationalist tension within Western civilization. Second, the nature of war now changed, with the advent of total war, and had more sweeping effects on societies involved in combat than earlier wars had. Propaganda bombarded civilians, often raising false hopes and encouraging new hatreds of foreign enemies as well as internal suspects, such as leftists or capitalist profiteers. The economy was massively enmeshed in the war effort, making subsequent recovery difficult. Also, the weaponry of war involved unprecedented capacity to kill and damage. Finally, weaknesses in Western democracy and industrialization, exacerbated by war, came home to roost. From an economic standpoint the Western economies tolerated too much poverty, in addition to depending too much on exports to poor countries, to be entirely secure; sales could easily plummet. From a social standpoint a number of groups continued to be suspicious of industrial conditions, eager in a crisis either to attack capitalism in the name of socialism or to urge a return to older values and authority.

Conditions of women continued to provoke fundamental disagreements. Some women were delighted with new consumer and life-style opportunities that opened up during the 1920s (along, in many countries, with the right to vote). Women began to smoke and drink in public and to enjoy new dance crazes and other leisure options. Yet other women continued to protest the limitations on women's roles and particularly their inequality in work opportunities, as a brief wartime surge of female employment was pushed back during the 1920s. These feminist grievances, though less pronounced than before World War I, could feed leftist sentiment. Still other Westerners were aghast at the changes that had arrived, urging that women return to more purely domestic roles and traditional, modest costumes and habits. This sentiment provided some support for fascist movements. The West, in sum, remained deeply affected by the innovations brought by industrialization, and the resultant divisions helped sharpen political dispute.

Industrialization, however, continued to advance. The interwar decades saw continued gains for assembly-line production and big-business forms. Huge combines developed in key industries, both in Europe and in the United States, and managers learned new ways to coordinate and discipline masses of workers in factories, offices, and sales outlets. Major new product lines developed with artificial fibers and other consumer goods, including British-pioneered television production in the 1930s. In terms of industrial development and big business, Nazi Germany, despite anticapitalist rhetoric, promoted change as well, somewhat ironically weakening many of the more conservative sectors of German society. Capitalist control of industry and marketing advanced under Hitler, further reducing the role of small shops and artisans, while peasant agriculture was squeezed by support for large estates. The Nazi regime

did dispute dominant Western cultural trends. It attacked modern art, urging more realistic, heroic styles (often in the classical mode), and even challenged scientific education with praise for sports and physical training over intellectual life.

ANALYSIS
THE DECLINE OF THE WEST?

At various points in the 20th century, influential Western thinkers and leaders have worried about the decline of Western society. Sometimes their concerns have focused on the undeniable relative decline of the West in the world, which sets the 20th century off from the periods in world history between the late 18th century and 1920. In the 1980s, for example, various U.S. news magazines began to trumpet the idea of an emerging "Pacific century," dominated by East Asian powers, that would replace the period of Western (and recently, U.S.) preponderance.

The idea of absolute decline has had its proponents as well. The West's relative loss of power over the past 60 years, with decolonization and the rise of Japanese exports, may produce absolute decline compared to earlier Western leadership. Some societies—such as the Roman Empire or the Ottoman Empire—depended on continued expansion to provide labor or booty for the upper class and then began to lose their vitality when further growth became impossible. The West no longer requires colonies to provide slaves, but it may have become so dependent on its ability to dominate other economies that relative decline will spell the beginning of a new period of internal woes.

Furthermore, there have been numerous periods in which developments in the West provoked gloom. Early in the 20th century the German philosopher Oswald Spengler, pondering the growing pleasure-seeking Western culture and its internal divisions, wrote *The Decline of the West,* in which he predicted that Western civilization was going the way of Rome. He argued that the West was doomed to fall before the onslaught of such vigorous but less civilized peoples as the Russians or the Americans. His book was hugely popular after World War I, when it looked as if Western nations had indeed inflicted grievous injury on their own civilization. Other historians, though somewhat less cosmically pessimistic than Spengler, have picked up the theme of what they see as an inevitable decline of societies following periods of vigor. The theme seemed to fit western Europe again immediately after World War II, when both victors and vanquished were suffering through the immense problems of reconstruction. It was revived again in the late 1980s, when the world dominance of the United States seemed in retreat.

Other observers, though less systematic, discerned internal decay. Some focused on cultural trends, bemoaning the lack of standards in art—the tendency to play with novel styles, however frivolous, simply to win attention. Or they might bemoan popular culture for what they claimed was a shallow, manipulable materialism and vulgar sexuality. Some critics saw analogies between modern Western commercialism and the Roman "bread and circuses" approach to the urban masses that, they argued, had weakened the empire's moral fiber and reduced its capacity for work and military valor.

Analogies, however, are inexact, and the role of moral decline in causing Rome's downfall is debatable in any event. One of the problems in comparing current Western trends to past cases of decline—even subtler cases, such as the gradual reduction of Arab vitality in the later postclassical era—is that modern conditions as shaped by industrialization may weaken the applicability of past standards.

Western demography is a case in point. There is no question that the demographic vitality of the West weakened in the late 19th and 20th centuries, with the baby boom era, from 1943 to 1963, a brief if interesting exception. Birthrates have gone down fairly steadily, in the 1930s and again by the 1980s, reaching a point close to bare reproduction. Indeed, some Western nations, such as Germany, were by the 1980s coming close to falling beneath reproduction levels, with birthrates so low that population decline would soon set in unless compensated by further immigration. Moreover, slow or zero population growth was accompanied by increased aging, the result of advancing life expectancy combined with the relatively small number of children being born. In most historic situations slowing population growth has signaled a general decrease in vitality, causing further decline as competition and the opportunity provided by population increase waned. Unquestionably, the West's demographic trends reduced its percentage of world population, which might relate to its relative decline and certainly opened it to new immigration from various parts of the world. But the total package was difficult to measure, for in the context of an industrial society,

which provided a variety of technical aids to human labor and was a heavy consumer of resources, stable populations might prove a source of strength, not weakness, whereas rapid population increase might be a fateful burden that limited effective development.

Judgments about decline, finally, are complicated by the cycles of Western history during the 20th century and the nature of modern Western expectations. Periods of great disarray, like the 1930s, have not thus far led to long-term chaos, as Western nations have seemed able to bounce back. Other decades roused anxieties mainly because of the heavy Western commitment to steady progress. Thus during the 1970s, when economic growth slowed, many polls showed that Americans had stopped believing that their society would advance in the future (though interestingly they still believed that their own lives would get better). Yet the 1970s brought no huge crisis, simply a slowing in the pace of improvement. The Western habit of expecting steady economic advance could easily lead to temporary exaggerations of what 1970s Americans called "malaise."

Clearly, to paraphrase Mark Twain, reports of the death of the West seemed, toward the end of the 20th century, premature. Yet past examples from world history suggest one other caution: Social decline, if it does set in, typically takes a long time to work through. Rome declined for three centuries before it "fell"; the Ottoman Empire began to turn downward two centuries before it became known as "sick." The first century of decline may be difficult to perceive yet particularly important to monitor in case restorative measures are necessary.

Questions: Has the West shown signs of cultural decline in the 20th century? What is the best case for arguing that 20th-century Western history does not suggest cultural decline? If the West is in decline by the late 20th century, what might be done about it? Does world history suggest that decline is reversible? ☉

WESTERN CULTURE: INNOVATIONS AND TENSIONS

Despite new political and economic tensions, or perhaps because of them, Western culture in the first half of the 20th century displayed important creativity and change. The early decades of the 20th century saw fundamental new developments in various facets of intellectual and artistic endeavor. Artists and composers stressed stylistic innovation, as against older traditions and even the efforts of the previous generation. Complex discoveries in science, such as the principle of relativity in physics, qualified older ideas that nature can be captured in a few sweeping scientific laws. And the sheer specialization of scientific research removed much of it from ready public understanding. Because no clear unifying assumptions captured the essence of formal intellectual activity in the contemporary West, neutral terms, such as *modern,* were used even in the artistic field. Disciplines that had once provided an intellectual overview, such as philosophy, declined in the 20th century or were transformed into specialized research fields; many philosophers, for example, turned to the scientific study of language, and sweeping political theory virtually disappeared. And although work in theology continued among both Catholic and Protestant thinkers, it no longer commanded center stage in intellectual life. No emphasis was placed on an integrated approach, as Western intellectual life developed with specialized branches, and no agreement was reached on what constitutes an essential understanding of human endeavor.

The dynamism of scientific research continued to form the clearest central thread in Western culture after 1920. Growing science faculties commanded greatest prestige in the expanding universities. Individual scientists made striking discoveries, and a veritable army of researchers cranked out more specific findings than scientists had ever before produced. In addition, the wider public continued to maintain a faith that science held the keys to understanding nature and society and to improving technology and human life. Finally, although scientific findings varied widely, a belief in a central scientific method persisted: Form a rational hypothesis, test through experiment or observation, and emerge with a generalization that will show regularities in physical behaviors and thus provide human reason with a means of systematizing and even predicting such behaviors. No other approach to understanding in Western culture has had such power or widespread adherence.

By the 1930s physicists began to experiment with bombarding basic matter with *neutrons,* or particles that carry no electric charge; this work culminated during World War II in the development of the atomic bomb. Astronomers made substantial progress in identifying additional galaxies and other phenomena in space; the debate also continued about the nature of matter.

Breakthroughs in biology primarily involved genetics. The identification in the 1860s of principles of inheritance received wide attention only after 1900. By the 1920s researchers who used the increasingly familiar fruit fly had exact rules for genetic transmission. Medical research advanced in a variety of areas, including new discoveries about human tissues.

Fundamental discoveries in physics and biology, though difficult for even the educated public to grasp, promoted the idea of science as penetrating the mysteries of the universe. They also furthered the relationship between science and technology. Physicists spearheaded research into atomic weaponry and atomic power. During and after World War II they helped develop missiles and other spacecraft. Biologists produced major improvements in health care. New drugs, beginning with penicillin in 1928, revolutionized the treatment of common diseases, and immunization virtually eliminated such scourges as diphtheria.

The new science displayed some troubling features, even apart from its use in the weapons of destruction or its sheer complexity. The physical world was no longer considered to be neatly regulated, as it had been by Newtonian physics. Many other phenomena came to be perceived as relative and unpredictable. Genetics made it clear that evolution proceeded by a series of random accidents, not through any consistent pattern. Use of the rational, scientific method thus has not produced the kind of tidy world view that was prevalent a century or so ago, and the resultant uncertainties have influenced some artists in their attempts to convey an irrational, relativist universe. Yet in the public mind, partly because the new science is so difficult to understand, the belief in progress, defined both as better technology and as rational penetration of nature, largely persists.

The rational method, broadly conceived, also advanced in the social sciences from 1920 onward. In economics, sweeping theories were downplayed while quantitative models of economic cycles or business behavior increasingly gained ground. Work by the British economist John Keynes, stressing the importance of government spending to compensate for loss of purchasing power during a depression, played a great role in the policies of the American New Deal. In psychology, the work by Sigmund Freud on the human unconscious and its role in mental disturbance gained increasing attention; although no single psychological theory predominated, the idea of using research to probe both conscious thought and irrational impulse won growing acceptance.

Like the physical sciences, the social sciences became increasingly diverse and specialized. Many individual researchers, like their scientific counterparts, worked on small problems of data gathering and manipulation. As in the sciences also, many social scientists sought practical applications for their work. Psychologists became involved, for example, not only in dealing with mental illness but also in trying to promote greater work efficiency.

The rise of anthropology in the 1920s and the development of social history as a branch of inquiry into human behavior swam against the social scientific current by pointing to the importance of diversity and chronology in understanding human life. Most leading social scientists, however, continued to emphasize the quest for consistency in human and social behavior.

Most 20th-century artists, concerned with capturing the world through impressions rather than through rea-

Marcel Duchamp, using a modified cubist style, sought dramatic visual effect in an approach characteristic of Western art from the 1920s onward.

son or the confinements of literal reality, worked against the grain of science and social science. Painting became increasingly nonrepresentational. The cubist movement, headed by Pablo Picasso, rendered familiar objects as geometrical shapes; after cubism, modern art moved even farther from normal perception, stressing purely geometrical design or wild swirls of color. The focus was on mood, the individual reaction of viewers to the individual reality of the artist. Musical composition involved the use of dissonance and experimentation with new scales. In poetry, the use of unfamiliar forms, ungrammatical constructions, and sweeping imagery continued the movement of the later 19th century. In literature, the novel remained dominant, but it turned toward the exploration of moods and personalities rather than the portrayal of objective events or clear story lines.

The arts in the 20th-century West were thus characterized by unprecedented diversity, by a conscious effort to seek new forms, and by a focus on the individual and mood rather than on some agreed-upon objective reality. These emphases provided the artistic equivalent of relativity, and they certainly stressed the importance of the unconscious. But a vast gulf grew between the scientific approach and the artistic framework as to how reality can be captured and even, to an extent, what constitutes reality.

Many people ignored the leading modern artists and writers in favor of more commercial artistic productions and popular stories. The gap that had opened earlier between avant-garde art and public taste generally continued. Some politicians, including Adolf Hitler, campaigned against what they saw as the decadence and immorality of modern art, urging a return to more traditional styles. And certainly art did not hold its own against the growing prestige of science.

Yet the artistic vision was not simply a preoccupation of artists. Designs and sculptures based on abstract art began to grace public places from the 1920s onward; furnishings and films also reflected the modernist themes. Most revealing of a blend of art, modern technology, and public taste was the development of a characteristic 20th-century architectural style, the "modern," or "international," style. Use of new materials, such as reinforced concrete and massive sheets of glass, allowed the abandonment of much that was traditional in architecture. Need for new kinds of buildings, particularly for office use, and the growing cost of urban space also encouraged the introduction of new forms, such as the skyscraper, pioneered in the United States. In general the modern style of architecture sought to develop individually distinct buildings—sharing the goal of modern art to defy conventional taste and cultivate the unique—while conveying a sense of space and freedom from natural constraints. Soaring structures, free-floating columns, and new combinations of angles and curves were features that described leading Western buildings in the 20th century.

Artistic innovation thus played an important role in Western society in the 20th century. Inherently controversial, it seemed to provide an alternative to the regularized world of mechanized industry and rationalistic science. The result has been no unified culture but rather a set of tensions and options that can be creative for society as a whole, as well as meaningful to many individuals.

There were a few unifying themes between the artistic and the scientific approaches, as both explored elements of the human unconscious or reflected a growing uncertainty about the benevolence and clear rationality of nature and human nature. A continual quest for the new was another feature, as artists sought new styles and scientists sought new discoveries. Furthermore, Western culture in the 20th century, both in art and in science, became increasingly secular. Individual artists, writers, and scientists might proclaim religious faith, but the churches generally lost control over basic style or content.

Western culture was not a monopoly of European civilization in the 20th century. Western art forms, particularly in architecture, spread widely, because of their practicality and their currency in what remained a highly influential society. The achievements of Western science, at least those related to technology and medicine, often had to be taken into account by societies seeking their own industrial development. Although the internationalization of 20th-century Western culture quickened after 1950, outreach developed in the interwar decades as well. No other culture, not even the Japanese, created quite the same balance between an overwhelming interest in science and a frenzied concern for stylistic innovation and individual expression in the arts.

THE NEW NATIONS OF EAST-CENTRAL EUROPE

Many of the problems and reactions visible in western Europe during the interwar period also affected the new nations of east-central Europe, though here the challenge of building new political regimes and the predominantly agrarian character of the economy complicated the situation even in the 1920s. Most of the new

nations looked to western Europe for political inspiration at first, and all were hostile to the new Communist regime in the Soviet Union. "Westernization," however, proved difficult, particularly when the West itself was so troubled.

Most of the new nations, from the Baltic states to Yugoslavia, were consumed by nationalist excitement at independence but also harbored intense grievances about territories they had not acquired. Hence there were bitter rivalries among the eastern European states, which weakened them both diplomatically and economically. Most of the new nations began the interwar period with some form of parliamentary democracy, in imitation of the West, but soon converted to authoritarian rule, either through a dictator (as in Poland) or by a monarch's seizure of new power (as in Yugoslavia, the new nation expanded from Serbia). This political pattern resulted from more underlying social tensions. Most eastern European countries remained primarily agricultural, heavily dependent on sales to western Europe. They were hard hit by the collapse of agricultural prices in the 1920s and then further damaged by the depression. Furthermore, most countries also refused to undertake serious land reform, despite widely professed intentions. Aristocratic estate owners thus sought desperately to repress peasant movements, which brought them to support authoritarian regimes, which often had vaguely Fascist trappings. Peasant land hunger and continued problems of poverty and illiteracy were simply not addressed in most cases.

The massive political and economic power of the landlords combined with low agricultural prices and economic pressure to maintain social tensions throughout the period. In Hungary 0.7 percent of the population owned 48.3 percent of the land; in Poland 0.6 percent owned 43 percent. Overall, 70 percent of the peasants in eastern Europe possessed less than 12.5 acres of land, enough for a bare subsistence at best. In Romania, the one non-Communist country where land reform did occur after 1918 (only 7 percent of the land remained in large holdings), 50 percent of the peasantry held less than 7.5 acres. Without capital or education, Romanian peasants were unable to produce for the market and returned to a near-subsistence economy. Here and elsewhere up to one-third of all children died before reaching two years of age, reflecting the impoverished housing and diet available.

Only Czechoslovakia stood as an exception to these regional patterns. Here an unusually advanced industrialization process and extensive urban culture, combined with substantial land reform, produced the basis for

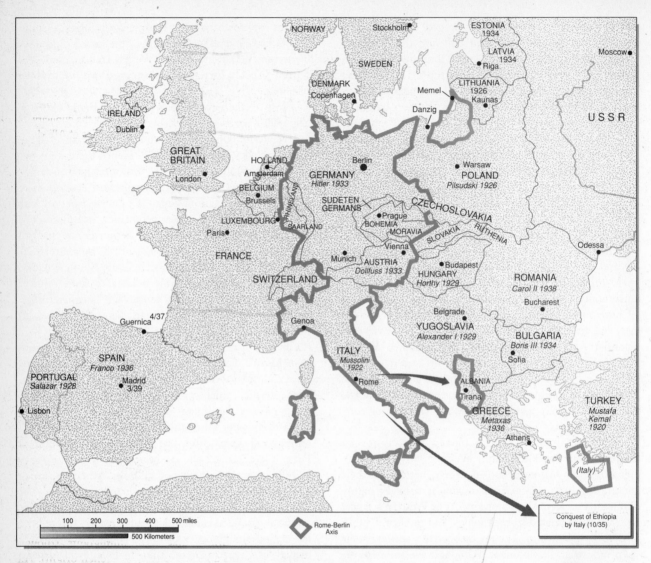

Central and Eastern Europe and the Spread of Fascism in the 1930s

an effective parliamentary-democratic regime. Only Czechoslovakia clearly maintained the east-central European borderland impulse to look primarily to the West for models and interaction. Most of the rest of eastern Europe remained caught between Western patterns that seemed impossible or irrelevant and a revolutionary Soviet Union now feared for both its communism and its Russian strength. The situation was predictably impossible. Although interwar experience served to enhance nationalist loyalties, it did not create a viable economic or diplomatic system for the region.

Then came the Nazi attack and ineffective Western response. Czechoslovakia, Poland, and Yugoslavia were overrun by German or Italian forces. Several other eastern European authoritarians allied directly with Hitler because of shared ideological leanings, a fear of the Soviet Union, and Germany's great economic voice as primary importer and exporter. One way or another, eastern Europe fell under Nazi control for four years. It was compelled to provide troops and labor service and was also involved in Hitler's attacks on the Jews. The next chapter in the region's troubled history came with the invasion of the Soviet armies in 1944, which led to new border changes and decisively new political regimes and social systems. Soviet armies were responsible for liberating all of eastern Europe and the eastern part of Ger-

Sober-faced and weeping Czechs watch the entry of the Nazi armies into Prague in the fall of 1938, as Hitler completes the takeover of the tiny democracy that was betrayed by the duplicity and cowardice of Allied leaders.

many to the Elbe river, except for Greece and Yugoslavia, thus remaking the Eastern European map. Throughout east-central Europe, the postwar years brought fundamental changes, even beyond the installation of new leadership and intensive involvement in the jockeyings of the cold war.

THE WEST OUTSIDE EUROPE: THE BRITISH COMMONWEALTH AND THE UNITED STATES

By 1900 societies profoundly shaped by Western institutions and culture had developed in several parts of the world distant from Europe. These extensions of the West were not, of course, mere European replicas. They embraced different populations, such as the native Maoris in New Zealand and both Native Americans and African-Americans in the United States, and were affected by their recent frontier experiences. Nevertheless, Canada, Australia, New Zealand, and the United States were Western in basic respects, beginning with the fact that the population majority in each case was of European origin; all aligned closely with the diplomatic and economic conflicts of Western society during the first

half of the 20th century. All, finally, came into new world prominence, starting with their roles in World War I, providing a vital new ingredient to both world and Western history.

Canada, Australia, and New Zealand had all been colonial territories of Great Britain and were heavily populated by British and Irish immigrants (though Canada also had a large minority of French origin). All three had developed increasing self-government during the 19th century. From this trend came the concept of a British commonwealth of nations, which would maintain the links that derived from a common British colonial background but adjust for effective national independence. This idea was first broached in an imperial conference in London in 1887 and discussed further at subsequent sessions. By 1914 all three regions had won effective independence—Australia, for example, became a unified and independent federation in 1901—with strong parliamentary governments. Their participation in World War I, at Britain's side, furthered the idea of a commonwealth, and another imperial conference in 1921 agreed that the self-governing dominions should be considered coequals with Britain in international affairs. A 1926 resolution defined the dominions as "au-

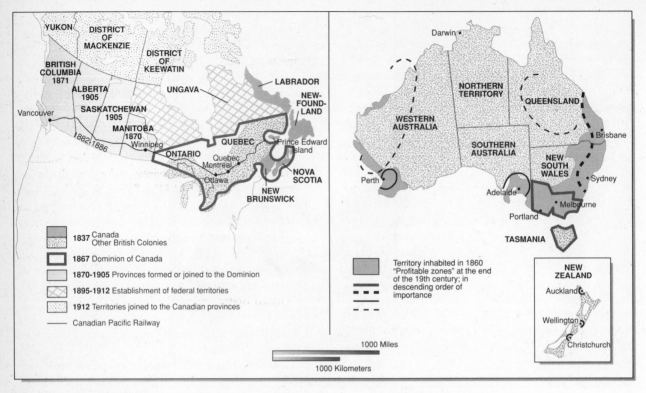

From Dominions to Nationhood: The Formation of Canada, Australia, and New Zealand

tonomous communities" within the British Empire, equal in status, in no way subordinate one to another in any aspect of their domestic or external affairs, though united by a common allegiance to the (British) crown, and freely associated as members of the British Commonwealth of Nations. British representation in the dominions, aside from the symbolic monarchy, consisted of a governor-general with no real authority.

Canada was developing not only its national politics but also an increasingly vibrant economy during the early years of the 20th century. Completion of the Canadian Pacific Railway by 1905 spurred rapid development in the western prairie provinces. Exploitation of mineral and forest resources joined with abundant production of wheat, as Canada exported food widely to Europe, as well as minerals and wood pulp to various areas, particularly the United States. Canadian development was marked also by rapid immigration, particularly from eastern Europe. Between 1903 and 1914, 2.7 million immigrants entered Canada, and as late as 1941, 40 percent of the population of the prairie provinces was of central or eastern European origin. French Canadians, centered in the province of Quebec, also increased their representation through one of the highest birthrates in the world, becoming a full quarter of the total Canadian population.

Vibrant as it was, the Canadian economy was overshadowed by that of its giant neighbor to the south. By 1914 almost one-quarter of all U.S. foreign investments were concentrated in Canada, and although British investments loomed larger, U.S. involvement cut a growing swath. Concentrated initially in Canadian mines and transportation, U.S. capital expanded into manufacturing during and after World War I. Canadian automobile production, for example, was simply an extension of U.S. corporations. Outright diplomatic relations with the United States eased in the same period. A joint commission was established between the two nations in 1909, charged with issuing binding decisions regarding water use (in shared lakes and rivers) and any other controversy referred to it by both countries. Boundary disputes, often contentious in the 19th century, virtually disappeared. Relations between Canada and the United States settled into a pattern of substantial harmony combined with a marked disparity in economic and cultural power that left many Canadians uneasy.

Canada's economic position suffered greatly during the Great Depression, precisely because it depended so heavily on sales of resources to industrial areas such as the United States. Exports fell by more than 65 percent. Serious political strife was averted, however, as Canada's major political parties were firmly committed to the parliamentary system.

World War I brought Canada international status as a mature democracy. The Ottawa government immediately backed Britain in the war, and 600,000 Canadians (of a population of nine million) served in the nation's military forces. Canada gained a seat at the Versailles peace conference and subsequently participated actively in the League of Nations. When World War II broke out, Canada again quickly allied with Britain, whose survival was seen as vital to Canadian interests. The Canadian economy also provided essential service in the war effort, as exports soared and manufacturing expanded. Canada contributed actively to the formation of the United Nations and other international measures at the war's end, though increasingly aligned more with U.S. than with British policy.

Australia's independence brought important developments in parliamentary institutions early in the 20th century. Like Canada, the new nation consisted of a federation of provinces. More than Canada, Australia strongly emphasized leadership in the field of social legislation. Welfare measures current in Britain and Germany were enacted during the 1890s and pressed forward in subsequent decades. A strong trade union movement prompted increasing attention to government-sponsored arbitration procedures. The government was also active in economic planning, for the country had limited arable land but depended heavily on agricultural exports. Government ownership included railways and shipping lines, banks, and power plants.

Participation in World War I gave Australia a new international role and a new sense of national pride. Rapid immigration contributed to a vigorous economy that was, however, severely damaged by the 1930s depression. World War II brought the realization that Britain was no longer capable of defending the nation, and Australians welcomed a new defensive alliance with the United States against the Japanese threat. The U.S. economic role in the nation increased as well, and a close diplomatic alliance persisted into the cold war decades after the war's end.

New Zealand's cultural and economic ties to Great Britain were particularly strong as the nation developed its independent parliamentary tradition. Until after World War II the nation served as Britain's garden, providing massive agricultural exports, particularly mutton

The skyline of Toronto, one of North America's most beautiful and livable cities, manifests the spurt of industrial growth that spread throughout much of Canada in the interwar decades.

and wool. The government committed early to political democracy and granted the vote to women in 1893—leading the Western world in this respect. The New Zealand government worked to promote small, independent farming and developed substantial social legislation. Spurred by the depression's impact, the Labor party came to power in 1935 and extended the protective measures and insurance systems covering urban workers.

THE RISE OF THE AMERICAN COLOSSUS

Outside the evolving British Commonwealth, the United States served as a final extension of many aspects of Western society. Because of its size, population, and economic strength, the growing international role of the United States had even greater significance than the emergence of Canada, Australia, and New Zealand. Like these nations, the United States had developed extensive agricultural exports to western Europe, based on its rich and highly mechanized farms. More than the other nations, however, the United States had also emerged as a formidable industrial power, rivaling and then surpassing the rise of Germany in the later 19th century. Active imperialism, in the acquisition of territory in the Caribbean and the Pacific during the 1890s, further revealed the new stature of the United States as a world power.

The United States was late entering World War I, reflecting strong traditions of isolation. The war catapulted the United States into a leadership position, and the nation guided many of the provisions of the Versailles treaty. But the U.S. Senate rejected the treaty, and the United States retreated into an isolationist policy between the world wars, leavened only by participation in international economic and disarmament conferences. Interventionism in Latin America continued, though in the 1930s the United States tried to improve its relations with its southern neighbors and to substitute negotiation for big-stick diplomacy.

The U.S. presence in world affairs accelerated during the 1920s, however, in the economic and cultural realms. After a brief postwar readjustment, the U.S. economy boomed during the 1920s. Industrial production doubled between 1921 and 1929. Republican administrations fostered business growth through high tariffs and low taxes on corporations and personal incomes. Many corporations merged into larger and more efficient conglomerates, and technological innovations spawned an increasing array of consumer goods for U.S. and world markets. Within the United States a new level of con-

sumerism developed, as growing numbers of the middle class bought automobiles and electric appliances. Radios and telephones spread even more widely. Humbler products, such as soap and cosmetics, won a growing mass market, and advertising reached new audiences to spur demand. Credit buying expanded, with enhanced reliance on installment buying.

Besides their sheer growth and their involvement in mass consumerism, U.S. corporations were innovators. Many corporations set up research and development programs, which helped generate new product lines, such as rayon and nylon—artificial fibers that soon rivaled silk in popularity. Organization of work systems combined with new technology to boost productivity. Henry Ford had introduced the assembly line in 1913, using conveyor belts to move automobile assembly through various routine stages, with semiskilled workers continuously repeating small tasks as the products moved toward completion. Engineers in the United States promoted efficiency studies, which treated workers like additional machinery to be rationalized as fully as possible. During the 1920s industrial psychologists found additional ways to boost output, studying the impact of piped-in music, for example, in unconsciously prompting workers to speed up their pace. Such methods were widely imitated abroad, not only in western Europe but also in the Soviet Union. With growing exports of grain and manufactured products, increasing international investment, and literal world leadership in organizational innovation, the international economic role of the United States gained ground steadily, in marked disparity to its isolationist diplomacy.

The 1920s also formed an important period in U.S. cultural development. For several decades U.S. artists had been participating actively in such Western painting styles as impressionism. This process continued, but U.S. artists increasingly experimented with abstraction. Major writers, such as T. S. Eliot and Ernest Hemingway, did most of their work in Europe, expressing a certain alienation from mainstream U.S. culture but also contributing to the national booklist. During the 1920s, as the Great Migration of African-Americans from southern farms to northern cities reached a crescendo, an important black cultural movement arose—the Harlem Renaissance. Poets and novelists, such as Langston Hughes, worked to capture the culture of their people. The rise of jazz, which originated in New Orleans, contributed a vital new musical genre. Architects also contributed new themes, building on the skyscrapers first introduced in Chicago before World War I.

Frank Lloyd Wright pioneered a variety of modern designs.

Its culture was increasingly exported, as the United States began to give as well as to receive in this vital area. Jazz quickly caught on in Europe; U.S. artists and writers participated in an increasingly internationalized Western culture. But it was in the area of popular culture that the United States made its greatest mark. As the first mass-consumer society, the United States led the way in a number of marketing and advertising developments. The dime store, for example, spread to England and was copied in France and Germany as a major outlet for low-cost mass merchandise. Hollywood became the world capital of the popular movie industry during the 1920s. Movies quickly began to play a vital role in U.S. culture, with 40 million viewers attending a film at least once a week in 1922; by 1929 that number had risen to 100 million. Hollywood stars—some born in Europe, such as Charlie Chaplin, Greta Garbo, and Rudolph Valentino—became symbols of comedy or sexuality throughout the Western world and beyond. Just as Britain had served as an international source of new sports in the later 19th century, so the United States now led in provision of commercial spectacles. Even its dance crazes, such as the Charleston, quickly spread to European centers, in an increasingly fad-conscious culture.

With all these signs of vigor, the United States also showed the symptoms of disturbingly rapid change. New relations between the genders were furthered by the granting of female suffrage in 1920. Women began to participate more fully in public entertainments, wearing new and more daring dresses and often smoking and drinking. Novel behaviors, such as teen-age dating, challenged 19th-century notions of strict sexual decorum in public. Although "going all the way" remained atypical, gradations of "necking" and "petting" became increasingly liberal. The continued growth of big cities posed another kind of challenge to rural and small-town populations. Emotional standards were changing as well. Nineteenth-century middle-class U.S. men had been urged toward assertiveness and courage. Now the emphasis on management harmony within a corporation and the growth of sales jobs stressed a more plastic, controlled personality. Dale Carnegie began a successful career in teaching Americans how to be cheerful salespeople in the 1920s, arguing that people-pleasing, not sincere conviction, was the key to the economic kingdom.

The interwar decades saw the rise of the star system in Europe and North America and the explosion of mass audiences for films, big bands, and (as this photo from a 1942 production attests) a succession of dance crazes.

Many people responded to change by casting about for new ways to slow the pace. The Ku Klux Klan, previously a southern organization directed mainly against political claims by blacks, now spread to other parts of the country as a means of shoring up more traditional values through intimidation and often violence. The United States acted to shut down immigration, with a restrictive law of 1923. A "red scare" focused new anxieties about political radicalism amid the aftermath of the Russian Revolution. Hostility to labor strikes and trade unionism, a common theme of Western capitalism in the 1920s, was particularly fierce in the United States. The Socialist movement, a small but promising third party before World-War I, withered in this attack against "un-American" politics. The United States became the only Western nation without a significant labor party. And, of course, isolationism expressed a fervent desire for a return to a simpler past—what in the 1920s was called "normalcy"—in foreign policy. A series of lackluster Republican presidents reassured the country that significant political and diplomatic change could be avoided.

The depression of 1929 brought change with a vengeance, however. President Herbert Hoover joined many business experts in first attributing little significance to the stock market crash—"I see nothing in the present situation that is either menacing or warranting pessimism." But several years of deepening economic chaos produced a major political realignment, as the Democratic party and Franklin Delano Roosevelt rode to power in 1932. As in Scandinavia, people in the United States showed themselves willing to combine commitment to the existing political system with new directions in government policy. Roosevelt's New Deal greatly expanded the role of the state. New economic planning boards, direct government public works projects, a social security system to assist the elderly and the unemployed all created a modest but definite U.S. version of the welfare state. The bargaining rights of labor unions received new protection, and trade unionism gained ground rapidly. The New Deal did not resolve the depression—only war-oriented employment would accomplish this feat, by 1940. It did, however, mark a milestone in U.S. political history, permanently changing the role of the state in U.S. society, and it allowed most people to retain basic confidence in their political and economic system.

This confidence, in turn, was fundamental to the U.S. ability to gear up for war, despite continued commitment to isolationism in official policy, and then to respond to the Japanese attack in 1941 with full-fledged entry into World War II in both the European and Asian theaters. And with U.S. success in the war, from late 1942 onward, the world power the nation had been projecting for years in the economic and cultural spheres was now joined with a dominant international military and diplomatic presence.

JAPAN AND ITS EMPIRE

One final area of the world participated in many of the same trends as did Western Europe, the Commonwealth nations, and the United States during the first decades of the 20th century. Japan was decidedly not a Western nation, either by origin or adoption. It had, however, become an industrial power and had replaced its traditional, feudal government with a regime in which ministers appointed by the emperor combined, sometimes uneasily, with a parliament. The Japanese government in 1900 was not totally unlike that of Germany, except that the vote was much more restricted. Like Germany and other Western nations, Japan would see its new political institutions tested by war and depression; like Germany and Italy its commitment to the parliamentary form would decline under this test. In the 1930s Japan turned to a more adventurous foreign policy in response to economic challenge and political change—again, like many nations in the West.

The interwar years were not simply a time of crisis for Japan, however. During the 1920s, particularly, new cultural developments, an expanding economy, and a growing commitment to liberal democracy produced important currents as well—ones that could be called on after the crisis period had ended.

During the initial decades of the 20th century, Japan concentrated heavily on diplomatic and military gains, as well as the difficult process of adjusting to the parliamentary, constitutional government established during the Meiji period. During the 1890s the various branches of the central government had faced serious problems of cooperation, as opposition parties in the Parliament tried to gain ground at the expense of the executive ministries. In 1900 the government leaders formed their own political party, winning a majority in the lower house of Parliament. Over the next 22 years the leadership party struggled to maintain a working majority against various opposition factions. Japan was by this point an expansionist power, having formally annexed Korea in 1910. Japan ruled its new Asian colonies firmly, exacting considerable taxes and raw materials while securing markets for its growing industrial output. In no sense did the new Japanese empire lead directly to a united or vigorous Pacific Rim, though the disruption of established dependence on China did add an important new ingredient to Korean development.

JAPAN'S ONGOING DEVELOPMENT

Along with international gains came continued industrial advance. Japanese industry continued to lag behind Western levels, relying heavily on low-wage labor and the export of a relatively small number of items, such as silk cloth; silk production, at 16 million pounds in 1900, soared to 93 million pounds in 1929. Agricultural productivity improved steadily, led by progressive landlords who introduced fertilizers and new equipment. Rice production more than doubled between the 1880s and the 1930s. Modern industry advanced more slowly, though it passed well beyond the pilot phase of the late 19th century. Great industrial combines—the *zaibatsu*—sponsored rapid expansion in such fields as shipbuilding, usually relying heavily on tight links with the government bureaucracy, but there were daring individual entrepreneurs as well. Between 1905 and 1918 Japan enjoyed a considerable industrial boom, with rapid advances not only in light industries, such as silk, but also in electrical power, iron, and coal. Japanese life ex-

pectancy began to improve, fueled by a higher standard of living. A popular consumer culture emerged, at least in the cities, as workers began to attend movies and read newspapers. Education advanced rapidly, with primary-school attendance universal in the relevant age groups by 1925. Enrollments in secondary schools and technical colleges swelled, improving the nation's capacity to assimilate the newer Western technologies.

Limits on Japanese economic advance included vulnerability to economic conditions abroad. Because Japan exported relatively few items to the West but continued to require considerable imports of raw materials, including fuels and sophisticated equipment, a slump in demand for a product such as silk cloth could be disastrous. In this sense Japan bore some resemblance to dependent economies in the world, despite industrial progress. Population growth was another burden, or at least a mixed blessing. Japan's population soared from 30 million in 1868 to 45 million in 1900 and then to 73 million by 1940. This was a tribute to agricultural advance, as the size of the farm population remained constant, and it facilitated a low-wage industrial economy. It also restricted further improvements in the standard of living and created considerable social dislocation in the crowded, migrant-filled cities. Periodic protests through strikes, demonstrations, and some Socialist agitation

Bright lights, neon signs, the big city. In outward appearance, at least, the Ginza district in Tokyo, Japan, in the 1920s shared much with the urban centers of Europe and North America.

were met with vigorous police response. Conditions worsened (see Chapter 5) in the first phase of the Great Depression of the 1930s. The economy recovered quickly, however, under the twin stimuli of a new export boom and government-organized military procurement as Japan began to beef up its war machine.

Indeed, Japan made a full turn toward industrialization after 1931, its economy growing much more rapidly than that of the West and rivaling the surge of the Soviet Union. Production of iron, steel, and chemicals soared. The spread of electric power was the most rapid in the world. The number of workers, mainly men, in the leading industries rose sevenfold during the 1930s. Quality of production increased as well, as Japanese manufacturing goods began to rival those of the West; assembly-line methods were introduced.

Japan also initiated a series of new industrial policies designed to stabilize the labor force and prevent social unrest. These paralleled the growing emphasis on mass patriotism and group loyalty developed by the government. Big companies began to offer lifetime contracts to a minority of skilled workers and to develop company entertainments and other activities designed to promote hard work and devotion. These distinctive Japanese policies, not part of its initial industrialization, proved to be a durable feature of Japanese society.

By 1937 Japan boasted the third largest and the newest merchant marine in the world. The nation became self-sufficient in machine tools and scientific equipment, the fruit of the growth in technical training. The quality of Japanese industrial goods rose, producing the first Western outcry against Japanese exports—even though in 1936 the Japanese controlled only 3.6 percent of world trade. The basis had been set for the more significant economic surge of the later 20th century, delayed by Japan's dash into World War II.

POLITICAL CRISIS

While the economy gained, however, political crisis seized center stage, leading in turn to a new and risky round of military and diplomatic experiments that culminated in World War II. Social tensions played a role in this transition, as Japan moved farther from its basic tradition of noninvolvement in elaborate foreign ventures. Tokyo was virtually destroyed by an earthquake in 1923, and 100,000 people died. Six years later the initial impact of the depression caused great misery, as exports fell by two-thirds. Half of all factories were idled by 1931. Widespread poverty and fears of social unrest helped produce an atmosphere in which new measures, including military aggression, seemed essential. In some

The Rise and Spread of the Japanese Empire to the Outbreak of World War II

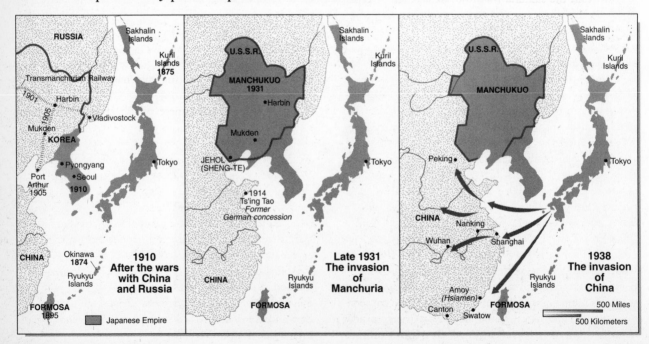

areas in 1931 children were reduced to begging for food from passing trains, and farmers were forced to eat the inner bark of pine trees. Despite these dire conditions, social protest did not surge to dangerous proportions, and the depression was soon successfully countered by an active government policy. As a result, Japan suffered far less than many Western nations did during the depression decade as a whole. Under the 1930s minister of finance, Korekiyo Takahashi, the government increased its spending to provide jobs, which in turn generated new demands for food and manufactured items, yielding not only the export boom but also the virtual elimination of unemployment by 1936. The same policy helped support government military purchasing, but it is not clear that this constituted an essential response.

The key to Japan's new initiatives rested rather with ongoing difficulties in assimilating a generally accepted political structure—difficulties that had not been resolved during the first decades of the 20th century. Military leaders began to take a growing role in setting general diplomatic policy from the mid-1920s onward, at the expense of the civilian parties and politicians. Japan's oligarchic political structure, in which elite groups negotiated with one another for appropriate policy rather than fully yielding to any single agency, such as Parliament, permitted this kind of realignment. From the Meiji period onward, military leaders, though largely weaned from the samurai tradition, had remained separate from the civilian bureaucracy. They were trained in separate schools and regarded themselves as true guardians of the modern Japanese state as well as older traditions. They reported not to civilian authority but directly to the emperor. Like military leaders in the West during the 1920s but with greater vigor, they resented what they regarded as the selfishness and accommodation to special interests of the political parties, as the latter increasingly resorted to mass political campaigns and vote-getting strategies. Reduction of military budgets during the 1920s hit military leaders hard, and army prestige declined to the point that officers wore civilian clothing when off base. Naval officers, at the same time, were appalled at decisions accepted from a Great Power naval conference in 1930 that limited fleet levels. In essence Japan experimented during the 1920s with a liberal political pattern, which seemed to give primacy to party maneuverings and electoral appeals but which also antagonized the military (and other conservative elite groups) while failing to subject them to new controls. This was the context in which military officials began to make separate decisions about Manchuria, leading to the 1931 seizure of this key Chinese region, while the civilian government tried to equivocate.

Then, as political divisions increased in response to the initial impact of the depression, a variety of nationalist groups emerged, some advocating a return to Shintoist or Confucian principles against the more Western values of urban Japan. This was more than a political response to the depression. As in Germany, a variety of groups used the occasion for a more sweeping protest against parliamentary forms; nationalism here seemed a counterpoise to alien Western values. Older military officers joined some bureaucrats in urging a more authoritarian state that could ignore party politics; some wanted further military expansion to protect Japan from the uncertainties of the world economy by providing secure markets.

In May 1932 a group of younger army officers attacked key government and banking officers and murdered the prime minister. They did not take over the state directly, but for the next four years moderate military leaders headed the executive branch, frustrating both the military firebrands and the political parties. Another attempted military coup in 1936 was put down by forces controlled by the established admirals and generals, but this group, including General Tojo Hideki, increasingly interfered with civilian cabinets, blocking the appointment of most liberal bureaucrats. The result, after 1936, was a series of increasingly militaristic prime ministers.

Japan gained a great deal of novel political experience during the 1920s and 1930s, and moderate political parties won widespread support. The Japanese people, though strongly nationalistic and loyal to the emperor, were not enthusiastic expansionists. These ingredients would re-emerge in Japanese politics after World War II. For the moment, however, the military superseded civilian politics, particularly when renewed wars broke out between Japan and China in 1937. By the end of 1938 Japan controlled a substantial regional empire, including Manchuria, Korea, and Taiwan, within which the nation sold half its exports and from which it bought more than 40 percent of all imports, particularly food and raw materials. Both the military leadership, eager to justify further modernization of Japan's weaponry and to consolidate political control, and economic leaders, interested in rich resources of other parts of Asia—such as the rubber of British Malaya or the oil of the Dutch East Indies—soon pressed for wider conquests as Japan surged into World War II.

DOCUMENT:
JAPAN AND THE
LOSS OF WORLD
WAR II

Japan's defeat obviously brought a great deal of moral as well as material confusion. The government was so uncertain of the intentions of the victorious Americans that it evacuated its female employees to the countryside. The following document, from the 1945 diary of Miss Hisako Yoshizawa, who became a writer on home economics, indicates something of more popular attitudes and the mixed ingredients that composed them. The passage also suggests how the U.S. occupation force tried to present itself and the reception it received.

August 15. As I listened to the Emperor's voice announcing the surrender, every word acquired a special meaning and His Majesty's voice penetrated my mind. Tears streamed down my cheeks. I kept on telling myself that we must not fight ourselves and work hard for our common good. Yes, I pledged myself, I must work [for Japan's recovery.]

The city was quiet.

I could not detect any special expression in people's faces. Were they too tired? However, somehow they seemed brighter, and I could catch an expression showing a sign of relief. It could have been a reflection of my own feelings. But I knew I could trust what I saw. . . .

The voluntary fighting unit was disbanded, and I was no longer a member of that unit. Each of us burned the insignia and other identifications.

I cannot foresee what kind of difficulty will befall me, but all I know is that I must learn to survive relying on my health and my will to live.

August 16. People do not wear expressions any different from other days. However, in place of a "good morning" or "good afternoon," people are now greeting each other with the phrase "What will become of us?"

During the morning, the city was still placed under air-raid alert.

My company announced that until everything becomes clearer, no female employees were to come to work, and urged all of us to go to the countryside, adding that we should leave forwarding addresses. This measure was taken to conform to the step already taken by governmental bureaus. Are they thinking that the occupation army will do something to us girls? There are so many important questions we have to cope with, I cannot understand why governmental officials are so worried about these matters.

We did not have enough power and lost the war.

The Army continued to appeal to the people to resist the enemy to the end. This poses a lot of problems. People can show their true colors better when they are defeated than when they win. I just hope we, as a nation, can show our better side now.

Just because we have been defeated, I do not wish to see us destroying our national characteristics when we are dealing with foreign countries.

August 17. It was rumored that a number of lower echelon military officers were unhappy with the peace, and were making some secret moves. There were other rumors, and with the quiet evacuation of women and children from the cities, our fear seemed to have intensified. After all we have never experienced a defeat before. Our fear may simply be the manifestation of fear of the unknown.

Our airplanes dropped propaganda leaflets.

One of the leaflets was posted at the Kanda Station which said: "Both the Army and Navy are alive and well. We expect the nation to follow our lead." The leaflet was signed. I could understand how those military men felt. However, we already have the imperial rescript to surrender. If we are going to rebuild, we must open a new path. It is much easier to die than to live. In the long history of our nation, this defeat may become one of those insignificant happenings. However, the rebuilding after the defeat is likely to be treated as a far more important chapter in our history.

We did our best and lost, so there is nothing we have to say in our own defense. Only those people who did not do their best may now be feeling guilty, though.

Mr. C. said that everything he saw in the city was so repugnant that he wanted to retreat to the countryside. I was amazed by the narrowness of his thought process. I could say that he had a pure sense of devotion to the country, but that was only his own way of thinking. Beautiful perhaps, but it lacked firm foundation. I wish men like him would learn to broaden their perspectives.

August 18. Rationed bread distribution in the morning. I went to the distribution center with Mrs. A.

August 21. We heard that the allied advance units will be airlifted and arrive in Japan on the 26th. And the following day, their fleet will also anchor in our harbors. The American Army will be airlifted and land in Atsugi airport.

According to someone who accompanied the Japanese delegation which went to accept surrender conditions, Americans behaved like gentlemen. They explained to the Americans that certain conditions were unworkable in light of the present situation in Japan. The Americans immediately agreed to alter those conditions. They listened very carefully to what the Japanese delegation had to say.

An American paper, according to someone, reported that meeting as follows: "We cooked thick beefsteak expecting seven or eight Japanese would appear. But seventeen of them came, so we had to kill a turkey to prepare for them. We treated them well before they returned. . . ." When I hear things like this, I immediately feel how exaggerated and inefficient our ways of doing things are. They say that

Americans will tackle one item after another at a conference table, and do not waste even 30 seconds.
. . .

In contrast, Japanese administration is conducted by many chairs and seals. For example when an auxiliary unit is asked to undertake a task for a governmental bureau, before anything can be done, twenty or thirty seals of approval must be secured. So there is no concept of not wasting time. Even in war, they are too accustomed to doing things the way they have been doing, and their many seals and chairs are nothing but a manifestation of their refusal to take individual responsibilities.

The fact of a defeat is a very serious matter and it is not easy to accept. However, it can bring some positive effects, if it can inculcate in our minds all the shortcomings we have had. I hope this will come true some day, and toward that end we must all endeavor. Even if we have to suffer hunger and other tribulations we must strive toward a positive goal.

Questions: How did Japanese attitudes in defeat help prepare Japan for postwar redevelopment? What other kinds of reactions might have been expected? How would you explain the rather calm and constructive outlook the passage suggests? Would American reactions to a Japanese victory have been similar?

JAPAN'S EMPIRE

The interwar decades and World War II were significant for the areas in eastern Asia brought under Japanese control. Japan's firm domination over Korea from 1910 onward created important resentments, and Japanese economic policies did little to stimulate major new developments in the Korean economy. The period of Japanese rule disrupted Korean traditions, including the tendency to look toward Chinese superiority and the fact of monarchy itself. Prior to full Japanese annexation in 1910, the Korean king had attempted to protest growing interference, but Western powers had ignored his appeals. The Japanese had replaced the monarch with his feebleminded son in 1908, and then, when a Korean patriot assassinated the resident general in 1909, they abolished the monarchy altogether. Korea's elabo-

rate court aristocracy was undermined in this process. Colonial status, which lasted until Japan's World War II defeat in 1945, prevented the generation of new, alternative institutions, but there was new potential for innovation after the long centuries of Yi dynasty rule.

Economically and culturally, the Japanese annexation of Korea ushered in an era of virtually unchecked exploitation of its land and people. For most of the three and one-half decades the Japanese ruled the peninsula, it was governed by military leaders, who put down all resistance quite brutally. Almost from the outset, the Japanese launched a concerted effort to suppress Korean culture and promote adoption of Japanese ways. Korean-language newspapers were banned; Korean teachers were required to wear Japanese uniforms and carry swords, and Japanese money, weights and measures, and language instruction were introduced throughout the coun-

During the early stages of World War II in Asia, the Japanese bombed Shanghai, China, in 1937.

try. Korean resources were put at the disposal of Japanese industrialists, many of whom invested in factories in the new colony. The Korean peasantry was compelled to concentrate on rice production for export to Japan and other foreign markets. With much of their labor devoted to producing rice for others to eat, the impoverished Koreans increasingly found that they could afford only millet (a grain they had traditionally considered quite inferior to rice) for their own consumption. In the Great Depression, when the world market for rice contracted rapidly and the price plunged as a consequence, the concentration on rice production proved disastrous. The long-suffering Korean peasant bore the brunt of the misery caused by Japanese miscalculations.

Peasants also bore the brunt of the Japanese effort to speed up exploitation of Korea's resources and labor as the Japanese advanced into China in the late 1930s and the Pacific war with the United States approached. Korea became the strategic pivot of Japanese empire-building in East Asia, a vast warehouse devoted to supplying Japanese military forces. Army officers instructed the dreaded Japanese military police to forcibly conscript increasing numbers of Korean youths for labor gangs and troops to support their expanding war effort. The population was exhorted to join the Japanese people in "training to endure hardship." Japanese military rituals were given great prominence, and the cult of the Japanese god-emperor was celebrated in schools and community centers across the colony. Throughout the 1930s and early 1940s, the Korean people were forced to endure hardships and the loss of tens of thousands of youths for an emperor who had usurped the powers of their own and a cause that had nothing to do with them. The state in which the long Japanese occupation left the country only prolonged the suffering and multiplied the casualties.

Overall, the first decades of the 20th century brought important changes to various parts of East Asia, largely though not exclusively as the result of new Japanese initiatives. China, long the dominant East Asian force, was consumed by its complex process of internal revolution and was of course itself beset by the Japanese; it lost much of its traditional regional hold in the process. Japan led the way in economic development, despite difficulties and setbacks, gaining new international and regional importance—witness its unusual ability to bounce back from the depression as most Western nations foundered. World War II obviously increased pressures for change in the region, as the Japanese temporarily dislodged Western colonial rule in such places as Malaya and Vietnam. Japan's defeat, and the hostility it had generated in its colonies along with admiration for its ability to defy the West, challenged the patterns that had developed by 1945, while ensuring the need for further change.

<hr>

CONCLUSION

THE INDUSTRIAL WORLD IN THE WAKE OF WORLD WAR II

The decades between 1914 and 1945 were disastrous in much of the industrial world. War now cost countless lives, destroyed confidence, and shattered economies. Promising new starts in Japan, Europe, and the United States alike, were shadowed in the 1920s by deep structural problems and a host of new uncertainties. The depression and renewed war confirmed the chaos of industrial society.

These troubled decades had permanent consequences, most obviously in steadily reducing western Europe's ability to control its colonial empires. Though the West ultimately accepted decolonization, more or less begrudgingly, there is no question that the process signaled a durable weakening of western Europe's world role or that many Westerners were agonizingly affected by the loss of cherished emblems of greatness. The advent of nuclear weaponry was another blatant threat, and many people in various parts of the world assumed that a major atomic war was virtually inevitable once the Soviet Union joined the United States in producing the dreaded bomb. Even optimistic Americans went through a period of several years of dread, under the ominous atomic shadow.

Yet the period of wars and depression did not produce the steady downward spiral for industrial societies that many had anticipated in the late 1930s. Indeed,

most industrial societies were doing much better by the mid-1950s than could have been anticipated in 1939 or 1945, as strong economic growth resumed and political tensions eased. Although most of these developments belong to the later 20th-century history of the West and Japan, their relationship to the decades of chaos can be clarified at this point.

Several societies, obviously, were directly strengthened by their role in World War II. The United States, Canada, and Australia suffered great strain in the war, but their economies boomed, as the Great Depression yielded to wartime military spending, and their people found new purpose in the defense of democracy against the Nazi and Japanese threat. The United States lost 300,000 troops in the war, which was deeply distressing, but overall population gained ground with the onset of a new surge in the birthrate—the famous baby boom, which lasted through the 1950s. The nation was unquestionably the world's leading power by 1945. By 1947 the U.S. had replaced Britain as the West's leading world policeman. The location of the new United Nations in New York expressed both U.S. determination to avoid the policy blunders of the post–World War I era and to maintain the role of the United States on the world scene.

The war produced great devastation in Japan and western Europe, and for several years agonizing reconstruction seemed to consume all available energy. The rise of the United States and the Soviet Union constituted yet another blow, as the new superpowers dwarfed the once proud states of western Europe militarily and diplomatically. Yet there were hopeful signs as well. On balance, the U.S. occupation of Japan proved constructive, leading to important changes in Japanese politics and society without destroying a distinctive national tone. The United States also contributed to the rebuilding of Europe, from a combination of generosity and a desire to support allies in a looming conflict with the Soviet Union. Germany, like Japan, benefited from this assistance and from accompanying pressures for reform.

The industrial societies also displayed a surprising capacity to rebuild on their own, and wartime destruction of property was not as great as military leaders—led by air force generals bent on arguing for the effectiveness of mass bombing raids—had proclaimed. Only 18 percent of Germany's industrial capacity had been wiped out, for example, though its transportation network was crippled.

More important still, new forces had been gathering during the 1930s and throughout the war itself that found expression in the years after 1945. Amid depression and political stalemate, new kinds of business leaders and politicians had been coming of age. In France, for example, these newcomers had been too young to take over the reins of leadership before the Nazi invasion but were ready to plan for a different future. Britain had been quietly building new economic sectors by the late 1930s, pioneering, for example, in the television industry, that would serve as the basis for economic growth later on. Japan's economy had prospered during the 1930s, as technology advanced. Even Nazi Germany inadvertently set the seeds for more constructive later change. The regime attacked traditional institutions, weakening the hold of old-line aristocrats and business magnates on the student bodies of universities and the offices of government. Continued economic growth undermined some backward sectors, such as the urban crafts and peasant agriculture, even though the Nazis voiced support for these traditional groups. Germany was poised for a newer kind of society, after the hideous Nazi interlude.

The war brought further sources of change. In Canada, the United States, and Britain, women gained new economic roles in the wartime economy. Although these gains would be briefly undermined at war's end, they proved to be the forerunners of a durable change in women's participation in the labor force. British coalition governments during the war planned a fuller version of the welfare state as a deliberate means of rewarding working-class loyalty to the war effort and preventing some of the disastrous social tensions that had marred the interwar decades. In France, the Netherlands, Denmark, and even Italy, movements of resistance to German occupation and to fascism enunciated new goals for postwar Europe. Again, the aim was to place new leaders at the helm and to attack the basic causes of collapse between the wars. Although resistance leaders hardly agreed on a single platform, most were committed to new economic and social welfare measures, and many pointed to a reduction of nationalist conflict in a new Europe as well.

The legacy of decades of conflict and collapse has not been easily wiped away. It lingers in the West and Japan even in the 1990s. Yet dreadful as the consequences were, they did not predict the next half century. Not only would the new world powers—the United States, Canada, and Australia—flourish but also Japan would resume its industrial advance, even while changing its political and diplomatic course. Western Europe would rise again, resuming, against widespread assumptions as World War II ended, a major economic, political, and cultural role in world affairs.

FURTHER READINGS

For an excellent general survey of European history in this period, see Robert Paxton's *Europe in the 20th Century* (1985). On Europe between the wars, Charles Maier's *Recasting Bourgeois Europe* (1975) is a penetrating comparative approach. On fascism and nazism, see F. Carsten's *The Rise of Fascism* (1980) and S. Payne's *Fascism: Comparison and Definition* (1984). David Schoenbaum's *Hitler's Social Revolution* (1980) is an excellent study of how nazism worked in practice. See also Gerald Fleming's *Hitler and the Final Solution* (1984), on the Holocaust. R. Stromberg's *Intellectual History of Modern Europe* (1966) and K. D. Bracher's *Age of Ideologies: A History of Political Thought in the Twentieth Century* (1989) provide a factual framework in a complex area. See also H. S. Hughes's *Consciousness and Society* (1976).

On the British Commonwealth nations, Roderick Cameron's *Australia, History and Horizons* (1971) is a useful overview; see also the essays in Stephen Graubard, ed., *Australia: Terra Incognita?* (1985). See also Colin MacInnes's *Australia and New Zealand* (1966). On Canada, see Gerald Craig's *The United States and Canada* (1968) and Mason Wase's *The French Canadians* (1955). Seymour M. Lipset, *North American Culture: Values and Institutions in Canada and the United States* (1990) is a comparative study. The best overview of the New Zealand experience remains Keith Sinclair's *A History of New Zealand* (1969).

For the United States, William Leuchtenburg's *The Perils of Prosperity* (1958) is an important account of the 1920s; for a more general view of basic changes, Morris Janowitz's *The Last Half Century: Political and Societal Change in the United States* (1970) is a useful account. For a case study of social and political change, see Lizabeth Cohen's *Making a New Deal: Industrial Workers in Chicago, 1919–1939* (1990). See also William Chafe's *Women and Equality: Changing Patterns in American Culture* (1984).

On Japan in the period, see P. Duus's *Party Rivalry and Political Change in Taisho Japan* (1968) on the 1910s and 1920s; also see R. H. Myers and M. R. Peattie, eds., *The Japanese Colonial Empire, 1895–1945* (1984); A. Ohkawa and H. Rosovsky, *Japanese Economic Growth: Trend Acceleration in the Twentieth Century* (1973).

Latin America

1920–1940 Mexican muralist movement active

1910–1920 Mexican Revolution
1910 Madero's revolt
1911 Zapata promises land reform
1914 Panama Canal opens

1917 Mexican Constitution includes revolutionary changes

1929 Women get the right to vote in Ecuador

Soviet Union

1918 Defeated Russia withdraws from World War I

1918–1919 Independent smaller nations in eastern Europe

1917 Russian Revolution; Bolshevik takeover (October)

1921 Lenin's New Economic Policy

1923 New constitution in Russia

1928 Beginning of collectivization of agriculture and five-year plans

1927 Stalin in full power

China and Vietnam

1912 Fall of the Qing dynasty in China

1921 Communist party of China founded

1919 May Fourth Movement begins; founding of Guomindang or Nationalist party

1911 Revolution in China

1929 Failed VNQDD-inspired uprising

1925 VNQDD founded in Vietnam; first Communist organization established in Vietnam

1927 Nationalists capture Shanghai; purge of Communists and workers

Forces of Revolution and Repression in Mexico, Russia, China, and Vietnam

7

INTRODUCTION. The agonies of the world's industrial societies during the middle phase of the 20th century constituted one crucial trend, with implications well beyond the borders of Europe, the United States, and Japan. Another dramatic pattern taking shape in roughly the same years also had profound global effects—the wave of revolutions that would periodically shake up domestic politics and especially international relations for much of the rest of the century. Beginning in Russia and China nearly a decade before the outbreak of World War I in 1914, revolutionary movements threatened one of the oldest dynasties in Europe, the Romanovs in Russia, and in China overthrew a civilization that had flourished and endured for more than two thousand years. Widespread revolution also engulfed Mexico from 1910 onward, and successive coups and renewed upheavals prolonged it into the late 1920s.

The awesome but seemingly senseless death and destruction of World War I gave new impetus to the revolutionary tide. It swept through eastern Europe, where the tsarist regime collapsed in early 1917 and the radical Bolsheviks seized power in late 1917. It gave rise to a Communist regime in

---

1934–1940 President Cárdenas enacts many of the reforms promised by the Mexican Revolution
1932 Women win voting rights in Cuba and Brazil
1938 Mexico nationalizes its petroleum resources
1933 Death of Augusto César Sandino, leader of Nicaraguan resistance to U.S. occupation
1942 Brazil joins the Allies; sends troops to Europe
1930 Revolution in Brazil brings Getúlio Vargas to power; Military takes control of the Argentine government

---

1936–1938 Stalin's great purges
1941–45 Yugoslav partisan resistance against fascist occupiers
1945 Victorious Soviet Union occupies eastern sectors of Germany
1939 Signing of Russo-German pact; Soviet invasion of eastern Poland and Finland
1943 Soviet army pushes west
1941 German invasion of Soviet Union

1931 Japanese invasion of Manchuria

1942 Japanese occupation of French Indochina

1930 Failed Communist uprising in Vietnam

1937 Japanese invasion of China proper

Hungary in 1919 that was crushed only with considerable outside intervention. The revolutionary wave threatened to engulf a defeated Germany in late 1918 and 1919 and struck China with renewed force after the May Fourth protests of 1919. Revolutionary slogans and sentiments—if not full-blown programs for social transformation—also fueled the anticolonial protest that spread through much of Africa and Asia. A new generation of more radical nationalist leaders emerged, epitomized by Gandhi in India and Zaghlul in Egypt, who are discussed in Chapter 8. Nationalist parties committed to violent resistance and more thoroughly revolutionary change than anticolonial movements elsewhere in Africa and Asia also arose in the 1920s in Vietnam. Though formally colonized by France, Vietnam shared much with its northern neighbor, China, in terms of revolutionary upheavals and persisting civil strife.

As these examples suggest, successful or attempted revolutions arose in a wide variety of societal situations during the first decades of the 20th century—former imperial powers (Russia and China), informally colonized societies (Mexico), and directly colonized areas (Vietnam). Revolutionary upheavals occurred in industrial, industrializing, and nonindustrial overwhelmingly agrarian societies. Notably, much of the industrial world was spared, despite wars and a global depression. Nonetheless, as we saw in Chapter 6, Italy and Germany and the only highly industrialized non-Western nation in this era, Japan, were captured by either Fascist demagogues or military dictators. In each case rightist reactionaries rose to power in part on promises to ward off the threat of revolution from the left. In these countries, as well as in France, Great Britain, and the United States, civil strife and related social disruption characterized this period, though not as much as in Mexico, Russia, and China, which all experienced massive and extended revolutionary transformations. In these and other societies engulfed by the revolutionary tide, the Great Depression and other international events were overshadowed by intense internal struggles until the late 1930s. From that point onward they, like both democratic and dictatorial industrialized powers, were caught up in the second round of catastrophic warfare that marked the end of three decades of profound global crisis.

Revolutionary forces invariably spilled over into neighboring and distant areas of the globe. Mexico's revolution was surprisingly isolated, given its scale and duration. But at various points the United States became deeply entangled; similarly, Britain and Germany sought to influence the direction of the Mexican explosion both before and during World War I. The Bolshevik victory in Russia had much more far-reaching implications for global history in the 20th century. To begin with, the Marxist-Leninist critique of capitalism and program for building a socialist society were for the first time enshrined in the ideology and policies of a powerful state. From the early 1920s the Bolshevik seizure of power and the Soviet programs for economic development and social change that followed proved key sources of inspiration for political dissidents in areas as diverse as the democracies of western Europe, strife-torn China, and Latin America. In addition, through a series of international organizations, the Soviets provided advice, training, and financial support for leftist political parties in other countries and the forces of anticolonialism throughout Africa and Asia. With the growing successes of the Communist party of China in the late 1930s and early 1940s, the Marxist-Leninist revolutionary vision, extensively reworked by Mao Zedong for preponderantly peasant societies like his own, took on a new relevance for the poverty-laden and technologically backward nations that emerged from Europe's former colonial empires.

The study of revolution has often focused on the violent struggles between dissident groups and the forces of the established order and the seizure of power by the former or the repression of protest by the latter. But the working through of revolutions requires much more extensive time periods. They are both a complex sequence of events and a persisting process that involve much more than a transfer of political power. Revolutions also lead to fundamental changes in the social structure, economic organization, and culture of the societies in which they occur. Thus different factions and social groups in Mexico continued to vie for power and concessions decades after the violent strife had ended. In fact, some observers argue that the revolution is still unfolding. Russia's revolutionary settlement extended at least into the 1930s, when Stalin systematically twisted revolutionary ideals and impulses into a brutal and highly bureaucratized police state. Though the Communists seized power in China in 1949, hard-fought, often violent struggles over revolutionary goals persisted, becoming particularly intense in the mid-1960s and 1970s. Again, many China watchers contend that they continue to the present day. Revolutions, in sum, represent long-term trajectories in the history of some of the world's most populous societies through much of the 20th century.

✠ REVOLUTION AND REACTION IN MEXICO AND LATIN AMERICA

Two cataclysmic events launched Latin America into the 20th century and set in motion trends that would determine much of the region's subsequent history. The first of these events was the Mexican Revolution, a ten-year civil war and political upheaval that erupted because of Mexico's internal situation. Eventually, however, the Mexican Revolution was also influenced by the other major event, the outbreak of World War I. Although most Latin American nations avoided direct participation in the Great War, as World War I was called at the time, the disruption of traditional markets for Latin American exports and the elimination of European sources of manufactures caused a realignment of the economies of a number of nations in the region. Forced to rely on themselves, a spurt of manufacturing continued the process begun after 1870, and some small steps were taken to overcome the traditional dependence on outside supply. Finally, at the end of World War I the United States emerged as the dominant foreign power in the region, replacing Great Britain in both economic and political terms. That position created a reality that Latin Americans could not ignore and that greatly influenced economic and political options in the region.

MEXICO'S UPHEAVAL

The event that announced a new age in Latin America and launched it into the 20th century was the Mexican Revolution of 1910. The regime of Porfirio Díaz had been in power since 1876 and seemed unshakable. During the Díaz dictatorship tremendous economic changes had been made, and foreign concessions in mining, railroads, and other sectors of the economy had created a sense of prosperity among the Mexican elite. This progress, however, had been bought at considerable expense. Foreigners controlled large sectors of the economy. The hacienda system of extensive landholdings dominated certain regions of the country. The political system was wholly corrupt, and any complaint was stifled. The government took repressive measures against workers, peasants, and Indians who opposed the alienation of their lands or the unbearable working conditions. Political opponents were often imprisoned or forced into exile. In short, Díaz ruled with an iron fist through an effective political machine.

By 1910, however, Díaz was 80 years old and seemed willing to allow some political opposition. Francisco Madero, a wealthy son of an elite family, proposed to run against Díaz. Madero was no radical, but he believed that some moderate democratic political reforms

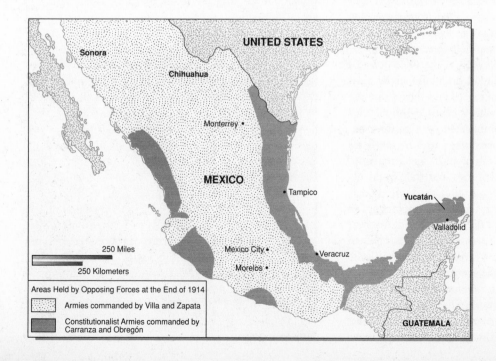

Mexico During the Early Stages of the 1911 Revolution

Areas Held by Opposing Forces at the End of 1914
☐ Armies commanded by Villa and Zapata
■ Constitutionalist Armies commanded by Carranza and Obregón

would relieve social tensions and allow the government to continue its "progressive" economic developments with a minimum of popular unrest. Madero's moderate challenge was more than Díaz could stand. Madero was arrested, a rigged election put Díaz back in power, and things returned to normal. When Madero was released from prison, he called for a revolt.

A general rebellion developed. In the north small farmers, railroaders, and cowboys coalesced under Pancho Villa, a colorful former bandit and able commander. In Morelos, an area of old conflicts between Indian communities and large sugar estates, a peasant-based guerrilla movement began under Emiliano Zapata, whose goal of land reform was expressed in his motto "Tierra y Libertad" (Land and Liberty). Díaz was driven from power by this coalition of forces, but it soon became apparent that Madero's moderate programs would not resolve Mexico's continuing social problems. Zapata rose in revolt, demanding a sweeping land reform, and Madero steadily lost control of his subordinates. In 1913, with at least tacit agreement of the U.S. ambassador in Mexico, a military coup removed Madero from government, and he was then assassinated.

General Victoriano Huerta sought to reimpose a Díaz-type dictatorship supported by the large landowners, the army, and the foreign companies, but the tide of revolution could not be stopped so easily. Villa and Zapata rose again against the government and were joined by other middle-class political opponents of Huerta's illegal rule. By 1914 Huerta was forced from power, but the victorious leaders now began to fight over the nature of the new regime and the mantle of leadership. An extended period of warfare followed as the tides of battle continually shifted. The railroad lines built under Díaz now moved large numbers of troops and their accompanying women *soldaderas,* who sometimes shouldered arms. Matters were also complicated by U.S. intervention and by diplomatic maneuverings after the outbreak of World War I in Europe. Villa and Zapata remained in control in their home territories, but they could not wrest the government from control of the more moderate political leaders in Mexico City. Alvaro Obregón, an able general who had learned the new tactics of machine guns and trenches from the war raging in Europe and had beaten Villa's cavalry in a series of bloody battles in 1915, emerged as leader of the government.

As much as the Mexican Revolution had its own internal dynamic, it is interesting to note that it was roughly contemporaneous with revolutions in other agrarian societies that had also just undergone a period of rapid and disruptive modernization. The Boxer Rebellion in China (1899–1901) and the toppling of the emperor in 1911, the 1905 revolution in Russia, and a revolution in Iran in the same year underlined the rapid changes in these societies, all of which had received large foreign investments from either the United States or western Europe. In each of these countries governments had tried to establish strong centralized control and had sought rapid modernization but in doing so had made their nations increasingly dependent on foreign investments and consequently on world financial markets. Thus a world banking crisis like that of 1907 and 1908 cut Mexico and these other countries off from their needed sources of capital and created severe strains on their governments. This kind of dependency, and the fact that in Mexico more than 20 percent of the nation's territory was owned directly by U.S. citizens or companies, fed a growing nationalism that spread throughout

The Mexican Revolution mobilized large segments of the population, both men and women. The Villista forces shown here included *soldaderas* among the railroad workers, peasants, cowboys, and townsfolk who took up arms in northern Mexico.

many sectors of society. That nationalist sentiment played a role in each of these revolutions.

By 1920 the period of civil war was ended, and Mexico began to consolidate the changes that had taken place in the previous confused and bloody decade. Obregón was elected president in that year, and he was then followed by a series of presidents from the new "revolutionary elite" seeking to consolidate the new regime. There was much to be done. The revolution had devastated the country; one-half million people had died, major industries were destroyed, and ranching and farming were disrupted. But there was great hope because the revolution also promised (although it did not always deliver) real changes.

What were some of these changes? A new constitution of 1917 promised land reform, limited the foreign ownership of key resources, guaranteed the rights of workers, placed restrictions on clerical education and Church ownership of property, and promised educational reforms. The workers who had been mobilized were organized in a national confederation and were given representation in the government. The promised land reforms were slow in coming, but under President Lázaro Cárdenas (1934–1940) more than 40 million acres were distributed, most of it in the form of *ejidos,* or communal holdings. The government launched an extensive program of primary and especially rural education.

CULTURE AND POLITICS IN POSTREVOLUTIONARY MEXICO

Nationalism and *indigenism,* or the concern for the Indians and their contribution to Mexican culture, lay beneath many reforms. Having failed to integrate the Indians into national life for a century, Mexico now sought to "Indianize" the nation through secular schools that emphasized nationalism and a vision of the Mexican past that glorified its Indian heritage and denounced Western capitalism. Artists, such as Diego Rivera and José Clemente Orozco, recaptured that past and outlined a social program for the future in stunning murals on public buildings designed to inform, convince, and entertain at the same time. The Mexican muralist movement had a wide impact on artists throughout Latin America even though, as Orozco himself stated, it sometimes created simple solutions and strange utopias by mixing a romantic image of the Indian past with Christian symbols and Communist ideology. Novelists, such as Mariano Azuela, found in the revolution itself a focus for the examination of Mexican reality. Popular culture celebrated the heroes and events of the revolution in scores of ballads that were sung to celebrate and inform. In literature, music, and the arts, the revolution and its themes provided a stimulus to a tremendous burst of creativity.

The gains of the revolution were not made without considerable opposition. Although it had preceded the

During and after the Mexican Revolution, David Alfaro Siqueiros and other artists called for murals in public places, worker neighborhoods, and sport stadiums, as well as on large buildings, to record the history of Mexico and to emphasize the actions of the people. Siqueiros's *Struggle for the Banner* (1957) portrays workers and peasants seizing the national flag from the hands of oppressors.

Russian Revolution of 1917 and had no single ideological model, many of the ideas of Marxist socialism were held by leading Mexican intellectuals and a few politicians. The secularization of society and especially education met strong opposition from the Church and the clergy, especially when in some states socialist rhetoric and anticlericalism were extreme. In the 1920s a conservative peasant movement backed by the Church erupted in central Mexico. These "Cristeros," backed also by conservative politicians, fought to stop the slide toward secularization. Fighting lasted for years until a compromise was reached.

The United States had intervened diplomatically and militarily during the revolution. An incident provoked a short-lived U.S. seizure of Veracruz in 1914, and when Pancho Villa's forces had raided across the border, the United States sent an expeditionary force into Mexico to catch him. The mission failed. For the most part, however, the war in Europe had distracted U.S. foreign policy until 1918. The United States was suspicious of the new government, and a serious conflict arose when U.S.-owned oil companies ran into problems with workers. The companies called for U.S. intervention or pressure when President Cárdenas expropriated the companies in 1934. An agreement was worked out, however, and Mexico nationalized its petroleum industry in a state-run monopoly. This nationalization of natural resources was considered a declaration of economic independence. It symbolized the nationalistic basis of many of the revolution's goals.

As in any revolution, the question of continuity arose when the fighting ended. The revolutionary leadership hoped to institutionalize the new regime by creating a one-party system. This organization, presently called the Party of the Institutionalized Revolution (PRI), developed slowly during the 1920s and 1930s into a dominant force in Mexican politics. It incorporated labor, peasant, military, and middle-class sectors and proved flexible enough to incorporate new interest groups as they developed. Although Mexico became in theory a multiparty democracy, in reality the PRI controlled politics and, by accommodation and sometimes repression, maintained its hold on national political life. Some presidents governed much like the strongmen in the 19th century had done, but the party structure and the need to incorporate various interests within the government coalition limited the worst aspects of caudillo, or personalist, rule. Presidents were strong, but the policy of limiting the presidency to a six-year term ensured some change in leadership. The question of whether a revolution could be institutionalized remained in debate. By the last decades of the century, many Mexicans believed that little remained of the principles and programs of the revolutionaries of 1910.

LATIN AMERICAN ECONOMIES AND WORLD WAR I

The Mexican Revolution had a limited immediate impact beyond the borders of Mexico, but the outbreak of World War I affected most of the region directly. Throughout much of Latin America, the effects of the economic boom of the late 19th century had continued into the first decades of the 20th century. Each nation

These graphs reflect PRI membership by sectors. Note that the population shifted away from rural areas and that labor remained fairly steady.

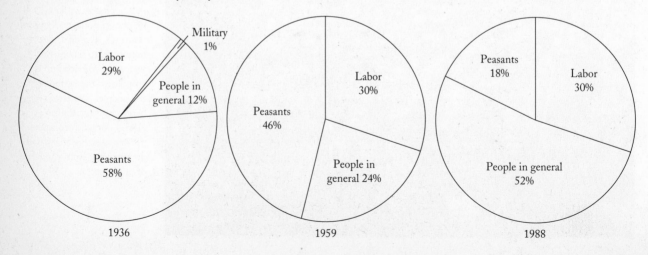

1936   1959   1988

had its specialized crop or set of exports—coffee for Colombia, Brazil, and Costa Rica; minerals from Bolivia, Chile, and Peru; bananas from Ecuador and other Central American nations; and sugar from Cuba. As long as European demand remained high, groups in control of these exports greatly profited.

For a while, World War I produced some immediate effects on the Latin American economies. Cut off from supplies of traditional imports, a spurt of industrial growth took place in what economists call "import substitution industrialization." Latin Americans had to produce for themselves some of what they had formerly imported. Most of this involved "light" industry, such as textiles. Latin America continued to suffer from a lack of capital, limited markets (because so many people had so little to spend), and low technological levels. Still, changes had taken place. Moreover, the war had increased European demand for some products. World War I had provided a stimulus to the economy, but it was a false start. A general inflationary trend after the war meant that the real wages of the working classes declined, and their worsening condition contributed to increasing political unrest.

That unrest also resulted from population growth, which was rapid in some countries. Immigrants continued to pour into Argentina, Brazil, and some of the other temperate countries, swelling the ranks of the rural and urban working classes. Cities grew in size and importance. Often the old pattern of a capital city and its port dominating the rest of the country became reinforced during this period. This has been a continuing problem in Latin America, where Lima, Montevideo, Quito, and Mexico City have so dominated the economic and political resources of their countries that growth outside the capital has been difficult. By 1920, for example, 20 percent of Argentina's total population lived in Buenos Aires; 14 percent of the population of Chile and Cuba lived in their capitals of Santiago and Havana. Latin America had had a strong urban tradition since colonial times, but in the 20th century rapid urban growth created a series of social problems that reflected the transformation of Latin America from basically agrarian to industrializing societies.

NEW POLITICAL ACTORS: LABOR AND THE MIDDLE CLASS

The rising importance of an urban labor force and the growth of an urban middle class led to changes in the political structure of some Latin American nations.

Latin America experienced industrial growth with light industries, such as textiles. This painting of a Mexican factory is from the mid-19th century.

The traditional landowning oligarchy in Argentina, Chile, and Brazil began to open up the political system in order to meet the desire of the growing middle class to share political power. In Argentina, for example, a new electoral law in 1912 led to the 1916 triumph of the middle-class-based Radical party. After some preliminary attempts to forge an alliance with workers, however, the party abandoned that strategy in favor of closer ties with the traditional elites. In Brazil, after the establishment of a republic in 1889, a series of conservative presidents from the Republican party in the wealthiest and most powerful states held control of the government. This alliance of traditional landed interests and urban middle classes maintained political stability and a business-as-usual approach to government, but it began to encounter a series of opponents during the 1920s. Reformist military officers, disaffected state politicians, social bandits, and millenarian peasant movements seeking a return to a golden age—all acted in different ways against the political system and the system of export-import capitalism that seemed to produce increasing inequality along with great wealth. Similar criticisms were voiced elsewhere throughout Latin America.

As in western Europe, the growing industrial and urban labor forces in Latin America began to exert some influence on politics in the first decades of the century. Not surprisingly, many of these workers were engaged in the production of exports or in related transportation activities. Immigrants from Spain, Italy, and elsewhere in Europe sometimes came with well-developed political goals and ideologies ranging from anarchism, which wished to smash the state entirely by using the weapon of the general strike to gain power, to syndicalism, which hoped to use the organization of labor to achieve that goal. Railroad, dock, and mining workers were often among the most radical and the first to organize and were usually met with force. Hundreds of miners in Iquique, Chile, striking against awful conditions in 1907, were shot down by government forces. Between 1914 and 1930 a series of general strikes and labor unrest swept through much of Latin America. Sometimes, as in Argentina in 1919 during the "Tragic Week," government reaction to "revolutionary workers," many of whom were foreign-born, led to brutal repression under the guise of nationalism.

A growing sense of class conflict developed in Latin America as it had in western Europe in this period. Some gains were made, however, as it became increasingly clear that governments now had to consider organized labor as a force that had to be confronted or incor-

porated. Unlike in western Europe, however, the vast majority of workers in Latin America were still agrarian and for the most part were not organized. Thus the history of the labor movement tells only a small part of the story.

IDEOLOGY AND SOCIAL REFORM. In the 1920s and 1930s the failures of liberalism were becoming increasingly apparent. A middle class had emerged and had begun to enter politics, but unlike its western European counterpart, it gained power only in conjunction with the traditional oligarchy or the military. In Latin America the ideology of liberalism was not an expression of the strength of this class but rather a series of ideas, "out of place," not particularly suited to the realities of Latin America, where large segments of the population were landless, uneducated, and destitute. Increasing industrialization did not dissolve the old class boundaries; nor did public education and other classic liberal programs produce as much social mobility as had been expected.

Disillusioned by liberalism and by the destruction of Europe in the Great War, artists and intellectuals who had looked to Europe for inspiration turned to Latin America's own populations and history for values and solutions to Latin American problems. During the 1920s intellectuals increasingly complained that Latin America was embarked on a race to nowhere. Books such as Paulo Prado's *Portrait of Brazil* (1928) or the Argentine Eziquiel Martínez's *X-Ray of the Pampa* (1933) examined the pseudo-European regimes, the corruption, and the seeming failure of these "co-optive democracies" that provided the forms of democratic government but little of the substance to the vast majority of the population. In literature and the arts the ideas of rationality, progress, and order associated with liberalism were under attack.

Ideas of reform and social change were in the air. University students in Cordoba, Argentina, began a reform of their university system that gave the university more autonomy and students more power within it. This movement soon spread to other countries. Movements for social reform gathered strength in Brazil, Chile, and Uruguay. Many of those who criticized the failure of the Liberal regimes claimed that Latin America should seek its own solutions and paths rather than import ideas and models from Europe. There were other responses as well. Socialist and Communist parties were formed or grew in strength in a number of Latin American nations in this period, especially after the Russian Revolution of 1917. The strength of these parties of the left originated in local conditions but was sometimes aided by the international Communist movement. Although criticism of existing governments and of liberalism as a political and economic philosophy came from these left-leaning parties, it also came from traditional elements in society such as the Roman Catholic church, which disliked the secularization a capitalist society represented.

POPULIST POLITICS: THE CASE OF PERU.   We can use Peru as an example of this ferment. That Andean nation, with its predominantly Indian population, had followed the general trend of export-oriented development based on nitrates and a few agricultural products. The foreign capital that was invested controlled many crucial transportation facilities and vital industries. The elites profited from economic expansion, but a war with Chile (the War of the Pacific, 1879–1883) led to the loss of territory and nitrate resources. Many peasants were landless, and government graft and corruption were rampant. By the 1920s critics had emerged. Essayist José Carlos Mariateguí (1895–1930) wrote nationalist analyses of Peru's ills from a socialist perspective that glorified the Indian past and denounced political and economic conditions in Peru. His *Seven Essays of Peruvian Reality* (1928) became a classic of social criticism.

Another young Peruvian, Victor Raul Haya de la Torre (1895–1979) created the American Popular Revolutionary Alliance (APRA) in 1924. This party, drawing on the models of the Mexican Revolution, socialism, and nationalism, as well as some aspects of Mussolini's fascism, aimed at being an international party throughout the hemisphere. Its greatest success, however, was in Peru itself, where by the 1930s its members had made an impact on politics. Antiimperialist, nationalistic, and in favor of nationalizing lands and basic industries, APRA's program won wide support. Haya de la Torre depended on his own personal charisma and on middle-class and proletarian support for the success of APRA. This mix of personal qualities and programs could be seen in a number of Latin American regimes in the period. Electoral battles and a virtual political war between right and left in the 1930s kept APRA from power. Although opposed by the military and other sectors of society, *Apristas* remained a force in Peruvian politics and finally gained the presidency in 1985 with the victory of Alan García, but the origins of the movement were tied to the political disillusionment of the period between the wars.

APRA represented the new populist political parties in Latin America that began to mobilize mass support among workers, small farmers, and urban sectors under the direction of personalist leaders. Populism was usually nationalist and seemingly antiestablishment. It gained broad support from urban masses and rural peasants, but it was often led by politicians from the military or the elites who channeled this support into policies that did not challenge the structure of government. With an emphasis on personal charisma, direct appeals to the masses, and the political mobilization of people previously excluded from politics, populist leaders, such as Juan Perón in Argentina, became powerful forces in the region.

THE GREAT CRASH AND LATIN AMERICAN RESPONSES.   The economic dependency of Latin America and the internal weaknesses of the Liberal regimes were made abundantly clear by the great world financial crisis of 1929. After the crash, the foreign investments so essential to the continued growth of the Latin American economies ceased, and purchases of the region's products declined. Unemployment and economic dislocation were general. The Liberal political and economic programs that had brought the changes of the late 19th and early 20th centuries were now literally bankrupt. Within three years, there were violent military coups in 12 countries. Among the new alternatives sought to the deepening crisis of the area were various adaptations of socialism or *corporatism*, a political ideology that emphasized the organic nature of society and made the state a mediator, adjusting the interests of different social groups. This philosophy often appealed to conservative groups in society and to the military because it stressed cooperation and the avoidance of class conflict and because it placed the state at the center of power. Moreover, the fact that corporatism was adopted by Catholic European regimes, such as Italy, Spain, and Portugal, contributed to its popularity in Latin America. Aspects of Italian and German fascism also appealed to conservatives in Latin America. During the 1930s Fascist groups, complete with their own militant rhetoric and uniforms, formed and sometimes gained considerable political power in Brazil, Mexico, and Chile.

Unrestrained capitalism had created deep social divisions. By the 1930s many Western societies, including Latin America, began to moderate the principles and policies of unbridled laissez-faire capitalism by attempting to provide some kind of social reform in order to provide a broader basis for governments. The New Deal in the United States and the corporatist governments of Italy and Spain were responses to the failures and problems of capitalism. Latin America also participated in this trend.

PROMISES OF SOCIAL REFORM

New regimes or a new concern with social problems characterized much of Latin America in the 1930s. One such reforming administration was that of President Cárdenas (1934–1940) in Mexico, when land reform and many of the social aspects of the revolution were finally initiated on a large scale. Cárdenas distributed over 40 million acres of land and created communal farms and a credit system to support them. He expropriated foreign oil companies that refused to obey Mexican law and created a state oil monopoly. He expanded rural education programs. These measures made him broadly popular in Mexico and seemed to give substance to the promises of the revolution.

Cárdenas was perhaps the most successful example of the new political tide in Latin America. In Cuba, for example, a nationalist revolution in 1933 aimed at social reform and breaking the tutelage of the United States took power, and although it soon was taken over by moderate elements, important changes and reforms did take place. To some extent such new departures underlined both the growing force of nationalism and the desire to integrate new forces into the political process. Nowhere was this more apparent than in the populist regimes of Brazil and Argentina.

THE VARGAS REGIME IN BRAZIL.   In Brazil a contested political election in 1929 in which the state elites could not agree on the next president resulted in a short civil war and the emergence of Getúlio Vargas (1872–1954) as the new president. The Brazilian economy, based on coffee exports, was a shambles due to the impact of the 1929 crash on coffee exports. Vargas had promised liberal reforms and elimination of the worst abuses of the old system. Once in power, he launched a new kind of centralized political program, imposing federal administrators over the state governments. He held off attempted coups by the Communists in 1935 and by the green-shirted Fascist "Integralists" in 1937. With the support of the military, Vargas then imposed a new constitution in 1937 that established the *Estado Novo* (New State), based on ideas from Mussolini's Italy. It imposed an authoritarian regime within the context of nationalism and economic reforms, limiting immigration and eliminating parties and groups that resisted national integration or that opposed the government.

For a while Vargas played off Germany and the Western powers in hopes of securing armaments and fa-

vorable trade arrangements. Despite Vargas's authoritarian sympathies, he eventually joined the Allies, supplied bases to the United States, and even sent troops to fight against the Axis powers in Italy. In return Brazil obtained arms, financial support for industrial development, and trade advantages. Meanwhile, Vargas ran a corporatist government, allowing some room for labor negotiations but only under strict government supervision. Little open opposition to the government was allowed. The state, moreover, organized many other aspects of the economy. Opposition to Vargas and his repressive policies was building in Brazil by 1945, but by then he was turning increasingly to the left, seeking support from organized labor and coming to terms with the Communist party leaders whom he had imprisoned.

In 1945 Vargas was deposed by a military coup, but he did not disappear from Brazilian political life. After an interim of five years, Vargas returned to the presidency, this time on a program of nationalism and with support from the left and from a new Workers' party (PTB). Under his supporter João Goulart, the party mobilized the urban labor force. Limitations were put on foreign profit making in Brazil. As in Mexico and Argentina, a state monopoly of petroleum was established. Vargas's nationalist and populist stance had a broad appeal, but his policies were often more conservative than his statements. Under attack and criticism from both the political right and left, Vargas committed suicide in 1954. His suicide note emphasized his populist ties and blamed his death on Brazil's enemies:

> Once more the forces and interests which work against the people have organized themselves again and emerge against me. . . . I was a slave to the people, and today I am freeing myself for eternal life. But this people whose slave I was will no longer be slave to anyone. My sacrifice will remain forever in their souls and my blood will be the price of their ransom. . . .

Much of Brazilian history since Vargas has been a struggle over his mantle of leadership. In death Vargas became a martyr and a nationalist hero even to those groups that he had repressed and imprisoned in the 1930s.

ARGENTINA: POPULISM, PERON, AND THE MILITARY.
Argentina was somewhat of an anomaly. In Argentina the middle-class Radical party that had held power dur-

ing the 1920s fell when the economy collapsed in 1929. A military coup backed by a strange coalition of nationalists, Fascists, and socialists seized power, hoping to return Argentina to the golden days of the great export boom of the 1890s. The coup failed. Argentina became more dependent, as foreign investments increased and markets for Argentine products declined. Industry, however, was growing, and with it grew the numbers and strength of industrial workers, many of whom had migrated from the countryside. By the 1940s the workers were organized in two major labor federations. Conservative governments backed by the traditional military held power through the 1930s, but in 1943 a military group once again took control of government.

The new military rulers were nationalists who wished to industrialize and modernize Argentina and make it the dominant power of South America. Some were admirers of the Fascist powers and their programs. Although many of them were distrustful of the workers, the man who became the dominant political force in Argentina recognized the need to create a broader basis of support for the government. Colonel Juan D. Perón (1895–1974) emerged as a power in the government. Using his position in the Ministry of Labor, he appealed to workers, raising their salaries, improving their benefits, and generally supporting their demands. Attempts to displace him failed, and he increasingly gained popular support, aided by his wife, Eva Duarte, known as Evita, who became a public spokesperson for Perón among the lower classes. During World War II Perón's admiration for the Axis powers was well known. In 1946, when the United States attempted to discredit him because of his pro-Fascist sympathies, Perón successfully manipulated anti-U.S. sentiment into nationalist support for his presidential campaign.

Perón forged an alliance of interest among the workers, the industrialists, and the military. Like Vargas, he learned the effectiveness of the radio, the press, and public speeches in mobilizing public support. He depended on his personal charisma and on repression of opponents to maintain his rule. The Peronist program was couched in nationalistic terms. The government nationalized the foreign-owned railroads and telephone companies, as well as petroleum resources. The foreign debt was paid off and for a while the Argentine economy boomed in the immediate postwar years. But by 1949 there were economic problems again. Meanwhile, Perón ruled by a combination of inducements and repression, and Evita became a symbol to the *descamisados,*

The populist politics of Juan Perón and his wife, Evita, brought new forces, especially urban workers, into Argentine politics. The Peróns' personal charisma attracted great support among groups formerly excluded from politics but eventually led to opposition from the Argentine military and Perón's overthrow in 1955.

or the poor and downtrodden, who saw in Peronism a glimmer of hope. Her death in 1952 at age 33 was the cause for national mourning.

Perón's regime was a populist government with a broader base than had ever been attempted before in Argentina. Nevertheless, holding the interests of the various components of the coalition together became increasingly difficult as the economy worsened. A democratic opposition developed and complained of Perón's control of the press and his violation of civil liberties. Industrialists disliked the strength of labor organizations. The military worried that Perón would arm the workers and would begin to cut back on the military's gains. The Peronist party became more radical and began a campaign against the Catholic church. In 1955 anti-Perón military officers drove him into exile.

For the next 20 years Argentina lived in the shadow of Perón. The Peronist party was banned, and a succession of military-supported civilian governments tried to resolve the nation's economic problems and continuing political instability. But Peronism could survive even without Perón, and the mass of urban workers and the strongly Peronist unions continued to agitate for his programs, especially as austerity measures began to affect living conditions of the working class. Perón and his new wife, Isabel, returned to Argentina in 1973, and they won the presidential election in that year (she as vice-president). When he died the following year, however, it was clear that Argentina's problems could not be solved by the old formulas. Argentina slid once more into military dictatorship.

WAR AND REVOLUTION IN RUSSIA

The currents of revolution in Russia emerged somewhat gradually. By 1900 a variety of groups were seriously aggrieved, and several erupted in recurrent protest. Peasants resented their continuing obligations under the terms of the Emancipation of the Serfs of 1861. Many had to make annual payments for their rights to the land. Many were subjected to community restrictions on buying or selling land or even leaving the village. Furthermore, aristocratic landlords continued to hold some of the richest land. Russia's peasantry, pressed by a growing population, sought new access to the land and to freedom from obligatory payments. Russia also had a growing urban working class, fed by migrations from the peasantry and absorbing some peasant discontents. Life in the factories and in the crowded cities was harsh, which generated grievances of another sort; strikes and illegal unions formed amid many groups. Business and professional people, a nascent middle class, often sought new political rights against a tsarist government that resolutely banned dissident political expression at the national level. Intellectuals, some of upper-class origin, espoused a variety of revolutionary doctrines, from anarchist yearnings to destroy all government to the newer Marxist ideas of working-class revolt. They organized illegal agitation groups and sought to disseminate their ideas to the lower classes.

These varied grievances erupted into revolution in 1905, triggered by Russia's shocking loss in a war with Japan. The tsar in turn created a national parliament, the Duma, and confirmed peasant land tenure, removing the hated community controls and obligatory redemption payments. Although peasant discontent was alleviated, prohibition of working-class parties and, soon, of trade unions only exacerbated urban discontent. The Duma was progressively stripped of any real power, becoming a hollow institution as tsarist autocracy resumed its hold. Many historians believe that renewed revolution was virtually inevitable. It certainly became inevitable when Russia's arduous participation in World War I led to new levels of material misery for the bulk of the population.

In March 1917 strikes and food riots broke out in Russia's capital, St. Petersburg (subsequently renamed Leningrad until 1991, when it was renamed St. Petersburg as a gesture of defiance against the revolutionary legacy). The outbursts, spurred by wartime misery, including painful food shortages, but more basically protesting the conditions of early industrialization set against incomplete rural reform and an unresponsive political system, quickly assumed revolutionary proportions. The rioters called not just for more food and work but for a new political regime as well. A council of workers, called a soviet, took over the city government and arrested the tsar's ministers, after some brutal attempts at military repression. Unable to rely on his own soldiers, the tsar abdicated, thus ending the long period of imperial rule.

LIBERALISM TO COMMUNISM

For eight months a liberal provisional government struggled to rule the country. Russia seemed thus to launch its revolution on a basis similar to France in 1789, where a liberal period set change in motion. Like Western liberals, Russian revolutionary leaders, such as Alexander Kerensky, were eager to see genuine parliamentary rule, religious and other freedoms, and a host of political and legal changes. But liberalism was not deeply rooted in Russia, if only because of the small middle class, so the analogies with the first phase of the French revolution cannot be pressed too far. Furthermore, Russia's revolution took place in much more adverse circumstances, given the pressures of participation in the world war. The initial liberal leaders were eager to maintain their war effort, which associated their link with democratic France and Britain. Yet the nation was desperately war weary, and prolongation drastically worsened economic conditions while public morale plummeted. Liberal leaders also held back from the massive land reforms expected by the peasantry, for in good middle-class fash-

Moscow workers guard the Bolshevik headquarters during the Russian Revolution of 1917.

ion they respected existing property arrangements and did not wish to rush into social change before a legitimate new political structure could be established. Hence serious popular unrest continued, and in November (October, by the Russian calendar) a second revolution took place, which expelled liberal leadership and soon brought to power the radical, Bolshevik, wing of the Social Democratic party (soon renamed the Communist party), and Lenin, their dynamic chief.

The revolution was a godsend to Lenin, who had long been writing of Russia's readiness for a Communist revolt because of the power of international capitalism and its creation of a massive proletariat, even in a society that had not directly passed through middle-class rule. Lenin quickly gained a strong position among the urban workers' councils in the major cities. This corresponded to his deeply rooted belief that revolution should come not from literal mass action but from tightly organized cells whose leaders espoused a coherent plan of action.

Once the liberals were toppled, Lenin and the Bolsheviks faced several immediate problems. One, the war, they handled by signing a humiliating peace treaty with Germany and giving up huge sections of western Russia in return for an end of hostilities. This treaty was soon nullified by Germany's defeat at the hands of the Western allies, but Russia was ignored at the Versailles peace conference—treated as a pariah by the fearful Western powers—and found considerable territory converted into nation-states. A revived Poland built heavily on land

Russia had controlled for more than a century, and new, small Baltic states cut into even earlier acquisitions. Still, although Russia's deep grievances against the Versailles treaty would later help motivate renewed expansionism, the early end to the war was vital to Lenin's consolidation of power.

Although Lenin and the Bolsheviks had gained a majority role in the leading urban soviets, they were not the most popular revolutionary party, and this situation constituted the second problem faced at the end of 1917. The November seizure of power had led to the creation of the Council of People's Commissars, drawn from soviets across the nation and headed by Lenin, to govern the state. But a parliamentary election had already been called, and this produced a clear majority for the Social Revolutionary party, which emphasized peasant support and rural reform. Lenin, however, shut down the parliament, replacing it with a Bolshevik-dominated Congress of Soviets. He pressed the Social Revolutionaries themselves to disband, arguing that "the people voted for a party which no longer existed." Russia was thus to have no Western-style, multiparty system but rather a Bolshevik monopoly in the name of the true people's will. Indeed, Communist control of the government apparatus persisted from this point to 1989, a record for continuity much different from the fate of revolutionary groups earlier in the Western past.

Russia's revolution did, however, produce a familiar backlash that revolutionaries in other eras would have

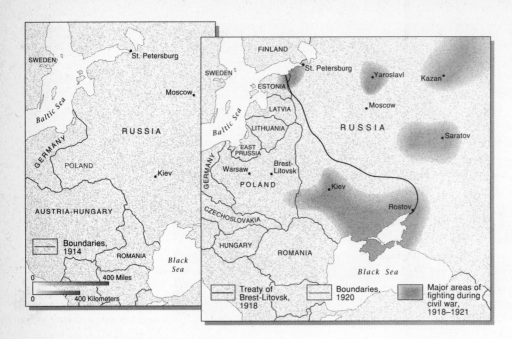

Eastern Europe and the Soviet Union, 1919–1939

recognized quite easily: foreign hostility and, even more important, domestic resistance. The world's leading nations—aside from Germany, now briefly irrelevant—were appalled at the Communist success, which threatened principles of property and freedom they cherished deeply. As settled regimes, they also disliked the unexpected, and some were directly injured by Russia's renunciation of its heavy foreign debts. The result was an attempt at intervention, recalling the attacks on France in 1792. Britain, France, the United States, and Japan all sent troops. But this intervention, although it heightened Russian suspicion of outsiders, did relatively little damage. The Western powers, exhausted by World War I, pulled out quickly, and even Japan, though interested in lingering in Asiatic Russia, stepped back fairly soon.

The internal civil war, which foreign troops slightly abetted, was a more serious matter, as it raged from 1918 to 1921. Tsarist generals, religiously faithful peasants, and many minority nationalities made common cause against the Communist regime. Their efforts were aided by continuing economic distress, the normal result of revolutionary disarray, but also heightened by earlier Communist measures. Lenin had quickly decreed a redistribution of land to the peasantry and also launched a nationalization, or state takeover, of basic industry. Many already landed peasants resented loss of property and incentive and in reaction lowered food production and the goods sent to markets. Industrial nationalization somewhat similarly disrupted manufacturing. Famine and unemployment created more economic hardship than the war had generated, which added fuel to the civil war fires. Even workers revolted in several cities, threatening the new regime's most obvious social base as well as ideological mainstay.

STABILIZATION OF THE NEW REGIME

Order was restored, however, on several key foundations. First, the construction of a powerful new army under the leadership of Leon Trotsky recruited able generals and masses of loyal conscripts. This Red Army was an early beneficiary of two ongoing sources of strength for Communist Russia: a willingness to use people of humble background but great ability who could rise to great heights under the new order but who had been doomed to immobility under the old system, and an ability to inspire mass loyalty in the name of an end to previous injustice and a promise of a brighter future. Next, economic disarray was reduced in 1921 when Lenin issued his New Economic Policy. Intended as a stopgap measure in recognition of the real-life barriers to immediate construction of communism, the NEP promised considerable freedom of action for small business owners and peasant landowners. The state continued to set basic economic policies, but its efforts were now combined with individual initiative. Under this temporary policy, food production began to recover, and the regime gained time to prepare the more durable structures of the Communist system.

By 1923 the Bolshevik revolution was an accomplished fact. A new constitution set up a federal system of socialist republics. This system recognized the multinational character of the nation, known now as the Union of Soviet Socialist Republics. The dominance of ethnic Russians was preserved in the central state apparatus, however, and certain groups, notably Jews, were given no distinct representation. Since the separate republics were firmly controlled by the national Communist party and since basic decisions were as firmly centralized, the impact of the new nationalities' policy was somewhat mixed; yet it was also true that direct nationalities' protest declined notably from the 1920s until the late 1980s.

The apparatus of the central state was another mixture of appearance and reality. The Supreme Soviet had many of the trappings of a parliament and was elected by universal suffrage. But competition in elections was normally prohibited, which meant that the Communist party easily controlled the body, which served mainly to ratify decisions taken by the party's central executive. Parallel systems of central bureaucracy and party bureaucracy further confirmed the Communist monopoly on power and the ability to control major decisions from the center. The Soviet political system was elaborated over time. A new constitution in the 1930s spoke glowingly of human rights. In fact, the Communists had quickly reestablished an authoritarian system, making it more efficient than its tsarist predecessor had been, complete with updated versions of political police to ensure loyalty.

Along with its political and constitutional construction, the Soviet regime grappled with other key definitional issues early in the 1920s. Rivalries among leaders at the top had to be sorted out. Lenin became ill and then died in 1924, creating an unexpected leadership gap. A number of key lieutenants jostled for power, including the Red Army's flamboyant Trotsky and a Communist party stalwart of worker origins who had taken the name Stalin, meaning steel. After a few years of jockeying, Joseph Stalin emerged as undisputed leader of the Soviet state, his victory a triumph also for party control over other branches of government. Stalin's accession was more than a personal bureaucratic issue, however. Stalin represented a strongly nationalist version of communism, in contrast to the more ideological and international visions of many of his rivals. At the revolution's outset Lenin himself had believed that the Russian

rising would be merely a prelude to a sweeping Communist upheaval throughout the Western industrial world. Many revolutionary leaders actively encouraged Communist parties in the West and set up a Comintern, or Communist International office, to guide this process. But revolution did not spill over, despite a few brief risings in Hungary and Germany right after World War I. Under Stalin, the revolutionary leadership, although still committed in theory to an international movement, pulled back to concentrate on Russian developments pure and simple—building "socialism in one country," as Stalin put it. Stalin in many ways represented the anti-Western strain in Russian tradition, though in new guise. Rival leaders were killed or expelled, rival visions of the revolution downplayed.

The Russian Revolution was one of the most successful risings in human history. Building on widespread if diverse popular discontent and a firm belief in centralized leadership, the Bolsheviks beat back powerful odds to create a new, though not totally unprecedented, political regime. They used features of the tsarist system but managed to propel a wholly new leadership group to power not only at the top but also at all levels of the bureaucracy and army. The tsar and his hated ministers were gone, mostly executed, but so was the overweening aristocratic class that had loomed so large in Russian history for centuries. And after the first years, the revolutionaries never had to look backward; they avoided even a partial restoration of the "old regime" as had occurred in England after its 17th-century Civil War and in France after Napoleon. The Bolsheviks, in contrast, managed to create a new political, economic, and cultural structure without serious internal challenge between the initial, chaotic years and the late 1980s.

Serious revolutions, however, do not end quickly. Although the formal revolutionary period consumed but a few vivid years, the force of the revolution continued easily until the middle of the 1930s—that is, through a period of fascinating experimentation during the 1920s and into the establishment of a full Stalinist regime from 1928 onward.

ANALYSIS
20TH-CENTURY REVOLUTIONS

Never in world history have there been as many revolutions in so many different civilizations as during the

20th century. The roster includes a minor and a major revolution in Russia; one or perhaps two major revolutions in China (the question concerns whether to view the entire span 1911–1947 as a single revolutionary process or a sequence of two outbreaks); a major upheaval in Mexico and then, much later, significant revolutions in Cuba, Bolivia, and Nicaragua; and, quite recently, Iran. In addition to these major cases, other possible candidates include the Philippines, where the replacement of strongman rule in 1986 had revolutionary overtones but where it remains too soon to judge whether significant changes in social arrangements are involved. And this does not count the important shifts to and from authoritarian and democratic regimes in other Latin American countries, Africa, and the Middle East, where the heavy popular involvement characteristic of a revolution as opposed to a coup d'etat was not fully present. Also omitted are the recent, largely nonviolent transformations in Eastern Europe.

The abundance of 20th-century revolutions raises vital questions about possible patterns and common causation—easier, however, to evoke than to answer. Contemporary revolutions occur in societies where significant changes are under way—like the earliest phases of industrialization in Russia, the economic development undertaken by the prerevolutionary regime in Iran, or initial political and educational changes in China—but where these changes have not yet had a chance to coalesce. The revolutionary moment, in other words, sees some groups antagonized by the shifts that have occurred and others eager for still more rapid change. Relatedly, 20th-century revolutions, like earlier revolts, always involve a number of different groups with diverse demands and diverse revolutionary attributes, some capable of assuming political controls and others willing to participate in street violence or rural risings. Most of the 20th-century revolutions have a strong peasant component and take place where landlord controls had helped spur rural grievances (in contrast to poor regions where peasant ownership predominated).

The wave of 20th-century revolutions has always involved a prior intellectual buildup. Doctrines of democracy and liberalism, nationalism, or some form of socialism (most often Marxism) have provided the most common ideological spurs, but the Iranian revolution—one of the most distinctive in the group—was dominated by Islamic fundamentalism. Revolutions also, of course, require an absence of effective political outlets for key groups together with a weakening of the established state; strong governments can repress discontent, though it is always possible that too many years of repression will raise new doubts and uncertainties and so lead to a softening of the established order. Most revolutions involve a government structure strong in principle but that had recently deteriorated due to weak new leaders (the tsarist case) or the aging of an authoritarian figure (as in Mexico, Cuba, and Iran).

Some historians have sought to develop a standard revolutionary dynamic, based on earlier Western models more than on 20th-century cases. In this model, revolutions begin with initially liberal impulses, seeking greater freedom and control from below. Then, however, as economic problems continue, often with civil strife and even foreign intervention, the liberal phase gives way to greater authority, even outright dictatorship. Elements of this pattern are visible in several 20th-century cases (China, Russia to an extent, Mexico, even Iran briefly), but the authoritarian strand in most instances emerges very quickly. This in turn often reflects an absence of a significant basis for liberalism in the host society, the decline of liberalism as a revolutionary doctrine, and the presence of more experienced revolutionary leaders who know that they must seize the state and use its power if the revolution is to have a chance.

Important common ingredients of 20th-century revolutions are the needs to come to terms with Western influence and often to reassert greater national autonomy. Mexico, Russia, and China all grappled with growing Western economic control and cultural influence in the early 20th century, and all tried to devise alternative development models. Though an array of internal issues is involved in each revolution, the problem of reacting to the West and objections to the responses developed by the existing regime (often, friendlier to Western involvement or at least weaker in its face than the revolutionaries desire) serves as a common bond. Many revolutions thus heighten anti-Western sentiment, at least for a time, and all try to reduce the Western power to interfere with internal affairs. Thus the Russian Revolution reduced foreign business involvement, and Stalinism attacked "decadent" Western cultural influence.

This revolutionary feature helps explain why 20th-century revolutions have generally occurred in societies that had not been outright Western colonies, at least in their recent past, for in such colonies national independence movements could serve some of the purposes that revolutions served elsewhere. Colonial administration often brought some of the changes revolutionaries sought elsewhere, in unseating old-fashioned monarchies, for example; independence movements brought new leaders to power and gave larger groups a sense of national pride that made revolution for a time less salient. This may explain why India and most of Africa have avoided revolution to date in the 20th century (just as Latin America did during its first century of independence after 1820).

No sense of a schema for 20th-century revolutions should, however, ignore two basic points: First, each revolution, including, of course, the Russian, had its own flavor—its own specific causes and outcomes. Individual flavor came from distinctive cultural traditions, distinctive social balances, and distinctive individual leadership. Not every revolution had a Lenin who could unify and galvanize the entire experience. Second, although 20th-century revolutions share some common ingredients, including previous government heavy-handedness, ideological buildup, peasant or other mass discontent, and anti-Western reactions, it remains impossible to predict where revolution will strike next. Understanding what revolutions are like once they occur—grasping certain common features, such as a period of radical isolation and truculence with foreign intervention—is possible on the basis of a sketch of the common revolutionary dynamic. And it is possible to suggest that certain societies are unlikely to face revolution, because of the strength of government, social balance, or recency of major change. But revolutions involve enough accident, a sufficiently unusual blend of factors, that precise forecasting defies expertise—whether the expertise comes from the historian or the intelligence community employed by one of the established powers fearful of revolutionary explosion. Right before World War I, an Austrian banker urged investment in the Russian Empire because it had endured so well, compared to the harassed regimes of western Europe; right before the Iranian revolution, the American Central Intelligence Agency sent back rosy reports of the government's solidity. Revolutions do have patterns, and these patterns suggest a great deal about the dynamic of 20th-century world history, in which the phenomenon of revolution has loomed so large. But revolutions must also attract through their accidental properties, their ability to make predictions look ridiculous.

Questions: How do 20th-century revolutions compare with "liberal" Western revolutions, 1789–1848? Will revolutions affect other societies in the 21st century, or has the revolutionary movement exhausted itself?   ☉

In his 1949 painting *Creative Fellowship,* Sheherbakov shows the cooperation of scientists and workers in an idealized factory setting.

FROM REVOLUTION TO POLICE STATE: THE TIME OF STALIN

The mid-1920s constituted a lively, experimental period in Soviet history, partly because of the jockeying for power at the top of the power pyramid. Despite the absence of Western-style political competition, a host of new groups found a voice. The Communist party, though not eager to recruit too many members lest it lose its tight organization and elite status, encouraged all sorts of subsidiary organizations. Youth movements, women's groups, and particularly organizations of workers all actively debated problems in their social environment and directions for future planning. Workers were able to influence management practices; women's leaders helped carve legal equality and new educational and work opportunities for their constituents.

The atmosphere of excited debate spilled over into such areas as family policy. At various points Soviet policy seemed to downplay the importance of family in favor of individual rights, thus making it easy to obtain divorces or abortions. Ultimately, by the 1930s the pendulum swung back toward greater conservatism, featuring protection of the family unit and an effort to encourage the birthrate, but only after some fascinating fluctuations and experimentalism. One key to the creative mood of these years was the rapid spread of education promoted by the government, as well as educational and propaganda activities sponsored by various adult groups. Literacy gained ground quickly. The new educational system was also bent on reshaping popular culture away from older peasant traditions and, above all, religion, and toward beliefs in Communist political analysis and science. Access to new information, new modes of inquiry, and new values encouraged controversy.

STALINISM

The experimental mood began to fade after 1927, when Joseph Stalin acquired full power over potential rivals. Stalin was eager both to have authoritarian control and to renew the momentum toward socialism, which had been deflected by the New Economic Policy and the surge of discussion among many mass organizations. By this point the bulk of the land lay in the hands of a minority of wealthy, commercially oriented peasants, the kulaks, who were particularly attuned to a profit-based market agriculture. Rural areas seemed inclined to parallel earlier Western experience, in dividing the peasantry among relatively innovative owners and a mass of laborers—and this was not socialism. Even in industry, state-run enterprises and planning had only limited effect, as opposed to small private businesses. Stalin devoted himself to a double task: to make the Soviet Union a fully industrial society and to do so under full control of the state rather than through private initiative and individual ownership of producing property. In essence, Stalin wanted modernization but with a revolutionary, noncapitalist twist. And although he was willing to borrow Western techniques and advice, importing a small number of foreign engineers, for example, he insisted on Soviet control and largely Soviet endeavor.

ECONOMIC POLICIES

A massive program to collectivize agriculture began in 1928. Collectivization meant the creation of large, state-run farms, rather than individual holdings as in the West. Communist party agitators pressed peasants to join in collectives. In addition to being distinctly socialistic, the collectives movement also further offered, at least in theory, the chance to mechanize agriculture most effectively, as collective farms could group scarce equipment, such as tractors and harvesters. Collectivization also allowed more efficient control over peasants themselves, reflecting, though in radical new form, a traditional reluctance to leave peasants to their own devices. Government and party control was desirable not only for political reasons, but also in case Stalin's hopes for a speedup of industrialization required that resources be taken from peasants, through taxation, in order to provide capital for industry.

The peasantry responded to collectivization with a decidedly mixed voice. Many laborers, resentful of kulak wealth, initially welcomed the opportunity to have more direct access to land. But most kulaks refused to cooperate voluntarily, often destroying livestock and other property rather than submit to collectivization. Devastating famine resulted from Stalin's insistence on pressing forward. In addition, millions of kulaks were killed or deported to Siberia during the early 1930s, in one of the most brutal oppressions of what turned out to be a brutal century in world history. Gradually, rural resistance collapsed and production began to increase once again; the decimation of the kulaks may indeed have weakened opportunities to oppose Stalin's increasingly authoritarian hold for a generation or more. But collectivization, though increasingly thorough, was not a smash success, for even those peasants who participated often seemed relatively unmotivated. Although the collective farms allowed peasants small plots of their own, as well as job security and considerable propagandizing by the omnipresent Party members, they created an atmosphere of factorylike discipline and rigid planning from above that antagonized many peasants. The centralized planning process allowed few incentives for special efforts and often complicated a smooth flow of supplies and equipment, a problem also exacerbated by the Stalinist regime's priority concentration on the industrial sector. Agricultural production remained a major weakness in the Soviet economy, demanding a higher percentage of the labor force than was common under industrialization.

The collective farms did, however, allow normally adequate if minimal food supplies once the messy transition period had ended, and they did free excess workers to be channeled into the ranks of urban labor. The late 1920s and early 1930s saw a massive flow of unskilled workers into the cities, as the Soviet Union's industrialization, already launched, shifted into high gear.

For if Stalin's approach to agriculture had serious flaws, his handling of industry was in most ways a stunning success. A system of five-year plans under the state planning commission began to set clear priorities for industrial development, including expected output levels and new facilities. The government constructed massive factories in metallurgy, mining, and electric power to make the Soviet Union an industrial country independent of Western-dominated world banking and trading patterns, with the productive infrastructure also suitable for modern war. There was more than a hint of Peter the Great's policies here, in updating the economy without really Westernizing it, save that industrialization constituted a more massive departure than anything Peter had contemplated. The focus, as earlier, was on heavy industry, which built on the nation's great natural resources and also served to prepare for possible war with Hitler's anti-Communist Germany. This distinctive industrialization, which slighted consumer goods production, was to remain characteristic of the Soviet version of industrial society. Further, Stalin sought to create an alternative not simply to private business ownership but also to the profit-oriented market mechanisms of the West. Thus he relied not on price competition but on formal, centralized resource allocation to distribute equipment and supplies. This led to many bottlenecks and considerable waste, as quotas for individual factories were set in Moscow, but there was no question that rapid industrial growth occurred. During the first two five-year plans, to 1937—that is, during the same period that the West was mired in the depression—Soviet output of machinery and metal products grew 14-fold. The Soviet Union had become the world's third industrial power, behind only Germany and the United States. A long history of backwardness seemed to have ended.

TOWARD AN INDUSTRIAL SOCIETY

For all its distinctive features, the industrialization process in the Soviet Union produced many results similar to those in the West. Increasing numbers of people were crowded into cities, often cramped in inadequate

In this example of socialist realism, heroic women workers labor at a bustling, productive factory. Their stalwart energy was an inspiration to the Soviet people.

housing stock—for Soviet planners, like earlier Western capitalists, were reluctant to put too many resources into mass housing. Factory discipline was strict, as Communist managers sought to instill new habits in a peasant-derived work force. Incentive procedures were introduced to motivate workers to higher production. Particularly capable workers received bonuses and also elaborate public awards for their service to society. At the same time, Communist policy quickly established a network of welfare services, surpassing the West in this area and reversing decades of tsarist neglect. Workers had meeting houses and recreational programs, as well as protection in cases of illness and old age. Soviet industrial society provided only modest standards of living at this point, but a host of collective activities compensated to some degree. Finally, although Soviet industry was directed from the top, with no legal outlet for worker grievances—strikes were outlawed, and the sole trade union movement was controlled by the Party—worker concerns were studied, and identified problems were addressed. The Soviet Union under Stalin used force and authority, but it also recognized the importance of maintaining worker support—so, informally, laborers were consulted as well.

TOTALITARIAN RULE

Stalin combined his industrialization program with a new intensification of government police procedures, as he used Party and state apparatus to monopolize power, even more thoroughly than Hitler's totalitarian state attempted. Real and imagined opponents of his version of communism were executed. During the great purge of Party leaders that culminated in 1937–1938, hundreds of people were intimidated into confessing imaginary crimes against the state, and most of them were then put to death. Many thousands more were sent to Siberian labor camps. Any possibility of vigorous internal initiative was crushed, as both state and Communist party were bent under Stalin's suspicious will. News outlets were monopolized by the state and the Party, and informal meetings also risked a visit from the ubiquitous secret police, renamed the MVD in 1934. Party congresses and meetings of the executive committee, or Politburo, became mere rubber stamps. An atmosphere of terror spread.

Stalin's purges, which included top army officials, ironically weakened the nation's ability to respond to growing foreign policy problems, notably the rising threat of Hitler. Soviet diplomatic initiatives after the Revolution had been unwontedly modest, given the nation's traditions, largely because of the intense concentration on internal development. Diplomatic relations with major nations were gradually reestablished, as the fact of Communist leadership was accepted, and the Soviet Union was allowed into the League of Nations. A few secret military negotiations, as with Turkey in the early 1920s, showed a flicker of interest in more active diplomacy, and of course the nation continued to encourage and often guide internal Communist party activities in many other countries.

Hitler's rise was a clear signal that more active concern was necessary. A strong Germany was inevitably a threat to Russia from the west, and Hitler was vocal about his scorn for Slavic peoples and communism, about his desire to create "living room" for Germany to the east. Stalin initially hoped that he could cooperate with the Western democracies in blocking the German threat. The Soviet Union thus tried to participate in a common response to German and Italian intervention during the Spanish Civil War, in 1936–1937. But France and Britain were incapable of forceful action and were in any event almost as suspicious of the Soviets as of the Nazis. So the Soviet Union, unready for war and greatly disappointed in the West, signed a historic agreement with Hitler in 1939. This pact bought some time for greater war preparation and also enabled Soviet troops to attack eastern Poland and Finland, in an effort to regain territories lost in World War I. Here was the first sign of a revival of Russia's long interest in conquest, which would be intensified by the experience of World War II.

The awkward honeymoon with Hitler did not last. The Nazis, having completed their sweep of France but blocked from invading Britain, quickly regained their eastern appetites, sharpened by concern about the Soviet Union's territorial gains. The invasion of the Soviet Union, launched in 1941 soon brought a new Soviet alliance with the Western powers, including, by the end of the year, the United States.

The war itself was both devastating and exhilarating for the Soviet Union. The nation's new industrial base, hastily relocated in the Ural Mountains and beyond, proved vital in providing the material needed for war, but the effort was extremely costly. The great cities of Leningrad and Stalingrad were besieged by the Germans for months, with huge loss of life. The war heightened Russia's age-old fear of invasion and foreign interference, already enhanced by World War I and Western intervention during the Russian Revolution. But as the Red army pressed westward after 1943, finally penetrating to the Elbe River in Germany, there was new opportunity for aggrandizement as well. Russia was able to regain its former western boundaries, at the expense of Poland; some small states, set up by the Treaty of Versailles, were swallowed entirely. Larger Eastern European states were allowed to remain intact, but their regimes were quickly brought under the control of Communist parties backed by the Soviet occupation forces. The Soviet Union was ready for a new era as a world superpower.

�֍ REMAKING MARX FOR THE PEASANTRY: REVOLUTIONARY STRUGGLES IN CHINA AND VIETNAM

The recent histories of China and Vietnam have had much in common with the rest of the Third World. Both China and Vietnam suffered heavily from the assaults and exploitive terms of exchange imposed by imperialist powers, both Western and Japanese. Each has had to contend with underdevelopment, overpopulation, poverty, and environmental degradation. Moreover, in contrast to most of the rest of the Third World, China and Vietnam have had to deal with these awesome challenges in the midst of the utter collapse of the patterns of civilized life each had followed for thousands of years.

However disruptive imperialist conquest and its effects proved in the rest of the Afro-Asian world, most colonized peoples managed to preserve much of their precolonial cultures and modes of social organization. The defense and revival of traditional customs, religious beliefs, and social arrangements played a key role in the struggle for decolonization. This was not the case in China and Vietnam, where a combination of external aggression and internal upheavals discredited and destroyed the Confucian system that had long been synonymous with the preservation of civilized life.

With their traditional order in shambles, the peoples of China and Vietnam had no choice but to embark on full-scale revolutions that would clear away the rubble of the failed Confucian system, remove the obstacles posed by imperialist dominance, and provide the means to build new and viable states and societies. In contrast to much of the rest of the colonized world, China and Vietnam derived few benefits from European domination, either informal or formal. Imperialist pressures eroded and smashed their political institutions rather than building up a bureaucratic grid and imparting political ideologies that could form the basis for nation building.

For differing reasons, neither China nor Vietnam developed a large middle class, though each had wealthy commercial groups. In each society the weakness of the bourgeoisie, coupled with the establishment of highly repressive regimes in the region in the late 19th and early 20th centuries, greatly constricted constitutionalist and nonviolent political options. The magnitude of the disruption and hardships the Chinese and Vietnamese peoples endured in this period also discredited gradualism and reformist democracy in the eyes of many emerging intellectuals and political leaders. Young students, such as Mao Zedong (Tsetung) and Nguyen Ai Quoc (alias Ho Chi Minh), became convinced that the salvation of their peoples and the restoration of civilized life in their lands could be won only through armed revolution and radical social transformations.

THE STRUGGLE FOR CHINA

The abdication of Puyi, the Manchu boy-emperor, in 1912 marked the end of a century-long losing struggle on the part of the Qing dynasty to protect Chinese civilization from foreign invaders and revolutionary threats from within, such as the massive Taiping movement. The fall of the Qing opened the way for an extended struggle over which leader or movement would be able to capture the mandate to rule the ancient society that had for millennia ordered the lives of one-fourth of the population of humankind. The loose alliance of students, middle-class politicians, secret societies, and regional military commanders that overthrew the Manchus quickly splintered into a number of hostile contenders for the right to rule China.

The military commanders, or warlords, who would play a leading role in Chinese politics for the next three decades were the best positioned of the contenders for power. Many of them combined in cliques or alliances, both to protect their own territories and to crush neighbors and annex their lands. The most powerful of these cliques was centered in north China and was headed by the unscrupulous Yuan Shikai, who hoped to seize the vacated Manchu throne and found a new dynasty. By virtue of their wealth, the merchants and bankers of coastal cities, such as Shanghai and Canton, made up a second power center in post-Manchu China. As had been the case in the late-Confucian era, their involvement in politics resulted from their eagerness to bankroll both favored warlords and Western-educated, middle-class politicians like Sun Yat-sen.

Sometimes supportive of the urban civilian politicians, sometimes wary of them, university students and their teachers, as well as independent intellectuals, pro-

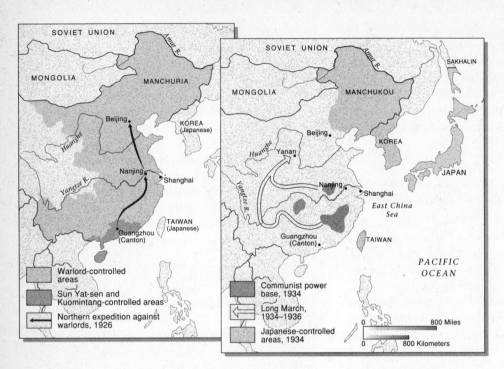

China in the Era
of Revolution and
Civil War

vided yet another factor in the complex political equation. Though the intellectuals and students played critical roles in shaping new ideologies to rebuild Chinese civilization, they were virtually defenseless in a situation in which force was essential to those who hoped to exert political influence. Deeply divided but very strong in some regions, the secret societies represented another contender for power. Like the military, they envisioned the restoration of monarchical rule but under a Chinese dynasty, not a foreign one like that of the Manchus. As if the situation were not already confused enough, it was further complicated by the continuing intervention of the Western powers eager to profit from China's divisions and weakness. Their inroads, however, were increasingly overshadowed by entry into the contest for the control of China by the newest imperialist power, Japan. From the mid-1890s, when the Japanese had humiliated their much larger neighbor by easily defeating China in war, until 1945, when Japan's surrender ended World War II, the Japanese were a major factor in the long and bloody contest for mastery of China.

THE MAY FOURTH MOVEMENT AND THE FAILURE OF LIBERALISM.   Sun Yat-sen, who headed the Revolutionary Alliance, a loose coalition of anti-Qing political groups that had spearheaded the 1911 revolt, claimed that he and the parties of the alliance were rightful suc-

cessors to the fallen Manchus. But he could do little to assert civilian control in the face of warlord opposition. The Revolutionary Alliance had little power and virtually no popular support outside the urban trading centers of the coastal areas in central and south China. Even in these areas they were at the mercy of the local warlords. The alliance formally elected Sun president at the end of 1911, set up a parliament modeled after those in Europe, and chose cabinets with great fanfare, but their decisions had little effect on warlord-dominated China.

Sun Yat-sen conceded this reality when he resigned the acting presidency in favor of the northern warlord Yuan Shikai in 1912. As the most powerful of the northern clique of generals, Yuan appeared to have the best chance to unify China under a single government. He at first feigned sympathy for the democratic aims of the alliance leaders but soon revealed his true intentions. He took foreign loans to build up his military forces and buy out most of the bureaucracy in the capital at Beijing. When Sun and other leaders of the Revolutionary Alliance called for a second revolution to oust Yuan in the years after 1912, he made full use of his military power and more underhanded methods, such as assassinations, to put down their opposition. By 1915 Yuan was well on his way to realizing his ambition of becoming China's next emperor. His schemes were foiled, however, by the continuing rivalry of other warlords, republican nationalists such as Sun, and the growing influence of Japan in China, which increased dramatically as a result of the First World War.

As England's ally according to terms of a 1902 treaty, Japan immediately entered the war on the side of the Entente powers. Moving much too quickly for the comfort of the British and the other Western powers, the Japanese seized German-held islands in the Pacific and occupied the Germans' concessionary areas in China. With all the great Powers except the United States embroiled in war, the Japanese seized the chance to establish a dominant hold over their giant neighbor. In early 1915 they presented Yuan's government with the so-called Twenty-One Demands, which, if accepted, would have reduced China to the status of a dependent protectorate. Though Sun and the Revolutionary Alliance lost much support by refusing to repudiate the Japanese demands, Yuan was no more decisive. He neither accepted nor rejected the demands but concentrated his energies on an effort to drum up popular enthusiasm for his accession to the throne. Disgusted by Yuan's weakness and ambition, one of his warlord rivals plotted his overthrow. Hostility to the Japanese won Yuan's rival widespread

support, and in 1916 Yuan was forced to retreat and then resign the presidency. His fall was the signal for a free-for-all power struggle among the remaining warlords for control of China.

As one of the victorious Allies, Japan managed to solidify its hold on northern China by winning control of the former German concessions in the Versailles Treaty of 1919, which ended the war. However, the Chinese had also allied themselves to the Entente powers during the war. Enraged by what they viewed as a betrayal by the Allied powers, students and nationalist politicians organized mass demonstrations in numerous Chinese cities on May 4, 1919. The demonstrations, which included strikes and mass boycotts of Japanese goods, began a prolonged period of protest against Japanese inroads. The date when the resistance began gave its name to a movement in which intellectuals and students played a leading role. Initially at least, the May Fourth movement was aimed at transforming China into a liberal democracy. Its program was enunciated in numerous speeches, pamphlets, novels, and newspaper articles. Confucianism was ridiculed and rejected in favor of a wholehearted acceptance of all the Western democracies

Spearheaded by students and intellectuals in China's urban areas, the May Fourth demonstrations in 1919 proclaimed the end of nearly two thousand years of Confucian dominance in China and the opening of the country to ideologies from the West, both democratic and Marxist.

had to offer. Noted Western thinkers, such as Bertrand Russell and John Dewey, toured China, extolling the merits of science, industrial technology, and democratic government and basking in the cheers of their packed Chinese audiences. Chinese thinkers called for the liberation of women, the simplification of the Chinese script in order to promote mass literacy, and the promotion of Western-style individualism. Many of these themes are captured in the literature of the period. In the novel *Family* by Ba Jin, for example, a younger brother audaciously informs his elder sibling that he will not accept the marriage partner the family has arranged for him. He clearly sees his refusal as part of a more general revolt of the youth of China against the ancient Confucian social code.

> Big Brother, I'm doing what no one in our family has ever dared do before—I'm running out on an arranged marriage. No one cares about my fate, so I've decided to walk my own road alone. I'm determined to struggle against the old forces to the end. Unless you cancel the match, I'll never come back. I'll die first. . . .

However enthusiastically Chinese urban youth adopted the program of the May Fourth movement, it was soon clear that mere emulation of the liberal democracies of the West could not provide effective solutions to China's prodigious problems. Civil liberties and democratic elections were meaningless in a China ruled by warlords; gradualist solutions were folly in a nation of destitute peasants, many of them malnourished or dying of starvation. Even if fair elections could be held and a Western-style parliament installed as China's effective rulers, China's crisis had become so severe that there was little time for legislators to squabble and debate. The ministers of an elected government with little military clout would hardly have been able to implement well-meaning programs for land redistribution and subsidies for the poor in the face of deeply entrenched regional opposition from the landlords and the military. It soon became clear to many Chinese intellectuals and students, as well as to some of the nationalist politicians, that more radical solutions were needed. In the 1920s this conviction gave rise to the Communist left within the Chinese nationalist movement.

THE RISE OF THE COMMUNIST ALTERNATIVE.   The example of the Russian Revolution, not careful readings of the writings of Karl Marx and Fredrich Engels, made a number of Chinese thinkers aware of possible Marxist solutions to China's ills. In fact, before the Russian upheavals of 1917 and Lenin's launching of a state-directed drive for the social and economic transformation of backward Russia, the few Chinese who knew about Marx or even less radical socialist theorists felt they had little to offer impoverished, agrarian societies like China. Marx, after all, had foreseen socialist revolutions occurring in the more advanced industrial societies with well-developed working classes and a strong proletarian consciousness. He had thought that there would be little chance for revolution in Russia. In China, with its overwhelmingly rural, peasant population (and Marx viewed the peasantry as a reactionary or at best a conservative, petty bourgeois social element), the prospects for revolution looked even more dismal. But the October revolution in Russia that brought Lenin and the Bolsheviks to power changed all of this. For the first time, a Marxist regime governed, and it had come to power in backward, largely peasant Russia, not in western Europe or North America.

The Bolshevik victory and the programs subsequently launched prompted Chinese intellectuals, such as Li Dazhao, to give serious attention to the works of Marx, Engels, Trotsky, and Lenin and to the potential they offered for the regeneration of China. A number of societies devoted to the study of Marxism developed just after the May Fourth movement around thinkers like Li, who headed the study circle at the University of Beijing. Li's borrowings from European Communist thinkers placed heavy emphasis on Marxism's capacity for renewal and its ability to harness the energy and vitality of a nation's youth. In contrast to Lenin, Li saw the peasants rather than the urban workers as the vanguard of the revolution. He justified this shift from the orthodox Marxist emphasis on the working classes, which made up only a tiny fraction of China's population at the time, by characterizing Chinese society as a whole as proletarian. All of China, he argued, had been exploited by the bourgeois, industrialized West. Thus the oppressed Chinese as a whole needed to unite and rise up against their exploiters.

Li's version of Marxism, with alterations or emphasis on elements that made it suitable for China, had great appeal for the students, including the young Mao Zedong, who joined his study circle. They too were angered by what they perceived as China's betrayal by the imperialist powers. In a throwback to the attitudes of the Confucian era, they shared Li's hostility to merchants and commerce, which appeared to dominate the West.

They too longed for a return to a political system, like the Confucian, in which those who governed were deeply committed to social reform and social welfare and an authoritarian state was expected to intervene in all aspects of the peoples' lives.

The societies that developed around Li Dazhao and other Marxist intellectuals soon spawned a number of more broadly based, politically activist organizations. The Marxists' capture of prominent periodicals, such as the *New Youth* magazine, did much to spread the ideas of Marx and Lenin among the politically active youth of China's coastal cities. With support from Sun Yat-sen, Marxist intellectuals established the Socialist Youth Corps in 1920, which was dedicated to recruiting the urban working classes to the revolutionary cause. Mao and other students returned to their provincial bases to win supporters for the leftist cause and foment resistance to the oppressive rule of the local warlords.

In an attempt to unify the growing Marxist wing of the nationalist struggle, a handful of leaders from various parts of China met secretly in the summer of 1921 in Shanghai. At this meeting, closely watched by the agents of the local warlord and rival political organizations, the Communist party of China was born. In Paris a year earlier, Zhou Enlai, who like Mao was later to become one of the main Communist leaders, and a number of other Chinese expatriot students founded the Communist Youth Corps. In Paris and inside China itself, the development of Communist organizations was supported by both the advisors and funds of the Comintern, the international arm of the Bolshevik, or Communist, party of the Soviet Union. Though they had few supporters and at this time were fixed on a revolutionary program fatally oriented to the working classes, the Communists at least offered a clear alternative to fill the ideological and institutional void left by the collapse of the Confucian order.

THE SEIZURE OF POWER BY THE GUOMINDANG, OR NATIONALIST PARTY. In the years when the Communist movement in China was being put together by urban students and intellectuals, the Guomindang, or Nationalist party, which was to prove the Communists' great rival for the mandate to rule in China, was struggling to survive in the deep south. Sun Yat-sen, who was the acknowledged head of the nationalist struggle from the 1911 revolution until the time of his death in early 1925, had gone into exile in Japan in 1914, while warlords, such as Yuan Shikai, consolidated their regional power bases. After returning to China, Sun and his followers sought in 1919 to join the diverse political organizations struggling for political influence in China by reorganizing the revolutionary movement and naming it the Nationalist Party of China (the Guomindang).

The Nationalists began the slow process of forging alliances with key social groups and building an army of their own, which they now viewed as the only way to rid China of the warlord menace. Sun strove to enunciate a nationalist ideology that gave something to everyone. It stressed the need to unify China under a strong central government, bring the imperialist intruders under control, and enact social reforms to alleviate peasant poverty and the oppressive working conditions of laborers in China's cities. Unfortunately for the great majority of the Chinese people, for whom social reforms were the main concern, the Nationalist leaders concentrated on political and international issues and neglected internal reforms.

In this early stage Sun and the Nationalists built their power primarily on the support provided by urban businesspeople and merchants in coastal cities, such as Canton. Though it received little publicity, the Nationalist party also drew support from local warlords and the criminal underworld, especially the notorious Green Gang headquartered in Shanghai. After extensive, time-consuming factional infighting, Sun had more or less secured control over the party, if not the warlords in the neighborhood of Canton. He forged an alliance with the Communists that was officially proclaimed at the first Nationalist party conference in 1924. For the time being, the Nationalist leaders were content to let the Communists serve as their major link to the peasants and the urban workers.

Disappointed in their early hopes of assistance from the Europeans and the United States, Nationalist leaders turned to Soviet Russia. Lenin and the Bolsheviks, eager to support a revolutionary movement in neighboring China, sent advisors, gave material assistance, and encouraged the fledgling Communist party to join with the larger and richer Nationalists in a common struggle to seize power.

From 1924, when the Whampoa Military Academy was founded with Soviet help and partially staffed by Soviet instructors, the Nationalists added a critical military dimension to their political maneuvering. The first head of the academy was an ambitious young military officer named Chiang Kai-shek. The son of a poor salt merchant, Chiang had fought his way up in the world through the military and by virtue of connections with powerful figures in the Shanghai underworld. He had received some military training in Japan and managed by the early 1920s to work his way into Sun Yat-sen's inner circle of advisors. Chiang was not happy with the Communist alliance but was willing to bide his time until he had the military strength to deal with both the Communists and the warlords, who remained the major obstacles to the Nationalist seizure of power.

Absorbed by all these political machinations, Sun and other Nationalist leaders had little time left for serious attention to the now severe deterioration of the Chinese economy and the huge population whose sufferings mounted as a result. Though urban laborers worked for pitiful wages and lived in appalling conditions, the social condition of the peasantry, which made up nearly 90 percent of China's population, was perhaps the most pressing issue facing China's aspiring national leaders. Patterns of landowning varied considerably in different parts of China. In many regions of China more than a century of corruption and weak Manchu rule, followed by the Manchu collapse in 1911 and the depredations of the warlords, had left the peasantry in misery. Big landlords and rich peasants rapaciously amassed great landholdings, which they rented out at exorbitant rates that left the tenants who worked them little with which to feed and clothe their families. In times of flood and drought when the crops failed, tenants, landless laborers, and even small landowners simply could not make ends meet. Tenants and smallholders were turned off their lands, and landless laborers could not find crops to harvest. Famine and disease stalked China's heavily populated provinces, while its ancient irrigation systems fell into disrepair. Corrupt warlords and bureaucrats, including those allied to the Nationalist party, colluded with the landlords to extract the maximum taxes and labor services from the peasantry.

As they had for millennia, dispossessed peasants took to banditry or vagabondage to survive. Many joined the hordes of beggars and unemployed in the towns; many more perished—swept away by floods, famine, disease, or the local warlord's armies. Parents sold their children into slavery so that both might have a chance to survive. A growing number of cases of cannibalism were reported, which occurred after the bark and leaves had been stripped off all the trees to make the scarcely digestible "stew" that the peasants ate to put something in their bellies. Many peasants were too poor to perform the most basic of social duties, such as burying their deceased parents, whose bodies were often left to be devoured by vultures and packs of wild dogs. Given the great reverence for family and parents that had been in-

stilled by Confucian teachings for millennia, the psychological scars left by the nonperformance of such critical obligations must have been deep and lasting.

Though rural China cried out for strong leadership and far-reaching economic and social reform, China's leaders bickered and plotted but did little. Sun gave lip service to the Nationalist party's need to deal with the peasant problem. But his abysmal ignorance of rural conditions was revealed by statements in which he denied that China had large landlords and his refusal to believe that there were "serious difficulties" between the great mass of the peasantry and the landowners. Communists such as Mao Zedong were an exception to the general Nationalist pattern of ignorance and neglect. But the numbers of peasants the Communists could as-

Though he received no formal military training, Mao Zedong's adoption of a soldier's uniform reflected the importance of force in the highly militarized and deeply divided society that China had become by the early 20th century.

sist were limited by the small size of the party at that time and the obstacles thrown up by the landlords and warlords. Nonetheless, Mao and his fellow Communists persisted in their work of rural reconstruction in areas such as Hunan in south-central China.

Though the son of a fairly prosperous peasant, Mao had rebelled early in his life against his father's exploitation of the tenants and laborers who worked the family fields. Receiving little assistance from his estranged father, Mao was forced to make his own way and educate himself in the history, philosophy, and economic theory that most other nationalist and revolutionary leaders mastered in private schools. Having made his way to Beijing in the post–May Fourth era, Mao came under the influence of thinkers such as Li Dazhao, who placed considerable emphasis on solutions to the peasant problem as one of the keys to China's survival. As the following passage from Mao's early writings reveals, almost from the outset he was committed to revolutionary solutions that depended on peasant support:

> A revolution is an insurrection, an act of violence by which one class overthrows another. A rural revolution is a revolution by which the peasantry overthrows the power of the feudal landlord class. Without using the greatest force, the peasants cannot possibly overthrow the deep-rooted authority of the landlords which has lasted for thousands of years.

Throughout most of the 1920s, however, Mao's vision of a rural revolution remained a minority and much repudiated position even with the Communist party. Rivals such as Li Lisan, who favored a more orthodox strategy based on the urban working classes that had formed the core of support for the Bolshevik revolutionaries in Russia, dominated party policy making. Ironically, the move by Chiang and the Nationalist leaders to destroy all of the Communists in the late-1920s would pave the way for Mao's rise to leadership in the party.

The Nationalists' successful drive for national power began only after Sun Yat-sen's death in 1925 opened the way for their counterparts among the warlords, Chiang Kaishek and his cronies, to seize control of the party. After winning over or eliminating the military chiefs in the Canton area, Chiang marched north with his newly created armies in a campaign that culminated in the Nationalists' seizure of the Yangtze River valley and Shanghai in early 1927. Later his forces also captured the capital at Beijing and the rest of the Yellow River basin. The refusal of most of the warlords to end their long-stand-

ing feuding meant that Chiang could defeat them or buy them out, one by one. By the late 1920s, he was the master of China—in name and international standing, if not in actual fact. He was, in effect, the head of a warlord hierarchy, but most political leaders within China and in the outside world recognized him as the new president of China.

Since there were no elections, the people had no say in the matter. Nor had Chiang's political rivals, whom he ruthlessly purged even while he was still settling scores with the warlords. The most fateful of these purges came while Chiang's armies were occupying Shanghai in the spring of 1927. After clearing the Communists out of the Nationalist Central Committee, where they had been represented since 1924, Chiang ordered his troops and gangster allies in Shanghai to round up the workers, despite the fact that their mass demonstrations had done so much to make possible the city's capture by the Nationalist armies. In some of the most brutal scenes of an era when violence and human suffering were almost commonplace, Chiang's soldiers and hired toughs machine-gunned and beheaded Communist supporters wherever they could be found throughout the city. Though the Communists' Soviet advisors continued to insist that they cooperate with the Nationalists, Chiang's extension of the bloody purge to other cities and into the countryside precipitated an open civil war between the two main branches of the nationalist movement that, despite temporary and halfhearted truces, ended only with the Communist victory in 1949.

REACTION VERSUS REVOLUTION: THE STRUGGLE FOR CHINA.   At the outset, all signs appeared to favor the Nationalist party in its violent contest with the Communists for control of China. Despite the fact that Chiang did not fully control the more powerful regional warlords, as the heir of Sun Yat-sen and as the architect of the victorious northern campaign, he had the support of the richest and most powerful social groups in China. These included the urban businesspeople and merchants, most of the intellectuals, and a large portion of the university students, the rural landlords, and the military. Chiang could also count on the services of the bureaucrats and police throughout China, and he launched a calculated public relations campaign to win sympathy in the United States and the other Western democracies. The urban workers, who preferred the Communists or other radical parties, had been beaten into submission. The peasants, who longed for stable government and state-sponsored relief, were willing, for the time being at

Even more than in the nationalist movements in colonized India and Egypt, women were drawn in large numbers into violent, revolutionary struggles in China and Vietnam. The breakdown of the polit-ical system and social order not only weakened the legal and family restrictions that had subordinated women and limited their career choices but also ushered in decades of severe crisis and brutal conflict in which the very survival of women depended on their assuming radically new roles and actively involving themselves in revolutionary activities. The following quotations are taken from Vietnamese and Chinese revolutionary writings and interviews with women involved in the revolutionary movements in each country. They express the women's goals, their struggle to be taken seriously in the uncharacteristic political roles they had assumed, and some of the many ways women found self-respect and redress for their grievances as a result of the changes wrought by the spread of the new social order.

1. Women must first of all be masters of themselves. They must strive to become skilled workers . . . and, at the same time, they must strictly observe family planning. Another major question is the responsibility of husbands to help their wives look after children and other housework. . . .

2. We intellectuals had had little contact with the peasants and when we first walked through the village in our Chinese gowns or skirts the people would just stare at us and talk behind our backs. When the village head beat gongs to call out the women to the meetings we were holding for them, only men and old women came, but no young ones. Later we found out that the land lords and rich peasants had spread slanders among the masses saying "They are a pack of wild women. Their words are not for young brides to hear."

3. . . . brave wives and daughters-in-law, untrammelled by the presence of their menfolk, could voice their own bitterness . . . encourage their poor sisters to do likewise, and thus eventually bring to the village-wide gatherings the strength of "half of China" as the more enlightened women, very much in earnest, like to call themselves. By "speaking pains to recall pains," the women found that they had as many if not more grievances than the men, and that given a chance to speak in public, they were as good at it as their fathers and husbands.

4. In Chingtsun the work team found a woman whose husband thought her ugly and wanted to divorce her. She was very depressed until she learned that under the Draft Law [of the Communist party] she could have her own share of land. Then she cheered up immediately. "If he divorces me, never mind," she said. "I'll get my share and the children will get theirs. We can live a good life without him."

Questions: On the basis of these quotations, what traditional roles and attitudes of women did those who opposed revolutionary movements in China and Vietnam seek to defend? Which of these roles and attitudes do the revolutionaries reject? What do they believe is essential if women are to gain equality with men? How similar and different are the demands of the women supporting these revolutionary movements in Asia to those of women's rights advocates in the United States?

least, to wait and see if the Nationalists would act to alleviate their distress.

Despite his ruthless betrayal of the Communists, Chiang continued to receive assistance from the Soviet Union, where Stalin had emerged as the unchallenged dictator of a totalitarian state. Possibly because he preferred a weak China under the Nationalist party to a revolutionary one under the Communists, Stalin gave little assistance to his alleged comrades and continued to push policies that left them at the mercy of Chiang and his henchmen. With what seemed to be insurmountable advantages, Chiang moved to eliminate what was left in the way of rivals for power, most especially the shattered remnants of the Communist party.

The Guomindang's brutal suppression of the workers' organizations in Shanghai in 1927 marked a watershed in the history of modern China. The Guomindang-Communist alliance was shattered, and Mao Zedong's call for a peasant-based revolution became imperative as the vulnerability of the small Chinese working class was exposed.

The smashing of the workers' movement in Shanghai and other urban centers greatly strengthened Mao's hand in his ongoing struggle with Li Lisan and other orthodox ideologues within the Communist party. Mao and much of what was left of the Communist leadership retreated into the countryside and set to work carrying out land reform and improving life in China's tens of thousands of impoverished villages.

In the late 1920s the center of Communist operations was the south-central province of Hunan, where the Communists established soviets (named after the revolutionary workers' and soldiers' organizations in Russia) and "liberated" zones. This area became the main target of a succession of military campaigns that Chiang launched against the Communists in the early 1930s. Though the Communists successfully resisted the early campaigns, Chiang's reliance on German military advisors and his command of the resources and labor of the rest of China eventually wore the Communists down. By the autumn of 1934, it was clear that if the remaining Communists did not break out of the Nationalist encirclement and escape from Hunan, they would be eliminated. At the head of more than 90,000 party stalwarts,

Mao set off on the Long March across thousands of miles of the most difficult terrain in China to Shaanxi in northwestern China, where a smaller number of peasant soviets had been established. At the end of the following year, Mao and only about 20,000 followers fought their way into the rugged, sparsely populated terrain of Shaanxi, which was the center of the Communist movement in China until the mid-1940s.

By the end of the Long March, Mao was firmly established as the head of the Chinese Communist party. The heroic and successful struggle for survival in the Long March by those who supported his peasant-based strategy of revolution greatly enhanced his stature and fired his followers with the conviction that whatever the odds, they could not be defeated. Chiang obviously did not agree. Soon after the Communists were established in Shaanxi, he launched a new series of extermination campaigns. Again, the peasant supporters of the Communists fought valiantly, but Chiang's armies were beginning to get the upper hand by early 1937.

Just as he was convinced that he was on the verge of total victory, Chiang's anti-Communist crusade was rudely interrupted by the all-out Japanese invasion of the

Chinese mainland. Obsessed with the Communists, Chiang had done little to block the steady advance of Japanese forces in the early 1930s into Manchuria and the islands along China's coast. Even after the Japanese launched their massive assaults aimed at the conquest of all of China, Chiang wanted to continue the struggle against the Communists. Forced by his military commanders to concentrate on the Japanese threat, Chiang grudgingly formed a military alliance with the Communists. Though he did all he could to undermine the alliance and continue the anti-Communist struggle by underhanded means, for the next seven years the war against Japan took priority over the civil war in the contest for control of China.

Though it brought yet further suffering to the Chinese people, the Japanese invasion proved enormously advantageous for the Communist party. This turned out to be so vital to the ultimate Communist victory that some writers have speculated that Mao chose Shaanxi in the northwest partly out of the calculation that it would put his forces in the probable path of the anticipated Japanese advance. Whatever his thinking, the war against the Japanese greatly strengthened his cause while weakening his Nationalist rivals. The Japanese invaders captured much of the Chinese coast, where the trading cities were the centers of the business and mercantile backers of the Nationalists. Chiang's conventional military forces were pummeled by the superior air, land, and sea forces of the Japanese. The Nationalists' attempts to meet the Japanese in conventional, set-piece battles led to disaster; their inability to defend the coastal provinces lowered their standing in the eyes of the Chinese people. Chiang's hasty and humiliating retreat to Chongqing deep in the interior of China further eroded his aura as the savior of the nation and rendered him more dependent than ever on his military allies and the rural landlords.

The Japanese invasion proved critical in the Communist drive to victory. But equally important were the Communists' social and economic reform programs that eventually won the great majority of the peasantry, the students and intellectuals, and even many of the bureaucrats to their side. Whereas Chiang, whatever his intentions, was able to do little to improve the condition of the great mass of the people, Mao made the peasants' uplift the central element in his drive for power. Land reforms, access to education, and improved health care gave the peasantry a real stake in Mao's revolutionary movement and good reason to defend the soviets against both the Nationalists and the Japanese. In contrast to

Chiang's armies, whose arrival meant theft, rape, and wanton murder to China's villagers, Mao's soldiers were indoctrinated with the need to protect the peasantry and win their support. Lest they forget, harsh penalties were levied, such as execution for stealing so much as an egg.

As guerrilla fighters, Mao's soldiers had a much better chance to survive and advance in the ranks than the forcibly conscripted, brutally treated rank-and-file Nationalists. Mao and the commanders around him, such as Lin Biao, who had been trained at Chiang's Whampoa Academy in the 1920s, proved far more gifted—even in conventional warfare—than the often corrupt and inept Nationalist generals. Thus though the importance of the Japanese invasion cannot be discounted, the Communists won the mandate to govern China because they offered solutions to China's fundamental social and economic problems, and they put their programs into action in the areas that came under their control. In a situation where revolutionary changes appeared to be essential, the Communists alone convinced the Chinese people that they had the leaders and program that could affect them.

ANTI-COLONIALISM AND REVOLUTION IN VIETNAM

Like most African and Asian peoples, the Vietnamese, as well as their neighbors in Laos and Cambodia, were brought under European colonial rule in the 19th century. But because the Vietnamese had long modeled their polity on the Confucian system of their giant neighbor to the north and borrowed heavily from China in the social and cultural spheres, their encounter with the expansive West had much in common with that of the Chinese. The Vietnamese were also shocked by the sudden and forcible intrusion into their formerly rather sheltered world by one of the European imperialist powers, France, bent on restoring its world empire after defeats in Europe. As in China, the failure of Vietnam's Confucian emperor and bureaucracy to successfully repel the foreign invaders discredited and eventually led to the complete collapse of the system around which the Vietnamese had organized civilized life for nearly two millennia.

As in China, the Vietnamese nationalists who emerged in the 1890s and early 1900s soon realized that their rejection of the traditional order meant that radical solutions rather than gradualist, reformist measures would be required to liberate Vietnam and build a viable social order for its people. The French refusal to encour-

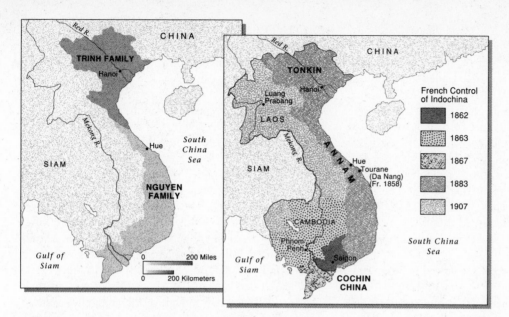

Vietnam: Divisions in the Nguyen and French Periods

age the growth of moderate political parties and to tolerate constitutional or peaceful mass agitation also served to channel Vietnamese political energies into revolutionary channels. The highly exploitive nature of French rule in Vietnam, which was excessive even by colonial standards, also gave rise to economic distress and social dislocations that rendered the status quo unbearable for most of the Vietnamese and won widespread support for those who offered revolutionary alternatives. Therefore, in contrast to much of the rest of the colonized world, the Vietnamese drive to win independence and build a new nation was dominated by violent insurrections, long decades of guerrilla warfare, and far-reaching social and economic transformations.

As if the struggle against the French and reactionary elements in Vietnam itself were not enough, the Vietnamese also had to contend with the intervention of the U.S. goliath in their affairs and nearly a decade of armed struggle against the world's leading military power. Though a tribute to their endurance and dedication, the ultimate victory of the Vietnamese in that struggle left the nation in shambles and isolated from much of the rest of the world.

THE NGUYEN DYNASTY AND THE RISE OF FRENCH COLONIAL DOMINANCE.   French interest in Vietnam reached back as far as the 17th century. Driven from Japan by the founders of the Tokugawa Shogunate, French missionaries fell back on coastal Vietnam. Vietnam attracted them both because its Confucian elite

seemed deceptively similar to that of the Japanese and because the continuing wars between rival dynastic houses in the Red River valley and central Vietnam gave the missionaries ample openings for their conversion efforts. From this time onward, French rulers, who styled themselves the protectors of the Catholic missions overseas, took an interest in Vietnamese affairs. As the numbers of converts grew into the tens of thousands and French merchants began to trade at Vietnamese ports, the French stake in the region increased.

By the last decades of the 18th century, French involvement had become distinctly political as a result of the power struggles that convulsed the region. In the south a genuine peasant rebellion, the Tayson, toppled the Nguyen dynasty in the late 1770s. In the following years the northern rival of the Nguyen, the Trinh dynasty, was also dethroned. The Tayson controlled most of the country, eliminated the Trinh, and all but wiped out the Nguyen. Seeing a chance to win influence in the ruling house, the French head of the Vietnam mission, the Bishop of Adran, threw his support behind the one surviving prince of the southern house, Nguyen Anh.

Anh had fled into the Mekong wilderness with a handful of supporters, thus escaping death at the hands of the Tayson. With the arms and advice of the French, he rallied local support for the dynasty and soon fielded a sizable army. After driving the Tayson from the south, Nguyen Anh launched an invasion of Tayson strongholds in the north. His task of conquest was made easier by bitter quarrels among the Tayson leaders. By 1802 the Nguyen armies had prevailed, and Nguyen Anh proclaimed himself the Gia Long emperor of Vietnam.

Nguyen Anh made the old Nguyen capital at Hue in central Vietnam the imperial capital of a unified Vietnam. His French missionary allies were rewarded with a special place at court, and French traders were given greater access to the port of Saigon, which was rapidly becoming the leading city of the Mekong River valley region in the south. The Nguyen dynasty was the first in centuries to rule all of Vietnam and the first to rule a Vietnamese kingdom that included both the Red River and Mekong deltas. In fact, the Mekong region had only begun to be settled extensively by Vietnamese in the century or so before Nguyen Anh rose to power.

Nguyen Anh and his successors proved to be archtraditionalists deeply committed to strengthening Confucianism in Vietnam. Their capital at Hue was intended to be a perfect miniature of the imperial palace at Beijing. The dynasty patronized Confucian schools and built its administration around scholar-bureaucrats well versed in Confucian learning. The second emperor, Minh Mang (1820–1841), prided himself on his knowledge of the Confucian classics and his mastery of the Chinese script. He even had the audacity to criticize the brushwork of the reigning Chinese emperor, who after all was not any more Chinese than Minh Mang but descended from Manchu nomads. All of this proved deeply disappointing to the French missionaries, who had been counting on baptizing Nguyen Anh and then carrying out the sort of top-down conversion of the Vietnamese the Jesuits had hoped for ever since their arrival in Asia. Things actually got worse. Gia Long's ultra-Confucian successor, Minh Mang, came to view the Catholics as something of a fifth column, which he believed posed a substantial danger to the dynasty. His persecution of the Vietnamese Catholic community not only enraged the missionaries but also contributed to the growing political and military intervention of the French government in the region.

Pushed by both political pressures at home and military defeats in Europe, French adventurers and soldiers exploited quarrels with the Nguyen rulers to justify the piecemeal conquest of Vietnam and neighboring Cambodia and Laos, beginning in the late 1840s. By the 1890s the entire country was under French control, and the Nguyen dynasty had been reduced to the status of puppet princes. In the following decades the French concentrated on drawing revenue and resources from Vietnam while providing very little in return.

The French determination to make Vietnam a colony profitable for the homeland exacerbated social and economic problems that were already bad under the Nguyen rulers. Most of the densely packed peasant population of the north lacked enough land to even eke out a subsistence livelihood. French taxes and the burden of obligatory purchases by each village of set amounts of government-sold opium and alcohol drove many peasants into labor in the mines. Even larger numbers left their ancestral villages and migrated to the Mekong region to work on the plantations established there by French and Chinese entrepreneurs or to become tenants on the great estates that had been carved out of sparsely settled frontier regions by Vietnamese and Chinese landlords. Migration brought little relief. Plantation workers were paid little and treated much like slave laborers. The unchecked demands of the Mekong landlords left their tenants with scarcely enough of the crops they grew to feed, clothe, and house their families. The blatantly exploitive nature of French colonialism in Vietnam was graphically revealed by the statistics the French themselves collected. These showed a sharp drop in the food consumed by the peasantry in all parts of the colony between the early 1900s and the 1930s—a drop that occurred despite the fact that Vietnam became, in these years, one of the world's major rice-exporting areas.

VIETNAMESE NATIONALISM: BOURGEOIS DEAD ENDS AND COMMUNIST SURVIVAL. The failure of the Nguyen rulers after Minh Mang to rally the forces of resistance against the French did much to discredit the dynasty. But from the 1880s into the first decades of the 20th century, guerrilla warfare was waged in various parts of the country in support of the Save the King movement. Because this resistance was localized and small-scale, the French were able to crush it on a piecemeal basis. In any case, French control over the puppet emperors who remained on the throne at Hue left the rebels with little cause worth fighting for. The failure of the Nguyen and the Confucian bureaucratic classes to defend Vietnam against the French did much to discredit the old order in the eyes of the new generations that came of age in the early decades of French rule. Perhaps because Confucianism was imported rather than homegrown, the Vietnamese were quicker than the Chinese to reject it once its failings were clear, and they did so with a good deal less trauma. But its demise left an ideological and institutional vacuum that the Vietnamese, again like the Chinese, would struggle decades to fill.

In the first years of the 20th century a new Western-educated middle class, similar to that found in other colonial settings was formed by the children of the traditional Confucian elite and the emerging landlord class in the Mekong region. Some, taking advantage of their parents' wealth, went to French schools and emerged speaking fluent French and with a taste for French fashions and frequent holiday jaunts to Paris and the French Riviera. Many of them went to work for the French as colonial administrators, bank managers, and even labor recruiters. Others pursued independent professional careers as lawyers, doctors, and journalists. Many who opted for French educations and French life-styles were soon drawn into nationalist organizations. Like their

Though violent Vietnamese resistance to French rule never really died out, this cartoon illustrates that some Vietnamese—mostly from the landlord and commercial middle classes—were willing not only to collaborate with the colonizers but also to adopt their dress and social conventions.

counterparts elsewhere in the colonies, the members of these organizations initially concentrated on protesting French racism and discrimination, improving their wages, and gaining access to positions in the colonial government held by the French.

As in other colonies, nationalist newspapers and magazines proliferated. These became the focal point of an extended debate regarding the approach that should be taken toward winning freedom from French rule and, increasingly, what needed to be done to rebuild Vietnam as a whole. Because the French forcibly repressed all attempts to mount peaceful mass demonstrations or organize constitutional agitation, those who argued for violent resistance eventually gained the upper hand. In the early 1920s the nationalist struggle was centered in the clandestine Vietnamese Nationalist party (Vietnamese Quoc Dan Dong, or VNQDD), which was committed to violent revolution against the French colonizers. Though the VNQDD made some attempt to organize urban laborers and peasant villagers, party members were drawn overwhelmingly from the children of the landlord elite and urban professional classes. Their secret codes and elaborate rituals proved little protection against the dreaded Sûreté, or French Secret Police. A series of failed uprisings, culminating in a 1929 attempt to spark a general revolution with the assassination of a hated French official in charge of labor recruitment, decimated the party. It was particularly hard-hit by the following all-out French campaign of repression, execution, and imprisonment. From that point onward the bourgeois nationalists were never again the dominant force in the independence struggle.

The demise of the VNQDD left its major rival, the Communist party, as the main focus of nationalist resistance in Vietnam. As in China and Korea, the Communist wing of the nationalist movement had developed in Vietnam during the 1920s, often at the initiative of leaders in exile. By the late 1920s the party was dominated by the charismatic young Nguyen Ai Quoc, later known as Ho Chi Minh. Ho had discovered Marxism while studying in France and Russia during and after World War I. Disillusioned by his failure to gain a hearing for his plea to the victorious Allies at the Versailles Peace Conference for the Vietnamese right to self-determination, Ho dedicated himself to a revolutionary struggle to drive the French from Indochina.

In the early 1930s the Communist party still held to the rigid, though unrealistic, orthodox vision of a revolution based on the urban working classes. Since the workers in Vietnam made up as small a percentage of the population as they had in China, the orthodox strategy made little headway. A sudden shift in the early 1930s to a peasant emphasis, in part to take advantage of widespread but non-Communist-inspired peasant uprisings in central Vietnam, led to a disaster almost as great as that which had overtaken the VNQDD a year before. French repression smashed the Communist party hierarchy and drove most of the major Communist leaders into exile. But the superior underground organization of the Communists and the support they received from Comintern helped them survive a French onslaught. Slowly, during the late 1930s, the discredited Ho reestablished his place in the party, and the party won growing peasant support due to its programs for land reform, higher wages for laborers, mass education, and health care. When the French were weakened by the Japanese invasion of Indochina in 1941, the Communists were ready to use the colonizers' setbacks to advance the struggle for national liberation.

CONCLUSION

A CENTURY OF REVOLUTIONS

Not since the late 18th and early 19th centuries has there been a succession of revolutions like that in the middle decades of the 20th century. In contrast to the revolutionary movements of the earlier period, however, the mid-20th century upheavals were just the first waves of a revolutionary tide that struck with renewed fury after 1945. Though the revolt against Spanish colonial rule continued to spread through Latin America in the early 1800s, revolutionary currents receded in Europe and elsewhere during the Napoleonic era (1798–1815). In addition, like the American Revolution that had begun the earlier phase of revolutionary struggle, the risings in Latin America were more wars of independence than full-scale revolutions. Thus of all of the earlier political upheavals only the French Revolution resulted in the sweeping social and economic transformations that are essential to the revolutionary process. Again by contrast, the successful and failed revolutions of the mid-20th century, from Mexico and Russia to Germany and China, were all aimed at these fundamental transformations, even if they often fell far short of the revolutionaries' goals.

A number of factors help to account for the sudden surge of the revolutionary tide in the 20th century. To begin with, vast increases in the power and reach of the state, which were made possible by industrial weaponry and communications systems, greatly reduced the effectiveness of the traditional tactics of resistance employed by key social groups, such as the peasantry. Larger, better-trained bureaucracies made cheating or running away from the tax collector increasingly difficult. Well-disciplined armies proved more and more able to foil such long-standing protest options as banditry, local riots, and rebellions. The ever greater growth of the commercial and working classes and their concentration in urban centers also contributed substantially to the propensity of disgruntled groups to confront what they viewed as the oppressive or ineffectual agents of the state, who were also concentrated in the cities. In addition, increases in the size and power of state bureaucracies and institutions themselves made them an increasingly obvious target. Somewhat ironically, dissident leaders and their followers increasingly counted on the seizure of the very state apparatus and national communications systems that they had once found so oppressive to carry out their revolutionary programs.

Equally fundamentally, the rise of revolutionary movements was fed by the underlying disruptions that had been caused by the spread of the Industrial Revolution and the Western-centered, global market system. Handicraft producers thrown out of work by an influx of machine-manufactured goods, and peasants who lost their land to moneylenders frequently rallied to calls to riot and ultimately became caught up in revolutionary currents. In the colonies, unemployed Western-educated African and Asian secondary school and college graduates became deeply committed to struggles for independence that promised them dignity and decent jobs. Urban laborers, enraged by the appalling working and living conditions that were characteristic of the early stages of industrialization in countries such as Russia, provided key support for revolutionary parties in many countries. Although global depression did much to fire the revolutionaries' longings, the world wars proved to be even more fertile seed beds of revolution. Returning soldiers and neglected veterans provided the shock troops for leftist revolutionaries and Fascist pretenders alike. Defeated states witnessed the rapid erosion of their power to suppress internal enemies and floundered as their armies refused to defend them or joined movements dedicated to their overthrow. Here the great increase in global interconnectedness was critical, as the economic competition and military rivalry of the industrialized powers drew them into unwanted wars that often proved beyond their capacity to wage successfully.

Another key factor that contributed to the sharp rise in the incidence of revolutions in the 20th century was the underlying intellectual climate. Notions of progress and a belief in the perfectibility of human society, which were widely held in the 19th century, deeply influenced the thinking of political theorists from such Communists as Marx and Lenin to such anarchists as Mikhail Bakunin. These and other revolutionary ideologues sought in part to overthrow existing regimes, which they viewed as exploitive. But they were also deeply committed to building radically new societies that would bring justice and a decent livelihood to previously downtrodden social groups, such as the working classes, the peasantry, and the urban poor. Visions of the good life in peasant communes or workers' utopias have proved a powerful driving force for revolutionary currents throughout the 20th century. One measure of their influence is the extent to which highly competitive capitalist societies have developed social welfare programs to curb social unrest that could spiral into revolutionary challenges to the existing order.

FURTHER READINGS

Good overall studies of revolution in the 20th century include Eric Wolf's *Peasant Wars of the Twentieth Century* (1965), Theda Skocpol's *States and Social Revolutions* (1979), and John Dunn's *Modern Revolutions* (1972).

Two good introductory texts to Latin American history in the 20th century are E. Bradfurd Burns's *Latin America: A Concise Interpretative History* (5th ed., 1990) and Thomas E. Skidmore and Peter H. Smith's *Modern Latin America* (1989). An excellent overview of Latin American literature and art is provided by Jean Franco's *The Modern Culture of Latin America* (2nd ed., 1970). The role of women is treated in June Hahner's *Women in Latin America* (1976). Among a large number of studies of the Mexican revolution, Alan Knight's *The Mexican Revolution*, 2 vols. (1986) and John M. Hart's *Revolutionary Mexico* (1987) provide two of the best overall analyses of that event.

On the Russian Revolution, Sheila Fitzpatrick's *The Russian Revolution, 1917–1932* (1982) is a recent overview with a rich bibliography. See also A. Rabinowich's *The Bolsheviks Come to Power* (1976) and E. H. Carr's *The Bolshevik Revolution,* 3 vols. (1978 ed.). On the Stalinist era, see Robert Tucker's *Stalin as a Revolutionary* (1972) and Robert Conquest's *The Great Terror: A Reassessment* (1990). Edmund Wilson's *To the Finland Station* (1972) offers a dramatic account of the Revolution's early phase and the philosophical currents that informed Bolshevik thinking. On specific social groups in the Revolution, see John Keep's *The Russian Revolution: A Study in Mass Mobilization* (1976) and Victoria Bonnell's *Roots of Rebellion: Workers' Politics and Organizations in St. Petersburg and Moscow, 1900–1914* (1983).

Some of the best general studies on China in the 20th century include Lucian Bianco's *The Communist Revolution in China* (1967), C. P. Fitzgearald's *The Birth of Communist China* (1964), Wolfgang Franke's *A Century of Chinese Revolution* (1970), and Jonathan Spence's *The Search for Modern China* (1990). For first-hand accounts of conditions in the revolutionary era, see especially Graham Peck's *Two Kinds of Time* (1950), Edgar Snow's *Red Star over China* (1938), and Theodore White and Analee Jacoby's *Thunder Out of China* (1946). Mark Selden's *The Yenan Way to Revolution in China* (1971) provides the fullest account of the development of the Communist movement after the Long March. Elizabeth Croll's *Feminism and Socialism in China* includes able surveys of women's roles in the decades of revolution.

There is substantial literature on Vietnamese history during the Nguyen and French period. Alexander Woodside's *Vietnam and the China Model* (1971) remains the place to start on the pre-French period, and Buttinger's *Political History of Vietnam* (1968) also remains useful for general background. Woodside, Huynh Kim Khanh, David Marr, Milton Osborne, William Duiker, and Hue Tam Ho-Tai have all made important contributions to the rise of nationalism and communism in Vietnam. Ho Tai's recent study of revolutionary currents in the 1920s and 1930s has fine sections on women's issues.

1876 Madras famine in India

1882 Orabi revolt in Egypt;
British occupation of Egypt

1885 Founding of
the Indian Con-
gress party

1890s First Egyptian political parties formed

1897 World Zionist Organization
founded; West African Aborigines
Rights Protection Society founded

1899–1901 Anglo-Boer War in
South Africa

1904–1905 Japanese victory over Russia; British
partition of the province
of Bengal in India

1906 Dinshawai
incident in Egypt;
Muslim League
founded in India

1909 Morley-
Minto political
reforms in India

1910 Union of South
Africa established

1913 Rabindranath Tagore wins
the Nobel Prize for literature

1914–1918 World War I; main theaters of war in European
colonies: Mesopotamia, Arabia and Palestine, and Africa

1915–1916 McMahon-
Hussein correspondence

1917 Balfour
Declaration

1919 Revolt in Egypt, women a major force
in demonstrations; Montagu-Chelmsford
reforms in India; Rowlatt Act in India; first
all-India civil disobedience movement

1920s Pan-African Congresses in Paris;
beginnings of the négritude movement

1921 René Maran wins the French
Prix Goncourt for *Batouala*

1922 British granted the League
of Nations mandate for Palestine; first stage in Egyptian
independence

1927 Simon Com-
mission in India

Decolonization and the Decline of the European World Order

8

INTRODUCTION. All of the great civilizations of Asia and Africa had been shaken to their foundations by Europe's rise to global hegemony in the 18th and 19th centuries. European political, economic, and later cultural dominance forced the thinkers and leaders of ancient centers of civilized development—from China and the Islamic heartlands to South Asia and Sudanic Africa—to reappraise their own beliefs, institutions, and traditions. However reluctantly, many of these thinkers and politicians came to the realization that if their civilizations were to be revitalized and freed from European domination, hard decisions had to be made as to what could be preserved of their own cultures and what could be rejected, what needed to be borrowed from the Europeans and what could be refused.

Most accounts of African and Asian solutions to these dilemmas stress ideas such as nationalism and modes of political organization that the colonized peoples borrowed from the Europeans. But African and Asian responses, which eventually forced the Europeans to relinquish their colonial empires, were also deeply rooted in their own religions, long-standing patterns of political mobilization, and other facets of their traditions of civilization. Reinvigorating and reformulating these distinctive civilized traditions has proved one of the central challenges for 20th-century African and Asian leaders, in both the era of decolonization and the postcolonial period that followed.

1941–1945 World War II; main theaters of war in European colonies: North Africa, Southeast Asia, and Pacific Islands

1930s Great Depression

1931 Gandhi-led Salt March revives Indian Nationalist movement; strikes and rebellion in Sierra Leone

1935 Government of India Act

1948 Israel-Palestine partition, first Arab-Israeli war; beginning of apartheid legislation in South Africa

1942 Cripps Mission to India; Quit India movement

1947 India and Pakistan gain independence

1936–1939 Arab risings in Palestine

1941 Fall of Singapore to the Japanese

1958 Afrikaner Nationalist party declares independence of South Africa

1962 Algeria wins independence

1957 Ghana established as first independent African nation

1960 Congo granted independence from Belgian rule

When Europe's global domination peaked in the decades at the end of the 19th century, forces were beginning to build that eventually led to the loss of its colonial empires and brought its world domination to an end. Some of these forces came from within the colonies, as a sense of community and common cause began to build among the Western-educated, middle-class groups that emerged in colonized Asia and Africa. The political organizations established by these groups and their efforts to arouse mass nationalist sentiments increasingly challenged the right of the Europeans to subjugate African and Asian lands and peoples.

Though violence was sometimes employed, particularly in colonial societies with settler populations, African and Asian nationalists relied mainly on peaceful mass demonstrations, economic boycotts, and constitutional maneuvers in their struggles for independence. Leaders in these struggles, such as Mohandas Gandhi and Kwame Nkrumah, deftly turned the Europeans' own principles and values, such as those stressing human dignity and civil rights, against the colonial overlords. At the same time, they employed indigenous religious beliefs and traditional symbols of legitimacy to rally mass support to their cause. The fact that European colonial regimes had been built in collaboration with indigenous elite groups—princes, landlords, and the new middle classes—and depended for their survival on these groups, as well as on soldiers and police officers recruited from the colonized peoples, rendered them particularly vulnerable to growing challenges from within.

In addition to internal forces that eroded the European colonial order, growing conflicts among the Western powers dealt heavy blows to the imperial edifice. Their rivalries, which helped cause the late-19th-century scramble for colonies, also contributed to the outbreak of the series of global conflicts that set the framework for 20th-century global history. Thus World War I cast doubt on the Europeans' claims that they were the fittest of all peoples to rule. It also strengthened the arguments of nationalist leaders who sought to disprove prevailing myths of European invincibility and superiority. Even before 1914 those myths had been badly damaged by the rise of Japan as an industrialized, global power. Japan's decisive victory over the Russians in the Russo-Japanese War of 1904 and 1905 thrilled nationalists from Vietnam to Egypt and gave them confidence that the European colonizers could be overcome.

The social and economic disruptions caused by the war in key colonies, such as Egypt, India, and the Ivory Coast, made it possible for nationalist agitators to build a mass base for their anticolonial movements. The Great Depression of the 1930s, which hit most of the colonies very hard, gave further strength to the nationalist cause. It also brought on harsh repression in many colonies on the part of European administrators, who became deeply worried about their capacity to preserve European dominance in Africa and Asia. Despite the ultimate victory of the old colonial powers over Nazi Germany and Japan, World War II dealt a series of crushing blows to the European colonial order. Within decades of the end of that conflict, most of Africa and Asia had been liberated from European rule.

This chapter explores each of these phases of the decolonization process, beginning with the first stirrings of nationalism in India and Egypt in the late 19th century. The sections that follow examine the interplay between international events, such as those associated with the two world wars and the Great Depression, and conditions and movements in the colonies. Since it is impossible to relate the history of the independence struggles in each of the colonies, key movements in India, Egypt, and British and French West Africa are considered in some depth. These specific movements are then related to broader patterns in African and Asian decolonization or, in the case of South Africa, the winning of independence for a small minority of the colonial population. The case of Vietnam, which makes an interesting comparison with its equally revolutionary neighbor, China, is considered in Chapter 7.

THE INDIAN PROTOTYPE: THE MAKINGS OF THE NATIONALIST CHALLENGE TO THE BRITISH RAJ

Because India and much of Southeast Asia had been colonized long before Africa, movements for independence arose in Asian colonies somewhat earlier than in their African counterparts. By the last years of the 19th century, the Western-educated minority of the colonized had been organized politically in India and the Philippines for decades, and they were beginning to form associations to give voice to their political concerns in Burma and the Netherlands Indies. Because of India's size, the pivotal role it played in the British Empire (by far the largest of the European imperialist empires) as a whole, and the large numbers and sophistication of India's Western-educated elite, the Indian nationalist movement pioneered patterns of nationalist challenge and European retreat that were later followed in many other colonies. Local conditions elsewhere in Asia and in Africa made for important variations on the sequence of decolonization worked out in India. But key themes, such as the lead taken by Western-educated elites, the importance of charismatic leaders in the spread of the anticolonial struggle to the peasant and urban masses, and a reliance on nonviolent forms of protest, were repeated again and again in other colonial settings, often in conscious emulation of strategies that had achieved great success in India.

The Indian Congress party, which led the Indians to independence and has governed through most of the postcolonial era, grew out of regional associations of Western-educated Indians that were more like study clubs than political organizations. These associations were centered in the cities of Bombay, Poona, Calcutta, and Madras. The Congress party that Indian leaders formed in 1885 had the blessing of a number of high-ranking British officials, who viewed it as a forum through which the opinions of educated Indians could be made known to the government, thereby heading off potential discontent and political protest.

For most of its first decades the Congress party served these purposes quite well. The organization had no mass base and very few ongoing staff members or full-time politicians who could sustain lobbying efforts on issues raised at its annual meetings. Some members of the Congress party voiced concern for the growing poverty of the Indian masses and the drain of wealth from the subcontinent to Great Britain. But the Congress party's debates and petitions to the government were dominated by elite-centric issues, such as the removal of barriers to Indian employment in the colonial bureaucracy and increased Indian representation in all-Indian and local legislative bodies. Most of the members of the early Congress party were firmly loyal to the British rulers and confident that once their grievances were made known to the government, they would be remedied.

Many Western-educated Indians were increasingly troubled, however, by the growing virulence of British racism, which they were convinced had much to do with their poor salaries and limited opportunities for advancement in the colonial administration. In their annual meetings members of the Congress party, who were now able to converse and write in a common language, English, discovered that from wherever they came in India, they were treated in a similar fashion. The Indians' common grievances, their similar educational and class backgrounds, and their growing contacts through the Congress party gave rise to a sense of common Indian identity that had never existed before among the diverse linguistic and religious groups in the Indian subcontinent.

SOCIAL FOUNDATIONS OF A MASS MOVEMENT

By the last years of the 19th century the Western-educated elites had also begun to search for causes that would draw a larger segment of the Indian population

British India in the Nationalist Era

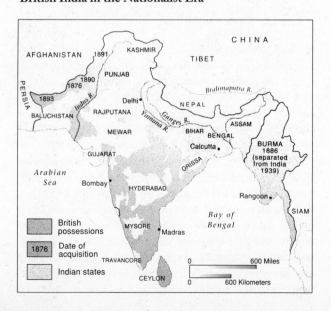

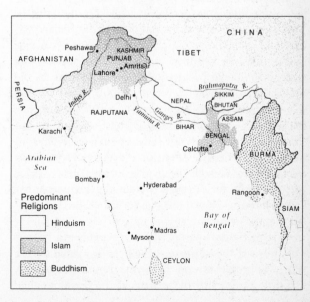

As this photograph of some of the leaders of the "Non-Cooperative" Congress party illustrates, by the early 1920s even moderate Indian nationalist leaders were moving away from loyalty to the British and extensive Anglicization. In the next decades the mix of Western coats and ties and Indian headgear and *dhotis* increasingly gave way to apparel that was entirely Indian, even among such highly Anglicized nationalist families as the Nehrus.

into their growing nationalist community. In many areas of India more than a century of British rule had generated the social and economic disruptions and the sort of discontent that produced substantial numbers of recruits for the nationalist campaigns. Indian business leaders, many of whom would become major financial backers of the Congress party, were angered by the favoritism the British rulers showed to British investors in establishing trade policies in India. Tariffs or taxes on British imports into India were set low, which kept the price of British goods down and made it difficult for Indian producers of such competing products as cotton textiles to shift to modern industrial techniques. Indian investors were also incensed by advantages, in the form of tax incentives and contracts, given to their British rivals. In their ever sharper attacks on British policies, Indian political leaders increasingly stressed these inequities and the more general loss to the Indian people resulting from what they termed the *drain* of Indian resources under colonial rule. Though the British rebutted that a price had to be paid for the peace and good government that had come with colonial rule, nationalist thinkers pointed out that the cost was very high indeed.

A large portion of the Indian government's budget went to cover the expenses of the huge army that fought wars mainly elsewhere in the British Empire—wars that had little to do with the welfare of the Indian people.

The Indian people also paid for the very high salaries and pensions of British administrators, who held posts that Indians themselves could have managed at much lower wages. Whenever possible, as in the purchase of railway equipment or steel for public works projects, the government bought goods manufactured in Great Britain. In addition to buttressing a British economy that was fast losing ground to the United States and Germany, this practice ensured the continuation of the classic colonial relationship between a manufacturing European colonizer and its raw-material-producing overseas dependencies.

In the villages of India the shortcomings of British rule were equally apparent by the last decades of the 19th century. The needs of the British home economy had often dictated policies that pushed the Indian peasantry toward the production of cash crops, such as cotton, jute, and indigo. The decline in food production that invariably resulted played a major role in the regional famines that struck repeatedly in the pre–World War I period. Radical Indian nationalists frequently charged that the British were callously indifferent to the suffering caused by food shortages or outbreaks of epidemic disease and that they did far too little to alleviate the suffering that resulted. In many areas landlessness and chronic poverty, already a problem before the establishment of British rule, increased markedly. In most places

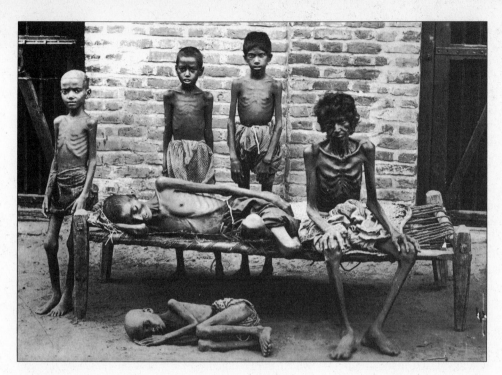

Despite widespread railway construction, government relief measures often proved too little and too late to avert horrific famines in the Indian countryside in the late 19th century. As in Ireland in the same period, British ineptitude in providing famine relief provided Indian nationalist leaders with compelling anticolonial arguments in the struggle to end alien rule.

British measures to control indebtedness and protect small landholders and tenants were too little and came too late.

One clear symptom of the worsening condition of the agrarian classes was the rash of localized riots and rebellions against moneylenders and landlords that shook the imperial peace in the late 19th century. Ironically, discontent among agrarian groups was most pronounced among the more prosperous smallholders and tenants, whose hard work and shrewdness had made them major beneficiaries of great increases in market production in the last half of the 19th century. When the global demand for many kinds of Indian agricultural produce fell at the end of the century, these groups began to rethink their loyalty to the British overlords and respond to the organizational appeals of the Indian nationalists. In many parts of India these market producers were to provide the key organizers and the ongoing core of the popular support aroused by Gandhi and other nationalist leaders in the war years and decades thereafter.

THE RISE OF MILITANT NATIONALISM

Although the issues that nationalist leaders selected, such as cow protection, in their campaigns to build a mass base had great appeal to devout Hindus, they often strongly alienated other religious groups, especially the Muslims, who made up nearly one-fourth of the Indian population. Some leaders, such as B. G. Tilak, were little concerned by this split; they believed that since Hindus were the overwhelming majority of the Indian population, nationalism should be built on appeals to Hindu religiosity. Tilak worked to promote the restoration and revival of what he believed to be the ancient traditions of Hinduism. He thus opposed women's education and the raising of the (very low) marriage age for women. Tilak also turned festivals for Hindu gods into occasions for mass political demonstrations. He broke with more moderate leaders of the Congress party by demanding (long before Gandhi) the boycott of British-manufactured goods and insisting that Indians refuse to serve in the colonial administration and military. He demanded full independence, with no deals or delays, and threatened violent rebellion if the British failed to comply.

Tilak's oratorical skills and religious appeals made him the first Indian nationalist leader with a genuine mass following, though that was confined mainly to his home base in Bombay and surrounding areas in western India. At the same time, his strong views alienated most of the moderates, and his promotion of a very reactionary sort of Hinduism offended and frightened Muslims, progressive Hindus, and the followers of other religions, such as Sikhism. When evidence was found connecting Tilak's writings to underground organizations that advocated violent revolt, the British, who had grown increasingly uneasy about his radical demands and mass appeal, arrested and imprisoned him. Though mass protests against Tilak's conviction and six-year jail term erupted in western India, they were quickly suppressed. Six years in a prison in Burma, as well as the death of his wife, took much of the fire out of India's first populist leader.

The other major threat to the British in India before World War I also came from Hindu communalists who advocated the violent overthrow of the colonial regime. But unlike Tilak and his followers, those who joined the terrorist movement favored clandestine operations over mass demonstrations. Though terrorists were active in several parts of India by the last decade of the 19th century, those in Bengal built perhaps the most extensive underground network. Considerable numbers of young Bengalis, impatient with the gradualist approach advocated by moderates in the Congress party, were attracted to secret societies led by quasi-religious, guru-style leaders who exhorted them to build up their physiques with Western-style calisthenics and learn how to use firearms and make bombs. British officials and government buildings were the major targets of terrorist assassination plots and sabotage, though on occasion the young revolutionaries also struck at European civilians and collaborators among the Indian population. But the terrorists' small numbers and limited support among the colonized populace as a whole rendered them highly vulnerable to British repressive measures. The very considerable resources the British devoted to crushing these violent threats to their rule had broken or greatly weakened the secret organizations by the outbreak of the First World War.

The alternative approaches to protest, which Gandhi developed first in South Africa in the early 1900s and then in India in the years after the war, further sapped the strength of violent populists, such as Tilak, as well as the communalist terrorists. Tilak's removal and the repression campaigns against the terrorists strengthened the hand of the more moderate politicians of the Congress party in the years before the war. Western-educated Indian lawyers became the dominant force in nationalist politics, and—as the careers of Gandhi, Jinnah, and Nehru demonstrated—they would provide many of the movement's key leaders throughout the struggle for independence.

The approach of those who advocated a peaceful, constitutionalist route to decolonization was given added appeal by timely political concessions on the part of the British. The Morley-Minto reforms of 1909 provided educated Indians with considerably expanded opportunities to elect and to serve on local and all-India legislative councils. The moderates also sought ways to expand their political base by both backing local protest movements and increasing their criticisms of the economic and social policies of the British colonizers. In addition, they dropped their loyalist attachment to the colonial overlords. By 1914, prominent moderate politicians were demanding Home Rule for India—but Home Rule within the larger British Empire. Though mass agitation that was genuinely nationalist rather than communalist emerged only with the rise of Gandhi after World War I, much of the organizational basis for Gandhi's early campaigns had been laid in the prewar decades.

EGYPT AND THE RISE OF NATIONALISM IN THE MIDDLE EAST

Egypt is the one country in the Afro-Asian world in which the emergence of nationalism *preceded* European conquest and domination. The risings touched off by the mutiny of Ahmad Orabi and other Egyptian officers, which led to the British occupation in 1882, were aimed at the liberation of the Egyptian people from both their alien Turkish overlords and the meddling Europeans. In contrast to the other peoples who shared an Arab and Islamic cultural tradition, the Egyptians long had a strong sense of separate identity that was anchored in their view of themselves as the descendants of the builders of the great ancient Egyptian civilizations. The concentration of the Egyptians along the Nile River and their geographical separation from other Islamic centers enhanced this sense of a distinctive identity. After the British occupation in 1882, this identity was further reinforced by railway and telegraph systems aimed at establishing communication links within the Nile valley rather than with other Islamic centers, such as those in Syria-Lebanon and the Fertile Crescent. Egyptian distinctiveness was also strengthened by the growing struggle against the British occupation, which other Arabs had not experienced, and the preoccupation of Arab leaders in Syria-Lebanon and the Fertile Crescent with opposition to Ottoman rule.

SOURCES OF EGYPTIAN NATIONALISM

For the Egyptian people British occupation meant, in effect, double colonization by the Turkish khedives (who

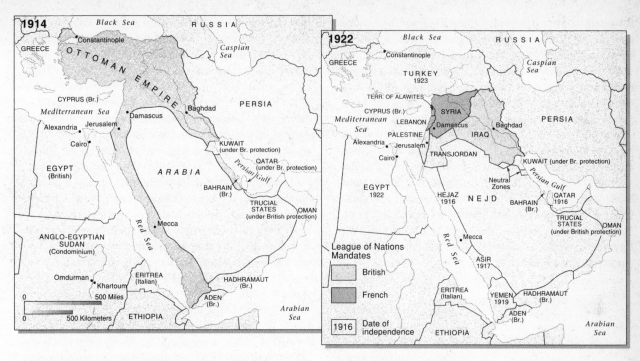

The Middle East, 1914–1922

were left in power) and their British advisors. In the decades following the British conquest, government policy was dominated by the strong-willed and imperious Lord Cromer, who pushed for needed economic reforms that reduced but could not eliminate the debts of the khedival regime, for sweeping reforms in the khedival bureaucracy, and for the construction of irrigation systems and other public works projects. But the prosperity the British congratulated themselves for having brought to Egypt by the first decade of the 20th century favored the tiny middle and elite classes, often at the expense of the mass of the population. The leading beneficiaries included foreign merchants, the Turco-Egyptian political elite, a small Egyptian bourgeoisie in Cairo and other towns in the Nile delta, and the ayan, the great landlords in the rural areas.

The latter were clearly one of the biggest gainers. The British had been forced to rely heavily on established local, estate-owning notables in extending their control into the rural areas. As a result, the ayan, not the impoverished mass of rural cultivators and laborers, received most of the benefits of the new irrigation works, the spread of the railway, and the increasing orientation of Egyptian agriculture to the production of raw cotton

for the export market. Unfettered by legal restrictions for decades, the ayan had greedily amassed ever larger estates by turning smallholder owners into landless tenants and laborers. As their wealth grew, the contrast between the landlords' estate houses and the thatch and mud-walled villages of the great mass of the peasantry became more and more pronounced. Bored by life in the provinces, the well-heeled landed classes spent most of their time in the fashionable districts of Cairo or in resort towns, such as Alexandria. Their estates were run by hired managers who, as far as the peasants were concerned, were little more than rent collectors.

With the khedival regime and the great landlords closely allied to the British overlords, resistance to the occupation was left mainly to the middle class that had been growing in the towns since the middle of the 19th century. With the memory of Orabi's revolt in 1882 still fresh, the cause of Egyptian independence was taken up mainly by the sons of the *effendi*, the prosperous business and professional urban families. Even nationalist leaders who came from rural ayan families built up their following from among the urban middle classes. In contrast to India, where lawyers predominated in the nationalist leadership, in Egypt journalists (a number of them educated in France) led the way. In the 1890s and early 1900s numerous newspapers in Arabic (and to a lesser extent French and English) vied to expose the mistakes of the British and the corruption of the khedival regime. Egyptian writers also attacked the British for their racist arrogance and their monopolization of well-paying positions in the Egyptian bureaucracy, which could just as well have gone to university-educated Egyptians. In the 1890s the first nationalist party was formed, but, again in contrast to India, where the Congress party dominated the nationalist movement from the outset, a variety of rival parties proliferated in Egypt. There were three main alternatives by 1907, and none could be said to speak for the great majority of the Egyptians, who were illiterate, poorly paid, and largely ignored urban laborers and rural cultivators.

NATIONALIST AGITATION BEFORE WORLD WAR I

Despite the failure of the nationalist parties to unite or build a mass base in the decades before the First World War, the extent of the Egyptian masses' hostility was demonstrated by the 1906 Dinshawai incident. Most Egyptian villages raised large numbers of pigeons, which served as an important supplement to the meager peasant diet. Over the years some of the British had turned the hunting of the pigeons of selected villages

into a holiday pastime. British officers on leave were hunting the pigeons of the village of Dinshawai in the Nile delta when they accidentally hit the wife of the prayer leader of the local mosque. The angry villagers mobbed the greatly outnumbered shooting party, which in panic fired on the villagers. In the scuffle both the villagers and the British soldiers suffered casualties. In reprisal for the death of one of the officers, the British summarily hung four of the villagers and publicly flogged or punished with hard labor numerous others.

The harsh British reprisals in turn aroused a storm of protest in the Egyptian press and among the nationalist parties. Some Egyptian leaders later recounted how the incident convinced them that cooperation with the British was totally unacceptable and fixed their resolve to agitate for an end to Egypt's occupation. Popular protests in a number of areas and the emergence of ayan support for the nationalist cause also suggested the possibility of building a mass base for anti-British agitation. In the years before the outbreak of World War I, heavy-handed British repression was necessary on several occasions to put down student riots or in reprisal for assassination attempts on high British and Turco-Egyptian officials. By 1913 the British had been sufficiently intimidated by the rising tide of Egyptian nationalism to grant a constitution and representation in a parliament elected indirectly by the men of wealth and influence. World War I and the British declaration of martial law

This contemporary photograph shows the hangings that were carried out in reprisal for the attacks on British soldiers at the village of Dinshawai. The conical tower in the distance behind the scaffold was the roost for the pigeons that were the original and intended targets of the ill-fated hunting party.

DOCUMENT
LESSONS FOR THE COLONIZED FROM THE SLAUGHTER IN THE TRENCHES

The prolonged and horrific slaughter of the youth of Europe in the trench stalemate on the western front did much to erode the image of Europeans as superior, rational, and more civilized beings that they had worked hard to propagate among the colonized peoples in the decades before the Great War. The futility of the seemingly endless slaughter cast doubts on the Europeans' rationality and fitness to rule themselves, much less the rest of the world. The destructive uses to which their science and technology were put brought into question the Europeans' long-standing claims that these material advancements tangibly demonstrated their intellectual and organizational superiority over all other peoples. The following quotations, taken from the writings of some of the leading thinkers and political leaders of the colonized peoples of Africa and Asia, reflect their disillusionment with the West as a result of the war and the continuing turmoil in Europe in the postwar era.

1. Rabindranath Tagore, Bengali poet, playwright, and novelist, who was one of the earliest non-European recipients of the Nobel Prize for literature:

Has not this truth already come home to you now when this cruel war has driven its claws into the vitals of Europe? When her hoard of wealth is bursting into smoke and her humanity is shattered on her battlefields? You ask in amazement what she has done to deserve this? The answer is, that the West has been systematically petrifying her moral nature in order to lay a solid foundation for her gigantic abstractions of efficiency. She has been all along starving the life of the personal man into that of the professional.

2. Mohandas Gandhi, who emerged in the years after the war as India's leading nationalist figure:

India's destiny lies not along the bloody way of the West, but along the bloodless way of peace that comes from a simple and godly life. India is in danger of losing her soul. . . . She must not, therefore, lazily and helplessly say, "I cannot escape the onrush from the West." She must be strong enough to resist it for her own sake and that of the world. I make bold to say that the Europeans themselves will have to remodel their outlooks if they are not to perish under the weight of the comforts to which they are becoming slaves.

3. Léopold Sédar Senghor, Senegalese poet and political leader, who is widely regarded as one of the finest writers in the *French* language of the 20th century:

Lord, the snow of your Peace is your proposal to a divided world to a divided Europe
To Spain torn apart. . . .
And I forget
White hands that fired the shots which brought the empires crumbling
Hands that flogged the slaves, that flogged You [Jesus Christ]
Chalk-white hands that buffeted You, powdered painted hands that buffeted me
Confident hands that delivered me to solitude to hatred
White hands that felled the forest of palm trees once commanding Africa, in the heart of Africa. . . .
(From *Snow Upon Paris*)

4. Aimé Cesaire, West Indian poet and founder of the *négritude*, or the assertion of black culture, movement in the late 1920s:

Heia [Praise] for those who have never invented anything
those who never explored anything
those who never tamed anything
those who give themselves up to the essence of all things
ignorant of surfaces but struck by the movement of all things
(From *Return to My Native Land*)

Questions: On the basis of this sample, what aspects of the West's claims to superiority would you say were called into question by the suicidal conflict of the leading powers within European civilization? What aspects of their own civilizations do these writers, both implicitly and explicitly, champion as alternatives to the ways of the West? Are these writers in danger of stereotyping both the West and their own civilizations?

put a temporary end to nationalist agitation. But as in India, the war unleashed forces in Egypt that could not be stopped and that would soon lead to the revival of the drive for independence with even greater strength than before.

WORLD WAR I AND THE POSTWAR CRISIS OF THE EUROPEAN EMPIRES

The nationalist struggle against European colonial domination was given a great boost by the long and devastating First World War. Though the European powers had frequently quarreled over colonial possessions in the late 19th century, during the war they fought one another in the colonies for the first time. Major theaters of conflict developed during the war in West and East Africa and especially in the Middle East. British naval supremacy denied the Germans access to their colonies in Africa and the Pacific. With the blockade on their side, the British, French, and Belgians were able to draw heavily on their colonies for soldiers, laborers, and raw materials.

Hundreds of thousands of African and Asian soldiers served both on the western front and in the far-flung theaters of war from Egypt, Palestine, and Mesopotamia to East Africa. The French recruited tens of thousands of African and Asian laborers to replace workers in French industrial centers who had been conscripted into the armies fighting on the western front. The colonies also supplied food for the home populations of the Entente powers and vital raw materials, such as oil, jute, and cotton. Contrary to long-standing colonial policy, the hard-pressed British even encouraged a considerable expansion of industrial production in India to supplement the output of their overextended home factories. Thus the war years contributed to the development in India of the largest industrial sector in the colonized world.

World War I presented the subjugated peoples of Africa and Asia with the spectacle of the self-styled civilizers of humankind sending their young men by the millions to be slaughtered in the horrific and barbaric trench stalemate on the western front. For the first time, African and Asian soldiers were ordered by their European officers to kill other Europeans. In the process the Europeans' deep divisions and the vulnerability of the seemingly invincible Europeans were starkly revealed. During the war years European troops in the colonies were withdrawn to meet the need for manpower on the many war fronts. The garrisons that remained were dangerously understaffed. The need to recall administrative personnel from both British and French colonies meant that colonial officials were compelled to fill their vacated posts with African and Asian administrators, many of whom enjoyed real responsibility for the first time.

To maintain the loyalty of their traditional allies among the colonized and to win the support of the Western-educated elites or new allies, such as the Arabs, the British and French made many promises regarding the postwar settlement. Because these concessions often seriously compromised their prewar dominance or plans for further colonial expansion, the leaders of victorious allies repeatedly reneged on them in the years after the war. The betrayal of these pledges understandably contributed a great deal to postwar agitation against the continuance and spread of European colonial domination.

INDIA: GANDHI AND THE NATIONALIST STRUGGLE

In the months after the outbreak of the war, the British could take great comfort from the way in which the peoples of the empire rallied to their defense. Though already well on the way to independence, their subjects in the White Dominions—Canada, Australia, and New Zealand—lost no time in declaring war on the Central Powers and raising armies. Dominion troops served with distinction in both the Middle Eastern and European theaters of war, though botched campaigns like those at Gallipoli and the costly offensives on the Somme severely strained relations between the British high command and the colonials. Of the many colonies in the "true" empire, none played as critical a role in the British war effort as India. The Indian princes offered substantial war loans; Indian soldiers bore the brunt of the war effort in East Africa and the Middle East; and nationalist leaders, including Gandhi and Tilak, toured India selling British war bonds. But as the war dragged on and Indians died on the battlefield or went hungry at home to sustain a conflict that had little to do with them, signs of unrest spread throughout the subcontinent.

Wartime inflation had adversely affected virtually all segments of the Indian population. Indian peasants were angered at the ceilings set on the price of their market produce, despite rising costs, and often their inability to sell it due to shipping shortages linked to the war. Indian laborers saw their already meager wages drop steadily in the face of rising prices. At the same time, their bosses grew rich from profits earned in war production.

Many localities suffered from famines that were exacerbated by wartime transport shortages that impeded relief efforts.

Moderate Indian politicians were frustrated by the British refusal to honor promises that if they continued to support the war effort, India would move steadily after the war to self-government *within the empire*, just as Canada had one-half century earlier. Indian hopes for the fulfillment of these promises were raised by the Montagu-Chelmsford reforms of 1919, which increased the powers of Indian legislators at the all-India level and placed much of the provincial administration of India under local ministries controlled by legislative bodies with substantial numbers of elected Indians. But the concessions granted in the reforms were offset by the passage later in the year of the Rowlatt Act, which placed severe restrictions on key Indian civil rights, such as freedom of the press. These conditions fueled localized protest during and immediately after the war; Gandhi soon built the protest into an all-India campaign directed against the policies of the colonial overlords.

Gandhi's remarkable appeal to the masses and the Western-educated nationalist politicians was due both to a number of personal traits and to the strategy for protest that had been worked out a decade earlier in opposing restrictive laws imposed on the Indian migrant community in South Africa. Gandhi combined the experience of a Western-educated lawyer, having considerable world exposure and a rather astute understanding of the British colonizers, with the attributes of a traditional Hindu holy man, which served as a reminder of the glories of India's past civilizations. The former made it possible for him to build up a strong following among middle-class, Western-educated Indians who, as we have seen, had long been the dominant force behind nationalist campaigns. Gandhi's stress on nonviolent but quite aggressive protest tactics endeared him to both the moderates and more radical elements within the nationalist movement. His advocacy of peaceful boycotts, strikes, noncooperation, and mass demonstrations—which he labeled collectively *satyagraha*, or truth force—proved a viable way of weakening British control while limiting opportunities for violent reprisals that would allow the British to make full use of their superior military strength.

These tactics also required the involvement of increasing numbers of the Indian people in the nationalist cause. The holy-man image Gandhi projected was

By the early 1920s Mohandas Gandhi had become a pivotal figure in Indian politics. The Mahatma attracted crowds whenever he appeared in public, and this mass appeal gave him unprecedented leverage in dealing with the British, as well as other nationalist politicians.

critical in arousing this mass support from peasants and laborers alike, many of whom walked for miles when Gandhi was on tour to do honor to a saint rather than listen to a political speech. Gandhi's widespread popular appeal in turn gave him even greater influence among nationalist politicians, who were very much aware of the leverage this mass base gave to them in their negotiations with British officials.

THE RISE OF COMMUNALISM AND THE BEGINNINGS OF POLITICAL FRAGMENTATION

Gandhi's holy-man side did, however, hamper his efforts to reach out to all Indians. Despite his constant stress on religious tolerance and communal harmony, many Muslims mistrusted this Hindu *guru* and the Congress party politicians who organized his civil disobedience campaigns. The less well-educated Muslim minority had been suspicious of the Hindu-dominated Congress party from the outset, even though a number of Muslims had been and continued to be prominent leaders in the organization. To better support their demands for separate electorates and legislative seats, a number of mostly well-educated and well-to-do Muslims founded a separate party, the Muslim League, in 1906. Though the League represented only a small percentage of even the Muslim minority until the 1940s, its presence signified a dangerous potential division within the Indian national movement. Its intransigence was matched on the Hindu side by a number of extremist, communalist parties that were equally mistrustful of united action and vehemently opposed to Gandhi's call for tolerance and Hindu power sharing with minority religious groups. All the charisma and wisdom Gandhi could muster were not sufficient to bring these fringe groups into the Congress party's mainstream. The Muslims would destroy his vision of a united India; a Hindu extremist would eventually take his life.

The success of Gandhian satyagraha tactics in a number of local protest movements paved the way for his sudden emergence as the central figure in the all-Indian nationalist struggle. The India-wide campaign to repeal the Rowlatt Act demonstrated both the strengths and the weaknesses of the Gandhian approach. Congress party organizers rallied mass support for boycotts, non-cooperation, and civil disobedience throughout the subcontinent that stunned the British and put them on the defensive. But a lack of time and sufficient numbers of trained followers to instruct protesters in the discipline of passive resistance led inevitably to violent reprisals for

police repression. Convinced that satyagraha could not be truly carried out under these conditions, Gandhi delighted the British and angered other nationalist politicians, such as Nehru, by calling off the anti-Rowlatt campaign. His withdrawal allowed the British to round up and imprison Gandhi and other nationalists whom they had identified as the ring leaders of the movement.

Although it would be nearly a decade before Gandhi and the Congress party could launch a campaign on a scale comparable to the postwar satyagraha, British relief at the successful repression of dissent was short-lived. Throughout the 1920s, urban lawyers and peasant associations used Gandhian tactics to protest colonial policies and local abuses by both British and Indian officials. By the early 1930s British insensitivity and the mounting effects of the global Great Depression paved the way for a revival of the civil disobedience campaign on an all-India basis. The establishment in 1927 of the all-white Simon Commission to consider future government responses to nationalist demands angered and unified, for a brief period, nationalist politicians on both the left and the right and those representing both Hindus and Muslims. The depression left openings for the revival of the mass struggle for decolonization. The sharp fall in the early 1930s in the price of agricultural products hit virtually all segments of the rural population, which made up well over 80 percent of the total Indian population.

Astutely gauging the mood of the Indian masses, Gandhi launched another round of all-India civil disobedience campaigns with the dramatic Salt March and satyagraha in early 1931. The British alternated between mass jailings and forcible repression and roundtable negotiations in the next half decade but ended by making major concessions to nationalist demands. These were embodied in the Government of India Act of 1935. Though retaining control of the central administration, the British agreed to turn the provincial governments over to Indian leaders who would be chosen by a greatly expanded electorate. Their assumption of office by 1937 brought an end to the already much diminished civil disobedience agitation and a British-nationalist accommodation that lasted until another global war shook the foundations of the European colonial order.

THE MIDDLE EAST: BETRAYAL AND THE GROWTH OF ARAB NATIONALISM

In the years after World War I, resistance to European colonial domination, which had been confined largely to Egypt in the prewar years, spread to much of the Middle East. With Turkish rule in the area ended by their defeat in the war, Arab nationalists in Beirut, Damascus, and Baghdad turned to face the new threat presented by the victorious Entente powers, France and Britain. Betraying promises to preserve Arab independence that Henry McMahon, the British High Commissioner in Egypt, had made in 1915 and early 1916 to Hussein, the *sherif* of Mecca, French and British forces occupied much of the Middle East in the years after the war. Because Hussein had used these promises to convince Arabs to rise in support of Britain's war against the Turks, who were fellow Muslims, their violation by the Allies humiliated and deeply angered Arabs throughout the Middle East. The occupying European powers faced stiff resistance from the Arabs in each of the mandates they carved out in Syria, Iraq, and Lebanon under the auspices of the League of Nations. The Arabs' sense of humiliation and anger was greatly intensified by the disposition of Palestine, where the British occupation was coupled with promises of a Jewish homeland.

The fact that the British had appeared to promise Palestine, for which they received a League of Nations mandate in 1922, to both the Jewish Zionists and the Arabs during the war greatly complicated an already confused situation. Zionist aspirations to return to their ancient Middle Eastern homeland had been nurtured by the Jews of the diaspora for millennia. But political organizations, created to restore the Jewish home in Palestine, were largely a product of the persecution of the Jews of eastern Europe in the last decades of the 19th century. Particularly vicious pogroms, or violent assaults on the Jewish communities of Russia and Romania in the 1860s and 1870s, convinced Jewish intellectuals, such as Leon Pinsker, that assimilation into or even acceptance by Christian European nations was impossible. Pinsker and other thinkers called for a return to the Holy Land. Like-minded individuals founded Zionist organizations, such as the Society for the Colonization of Israel, to promote Jewish migration to Palestine in the last decades of the 19th century. Until World War I the numbers of Jews returning were small—in the tens of thousands—though Zionist communities were established on lands purchased in Palestine.

Until the late 1890s the Zionist effort was generally opposed by Jews in Germany, France, and other parts of western Europe, who enjoyed citizenship and extensive civil rights; many of them had grown prosperous and powerful in their adopted lands. A major defection to the Zionists occurred in 1894 after Theodor Herzl, an established Austrian journalist, witnessed angry mobs shouting "Death to the Jews" as they taunted the hapless French army officer Alfred Dreyfus, a Jew who had been falsely accused of passing military secrets to the Germans. Soon after this incident, Herzl and a number of other western European Jews joined with prominent eastern Jews in forming the World Zionist Organization in 1897. As Herzl made clear in his writings, the central aim of his increasingly well-funded organization was to promote Jewish migration to and settlement in Palestine until a Zionist state could be established in the area. Herzl's nationalist ambitions, as well as his indifference to the Arabs already living in the area, were captured in his often quoted view that Palestine was "a land without people for a people [the Jews] without a land."

British motivations for claiming Palestine in the postwar settlement arose from the dangers posed by Turkish offensives during the war against Britain's crucial lifeline at Suez. These offensives convinced the British of the need to occupy Palestine as an additional buffer zone. The situation was further complicated in 1917 when Lord Balfour, the British foreign secretary, assured prominent Zionist leaders that the British would promote the establishment of a Jewish homeland in the region after the war. Lord Balfour's promises to the Zionists and the British takeover of Palestine struck the Arabs as a double betrayal of McMahon's assurances that Arab support for the Entente powers against the Turks would guarantee them independence after the war. This sense of betrayal was a critical source of the growing hostility the Arabs felt toward Jewish emigration to Palestine and their purchase of land in the area.

Rising Arab opposition convinced many British officials, especially those who administered Palestine, to constrict severely the rather open-ended pledges that had been made to the Zionists during the war. This shift led to Zionist mistrust of and open resistance to British policies, as well as to a determination to build up their own defenses against the increasingly violent Arab resistance to the Zionist presence in Palestine. But British attempts to limit Jewish emigration and settlement were not matched by efforts to encourage, through education and consultation, the emergence of strong leadership within the Arab population of Palestine. Consequently in the critical struggles and diplomatic maneuvers of the 1930s and 1940s, the Arabs of Palestine rarely spoke for themselves. They were represented by Arab leaders from neighboring lands, who did not always understand their needs and desires and who often acted more in the interest of Syrian or Lebanese Arabs than that of the Arabs of Palestine.

REVOLT IN EGYPT

Because Egypt was already occupied by the British when the war broke out and had been formally declared a protectorate in 1914, it was not included in the promises made by McMahon to the sherif Hussein. As a result the anticolonial struggle in Egypt was rooted in earlier agitation and the heavy toll the war had taken on the Egyptian people, particularly the peasantry. During the war the defense of the Suez Canal was one of the top priorities for the British. To guard against possible Muslim uprisings in response to Turkish calls for a holy war, martial law was declared soon after hostilities began, and throughout the war large contingents of Entente and empire forces were garrisoned in Egypt. These proved a heavy drain on the increasingly scarce food supplies of the area. Forced labor and confiscations by the military of the precious draft animals of the peasantry also led to widespread discontent. As the war dragged on, this dissidence was further inflamed by spiraling inflation and by food shortages and even starvation in some areas. The wartime cotton boom enriched a tiny mercantile elite, which included many Europeans and Egyptian Christians, and further alienated the mass of peasants and workers from the British and their loyal khedival allies.

By the end of the war Egypt was ripe for revolt. Mass discontent strengthened the resolve of the educated nationalist elite to receive a hearing at Versailles, where the victorious Allies were struggling to reach a postwar settlement. Like many of the leaders of the colonial world, the Egyptians were also inspired by Woodrow Wilson's principle of self-determination. What they failed to understand was that Wilson's belief that subjugated ethnic groups should have the right to freely elect their own leaders and form their own nations was intended only for Poles and Czechs, not Arabs, Indians, or Africans. When a delegation, or *Wafd* in Arabic, of Egyptian leaders was denied permission to travel to France to put the case for Egyptian self-determination to the peacemakers at Versailles, most Egyptians resigned from the government and called for mass demonstrations. What followed shocked nervous British officials. Student-led riots touched off outright insurrection over much of Egypt. At one point Cairo was cut off from the outside world, and much of the countryside was hostile territory for the occupying power. Though the British army was able, at the cost of scores of deaths, to restore control, it was clear that some hearing had to be given to Egyptian demands. The emergence of the newly formed Wafd party under its hard-driving leader Sa'd Zaghlūl provided the nationalists with both unity and a mass base that far excelled any they had attracted in the prewar decades.

When a special British commission, sent to inquire into the causes of the upheaval in Egypt, met with widespread civil disobedience and continuing violent opposition, it recommended that the British begin negotiations for an eventual withdrawal from Egypt. Years of bargaining followed, which led to a highly qualified independence for the Egyptians that came in stages beginning in 1922 and culminating in the British withdrawal to the Suez Canal zone in 1936. Although the British pulled out of Egypt, the khedival regime was preserved, and the British reserved the right to reoccupy should Egypt be threatened by a foreign aggressor.

Though they had won a significant degree of political independence, the Egyptian leaders of the Wafd party, as well as its rivals in the Liberal Constitutionalist and Union parties that were formed in the 1920s, did little to relieve the increasing misery of the great majority of the Egyptian people. Most Egyptian politicians regarded the winning of office as an opportunity to increase their own and their families' fortunes. Many politicians, both those from ayan households and those from the professional and merchant classes, used their influence and growing wealth to amass huge estates, which were worked by landless tenants and laborers. Locked in personal and interparty quarrels, as well as the ongoing contest with the khedival regime for control of the government, few political leaders had the time or inclination to push for the land reforms and public works projects that the peasantry so desperately needed. Though entrepreneurs and landlords were adversely affected by the slump in the cotton market that hit Egypt during the Great Depression, most were able to pass along their losses to laborers and tenants, who had no choice but to accept lower wages or pay higher rents.

The utter social bankruptcy of the 40 years of nationalist political dominance that preceded Nasser's revolution in 1952 is suggested by some revealing statistics compiled by the United Nations in the early 1950s. By that time, nearly 70 percent of Egypt's cultivable land was owned by 6 percent of the population. Some 12,000 families alone controlled 37 percent of the farmland. As for the mass of the people, 98 percent of the peasants were illiterate; malnutrition was chronic among both the urban and rural population; and an estimated 95 percent of rural Egyptians suffered from eye diseases. Such was the legacy of the very unrevolutionary process of decolonization in Egypt.

THE BEGINNINGS OF THE LIBERATION STRUGGLE IN AFRICA

Although most of Africa had come under European colonial rule in the decades just before the outbreak of World War I, precolonial missionary efforts had produced small groups of Western-educated Africans in parts of west and south-central Africa by the end of the 19th century. Like their counterparts in India, most Western-educated Africans were staunchly loyal to their British and French overlords during the First World War. With the backing of both Western-educated Africans and the traditional rulers, many of whom found that their powers increased under colonial rule, the British and especially the French were able to draw on their African possessions for manpower and raw materials throughout the war. But this reliance took its toll on their colonial domination in the long run. In addition to local rebellions in response to the forcible recruitment of African soldiers and laborers, the war effort seriously disrupted newly colonized African societies. African merchants and farmers suffered from shipping shortages and the sudden decline in demand for crops, such as cocoa, some of which had been heavily dependent on German markets before the war. African villagers were not happy to go hungry so that their crops could feed the armies of the Allies. The sudden removal of European administrators and police officers from the colonies led to widespread and dangerous rumors that the Europeans were withdrawing for good or that they had run out of human resources in Europe. As Lord Lugard pointed out, the desperate plight of the British and French also forced them to teach tens of thousands of Africans

> how to kill white men, around whom [they had] been taught to weave a web of sanctity of life. [They] also know how to handle bombs and Lewis guns and Maxims—and [they have] seen the white men budge when [they have] stood fast. Altogether [they have] acquired much knowledge that might be put to uncomfortable use someday.

The fact that the Europeans kept few of the promises of better jobs and public honors after the war, which they had made to induce young Africans to enlist in the armed forces or serve in the colonial administration, contributed a good deal to the unrest of the postwar years. In the French colonies—where opportunities for political organization, much less protest, were severely constricted—there were major strikes and a number of riots in the interwar period. In the British colonies, where there was considerably more tolerance for political organization, there were also strikes and a major uprising in Sierra Leone in 1931, protesting colonial taxes and the hardships caused by the sharp fall in prices paid for cash crops due to the Great Depression. The economic slump brought on by the depression also contributed to the refusal of cocoa producers in the Gold Coast colony (later called Ghana) to market their crops for the greatly reduced prices offered by the merchants in the port towns. The growing political involvement of the cocoa farmers and other cash-crop producers was to prove a major factor in the nationalists' ability to build a popular base for anticolonialism in the post–World War II era.

Though Western-educated politicians did not link up with urban workers or peasants in most African colonies until the 1940s, disenchanted members of the emerging African elite began to organize in the 1920s and 1930s. In the early stages of this process, charismatic black American political figures, such as Marcus Garvey and W. E. B. Du Bois, had a major impact on emerging African nationalist leaders, including those who were delegates to international conferences in Paris and other Western capitals. Unlike Indian or Egyptian nationalist leaders, African nationalists had to struggle with the question of the level at which their political energies ought to be focused. In the 1920s much effort was placed into attempts to arouse all-Africa loyalties and build pan-African organizations. The fact that the leadership of these organizations was more American and West Indian than African, and that African delegates faced very different challenges in different colonies, rendered pan-Africanism unworkable. But its well-attended conferences did much to arouse anticolonial sentiments among Western-educated Africans.

By the mid-1920s nationalists from French and British colonies were pretty much going separate ways. Due to restrictions in the colonies and the fact that small but well-educated groups of Africans were represented in the French Parliament, French-speaking West Africans concentrated their organizational and ideological efforts in Paris in this period. The négritude literary movement nurtured by these exiles did much to combat the racial stereotyping that had so long held the Africans in psychological bondage to the Europeans. Writers such as L. S. Senghor, Léon Damas, and the West Indian Aimé Cesaire celebrated the beauty of black skin and the African physique. They argued that in the precolonial era African peoples had built societies where women were freer, old people were better cared for, and attitudes toward sex were far healthier than they had ever been in the so-called civilized West. Though there was no literary movement comparable to négritude in the British colonies, authors such as Edward Blyden and J. E. Casely Hayford stressed Africa's contributions to the civilized development of all humankind in their books and essays. These and other writers made good use of the press, which was a good deal freer in the British colonies.

Western-educated Africans in British colonies were also given greater opportunities to organize political as-

In the post–World War I era African and African-American intellectuals, such as Léopold Sédar Senghor (pictured here), W. F. B. Du Bois, and Aimé Cesaire explored in their writings the ravages wrought by centuries of suffering inflicted on the people of Africa by the slave trade and the forced diaspora that resulted. These intellectuals sought to affirm the genius of African culture and patterns of social interaction.

sociations within Africa. Early organizations that linked the emerging nationalists of various British colonies, such as the National Congress of British West Africa, gave way in the late 1920s to political groupings concerned primarily with issues confined to single colonies, such as Sierra Leone, the Gold Coast, or Nigeria. After the British granted some representation in colonial advisory councils to Western-educated Africans in this period, these types of political groupings became even more pronounced. Though most of these early political organizations were too loosely structured to be considered true political parties and their members spent most of their energies getting elected to the colonial legislative councils, some leaders increasingly recognized the need to build a mass base. In the 1930s a new generation of leaders not only made much more vigorous attacks on the policies of the British but also, through their newspapers and political associations, sought to reach out to the ordinary African villagers and the young, who had hitherto played little role in nationalist agitation. The disruptions of yet another world war and the emergence of a new generation of much more radical nationalist leaders would turn these early efforts at outreach to the masses into the more broadly supported movements that won independence in both British and French Africa in the 1950s and 1960s.

ANALYSIS

WOMEN IN ASIAN AND AFRICAN NATIONALIST MOVEMENTS

One important but often neglected dimension of the liberation struggles that Asian and African peoples waged against their colonial overlords was the emergence of a stratum of educated, articulate, and politically active women in most colonial societies. In this process the educational opportunities provided by the European colonizers often played as vital a role as they had in the formation of male leadership in nationalist movements. Though confined in the early stages of European involvement in Africa and Asia to the daughters of low-class or marginal social groups, missionary girls' schools had by the end of the 19th century become quite respectable for women from the growing Westernized business and professional classes. In fact, in many cases some degree of Western education was essential if Westernized males were to find wives with whom they could share their career concerns and intellectual pursuits.

The seemingly insurmountable barriers that separated Westernized Asian and African males from their traditional—and thus usually without formal education—wives became a stock theme in the novels and short stories of the early nationalist era, a theme perhaps best exemplified by the works of Rabindranath Tagore. The problem was felt so acutely by the first generation of Indian nationalist leaders that many took up the task of teaching their wives English and Western philosophy and literature at home. Thus for many upper-class Asian and African women colonization proved a liberating force. This trend was often offset by the male-centric nature of colonial education and the "domestic" focus of much of the curriculum in women's schools.

Although women played little role in the early, elitist stages of Asian and African nationalist movements, they frequently became more and more prominent as the early study clubs and political associations reached out to build a mass base. In India women who had been exposed to Western education and European ways, such as Tagore's famous heroine in the novel *The Home and the World,* came out of seclusion and took up supporting roles, though still usually behind the scenes. Gandhi's campaign to supplant imported, machine-made British cloth with homespun Indian cloth, for example, owed much of whatever success it had to female spinners and weavers. As nationalist leaders moved their anticolonial campaigns into the streets, women became involved in mass demonstrations. Throughout the 1920s and 1930s Indian women braved the *lathi,* or billy club, assaults of the Indian police, suffered the indignities of imprisonment, and launched their own newspapers and lecture campaigns to mobilize female support for the nationalist struggle.

In Egypt the British made special note of the powerful effect that the participation of both traditional veiled women and more Westernized upper-class women had on mass demonstrations in 1919 and the early 1920s. These outpourings of popular support did much to give credibility to the Wafd's demands for British withdrawal. In both India and Egypt female nationalists addressed special appeals to British and American suffragettes to support their peoples' struggles for political and social liberation. In India in particular, their causes were advanced by feminists, such as the English champion of Hinduism, Annie Besant, who became a major figure in the nationalist movement both before and after the First World War.

When African nationalism became a popularly supported movement in the post–World War II period, women, particularly the outspoken and fearless market women in West Africa, emerged as a major political force. In settler colonies, such as Algeria and Kenya, where violent revolt proved necessary to bring down deeply entrenched colonial regimes, women took on the dangerous tasks of messengers, bomb carriers, and guerrilla fighters. As Frantz Fanon argued decades ago and as it was later beautifully dramatized in the film *The Battle of Algiers,* this transformation was particularly painful for women who had been in seclusion right up until the time of the revolutionary upsurge. Cutting their hair and wearing lipstick and Western clothes often alienated them from their own fathers and brothers, who equated such practices with prostitution.

In many cases women's participation in struggles for the political liberation of their people was paralleled by campaigns for female rights in male-dominated societies. Upper-class Egyptian women founded newspapers and educational associations that pushed for raising the age of marriage, educational opportunities for women, and an end to seclusion and veiling. Indian women took up many of these causes and also sought to develop programs to improve hygiene and employment opportunities for lower-caste women. These early efforts, as well as the prominent place of women in nationalist struggles, had much to do with the granting of rights to women, including suffrage and legal equality that were key features of the constitutions of many newly independent Asian and African nations. Though the great majority of women in the new states of Africa and Asia have yet to enjoy most of these rights, their recognition in constitutions and laws provides crucial backing for the struggle for women's liberation in much of the present-day Third World.

Questions: Why might missionary education for women in the colonies have stressed domestic skills? In what ways do you think measures to "modernize" colonial societies might have been oriented to males? Can you think of women who have been or are major political figures in the contemporary Third World? Why have there not been more? What sorts of traditional constraints hamper the efforts of women to achieve economic and social equality and major political roles in the Third World today?   ❂

✣ ANOTHER GLOBAL WAR AND THE COLLAPSE OF THE EUROPEAN WORLD ORDER

The effects of a second global conflict, brought on by the expansionist ambitions of Hitler's Germany and imperial Japan, proved fatal to the already badly battered European colonial empires. The Nazi rout of the French and the stunningly rapid Japanese capture of the French, Dutch, British, and U.S. colonies in Southeast Asia put an end to whatever illusions the colonized peoples of Africa and Asia had left about the strength and innate superiority of the colonial overlords. Because the Japanese were non-Europeans, their early victories over the Europeans and Americans played a particularly critical role in destroying the myth of white invincibility. The fall of the "impregnable" fortress at Singapore on the southern tip of Malaya and the U.S. reverses at Pearl Harbor and in the Philippines proved to be blows from which the colonizers never quite recovered, even though they went on to eventually defeat the Japanese. The sight of tens of thousands of British, Dutch, or American troops struggling under the supervision of the victorious Japanese to survive the death marches to prison camps in their former colonies left an indelible impression on the Asian villagers who saw them pass by. The colonized peoples were also disenchanted by the feeble defense against the Japanese invaders put up by their former masters. The harsh regimes and heavy demands the Japanese conquerors imposed on the peoples of Southeast Asia during the war further strengthened their determination to fight for self-rule and look to their own defenses after the conflict was over.

The devastation of World War II—a total war fought in the cities and countryside over much of Europe—drained the resources of the European powers and sapped their citizens' will to hold increasingly resistant African and Asian peoples in bondage. The war also greatly enhanced the power and influence of the two giants on the European periphery, the United States and the Soviet Union. In Africa and the Middle East, as well as in the Pacific, the United States approached the war as a campaign of liberation. American propagandists made no secret of Franklin Roosevelt's hostility to colonialism in their efforts to win Asian and African support for the Allied war effort. In the Atlantic Charter of 1941, which sealed an alliance between the United States and Great Britain that the latter desperately needed to survive, Roosevelt persuaded a reluctant Churchill to include a clause that recognized the "right of all people to choose the form of government under which they live." The Soviets were equally vocal in their condemnation of colonialism and even more forthcoming with material support for nationalist campaigns after the war. In the cold war world of the superpowers that emerged after 1945, there was little room for the domination the greatly reduced powers of western Europe had once exercised over much of the globe.

THE WINNING OF INDEPENDENCE IN SOUTH AND SOUTHEAST ASIA

The outbreak of the Second World War soon put an end to the accommodation between the Indian Congress party and the British in the late 1930s. Congress party leaders offered to support the British war effort if the British would give them a significant share of power at the all-India level and commit themselves to Indian independence once the conflict was over. These conditions were staunchly rejected both by the viceroy in India and at home by Winston Churchill, who headed the coalition government that led Britain through the war. Labour members of the coalition government, however, indicated that they were quite willing to negotiate India's eventual independence. As tensions built between the nationalist leaders and the British rulers, hard-pressed in the early 1940s by their defeats both in Southeast Asia and the Mediterranean, Sir Stafford Cripps was sent to India in early 1942 to see if a deal could be struck to bring the Indians fully behind the British in the war effort. Indian divisions and British intransigence led to the collapse of Cripps's initiative and the renewal of mass civil disobedience campaigns under the guise of the Quit India movement, which began in the summer of 1942.

The British responded with repression and mass arrests, and for much of the remainder of the war Gandhi, Nehru, and other major Congress party politicians were imprisoned. Of the Indian nationalist parties, only the Communists—who were committed to the anti-Fascist alliance and, more ominously, the Muslim League—rallied to the British cause. The League, now led by a former Congress party politician, the dour and uncompromising Muhammad Ali Jinnah, won much favor from the British for its wartime support. As their demands for a separate Muslim state in the subcontinent hardened, the links among the British, Jinnah, and other League leaders became a key factor in the struggle for decolonization in South Asia.

The Second World War brought disruptions to India similar to those caused by the First World War. Inflation stirred up urban unrest, and a widespread famine in 1943 and 1944, brought on in part by wartime transport shortages, engendered much bitterness in rural India. Though successful, the repression of the nationalists during the war convinced many British politicians and even the viceroy of India in the mid-1940s that they had neither the resources nor the will to hold India by force. Churchill's defeat in the 1945 elections, in large part because of his determination to resist India's move toward independence, brought to power a Labour government ready to deal with the nationalist leaders. With independence in effect conceded in the near future, the process of decolonization between 1945 and 1947 focused on what sort of state or states would be carved out of the subcontinent after the British withdrawal. Jinnah and the Muslim League had begun to build a mass following among the Muslims on the basis of their claims that a single Indian nation would be dominated by the Hindu majority, with the Muslims an oppressed minority. It was therefore essential, they insisted, that a separate Muslim state called Pakistan be created from those areas in northwest and east India where Muslims were in the majority.

As communal rioting, which only the physical presence of Gandhi was capable of checking, spread throughout India, the British and key Congress party politicians reluctantly concluded that only partition— the creation of two nations in the subcontinent, one secular, one Muslim—could avert a bloodbath. Thus in the summer of 1947 the British handed power over to the leaders of the majority Congress party, who headed the new nation of India, and to Jinnah, who became the first president of Pakistan. In part because of the haste with which the British withdrew their forces from the deeply divided subcontinent, a bloodbath occurred anyway. Vicious Hindu-Muslim and Muslim-Sikh communal rioting, in which neither women nor children were spared, took the lives of hundreds of thousands in the searing summer heat of the plains of northwest India. Whole villages were destroyed; trains pulling into railway stations were packed with corpses that had been hacked to death by armed bands of rival religious adherents. These atrocities fed a massive exchange of refugee populations between Hindu-Sikh and Muslim areas that may have totaled ten million people. Those who fled were so terrified that they were willing to give up their land, their villages, and most of their worldly possessions.

Partition was compounded by the fact that there was soon no longer a Gandhi to preach tolerance and communal coexistence. On January 30, 1948, Mohandas Gandhi was shot by a Hindu fanatic while on his way to one of his regular prayer meetings. Ironically, Gandhi's prayer sessions had always begun with prayers from each of the many faiths observed by the peoples of the Indian subcontinent.

In granting independence to India, the British in effect removed the keystone from the arch of an empire that spanned three continents. Burma (known today as Myanmar) and Ceylon (now named Sri Lanka) won their independence peacefully in the following years. India's independence and Gandhi's civil disobedience campaigns, which had done so much to win a mass following for the nationalist cause, also inspired African leaders, such as Nkrumah, Kenyatta, and Nyerere in the 1950s and 1960s.

The retreat of the greatest of the imperial powers could not help but contribute to the weakening of the lesser Dutch, French, and U.S. empires. In fact, the process of the transfer of power from U.S. officials to moderate, middle-class Filipino politicians was well under way before the Second World War broke out. The loyalty to the United States that most Filipinos displayed during the war, as well as the stubborn guerrilla resistance they put up against the Japanese occupation, did much to bring about the rapid granting of independence to the Philippines once the war was ended. The Dutch and French were less willing to follow the British example and relinquish their colonial possessions in the postwar era. From 1945 to 1949, the Dutch fought a losing war to destroy the nation of Indonesia, which nationalists in the Netherlands Indies had claimed when the Japanese hold over the islands broke down in mid-1945. No sooner had the European colonizers suffered those losses than they were forced to deal with new threats to the last bastions of the imperial order in Africa.

THE LIBERATION OF NONSETTLER AFRICA

The Second World War proved even more disruptive to the colonial order imposed on Africa than had the first global conflict of the European powers. Forced labor and confiscations of crops and minerals returned, and inflation and controlled markets again cut down on African earnings. African recruits in the hundreds of thousands were drawn once more into the conflict and had even greater opportunities to use the latest European weapons to destroy Europeans. African soldiers, who had witnessed British and French defeats in the

Middle East and Southeast Asia and fought bravely only to experience again racial discrimination once they returned home, became in some colonies the staunchest supporters of postwar nationalist campaigns. The swift and humiliating rout of the French and Belgians by Nazi armies in the spring of 1940 shattered whatever was left of the colonizers' reputation for military prowess. It also led to a bitter and, in the circumstances, embarrassing struggle between the forces of the puppet Vichy regime and those of de Gaulle's Free French, or those who continued fighting the Nazis, which was fought out mainly in France's North and West African colonies.

The wartime needs of both the British and the Free French led to major departures from long-standing colonial policies that had restricted industrial development throughout Africa. Factories to process urgently needed vegetable oils, foods, and minerals were established in West and south-central Africa. These in turn contributed to a growing migration on the part of African peasants to the towns and a sharp spurt in African urban growth. The inability of many of those who moved to the towns to find employment resulted in a reservoir of disgruntled, idle workers that would be skillfully tapped by nationalist politicians in the postwar decades.

There were essentially two main paths to decolonization in nonsettler Africa in the postwar era. The first was pioneered by Kwame Nkrumah and his followers in the British Gold Coast colony, which, as the nation of Ghana, became the first independent black African state in 1957. Nkrumah epitomized the more radical sort of African leader that emerged throughout Africa after the war. Educated in African missionary schools and the United States, he had established wide contacts with nationalist leaders in both British and French West Africa and civil rights leaders in the United States prior to his return to the Gold Coast in the late 1940s. He returned to a land in ferment. The restrictions of government-controlled marketing boards and their favoritism for British merchants had led to protests and then, after the police fired on a peaceful demonstration of former soldiers, to widespread rioting in 1948. Though both urban workers and cash-crop farmers had supported the unrest, Western-educated African leaders were slow to organize their dissidents into a sustained mass movement. Their reluctance arose in part from their fear of losing major political concessions, such as seats on colonial legislative councils, that the British had just made. Sweeping aside the fears of more established political leaders regarding the radical nature of the popular protest, Nkrumah resigned his position as chairman of the dom-

inant political party in the Gold Coast and established his own Convention Peoples Party (CPP). Even before the formal break, Nkrumah had signaled the arrival of a new style of politics by organizing mass rallies, boycotts, and strikes—inspired, as he readily admitted, by the tactics of Gandhi and the Indian nationalists. In the mid-1950s Nkrumah's growing stature as a leader who would not be deterred by imprisonment or British threats and his mass following won repeated concessions from the British. Educated Africans were given more and more representation in legislative bodies, and gradually they took over administration of the colony. The British acknowledgement of Nkrumah as the prime minister of an independent Ghana in 1957 simply concluded a transfer of power from the European colonizers to the Western-educated African elite that had been under way for nearly a decade.

The peaceful devolution of power to African nationalists—often led by charismatic figures, such as Nkrumah, who were capable of mobilizing mass protest when the British stalled—led to the independence of the British nonsettler colonies in black Africa by the mid-1960s. Independence in the comparable areas of the French and Belgian empires in Africa came in a somewhat different way. Pressed by costly military struggles to hold on to their colonies in Indochina and Algeria, the French took a much more conciliatory line in dealing with the many peoples they ruled in West Africa. Ongoing negotiations with Senegal's Senghor and the Ivory Coast's Felix Houphouët-Boigny led to reforms and political concessions that ensured that moderate African leaders, who were eager to retain French economic and cultural ties, dominated the nationalist movement in French West Africa. Between 1956 and 1960 the French colonies moved by stages toward nationhood, a process that accelerated after de Gaulle's return to power in 1958. By 1960 all of France's African colonies, with the exception of Algeria, where there was a European settler community nearly one million strong, had been granted their independence.

In the same year, the Belgians completed an even hastier retreat from their huge colonial possession in the Congo (now called Zaire). Their rapid retreat is evidenced by the fact that there was little in the way of an organized nationalist movement to pressure them into concessions of any kind. In fact, by design there were scarcely any well-educated Congolese to lead resistance to Belgian rule. At independence in 1960, there were only 16 African college graduates in a Congolese population that exceeded 13 million. Though the Portuguese

The scene depicted in this photo was played out tens of times in the decades after World War II. British Home Secretary R. A. Butler is greeted by Kwame Nkrumah, whom Butler soon installs as the leader of the first independent nation, Ghana, to be carved out of Britain's African colonies.

still clung to their impoverished and scattered colonial territories, by the mid-1960s the European colonial era had come to an end.

REPRESSION AND GUERRILLA WAR: THE STRUGGLE FOR THE SETTLER COLONIES

The pattern of relatively peaceful withdrawal by stages, which characterized the process of decolonization in most of Asia and Africa, proved unworkable in Algeria, Kenya, and Southern Rhodesia, where substantial numbers of Europeans had gone to settle permanently in the 19th and early 20th centuries, and in South Africa, which had begun to be settled by Europeans centuries earlier. In each case the presence of European settler communities, varying in size from millions of whites in South Africa and Algeria to tens of thousands in Kenya and Southern Rhodesia, blocked both the rise of indigenous nationalist movements and concessions on the part of the colonial overlords. Because the settlers regarded the colonies to which they had emigrated as their per-

manent homes, they fought all attempts to turn political control over to the African majority or even to grant them civil rights. They also doggedly refused all reforms by colonial administrators that required them to give up any of the lands they had occupied, often dispossessing the indigenous Africans in the process. Unable to make headway through nonviolent protest tactics, which were forbidden, or negotiations with British or French officials, who were fearful of angering the highly vocal settler minority, many African leaders turned to violent, revolutionary struggles to win their peoples' independence.

The first of these erupted in Kenya in the early 1950s. Impatient with the failure of the nonviolent approach adopted by Jomo Kenyatta and the leading nationalist party, the Kenya African Union (KAU), an underground organization, coalesced around a number of more radical leaders to win meaningful concessions from the settler-dominated regime. Some of these leaders had fought with the British in Burma and were disgusted by the British failure to reward their services with a fair hearing on such key issues as land confiscations by the settlers. After forming the Land Freedom Army, they mounted, beginning in 1952, a campaign of terror and guerrilla warfare against the British, the settlers, and Africans who were considered collaborators. At the height of the struggle, in 1954, some 200,000 rebels were in action in the capital at Nairobi and in the forest reserves of the central Kenyan highlands. The British responded with an all-out effort to crush the guerrilla movement—which was dismissed as an explosion of African savagery and labeled, menacingly, the Mau Mau. In the process they imprisoned Kenyatta and his KAU organizers, thus eliminating the nonviolent alternative to the guerrillas.

Though the rebel movement had been militarily defeated by 1956 at the cost of thousands of lives, the British were now in a mood to negotiate with the nationalists, despite strong objections from the European settlers. Kenyatta was released from prison, and he emerged as the spokesman for the Africans of Kenya. By 1963 a multiracial Kenya had won its independence, and under virtually one-party rule it remained until the mid-1980s one of the most stable and more prosperous of the new African states.

The struggle of the Arab and Berber peoples of Algeria for independence was longer and even more vicious than that in Kenya. Algeria had for decades been regarded by the French as in integral part of France, a department just like Province or Brittany. The presence of more than one million European settlers in the colony only bolstered the resolve of French politicians to retain it at all costs. When sporadic rioting in the years after the war turned to sustained guerrilla resistance, led by the National Liberation Front (FLN) in the mid-1950s, the French army saw the defeat of the movement as a way to restore a reputation that had been badly tarnished by recent defeats in Vietnam. As in Kenya, the rebels were defeated in the field, but they gradually negotiated the independence of Algeria after de Gaulle came to power in 1958. The French people soon wearied of the seemingly endless war, and de Gaulle became convinced that he could not restore France to Great Power status as long as its resources were drained by the Algerian conflict.

In contrast to Kenya, the Algerian struggle was prolonged and brutalized by a violent settler backlash, led after 1960 by the Secret Army Organization (OAS), directed against the Arabs and Berbers as well as French people who favored independence for the colony. With strong support from elements in the French military,

earlier settler resistance had managed to topple the government in Paris in 1958, thereby putting an end to the Fourth Republic. In the early 1960s, the OAS came close to assassinating de Gaulle and overthrowing the Fifth Republic, which his accession to power brought into existence. In the end Algeria was granted its independence in 1962. After the bitter civil war, the multiracial accommodation worked out in Kenya appeared out of the question for the settlers. Over 900,000 left the new nation within months after its birth.

In southern Africa violent revolutions had also put an end to white settler dominance in the Portuguese colonies of Angola and Mozambique in 1975 and in Southern Rhodesia (now Zimbabwe) by 1980. Only in South Africa did the white minority manage to maintain its position of supremacy. Its ability to do so was based on a number of factors that distinguished it from other settler societies. To begin with, the white population of South Africa, roughly equally divided between the Dutch-descended Afrikaners and more recently arrived English speakers, was a good deal larger than that of any of the other settler societies. Though only a small minority in a country of 23 million black Africans and 3½ million East Indians and coloreds (mulattos), by the mid-1980s South Africa's settler-descended population had reached 4½ million. Unlike the settlers in Kenya and Algeria, who had the option of retreating to Europe as full citizens of France or Great Britain, the Afrikaners in particular have no European homeland to fall back on. They have lived in South Africa as long as Europeans have lived in North America and consider themselves quite distinct from the Dutch. Over the centuries the Afrikaners had also built up what was for them a persuasive ideology of white racist supremacy, which, though crude by European or U.S. standards, is much more explicit and elaborate than that developed by the settlers in any other colony. The Afrikaner ideology, grounded in selected biblical quotations, celebrated their historic struggle to "tame a beautiful but hard land" in the face of opposition from both the African "savages" and the British "imperialists."

Ironically, their defeat by the British in the Boer War (1899–1902) also contributed much to the capacity of the white settler minority to maintain its place of dominance in South Africa. A sense of guilt, arising especially from their treatment of Boer women and children during the war—tens of thousands of whom died of disease in what the British called "concentration camps"—led the British to make major concessions to the Afrikaners in the postwar decades. The most important

Algerians celebrate in Oran as French barricades, designed to confine the Arab-Berber population to non-European quarters of the city, are torn down by the local militia and civilians just after independence is announced in July 1962.

of these was internal political control, which included turning over the fate of the black African majority to the openly racist supremist Afrikaners. Not surprisingly, the continued subjugation of the black Africans became a central aim of the Afrikaner political organizations that emerged in the 1930s and 1940s, culminating in the Afrikaner National party. From 1948, when it emerged as the majority party in the all-white South African legislature, the National party devoted itself to winning complete independence from Britain (which came without violence in 1961) and to establishing lasting white domination over the political, social, and economic life of the new nation.

A rigid system of racial segregation, called *apartheid* by the Afrikaners, was established after 1948 through the passage of thousands of laws. Among other things, this legislation reserved the best jobs for whites and carefully defined the sorts of contacts permissible between different racial groups. The vote and political representation were denied to the black Africans and ultimately to the coloreds and Indians; it was illegal for them to hold mass meetings or to organize political parties or labor unions. These restrictions, combined with

very limited opportunities for higher education for black Africans, obviously hampered the growth of black African political parties and mass mobilization for decolonization efforts. The Afrikaners' establishment of a vigilant and brutal police state to uphold apartheid and their opportunistic cultivation of divisions between the diverse peoples in the black African population also contributed to their ability to preserve a bastion of white supremacy in a liberated continent. Thus far, despite the opening of political dialogue under the current de Klerk regime, decolonization in South Africa has been meaningful only for the privileged white majority.

CONFLICTING NATIONALISMS: ARABS, ISRAELIS, AND THE PALESTINIAN QUESTION

Though virtually all Arab peoples who were not yet free by the end of the Second World War were liberated by the early 1960s, the fate of Palestine continued to present special problems. Hitler's campaign of genocide against the European Jews had provided powerful support for the Zionists' insistence that the Jews must have their own homeland, which increasingly was conceived in terms of a modern national state. The brutal persecution of the Jews also won international sympathy for the Zionist cause—in part because the leaders of many nations were reluctant to admit Jews fleeing the Nazi terror into their own countries. As Hitler's henchmen stepped up their race war against the Jews, the tide of Jewish immigration to Palestine rose sharply. But growing Arab resistance to Jewish settlement and land purchases in Palestine, which was often expressed in communal rioting and violent assaults on Zionist communities, led to increasing British restrictions on Jewish entry into the colony. A major Muslim revolt between 1936 and 1939, which the British managed to put down only with great difficulty, both decimated the leadership of the Palestinian Arab community and further strengthened the British resolve to stem the flow of Jewish immigrants to Palestine. Government measures to keep out Jewish refugees from the Holocaust led in turn to violent Zionist resistance to the British presence in Palestine. The Zionist assault was spearheaded by several underground terrorist organizations, including the Stern Gang and the Irgun.

By the end of World War II the major parties claiming Palestine were locked into a deadly stalemate. The Zionists were determined to carve out a Jewish state in the region. The Palestinian Arabs and their allies in neighboring Arab lands were equally determined to transform Palestine into a multireligious nation, in which the position of the Arab majority would be ensured. Having badly bungled their mandatory responsibilities and under attack from both sides, the British wanted more than anything else to scuttle and run. The 1937 report of a British commission of inquiry supplied a possible solution—partition—and the newly created United Nations provided an international body that could give a semblance of legality to the proceedings. In 1948, with sympathy for the Jews running high due to postwar revelations of the horrors of Hitler's Final Solution, the member nations of the United Nations, with the United States and the Soviet Union in rare agreement, approved the partition of Palestine into Arab and Jewish states.

The Arab states that bordered on the newly created nation of Israel had vehemently opposed the U.N. action and attacked from all sides. Though heavily outnumbered, the Zionists proved to be better armed and much better prepared to defend themselves than almost anyone could have expected. They not only held on to the tiny, patchwork state they had been given by the United Nations, but also they expanded it at the Arabs' expense.

The brief but bloody war that ensued created hundreds of thousands of Arab refugees from Palestine and engendered the abiding hostility between Arabs and Israelis that has been the all-consuming issue in the region and a major international problem throughout the postwar era. In Palestine conflicting strains of nationalism had collided, and the legacy of colonialism proved even more of a liability to social and economic development than in the rest of the newly independent Third World.

CONCLUSION

THE LIMITS OF DECOLONIZATION

Given the fragile foundations on which it rested, the rather rapid demise of the European colonial order is not really surprising. The winning of political freedom in Asia and Africa also represented less of a break with the colonial past than the appearance of many new nations on the map of the world might lead one to assume. The decidedly nonrevolutionary, elite-to-elite transfer of power that was central to the decolonization process in most colonies, even those where there were violent guerrilla movements, limited the amount of change that accompanied the decolonization process. The Western-educated African and Asian classes moved into the offices and jobs, and often the former homes, of the European colonizers. But social gains for the rest of the population in most new nations were minimal or nonexistent. In Kenya, Algeria, and Zimbabwe (formerly Southern Rhodesia), abandoned European lands were distributed to Arab and African peasants and laborers, but in most former colonies, especially in Asia, the big landholders were indigenous, and they have held on tenaciously to their holdings. Though educational reforms were carried out to include more sciences in school curricula and the history of Asia or Africa rather than Europe, Western cultural influences have remained strong in almost all of the former colonies. Indians with a higher education continue to communicate in English; some of the most prominent of the leaders of West African states continue to pride themselves on their impeccable French, decorate their presidential palaces with French antiques, and keep in close touch with trends in French intellectual circles.

The liberation of the colonies also did little to disrupt Western dominance of international trade or the global economic order more generally. In fact, in the negotiations that led to decolonization Asian and African leaders often explicitly promised to protect the interests of Western merchants and businesspeople in the postindependence era. These and other limits that sustained Western influence and often dominance, even after freedom was won, greatly reduced the options open to nationalist leaders struggling to build viable and prosperous nations. Though new forces have also played important roles, the postindependence history of the Third World cannot be understood without taking into account the lingering effects of the colonial interlude.

FURTHER READINGS

The best introduction to the extensive literature that has developed on the Indian nationalist movement, as well as a good general historical chronology of the struggle for independence, can be found in Sumit Sarkar's *Modern India 1885–1947* (1983). Louis Fischer's biography, *Gandhi* (1950), still yields valuable insights into the personality of one of the great nationalist leaders and the workings of nationalist politics; Judith Brown's studies of Gandhi's political career, including *Gandhi's Rise to Power* (1972), provide an approach more in tune with current research. The poems and novels of Tagore yield wonderful insights into the social and cultural life of India through much of this era.

P. J. Vatikiotis's *The History of Egypt* (especially the 1985 edition) has excellent sections on the nationalist era in that country. Interesting but less reliable is Jacque Berque's *Colonialism and Nationalism in Egypt* (1972). George Antonius's *The Arab Awakening* (1946) is essential reading on the Palestine question. It can be balanced by Aaron Cohen's *The Arabs and Israel* (1970) and Fred Khouri's survey of the roots of *The Arab-Israeli Dilemma* (1968). The early stages of the nationalist struggle in West Africa are covered by Michael Crowder's *West Africa under Colonial Rule* (1982); the final drives for decolonization are surveyed by Ali A. Mazrui and Michael Tidy in *Nationalism and New States in Africa* (1984), J. D. Hargreaves's *Decolonization in Africa* (1988), and W. R. Louis and P. Gifford, eds., *Decolonization in Africa* (1984). On specific movements, see Alstair Horne's *A Savage War of Peace* (1977) on Algeria, C. Rosberg and J. Nottingham's *The Myth of 'Mau Mau'* (1966) on Kenya, and the writings of Terrence Ranger on Rhodesia. Of the many works on South Africa, the general histories by S. Throup, B. Bunting, T. D. Moodie, and L. Thompson provide a good introduction to the rise of Afrikaner power.

1946–1974 Decolonization in Asia, Africa, and Oceania
1948 Division of Korea
1945 Formation
of United Nations **1949** Formation of NATO
1948 Israel-Palestine partition; first Arab-Israeli war

1950–1953 Korean War
1951 End U.S. occupation of Japan
1945–1948 Soviet takeover of Eastern Europe

1947 India and Pakistan gain independence
1945 Atomic bomb **1949** Communist victory in China

1947–1975 Cold war; Marshall Plan
1946 Philippines proclaim independence
1945 Communists proclaim Vietnam independence
1947 Peronism in Argentina

1960s Civil rights movement
in U.S.; revival of feminism **1968–1973** Student
1959 Cuban Revolution protests in West

1957 Ghana becomes first
independent African nation **1965–1968** Cultural
revolution in China

1955 Bandung conference; nonaligned movement
1956 Partial end of Stalinism

1957 European Economic
Community (Common Market)
1955 Warsaw Pact

1965–1973 U.S. military
intervention in Vietnam
1962 Algeria declares independence

Cold War Transformations and the Transition to a New Era

9 THE WEST IN THE ERA OF
THE COLD WAR

10 THE SOVIET UNION AND
EASTERN EUROPE: THE
COLD WAR AND ITS
AFTERMATH

11 UP FROM THE ASHES: JAPAN
AND THE PACIFIC RIM IN THE
POST–WORLD WAR II ERA

12 AFRICA AND ASIA IN THE
ERA OF INDEPENDENCE

13 COLD WAR CONFRONTATIONS
AND THE RESURGENCE OF
REVOLUTION IN THE
"THIRD WORLD"

Nearly three decades after its construction, the Berlin Wall, one of the most evocative symbols of the Cold War, was destroyed in the popular risings that toppled the East German government in the fall of 1989.

PART III

After the Deluge: World History from 1945 to the End of the 20th Century

COLD WAR TRANSFORMATIONS AND THE TRANSITION TO A NEW ERA. By the end of the "30 years war," which dominated global history in the middle decades of the 20th century, much of Europe and Asia was in ruins. From Great Britain to Japan some of the key industrial and trading centers of the world had been reduced to smoldering rubble. A vast swath of death and destruction stretched from the Rhineland in Germany through central and southern Europe and the heartlands of the Soviet Union across northern and coastal China to the islands of the vanquished Japanese empire. The Middle East and much of Southeast Asia, which had been secondary theaters of World War II, had also suffered heavy losses of life and property. Areas that had not been sites for the massive campaigns of the war, such as the United States, Australia, India, and much of sub-Saharan Africa, had nonetheless poured vast amounts of resources and suffered sobering losses of young men and women sent overseas to wage war against the Axis powers. The burden of these losses was compounded by revelations of the brutal excesses that had accompanied the war on virtually all fronts. This was especially true in eastern Europe and in the Pacific, where the struggle had degenerated into a race war, and in the concentration camps of the Nazi empire, where racist ideologies had inspired state-directed genocide that had claimed millions of defenseless civilian victims.

By conservative estimates, more than 100 million people were dead, injured, or missing. A sizable majority were civilians, who were either direct casualties of bombing and enemy assaults or victims of the death camps, epidemics, forced-labor schemes, and famines spawned by the greatest of all conflicts in human history. Tens of millions more were homeless and displaced persons, the latter often uprooted forever from the lands of their birth. Throughout much of eastern Europe, the Middle East, South and Southeast Asia, and China, the collapse of the Axis regimes gave rise to costly civil wars or gave new impetus to sometimes violent struggles for liberation from European colonial rule. These conflicts were almost invariably caught up in a larger postwar confrontation between the Soviet Union and its Western allies that the fall of their common Axis adversaries also made possible.

The World After 1972

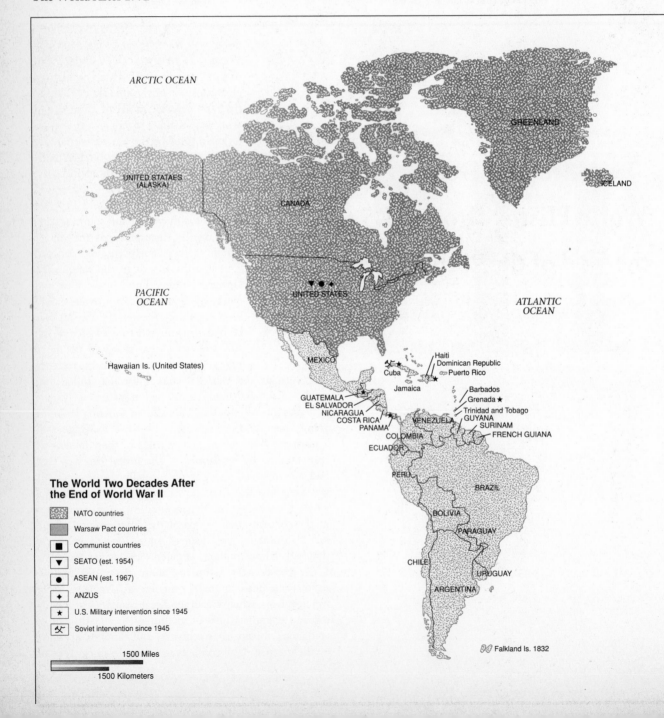

The World Two Decades After the End of World War II

- NATO countries
- Warsaw Pact countries
- ■ Communist countries
- ▼ SEATO (est. 1954)
- ● ASEAN (est. 1967)
- ✦ ANZUS
- ★ U.S. Military intervention since 1945
- Soviet intervention since 1945

1500 Miles

1500 Kilometers

THE COLD WAR AND SHIFTS IN THE BALANCE OF GLOBAL POWER

Even before the guns had quieted and the bombs ceased to fall, a new kind of global war—a "cold war"—between the Soviet-built Communist bloc and the capitalist West had begun. Though direct military clashes were for the most part avoided, none could rest easy as the tensions mounted between the emerging superpowers. The specter of unimaginable devastation caused by U.S. atomic bombs dropped in the last month of the war on Hiroshima and Nagasaki made the mounting contest between the United States and the Soviet Union an immediate concern for all the peoples of the globe. Incredibly,

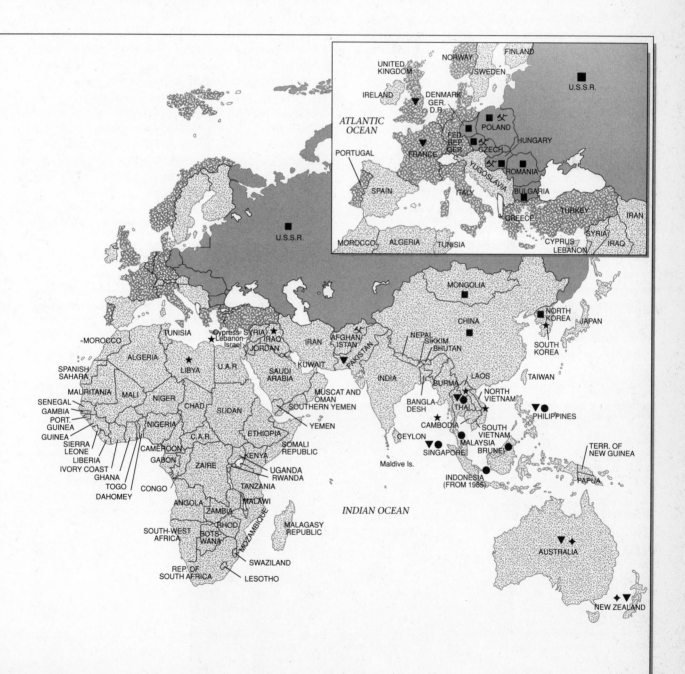

an even more destructive war than World War II was now possible—truly the war that would end war and perhaps human history itself.

Though the tense global contest for supremacy between the United States and the Soviet Union and their respective allies dominated the headlines in the decades after 1945, some of the more virulent sources of human misery and destructiveness had been removed or discredited. Isolated fascist regimes remained in Spain, Portugal, and Argentina, but the global threat of this strain of totalitarianism abated. Nazi excesses, revolt by colonized peoples, and civil rights struggles in the United States and elsewhere dealt crippling blows to racist ideologies that had been prominent in the first two phases of the 20th century. Racist sentiments continued to underlie discrimination and spark social conflict in many areas of the globe. But anthropologists and scientists alike rejected the so-called scientific proofs of biological superiority or inferiority that racist thinkers had pushed throughout the 19th and early 20th centuries. The struggles for human rights and dignity on the part of minorities and disadvantaged groups, such as women, which had surfaced in the first decades of the 20th century, were revitalized after 1945. In the United States, for example, President Truman's executive order of 1948 ended formal segregation in the military, and a civil rights movement aiming to end discrimination in U.S. society more generally gained momentum in the 1950s. At the same time, ancient ethnic rivalries and hatreds in many regions, particularly eastern and central Europe,

where communist regimes came to power, were submerged by monolithic regimes and the overarching ideological confrontations of the cold war adversaries.

In addition, within the global framework shaped by the cold war struggles between the capitalist and communist blocs, potent new forces of renewal and creativity soon emerged from the ruins of decades of war and turmoil. Though the settlement that followed World War II was dominated by the growing divisions between the Soviet Union and the United States, which had only recently been allies against the Axis powers, determined efforts were made to strengthen international organizations aimed at keeping the peace. Even before the war had ended, the partners of the victorious allied coalition had drawn up plans for and convened the first meetings of a new security organization, the United Nations. With Soviet and U.S. participation and possessing greater powers in such critical areas as peacekeeping and economic assistance, the United Nations was a much more effective and comprehensive force in world affairs than its failed predecessor, the League of Nations, which had been established after World War I. Though its initiatives have often been frustrated by the opposition of one or both of the superpowers, at critical junctures—as, for example, in the Cuban missile crisis of 1962—the UN has provided a forum for debate and negotiation that has helped to head off violent clashes and on several occasions global nuclear war.

Perhaps the most remarkable rebirths after 1945 came in war-shattered Europe and Japan. Determined

The long struggle for desegregation and African-American civil rights reached its climax in August 1963, when Martin Luther King, Jr. (front center, looking to his right), led a massive march on Washington, D.C.

to avoid the devastating backlash that had resulted from the punitive peace forced on Germany after World War I and eager for an ally in the emerging cold war, the United States sought to bring the defeated Axis powers—Germany, Japan, and Italy—back into a reconstructed world community rather than isolate them as pariahs. Fearing that communism might readily spread to these shattered and impoverished societies, the United States also provided massive economic support and technical assistance to spur their redevelopment as democracies within the Western capitalist camp. Of all of the international projects undertaken by the United States in the last phase of the 20th century, these were by far the most successful. In the decade after 1945 the leaders of the revitalizing economies and stabilized polities of western Europe took steps to forge an economic union, the European Economic Community (EEC), that it was hoped would put an end to the recurring wars that had plagued western European civilization from its inception.

Buoyed by the Common Market that resulted, western Europe entered into an era of unprecedented prosperity and launched a cultural renaissance that defied its greatly reduced position in global politics. Drawn into political and military alliance under the U.S.-led North Atlantic Treaty Organization (NATO), the nations of Western Europe have enjoyed decades of internal peace that have in turn fed hopes of a lasting union of the European continent. The economic "miracle" of postwar Europe's revival and its cultural ramifications are the focus of Chapter 9, which leads off Part III, on the third and last phase of 20th-century history.

The revival of Japan in the last third of the 20th century, which is treated in Chapter 11, has been equally impressive. By 1945 Japan's industries and urban centers had been shattered by Allied bombings. Much of Japan's navy and merchant marine, which provided its resource-poor islands with essential links to overseas resources and markets, had been sunk or captured. Though the Allies demanded Japan's unconditional surrender, the fact that the emperor (shorn of his claims of divinity) was allowed to remain as a symbol of Japan's history and identity signaled that the postwar settlement would be constructive rather than punitive. Again, in part in response to the spread of communism in East Asia but also out of a genuine concern to promote democracy in Japan, the United States provided economic assistance and political security.

Like the Germans, the Japanese were forced to rebuild their industrial base. Both peoples strove, with ample government support, to introduce and increasingly to develop themselves the most advanced technologies available. Japan soon regained its prewar markets and levels of industrial production. By the late 1960s the Japanese had achieved a standard of living that would have been unimaginable in the prewar decades, and Japan was well on the way to becoming the world leader in the manufacture and sale of such hallmark, late-20th-century consumer goods as transistor radios and television sets. Less than a decade later Japan was vying with the United States and Germany for supremacy in such critical areas as automobile production and, increasingly, computer technology. As in western Europe, these gains were made under a democratic political system, though in contrast to most western European nations, Japan's democracy was dominated by a single political party for nearly forty years after 1945. Only a revolt *within* the ruling Liberal Democratic party in 1993 opened the way for an election that brought opposition groups to power, though in alliance with splinter groups from the Liberal Democrats.

The emergence of Japan as one of the world's wealthiest societies and industrial giants was symptomatic of a more fundamental trend in the last phase of the 20th century—the growing importance of the Pacific Rim (countries, including portions of the United States, around the Pacific Ocean) in world affairs. Growing economic dynamism in South Korea, Singapore, and Malaysia joined with Japan's surge to create a new zone of rapid industrial growth in the 1970s and 1980s. The emergence of these new rivals for the older industrial powers formed one index of the declining relative position of western Europe since World War II. After the 1960s the relative position of the United States in the global economy was also increasingly challenged. In terms of population, this trend had begun in the first decades of the 20th century as family planning and the availability of modern contraceptives led to a slowing or leveling off of population growth in the industrialized nations flanking the north Atlantic. This meant a declining share of world population overall. In the decades after 1945, the revolt against Western colonial dominance in Africa and Asia and the consequent formation of tens of newly independent nations in these regions greatly diminished the global political influence of the former European powers, most notably France and Great Britain.

As we see in Chapter 12, however, on the era of independence in the Third World, despite the fall of the colonial empires, the economic and cultural influence of the

West has, if anything, increased markedly. Not only have the new nations of Africa and Asia become even more dependent on a global market system, which is dominated by the West and in recent decades by Japan, but also none has found a viable path to development that diverges substantially from those pioneered in western Europe and the United States. In addition, from Levi's jeans and Coca Cola to rock music and stream-of-consciousness novels, the cultural hold of the West has grown steadily stronger as indigenous crafts and artistic traditions have been marginalized in many non-Western areas.

Efforts by African, Asian, or Latin American peoples to forge independent paths to development have also been greatly hampered by the fact that these regions have been repeatedly drawn into cold war rivalries between the superpowers and their ideological allies. Attempts in the 1950s and 1960s by leaders, such as Egypt's Nasser and India's Nehru, to build a meaningful bloc of nonaligned nations between the Western alliance and the Warsaw Pact nations floundered due to divisions within and pressing economic needs of much of the Third World. Throughout the cold war era, the communist and capitalist global rivalry repeatedly spilled over into the power struggles within and between Third World nations. Third World countries have provided major outlets for the armaments industries of both West

and East. Foreign aid and the assistance of international lending agencies, such as the International Monetary Fund (IMF) and the World Bank, have often been contingent on political and economic policies of Third World leaders that are in line with communist or capitalist strategies. Attempts by Third World producers of raw materials, such as that by OPEC (the Organization of Petroleum Exporting Countries), to band together to gain leverage in international markets have been limited to specific products and a handful of countries and undermined by divisions within. Revolutionary movements in Africa, Asia, and Latin America have also frequently, and at the cost of countless lives, become caught up in cold war calculations and prolonged military interventions in Third World countries by the superpowers or their surrogates. Several of these key confrontations, including the U.S. debacle in Vietnam and the ill-fated Soviet involvement in Afghanistan, are considered in Chapter 13.

PORTENTS OF THE FUTURE OF THE GLOBAL COMMUNITY

For much of the third phase of 20th-century history, the cold war maneuvers of the superpowers and the continuing nuclear arms race obscured other shifts in global

The letter sweaters, "box," and rock-and-roll dancing of these Japanese teenagers are all hallmarks of a youth culture that spread across the globe in the decades after 1945. Much of this culture originated in the United States, but rock groups, such as Great Britain's Beatles, and Japanese electronics shaped it in major ways.

history that may eventually been seen as more decisive. Beginning in the late 1960s there was an increasing awareness of the adverse environmental consequences of nearly two centuries of unchecked scientific experimentation and industrial growth. Subsequent revelations about the acceleration of plant and animal species' extinction in recent decades and the ecological devastation wrought by the "development" of hitherto sparsely populated regions—most dramatically the rain forests of the tropics—have underscored the global perils of pollution and resource exhaustion. Though still hotly debated, environmental trends, such as global warming and the depletion of the ozone layer, have become major concerns for government policymakers and ordinary citizens throughout the world. The environmental toll of Western-style development has raised doubts about the capacity of the planet to withstand the global spread of industrialization, particularly since few Third World countries can afford the antipollution devices deployed in Europe, Japan, and the United States. At the very least it has become essential to include environmental costs in schemes promoting economic growth.

These concerns are heightened by another global trend, the spiraling growth of the human population. Though birthrates in industrialized societies have fallen or leveled off and those in the largest countries, China and India, have abated somewhat, very high levels of net population increase persist in Africa, much of the Middle East, Latin America, and other regions of the world. Though it had taken humankind tens of thousands of years to reach a population of six billion by 1990, nearly four of that six billion had been added in the six decades since 1930, and by conservative estimates another four billion will be added by about the year 2020.

In a world that is already threatened by overpopulation, pollution, and dwindling resources, these are daunting trends. They are complicated by what appear to be countervailing tendencies of the most brutal Malthusian variety. Despite the great 20th-century advances in medicine and scientific farming, the spread of epidemic disease and the persistence of massive famines have figured prominently in the last decades of the century. The resurgence of disease is epitomized by the AIDS epidemic, which is much more widespread in Africa and parts of the Caribbean than in more publicized areas like the United States and western Europe. Less spectacular, but perhaps equally threatening, has been the reemergence of tuberculosis and smallpox, which international health agencies had once predicted

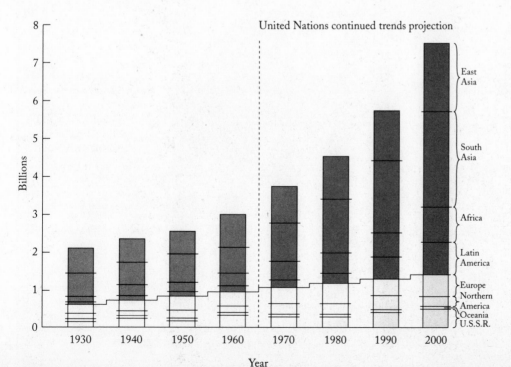

Numerical growth of world population, 1930–2000

would soon be eradicated. In addition, new strains of crop and animal diseases have surfaced, which may be linked to broader processes of environmental degradation. Shifting global weather patterns and inappropriate farming techniques, often based on those in the West, have done much to accelerate the spread of the desert and to precipitate famine in Third World areas. In Somalia, Ethiopia, and Mozambique these conditions have been greatly exacerbated by local civil wars, which have disrupted food production and distribution and often frustrated international relief efforts.

The world's history since World War II was long dominated by the cold war. The first few postwar years highlighted the most basic kinds of recovery from wartime dislocations and destruction, particularly but not exclusively in Europe. Then as the rivalry between the United States and the Soviet Union and their respective allies intensified in 1947–1948, a number of other basic trends surfaced. Key among these were the decolonization struggle, which continued through the

1970s, the revival of western Europe and Japan, and the growing influence of consumer cultures developed in the United States and Europe. Finally, underlying patterns of a global population explosion, environmental degradation, and the spreading hold of a world economy dominated by the industrial leaders took shape as well. The cold war itself, though most dangerous from the late 1940s to the 1960s, still maintained an ominous presence into the 1980s.

In the late 1980s and early 1990s a number of more positive but equally decisive shifts occurred that can be seen as part of a larger transition from the 20th to the 21st century. The collapse of the Communist regimes of eastern Europe and the Soviet Union, which are covered in Chapter 10, and major new moves for detente between Russia and the West rather suddenly and dramatically brought about the winding down of the cold war. For the first time since 1945, the nuclear balance of terror began to recede as the adversary superpowers and their allies began to dismantle their atomic arsenals. The

Eastern Europe After 1989

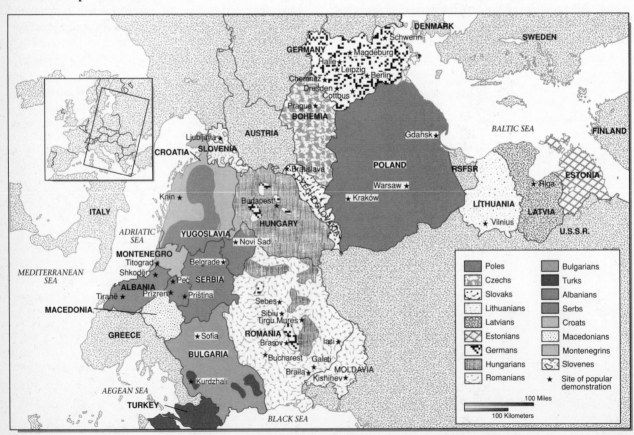

nations of the former Soviet bloc also began to be fully integrated into the world market system, which had been dominated for some decades by multinational corporations. The popular uprisings that brought down communist regimes in East Germany, Poland, Czechoslovakia, Hungary, and Romania and that helped to preserve the program of reform that Mikhael Gorbachev had initiated in the Soviet Union represented further advances for the cause of human rights in the closing years of the 20th century. The fall of dictatorships over much of Latin America in the 1980s and the unraveling of the system of apartheid in South Africa at the end of the decade also marked major progress in the liberation of oppressed peoples and in efforts to build viable democracies.

These very encouraging political trends signaled the end of the cold war and with it the third and final phase of the 20th century. But these forces for reconciliation and liberation need to be set against more troubling developments that will pose major challenges for the world's leaders in the 21st century. The collapse of the Communist regimes of eastern Europe has not only revealed the appalling ecological damage done by the command economies of the Soviet bloc but also removed what appeared to be one of the most effective paths to development for the poor nations of the globe. The fall of communism has also unleashed long-simmering ethnic and religious rivalries that have erupted into vicious warfare in many parts of the former Soviet Union and, perhaps most brutally, in the former nation of Yugoslavia. Civil strife, based on similar subnational struggles for political power and control over dwindling resources, has also spread through much of Africa, the Middle East, and South and Southeast Asia. In these areas the artificial nations carved out of the former European colonial empires have often proved unworkable and much less able to generate popular allegiance than have religious and ethnic affiliations.

With the apparent demise of communism as a major global force, alternative movements for social reform and political revival, most notably various strains of religious fundamentalism and liberation theology, have gained greatly in appeal and popular support. Though these movements often provide a source of hope and genuine assistance to impoverished and politically disenfranchised people throughout the world, they also raise the prospect of heightened prejudice, discrimination, and social strife in the coming decades. Neither their proponents nor many of the regimes now in power over much of the globe have shown great concern to limit runaway population growth or to check the ecological degradation that is pervasive in both the industrial and developing worlds. These trends and those sketched above suggest that the turbulent passage that provides an apt metaphor for global history in the 20th century will continue in the 21st.

1947–1974 Decolonization

1947–1960s Emergence and
most intense phase of cold war

1945 End of World War II

1945–1948 New constitutions in Italy, Germany, and France; Labour party victory in
Britain; basic measures of welfare states

1947 Marshall Plan
1948 Publication of *The Second Sex*

1948 East and West German regimes established
1949 North Atlantic Treaty Organization established

1960s Civil rights
movement in U.S.

1958 De Gaulle's Fifth Republic
in France

1957 Establishment of European Economic Community (Common Market)

1960s Emergence of new feminist movement

1973, 1979
Oil crises

1970s Democratic
regimes in Spain,
Portugal, and
Greece

1968–1973 Massive
student protests

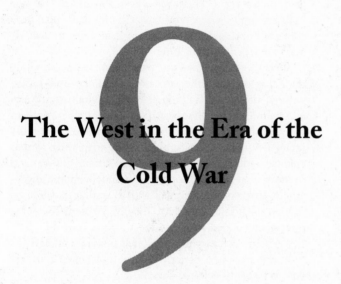

The West in the Era of the Cold War

INTRODUCTION. Amid the ashes of World War II, almost any observer of the West in 1947 would have been filled with dire forebodings about the region's future. After a previous war a scant 30 years before, European society had proved unable to invigorate an ailing economy or to deal with massive internal tensions among the major classes; political leadership had failed, and the only major innovations pointed toward the belligerence of fascism and renewed bloodshed. How could the results of this second devastating war be any better? Europe seemed prostrate, perhaps permanently crippled.

Yet after a brief recovery period, European society, along with its cousins in North America, moved into a new phase. Novel diplomatic policies joined with new domestic roles for the state. Older conflicts, though still present, eased. Though its world role was considerably revised and in important ways reduced, Europe rebounded from the 1940s onward, remaining one of the key international players in terms of economic and cultural influence and even military outreach.

As Europe established new directions, the United States, Australia, and Canada continued their own development, with the United States becoming the single most important military and, for a time, economic power in the world. Adjustments to new global responsibilities and interests pushed the United States toward innovations of its own, though economic and political policies internally were in some ways more conservative than those staked out in Western Europe.

1979 Thatcher and new conservatism in Britain

1993 Division of Czechoslovakia; Clinton inauguration ends three-term Republican tenure in White House

1981 Reagan president in U.S.

1992 End of economic restrictions within Common Market; disintegration of Yugoslavia; prolonged war over a fragmented Bosnia

1979 Significant recession

Europe's new lease on life and the firm establishment of the United States as the leading superpower formed key themes in the overall postwar history of Western society. Much of the West, furthermore, developed a new version of industrial society. The manufacturing sector declined in importance, in favor of the rise of service activities, such as information exchange and medical care. Gender roles were substantially altered by the new entry of women in the labor force. Popular culture reached for new expressions, from Europe's mania for vacations to the rock music that emerged from both sides of the North Atlantic. The striking and fundamental changes in the West's social forms constituted a final focus of the second half of the 20th century, emerging gradually amid initial postwar experimentation, then blossoming during the 1960s and 1970s.

❧ AFTER WORLD WAR II: INTERNATIONAL SETTING FOR THE WEST

World War II was fully as total a war as its predecessor, and it left western Europe in shambles. The sheer physical destruction, caused particularly by bombing raids, disrupted housing and transportation. Downed bridges and rail lines complicated food shipments, leaving many people in France and Germany ill-fed and unable to work at full efficiency. German use of forced foreign labor, as well as the many boundary changes resulting from the war, generated hundreds of thousands of refugees trying to return home or find a new home. For at least two years after 1945 it was unclear that recovery would be possible, as sheer survival proved difficult enough. In the long run Europe's postwar weakness after three decades of strife helped trigger in the former colonial areas a crescendo of nationalist sentiment directed against the West, as well as the fuller emergence of the United States and the Soviet Union, whose size and building industrial strength finally overshadowed Europe's proud nation-states.

EUROPE AND ITS COLONIES

The two larger changes provoked by the war—decolonization and the cold war—quickly intruded on the West. Colonies outside Europe, roused by the war, became increasingly restive. When the British returned to Malaya and the Dutch to Indonesia—areas from which they had been dislodged—they found a more hostile climate, with well-organized nationalist resistance. It was soon clear that many colonies could be maintained only

at great cost, and in the main the European nations decided that the game was not worth the candle. A few cases proved messy. France tried to defend its holdings in Vietnam against Communist guerrillas, yielding only in 1954 after some major defeats. The French clung even more fiercely to Algeria, its oldest African colony and one with a large European minority. The French military joined Algerian settlers in insisting on a war to the death against nationalist forces, and bitter fighting went on for years. The tension even threatened civil war in France, until a new president, Charles de Gaulle, realized the hopelessness of the struggle and negotiated Algeria's independence in 1962.

Overall, decolonization proceeded more smoothly than this between the late 1940s and the mid-1970s, without prolonged fighting that might drain the Western nations themselves, with Kenya and the Algerian morass bitter exceptions. Western governments typically retained important cultural relations with their former colonies and sometimes provided administrative and military help as well. Both France and Belgium, for example, frequently intervened in Africa after decolonization was officially complete. Finally, Western economic interests remained strong in most former colonies—particularly in Africa, which exploited mineral and agricultural resources in a pattern of trade not radically different from that of colonial days.

The impact of decolonization on the West should not, however, be minimized. Important minorities of former settlers and officials came home embittered, though, except briefly in France, they were not a significant political force. Europe's overt power in the world was dramatically reduced. Efforts by Britain and France to attack independent Egypt in 1956, to protest Egypt's nationalization of the Suez Canal, symbolized the new state of affairs. The United States and the Soviet Union forced a quick end to hostilities, and what was once a colonial lifeline came into non-Western hands. Yet although decolonization was a powerful change in world affairs, it did not, at least in the short run, overwhelm the West, as neither economic growth nor internal political stability suffered greatly.

THE COLD WAR

The final new ingredient of Europe's diplomatic framework, the cold war between the United States and the Soviet Union, had a more durable ongoing influence on politics and society within the West. The conflict took shape between 1945 and 1947. The last wartime meetings among the leaders of Britain, the United States, and the Soviet Union had rather vaguely staked out the boundaries of postwar Europe, which were certainly open to varied interpretations. By the war's end Soviet troops firmly occupied most eastern European countries, and within three years the Soviets had installed Communist regimes to their liking, while excluding opposition political movements. Thus an *eastern bloc* emerged that included Poland, Czechoslovakia, Bulgaria, Romania, and Hungary. And Soviet boundaries themselves had pushed west, reversing the decisions of the post–World War I Versailles conference. The Baltic states disappeared, and Poland lost territory to Russia, gaining some former German lands as compensation. Finally, Soviet occupation of the eastern zone of Germany gave Russia a base closer toward the heart of Europe than the tsars had ever dreamed possible.

Offended by the Soviet Union's heavy-handed manipulation of eastern Europe, U.S. and British policymakers tried to counter. The new American president, Harry Truman, was less eager for smooth relations with the Soviets than Franklin Roosevelt had been; Truman was emboldened by the U.S. development in 1945 of the atomic bomb. Britain's wartime leader, Winston Churchill, had long feared Communist aggression; it was he who in 1946 coined the phrase *iron curtain* to describe the division between free and repressed societies that he saw taking shape in Europe. But Britain frankly lacked the power to resist Soviet pressure, and under the Labour government it explicitly left the initiative to the United States.

The United States responded to Soviet power plays with vigor. It criticized Soviet policies and denied Soviet applications for reconstruction loans. It bolstered regimes in Iran, Turkey, and Greece that were under Soviet pressure. In Greece, particularly, the United States took over British resistance to a powerful Communist guerrilla campaign. Then in 1947 the United States proclaimed its Marshall Plan, a program of substantial loans that was designed to aid Western nations rebuild from the war's devastation. In Soviet eyes the Marshall Plan was a vehicle for U.S. economic dominance, and indeed there is little question that in addition to humanitarian motives the United States intended to beat back domestic Communist movements in countries such as France and Italy by promoting economic growth.

The focal point of the cold war in these early years was in Germany. Soviet policy in Germany initially concentrated on seizing goods and factories as reparation. The Western Allies soon prevented Soviet intervention in their own zones and turned to some rebuilding efforts in the interests of playing a modest "German card" against growing Soviet strength in the east. That is, although the West, led by the United States, did not intend to resurrect a powerful Germany, it soon began to think in terms of constructing a viable political and

The Common Market and its Growth; NATO Boundaries and Neutral

economic entity. Allied collaboration started building a unified West Germany in 1946, and local followed by more national political structures were established through elections. When in 1947 the West moved to promote German economic recovery by creating a stable currency, the Soviet Union responded by blockading the city of Berlin, the divided former capital that sat in the midst of the Soviet zone. The United States responded with a massive airlift to keep the city supplied, and the crisis finally ended in 1948, with two separate Germanies—East and West—beginning to take clear shape along a tense, heavily fortified frontier.

Cold war divisions spread from Germany to Europe more generally with the formation of two rival military alliances. The North Atlantic Treaty Organization (NATO) was formed in 1949, under U.S. leadership, to group most of the western European powers and Canada in a defensive alliance against possible Soviet aggression. The NATO pact soon legitimated some rearmament of West Germany in the context of resistance to

German workers present their passports at a checkpoint between East and West Berlin in 1948. The division of Berlin was mirrored in the partition of defeated Germany and the broader division of European nations between NATO and the Warsaw Pact.

communism, as well as the continued maintenance of a substantial U.S. military presence in Germany and in other member nations. In response the Soviet Union organized the Warsaw Pact among its eastern European satellites. When in 1949 the Soviets developed their own nuclear capability, the world—particularly the European world—seemed indeed divided between two rival camps, each in turn dominated by its own superpower. Numerous U.S. and Soviet military units were permanently stationed in Europe on either side of the cold war divide.

The cold war had a number of implications for western Europe. It brought new influences from the United States on internal as well as foreign policy. Through the 1950s and beyond, the United States pressed for acceptance of German rearmament (though under some agreed on limits); it lobbied for higher military expenditures in its old allies France and Britain; and it pressed for acceptance of U.S. forces and weapons systems. The Americans' wishes were not always met, but the United States had vital negotiating leverage in the economic aid it offered (and might withdraw), in the troops it stationed in Europe, and in the nuclear "umbrella" it developed (and might, in theory, also withdraw). The nuclear weapons seemed to offer the only realistic protection should the Soviet Union venture direct attack. The Soviets, for their part, influenced western Europe not only through perceived aggressive intent but also by funding and supporting substantial Communist movements in France and Italy, which in turn affected but did not overwhelm the political process.

The cold war did not maintain the intensity it reached in its early years. Centers of conflict shifted in part outside Europe as Korea, then Vietnam, and recurrently the Middle East became flashpoints. In special circumstances a few European states managed to stay out of strict cold war alignment. Sweden and Switzerland maintained traditions of neutrality; Finland, a capitalist democracy on Soviet borders, was neutral perforce. Austria regained independence in 1956—in a period of lessening cold war dispute—on condition of neutrality; and Yugoslavia, though Communist, increasingly pulled away from the Soviet camp. Finally, the main Western powers themselves, once launched on recovery, found increasing room to maneuver. After 1958, France became more and more restive under what it viewed as Anglo-U.S. dominance of NATO, and it finally withdrew its forces from the joint NATO command, requiring also that U.S. troops leave French soil. In the 1970s Germany opened new negotiations with the Soviet Union and eastern bloc countries, wanting increased export opportunities and reduced diplomatic tension.

The fact was that the cold war and the resultant alliance system continued to describe much of the framework of East-West relations in Europe from the end of World War II into the 1990s. France might gain partial independence from NATO, but it did not withdraw entirely. Although tensions often receded after the high point of the late 1940s, fear of possible Soviet aggression remained; for this reason the U.S. military presence was deemed essential by leading policymakers, if not the entire European public. Western Europe could no longer plan on defending itself against a major outside enemy. Although Great Britain and, after 1958, France developed small nuclear capabilities, they simply could not afford the massive stockpiles and rockets of the two superpowers. To some extent, indeed, Europeans ultimately grew rather comfortable in their reliance on the United States for protection. Not only during the lean postwar recovery years but also after prosperity returned, European nations kept military budgets relatively modest, compared to U.S. or Soviet spending, which meant a degree of vulnerability to outside military and diplomatic pressures that had no precedent in modern European history. Even when Soviet-Western tensions virtually disappeared, early in the 1990s, most western European nations still approved of U.S. military involvement in the region through NATO.

A vital feature of this diplomatic configuration obviously involved the rise of the United States to preeminence within the West. This development was long in the making. Its industrial surge had already brought the United States new influence by the late 19th century, as key U.S. firms—such as Singer, manufacturer of sewing machines—quickly established a worldwide base with branches heavily influencing the economies of several European nations. Economic power was enhanced by agricultural exports and, after World War I, the power of U.S. banking and credit. Following World War II, when the dollar became standard international currency, the economic supremacy of the United States among the Western nations seemed assured, and for a time many experts worried that Europe would never regain economic autonomy, doomed always to poor-relative status vis-à-vis its giant U.S. cousin. This situation proved temporary, as we will see, but even in the 1980s the economic power of the United States continued to surpass that of western Europe.

After 1941 the diplomatic and military ascendancy of the United States matched its economic power for the

first time, save for the brief flicker between 1917 and 1919. The U.S. leadership role in the postwar Western alliance was never seriously challenged, although it produced grievances and protests within Europe from various groups, both conservative nationalists and leftist supporters of nuclear disarmament. The rise of the United States qualified the general pattern of declining world power for the West, though some by the late 1980s argued that this nation, too, had become overcommitted and was destined to pull back. This same rise signaled the reduced status of what had been the Western heartland in Europe and raised questions about whether the West would remain coherent, not just diplomatically but also culturally, under unfamiliar U.S. leadership.

The shifting balance between the United States and Europe produced a crisscrossing of military relationships, whatever the larger implications of the shift. As western Europe abandoned military preeminence, the United States, never before a major peacetime military power, devoted growing resources to its military capacity and gave an increasing voice to its military leaders. Regardless of the political party in power, the percentage of the U.S. government budget going to the military remained stable from the 1950s to the 1980s—when it went up. In contrast, some European leaders boasted that their societies had made a transition toward preeminence of civilian values and goals. Although U.S. and European values and institutions became more similar in key respects after World War II, the difference in military roles signaled ongoing distinctions within Western society.

THE RESURGENCE OF WESTERN EUROPE

Although the shifts in the West's external environment triggered by World War II were not catastrophic, they constituted major readjustments. Ironically, western Europe's domestic development in this same period was considerably more positive, a strong contrast not only to its reduction in world status but also to the massive troubles that had followed World War I. Immediately after the war, western Europe suffered tremendous dislocation, amid grinding poverty and painful rebuilding, made worse by the new cold war division of the European map and strong fears of a new superpower clash.

But though postwar problems left their mark, western Europe demonstrated surprising resiliency. A new set of leaders emerged in many countries, some from wartime resistance movements, eager to avoid the mistakes that had led to depression and war. Although their vision was not always realized, from 1945 onward western Europe did move forward on three important fronts: the extension of democratic political systems, a modification of nation-state rivalries within Europe, and a commitment to rapid economic growth that reduced previous social and gender tensions.

THE SPREAD OF LIBERAL DEMOCRACY

In politics, defeat in war greatly discredited fascism and other rightist movements that had opposed parliamentary democracy. Vestiges of these movements continued, periodically surfacing in France and Italy but rarely with much muscle. At the same time, key leftist groups, including the strong Communist movements that emerged from the war in France and Italy, were committed to democratic politics. Although social protest continued, outright revolutionary sentiment declined. Finally, several new political movements surfaced, notably an important Christian Democratic current, which was wedded to democratic institutions and moderate social reform. Despite national variations, in general western Europe experienced a shift in the political spectrum toward fuller support for democratic constitutions and greater agreement on the need for government planning and welfare activities.

New regimes had to be constructed in Germany and Italy after the defeat of Fascist and Nazi leadership; France established a new republic once occupation ended. In Germany political reconstruction was delayed by the division of the nation by the victorious Allies. As the cold war took shape, however, France, Britain, and the United States progressively merged their zones into what became the Federal Republic of Germany (West Germany), encouraging a new constitution that would avoid the mistakes of Germany's earlier Weimar Republic by outlawing extremist political movements. The new constitutions set up after 1945 in many European countries varied in particulars but uniformly established effective parliaments with universal (now always including female) suffrage. And the regimes endured. Only France, pressed by the Algerian War, changed its constitution in 1958, forming a Fifth Republic, still democratic but with stronger presidential authority.

Western Europe's movement toward more consistent democracy continued in the 1970s, when Spain and Portugal moved from their authoritarian, semi-Fascist constitutions (following the deaths of longtime strongmen) to democratic, parliamentary systems. Greece, increasingly linked to the West, followed the same pattern. By the 1980s western Europe had become more politically uniform than ever before in history. Party dominance shifted, with conservatives, including Christian Democrats, alternating with Socialist coalitions, but all major actors agreed on the constitutional system itself.

THE WELFARE STATE

The consolidation of democracy also entailed a general movement toward a welfare state. Resistance ideas and the shift leftward of the political spectrum helped explain the new activism of the state in economic policy and welfare issues. Wartime planning in the British government had pointed to the need for new programs to reduce the impact of economic inequality and to reward the lower classes for their loyalty. Not surprisingly, the governments that emerged at the war's end—Britain's Labour party and Communist-Socialist–Christian Democrat coalitions in France and Italy—quickly moved to set up a new government apparatus that would play a vigorous role in economic planning and develop new social activities as well. By 1948 the basic nature of the modern welfare state had been established throughout western Europe, as not only the new regimes but also established reformists (as in Scandinavia) extended a variety of government programs. The United States, though somewhat more tentative in welfare measures, added to its New Deal legislation in the 1960s, under President Lyndon Johnson's Great Society programs, creating medical assistance packages for the poor and the elderly. Canada enacted an even more comprehensive medical insurance plan.

The welfare state elaborated a host of social insurance measures. Unemployment insurance was improved. Medical care was supported by state-funded insurance or, as in Britain where it became a centerpiece to the new Labour program, the basic health care system was nationalized. State-run medical facilities provided free care to the bulk of the British population from 1947 onward, although some small fees were later introduced. Family assistance was another category, not entirely new, that was now greatly expanded. All western European governments provided payments to families with several children, the amount increasing with family size. Because the poor now tended to have the largest families, family-aid programs both encouraged population growth—of particular concern to countries such as France—and helped redistribute some of the general tax revenues toward the neediest groups. In the 1950s a

French worker family with low earnings and five children (admittedly an unusual brood by this point) could improve its income by as much as 40 percent through family aid. Governments also became more active in the housing field—a virtual necessity given wartime destruction and postwar population growth. Britain embarked on an ambitious program of "council housing," providing many single-family units that deliberately mixed working-class and middle-class families in new neighborhoods. By the 1950s over one-fourth of the British population was housed in structures built and run by the government.

The welfare state that emerged in the postwar years was a compromise product. It recognized a substantial private sector and tried to limit and cushion individual initiative rather than replacing it with state action alone, as in the Communist system. It provided aid for citizens at many income levels. Middle-class people might bene-

The great sacrifices of the ordinary people in World War II brought great pressure for the establishment of welfare states at war's end. Here orange juice and vitamins are distributed to children and mothers at a British health clinic in the mid-1950s.

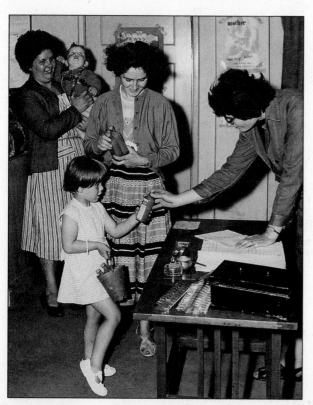

fit from family assistance, and they certainly used state medical insurance. They also disproportionately benefited from the expanded educational systems and university scholarships that developed along with the welfare state. In other words, although the welfare state focused particularly on problems of workers and the poor, it won support from other groups by dealing with some of their special needs as well.

Relatedly, although some aspects of the welfare state redistributed income, the welfare state did not generally make a huge dent on western Europe's unequal class system. Though taxes rose, they were not always steeply graduated. Furthermore, starting with France, a supplementary tax system was installed, beginning in the late 1950s, that was not graduated at all. This value-added tax system, which quickly spread through Europe, levied taxes on each stage of the production process, operating essentially as a supra–sales tax ultimately paid by consumers. Here was a potent source of revenue that had little redistributive effect.

The welfare state was, in sum, an important new definition of government functions but hardly a device for social revolution. It cushioned citizens against major expenses and unusual hardships rather than rearranging overall social structure. It protected the purchasing power of the very poor against catastrophe, and it contributed to improved health conditions generally. It also, of course, increased contacts between government and citizen, and it produced a host of new regulations that framed European life.

Despite many criticisms from both the left and the right, the welfare state won wide acceptance from its inception. The British, for example, became quickly attached to their new health system, making major revision impossible. For the most part political debate centered on tinkering with the welfare state, not revolutionizing it in any particular direction. Socialist parties, when in power, extended welfare measures by expanding their coverage and benefits. Conservative parties, for their part, often cut back a bit and promised more efficient administration. Into the 1970s no major political movement attacked the new state root and branch.

The welfare state was undeniably expensive. It greatly enlarged government bureaucracies, in addition to channeling tax monies to new purposes. By the 1950s up to 25 percent of the gross national product of France and Holland was going to welfare purposes, and the figure tended to rise with time. As military expenses began to stabilize, welfare commitments became far and away the largest component of Western government budgets outside the United States. Here was a clear indication of the extent to which the western European state had altered its relationship to the wider society.

An increased governmental role in economic policy paralleled the welfare state. Most postwar governments nationalized some sectors of industry outright. Most European countries also set up new planning offices, responsible for developing multiyear economic projections and for setting goals and the means to meet them. By coordinating tax concessions and directing the flow of capital from state banks, government planners had genuine power to shape, although not directly to run, economic activity. Planning extended to both agriculture and industry. Planning offices regulated crop sizes and encouraged consolidation of land for greater efficiency, and they could require farmers to participate in cooperatives that would improve marketing and purchasing procedures.

Planning involved European governments more directly than ever before in commitments to economic growth, full employment, and avoidance of damaging recessions. It was also aimed at improving the economic development of laggard regions. Italy thus tried to direct increasing industrialization toward the south, whereas France industrialized toward the west, in both cases with partial success.

Of the Western nations, only the United States shunned an economic planning office, though it maintained government regulation of the financial system. Rather, government growth consisted more of expanding military activities and piecemeal welfare measures, though U.S. elections, like European, usually hinged on the electorate's judgment of how well the nation was doing economically.

Despite important variations, the role of the state loomed unprecedentedly large throughout the West from the 1940s onward. A new breed of bureaucrat, often called a technocrat because of intense training in engineering or economics and because of a devotion to the power of national planning, came to the fore in the offices of the government. Some state initiatives undoubtedly reflected the potential overzealousness of the new breed. Housing authorities forced workers out of old but comfortable slums into anonymous high-rise structures that, however elegant on paper, never felt right to residents. Peasants, no friend of distant central governments even before, often lamented heavy-handed requirements. Yet here too, as with the welfare state, no particularly coherent political disputes took shape, at least until the 1960s. The new state seemed to work well enough that it was difficult to attack categorically.

POLITICAL STABILITY AND THE QUESTION MARKS

The fact was that big, contentious political issues were notable for their absence through most of Europe during the 1950s and 1960s, except for the polarizing experience in France of the Algerian War. Reformist governments of the immediate postwar years tended to give way to more conservative regimes during the 1950s. Labour, for example, lost the 1951 election in Britain; even earlier, Communists had been forced out of coalitions in France and Italy. But the conservative regimes were generally content to support the existing definition of state functions. Also, when socialist or labor governments gained renewed access to power, as in Britain in the 1960s, they, too, typically had no dramatic new programs to offer. For better or worse, Europeans seemed to accept the state's new social and economic role as well as its constitutional structure. Political debates were often fierce, and partisan loyalties intense, but few sweeping issues were raised.

The Western pattern of political compromise around the mechanisms of parliamentary democracy and the welfare state were, however, severely jolted by a series of student protests that developed in the late 1960s. Even before this, in the United States a vigorous civil rights movement had developed to protest unequal treatment of African-Americans. Massive demonstrations, particularly in Southern cities, attacked segregation and limitations on African-American voting rights.

Campus unrest was a Western-wide phenomenon in the 1960s. At major American universities, campus unrest focused on the nation's involvement in the war in Vietnam. Young people in Europe and the United States also targeted the materialism of their societies, including the stodginess of the welfare state, seeking more idealistic goals and greater justice. Student uprisings in France in 1968 created a near revolution. By the early 1970s new rights for students and other reforms, combined with police repression, ended the most intense student protests, whereas passage of civil rights legislation in the United States ultimately reduced urban rioting and demonstrations. The flexibility of postwar Western democracy seemed triumphant. Some additional political concerns, including a new wave of feminism focusing on economic rights and dignity for women, and environmentalist movements entered the arena during the 1970s, partly as an aftermath of the student explosion. The rise of the Green movement in several countries in the 1970s signaled a new political tone, hostile to uncontrolled economic growth. Green parliamentary deputies in Germany even refused to wear coats and ties in their efforts to defy established political habits.

Observers in many countries speculated that a shift in basic political alignments might be in the making if old parties failed to deal adequately with the new issues. In some western European countries, also, a terrorist movement, targeting political and business leaders, caused recurrent anxiety. As economic growth slowed in the 1970s and the Western world faced its greatest economic recession since the immediate postwar years, other signs of political change appeared. New leadership sprang up within the British Conservative party and the U.S. Republican party, seeking to reduce the costs and coverage of the welfare state. In 1979 British Conservative leader Margaret Thatcher began the longest-running prime-ministership in history, working to cut welfare and housing expenses and to promote free

enterprise. Neither she nor her U.S. counterpart, Ronald Reagan, fully dismantled the welfare state, but they did reduce its impact.

Despite all the portents of change, however, the main lines of postwar government persisted into the 1990s. Democratic institutions often failed to command great excitement, as voting levels went down throughout the West (particularly in the United States), but they roused no widespread, coherent resistance either. New political movements, although interesting, had yet to dislodge mainstream conservative and socialist (or, in the United States, liberal) parties. The Western world has unquestionably remained freer from major political upheavals than have most other civilizations in the postwar decades and freer than Western society itself had been during the 1920s and 1930s. Has Western society achieved a durable new harmony, or were the postwar decades a period of deceiving tranquility before some yet-to-be-defined storm?

DOCUMENT
YOUTH CULTURE IN THE 1960s

The explosion of youth unrest throughout the West in the 1960s was directed against a host of grievances—problems in finding jobs, opposition to the Vietnam War, concerns about the basic trends of corporate life and consumerism in Europe and the United States alike. Some observers predicted that youth would become the central protest group of advanced industrial society, replacing the working class. In key respects, however, youth protest turned out to be a vivid but short-lived phenomenon. It generated larger cultural outlooks and new behaviors that continued to excite young people and that outlasted the protest current itself. Rock music, for example, maintained high levels of popularity. New kinds of sexual behavior, involving earlier ages of sexual intercourse, exploded in the 1960s and substantially continued thereafter, though modified in the early 1990s by new disease concerns.

The following three selections deal with the two kinds of youth rebellion. The first is a recollection by a former U.S. student radical, reflecting after the fact on his protest activities during his college years. The

second selection offers a different kind of evidence: statistics on youth political attitudes, also in the United States, during the same time period. The third selection, also statistical, moves to one of the other areas of innovation—sexuality, picking up on trends that had begun during the 1960s but continued to amplify during the 1970s.

When I felt really good was during a sit-in, when there was a drawing together, a unity . . . The marches I went on, they made me feel like I was doing something. When I saw it wasn't going anywhere it started turning me off. All I was doing was stretching my legs. People would yell and shake their fist, and the government would once in a while come out and throw them a bone or push them around, then pass them off.

From the way that I felt when I was on acid, I thought that everyone else would feel like that, too. So if we all felt like that, how could there be any violence or evil? Because when I was on acid, I didn't feel like being hassled. All I wanted to do was sit and rap or just think about something. Just sit down between the stereo speakers and put on Janis [Joplin] singing "Summertime" and just watch the fish swim in the aquarium. That was the most mellow state I could be in.

I didn't know what I wanted. No, I wanted happiness, but I didn't know what it was. I thought it was being high twenty-four hours a day, and I couldn't get it. Now I know it's being contented. In the world that's impossible—there's always something wrong with you, but the Lord takes you just the way you are and if you've got something wrong in your heart, he'll deliver you from it. All you have to do is obey His Word.

From: Steven M. Tipton, *Getting Saved from the Sixties.* Berkeley: University of California Press, 1982, pp. 86, 39, 1.

A 1968 Poll on Political Attitudes:
(Note: This poll divided American college students into two groups: "high prestige" students from upper-middle-class backgrounds and "vocationals," students from lower status families, who looked on college as providing a set of job-relevant skills.)

Beliefs	Percentages "Vocational" Students	"High Prestige" Students
U.S. a "sick" society	32	50
Against war in Vietnam	43	69
Civil disobedience may be justified	32	68
Too little done for blacks	38	71
Dislike business	26	46
Containing communism worth fighting for	59	28
Need more law and order	78	39
More respect for authority	73	41
Should prohibit marijuana	69	37
Technology good	75	56
Factors in career choice:		
Family	48	25
Money	58	21
Job prestige	33	13

This table is adapted from "What They Believe: A Fortune Yankelovich Survey," *Fortune*, January 1969. Copyright Time Inc.

The Sexual Revolution:
Percent of women 15–19 years of age who had premarital intercourse

Current Age	1971 %	1976 %
15	14.2	18.5
16	22.3	27.9
17	28.6	43.6
18	40.7	54.0
19	49.5	60.4
15–19	30.1	40.9

Adapted from Melvin Zelnik, John F. Kantner, Kathleen Ford, *Sex and Pregnancy in Adolescence.* Beverly Hills: Sage, 1981, p.65

Questions: What were the common themes of youth culture that emerged in the 1960s? Was sex related to politics? What were some of the divisions among youth? How can the new youth culture be explained? Why did it ultimately turn away from collective protest? How much of it survives in the West today?

THE DIPLOMATIC CONTEXT

Along with the extension of democracy and the development of the welfare state, the West showed postwar vigor in addressing some traditional diplomatic problems, notably recurrent nationalistic rivalry, as well as specific manifestations, such as French-German enmity. U.S. guidance combined with innovative thinking in the new European governments.

During the war, many resistance leaders had tempered their hatred of nazism with a plea for a reconstruction of the European spirit. The Christian Democratic movement, particularly, produced important new advocates of harmony among European nations. Early postwar reforms, however, concentrated primarily on internal changes. Although cold war rivalries prevented a formal European peace settlement, initial impulses by the victorious Allies suggested a harsh treatment of Germany, possibly a permanent dismemberment, in order to avoid a repetition of the two previous world wars—not a more fundamental rethinking of Western conventions.

Yet the demands of the cold war and pressure from the United States forced second thoughts, which ultimately revived elements of resistance idealism. By 1947 U.S. leaders were eager to spur western Europe's economic recovery, for which they judged coordination across national boundaries an essential precondition. Thus the resulting Marshall Plan required discussion of tariffs and other development issues among recipient nations. With simultaneous U.S. insistence on the partial rearmament of Germany and German participation in NATO, the framework for diplomatic reform was complete.

Faced with these pressures and aware of the failure of nationalistic policies between the wars, several French statesmen took a lead in proposing coordination between France and Germany as a means of setting up a new Europe. The nations of the Low Countries and Italy were soon linked in these activities. The idea was to tie German economic activity to an international framework so that the nation's growing strength would not again threaten European peace. Institutions were established to link policies in heavy industry and later to develop atomic power. A measure to establish a united European military force proved too ambitious and collapsed under nationalist objections. But in 1958 the six western European nations (West Germany, France, Italy, Belgium, Luxembourg, and the Netherlands) set up the European Economic Community, or Common Market, to begin to create a single economic entity across national political boundaries. Tariffs were progressively reduced among the member nations, and a common tariff policy was set for the outside world. Free movement of labor and investment was encouraged. A Common Market bureaucracy was established, ultimately in Brussels, to oversee these operations. The Common Market set up a court system to adjudicate disputes and prevent violations of coordination rules; it also administered a development fund to spur economic growth in such laggard regions as southern Italy and western France.

One of the most dynamic and farseeing of the so-called technocrats who became a major force in national policymaking after 1945, Jean Monnet first engineered France's economic recovery from the war and then helped formulate the Schuman Plan in 1950, which provided the first steps toward the creation of the European Economic Community.

The Common Market did not move quickly toward a single government. Important national disputes limited the organization's further growth. France and Germany, for example, routinely quarreled over agricultural policy, with France seeking more payments to farmers as a matter of obvious self-interest. The establishment of the Fifth Republic in France, under Charles de Gaulle, indeed signaled an increase of French nationalism. But although the Common Market did not turn into full unity, it did survive and, on the whole, prosper. It even established an advisory international parliament, ultimately elected by direct vote. Further, in the 1980s firm arrangements were made to dismantle all trade and currency exchange barriers among member states in 1992, creating essentially complete economic unity. The Common Market's success expanded its hold within western Europe. After long hesitations Britain, despite its tradition of proud island independence, decided to join, as did Ireland, Denmark, and later Greece, Spain, and Portugal. Nationalist tensions within Europe receded to a lower point than ever before in modern European history. After the worst scares of the cold war, focused mainly on the division between Communist East and semicapitalist West, Europe became a diplomatically placid continent, enjoying one of the longest periods of complete internal peace in its history. Plans to press unity further, for example by establishing a single currency, though hotly debated in 1992–1993, testified to the impact of the postwar reorientation in diplomatic policy.

ECONOMIC EXPANSION

After a surprisingly short, if agonizing, postwar rebuilding, striking economic growth accompanied political and diplomatic change. The welfare state and the Common Market may have encouraged this growth by improving purchasing power for the masses and facilitating market expansion across national boundaries; certainly economic growth encouraged the success of new political and diplomatic systems.

There was no question that by the mid-1950s western Europe had entered a new economic phase. Agricultural production and productivity increased rapidly as peasant farmers, backed by the technocrats, adopted new equipment and seeds. European agriculture was still less efficient than that of North America, which necessitated some much resented tariff barriers by the Common Market. But food production easily met European needs, often with some to spare for export. Retooled industries poured out textiles and metallurgical products. Expensive consumer products, such as automobiles and appliances, supported rapidly growing factories. Western Europe also remained a leading center of weapons production, trailing only the United States and the Soviet Union in exports.

Overall growth in gross national product surpassed the rates of any extended period since the Industrial Revolution began; it also surpassed the growth rates of the U.S. economy during the 1950s and 1960s. The German economy, after some basic reconstruction and a currency stabilization in 1948, expanded at 6 percent a year during the 1950s; with few modest setbacks this pace continued into the early 1970s. France's growth rate reached 8 percent by the late 1950s, maintained almost this level during the 1960s, and returned to rates of over 7 percent annually by the early 1970s. By 1959 the Italian economy, a newcomer to the industrial big leagues, was expanding at an annual rate of 11 percent. These were, admittedly, the clearest success stories. Scandinavian growth was substantial but more modest, and Britain, also expanding but falling rapidly in rank among the European national economies, managed an annual increase of 4 percent at best. Even this, however, contrasted markedly with the stagnation of the 1920s and early 1930s.

Growth rates of the sort common in western Europe, their impact heightened by the absence of major depressions, depended on rapid technological change. Europe's rising food production was achieved with a steadily shrinking agricultural labor force. France's peasant population—16 percent of the labor force in the early 1950s—fell to 10 percent two decades later, but overall output was much higher than before. During the 1950s the industrial work force grew as part of factory expansion, but by the 1960s, the relative proportion of factory workers also began to drop, despite rising production. Workers in the service sector, filling functions as teachers, clerks, medical personnel, insurance and bank workers, and performers and other "leisure industry" personnel, rose rapidly in contrast. Europe, like the United States, began to convert technological advance into the provision of larger bureaucracies and service operations without jeopardizing the expanding output of goods. In France half of all paid workers were in the service sector by 1968, and the proportion rose steadily thereafter.

The high rates of economic growth also ensured relatively low unemployment after the immediate postwar dislocations passed. Even Britain, with lagging development, averaged no more than 4 percent unemployment a year during the 1950s and 1960s, whereas France and Germany featured rates of 2 percent to 3 percent a year.

Indeed, many parts of the Continent were labor-short and had to seek hundreds of thousands of workers from other areas—first from southern Europe, then, as this region industrialized, from Africa, the Middle East, and parts of Asia. The rise of immigrant minorities was a vital development in western Europe and also the United States, where the influx of Asian and Latin American immigrants stepped up markedly.

Unprecedented economic growth and low unemployment meant unprecedented improvements in incomes, even with the taxation necessary to sustain welfare programs. Per capita disposable income rose 117 percent in the United States between 1960 and 1973 and soared 258 percent in France, 312 percent in Germany, and 323 percent in Denmark. Indeed, Scandinavia, Switzerland, and the Federal Republic of Germany surpassed the United States in standards of living by the 1980s, whereas France, long an apparent laggard in modern economic development, pulled even. New spending money rapidly translated into huge increases in the purchase of durable consumer goods, as virtually the whole of Western civilization became an "affluent society." By 1969 two of every ten people in Britain, Sweden, West Germany, and France owned an automobile. Ownership of television sets became virtually universal. France and other countries indulged in a mania for household appliances. Shopping malls and supermarkets, the agents of affluence and extensive but efficient shopping that had first developed in the United States, spread widely, at the expense of more traditional, small specialty shops. A West German company, in fact, took over a key U.S. grocery chain in the late 1970s, on grounds that Europeans now knew mass marketing as well as or better than the U.S. consumer pioneers.

Europe had unquestionably developed a framework of affluent consumerism as fully as had the United States, with at least as much impact on basic social patterns and habits of thought. Advertising was not quite as ubiquitous in Europe as across the Atlantic, particularly because most television channels were state-run and noncommercial. But promptings to buy, to smell good, to look right, to express one's personality in the latest car style began quickly to describe European life. The frenzy to find good vacation spots was certainly intense. Literally millions of Germans poured annually into Italy and Spain, seeking the sun. Britons thronged to Spanish beaches. Europeans were bent on combining efficient work with indulgent leisure.

The West's economic advance was not without some dark spots. Inflation was a recurrent headache when demand outstripped production. Inflation in the 1970s, af-

TABLE 9.1
Two Measures of Rising Consumer Prosperity in Europe, 1957 and 1965

Automobiles	1957	1965
France	3,476,000	7,842,000
Germany (Federal Republic)	2,456,288	8,103,600
Italy	1,051,004 (1956)	5,469,981
The Netherlands	375,676	1,272,890
Sweden	796,000	1,793,000

Televisions	1957	1965
France	683,000	6,489,000
Germany	789,586	11,379,000
Italy	367,000	6,044,542
The Netherlands	239,000	2,113,000
Sweden	75,817	2,110,584

Sources: Adapted from *The Europa Year Book 1959* (London: Europa Publication, 1959) and *The Europa Year Book 1967*, vol. I (London: Europa Publications, 1967).

fecting even the cautious Germans, who were particularly eager to avoid this specter from the past, caused serious dislocation. Pockets of unemployment were troubling. Many immigrant workers from Turkey, North Africa, Pakistan, and the West Indies suffered very low wages and unstable employment. These immigrants, euphemistically labeled "guest workers," were often residentially segregated and victims of discrimination by employers and police, as racism continued to be an important factor in Western society.

More troubling still was the slowing of economic growth in the 1970s. In 1973 the oil-producing states of the Middle East cut their production and raised prices, initially in response to a Middle Eastern war with Israel. Many nations were hit hard by higher energy prices, but western Europe, heavily dependent on imports, was particularly pressed. A second orchestrated oil crisis in 1979 led to a severe recession throughout Western society, with unusually high rates of unemployment. By now growing competition from East Asia and other areas cut into traditional staples, such as steel and automobile production, making it difficult to recover the dynamism of the two postwar decades.

Western leaders were able to respond to new crises with some success. Conservation measures reduced dependence on imported oil, and by the 1980s energy prices fell back. Several European nations embarked on rapid development of nuclear energy production. European productivity rates continued to improve; some nations, such as France, introduced the use of robots on assembly lines at a particularly rapid pace. The economic climate had become tighter, however. This spurred some renewed labor agitation, directed, for example, at governments that closed inefficient factories. Yet even by 1990 the ongoing impact of dramatic economic growth lingered, giving both western Europe and the United States a source of new satisfactions and interests, as well as a vigorous presence in the world power structure even as colonies disappeared and sheer military dominance receded.

THE SOURCES OF WESTERN VITALITY

No single factor explained the post-1945 vigor of Western society in political, diplomatic, and economic structure. The West, including the United States, continued to benefit from technological leadership in the world economy even as it faced new competition from Japan, and the Pacific Rim (see Chapter 11). It built on its existing industrial base, in contrast to most other societies, which were still trying to industrialize for the first time. It also spread and adapted democratic and parliamentary traditions, another heritage from the 19th century and before. Emphasis on scientific training, particularly strong in Europe, followed from prior intellectual change; it made Westerners open to new ideas and techniques.

The West, in other words, was not involved in revolutionary adaptation, even as it pulled out of the doldrums of the decades from 1914 to 1945. Yet there were major changes resulting from innovative leadership in various fields—the fruit of new groups ascending to power after World War II, as well as the role of the United States in influencing key adjustments. The reduction of nationalism in favor of regional cooperation was a basic step. So was the more active posture of the state in promoting and guiding change. Even as Western politics became less contentious, political leadership became more central in shaping the patterns of Western society.

❀ COLD WAR ALLIES: THE UNITED STATES, CANADA, AUSTRALIA, AND NEW ZEALAND

Developments in the so-called overseas West in many ways paralleled those in western Europe, but without the

sense of grappling with prior collapse. The sheer level of innovation in domestic policy was less great, in part because the crises of the first half of the 20th century had been less severe. Crucial adjustments occurred, however, in foreign policy. The United States led the way in making the changes in its own traditions that were necessary to develop a massive peacetime military force and a global set of alliances. With the decline of European, and particularly British, international power and the emergence of the cold war context, Australia, New Zealand, and Canada tightened their links with the United States and developed new contacts with other areas of the world.

THE FORMER DOMINIONS

Canada forged ahead in welfare policies after World War II, establishing a greater stake in economic planning and in state-run medical insurance than did the United States. At the same time, however, Canadian economic integration with the United States continued, with U.S. investments in Canadian resources and mutual exports and imports soaring steadily into the 1970s. By 1980 the Canadian government took some measures to limit further U.S. penetration, and a sense of Canadian nationalism sparked resentment of the giant to the south. In 1988, however, the two nations signed a free-trade agreement, creating a North American trading bloc at a time when European economic unity was increasing rapidly.

Continued emigration to Canada pointed in new directions also, with growing numbers of people arriving from various parts of Asia. Canada's most distinctive issue, however, involved growing agitation by French Canadians in Quebec for regional autonomy or even national independence. A new separatist party, founded in 1967, took control of the provincial government during the 1970s. Subsequent legislation limited the use of the English language in Quebec's public and commercial life, though referendums for full independence failed during the 1980s. A new constitution in 1982, however, granted greater voice to the provinces, both to counter French Canadian demand and also to recognize the growing economic strength of the resource-rich western provinces. Separatist tensions continued to simmer, however, into the 1990s.

From 1945 onward Australia and New Zealand moved steadily away from their traditional alignment with Great Britain and toward horizons around the Pacific. The two commonwealths joined a mutual defense pact with the United States in 1951, directed against potential Communist aggression in the Pacific. Both nations cooperated with the United States in the Korean War, and Australia backed U.S. intervention in Vietnam. In 1966 the Australian prime minister declared, "Wherever the United States is resisting aggression . . . we will go a-waltzing Matilda with you." In the later 1970s and 1980s Australia and especially New Zealand began to distance themselves somewhat from U.S. foreign policy. New Zealand barred U.S. nuclear-armed vessels in 1985.

As Great Britain aligned with the Common Market, Australian and New Zealand exports were increasingly directed toward other Pacific nations, notably Japan, whereas investment capital came mainly from the United States and Japan. Indeed, Australia became Japan's chief raw-materials supplier aside from oil. Asian emigration also increasingly altered the population mix, again particularly in Australia. Despite a long-held whites-only immigration policy, the Australian government was powerless to resist growing regional emigration, particularly from Indochina. By 1983 Asians accounted for 60 percent of the total immigrant population in Australia.

THE "U.S. CENTURY"?

Amid a host of domestic issues, the big news in U.S. history after 1945 was its assumption—in many ways, its eager assumption—of the superpower mantle, opposing the Soviet Union and serving as the world's leading defender of democratic and capitalistic values. The United States hesitated briefly after 1945, demobilizing its World War II forces rather quickly with some hope that world peace would provide some respite from further international engagement. However, Great Britain's inability to continue to police the world for the West, together with rapid Soviet successes in installing Communist governments in eastern Europe, prompted a decisive U.S. stance. In 1947 President Harry Truman promised support for "free peoples who are resisting subjugation by armed minorities or by outside pressures." The doctrine, specifically directed against Communist pressures on Greece and Turkey, it soon extended into the elaboration of Marshall Plan aid to rebuild the economies of western Europe against the possibility of Communist subversion in these war-torn countries. The Republican party was initially tempted to resist these new international engagements, but the 1948 Communist takeover of Czechoslovakia checked that impulse.

For many decades basic U.S. foreign policy proceeded amid wide bipartisan agreement.

The plunge into the cold war took a toll on the home front, however. The United States entered a period of intense, even frenzied, concern about internal Communist conspiracies, ferreting out a host of suspected spies and subjecting people in many fields to dismissals from their jobs on grounds of suspected radical sympathies.

Cold war engagement prompted other policy changes in the federal government. The Defense Department was set up in 1947 to coordinate military policy, and the Central Intelligence Agency was established to organize a worldwide information-gathering and espionage network. Military spending increased considerably, with the formation of the Strategic Air Command to stand in constant readiness in case of a Soviet bombing attack. A massive U.S. airlift thwarted Soviet pressure on the western sectors of occupied Berlin. The United States resisted the invasion of South Korea by the Communist North, beginning in 1950; U.S. troops stationed in Japan were sent in to support the South Koreans. Under General Douglas MacArthur and backed by several allies under a hastily arranged UN mandate, the North Korean invasion was repulsed within a few months. The United States then authorized an invasion into North Korea, which brought a retaliatory intervention from Communist China. The United States was pushed back, and more than two years of additional fighting ensued before peace was negotiated in 1953—with the earlier boundary line between the two Koreas restored. In the meantime annual U.S. spending on the military had increased further, from $13.5 billion to $50 billion.

During the 1950s, under the presidency of Dwight D. Eisenhower, the United States settled into a policy of containment of the Soviet Union, which involved maintenance of large peacetime military forces. The United States also arranged alliances not only with western Europe, in NATO, but also with Australia and New Zealand, with several southeast Asian nations, and with several nations in the Middle East; this alliance system virtually surrounded the Soviet Union. Less novel was recurrent U.S. intervention in Central America against suspected Communist movements; thus U.S. aid toppled a new Guatemalan government in 1954. The United States was unable to prevent a takeover in Cuba that eventually propelled Cuba into the Communist camp, despite a U.S.-backed invasion attempt by anti-Communist Cuban rebels. Nonetheless, the United States maintained its policy of vigilance (under President John

Kennedy, in 1962) by forcing the Soviet Union to back down on plans to install missile sites on the island.

The U.S. containment policy yielded a final test that took shape during the 1960s, when intervention against Communist revolutionaries in South Vietnam gradually escalated. The United States air force began bombing Communist North Vietnam in 1965. Later that year troops were sent in, reaching a total of 550,000 by 1968. By this time the United States was spending $2 billion a week on a war that never produced convincing success and gradually bogged down in horrendous bloodshed on both sides. By 1970 more bombs had been dropped on Vietnam than had been dropped by anyone, anywhere previously in the 20th century. By 1968 domestic pressure against the war, centered particularly on U.S. college campuses, began to force changes in strategy. A new U.S. president, Richard Nixon, tried to expand the war to other parts of Indochina, to increase pressure on North Vietnam. Simultaneously, peace negotiations with North Vietnam were launched, resulting finally, in 1973, in agreement on a ceasefire. By 1975, as the United States speedily withdrew, all Vietnam lay in Communist hands.

Furor over the Vietnam War led to agonizing policy reassessments in the United States. Some observers judged that new directions might be forged, as the United States had discovered that its massive military might could be stalemated by fervent guerrilla tactics. Both the U.S. military and the public grew more wary of regional wars. Although the national mood sobered, however, decisive policy changes did not ensue. A socialist government in Chile, for example, was ousted with the aid of covert U.S. pressure even as the Vietnam conflict wound down. The socialist government was replaced by a brutal military regime. Then in 1980 the United States overwhelmingly elected a new president, Ronald Reagan, who combined conservative domestic policies with a commitment to bolster military spending and make sure that the United States would "ride tall" again in world affairs. The 1980s saw no major new international involvements, but several punitive raids were conducted against suspected terrorists in the Middle East, and the small West Indian island of Grenada was invaded to topple a leftist regime. President Reagan sponsored a number of expensive new weapons systems, which helped press an afflicted Soviet economy to virtual collapse as its leaders attempted to keep pace. The next president, George Bush, continued an interventionist policy by sending U.S. troops into Panama to evict and arrest an abrasive dictator and then by spearheading a

Hardly the hippie radicals despised by champions of the Vietnam war, these demonstrators, young and old women, reflect the widespread disenchantment with the war that swept U.S. society in the late 1960s.

Western and moderate Arab alliance against Iraq's invasion of Kuwait, in 1990–1991.

DOMESTIC DISLOCATIONS

Amid the extensive overseas commitments and recurrent crises linked to the new U.S. role as anti-Soviet leader and self-appointed world police officer, domestic innovations took something of a back seat. In the ongoing economic prosperity of the 1950s and 1960s the United States had been able to combine its growing military budget with several new initiatives: a massive highway program and then the extension of the limited welfare state under Great Society initiatives in the mid-1960s. Federal involvement in preschool programs and health assistance to the needy and elderly expanded notably. New civil rights legislation was introduced in the mid-1960s, following a decade of mounting pressure from various African-American organizations and inspired particularly by the leadership of Martin Luther King, Jr. Dr. King's preaching of nonviolence moved many people to support the cause of racial equality; a series of major urban riots between 1965 and 1968 pressed the need for change as well. Protection for blacks' voting rights in the South and new legislation against discrimination in housing and public facilities combined with court-sponsored school integration measures to ease racial tensions somewhat.

With more difficult economic times in the 1970s, however, domestic initiatives dwindled. Many observers faulted not only government but also private business for insufficient attention to research and development and even to application of existing technologies. Concern mounted that the United States, though still a massive economic powerhouse, was lagging behind its industrial competitors both in western Europe and on the Pacific Rim. Material standards suffered as well; from 1973 onward families improved their average standard of living only through additional work of family members, usually a wife and mother. Individual real wages stagnated into the 1990s. Certain groups, including inner-city African-Americans, suffered particularly, as outright unemployment mounted. However, little collective violence resulted after both civil rights and youth unrest subsided in the early 1970s. Under conservative presidents in the 1980s, government protections were scaled back, especially for the unemployed and for impoverished children—as one-third of all the nation's children now fell below the poverty line. The United States entered the final decade of the

century as the world's unquestioned military leader, apparently tranquil at home but more than slightly troubled by signs of economic lethargy and social neglect.

ANALYSIS
THE UNITED STATES AND WESTERN EUROPE: CONVERGENCE AND COMPLEXITY

The relationship between the United States and western Europe has been important both historically and analytically for at least two centuries. Many people in the United States have tried to establish a distinctive identity while acknowledging special relationships with Europe; isolationism was one response earlier in this century. Europeans, for their part, have groped for definition of their U.S. "cousins," particularly as U.S. military and cultural influence grew in the 20th century. Were U.S. innovations to be welcomed, as stemming from a kindred society with a special flair for technology and modern mass taste, or should they be resisted as emblems of a superficial, degenerate, and essentially un-European society?

Analytically, comparison of the United States and western Europe is essential in order to organize a civilization roster for world history. If the United States forms a separate civilization, related to but different from the West, the list of important civilizations obviously grows. If, however, the United States is "Western," albeit with some undeniably distinctive features, the civilization roster is simpler. Both cases can be argued; both depend, however, on careful comparison.

The United States–western Europe relationship is, furthermore, not a constant. It is easy to draw distinctions at some points, as when the United States established universal male suffrage for nonslaves in the early 19th century but Europe remained locked in older political systems; when the aristocracy still loomed large in European society but not U.S. or when there was slavery in U.S. society but not European. Over time, however, and particularly since 1945, U.S. and European societies have in many important respects converged. Because of heightened imitation and shared advanced industrial economies, some earlier differences have receded.

Western Europe, for example, no longer has a very distinct peasantry. Its farmers, though smaller scale than their U.S. agribusiness counterparts, are commercialized and simply so few in numbers that they no longer set their society apart. European workers, though less likely than those in the United States to call themselves middle class, are now relatively prosperous. They have moved away from some of the political radicalism that differentiated them from their U.S. counterparts earlier in the 20th century. Europe does not, to be sure, have as deep-seated a racial issue as the United States inherited from slavery, but the growing influx of people from the West Indies, North Africa, and Asia has duplicated in Europe some of the same racial tensions and inner-city problems that bedevil the United States. At the other end of the social scale, trained managers and professionals now form a similar upper class in both societies, the fruit of systems of higher education that differ in particulars but resemble each other in producing something of a meritocratic elite.

A shared popular culture has certainly emerged. Although it stemmed mainly from U.S. innovations before World War II, more recently it has involved mutual borrowing. The United States, for example, embraced miniskirts and rock groups from Britain in the 1960s, and not only British but also French youth raced to buy the latest style in blue jeans.

Differences remain, of course, some of them going back to earlier historical traditions. The United States has relied more fully on free-market capitalism than did western Europe, with the United States possessing a less complete planning and more modest welfare apparatus. The United States proved much more religious than did western Europe. Only a minority of people in most western European countries professed religious belief by the 1990s, with less than 10 percent in most cases attending church with any regularity. In contrast the United States remains highly religious, with up to 40 percent regular church attendance and 70–80 percent of its people professing religious belief. The United States made a less complete conversion to a new leisure ethic after World War II than did western Europe; European vacation time advanced toward more than a month a year, whereas the average in the United States remained two weeks or less. Europeans were franker also about teenage sexuality, following the 1960 sexual revolution. They distributed birth control materials to adolescents much more commonly than did their more prudish U.S. counterparts, reducing rates of teen-age pregnancy in the process. In certain important respects, then, the United States constituted a more traditional society, in terms of values, in the later 20th century than did western Europe. Some of the variation between the two societies related to long-established distinctions (as in the degree of suspicion of government power); others emerged for the first time, sometimes surprisingly, after World War II.

The biggest distinctions between the two societies in recent decades, however, followed from their increasingly divergent world roles. Western Europe, though still highly influential in culture and trade on a global scale, concentrated increasingly on its own regional arrangements, including the Common Market trading bloc, and decreasingly on military development. The United States moved in the opposite direction. Thus a traditional distinction was reversed; the United States became the more military (and, some would argue, militaristic) society, and many Europeans became committed to more strictly civilian goals.

Questions: Why did the United States and western Europe converge in new ways during the 20th century? Do the two societies remain part of a common civilization? What are the most important issues to resolve in making this judgment? ✥

CULTURE AND SOCIETY IN THE WEST

Political and economic changes in Western society progressively altered the contours of earlier industrial development. These were the changes, also, that smoothed out a number of earlier differences within Western society, particularly between the United States and western Europe, as the two key Western spaces converged in many respects. The West became the first example of an advanced industrial society, especially from the 1950s onward, and both the United States and western Europe shared in leading facets of change.

SOCIAL STRUCTURE

Economic growth, bringing increasing prosperity to most groups, eased some earlier social conflicts throughout the West. Workers were still propertyless, but they had substantial holdings as consumers, and their sense of social inferiority often declined as a result. Social lines were also blurred by increasing social mobility, as educational opportunities opened further and the size of the white-collar sector expanded. Much unskilled labor was left to immigrants. Economic and political change also altered conditions for western Europe's peasantry and not only by cutting its size. Peasants became increasingly commercial, eager for improvements in standards of living, and participant, through car trips and television, in urban culture. They also became more attuned to bureaucracies, as state regulations pushed them into cooperative organizations.

Social distinctions remained. Middle-class people had more abundant leisure opportunities and a more optimistic outlook than did most workers. Signs of tension continued. Crime rates went up throughout Western society after the 1920s, though the levels were particularly high in the United States. Race riots punctuated U.S. life in the 1950s and 1960s and exploded in immigrant sections of British cities in the 1980s and Germany in the early 1990s.

There were strong signs that what was happening in Western society, at least by the 1960s, was not so much a resolution of older issues—how to fit peasants into modern society or what to do about worker grievances—as the establishment of a new social system, a second version of industrial society or, as some held, a postindustrial society. The majority of the labor force in the West was now engaged in services and management hierar-

chies, not working as producers in either farm or factory. The new labor force was drawn less to the older ethic of hard work than to new ideas of high consumption and expressive leisure. The West, in sum, continued to change, whether for good or ill.

THE WOMEN'S REVOLUTION

A key facet of postwar change involved women and the family, and again both western Europe and the United States participated fully in this upheaval. Although family ideals persisted in many ways—with workers, for example, urging that "a loving family is the finest thing, something to work for, to look to and to look after"—the realities of family life changed in many ways. Family leisure activities expanded. Extended family contacts were facilitated by telephones and automobiles. More years of schooling increased the importance of peer groups for children, and the authority of parents undoubtedly declined.

The clearest innovation in family life came through the new working patterns of women. World War II

The greatly accelerated entry of women into business and the professions marked one of the key social transformations of the postwar era. Often in very different ways, women in Western nations have organized to assert their rights to fulfilling careers and legal equality with males.

brought increased factory and clerical jobs for women, as the earlier world war had done. After a few years of downward adjustment, the trends continued. From the early 1950s onward, the number of working women, particularly married women, rose steadily in western Europe, the United States, and Canada. Women's earlier educational gains had improved their work qualifications; the growing number of service jobs created a need for additional workers—and women, long associated with clerical jobs and paid less than men, were ideal candidates. Many women also sought entry into the labor force as a means of adding to personal or family income, to afford some of the consumer items now becoming feasible but not yet easy to buy, or as a means of personal fulfillment in a society that associated worth with work and earnings.

The growing employment of women, which by the 1970s brought the female segment of the labor force up to 44 percent of the total in most Western countries, represented particularly the employment of adult women, most of them married and many with children. Teen-age employment dropped as more girls stayed in school, but long-term work commitments rose steadily. This was not, to be sure, a full stride to job equality. Women's pay lagged behind men's pay. Most women were concentrated in clerical jobs rather than spread through the occupational spectrum, despite a growing minority of middle-class women who were entering professional and management ranks. Clearly, however, the trends of the 19th-century Industrial Revolution, to keep women and family separate from work outside the home, had yielded to a dramatic new pattern.

Other new rights for women accompanied this shift. Where women had lacked the vote before, as in France, they now got it; of the west European nations, only Switzerland doggedly refused this concession at the national level until 1971. Gains in higher education were considerable, though again full equality remained elusive. Women constituted 23 percent of German university students in 1963, and under Socialist governments in the 1970s the figure rose. Preferred subjects, however, remained different from those of men, as most women stayed out of engineering, science (except medicine), and management. Family rights improved, at least in the judgment of most women's advocates. Access to divorce increased, which many observers viewed as particularly important to women. Abortion law eased, though more slowly in countries of Catholic background than in Britain or Scandinavia; it became increasingly easy for women to regulate their birthrate. Development of new birth control methods, such as the contraceptive pill introduced in 1960, as well as growing knowledge and acceptability of birth control, decreased unwanted pregnancies. Sex and procreation became increasingly separate considerations. Although women continued to differ from men in sexual outlook and behavior—more than twice as many French women as men, for example, hoped to link sex, marriage, and romantic love, according to 1960s polls—more women than before tended to define sex in terms of pleasure.

Predictably, of course, changes in the family, including the roles of women, brought new issues and redefined ideals of companionship. The first issue involved children. A brief increase in the Western birthrate ended in the early 1960s, and a rapid decline ensued. Women working and the desire to use income for high consumer standards mitigated against children, or very many children, particularly in the middle class, where birthrates were lowest. Those children born were increasingly sent, often at an early age, to day-care centers, one of the amenities provided by the European welfare state and particularly essential where new fears about population growth began to surface. European families had few hesitations about replacing maternal care with collective care, and parents often claimed that the result was preferable for children. At the same time, however, some observers worried that Western society, and the Western family, were becoming indifferent to children in an eagerness for adult work and consumer achievements. American adults, for example, between the 1950s and 1980s, shifted their assessment of family satisfaction away from parenthood by concentrating on shared enjoyments between husbands and wives.

Family stability also opened new cracks. Pressures to readjust family roles, women working outside the family context, and growing legal freedoms for women caused men and women alike to turn more readily to divorce. In 1961, 9 percent of all British marriages ended in divorce; by 1965 the figure was 16 percent and rising. By the late 1970s, one-third of all British marriages ended in divorce, and the U.S. rate was higher still.

Finally, even aside from divorce, the changing roles of women raised questions about family values. Expectations lagged behind reality. Polls taken of German women in the 1960s indicated that a solid majority believed that mothers with children under 12 should stay home; yet in fact a solid majority of such mothers were working. Gaps of this sort, between ideals and practice, suggested that, like Western society generally, the family was in a new transition, its end state far from clear.

The development of a new surge of feminist protest, although it reflected much wider concerns than family life alone, showed the strains caused by women's new activities and continued limitations. Growing divorce produced many cases of impoverished women combining work and child care. New work roles revealed the persistent earnings gap between men and women. More generally, many women sought supporting values and organizations as they tried to define new identities less tied to the domestic roles and images of previous decades.

A new feminism began to take shape with the publication in 1949 of *The Second Sex* by the French intellectual Simone de Beauvoir. Echoed in the 1950s and 1960s by other works, such as *The Feminine Mystique,* by Betty Friedan of the United States, a new wave of women's rights agitation arose after three decades of relative calm. The new feminism tended to emphasize a more literal equality that would play down special domestic roles and qualities; therefore, it promoted not only specific reforms but also more basic redefinitions of what it meant to be male and female.

The new feminism did not win all women, even in the middle class, which was feminism's most avid audience. It also did not cause some of the most sweeping practical changes that were taking place, as in the new work roles. But it did support the revolution in roles. From the late 1960s onward it pressed Western governments for further change, raising issues that were difficult to fit into established political contexts. The movement both articulated and promoted the gap between new expectations and ongoing inequalities in gender. And the new feminism expressed and promoted some unanswered questions about family functions. In a real sense later 20th-century feminism seemed to respond to the same desire for individuality and work identity in women that had earlier been urged on men as part of the new mentality suitable for a commercialized economy. Family remained important in the evolving outlook of women, although some feminist leaders attacked the institution outright as hopelessly repressive. Even for many less ideological women, however, family goals were less important than they had been before.

OTHER SOCIAL DISTINCTIONS IN THE WEST

By the 1960s and 1970s what seemed to be happening in the West was a major realignment of protest issues and groups, accompanying the larger structural changes in society and economy. Working-class unrest persisted but at a reduced rate. Aside from a brief surge at the end of the 1960s, strike rates and union membership fell from 1958 onward, both in Europe and the United States. Class-based politics also became less divisive, as working-class parties accepted moderate reforms and middle-class groups accepted basic premises of the welfare state. There was no guarantee that class division would not surge again in the future, if economic growth stagnated, for example, but for the moment, at least, other currents seemed more vigorous.

Feminism was one of these; environmentalism was another. Although youth unrest had declined by the early 1970s, it left a legacy of concern about aspects of industrial society and rampant consumerism that spawned more durable protest movements. In many European countries, and to a slightly lesser extent in the United States, environmental issues moved steadily forward on the social and political agenda. Environmentalists in Germany, Austria, and Scandinavia, as well as the United States, forced curtailment of nuclear power programs, for example.

Ethnic nationalisms generated another set of protest issues, as regional minorities pressed for greater autonomy from the pressures of political and cultural centralization, sometimes using violence to drive their point home. Ethnic conflicts in Northern Ireland, Quebec, and the Basque region of Spain formed recurrently bitter centers of unrest, but there were other movements as well. Old identities combined with new grievances about the homogenizing, impersonal qualities of modern industrial society.

Finally, racial issues generated important conflict. By the 1980s western Europe housed about 15 million immigrant workers. Since the early 1960s the United States had witnessed the largest immigration in its history, and like western Europe, most of its newcomers came from non-Western sources. A disproportionate number of immigrants, together with the African Americans in U.S. inner cities, constituted a largely segregated labor force, holding low-paying, transient, unskilled jobs. African Americans in Chicago, for example, were 40 percent less likely than working-class whites to be employed by the 1980s, although a decade earlier their rates had been roughly equal. The decline in the number of factory jobs, racism on the part of employers, and increased competition from immigrants led to a new structure within the labor force and a new set of problems. The result was recurrent unrest in the cities, as in the British race riots of the 1980s. Another result was the formation of new anti-immigrant and racist organizations. Many Germans turned against the Muslim minority in the country. According to one extremist faction: "Two million foreign workers equals two million German unemployed, so send them all home." A new political party in France argued for expulsion of many immigrants; by 1984 it was winning 11 percent of the total French vote. Here, clearly, was a set of issues of vital importance for the future of the West and, more broadly, for the future of the West's relationship to the wider world.

WESTERN CULTURE

Amid great innovations in politics, the economy, and social structure—including some pressing new problems—Western cultural life in many respects proceeded along established lines. A host of specific new movements arose, and a wealth of scientific data was assimilated, but basic frameworks had been set earlier, often in the more turbulent but intellectually creative decades of the early 20th century. The partial cooling of Western intellectual life raised interesting issues for those who judge that cultural creativity is ultimately the most accurate measurement of a society and its prospects. It is also possible that intellectual life reflected a channeling of creative energies in other directions, including those of mass culture, where Europe in fact displayed new spark.

One key factor in Europe's relative intellectual lag was a shift of focus toward the United States. Greater political stability in the United States during the 1930s and 1940s, as well as Hitler's persecutions, had driven many prominent intellectuals to U.S. shores, where they often remained even as western Europe revived. As U.S. universities expanded, their greater wealth fueled more scientific research; what was called a "brain drain," based on dollar power, drew many leading European scientists to the United States even during the 1950s and 1960s. European science remained active, but the costliness of cutting-edge research produced a durable U.S. advantage. Money also mattered in art, as patronage became increasingly important, and thus New York replaced Paris as the center of international styles.

Europeans did participate in some of the leading scientific advances of the postwar years. Francis Crick, of Cambridge University in England, shared with the American James Watson key credit for the discovery of the basic structure of the genetic building block deoxyribonucleic acid (DNA), which in turn opened the way for rapid advances in genetic knowledge and industries based on artificial synthesis of genetic materials. Europeans also participated in nuclear research, often through laboratories funded by Common Market or other inter-European agencies. European space research, slower to develop than Soviet or U.S. initiatives, nevertheless also produced noteworthy achievements by the 1970s, and again there were important commercial spinoffs in communications satellites and other activities. By the 1980s European space research in unmanned vehicles in some respects seemed more solidly based than that of the United States, where greater emphasis had been given to showy—and much more costly—manned space programs.

The Western commitment to science certainly did not flag. Scientific research everywhere consisted increasingly of largely incremental additions to the knowledge store, rather than sweeping breakthroughs of the Newtonian or Einsteinian sort. It remained true that the clear European leadership, a fact of scientific life since the 16th century, seemed to have passed.

Developments in the arts maintained earlier 20th-century themes quite clearly. Most artists continued to work in the "modern" modes set before World War I, which featured unconventional self-expression and a wide array of nonrepresentational techniques. The clearest change involved growing public acceptance of the modern styles, as the shock that had greeted earlier innovations disappeared and the public, even when preferring older styles displayed in museums or performed by symphony orchestras devoted to the classics, now seemed reconciled to the redefinition of artistic standards. New names were added to the roster of leading modern artists. In Paris Bernard Buffet scored important successes with gaunt, partially abstract figures. The British sculptor Henry Moore produced rounded figures and outright abstractions that conveyed some of the horrors of wartime life and postwar dislocations. A new group of "pop" artists in the 1960s tried to bridge the gap between art and commercial mass culture by incorporating cans and other products, comic strips, and advertisements into paintings, prints, and collages. As also held true in the realm of fully abstract painting, U.S. artists increasingly took the lead.

Europeans retained clearer advantages in artistic films. Italian directors produced a number of gripping, realistic films in the late 1940s, portraying both urban and peasant life without frills. Italy, France, and Sweden became centers of experimental filmmaking again in the 1960s. Jean-Luc Godard and Michelangelo Antonioni portrayed the emptiness of urban life, and Swedish director Ingmar Bergman produced a series of dark psychological dramas. Individual directors in Spain, Britain, and Germany also broke new ground, as Europeans re-

The skyscraper, which appeared first on the U.S. horizon, became a major expression of artistic innovation and dramatic new structural materials, including novel uses of glass. This Chicago tower was designed by European master Ludwig Mies van der Rohe.

mained more comfortable than their U.S. counterparts in producing films of high artistic merit, relatively free from commercial distractions.

Developments in literature and in painting generally continued prewar directions. A variety of French writers concocted the "new novel," which focused on concrete details and descriptions of surfaces and objects, without plot, character development, or a clear sense of the observer's identity. Some German novelists were more realistic, using the novel to satirize the frenzied commercial society around them. In music, composers continued to search for new sounds to liberate themselves from conventional tone and harmony. New electronic techniques were added to earlier experimentation, as computers and synthesizers joined instrumentation developed in Europe in the 1930s.

Overall, the arts reflected significant levels of activity, but in general a substantial acceptance of stylistic statements developed as much as a century before. In several fields Europeans at least shared eminence with practitioners in the United States, in what was increasingly a transatlantic high culture.

Fragmentation also occurred in the social sciences, with no commanding figure arising to succeed the Marxes or Webers of previous generations, willing to posit fundamental social dynamics or sweeping theories. Many specific fields in the social sciences turned to massive data collections and pragmatic, detailed observations; in many of these, in turn, U.S. practitioners developed a decided advantage. Economics, in particular, became something of an American specialty in the post-Keynesian decades and focused on massive quantitative studies of economic cycles and money supplies.

Basic innovation and European leadership did conjoin in the structuralist movement in the social sciences and related literary criticism. Here the leading figure was the French anthropologist Claude Lévi-Strauss. Starting with field work among Indian tribes in Brazil, Lévi-Strauss set out to discover basic, common ingredients in thought processes among primitive peoples generally. By analyzing rituals and myths concerning food and other fundamental activities, Lévi-Strauss believed he could decipher and catalog a limited number of standard thought processes applicable to all human societies, primitive or not, featuring the logic of pairing, determining opposites, and similar activities.

French intellectuals also contributed to a redefinition of historical study, building on innovations launched between the world wars. Social history, or the focus on changes in the lives of ordinary people, became increasingly the order of the day, giving a great spur to historical research throughout western Europe and the United States. Some French social historians were attracted to a structural approach that downplayed fundamental change, but others retained a lively interest in periodization and the discovery of basic alterations of human and social modes.

A LIVELY POPULAR CULTURE

Western society displayed more vitality in its popular culture than in formal intellectual life, which reflected the concentration on economic and social change. Here too, as in previous decades and as in high culture, U.S. influence was strong in what was in so many respects a common North Atlantic pattern. As European economies struggled to recover from the war and as U.S. military forces spread certain enthusiasms more widely than before, some observers indeed spoke of a U.S. "Coca-cola-nization" of Europe. U.S. soft drinks,

blue-jeaned fashions, chewing gum, and other artifacts became increasingly common. U.S. films continued to wield substantial influence, although the lure of Hollywood declined somewhat. More important was the growing impact of U.S. television series. Blessed with a wide market and revenues generated from advertising, American television was quite simply "slicker" than its European counterparts, and the western drama "Bonanza," the soap opera "Dallas," and many other shows appeared regularly on European screens to define, for better or worse, an image of the United States.

In contrast to the interwar decades, however, European popular culture had its own power, and it even began to influence the United States as well. The most celebrated figures of popular culture in the 1960s were unquestionably the Beatles, from the British port city of Liverpool. Although they adopted popular music styles of the United States, including jazz and early rock, the Beatles added an authentic working-class touch in their impulsiveness and their mockery of authority. They also expressed a good-natured desire to enjoy the pleasures of life, which is characteristic of modern Western popular culture regardless of national context. British popular music groups continued to set standards in the 1970s and had wide impact on western Europe more generally.

Other facets of popular culture displayed a new vigor. Again in Britain, youth fashions, separate from the standards of the upper class, showed an ability to innovate and sometimes to shock. Unconventional uses of color and cut, as in punk hairstyles of the later 1970s, bore some resemblance to the anticonventional tone of modern painting and sculpture.

Sexual culture also changed in the West, building on earlier trends that linked sex to a larger pleasure-seeking mentality characteristic of growing consumerism and to a desire for personal expression. Films and television shows demonstrated increasingly relaxed standards about sexual display. In Britain, Holland, and Denmark sex shops sold a wide array of erotic materials and products.

Like the United States, western Europe experienced important changes in sexual behavior starting around 1960, particularly among young people. Premarital sex became more common. The average age of first sexual intercourse began to go down. For a time as a result, rates of illegitimate births began to rise once more, after a long period of stability since 1870. But Europeans adjusted relatively easily to the new habits and began urging teen-agers to use birth control devices; in contrast, reactions in the United States were more tentative and prudish, with the result that teen-age ignorance of birth control measures remained more widespread. Expressive sexuality in western Europe was also evident in the growing number of nude bathing spots, again in interesting contrast to more hesitant initiatives in the United States. Although the association of modern popular culture with sexuality and body concern was not novel, the openness and diversity of expression unquestionably reached new levels and also demonstrated western Europe's new confidence in defining a vigorous, nontraditional mass culture of its own.

Cultural innovation, like social change, brought disturbance as well as enthusiasm. Although critics of changing tastes were less numerous and less political than between the wars—there was no counterpart to the Nazi attack on modern styles or women's fashions—there was concern about the disparity between formal intellectual life, where energies might be flagging, and the vibrancy of youth-oriented popular styles. Other observers wondered whether enthusiasms for new fashions and antiestablishment lyrics misleadingly distracted ordinary people in what was still a hierarchical society—but this, of course, was a complex subject that had emerged with the birth of modern popular culture itself.

CONCLUSION

ADJUSTING TO ADVANCED INDUSTRIAL SOCIETY

To some observers the West in the 20th century was dominated by the futilities and barbarianisms of the interwar years; no superficial recovery could undo these wounds or make good these failures. This despairing judgment might be compounded by the renewed uncertainties of Western life in the 1970s and 1980s and the growing impact of the decline in world dominance that the interwar years had launched.

Other observers saw Western trends in terms of some ongoing dilemmas raised by industrialization. They noted the dualism present in formal culture and popular outlook since the 19th century. Western intellectuals thus insisted on the primacy of rational inquiry, while relying on artistic forms that seemed bent on portraying a world gone mad. Ordinary Europeans and Americans accepted a disciplined work environment that stressed control over emotion but reveled in scenes of violence and sexual ecstasy in their leisure hours, sometimes embellished as well by the use of drugs.

Contemporary Western society reflected tensions between industrial values and Western traditions that were exacerbated in the 20th century. On the one hand, the society encouraged children to think of themselves as individuals, to rise above their parents' achievements if possible, to adjust to new work opportunities. Leisure interests appealed to individual pleasure seeking. But individualism was severely curtailed by the growing bureaucratization of society. Most jobs involved routine activities, controlled by an elaborate supervisory apparatus; individual initiative counted for little in factories or in the offices of giant corporations. Leisure, appealing to individual self-expression in one sense, generally meant mass, commercially manipulated outlets for all but a handful of venturesome souls. By the 1950s television watching had become far and away the leading recreational interest of Western peoples, and most television fare was deliberately standardized. Ironically, individual-

In the United States, Japan, and Western Europe, advertisements increasingly evoked a good life to be fulfilled through buying the right goods. The newest car was associated with a prosperous home, a loving family, and even happy pets.

ism and its outlets in consumer behavior often made collective protest against bureaucratization and routine extremely difficult. One reason for the decline of organized labor throughout the West was workers' growing need to spend time earning money for a new car or using the new car they had.

To Western and non-Western critics alike, Western society at times seemed badly confused. Poverty and job boredom coexisted with affluence and continued appeals to the essential value of work. Youth protest—including defiant costumes and pulsating rock music—family instability, and growing crime might be signs of a fatally flawed society. The rising rates of suicide and increasing incidence of mental illness were other troubling symptoms. At the least, Western society continued to display the strains of change.

Western civilization, in sum, continued to be distinctive for a mixture of old and new reasons. Headed by the United States, by the 1960s it led the world in the use of mind-altering drugs. The burgeoning leisure culture involved many Westerners with an interest in sexuality and sexual symbolism profoundly shocking to people from many other societies. The West also maintained a distinctive commitment to liberal democracy, and when Latin America and then Eastern Europe looked to political change in the 1970s and 1980s, they turned largely to Western models. Germany reunited in 1990, for example, as East Germans sought both the affluence and the political freedom they saw among their Western cousins.

The West also remained closely tied to larger world currents. It continued to organize much world trade, as its economy expanded fairly steadily. Western developments in technology, science, and popular culture continued to have international impact. Western feminism, a newer force, helped inspire feminist interests in other societies, such as Japan. At the same time, growing rates of emigration to the West and the increasing impact of economic competition from industry in other societies made it clear that the West's links to the rest of the world were not determined solely by the West.

Many people in Western society believe that they are facing greater changes than ever before, whether for better or for worse. By the late 1960s a new concept of a postindustrial society took shape both in western Europe and in North America. The idea was that Western society was leading in a transformation as fundamental as the Industrial Revolution had been. The rise of a service economy, according to this argument, promised as many shifts as the rise of an industrial economy had

done. Control of knowledge, rather than control of goods, would be the key to the postindustrial social structure. Technology would allow expansion of factory production with a shrinking labor force, and attention would shift to the generation and control of information. The advent of new technology, particularly the computer, supported the postindustrial concept by applying to knowledge transmission the same potential technological revolution the steam engine had brought to manufacturing.

Changes in the role of women paralleled the postindustrial concept, and some observers began to talk of a postindustrial family in which two equal spouses would pool their earnings in a high-consumption life-style. Postindustrial cities would increasingly become entertainment centers, as most work could now be decentralized in suburbs, linked by the omnipresent computer. Postindustrial politics were less clearly defined, though some commentators noted that the old party structure might loosen as new, service-sector voters sought issues more appropriate to their interests. The rise of environmental and feminist concerns, which cut across older political alignments, thus might prove an opening wedge to an unpredictable future for the West.

The postindustrial society is not established fact, of course. Important continuities with earlier social forms, including political values and cultural directions, suggest that new technologies might modify rather than revolutionize Western industrial society. It is clear, however, that Western society has taken on important new characteristics, ranging from age brackets to occupational structure, that differentiate it from the initial industrial patterns generated in the 19th century. And this fact, even if more modest than the visions of some postindustrial forecasters, raises a vital question for the West and the world: How would a rapidly changing, advanced industrial society fit in a world that has yet fully to industrialize? How could the concerns of an affluent, urban, fad-conscious Westerner coexist with the values of the world's peasant majority?

FURTHER READINGS

Important overviews of recent European history are Walter Laqueur's *Europe since Hitler* (1982), John Darwin's *Britain and Decolonization* (1988), Helen Wallace and others' *Policy-Making in the European Community*

(1983), and Alfred Grosser's *The Western Alliance* (1982).

Some excellent national interpretations provide vital coverage of events since 1945 in key areas of Europe. See A. F. Havighurst's *Twentieth-Century Britain* (1982) and John Ardagh's highly readable *The New French Revolution: A Social and Economic Survey of France* (1968) and *France in the 1980's* (1982). Volker Berghahn's *Modern Germany: Society, Economy and Politics in the 20th Century* (1983) is also useful.

On post–World War II social and economic trends, see C. Kindleberger's *Europe's Postwar Growth* (1967), V. Bogdanor and R. Skidelsky, eds., *The Age of Affluence* (1970), R. Dahrendorf, ed., *Europe's Economy in Crisis* (1982), and Peter Stearns and Herrick Chapman's *European Society in Upheaval* (3rd ed., 1991). On the welfare state, see Stephen Cohen's *Modern Capitalist Planning: The French Model* (1977) and E. S. Einhorn and J. Logue's *Welfare States in Hard Times* (1982).

On the relevant Commonwealth nations, see Charles Doran's *Forgotten Partnership: U.S.-Canada Relations Today* (1983), Edward McWhinney, *Canada and the Constitution, 1979–1982* (1982), and Stephen Graubard, ed., *Australia: Terra Incognita?* (1985).

On the United States in the cold war decades, see Walter LaFeber's *America, Russia and the Cold War, 1945–1980* (4th ed., 1980), Thomas Patterson, *On Every Front: The Making of the Cold War* (1979), David Oshinsky, *A Conspiracy So Immense: The World of Joe McCarthy* (1983), Richard Polenberg, *One Nation Divisible: Class, Race and Ethnicity in the United States since 1938* (1980), Harvard Sitkoff, *The Struggle for Black Equality, 1954–1980* (1981), and William Chafe, *The American Woman: Her Changing Social, Economic and Political Roles* (1972).

1945–1948 Soviet takeover of Eastern Europe

1949 Soviet Union develops atomic bomb

1953 Stalin's death

1955 Formation of Warsaw Pact

1956 Stalinism attacked by Khrushchev

1956 Hungarian revolt and its suppression

1961 Berlin Wall erected

1962 Cuban missile crisis

1968 Revolt in Czechoslovakia and its repression; Soviet policy (Brezhnev doctrine) proclaims right to intervene in any Socialist country

1979 Uprisings in Poland and their suppression

1979 Soviet invasion of Afghanistan

The Eastern Bloc to the Collapse of the Soviet Union

10

INTRODUCTION. The history of Eastern Europe in the 20th century has been dominated by the glare of Russia's 1917 revolution, one of the great upheavals of modern times. Much of Russian history thereafter, especially during the 1920s and 1930s but to some extent into the 1990s as well, derived from the working out of the revolution and the attempt to build a society on new, Communist principles. The Communist regime had consolidated under Stalin in the late 1920s and 1930s and had survived the great strains of World War II, but new questions arose in the 1950s. Renewed upheaval after 1985 made it clear that neither the Soviet Union nor the nations of Eastern Europe had devised a definitive political and economic system—even for the remainder of the 20th century. Russia's history merged unprecedentedly with that of the rest of Eastern Europe after 1945, as Soviet-dominated regimes were installed in most of the smaller countries after a confused interwar period. Soviet control was not complete, and important discontents boiled to the surface, particularly after 1985. But there were more common directions in Eastern European institutions than ever before in the region's history.

Soviet history also had an unprecedented importance in wider world history during the 20th century, for two reasons. The Russian Revolution and the success of the Soviet state seemed to many people, in many parts of the world, a vital beacon. The example of the revolution and the rise of Communist movements to some extent patterned after and guided by Russian leadership played a vital role in world history both before and after 1945. China and Cuba used Russian models, though adding their own twists. Revolutionaries elsewhere in Latin America, Asia, Africa, and the West drew inspiration from the Soviet system.

1988–1989 Liberalization movements throughout Eastern Europe; new constitutions, economic reforms; nationalist agitation in Soviet Union

1990 Gorbachev selected as President; new elections throughout much of Eastern Europe; economic unification in Germany

1991 Failed coup against Gorbachev; Yeltsin emerges as premier leader in Russia

1985 Gorbachev to power

1992–1993 Russia's deepening economic crisis leads to growing assistance from the West; Yeltsin struggles with a communist-dominated parliament for power

1988 New Soviet constitution; establishment of the Congress of People's Deputies

Spurred by the revolution and ongoing industrialization, the new Soviet Union also emerged, after 1945, as one of the two great world powers. Soviet economic and military influence burst beyond Europe and Asia, to have direct effects literally round the globe, as the rivalry between the Soviet Union and the United States set a basic framework for world diplomacy in the post–World War II decades. The Soviet role must thus be added to the factors considered in the intensifying world exchange of the 20th century. For several decades after 1945, as Western colonial controls receded, Soviet ideological influence seemed to rival the West's cultural outreach in the world at large.

Soviet history during the later 20th century involves several major themes. The issues raised by Soviet attempts to rebuild after the revolution require analysis in their own right as key phenomena in contemporary history. The success of Soviet industrialization, with such ramifications as the periodic Soviet leads in space programs, demands attention as an important non-Western example of economic and technological reorientation. The Soviet role as world power must also be assessed. Finally, an explosion of new uncertainties, opening up after 1985, raises vital questions not only about the Soviet Union but also about the cold war, Eastern Europe, and the future of revolution.

One means of sorting out the complex history of the Soviet Union and its global impact after 1945 involves division into three subperiods. Between 1945 and 1955 the Soviet Union seized on new opportunities as a World War II victor, while also attempting to prevent a recurrence of outside attack and grappling with the superpower activities of United States. Stalinism survived, but it was altered by the growing international role. The years 1956–1985, as Stalinism was modified, saw the consolidation of the Soviet Union as world superpower and the development of Eastern Europe into what was effectively a new Soviet empire. Finally, since 1985 a host of innovations and uncertainties have shaken the Soviet system, dissolved its empire, and raised questions about the survival of the Russian state itself.

THEMES IN EASTERN EUROPEAN HISTORY SINCE 1945

The consolidation of the Russian Revolution and the spread of communism throughout most of Eastern Europe after World War II embraced several subsidiary themes. The revolution redefined Russia's relationship with Western civilization, but it did not end the ambivalent attraction-rejection reactions that had surfaced earlier. The theme of Russian expansion resumed in the postrevolutionary decades, after a retreat during an initial consolidation period. To Western eyes Russian expansion seemed an obvious resumption of older tsarist goals, though to Soviet leaders a different set of criteria, including the importance of spreading revolutionary truth and the need to prevent a recurrence of German attack, seemed more salient.

Ongoing industrialization produced some social results similar to those in other industrial societies, including the rapid growth of cities, changes in family styles, even the rise of a managerial class. But it was also a unique product, concentrating unusually on heavy industry and government control. It was also designed to protect Russia's independence from the world economy and Western modes of exchange rather than to gain new power within the world commercial network. As the Soviets built their society and completed the basic industrialization framework, they greatly enhanced their strength in world affairs but on somewhat distinctive foundations. Thus during the 1980s serious questions arose about the viability of the Soviet version of an industrial economy.

Soviet and East European Boundaries by 1948

The theme of change dominates Eastern European history during the late 20th century because of the great revolution that opened the contemporary era in this region and then the extension of Russian influence to virtually the entire area. Yet even great changes must be balanced against continuities from the past. Earlier politics and foreign policy traditions intertwined with the effects of revolution within the Soviet Union. Communist rule and industrialization greatly altered the lives of Russian peasants, but a peasant problem remained, in an interesting if muted echo from tsarist days. Aspects of Western culture were embraced more eagerly than before, particularly in scientific areas, but new ambiguities surfaced in relation to Western art and popular culture—again a redefinition of an older theme. The smaller Eastern European nations also recalled their past, in different kinds of relationships with Soviet military dominance and political guidance. Seldom had conditions of life changed as rapidly in Eastern Europe as they did in the decades after 1945, yet inevitably upheaval included a reworking of earlier values and institutions as well as brand new construction. The ferment after 1985 showed how many traditional impulses had survived, even as another new era dawned.

THE SOVIET UNION AS SUPERPOWER

By 1945 Soviet foreign policy had several ingredients. Desire to regain tsarist boundaries (though not carried through regarding Finland) joined with traditional interest in expansion and in playing an active role in European diplomacy. Genuine revulsion at Germany's two invasions prompted a feverish desire to set up buffer zones, under Soviet control. As a result of Soviet industrialization and its World War II push westward, the nation also emerged as a world power, like the newcomer United States. Continued concentration on heavy industry and weapons development, combined with strategic alliances and links to Communist movements in various parts of the world, helped maintain this status.

Soviet participation in the late phases of the war against Japan provided an opportunity to seize some islands in the northern Pacific. The Soviet Union established a protectorate over the Communist regime of North Korea, to match the U.S. protectorate in South Korea. Soviet aid to the victorious Communist party in China brought new influence in that country for a time, and in the 1970s the Soviet Union gained a new ally in Communist Vietnam, which provided naval bases for the Soviet fleet. Its growing military and economic strength gave the postwar Soviet Union new leverage in the Middle East, Africa, and even parts of Latin America; alliance with the new Communist regime in Cuba was a key step here, during the 1960s. The Soviet Union's superpower status was confirmed by its development of the atomic and then hydrogen bombs, from 1949 onward, and by its deployment of missiles and naval forces to match the rapid expansion of U.S. arsenals. The Soviet Union had become a world power.

THE NEW SOVIET EMPIRE IN EASTERN EUROPE

As a superpower, the Soviet Union developed increasing worldwide influence, with trade and cultural missions on all inhabited continents and military alliances with several Asian, African, and Latin American nations. But the clearest extension of the Soviet sphere developed right after World War II, in Eastern Europe. Here the Soviets made it clear that they intended to stay, pushing the Soviet effective sphere of influence farther to the west than ever before in history. Soviet insistence on this empire helped launch the cold war, as the Soviet Union made clear its willingness to confront the West rather than relax its grip.

The small nations of Eastern Europe, mostly new or revived after World War I, had gone through a troubled period between the world wars. Other than democratic Czechoslovakia, they had failed to establish vigorous, independent economies or effective political systems. Then came the Nazi attack and ineffective Western response, as Czechoslovakia, Poland, and Yugoslavia were seized by German or Italian forces. Eastern Europe fell under Nazi control for four years. Although anti-Nazi governments formed abroad, only in Yugoslavia was a resistance movement strong enough to seriously affect postwar results.

By 1945 the dominant force in Eastern Europe was the Soviet army, as it pushed the Germans back and remade the map of Eastern Europe. Through the combination of Soviet military might and collaboration with local Communist movements in the nations that remained technically independent, opposition parties were crushed and non-Communist regimes forced out by 1948. The only exceptions to this pattern were Greece, which moved toward the Western camp in diplomatic alignment and political and social systems; Albania, which formed a rigid Stalinist regime that ironically brought it into disagreement with Soviet post-Stalinist leaders; and Yugoslavia, where a Communist regime formed under the resistance leader Tito quickly proclaimed its neutrality in the cold war, resisting Soviet direction and trying to form a more open-ended, responsive version of the Communist economic and social system.

After what was in effect the Soviet takeover, a standard development dynamic emerged throughout most of Eastern Europe by the early 1950s. The new Soviet-sponsored regimes attacked possible rivals for power, including, where relevant, the Roman Catholic church. Mass education and propaganda outlets were quickly developed. Collectivization of agriculture ended the large estate system, without creating a property-owning peasantry. Industrialization was pushed through successive five-year plans, though with some limitation due to Soviet insistence on access to key natural resources (such as Romanian oil) on favorable terms. Finally, a Soviet–Eastern European trading zone became largely separate from the larger trends of international commerce.

After the formation of NATO in western Europe, the relevant Eastern European nations were also enfolded in a common defense alliance, the Warsaw Pact, and a common economic planning organization. Soviet troops continued to be stationed in most Eastern European states both to confront the Western alliance and to ensure the continuation of the new regimes and their loyalty to the common cause.

Although it responded to many social problems in the smaller nations of Eastern Europe, as well as to the desire of the Soviet Union to expand its influence and guard against German or more general Western attack, the new Soviet system created obvious tensions. Dissatisfaction with particularly tight controls in East Germany brought a workers' rising in 1953, vigorously repressed by Soviet troops, and widespread exodus to West Germany until a wall was built in Berlin in 1961 to stem the flow. All along the new borders of Eastern Europe, barbed wire fences and armed patrols kept the people in. In 1956 relaxation of Stalinism within the Soviet Union created new hopes that controls might be loosened. More liberal Communist leaders arose in Hungary and Poland, with massive popular backing, seeking to create states that, although Communist, would permit greater

As Soviet troops moved into Hungary to crush the revolt of 1956, freedom fighters in Budapest headed for the front with whatever weapons they could find.

diversity and certainly more freedom from Soviet domination. In Poland the Soviets accepted a new leader more popular with the Polish people. Among other results, Poland was allowed to halt agricultural collectivation, establishing widespread peasant ownership in its place, and the Catholic church, now the symbol of Polish independence, gained greater tolerance. But a new regime in Hungary was cruelly crushed by the Soviet army and a hard-line Stalinist leadership set up in its place.

Yet Soviet control over Eastern Europe did loosen slightly overall, for the heavy-handed repression cost considerable prestige. Eastern European governments were given a freer hand in economic policy and were allowed limited room to experiment with greater cultural freedom. Several countries thus began to outstrip the Soviet Union in industrialization levels and consumer prosperity. Contacts with the West expanded in several cases, with greater trade and tourism. Eastern Europe remained with the Soviet Union as a somewhat separate economic bloc in world trade, but there was room for limited diversity. Individual nations, such as Hungary, developed new intellectual vigor and experimented with slightly less centralized economic planning. The Communist political system remained in full force, however, with its single-party dominance and strong police controls; diplomatic and military alignment with the Soviet Union remained essential.

The limits of experimentation in Eastern Europe were brought home again in 1968, when a more liberal regime came to power in Czechoslovakia. Again the Soviet army responded, expelling the reformers and setting up a particularly rigid leader. A challenge came again from Poland in the late 1970s, in the form of widespread Catholic unrest and an independent labor movement called Solidarity, all against the backdrop of a stagnant economy and low morale. Here response was slightly more muted, though key agitators were arrested; the Polish army took over the state, under careful Soviet supervision.

By the 1980s Eastern Europe had been vastly transformed by several decades of Communist rule. Important national diversity remained, visible both in industrial levels and in political styles. Catholic Poland thus differed from hard-line, neo-Stalinist Bulgaria or Romania. Important discontents remained as well. Yet a Communist-imposed social revolution had brought considerable economic change and real social upheaval, through the abolition of the once-dominant aristocracy and the remaking of the peasant masses through collectivization, new systems of mass education, and industrial, urban

growth. Earlier cultural ties with the West, though still greater than in the Soviet Union itself, had been lessened; Russian, not French or English, was the first foreign language learned.

The expansion of Soviet influence answered important Soviet foreign policy goals, both traditional and new. The Soviets retained a military presence deep in Europe, which among other things reduced very real anxiety about yet another German threat. Eastern European allies aided Soviet ventures in other parts of the world, providing supplies and advisors for activities in Africa, Latin America, and elsewhere. Yet the recurrent unrest in Eastern Europe served as something of a check on Soviet policy as well. The need for continued military presence may have diverted Soviet leaders from emphasizing expansionist ambitions in other directions, particularly where direct commitment of troops might be involved.

EVOLUTION OF DOMESTIC POLICIES

Within the Soviet Union the Stalinist system remained intact during the initial postwar years. The war encouraged growing use of nationalism as well as appeals for Communist loyalty, as millions of Russians responded heroically to the new foreign threat. Elements of this mood were sustained as the cold war with the United States developed after 1947, with news media blasting the United States as an evil power and a distorted society. Many Soviets, fearful of a new war that U.S. aggressiveness seemed to them to threaten, agreed that strong government authority remained necessary. This attitude helped sustain the difficult rebuilding efforts after the war, which proceeded rapidly enough for the Soviet Union to regain its prewar industrial capacity and then proceed, during the 1950s, to impressive annual growth rates. The attitude also helped support Stalin's rigorous efforts to shield the Soviet population from extensive contact with foreigners or foreign ideas. Strict limits on travel, outside media, or any uncensored glimpse of the outside world kept the Soviet Union unusually isolated in the mid-20th-century world—its culture, like its economy, largely removed from world currents.

Stalin's political structure continued to emphasize central controls and the omnipresent party bureaucracy, leavened by the adulation accorded to Stalin and by the aging leader's endemic suspiciousness. Moscow-based direction of the national economy, along with the steady extension of education, welfare, and police operations, expanded the bureaucracy both of the government and of the parallel Communist party. Recruitment from the ranks of peasant and worker families continued into the 1940s, as educational opportunities, including growing secondary school and university facilities, allowed talented young people to rise from below. Party membership, the ticket to bureaucratic promotion, was deliberately kept low, at about 6 percent of the population, to ensure selection of the most dedicated elements. New candidates for the Party, drawn mostly from the more broadly based Communist youth organizations, had to be nominated by at least three Party members. Party members vowed unswerving loyalty and group consciousness. A 1939 Communist party charter stated the essential qualities:

> The Party is a united militant organization bound together by a conscious discipline which is equally binding on all its members. The Party is strong because of its solidarity, unity of will and unity of action, which are incompatible with any deviation from its program and rules, with any violation of Party discipline, with fractional groupings, or with double-dealing. The Party purges its ranks of persons who violate its program, rules or discipline.

Through the Party apparatus, the Soviet system became one of careful hierarchy and elaborate bureaucracy. The Communist party itself was run by a top committee, the Political Bureau (Politburo), consisting of 20 people who were the real power brokers in the nation—operating, of course, under Stalin's watchful eye. Most Politburo members also held key ministries or top positions in the secret police or army. The Politburo apparatus helped coordinate these various branches and balance their interests and ambitions. Both Party and state, as overlapping governing bodies, spread gradations of authority from the top committees through the state governments to local industries, cities, and collective farms. Decisions were made at the top, often in secret, and then transmitted to lower levels for execution; little reverse initiative, with proposals coming from lower bureaucratic agencies, was encouraged.

The Stalinist version of this system, indeed, engendered particular bureaucratic caution. Innovative proposals, much less criticisms, were risky. Top officials who kept their posts tended to be colorless figures, competent but above all extremely loyal both to official ideology and to Stalin as leader. One durable foreign minister, for example, Molotov, was described by Stalin himself as having a "mind like a file clerk."

The Communist government built on the precedent of tsarist authoritarianism. As with the tsars, political contests and open-ended agencies, much less multiparty parliaments, were shunned. Carefully worded constitutions gave citizens the vote, and indeed required participation in elections, but mainly to rubber-stamp official candidates and policies. The Supreme Soviet, like the earlier Duma, had no power to initiate legislation or block official decisions; it served to ratify and praise.

ANALYSIS
THE NATURE OF TOTALITARIANISM

At the height of the cold war, in the 1950s, many analysts and many ordinary U.S. citizens worried about the almost superhuman capacities of a totalitarian state. Spy stories reflected the cruel resolve of the Soviet totalitarian system, though plucky Westerners were supposed to win out after incredible difficulties. Sober political science analysis sought to contrast totalitarian systems with 20th-century democracies as decisively modern, but decisively different, forms of government.

Totalitarianism differed from democracy in repressing free expression of opinion and preventing real choice of leadership. Decisions came from above, and voting merely confirmed what had already been decided. Parliaments were rubber stamps, elections presented no alternative parties or candidates; all competing political movements were swept away.

Totalitarianism also, however, differed from more traditional authoritarian regimes, such as the tsarist government of prerevolutionary Russia. Totalitarianism depended on modern, industrial technology to organize an extensive bureaucracy, monitor the population, and reach the people with bombardments of propaganda. It wanted active popular loyalty to the government, and it wanted the state not simply to maintain order but to change the society as well—and this meant extensive controls. Vastly expanded police; mass meetings; radio, film, and poster notices that glorified the leader and blasted the enemies of the state; and elections that provided seeming and sweeping popular endorsement—these were the hallmarks of the totalitarian system. Finally, totalitarian regimes were held to be supremely efficient, badgering and forcing the people into line. With opposition leaders killed or jailed, police forces omnipresent, churches and other institutions attacked, totalitarian regimes pushed the concept of a police state to new heights.

These judgments of totalitarianism, and its newness and importance in the 20th century, retain great validity. But with the Nazi totalitarian system crushed in war and now the Soviet system crumbling from within, some questions arise about the totality of totalitarianism. Historians are taking some second looks.

Totalitarian states could not be oblivious to certain interest groups within the society. They did not grind every element uniformly beneath the state, and they did sometimes listen, informally, to pressures from below. Hitler thus attacked Protestant churches, forcing revisions in their presentations to include a more Germanic image of Christ, more thoroughly than he did the internationally powerful Catholic church, though he forced some concessions from it as well. The Stalinist regime listened for complaints from factory worker groups in the later 1930s, even though it banned independent unions and crushed outright dissidence.

Totalitarian states also did not force uniform compliance from ordinary citizens, though they made protest very difficult. They did create widespread fear. But they were much less successful in generating new beliefs than was often imagined. Seventy years of Communist rule in the Soviet Union thus did not eliminate religion, though it did manage to limit religious practice. When Communist rule eased in the later 1980s, religious interests turned out to be significant among many groups. Minority nationalisms obviously had not been crushed.

Communist China offers yet a final example; by 1991 it was increasingly clear that massive state campaigns to persuade peasants to adopt a low birthrate were not succeeding as planned, for peasants either evaded restriction or expressed traditional values by getting rid of daughters in order to try to ensure a male heir. Here, too, the capacity of a totalitarian state to restructure deep-seated habits was far from infinite.

The totalitarian state was a very real phenomenon, and it expresses important features of 20th-century world history. It is, however, more complex than the simplest textbook definitions can convey.

One other impact of totalitarianism does command attention in the 1990s: experience with a totalitarian state, although not forcing a robotlike conformity, may tend to freeze opinions in certain respects. Although East Germans, for example, did not accept Communist ideology fully or uniformly, they did retain more remnants of Nazi thinking than did their counterparts in the West; there was less opportunity for them to discuss and reconsider. Bulgarians who used new-found freedom to belabor their Turkish minority, expressing ethnic nationalism of an early 20th-century variety, may have similarly reflected a tendency to rely on older beliefs as a fallback against the pressures of a totalitarian state. This impact of totalitarianism, in constraining the evolution of beliefs, raised some obvious issues for areas emerging into new, less rigid political forms in the 1990s.

Questions: How is a totalitarian state different from a more conventional authoritarian regime? Why is it difficult to dislodge an established totalitarian state? Did Nazi Germany and Soviet Russia develop the same kinds of totalitarianism, despite their different ideologies? 🕸

SOVIET CULTURE: PROMOTING NEW BELIEFS AND INSTITUTIONS

The Soviet government was also an impressive new product, not just a renewal of tsarist autocracy. It carried on a much wider array of functions than the tsars had ventured, not only in fostering industrialization but also in reaching out for the direct loyalties of individual citizens. The government and Party also maintained an active cultural agenda, and although this had been foreshadowed by the church-state links of tsarist days, it had no full precedent. The regime declared war on the Orthodox church and other religions soon after 1917, seeking to shape a secular population that would maintain a Marxist, scientific orthodoxy; vestigial church activities remained but under tight government regulation. Artistic and literary styles, as well as purely political writings, were carefully monitored to ensure adherence to the Party line. The educational system was used not only to train and recruit technicians and bureaucrats but also to create a loyal, right-thinking citizenry. Mass ceremonies, such as May Day parades, stimulated devotion to the state and to communism.

Although the new regime did not attempt to abolish the Orthodox church outright, it greatly limited the church's outreach. Thus the church was barred from giving religious instruction to anyone under 18, and state schools vigorously preached the doctrine that religion was mere superstition. Although loyalties to the church persisted, they now seemed concentrated in a largely elderly minority. The Soviet regime also limited freedom of religion for the Jewish minority, often holding up Jews as enemies of the state in what was in fact a

The grim-faced collection of leaders reviewing military parades from atop Lenin's tomb in Moscow became a fixture of the cold war decades. Here Khrushchev's central position indicates that he has moved to the apex of the ruling Communist party pyramid.

manipulation of traditional Russian anti-Semitism. The larger Muslim minority was given greater latitude, on condition of careful loyalty to the regime. On the whole, the traditional religious orientation of Soviet society declined in favor of a scientific outlook and Marxist explanations of history in terms of class conflict. Church attendance dwindled under government repression; by the 1950s only the elderly seemed particularly interested.

The Soviet state also continued to attack modern Western styles of art and literature, terming them decadent, but maintained some earlier Western styles, which were appropriated as Russian. Thus Russian orchestras performed a wide variety of classical music, and the Russian ballet, though rigid and conservative by 20th-century Western norms, commanded wide attention and enforced rigorous standards of excellence. Soviet culture emphasized a new style of "socialist realism" in the arts, bent on glorifying heroic workers, soldiers, and peasants through grandiose neoclassical paintings and sculpture. Soviet architecture, though careful to preserve older buildings, emphasized functional, classical lines, with a pronounced taste for the monumental. Socialist realist principles spread to Eastern Europe after World War II, particularly in public displays and monuments. With some political loosening and cold war thaw after 1950, however, Soviet and Eastern European artists began to adopt to some extent Western styles. At the popular level, jazz and rock music bands began to emerge by the 1980s, though official suspicion persisted.

Literature in the Soviet Union remained diverse and creative, despite official controls sponsored by the Communist-dominated Writers' Union. Leading authors wrote movingly of the travails of World War II, maintaining the earlier tradition of sympathy with the people, great patriotism, and a concern for the Russian soul. The most creative Soviet artists, particularly the writers, often skirted a fine line between conveying some of the sufferings of the Russian people in the 20th century and courting official disapproval. Their freedom also depended on leadership mood; thus censorship eased after Stalin and then tightened again somewhat in the late 1960s and 1970s, though not to previous levels. Yet even authors critical of aspects of the Soviet regime maintained distinctive Russian values. Aleksandr Solzhenitsyn, for example, exiled to the West because of publication of his trilogy on Siberian prison camps, *The Gulag Archipelago,* found the West too materialistic and individualistic for his taste. Though barred from his homeland, he continued to seek an alternative both to Communist policy and to Westernization, with more than a hint of a continuing belief in the durable solidarity and faith of the Russian common people and a mysterious Russian national soul.

Along with interest in the arts and a genuine diversity of expression despite official party lines, Soviet culture continued to place great emphasis on science and social science. Scientists enjoyed great prestige and wielded considerable power. Social scientific work, heavily colored by Marxist theory, nonetheless produced important

Successful competition in international athletic events, such as those at the Olympics, were among the great accomplishments of the states of the Soviet bloc. At the 1988 Summer Olympics in Seoul, the Soviet men's gymnastic team celebrates its long-standing monopoly of the team gold medals.

analyses of current trends and of history. Scientific research was even more heavily funded, and Soviet scientists generated a number of fundamental discoveries in physics, chemistry, and mathematics. At times scientists themselves felt the heavy hand of official disapproval. Biologists and psychiatrists, particularly, were urged to reject Western theories that called human rationality and social progress into question, though here as in other areas controls were most stringent in the Stalinist years. Thus Freudianism was banned, and under Stalin biologists who overemphasized the uncontrollability of genetic evolution were jailed. But Soviet scientists overall enjoyed considerable freedom and great prestige. As in the West, their work was often linked with advances in technology and weaponry. After the heyday of Stalinism, scientists gained greater freedom from ideological dictates, and exchanges with Western researchers became more common in what was, at base, a common scientific culture.

Shaped by substantial state control, 20th-century Soviet culture overall proved neither traditional nor Western. Considerable ambivalence about the West remained, as Soviets continued to utilize many art forms they developed in common with the West, such as the ballet, while instilling a comparable faith in science. Fear of cultural pollution—particularly, of course, through non-Marxist political tracts but also through modern art forms—remained lively, as Soviet leaders sought a culture that would enhance their goals of building a socialist society separate from the capitalist West.

ECONOMY AND SOCIETY

The Soviet Union became a fully industrial society between the 1920s and the 1950s. Rapid growth of manufacturing and the rise of urban populations to more than 50 percent of the total were measures of this development. Most of the rest of Eastern Europe was also fully industrialized by the 1950s. Eastern European modernization, however, had a number of distinctive features. State control of virtually all economic sectors was one key element; no other industrialized society gave so little leeway to private initiative. The unusual imbalance between heavy industrial goods and consumer items was another distinctive aspect. The Soviet Union lagged in the priorities it placed on consumer goods— not only such Western staples as automobiles but also housing construction and simple items, such as bathtub plugs. Consumer-goods industries were poorly funded and did not achieve the advanced technological level that characterized the heavy-manufacturing sector. The Soviet need to amass capital for development in a traditionally poor society helped explain the inattention to consumer goods; so did the need to create, in a society that remained poorer overall, a massive armaments industry to rival that of the United States. Thus despite an occasional desire to beat the West at its own affluent-society game, Eastern Europe did not develop the kind of consumer society that came to characterize the West. Living standards improved greatly, and extensive welfare services provided security for some groups not similarly supported in the West, but complaints about poor consumer products and long lines to obtain desired goods remained a feature of Soviet life.

The Communist system throughout Eastern Europe also failed to resolve problems with agriculture. Capital that might have gone into farming equipment was often diverted to armaments and heavy industry. The arduous climate of northern Europe and Asia was a factor as well, dooming a number of attempts to spread grain production to Siberia, for example. But it seemed clear that the Eastern European peasantry continued to find the constraints and lack of individual incentive in collectivized agriculture deterrents to maximum effort. Thus Eastern Europe had to retain a larger percentage of its labor force in agriculture than was true of the industrial West, but it still encountered problems with food supply and quality.

Despite the importance of distinctive political and economic characteristics, Eastern European society echoed a number of the themes of contemporary Western social history—simply because of the shared fact of industrial life. Work rhythms, for example, became roughly similar. Industrialization brought massive efforts to speed the pace of work and to introduce regularized supervision. The incentive systems designed to encourage able workers resembled those used in Western factories. Along with similar work habits came similar leisure activities. For decades, sports have provided excitement for the peoples of Eastern Europe, as have films and television. Family vacations to the beaches of the Black Sea became cherished respites. Here too there were some distinctive twists, as the Communist states boosted sports efforts as part of their political program (in contrast to the Western view of sports as a combination of leisure and commercialism). East Germany, along with the Soviet Union, developed particularly extensive athletic programs under state sponsorship, winning international competitions in a host of fields.

Eastern European social structure also grew closer to that of the West, despite the continued importance of the rural population and despite the impact of Marxist theory. Particularly interesting was a tendency to divide urban society along class lines—between workers and a better-educated, managerial middle class. Wealth divisions remained much less great than in the West, to be sure, but the perquisites of managers and professional people—particularly for Communist party members— set them off from the standard of living of the masses.

Finally, the Soviet family reacted to some of the same pressures of industrialization as did the Western family. Massive movement to the cities and crowded housing enhanced the nuclear family unit, as ties to a wider network of relatives loosened. The birthrate dropped. Official Soviet policy on birthrates varied for a time, but the basic pressures became similar to those in the West: falling infant death rates, with improved diets and medical care, together with increasing periods of schooling and some increase in consumer expectations, made large families less desirable than before. Wartime dislocations contributed to birthrate decline at points as well. By the 1970s the Soviet growth rate was about the same as that of the West. As in the West, also, some minority groups—particularly Muslims in the southern Soviet Union—have maintained higher birthrates than the majority ethnic group—in this case, ethnic Russians—a differential that has caused some concern about maintaining Russian cultural dominance.

Patterns of child rearing showed some similarities to those in the West, as parents, especially in the managerial middle class, devoted great attention to promoting their children's education and ensuring good jobs for the future. At the same time children were more strictly disciplined than in the West, both at home and in school, with an emphasis on authority that had political implications as well. Soviet families never afforded the domestic idealization of women that had prevailed in the West during industrialization. Most married women worked, an essential feature of an economy struggling to industrialize and offering relatively low wages to individual workers. As in the peasant past, women performed many heavy physical tasks. They also dominated some professions, such as medicine, though these professionals were much lower in status than were their male-dominated counterparts in the West. Soviet propagandists took pride in the constructive role of women and their official equality, but there were signs that many women were suffering burdens from demanding jobs with little help from their husbands at home.

The features that Soviet society shared with the West because of common urban and industrial experience showed in aspects of popular culture. Concerns about acquisition, romance, and school success can have a very Western, or more properly modern-industrial, ring. Thus graffiti—a traditional site of wish lists since late tsarist days—on a Leningrad church wall in the 1970s displayed familiar personal aspirations:

> "Lord, grant me luck, and help me to be accepted into the Art Academy in four years."—"Happiness and health to me and Volodya."—"Lord strangle Tarisyn."—"Lord, help me get rid of Valery."—"Lord, help me in love."—"Lord make Charlotte fall in love with me."—"Lord, I'm hungry."—"Lord, help me pass the exam in political economics."—"Lord, help me pass the exam in: (1) electrical technology; (2) electrical vacuum instruments; (3) Marxism-Leninism."—"Help me pass my driver's license test, Lord."—"Lord, take the arrogance out of my wife."—"Lord, help me win a transistor radio, model AP–2–14, in the lottery." (Added on by another person:) "All we have is P–20–1. Archangel Gabriel."

Overall, Soviet society and culture displayed a distinctive blend of basic features. Several key traditions persisted, like belief in a Russian soul. Revolutionary emphases produced unique artistic forms (though later imitated in other Communist societies) and a large bureaucratic class. Industrialization generated many familiar forms of urban life, even in such intimate areas as family behavior and personal aspirations.

DE-STALINIZATION

The rigid government apparatus created by Stalin and sustained after World War II by frequent arrests and exiles to forced labor camps was put to a major test after Stalin's death in 1953. The results gradually loosened, without totally reversing, Stalinist cultural isolation. Focus on one-man rule might have created immense succession problems, and indeed frequent jockeying for power did develop among aspiring candidates. Yet the system held

together. Years of bureaucratic experience had given most Soviet leaders a taste for coordination and compromise, along with a reluctance to strike out in radical new directions that might cause controversy or arouse resistance from one of the key power blocs within the state. Stalin's death was followed by a ruling committee that balanced interest groups, notably the army, the police, and the Party apparatus. This mechanism encouraged conservatism, as each bureaucratic sector defended its existing prerogatives, but it also ensured fundamental stability.

In 1956, however, Nikita Krushchev emerged from the committee pack to gain primary power, though without seeking to match Stalin's eminence. Indeed, Krushchev attacked Stalinism for its concentration of power and arbitrary dictatorship. In a stirring speech delivered to the Party congress, Krushchev condemned Stalin for his treatment of political opponents, for his narrow interpretations of Marxist doctrine, even for his failure to adequately prepare for World War II. The implications of the de-Stalinization campaign within the Soviet Union suggested a more tolerant political climate and some decentralization of decision making. In fact, however, despite a change in tone, little concrete institutional reform occurred. Political trials became less common, and the most overt police repression eased. A few intellectuals were allowed to raise new issues, dealing, for example, with the purges and other Stalinist excesses. Outright critics of the regime were less likely to be executed and more likely to be sent to psychiatric institutions or, in the case of internationally visible figures, exiled to the West or confined to house arrest. Party control and centralized economic planning remained intact. Indeed, Khrushchev planned a major extension of state-directed initiative by opening new Siberian land to cultivation; his failure in this costly effort, combined with his antagonizing of many Stalinist loyalists, led to his quiet downfall.

After the de-Stalinization furor and Khrushchev's fall from power, patterns in the Soviet Union remained stable into the 1980s, verging at times on stagnant. Economic growth continued but with no dramatic breakthroughs and with recurrent worries over sluggish productivity and especially over periodically inadequate harvests, which compelled expensive grain deals with Western nations, including the United States. A number of subsequent leadership changes occurred, but the transitions were handled smoothly.

Cold war policies eased somewhat after Stalin's death. Khrushchev vaunted the Soviet ability to outdo the West at its own industrial game, bragging on a visit to the United States that "we will bury you." The Khrushchev regime also produced one of the most intense moments of the cold war with the United States, as he probed for vulnerabilities. Exploiting the new alliance with Cuba, the Soviets installed missiles in Cuba, yielding only to a firm U.S. response in 1962 by removing the missiles but not their support of the Communist regime on the island. Khrushchev had no desire for war, and overall he promoted a new policy of peaceful coexistence. He hoped to beat the West economically and actively expanded the Soviet space program; Sputnik, the first space satellite, was sent up in 1957, well in advance of its U.S. counterpart. Khrushchev maintained a competitive tone, but he shifted away from an exclusive military emphasis. Lowered cold war tensions with the West permitted a small influx of Western tourists by the 1960s, as well as greater access to the Western media and a variety of cultural exchanges, which gave some Soviets a renewed sense of contact with a wider world and restored some of the earlier ambiguities about the nation's relationship to Western standards.

At the same time, the Soviet leadership continued a steady military buildup, adding increasingly sophisticated rocketry and bolstered by its unusually successful space program. The Soviets maintained a lead in manned space flights into the late 1980s. Both in space and in the arms race, the Soviet Union demonstrated great technical ability combined with a willingness to settle for somewhat simpler systems than those the United States attempted, which helped explain how it could maintain superpower parity even with a less prosperous overall economy. An active sports program, resulting in a growing array of victories in Olympic Games competition, also showed the Soviet Union's new ability to compete on an international scale and its growing pride in international achievements.

The nation faced a number of new foreign policy problems, although maintaining superpower status. From the mid-1950s onward the Soviet Union experienced a growing rift with China, a Communist nation with which it shared a long border. Successful courtship of many other nations—such as Egypt, a close diplomatic friend during the 1960s—often turned sour, though these developments were often balanced by new alignments elsewhere. The rise of Muslim awareness in the 1970s was deeply troubling to the Soviet Union, with its own large Muslim minority. This prompted an

Soviet advances in science and technology both surprised and threatened the United States and western Europe. Manned space flights were but one area in which the Soviets challenged the material supremacy of the West.

invasion of Afghanistan, to promote a friendly puppet regime, which bogged down amid guerrilla warfare into the late 1980s. On balance, the Soviet Union played a normally cautious diplomatic game, almost never engaging directly in warfare but maintaining a high level of preparedness.

Problems of work motivation and discipline loomed larger in the Soviet Union than in the West by the 1980s, after the heroic period of building an industrial society under Stanlinist exhortation and threat. With highly bureaucratized and centralized work plans and the absence of abundant consumer goods, many workers found little reason for great diligence. High rates of alcoholism, so severe as to cause an increase in death rates, particularly among adult males, also burdened work performance and caused great concern to Soviet leaders. More familiar were problems of youth agitation. Although Soviet statistics tended to conceal crime problems, it is clear that many youth became impatient with the disciplined life and eager to have greater access to Western culture, including rock music and blue jeans.

Soviet output continued to grow, though the economy by the 1980s was lagging behind the West and Japan in adopting new technologies, such as computers (aside from military applications). Military and space technology still kept pace with Western levels, as both sides fed the arms race. But a higher percentage of Soviet output had to go to military uses than in the West, because of the continued differential in per capita wealth. Despite the consumer shortages that resulted, most Soviet citizens seemed to accept the necessity, given what they were told about the West's aggressive intentions and their own memory of invasion in World War II. Some skepticism about the existing system, however, showed in the minority of beleaguered intellectuals who occasionally ventured criticism of domestic and foreign policies, including armaments policies. Cynicism cropped up also in humor magazines and popular jokes, which poked fun at the luxurious living of Communist officials and the inefficiencies of the bureaucracy. Humor may at the same time have provided some outlet for grievances that might otherwise have festered.

DOCUMENT
KHRUSHCHEV'S 1956 SPECIAL REPORT TO THE COMMUNIST PARTY

This report, a step in Khrushchev's successful bid to become leader of the Soviet Union, seemed to be a milestone in Soviet political history after the long era of Stalin's rule and then an interlude of collective leadership following his death in 1953. Leaders in the smaller Eastern European states particularly were encouraged to believe that significant policy change was in the offing. In fact, Khrushchev, who had previously docilely followed Stalin's wishes, intended no major policy changes, yet the speech prompted a certain evolution even so.

When we analyze the practice of Stalin in regard to the direction of the party and of the country, when we pause to consider everything which Stalin perpetrated, we must be convinced that Lenin's fears were justified. The negative characteristics of Stalin, which, in Lenin's time, were only incipient, transformed themselves during the last years into a grave abuse of Power by Stalin, which caused untold harm to our party. . . .

Stalin acted not through persuasion, explanation and patient cooperation with people, but by imposing his concepts and demanding absolute submission to his opinion. Whoever opposed this concept or tried to prove his viewpoint and the correctness of his position was doomed to removal from the leading collective and to subsequent moral and physical annihilation. . . .

Stalin originated the concept "enemy of the people." This term automatically rendered it unnecessary that the ideological errors of a man or men engaged in a controversy be proven; this term made possible the usage of the most cruel repression, violating all norms of revolutionary legality, against anyone who in any way disagreed with Stalin, against those who were only suspected of hostile intent, against those who had bad reputations. This concept "enemy of the people" actually eliminated the possibility of any kind of ideological fight or the making of one's views known on this or that issue, even those of a practical character. In the main, and in actuality, the only proof of guilt used, against all norms of current legal science, was the "confession" of the accused himself; and, as subsequent probing proved, "confessions" were acquired through physical pressures against the accused. This led to glaring violations of revolutionary legality and to the fact that many entirely innocent persons, who in the past had defended the party line, became victims. . . .

During Lenin's life, party congresses were convened regularly; always, when a radical turn in the development of the party and the country took place, Lenin considered it absolutely necessary that the party discuss at length all the basic matters pertaining to internal and foreign policy and to questions bearing on the development of party and government. . . .

So it was during Lenin's life. Were our party's holy Leninist principles observed after the death of Vladimir Ilyich?

Whereas, during the first few years after Lenin's death, party congresses and Central Committee plenums took place more or less regularly, later, when Stalin began increasingly to abuse his power, these principles were brutally violated. This was especially evident during the last 15 years of his life. Was it a normal situation when over 13 years elapsed between the 18th and 19th Party Congresses, years during which our party and our country had experienced so many important events? . . .

Having at its disposal numerous data showing brutal willfulness toward party cadres, the Central Committee has created a party commission under the control of the Central Committee Presidium: it was charged with investigating what made possible the mass repressions against the majority of the Central Committee members and candidates elected at the 17th Congress of the All-Union Communist Party. . . .

It was determined that of the 139 members and candidates of the party's Central Committee who were elected at the 17th Congress, 98 persons, i.e., 70 per cent, were arrested and shot (mostly in 1937–38). . . .

A large part of these cases are being reviewed now and a great part of them are being voided because they were baseless and falsified. Suffice it to say that from 1954 to the present time the Military Collegium of the Supreme Court has rehabilitated 7,679 persons, many of whom were rehabilitated posthumously. . . .

The power accumulated in the hands of one person, Stalin, led to serious consequences during the Great Patriotic War. . . .

During the war and after the war, Stalin put forward the thesis that the tragedy which our nation experienced in the first part of the war was the result of the "unexpected" attack of the Germans against the Soviet Union. But, comrades, this is completely untrue. As soon as Hitler came to power in Germany he assigned to himself the task of liquidating Communism. The fascists were saying this openly; they did not hide their plans. . . .

When there developed an exceptionally serious situation for our army in 1942 in the Kharkov region, we had correctly decided to drop an operation whose objective was to encircle Kharkov, because the real situation at that time would have threatened our Army with fatal consequences if this operation were continued.

We communicated this to Stalin, stating that the situation demanded changes in operational plans so that the enemy would be prevented from liquidating a sizable concentration of our Army.

Contrary to common sense, Stalin rejected our suggestion and issued the order to continue the operation aimed at the encirclement of Kharkov, despite the fact that at this time many Army concentrations were themselves actually threatened with encirclement and liquidation.

I telephoned to Vasilevsky and begged him: "Alexander Mikhailovich, take a map"—Vasilevsky is present here—"and show Comrade Stalin the situation which has developed." We should note that Stalin planned operations on a globe. [Animation in the hall.] Yes, Comrades, he used to take the globe and trace the front line on it. I said to Comrade Vasilevsky: "Show him the situation on a map; in the present situation we cannot continue the operation which was planned. The old decision must be changed for the good of the cause." . . .

After "listening" . . . to our plea, Stalin said: "Let everything remain as it is!"

And what was the result of this? The worst that we had expected. The Germans surrounded our army concentrations and consequently we lost hundreds of thousands of our soldiers. This is Stalin's military "genius"; this is what it cost us. . . .

We must state that, after the war, the situation became even more complicated. Stalin became even more capricious, irritable and brutal; in particular his suspicion grew. His persecution mania reached unbelievable dimensions. Many workers were becoming enemies before his very eyes. After the war, Stalin separated himself from the collective even more. Everything was decided by him alone without any consideration for anyone or anything. . . .

Let us also recall the "affair of the doctor-plotters." [Animation in the hall.] Actually there was no "affair" outside of the declaration of the woman doctor Timashuk, who was probably influenced or ordered by someone (after all, she was an unofficial collaborator of the organs of state security) to write Stalin a letter in which she declared that doctors were applying supposedly improper methods of medical treatment.

Such a letter was sufficient for Stalin to reach an immediate conclusion that there are doctor-plotters in the Soviet Union. He issued orders to arrest a group of eminent Soviet medical specialists. . . .

Shortly after the doctors were arrested, we members of the Political Bureau received protocols with the doctors' confessions of guilt. After distributing these protocols, Stalin told us, "You are blind like young kittens: what will happen without me? The country will perish because you do not know how to recognize enemies." . . .

Comrades: the cult of the individual acquired such monstrous size chiefly because Stalin himself, using all conceivable methods, supported the glorification of his own person. . . .

Comrades! We must abolish the cult of the individual decisively, once and for all; we must draw the proper conclusions concerning both ideological-theoretical and practical work. It is necessary for this purpose:

First, in a Bolshevik manner to condemn and to eradicate the cult of the individual as alien to Marxism-Leninism and not consonant with the principles of party leadership and the norms of party life. . . .

Secondly, to continue systematically and consistently the work done by the party's Central Committee during the last years, a work characterized by minute observation in all party organizations, from the bottom to the top, of the Leninist principles of party leadership, characterized, above all, by the main principle of collective leadership. . . .

Thirdly, to restore completely the Leninist principles of Soviet socialist democracy, expressed in the Constitution of the Soviet Union, to fight willfulness of individuals abusing their power. . . .

Long live the victorious banner of our party—Leninism!

(From *The Crimes of the Stalin Era*, annotated by Boris I. Nicolaevsky, in *The New Leader*, New York, 1956, S12–15, S19–20, S32, S36, S38, S41, S45, S48, S54, S64–65. Reprinted by permission of *The New Leader*.)

Questions: Why did the 1956 speech seem so shocking and potentially liberating in Eastern Europe and the Soviet Union? What changes did Kruschchev suggest in Soviet politics? How did he contrast communism and Stalinism? How does his approach compare with more recent changes in Russian politics?

THE EXPLOSION OF THE 1980s AND 1990s

From 1985 onward the Soviet Union entered a period of intensive reform, soon matched by new political movements in Eastern Europe that effectively dismantled the Soviet empire. The initial cause of this extraordinary and unanticipated upheaval lay in the deteriorating Soviet economic performance, intensified by the costs of military rivalry with the United States. There were reasons for pride in the Soviet system as well, and many observers believed that public attitudes by the 1980s were shaped much less by terror than by satisfaction with the Soviet Union's world prestige and the improvements the Communist regime had fostered in education and welfare. But to a degree unperceived outside the Soviet Union, the economy was grinding to a standstill. Forced industrialization had produced extensive environmental deterioration throughout Eastern Europe. According to Soviet estimates, half of all rivers were severely polluted, and more than 40 percent of all agricultural land was endangered by late 1980s; more than 20 percent of Soviet citizens lived in regions of ecological disaster. Rates and severity of respiratory and other diseases rose, impairing both morale and economic performance. Infant mortality rates also rose in several regions, sometimes to among the highest levels in the world.

More directly, industrial production began to stagnate and even drop as a result of rigid central planning, health problems, and poor worker morale. Growing inadequacy of housing and common goods resulted, further lowering motivation. As economic growth stopped, the percentage of resources allocated to military production escalated, toward a third of all national income.

This reduced funds available for other investments or for consumer needs. At first only privately, younger leaders began to recognize that the system was near collapse.

THE AGE OF REFORM

Yet the Soviet system was not changeless, despite its heavy bureaucratization. Problems and dissatisfactions, though controlled, could provoke response beyond renewed repression. After a succession of leaders whose age or health precluded major initiatives, the Soviet Union in 1985 brought a new, younger official to the fore. Mikhail Gorbachev quickly renewed some of the earlier attacks on Stalinist rigidity and replaced some of the old-line Party bureaucrats. He conveyed a new and more Western style, dressing in fashionable clothes (and accompanied by his stylish wife), holding relatively open press conferences, and even allowing the Soviet media to

More than any other leader, Mikhail Gorbachev effected the changes that brought an end to the cold war. Here he works to convince independence-minded Lithuanians of the advantages of staying in the Soviet Union.

engage in active debate and reports on problems as well as successes. Gorbachev also further altered the Soviet Union's modified cold war stance. He urged a reduction in nuclear armament, and in 1987 he negotiated a new agreement with the United States that limited medium-range missiles in Europe. He ended the war in Afghanistan, bringing Soviet troops home.

Internally, Gorbachev proclaimed a policy of *glasnost*, or openness, which implied new freedom to comment and criticize. He pressed particularly for a reduction in bureaucratic inefficiency and unproductive labor in the Soviet economy, sketching more decentralized decision making and the use of some market incentives to stimulate greater output. The sweep of Gorbachev's reforms, as opposed to an undeniable new tone in Soviet public relations, remained difficult to assess. Strong limits on political freedom remained, and it was unclear whether Gorbachev could cut through the centralized planning apparatus that controlled the main lines of the Soviet economy. There was also uncertainty about how well the new leader could balance reform and stability.

Indeed, questions about Gorbachev's prospects recalled many basic issues in Soviet history. In many ways Gorbachev's policies constituted a return to a characteristic ambivalence about the West as he reduced Soviet isolation while continuing to criticize aspects of Western political and social structure. Gorbachev clearly hoped to use some Western management techniques and was open to certain Western cultural styles without, however, intending to abandon basic controls of the Communist state. Western analysts wondered if the Soviet economy could improve worker motivation without embracing a Western-style consumerism or whether computers could be more widely introduced without admitting freedom for information exchange.

Gorbachev also sought to open the Soviet Union to fuller participation in the world economy, recognizing that isolation in a separate empire had restricted access to new technology and limited motivation to change. Although the new leadership did not rush to make foreign trade or investment too easy—considerable suspicion persisted—the economic initiatives brought symbolic changes, such as the opening of a McDonald's restaurant in Moscow and a whole array of new contacts between Soviet citizens and foreigners.

Gorbachev's initial policies did not quickly stir the Soviet economy, but they had immediate political effects, some of which the reform leader had almost certainly not anticipated. The keynote of the reform program was *perestroika*, or economic restructuring, which Gorbachev

translated into more leeway for private ownership and decentralized control in industry and agriculture. Farmers, for example, could now lease land for 50 years, with rights of inheritance, and industrial concerns were authorized to buy from either private or state operations. Foreign investment was encouraged. Gorbachev pressed for reductions in Soviet military commitments, particularly through agreements with the United States on troop reductions and limitations on nuclear weaponry, in order to free resources for consumer-goods industries. He urged more self-help among the Soviets, including a reduction in drinking, arguing that he wanted to "rid public opinion of . . . faith in a 'good Tsar,' the all powerful center, the notion that someone can bring about order and organize perestroika from on high." Politically, he encouraged a new constitution in 1988, giving considerable power to a new parliament, the Congress of People's Deputies, and abolishing the Communist monopoly on elections. Important opposition groups developed both inside and outside the Party, pressing Gorbachev between radicals who wanted a faster pace of reform and conservative hard-liners. Gorbachev himself was elected to a new, powerful presidency of the Soviet Union in 1990.

Reform amid continued economic stagnation provoked agitation among minority nationalities in the Soviet Union, from 1988 onward. Muslims and Armenian Christians rioted in the south, both against each other and against the central state. Baltic nationalists and other European minorities also stirred, some insisting on independence (notably in Lithuania), some pressing for greater autonomy. Again, results of this diverse unrest were difficult to forecast, but some observers predicted the end of Soviet control of Central Asia and the European borderlands.

Even social issues were given uncertain new twists. Gorbachev noted that Soviet efforts to establish equality between the sexes had burdened women with a combination of work and household duties. His solution—to allow women to "return to their purely womanly missions" of housework, childrearing, and "the creation of a good family atmosphere"—had a somewhat old-fashioned ring to it.

DISMANTLING THE SOVIET EMPIRE

Gorbachev's new approach, including his desire for better relations with Western powers, prompted more definitive results outside the Soviet Union than within, as the smaller states of Eastern Europe uniformly moved for greater independence and internal reforms. Bulgaria moved for economic liberalization in 1987 but was held back by the Soviets; pressure resumed in 1989 as the Party leader was ousted and free elections were arranged. Hungary changed leadership in 1988 and installed a non-Communist president. A new constitution and free elections were planned, as the Communist party re-named itself Socialist. Hungary also reviewed its great 1956 rising, formally declaring it "a popular uprising . . . against an oligarchic system . . . which had humiliated the nation." Hungary moved rapidly toward a free-mar-ket economy. Poland installed a non-Communist gov-ernment in 1988 and again moved quickly to dismantle the state-run economy; prices rose rapidly as govern-ment subsidies were withdrawn. The Solidarity move-ment, born a decade before through a merger of non-Communist labor leaders and Catholic intellectuals, became the dominant political force. East Germany dis-placed its Communist government in 1989, expelling

key leaders and moving rapidly toward unification with West Germany. The Berlin wall was dismantled, and in 1990 non-Communists won a free election. German unification occurred in 1991, a dramatic sign of the col-lapse of postwar Soviet foreign policy. Czechoslovakia installed a new government in 1989, headed by a play-wright, and sought to introduce free elections and a more market-driven economy.

Although mass demonstrations played a key role in several of these political upheavals, only in Romania was there outright violence, as an exceptionally authoritarian Communist leader was swept out by force. As in Bulgar-ia, the Communist party retained considerable power, though under new leadership, and reforms moved less rapidly than in Hungary and Czechoslovakia. The same held true for Albania, where the unreconstructed Stalin-ist regime was dislodged and a more flexible Communist leadership installed.

During the revolts of the late 1980s Lithuanians demonstrated in the capital city of Vilnius for national independence from the Soviet Union.

New divergences in the nature and extent of reform in Eastern Europe were exacerbated by clashes among nationalities, as in the Soviet Union. Change and uncertainty brought older attachments to the fore. Romanians and ethnic Hungarians clashed; Bulgarians attacked a Turkish minority left over from the Ottoman period. In 1991 the Yugoslavian Communist regime, though not Soviet-dominated, also came under attack, and a civil war boiled up from disputes among nationalities. Minority nationality areas, notably Slovenia, Croatia, and Bosnia-Herzogovinia, proclaimed independence, but the national, Serbian-dominated army applied massive force to preserve the Yugoslav nation.

Amid this rapid and unexpected change, prospects for the future were in many ways very unpredictable. Few of the new governments fully defined their constitutional structure, and amid innovation the range of new political parties almost compelled later consolidations. Like the Soviet Union itself, all the Eastern European states suffered from sluggish production and massive pollution, and economic problems might well lead to new political discontents.

With state controls and protection abruptly withdrawn by 1991, tensions over the first results of the introduction of the market economy in Poland brought rising unemployment and further price increases. These in turn produced growing disaffection from the Solidarity leadership. Diplomatic linkages among small states— a critical problem area between the two world wars— also had yet to be resolved.

The massive change in Soviet policy was clear. Gorbachev reversed postwar imperialism completely, stating that "any nation has the right to decide its fate by itself." In several cases, notably Hungary, Soviet troops were rapidly withdrawn, and generally it seemed unlikely that a change of heart, toward a repressive attempt to reestablish empire, would be possible. New contacts with Western nations, particularly in the European Economic Community, seemed to promise further realignment in the future.

RENEWED TURMOIL IN 1991–1992

The uncertainties of the situation within the Soviet Union were confirmed in the summer of 1991, when an attempted coup was mounted by military and police elements. Gorbachev's presidency and democratic decentralization were both threatened. Massive popular demonstration, however, asserted the strong democratic current that had developed in the Soviet Union since

1986. The contrast with earlier Soviet history and with the suppression of democracy in China two years before was striking.

In the aftermath of the attempted coup, Gorbachev's authority weakened. Leadership of the key republics, including the massive Russian Republic, became relatively stronger. The three Baltic states used the occasion to gain full independence, though economic links with the Soviet Union remained. Other minority republics proclaimed independence as well, but Gorbachev struggled to win agreement on continued economic union and some other coordination. By the end of 1991 leaders of the major republics, including Russia's Boris Yeltsin, proclaimed the end of the Soviet Union, projecting a commonwealth of the leading republics, including the economically crucial Ukraine, in its stead.

Amid the disputes Gorbachev fell from power, doomed by his attempts to salvage a presidency that depended on some survival of a greater Soviet Union. His leadership role was taken over by Boris Yeltsin, who as president of Russia and an early renouncer of communism now emerged as the leading, though quickly beleaguered, political figure.

The resulting Commonwealth of Independent States won tentative agreement from most of the now independent republics. But tensions immediately surfaced about economic coordination amid rapid dismantling of state controls; about control of the military, where Russia— still by far the largest unit—sought predominance, including nuclear control amid challenges from the Ukraine and from Kazakhstan (two of the other republics with nuclear weaponry on their soil); and about relationships between the European-dominated republics, including Russia, and the cluster of Central Asian states. How much unity might survive in the former Soviet Union was very unclear.

The fate of economic reform was also uncertain, as Russian leaders hesitated to convert to a full market system lest transitional disruption further antagonize the population. Here again, more radical plans emerged at the end of 1991, calling for removal of most government price controls.

Nor, finally, was it clear what role remained for the once proud Communist party or what political movements would replace it. Russian leaders sought to outlaw the Party for its leadership of the failed coup, but an alternative party system emerged only slowly. Citizens took new delight in tearing down the old emblems of the revolution, including massive socialist realist statues of Lenin. Even old tsarist flags and uniforms were trotted out for display. But effective new emblems had yet to be generated. Nonetheless, in some republics, including Central Asia, Party leadership retained considerable vigor.

CONCLUSION

UNCERTAIN FUTURES IN EASTERN EUROPE

Inevitably, Soviet and Eastern European history in the 1990s has been dominated by the surprising events of the most recent periods and by huge uncertainties about their consequences. Recent events made clear that much less had changed in this region during the 20th century than had been recognized—even by Soviet citizens. Soviet law had long trumpeted women's equality, and indeed Soviet women played vital roles in the labor force, but inequality in household chores continued, and the unavailability of reliable birth control devices—a result of shoddy consumer-goods production—forced a high rate of abortions. Soviet constitutions had featured a system of federated republics, but in fact central government control and Russian ethnic dominance spurred minority nationalism, and nationalist hostilities burned brightly. Nationalism in the Soviet Union and among newly independent Eastern European nations threatened to divide the region profoundly. Religion also remained a vital force, despite decades of secularization. Catholicism in the smaller nations and in the western republics of the Soviet Union, Judaism and Islam in Central Asia provided important loyalties for citizens.

Revolution and a totalitarian state had exerted only a limited impact, despite theories of absolute control and undeniable police terror in key periods. The same system had done less to diminish a traditional attraction to Western values and standards than might have been imagined. Several Eastern European states rushed to proclaim a Western-style devotion to individual liberty as well as a market economy. Though nationalist loyalties and economic lags might well limit openness to Westernization in the long run, it seemed unlikely that isolation could be resumed—a sign both of older Eastern European interests in the West and the new intensity of international contacts.

The excitement of recent change, however, and the enormous uncertainties of Eastern Europe's future are not the entire story of the later 20th century, for the Soviet Union had been an expansionist state building on an older Russian tradition of expansionism. The Soviet Union had been a cautious superpower in most respects, avoiding outright war after 1945 save in Afghanistan—more careful in this respect than the United States. Economic problems prompted outright pullback under Gorbachev, but questions inevitably remained about the permanence of this reorientation. Concern about outside threats, combined with the temptation to use military means to defend a beleaguered empire, might change that moderation, and undue rigidity by the United States might cause the same effect.

Communist domestic policies might also survive the turmoil of transition. The conservative bureaucracy remained suspicious of loss of control. Gorbachev constructed a powerful presidency, legally protected from public "insult," to balance greater political freedom, thus displaying strong attachment to authoritarian structures, as did new leaders in Bulgaria and Romania. Even other areas, such as Poland, might return to authoritarianism, as they had before World War II, if economic pressures persisted, because liberal experience was limited. Several of the newly autonomous republics, particularly in Muslim Central Asia, favored strong leadership over any democratic structures.

Continuities or potential continuities were not confined to leadership. Eastern Europeans and Soviet citizens valued the welfare protections of Communist society and the limitations on social inequality. Many hoped to combine elements of collective protection with a larger dollop of capitalism. Many continued to attack aspects of Western individualism that seemed unattractive, such as high crime rates and youth unrest, even as these very trends gained ground in Eastern European society. And many could appreciate the earlier achievements of the Soviet system in destroying the landlord class, for example, and in revolutionizing educational access.

Prospects in Eastern Europe remained unclear not only because of the shock of recent changes and the magnitude of economic and environmental issues but also because of probable holdovers from earlier revolutionary institutions and the expectations they had fostered. The social, political, and cultural restructuring of the 20th century was open to drastic change, but it was unlikely to be obliterated. Tensions in relationships with Western values, an old theme redefined under communism, might persist as well.

Eastern Europe had been a dynamic factor in world history for centuries, which meant that the questions about its future, answerable in the early 1990s, affected far more than the region itself. Throughout the turmoil of 20th-century war and revolution, the Soviet Union had retained a pivotal position in European and Asian power balances and ultimately in world affairs more widely. Clearly this role was being redefined, and probably it would recede, but with what consequences to the Soviet Union and to the world at large?

FURTHER READINGS

Recent Soviet history is treated in Richard Barnet's *The Giants: Russia and America* (1977), A. Rubinstein's *Soviet Foreign Policy Since World War II* (1981), Alec Nove's *The Soviet Economic System* (1980), Stephen Cohen et al., eds., *The Soviet Union Since Stalin*, and Ben Eklof's *Gorbachev and the Reform Period* (1988).

Other parts of Eastern Europe are treated in H. Setson Watson's *Eastern Europe between the Wars* (1962), F. Fetjo's *History of the People's Democracies: Eastern Europe since Stalin* (1971), J. Tampke's *The People's Republics of Eastern Europe* (1983), Timothy Ash's *The Polish Revolution: Solidarity* (1984), H. G. Skilling's *Czechoslovakia: Interrupted Revolution* (1976) (on the 1968 uprising), and B. Kovrig's *Communism in Hungary from Kun to Kadar* (1979).

On the early signs of explosion in Eastern Europe, see K. Dawisha's *Eastern Europe, Gorbachev and Reform: The Great Challenge* (1988). Bohdan Nahaylo and Victor Swoboda's *Soviet Disunion: A History of the Nationalities Problem in the USSR* (1990) provides important background. On women's experiences, see Barbara Engel and Christine Worobec, eds., *Russia's Women: Accommodation, Resistance, Transformation* (1990).

1946–1948 Kuomintang (Nationalist) regime consolidates in Taiwan   **1965** Growing Hong Kong autonomy

1955 Japanese production reaches prewar levels

1948 Korea   **1951** American occupation
divided   ends in Japan   **1959** Singapore declares independence

1961 Military regime in South Korea

1945 Japan defeated;   **1954** U.S.-Taiwan defense treaty
American occupation   **1955** Merger forms Liberal Democratic party in Japan

1950–1953 Korean War after invasion by North Korea

Up from the Ashes: Japan and the Pacific Rim in the Post–World War II Era

11

INTRODUCTION. The rise of coastal areas in eastern Asia to world importance forms one of the major facets of the rebalancing of major societies in the last phase of the 20th century. Unmarked by formal revolution—in contrast to Russia—the Pacific Rim gained momentum as an economic rather than as a military superpower following the upheaval of World War II. The dynamism of Asia's Pacific coast centered in several societies long in China's shadow, as eastern Asian civilization was redivided and redefined, and the same societies began to influence international patterns in unprecedented ways. Societies that had been shaped by Confucian influence began to take very different paths.

This chapter covers several political units in eastern Asia—Japan, Korea, Taiwan, and the city-states of Singapore and Hong Kong—that are joined by their common ability to generate unusual economic growth during the second half of the 20th century. The Pacific Rim states also reflect some common heritage that had included considerable Chinese influence. The Pacific Rim category was still tentative by the 1990s, for it was not clear how much these nations would prove to have in common or how permanent their splitting away from other eastern Asian societies would be, notably China and Vietnam (see Chapter 13). Yet the Pacific Rim states were undeniably important in their own right, becoming, along with the West, the center of the world's greatest economic strength and challenging the West through new competition. The Pacific Rim states also shared a fascinating effort to blend successful industrial forms with a distinctive cultural and political tradition—providing the clearest alternative to the West of what a vigorous modern society might look like.

The key actor was Japan, which had diverged from Chinese patterns in the previous period. Japan's rise to

---

1988–1989 Growing student agitation for liberal political reform in South Korea; elected civilian government installed

1992–1993 Stock market decline and economic slowdown in Japan

1980 End of U.S.-Taiwan treaty alliance

1984 British-Chinese agreement to return Hong Kong to China in 1997

1993 Liberal Democratic party defeated in Japanese elections; coalition government takes power

new eminence had begun in the 19th century with the reforms of the Meiji era, the beginnings of industrialization, and then the military push that brought Japanese victories over China and Russia and profitable participation on the Allied side in World War I. After defeat in World War II and a new series of internal reforms, Japanese influence returned, this time in the guise of dynamic economic growth that by the 1960s made Japan a leading world competitor—the first Asian nation to reach this position since the onset of the Industrial Revolution. On the basis of its export surge, Japan became a major factor in international markets of all sorts—in banking, in foreign investment both in raw-materials areas and in the United States, and in foreign economic aid—as the relatively small, resource-poor island nation reached toward control of almost one-fifth of total world trade. Japanese competition challenged the United States and western Europe, and its demand for raw materials figured prominently in Canada, Latin America, Australia, and the Middle East as well as Asia.

After World War II Japan's success was mirrored by the rapid rise of other centers in eastern Asia, some of which became the first successful entrants to the ranks of industrial economies for virtually a century—since Japan and Russia had begun their surge. South Korea, Taiwan, and the city-states of Hong Kong and Singapore, though not yet attaining Japanese levels of prosperity and influence, gained ground rapidly, challenging the Japanese lead in certain export sectors and making a profound impact on international markets.

The rise of the Pacific Rim nations commands attention in 20th-century history because of their success in breaking the previous Western monopoly on industrial leadership—not only in sheer volume of production and export trade but in technological innovation as well. Many observers predicted that coastal eastern Asia, perhaps joined by parts of China and other areas, would replace the West in world leadership. This had not yet occurred by the 1990s, though the Pacific Rim unquestionably generates significant new competition and shares in world economic leadership. It was revealing, nevertheless, that many Western businesses and political leaders advocated imitation of certain Japanese methods of organization and personality style on grounds that the Japanese had leapfrogged over the West in the habits essential to successful modern life. "Japanization" has not become a word, and Japan's ability to provoke imitation has not yet reached Westernization levels in the world at large; indeed, Japan continues its earlier interest in selective adoption of Western attributes even as it serves as a

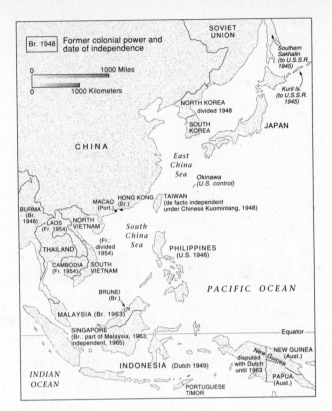

The Pacific Rim Areas by 1960

model in other respects. Nevertheless, the Pacific Rim's presence seems to have increased with every passing year during the final quarter of the 20th century. Japan has begun to earn the combination of envy and resentment the West had produced during its period of growing influence.

The emergence of the Pacific Rim also commands interest because it has formed such a challenging exception to the general difficulty faced by 20th-century societies that were still to enter into a genuine industrial revolution. Here, South Korea and other areas that successfully industrialized after 1960 were even more interesting than Japan, where the Pacific Rim process of change had been launched so much earlier. Japan included, the Pacific Rim commands interest because successful industrialization has not led to full Westernization. In political styles and a host of personal values the Pacific Rim states, headed by Japan, have provided a laboratory for testing what social features were inherent in industrial advance and what features could diverge from Western patterns on the basis of distinctive traditions and ongoing experience. Japan and increasingly other nations, such as South Korea, were at once highly industrial, setting new standards for the most advanced versions of industrial society, and highly Asian, adapting a host of regional traditions quite different from contemporary Western patterns.

Overall, the Pacific Rim has formed a distinctive grouping of societies amid the larger patterns of the 20th-century world, particularly after the upheavals of World War II and its immediate aftermath. Pacific Rim societies differ from the West, from Eastern Europe, and from most of the rest of Asia. Their influence steadily expanded, introducing a host of new factors into world dynamics.

⚘ THE AFTERMATH OF WAR IN EASTERN ASIA

The victors in World War II had some reasonably clear ideas about how eastern Asia was to be restructured as part of the dismantling of the short-lived Japanese empire. Korea, freed from Japanese control, was divided between a Soviet zone of occupation in the north and a U.S. zone in the south. Taiwan was restored to China, which was in principle and to some extent in fact ruled by a Kuomintang government headed by Chiang Kai-shek. The United States regained the Philippines but pledged to grant independence quickly—save for retaining some key military bases. European powers restored colonial controls over their former holdings in Vietnam, Malaya, and Indonesia. Japan was occupied by U.S. forces bent on introducing major changes that would prevent a recurrence of military aggression.

NEW DIVISIONS AND THE END OF EMPIRES

Not surprisingly, given the complex impact of the war and the complication of the new cold war struggle between the United States and the Soviet Union, the Pacific regions of Asia did not quickly settle into agreed-on patterns. A decade after the war's end, the Philippines, Indonesia, and Malaya were independent—part of the postwar tide of decolonization. Taiwan was still ruled by Chiang Kai-shek, but the Chinese mainland was in the hands of a new and powerful Communist regime. Chiang's Nationalist regime claimed a mission to recover China, but in fact Taiwan was now a separate republic. Korea remained divided but had undergone a brutal north-south conflict in which only U.S. intervention preserved South Korea's independence. Japan, rather ironically, was one of the few Pacific regions where mat-

ters had proceeded somewhat according to plan, as the nation began to recover while also adjusting to a considerably altered political structure.

Eastern Asia's postwar turmoil forms a complex story, only part of which is directly relevant to the emergence of the Pacific Rim economy. The Communist phase of China's revolution maintained a separation between China and the parts of its traditional regional hinterland that showed little interest in communism; Vietnam's decolonization struggles also demand special attention. The Pacific Rim turned out to be composed of areas traditionally influenced to some degree by Chinese culture but not brought under Communist control. This somewhat complex definition was forged in part by the actual experience of key Pacific regions during the period of postwar confusion.

JAPANESE RECOVERY

Japan in 1945 was in shambles. Its cities were burned, its factories destroyed or idle, its people impoverished and shocked by the fact of surrender and by the trauma of bombing, including the atomic devastation of Hiroshima and Nagasaki. However, like the industrial nations of the West, Japan was capable of reestablishing a vigorous economy with surprising speed. And its occupation by U.S. forces, eager to reform Japan but to avoid punitive measures, provided an opportunity for a new period of selective Westernization.

The U.S. occupation government, headed by General Douglas MacArthur, worked quickly to tear down Japan's wartime political structure. The military forces were disbanded, the police decentralized, some officials removed, and political prisoners released. For the long run U.S. authorities pressed for a democratization of Japanese society by giving women the vote, encouraging labor unions, and abolishing Shintoism as a state religion. Several economic reforms were also introduced, breaking up landed estates for the benefit of small farmers, who quickly became politically conservative, and dissolving the holdings of the zaibatsu combines, a measure that had little lasting effect, as Japanese big business quickly regrouped.

A new constitution tried to cut through older limitations by making Parliament the supreme government body from which the cabinet was appointed; various civil liberties were guaranteed, along with gender equality in marriage and collective bargaining rights; military forces with "war potential" were abolished forever, making Japan a unique major nation in its limited military

The signing on the battleship *Missouri* of the terms of surrender by the Japanese foreign minister, Namoru Shigemitsu, brought the official end to a long and bloody global conflict. General Douglas MacArthur, who accepted the Japanese surrender, strove to establish democratic institutions and to rebuild the Japanese economy in the years of U.S. military occupation following the war.

strength; and the emperor was made a symbolic figure-head, without political power and with no claims to Shinto divinity. Even as Japan accepted many political and legal concepts, it inserted its own values into the new constitution. Thus a 1963 law defined special social obligations to the elderly, in obvious contrast to Western approaches to this subject, at the statutory level: "The elders shall be loved and respected as those who have for many years contributed toward the development of society, and a wholesome and peaceful life shall be guaranteed to them. . . ."

These new constitutional measures were in the main embraced by the Japanese people, many of whom became avid opponents of any hint of military revival. Japan did ultimately create a self-defense force, and military capacity quietly grew well beyond what the constitution intended, but military expenditures remained a minuscule part of the overall budget. The United States retained military power and responsibility in the region

long after the occupation period, keeping important bases in Japan. Many of the political features of the new constitution worked smoothly, in large part, of course, because the Japanese had experienced parliamentary and political party activity for extended periods in previous decades. Two moderate parties, both with substantial prewar traditions, vied for power during the late 1940s, with the Liberal party holding sway; in 1947 a minority Socialist party gained ground by winning 26 percent of the vote in the first postwar elections. The Socialist threat indeed spurred a 1955 merger of the moderate parties into the new Liberal Democratic party, which monopolized Japan's government into the 1990s.

Amid political reconstruction, Japan's economy gradually recovered, a process that required about ten years. By 1955 production in the major industrial branches regained prewar levels. At that point many experts anticipated a moderation of growth, but in fact a huge surge ensued—the surge that propelled Japan into the first rank of world industrial powers. By this point, of course, the postwar adjustment period was clearly past, a fact expressed by the signing in 1951 of a peace treaty between Japan and 48 of its former wartime opponents; U.S. occupation ended in the following year, with an agreement on postwar bases. The Soviet Union, now locked in the cold war (which in fact had spurred the United States to convert Japan from defeated enemy to dependent ally) did not officially make peace, and its continued occupation of former Japanese islands was a source of serious friction. Nevertheless the Soviets acquiesced in the new arrangements, leaving Japan free from major diplomatic distractions.

KOREA: INTERVENTION AND WAR *

Korea's postwar adjustment period was far more troubled than Japan's. Leaders of the Allied powers during World War II had agreed in principle that Korea should be restored as an independent state. But U.S. eagerness to obtain Soviet help against Japan, combined with long-standing Soviet interest in the area, determined that the northern part of the peninsula was occupied by the Soviet Union after the war. As the cold war intensified, U.S. and Soviet authorities could not agree on unification of the zones, and in 1948 the United States sponsored the Republic of Korea in the south, matched by the Soviet-dominated People's Democratic Republic of Korea in the north. North Korea's regime drew on an earlier Korean Communist party founded in exile in the 1920s. North Korea quickly became a Communist state with Stalinist-type emphasis on the power of the leader, Kim Il-Sung. The South Korean regime, bolstered by ongoing U.S. military presence, was headed by the nationalist Syngman Rhee, another politician who had earlier worked in exile against Japanese occupation. Rhee's South Korea developed parliamentary institutions in form but maintained a strongly authoritarian tone.

In June 1950 North Korean forces attacked the south, hoping to impose unification on Communist terms. The United States, eager to maintain South Korea as protection for its deeper interests in Japan, reacted quickly (after some confusing signals about whether or not South Korea was inside the U.S.' "defense perimeter"). President Truman insisted on drawing another line against Communist aggression and orchestrated U.N. sponsorship of a largely U.S. "police action" in support of South Korean troops. Under General MacArthur's leadership Allied forces pushed North Korea back, driving on toward the Chinese border; this in turn roused concern on the part of China's Communist regime, whose "volunteers" drove U.S. troops back toward the south. The front stabilized in 1952 near the original north-south border. The stalemate dragged on until 1953, when a new U.S. administration was able to agree to an armistice.

Korea then continued its dual pattern of development. North Korea produced an unusually isolated version of one-man rule, as Kim concentrated powers over the only legal political party, the military, and the government. Even Soviet liberalization in the late 1980s brought little change. South Korea and the United States concluded a mutual defense treaty in 1954; U.S. troops levels were reduced, but the South Korean army gained more sophisticated military equipment and the United States poured considerable economic aid into the country, initially to prevent starvation in a war-ravaged land. The political tenor of South Korea continued to be authoritarian but with sporadic protests in behalf of a more genuine democracy. In 1961 army officers took over effective rule of the country, though sometimes a civilian government served as a facade. Economic change, however, began to gain ground in the south, ushering in a new phase of activity and international impact. Tensions between the two Koreas continued to run high, with many border clashes and sabotage, but outright warfare was avoided.

TAIWAN, HONG KONG, AND SINGAPORE

Postwar adjustments in Taiwan involved yet another set of issues. As the Communist revolutionary armies gained the upper hand in mainland China, between 1946 and 1948 the Kuomintang (Nationalist) regime prepared to fall back on its newly reacquired island, which the Communists could not threaten because they had no navy. The result was imposition over the Taiwanese majority of a new leadership, bureaucracy, and massive military force drawn from the mainland and, particularly in its early years but in principle for several decades, devoted to the task of regaining mainland authority from the Communists.

The authoritarian political patterns the Nationalists had developed in China, centered on Chiang Kai-shek's personal control of the government, were amplified by the need to keep disaffected Taiwanese in check. Tensions with the Communist regime across the Taiwan Strait ran high. In 1950 the United States sent its Seventh Fleet to protect the island, and in 1954 a mutual defense treaty was signed (ended only in 1980, in the aftermath of U.S. diplomatic recognition of the Communist regime). In 1955 and 1958 the Communists bombarded two small islands controlled by the Nationalists, Quemoy and Matsu, and wider conflict threatened as the United States backed up its ally. Tensions were defused when China agreed to fire on the islands only on alternate days; U.S. ships supplied them on the off-days, thus salvaging national honor. Finally, the United States induced Chiang to renounce any intentions of attacking the mainland, and conflict eased into mutual bombardments of propaganda leaflets. During this period, as in South Korea, the United States devoted considerable economic aid to its Taiwanese ally, ending assistance only in the 1960s, when growing prosperity (and increasing competition with U.S. firms in the manufacture of inexpensive consumer items) seemed assured.

Two other ultimate participants in Pacific Rim economic advance were distinguished by special ties to Britain. Hong Kong, leased from China under British pressure in 1898, remained a British colony after World War II; only in the 1980s was an agreement reached between Britain and China for its 1997 return to the Chinese fold. Hong Kong gained increasing autonomy from direct British rule. Its Chinese population, already considerable, swelled at various points after 1946 as a result of flights from Communist rule. Singapore, a city founded by British imperialists in the 19th century, retained a large British naval base until 1971, when Britain abandoned all pretense of significant power in eastern Asia. An even earlier merger with independent Malaya (granted self-government in 1957) collapsed on racial grounds in tensions between multiethnic Malaysia and Chinese-dominated Singapore. Because Singapore's presence made the Chinese in Malaysia a plurality (44 percent to the Malay 41 percent), Malay nationalists rejected the association with Singapore, which gained independence as a vigorous free port in 1959.

Overall, by the end of the 1950s a certain stability had emerged in the political situation of the smaller eastern Asian nations, with the vital exception of Vietnam and its neighbors in Indochina. Despite unresolved problems, such as a divided Korean or Taiwanese-Chinese relations, a number of nations had acquired de facto independence or, like Japan, had accepted important alterations in previous political and military structures. Several of these nations in turn had received special Western attention and economic support during this same adjustment period. It was from the 1960s onward that some of these same areas, combining Western contacts with important earlier traditions of group activity

and vigorous group loyalty, moved from impressive economic recovery to new international influence on the basis of manufacturing and trade.

JAPAN, INCORPORATED

As Japanese politics developed under its postwar constitution, its chief emphasis lay in a rather conservative stability. The Liberal Democratic party, formed by the merger of two conservative units in response to Socialist challenge, held the reins of government from 1955 onward. This meant that Japan, uniquely among the democratic nations of the postwar world, had no experience with shifts in party administration. Changes in leadership, which at times were frequent, were handled through negotiations among the Liberal Democratic elite, not directly as a result of shifts in voter preference.

THE DISTINCTIVE POLITICAL STYLE

Clearly, this system revived many of the oligarchic features of Meiji Japan and the Japan of the 1920s, in which parliamentary rule was mediated through the close ties among the members of the elite. The system also encouraged cooperation between government bureaucracy and big-business combines, based on shared participation in the leadership group. The Liberal Democrats also revived some other features of Japan's previous political tradition. In the late 1950s, for example, it recentralized the police force. Socialist opponents of these programs reacted bitterly, protesting what they termed a revival of authoritarianism; Japan's political atmosphere for a time turned venomous, and there were many strikes and street demonstrations to protest government policies. During the 1960s, however, the Liberal Democrats shifted to avoid needless confrontations, and they strongly emphasized policies of economic development. During the prosperous 1970s and 1980s economic progress and the Liberal Democrats' willingness to consult opposition leaders about major legislation reinforced Japan's effective political unity. Only at the end of the 1980s, when a number of Liberal Democratic leaders were branded by corruption of various sorts and Socialist strength revived somewhat, were new political questions raised. In 1993, the ruling party split, losing its majority for the first time in the general elections. The possibility of a more competitive political atmosphere opened up with uncertain prospects for the future.

Japan's distinctive political atmosphere, even under a Western-influenced constitution, showed clearly in the array of functions the government undertook in cooperation with business leaders. Economic planning was extensive, and the state set production and investment goals in many sectors while actively lending public resources to encourage investment and limit imports. There was scant sense of division between public and private spheres, another reminder of older Japanese traditions, in this case encouraged by Confucian principles. The government-business coordination to promote economic growth and export expansion prompted the half-admiring, half-derisory Western label of "Japan, Incorporated."

Close business and political interaction resulted in part from the needs of postwar reconstruction and from Japan's precarious resource position, as the nation needed to import petroleum and most other vital raw materials and so depended on success in the export sector to an unusual degree. Government initiative extended also to the demographic sphere, as postwar leaders realized that with Japanese imperial expansion ended, it was vital to control population size. The government actively campaigned to promote birth control and abortion, and demographic growth, though still somewhat higher than Western levels, slowed notably. Here again was a product of the strong national tradition of group cohesion; although it did not prevent strong political party differences, this tradition united many Japanese in a sense of common purpose with the government. Later, however, Japan's aging population prompted the government to try to limit birth control by making a number of common methods illegal; here Japan's people proved more recalcitrant, as high costs of living kept families small.

Expansion of the educational system was another practical contact between state and citizens. The extensive school system developed from the Meiji era was further expanded, giving many more Japanese an opportunity to attend secondary schools and universities, which in turn were strongly oriented toward technical subjects. Japanese children were encouraged to achieve academic success, with demanding examinations for entry into universities defining much of the youth of ambitious men and women. The scientific and technical focus encouraged further secularization in Japanese culture, with strong emphasis on rational inquiry and practical knowledge. The deep impact of this cultural focus was evident in not only growing creativity in science and technology, as Japan began to generate innovative discoveries instead of specializing in clever imitation of ideas developed elsewhere, but also the unusually high I.Q. scores of Japanese children. Again, traditional elements entered

the picture, as education stressed somewhat mechanical group learning, based on disciplined memorization, over more eccentric individual achievements.

Japanese culture more generally preserved other important traditional elements that provided aesthetic and spiritual satisfactions amid rapid economic change and an ongoing interest in Western forms. Customary styles in poetry, painting, tea ceremonies, and flower arrangements continued; each New Year's Day, for example, the emperor presided at a poetry contest, and masters of traditional arts were honored by being designated "Living National Treasures." Kabuki and No theater also flourished. Japanese films and novels often recalled earlier history, including the age of the samurai warriors; they also stressed group loyalties, as opposed to individuality or strong assertions of will. Japanese painters and architects participated actively in the "international style" pioneered in the West, but they often infused it with earlier Japanese motifs, such as stylized nature painting. City orchestras played the works of Western composers, both classical and contemporary, and also native compositions

Traditional settings are found in modern Japan. The *yomeimon* gateway, at the mausoleum of Ieyasu in Nikko, is a traditional place for contemplation.

with passages played on the Japanese flute and zither. Both Buddhism and Shintoism remained significant forces in Japanese life as well, despite the strong secular emphasis.

Overall, Japan in the later 20th century blended new cultural interests, which allowed the Japanese to incorporate many Western forms, with distinctive recollections of strictly national ways. At the same time, aside from interior decoration and film, Japanese contributions to world culture were negligible; this was not where national creativity showed an international face.

DOCUMENT
WARINESS OF THE WEST AND DEFENSE OF JAPANESE TRADITIONS

Since the tumultuous 1850s, when Japanese society was forced by the United States and the European powers to open itself to the outside world, leading Japanese thinkers and writers have expressed the ambivalent, often anxious, responses of their people to the increasing influences from the West. In the present day best-selling Japanese novelists and social commentators deplore the erosion of traditional Japanese values and sensibilities as a result of U.S.-induced corporate commercialism, consumerism, and democratization following Japan's defeat in World War II. Wide media coverage is given to gatherings in which Japanese intellectuals lament the demise of Japan's ancient culture in the face of the Western onslaught. Japan-bashing ads and books in the United States are countered in Japan by politicians and writers who are highly critical of U.S. society, which many regard as violence-ridden, lazy, and clearly in decline.

Each of the following selections was written by a prominent post–World War II novelist. The first passages, taken from the novel *Runaway Horses* (first published in 1969) by Yukio Mishima, reflect Japanese uneasiness or open hostility to Western influences in the 1920s and 1930s, when Japan emerged as a global power for the first time in history. Mishima's novel focuses on the training of the paramilitary forces of an ultrapatriotic secret society whose young adherents seek to overthrow Japan's democratically elected civilian government and turn all power over to the emperor and his advisors. The incidents in the novel are often loosely based on historical events. In the following passage from *Runaway Horses*, an officer in the Japanese army lectures several of the paramilitary youths about the threats from abroad and Japan's dismal domestic situation in the depths of the Great Depression.

Once he had abandoned his subtle questions, Lieutenant Hori's conversation became both interesting and profitable, quite capable of arousing their zeal. The shameful state of foreign affairs, the government's economic program which was doing nothing to relieve rural poverty, the corruption of politicians, the rise of communism, and then the political parties' halving the number of Army divisions and, by championing the cause of arms cutbacks, bringing constant pressure to bear upon the military. In the course of this conversation, the Shinkawa *zaibatsu's* [big industrialists'] exertions in purchasing American dollars came up, something of which Isao [the novel's protagonist] had already heard from his father. According to the Lieutenant, Shinkawa's groups had been making a great show of restraint ever since the May Fifteenth Incident [in May 1932 extremist plotters assassinated the Japanese Prime Minister, Inukai Tsuyoshi, as part of a broader assault on the parliamentary government]. However, the Lieutenant went on to say, there were not grounds at all for placing any trust in the self-control of people of that sort.

Japan was sorely beset. Storm clouds were piling up in an ever-growing mass, and the situation was enough to make a man despair. Even the august person of His Sacred Majesty was affronted. The boys' knowledge of current evils to be deplored was greatly expanded.

The fears and targets of the young extremists in Mishima's novel can be contrasted with the very different critique of outside influences expressed in Kenzaburo Oë's novel *A Personal Matter* (first published in 1964). Reflecting major post–World War II social concerns in Japanese society, the novel focuses on the personal struggles of a student named Bird. Once a member of a gang of juvenile delinquents, Bird, now in his late twenties, unwillingly confronts the responsibilities of adulthood, including an unhappy marriage and the birth of a deformed child. Bird's sense of isolation and alienation is sharpened throughout the story by the ugly, Westernized cityscapes that form the backdrop for his attempts to cope with urban life in modern Japan.

> Bird was looking for a drugstore when an outlandish establishment on a corner stopped him short. On a giant billboard suspended above the door, a cowboy crouched with a pistol flaming. Bird read the legend that flowered on the head of the Indian pinned beneath the cowboy's spurs: Gun Corner. Inside, beneath paper flags of the United Nations and strips of spiraling green and yellow crepe paper, a crowd much younger than Bird was milling around the many-colored, box-shaped games that filled the store from front to back. Bird, ascertaining through the glass doors rimmed with red and indigo tape that a public telephone was installed in a corner at the rear, stepped into the Gun Corner, passed a Coke machine and a juke box howling rock-n-roll already out of vogue, and started across the muddy wooden floor. It was instantly as if skyrockets were bursting in his ears. Bird toiled across the room as though he were walking in a maze, past pinball machines, dart games, and a miniature forest alive with deer and rabbits and monstrous green toads that moved on a conveyor belt; as Bird passed, a high-school boy bagged a frog under the admiring eyes of his girlfriends and five points clicked into the window on the side of the game.

Questions: What foreign threats does the Lieutenant in Mishima's *Runaway Horses* directly and indirectly seek to impress on his youthful listeners? What within Japan is threatened? What sorts of Japanese collaborate with the foreigners? What solutions does the Lieutenant advocate? How has the foreign threat changed in Oë's novel about postwar Japan? What sort of view of U.S. society do the artifacts in the game parlor convey to the reader? Who does Oë suggest is being corrupted by these cultural imports? What items in Oë's description suggest that the setting is the 1950s or perhaps the early 1960s?

THE ECONOMIC SURGE

Particularly after the mid-1950s rapid economic growth produced Japan's clearest mark internationally and commanded the most intense energies at home. By 1983 the total national product was equal to the combined totals of China, both Koreas, Taiwan, India, Pakistan, Australia, and Brazil. Per capita income, though still slightly behind such leading Western nations as West Germany, had passed that of many centers, including Britain. Annual economic growth reached at least ten percent regularly from the mid-1950s onward, surpassing the regular levels of every other nation during the 1960s and 1970s, as Japan became one of the top two or three economic powers in the world. Leading Japanese corporations, such as the great automobile manufacturers and electronic equipment producers, became known for both their volume of international exports and the high quality of their goods.

A host of factors fed this astounding economic performance. Active government encouragement was a vital ingredient, as the government made economic growth its top priority. Cheap loans for technological innovations and direct technical research in government laboratories, as well as carefully favorable international trade policies, translated this priority directly. Educational expansion played a vital role, as Japan began to turn out far more engineers than did more populous competitors, such as the United States. Foreign policy also figured prominently. Japan was able to devote virtually its entire capital to investment in productive technology, for its military expenses were negligible given reliance on U.S. protection. Labor was a central feature. Japan had a growing available labor force based on continued if slower population growth and a rapid reduction of the agricultural population (from 47 percent in 1945 to the standard advanced-industrial rate of about ten percent by the mid-1980s).

Workers were abundant and highly organized, mainly in company unions that engaged in important social activities and some serious bargaining for improved benefits; the unions, however, remained careful not to impair their companies' productivity. Leading corporations solidified this cooperation, which spurred zealous work from most employees. Few days were lost to strikes, because paternalistic policies provided important benefits to workers despite wages that remained somewhat low by Western standards. Social activities promoted and expressed group loyalty (including group exercise sessions before the start of the working day), and managers displayed active interest in suggestions by employees. The Japanese system also ensured lifetime employment for an important part of the labor force, a policy aided by economic growth, low average unemployment rates, and a relatively early retirement age. This network of policies and attitudes made Japanese labor seem both less class-conscious and less individualistic than labor forces in the advanced industrial nations of the West; it reflected older traditions of group solidarity in Japan, going back to feudal patterns. Other popular habits encouraged economic growth, including a high (20 percent) savings rate born of a cautious attitude toward materialist acquisitiveness and the need to set aside money for old age. The result was considerable capital for investment in further innovation.

Japanese management displayed a distinctive spirit, again the result of adapting older traditions of leadership. There was more group consciousness, including a willingness to abide by collective decisions once made and less concern for quick personal profits than was characteristic of the West and particularly the United States. Few corporate bureaucrats changed firms, which meant that their own efforts concentrated on their company's success.

Japan, in other words, produced a distinctive economic culture that was clearly compatible with impressive results, that responded to particular Japanese needs and traditions, and that differed in important ways from Western norms. It had costs, however. Workers faced intense pressure to produce and were deprived of much protest outlet. Personal consumer standards did not rise as rapidly as national output did, because of the concentration on savings and group benefits and the government-sponsored push to promote exports rather than drain output toward internal use. Leisure life remained meager by Western standards, and many Japanese even proved reluctant to take regular vacations.

Not surprisingly, the society that developed under the rapid industrial spurt showed features similar to the West's slightly earlier experience. Japanese women, though increasingly well educated and experiencing an important decline in birthrates, did not follow Western patterns precisely. A feminist movement was confined to a small number of intellectuals. Women's work outside the home was slightly less common and considerably more segregated than in the postwar West. Within the family, women shared fewer leisure activities with their husbands, concentrating more heavily on domestic duties and intensive child rearing than was true in the West by the 1970s. Divorce rates were lower (merely one-third of U.S. levels), a sign of Japanese family stability after the disruptions of earlier stages of modernization, but this stability was predicated on the acceptance of considerable differences in gender roles and power.

Japanese methods of child rearing reflected distinctive family values. Conformity to group standards was emphasized far more than in the West or in Communist China. A comparative study of nursery schools thus showed Japanese teachers bent on effacing their own authority in the interests of developing strong bonds among the children themselves. Shame was directed toward nonconformist behaviors—a disciplinary approach the West had largely abandoned in the early 19th century. Japanese television game shows, superficially copied from the West, accordingly imposed elaborate, dishonoring punishment on losing contestants.

The same group-oriented culture shone through in diverse facets of Japanese life. The nation had few lawyers, for it was assumed that people could make and abide by firm arrangements through mutual agreement. Japanese psychiatrists reported far fewer problems of loneliness and individual alienation than in the West, as the Japanese remained devoted to group activities. Conversely, situations that promoted competition among individuals, such as the university entrance tests, produced far higher stress levels than did analogous Western experiences. The Japanese had particular ways to relieve tension; bouts of heavy drinking were more readily tolerated than in the West, as a time when normal codes of conduct could be suspended under the helpful eyes of friends. Businessmen and some politicians had recourse to traditional geisha houses for female-supplied pampering, as a normal and publicly accepted activity. Japanese teenagers participated in higher rates of sexual activity than was common in the West, another sign, perhaps, of a distinctive Japanese combination of hard work with recreational release.

Japanese popular culture was not static, because of both ongoing attraction to Western standards and rapid urbanization and economic growth. The U.S. presence after World War II brought a growing fascination with baseball, and a number of professional teams were set up. Individual Japanese athletes began also to excel in such sports as tennis and golf. In popular as well as more formal culture, change and Westernization continued to cause concern among conservatives who worried that vital traditions might be lost for good. In the mid-1980s the government, appalled to discover that a majority of Japanese children preferred knives and forks in order to eat more rapidly, invested considerable money to promote chopstick training in the schools—a minor development but indicative of the ongoing tension between change, with its Western connotations, and a commitment to Japanese identity. At the end of the 1980s a new assertion of women's political power against some Japanese politicians who kept mistresses suggested the possibility that a more Western-style feminist consciousness might gain ground as part of Japan's ongoing evolution and its growing awareness, through cultural imports and also growing tourism abroad, of the standards of other societies. Veneration of old age was challenged by some youthful assertiveness and also by the sheer cost of the rapidly growing percentage of older people—for Japan relied heavily on family support for elders. Questions abounded about how Japan would combine distinctiveness with its industrial achievement in the future, but to Western eyes the Japanese ability to adapt traditions to change and imitation remained the most striking characteristic of the nation as the end of the 20th century neared.

Japan's continued success in international competition remained the dominant theme. Many nations in the West and in Asia resented Japanese competition and the Japanese reluctance to open their own markets to outside goods. Calls for retaliation by erecting tariff barriers against Japan were a recurrent threat, and the Japanese tried to respond—for example by increasing their economic aid to developing nations and by investing directly in the United States and Europe—without changing their policies entirely. By the 1960s pollution became a serious problem as cities and industry expanded rapidly; traffic police, for example, sometimes wore protective masks, though the government (eager to preempt a potential opposition issue) paid increasing attention to environmental issues after 1970. Some Japanese experts,

worried that the nation's economic vigor would prove fragile amid such problems as growing fuel costs, foreign hostility, and internal problems, wrote articles with such titles as "The Short, Happy Life of Japan as a Superpower." Western observers continued at times to expect that Japan would soon become like the West, that is, would experience the same level of crime, strikes, individualism, family instability, youth unrest, and feminist assertiveness as the West had come to know. This expectation combined a certain amount of wishful thinking— that a wider array of problems would slow Japan up— with an implicit belief that industrialization must in the long run produce the same kinds of society regardless of the starting point.

Increasing recognition developed, however, that Japan must be understood in its combination of change with distinctiveness. Some observers even advocated

The hot sand baths at Kyushu exemplify traditional practices of health and relaxation in Japan.

that the West copy key Japanese values, particularly in the areas of diligence and group loyalty. Quite possibly, now that advanced industrialization had ceased being a Western monopoly, Japanese models would gain an increasing audience, though how much the West could or would imitate remained unclear. What was obvious, though confusing to many in the West, was Japan's achievement in reaching full economic equality—in becoming a genuine economic superpower—without adopting all Western forms of politics, family life, or personal values.

THE PACIFIC RIM: NEW JAPANS?

Economic and to some extent political developments in several other middle-sized nations and city-states on Asia's Pacific coast mirrored important elements of Japan's 20th-century history, though at a slightly later date. Political authoritarianism was characteristic, though usually with periodic bows to parliamentary forms and with recurrent protest from dissident elements that wanted greater freedom. Government functions extended to careful economic planning and promotion and to rapid expansions of the educational system, with the emphasis on technical training. Group loyalties promoted diligent labor and a willingness to work hard for relatively low wages. Economic growth burgeoned.

THE KOREAN MIRACLE

South Korea was the most obvious exemplar of the spread of new economic dynamism to other parts of the Pacific Rim. The Korean government rested normally in the hands of a political strongman, usually from army ranks. Syngman Rhee was forced out of office by massive student demonstrations in 1960, but a year later a military general, Chung-hee, seized power. He retained his authority until his assassination in 1979 by his director of intelligence. Then another general seized power. Intense student protest, backed by wider popular support, pressed the military from power at the end of the 1980s, but a conservative politician won the ensuing general election, and it was not clear how much the political situation had changed. Opposition activity was possible in South Korea, though usually heavily circumscribed, with many leaders jailed. There was some freedom of the press except for publications from Communist countries.

As in postwar Japan the South Korean government from the mid-1950s onward placed its primary emphasis on economic growth, which in this case started from a much lower base after the Korean War and previous Japanese exploitation. Huge industrial firms were created by a combination of government aid and active entrepreneurship. Exports were actively encouraged; by the 1970s, when Korean growth rates began to match those of Japan, Korea was competing successfully in the area of cheap consumer goods, steel, and automobiles in a variety of international markets. In steel Korea's surge—based on the most up-to-date technology, a skilled engineering sector, and low wages—indeed pushed past Japan. The same held true in textiles, where Korean growth (along with that of Taiwan) erased almost one-third of the jobs held in the industry in Japan.

Huge industrial groups, such as Daewoo and Hyundai, resembled the great Japanese holding companies before and after World War II and wielded great political influence. Hyundai, for example, is the creation of the entrepreneur Chung Ju Yung, a modern folk hero who walked 150 miles to Seoul, South Korea's capital, from his native village to take his first job as a day laborer at the age of 16. By the 1980s, when Chung was in his sixties, his firm had 135,000 employees and embraced 42 overseas offices throughout the world. Hyundai virtually governed Korea's southeastern coast. It built ships, including petroleum supertankers; it constructed thousands of housing units given to relatively low-paid workers at below-market rates; it built schools, a technical college, and an arena for the practice of the traditional Korean martial art, Tae Kwon Do. With their lives carefully provided for, Hyundai workers responded in kind, putting in six-day weeks with three vacation days a year and participating in almost worshipful ceremonies when a fleet of cars was shipped abroad or a new tanker launched.

South Korea's rapid entry into the ranks of newly industrialized countries produced a host of more general changes. Population growth soared, as by the 1980s over 40 million people lived in a nation about the size of the state of Indiana, producing the highest population density on earth, about 1000 people a square mile. Here was one reason that even amid growing prosperity, many Koreans emigrated, and the government gradually began to encourage couples to limit their birthrates. Seoul expanded to embrace nine million people, with intense air pollution and a hothouse atmosphere of deals and business maneuvers. Per capita income advanced despite demography, rising almost ten times from the early 1950s to the early 1980s—but to a level still only one-ninth of that of Japan. Huge fortunes coexisted with massive poverty in this setting, though the poverty itself had risen well above levels characteristic of less-developed nations.

ADVANCES IN TAIWAN AND THE CITY-STATES

The Republic of China, as the government on Taiwan came to call itself, experienced a rate of economic development similar to that in Korea, though slightly less impressive in terms of outright industrialization. Productivity in both agriculture and industry increased rapidly, the former spurred by substantial land reform that benefited small commercial farmers. The government concentrated increasingly on economic gains, as its involvement in plans for military action against the mainland Communist regime declined. As in Japan and Korea, formal economic planning reached high levels, though not at the expense of considerable latitude for private business. Massive investments were also poured into education, with basic literacy rates and levels of technical training rising rapidly. The result was important cultural and economic change for the Taiwanese people. Traditional medical practices and ritualistic popular religion remained lively but expanded to allow simultaneous use of modern, Western-derived medicine and some of the urban entertainment forms popular elsewhere.

The assimilation of rapid change gave the Taiwanese government considerable stability despite a host of new concerns. With the U.S. recognition of the People's Republic of China came a steadily decreasing official commitment to Taiwan. In 1978 the United States severed diplomatic ties with the Taiwanese regime, though unofficial contacts—through the American Institute in Taiwan and the Coordination Council for North American Affairs established by the republic in Washington—remained strong. The Taiwanese also built important regional contacts with other governments in eastern and southeastern Asia that facilitated trade; Japan, for example, served as the nation's most important single trading partner, purchasing foodstuffs, manufactured textiles, chemicals, and other industrial goods.

Taiwan also developed some informal links with the Communist regime in Beijing, though the latter continued to claim the island as part of its territory. The republic survived the death of Chiang Kai-shek and the accession of his son, Chiang Ching-kuo, to power in 1978. The young Chiang emphasized personal authority less than his father had and reduced somewhat the gap between mainland-born military personnel and native Taiwanese in government ranks. A strong authoritarian strain, however, continued, and political diversity was not encouraged.

Conditions in the city-state of Singapore, though less enveloped in echoes of Great Power politics, resembled those in Taiwan in many ways. The prime minister, Lee Kuan Yew, took office in 1959, when the area first gained independence, and held power for the next three decades. The government established tight controls over its citizens—here going beyond anything attempted elsewhere in the Pacific Rim. Sexual behavior and potential economic corruption, as well as more standard aspects of municipal regulation and economic planning, were carefully scrutinized, as the government proclaimed the necessity of unusual discipline and restraint given a large population crowded into limited space. Among the results were unusually low reported crime rates, limited tensions between the Chinese majority and other ethnic groups, and the virtual impossibility of serious political protest. The authoritarian strain in politics developed increasingly, after an initially democratic constitution; the dominant People's Action party suppressed opposition movements, though there was some easing in the late 1980s. Authoritarian politics were rendered somewhat more palatable by extraordinarily successful economic development, based on a combination of government controls and initiatives and free enterprise. Already the world's fourth largest port, Singapore saw manufacturing and banking surpass shipping as sources of revenue. Electronics, textiles, and oil refining joined shipbuilding as major sectors. By the 1980s Singapore's population enjoyed the second highest per capita income in Asia, though well after Japan. Educational levels and health conditions improved commensurately. Government regulation and propaganda combined to reduce population growth, which leveled off notably.

Finally, Hong Kong retained its status as a major world port and branched out increasingly as a center of international banking, serving as a bridge between the Communist regime in China and the wider world. Export production, particularly in textiles, combined high-speed technology with low wages and long hours for the labor force, yielding highly competitive results. Although textiles and clothing formed 39 percent of total exports by the 1980s, other sectors, including heavy industry, had developed impressively as well. As in other Pacific Rim nations, a large and prosperous middle class had developed, with cosmopolitan links to many other parts of the world, Western and Asian alike.

✥ COMMON THEMES IN THE PACIFIC RIM

Overall, the Pacific Rim states, including Japan as a special case of advanced industrial success, had more in common than their rapid growth rates and expanding exports. They all stressed group loyalties against excessive individualism and in support of hard work and somewhat limited consumer demands. Confucian morality was often used, implicitly or explicitly, as part of this effort, for all the Pacific Rim states were either ethnically Chinese or had been strongly influenced by Chinese values. Pacific Rim areas thus sought to merge rapid change and considerable imitation of Western ways with preservation of core standards that were distinctly eastern Asian. Pacific Rim states also shared, despite diverse specific political systems, considerable reliance on government planning and direction, amid limitations on dissent and instability.

ANALYSIS
THE PACIFIC RIM AS A U.S. POLICY ISSUE

Whenever power balances change among nations or larger civilizations, policy issues arise for all parties involved. The rise of the Pacific Rim economies posed some important dilemmas for the West, particularly for the United States, because of its military role in the Pacific and its world economic role. The United States had actively promoted economic growth in Japan, Korea, and Taiwan as part of its desire to sponsor solid regional development that would discourage the spread of communism. Although U.S. aid was not alone responsible for Pacific Rim advance and although it tapered off by the 1960s, the United States took some satisfaction in the fruits of its efforts and in the demonstration of the vitality of non-Communist economies. The United States was also not eager to relinquish its military superiority in the region, which gave it a stake in continued conciliation of Asian opinion; it did not want to see tensions translated into outright hostility that might threaten U.S. bases (as in South Korea) or lead to independent military efforts (a potential in the case of Japan).

Yet the threats posed by growing Pacific Rim economic competition, if more subtle than the military challenges more characteristic of changing power balances, were real and growing. Japan seemed to wield a permanent superiority in balance of payment; exports to the United States regularly exceeded imports by the 1970s and 1980s, which contributed greatly to the U.S. unfavorable overall trade balance between the United States and Japan. Japanese investment in U.S. companies and real estate, although helping to bridge the international payments deficit by bringing yen for dollars, increased the growing indebtedness of the United States to foreign nations. Symbolic problems existed as well. Japanese observers pointed out with some justice that the United States seemed more worried about Japanese investments than about larger British holdings in the United States, an imbalance that smacked of racism. Certainly the United States found it more difficult to accept Asian competition than European, if only because it was less familiar. Thus a Korean advertisement for a major firm, placed in a 1984 copy of *Fortune* magazine, featured tales of technological prowess and also pictures of three leading executives wearing the sweatshirt of their U.S. alma maters (MIT, Wisconsin, and Cal Tech)—a combination that rankled many in the United States both because of the boasts and because of the partially justified sense that U.S. know-how was being used against it. More concretely, Japanese ability to gain near monopolies in key industries, such as electronic recording systems—in some of which initial inventions still came from the United States, but their successful implementation shifted to Asia—and the growing Korean challenge in steel and automobiles meant or seemed to mean loss of jobs and perhaps a threat of more fundamental economic decline in years to come.

Several general lines of response were suggested to deal with the new competitive balance between the United States and the Pacific Rim. Some observers downplayed any sense of crisis. They argued that some readjustment was acceptable— the United States did not have to maintain its brief economic superiority worldwide and could not indeed do so. They urged that acceptance of Japanese economic vigor in tandem with U.S. military strength in eastern Asia was a viable combination—each society specialized in areas it had talent for, to the benefit of both.

Other observers, far more concerned about a worsening economic imbalance, urged that the United States imitate the bases of Pacific Rim success by opening more partnerships between government and private industry and doing more economic planning; it should teach managers to commit themselves to group harmony rather than to individual profit seeking and it should build a new concord between management and labor based on mutual respect, greater job security, and cooperative social programs. Some U.S. firms did introduce certain Japanese management methods, including more consultation with workers, with some success.

A final set of observers, also concerned about long-term erosion of U.S. power on the Pacific Rim, urged a more antagonistic stance. A few wanted the United States to pull out of costly Japanese and Korean bases so that the Pacific Rim would be forced to shoulder more of its own defense costs. Others wanted to mount tariffs against Asian goods, at least until Pacific Rim nations made it easier for U.S. firms to compete in Asian markets. Some limits on Asian competition were introduced by law during the 1980s, and Japan occasionally agreed to stabilize exports lest more hostile restrictions ensue. Aggrieved U.S. workers sometimes smashed imported cars and threatened Asian immigrants, though many U.S. consumers continued to prefer Pacific Rim products, and many U.S. firms set up production in Japan or

Crowding and commerce in contemporary Japan are depicted in this photo of the lively Shinjuku district of Tokyo at night.

Korea—with an eye toward export back to the home market—in order to maintain profits while using superior Pacific Rim technology and advantageous labor costs. Clearly, the options were complex, and U.S. policy continued to veer among them.

Pacific Rim nations also faced choices about orientation toward the West, particularly the United States. Questions that had arisen earlier about what Western patterns to copy and what to avoid continued to be important, as the Japanese concern about forks and chopsticks suggests. Added now were issues about how to express pride and confidence in modern achievements against what was seen as Western tendencies to belittle and patronize. In 1988 the summer Olympic Games were held in South Korea, a sign of Korea's international advance and a source of great national satisfaction. During the games a great deal of Korean nationalism flared against U.S. athletes and television commentators, based on real or imagined tendencies to seek out faults in Korean society. South Korea, like Japan, continued to look heavily toward Western markets and U.S. military assistance, but there was clearly a desire to put the relationship on a new and more fully equal footing. This desire reflected widespread public opinion, and it could also have policy implications.

Finally, continued economic growth virtually ensured pressures for further change in the policy arena. In 1991 a new prime minister of Japan vowed to reconsider Japan's diplomatic and military policies, to bring them more in line with the nation's international economic surge. This shift reflected, among other things, Japanese annoyance with Western complaints that the nation had not done enough during the war against Iraq earlier in the year, when a U.S.-led alliance had attacked Iraqi efforts to gain greater control over Middle Eastern oil. Japan contributed $13 billion to the war effort, somewhat grudgingly, but encountered criticism for inactivity as others shouldered the burden of ensuring the flow of Middle Eastern oil—oil on which Japan depended. Here was a dramatic illustration of the tensions between massive economic power and a rather limited diplomatic role. Constitutional limitations prohibiting Japan from sending troops abroad now passed under new review. A total restructuring of Japanese policy seemed unlikely, but a more activist, assertive stance, more in line with international economic realities, seemed likely. New leadership emerging from the 1993 political crisis groped for new trade policies as well. This, too, raised questions of appropriate response for the various societies Japan affected—as buyer of raw materials or export competitor. Although the United States professed to favor a less passive Japan, there was no assurance it would be pleased with the results of change.

Questions: How great were the challenges posed by the Pacific Rim to the U.S. world position and well-being? What are the most likely changes in American–Pacific Rim relations over the next two decades? 🏵

THE REGIONAL IMPACT OF THE PACIFIC RIM

By the 1980s the steady economic growth of the Pacific Rim states, headed of course by Japan, drew in other parts of eastern and southeastern Asia. Economic growth rates accelerated in Malaysia, for example. During the early 1960s the Malaysian government launched a program of diversification of its export crops, to improve foreign earnings. The manufacturing sector, in 1960 responsible for only about 15 percent of total national income, began to expand as well. Malaysia began to develop a consistent export surplus, as it targeted raw materials (including newly discovered petroleum reserves) and inexpensive manufactured products to Japan. Tourist facilities expanded as well, again directed toward Japanese and Western resort goers. Malaysia was not yet experiencing an industrial revolution; its economic status lagged behind that of South Korea or Taiwan. But there was no question that significant change was occurring, as the region benefited from Japan's expanding market. Some observers believed that full industrialization was imminent and that equal participation in an expanding Pacific Rim was assured.

Thailand was another entrant to the region's rapid-growth sector. A significant stream of Thai workers labored in Japan (joining workers from the Philippines and Korea, as Japan's labor force no longer sufficed for all the nation's needs). Exports from Thailand expanded, and again the manufacturing segment grew. Though it grew at a slightly slower pace, Indonesia was also drawn into the expanding trade zone of the Pacific Rim.

The rise of the Pacific Rim inevitably had an impact on regional economic policy. Communist China, turning to a more open trade policy after 1978, called extensively on Japanese expertise. The same held true for Vietnam, where economic reforms were introduced to spur growth in 1987. In 1990 Mongolia, China, and North and South Korea signed a trade and development agreement, another sign of the growing openness of the Communist

regimes to a commitment to market reforms and economic growth. It also reflected the power of the Pacific Rim example—in this case, that of South Korea—in prompting new, if limited, regional alignments. Mongolia, for example, had been a virtual protectorate of the Soviet Union for decades, but now it turned to a Pacific Rim state for cooperation. A 1991 pacification plan in Cambodia, long a troubled state in southeast Asia, called for a massive Japanese role in financing and economic reconstruction. Clearly, the regional spillover of the Pacific Rim, throughout eastern Asia, grew steadily greater.

Finally, Pacific Rim dynamism prompted new trade discussions among eastern Asian states, Canada, the United States, Australia, New Zealand, and some of the Pacific coastal nations of Latin America, including Mexico. A new association was established to sponsor these discussions. With the Asian market growing steadily because of not only Pacific Rim prosperity but also the new expansion of such states as Malaysia, and with new regional economic blocs forming in Europe and, possibly, the Americas, discussions of trade policies on both sides of the Pacific seemed increasingly vital. Some Asian and U.S. experts urged a new orientation toward Pacific trade partnerships, along with, and possibly instead of, the historic orientation of nations such as Canada, the United States, and Australia to trade with Europe. Future prospects were by no means clear, but the importance of Pacific Rim trade connections promised further impact on policy.

CONCLUSION

THE PACIFIC RIM AS EXCEPTION OR AS MODEL

The rise of the Pacific Rim nations was based on a combination of factors. First, the nations shared aspects of the Chinese cultural and political heritage, mediated, as in Japan, by many prior adaptations and additions. A roughly common culture helped account for similar tendencies to emphasize cooperation, to build tight links between state and society, and to seek to maintain distinctive identity even amid change and imitation of aspects of Western technical and social forms. Second, the Pacific Rim nations shared some special contacts with the West through unusually intense interaction with the British or through postwar dealings with the United

States. These contacts provided a certain amount of economic or military support at key junctures and also some unusual opportunities to grasp aspects of the West's technology, politics, and even popular culture. Finally, the principal Pacific Rim centers, including Japan, had been rocked by 20th-century events, which virtually forced considerable rethinking and innovation.

The shared features of the Pacific Rim were very general. The region was not unified geographically or in any other way, though growing mutual trade provided an important bond in some instances. Japan was far more advanced industrially than the rest of the Pacific Rim. Political structures and diplomatic and military contexts varied considerably. The apparent similarities of Pacific Rim nations might therefore prove temporary. Certainly, even in the short run, there was substantial mutual rivalry, most obviously in the economic competition between Japan and Korea, exacerbated by mutual memories of Japanese occupation.

At least for an important moment in the later 20th century, however, the emergence of the Pacific Rim nations involved important innovations both in the cultural and political maps of eastern Asia, newly divided between Communist and other, and in the economic map of the world as a whole. The Pacific Rim, headed by Japan but joined by the self-sustaining industrializations achieved elsewhere, provided the clearest challenge to the West's long international economic leadership. Though not wedded to commensurate military process, the Pacific Rim's economic surge might foreshadow wider international influence later on, as cultural forms and values, for example, begin spreading both ways instead of primarily mainly west to east. And what of China, and possibly Vietnam, where different issues dominated much of the 20th century but where many features were shared or could be resurrected that would mesh with the factors responsible for Pacific Rim dynamism? As China experimented with new economic forms in the late 1970s and early 1980s, many observers wondered if this Asian giant, or at least its coastal cities, would soon join in the Pacific Rim ascendancy. What will happen, for example, when Hong Kong is rejoined to China in 1997, assuming the Communist regime keeps its pledge to give the city-state considerable latitude? Would this encourage more general Chinese adaptation to a more mixed economic structure that in turn could propel more rapid economic growth?

Certainly the success of the Pacific Rim states after World War II raised substantial questions about the contrast to China, questions that linked history to present patterns. Confucian traditions were clearly not only compatible with rapid industrial advance but also could contribute to it. Chinese zest for commerce showed directly in Hong Kong, Taiwan, and Singapore. Huge population pressure and a long period of foreign exploitation did not hold South Korea back. Was eastern Asia durably divided between industrial states and societies that, although changing, remained largely agricultural, or between non-Communist and Communist? Here is a key question for Hong Kong as it prepares to accept Chinese rule in 1997. And here is a larger question for the future, where recent experience and long-term tradition suggest different answers.

Ongoing evolution within the Pacific Rim states and the expansion of Pacific Rim dynamism to include such nations as Malaysia raises a final set of questions. Both Japan and South Korea continue to express tension between change and considerable imitation of Western forms on the one hand and periodic traditionalist-nationalist reactions on the other. Usually, to be sure, a compromise has prevailed that maintains distinctive social forms without preventing rapid change. Japan's interwar experience, as well as some of the political frustrations visible in South Korea late in the 1980s, remind us that adaptive compromise might not always be successful.

Even without these speculations for the future, the entry of the Pacific Rim into the mainstream of international trade represented a vital new development both for the region and for the world economy. Unsupported by military might after World War II and not joined as yet by any missionary culture of the sort that helped propel the Arabs or western Europeans in the past, the rise of the Pacific Rim was an unusual development in world history, quite apart from its contrast with the region's substantial isolation in earlier eras. It is not surprising that it provokes questions about a wider ultimate international role. If a choice has to be made for the next internationally dominant region—and it is not clear that it is sensible to project a choice in the early 1990s—eastern Asia seems the most obvious single candidate.

FURTHER READINGS

The best account of contemporary Japanese society and politics is E. O. Reischauer's *The Japanese* (1988). For a recent history, see M. Howe's *Modern Japan: A*

Historical Survey (1986). On the economy, consult H. Patrick and H. Rosovsky's *Asia's New Giant: How the Japanese Economy Works* (1976); E. F. Vogel's *Japan as Number One: Lessons for America* (1979); and K. Ohkawa and H. Rosovsky's *Japanese Economic Growth: Trend Acceleration in the Twentieth Century* (1973).

Several novels and literary collections are accessible and useful. J. Tanizaki's *The Makioka Sisters* (1957) deals with a merchant family in the 1930s; see also H. Hibbett, ed., *Contemporary Japanese Literature: An Anthology of Fiction, Film and Other Writing Since 1945* (1977). An important study of change, focusing on postwar rural society, is G. Bernstein's *Haruko's World: A Japanese Farm Woman and Her Community* (1983). Another complex 20th-century topic is assessed in R. Storry's *The Double Patriots: A Story of Japanese Nationalism* (1973).

On the Pacific Rim concept and its implications in terms of the world economy, see David Aikman's *Pacific Rim: Area of Change, Area of Opportunity* (1986); Philip West et al., eds., *Pacific Rim and the Western World: Strategic, Economic and Cultural Perspectives* (1987); Stephen Haggard and Chung-in Moon's *Pacific Dynamics: The International Politics of Industrial Change* (1988); Ronald A. Morse et al., *Pacific Basin: Concept and Challenge* (1986); and Staffan B. Linder's *Pacific Century: Economic and Political Consequences of Asian-Pacific Dynamism* (1986).

Excellent introductions to recent Korean history are Bruce Cumings's *The Two Koreas* (1984) and David Rees's *A Short History of Modern Korea* (1988). A variety of special topics are addressed in Marshall R. Pihl, ed., *Listening to Korea* (1973). See also David Steinberg's *The Republic of Korea: Economic Transformation and Social Change* (1989), Paul Kuznets's *Economic Growth and Structure in the Republic of Korea* (1977), and Dennis McNamara's *The Colonial Origins of Korean Enterprise 1910–1945* (1990).

For a fascinating exploration of cultural change and continuity in Taiwan around issues in health and medicine, see Arthur Kleinman's *Patients and Healers in the Context of Culture* (1979). On Singapore, Janet W. Salaff's *State and Family in Singapore* (1988) is an excellent study; see also R. N. Kearney, ed., *Politics and Modernization in South and Southeast Asia* (1975).

1947 India and
Pakistan achieve
independence

1948 First Arab-Israeli War; Afrikaner
Nationalist party to power in South
Africa; beginnings of apartheid legislation

1949 Hassan al-Banna assassinated in Egypt

1951 India's first Five-Year Plan for
economic development launched

1952 Farouk and khedival regime overthrown
in Egypt; Nasser and Free Officers to power

1955 Bandung Conference; beginning of Non-Aligned movement

1956 Abortive British-French intervention in Suez

1958 South Africa completely
independent of Great Britain

1960 Sharpeville shootings
in South Africa

1966 Nkrumah over-
thrown by a military
coup in Ghana

1967 Six-Day War
between Israel and
the Arabs

1966–1970 Biafran se-
cessionist war in Nigeria

Africa and Asia in the Era of Independence

12

INTRODUCTION.   In *The Battle of Algiers*, Gillo Pontecorvo's moving film on the struggle for independence in Algeria, one member of the high command of the National Liberation Front (FLN) reflects on the nature of the revolutionary struggle in a conversation with a young guerrilla fighter, the film's protagonist. When the young man expresses his anxieties about the outcome of the general strike then taking place in the city of Algiers, the thoughtful leader of the FLN seeks to put the immediate crisis in a larger perspective. Revolutions, he muses, are difficult to get going and even more difficult to sustain. But the real test, he concludes, will come when the revolutionary struggle has been successfully concluded, when the makers of the movement must assume power and face the greatest challenges of all—those involved in building viable nations and prosperous societies for peoples disoriented and deprived by decades or in many cases centuries of colonial rule.

These reflections on the process of decolonization anticipated the experience of the peoples in the new nations carved out of the ruins of the European colonial empires. Once the European colonizers had withdrawn and the initial euphoria of freedom had begun to wear off, Western-educated nationalist leaders were forced to confront the sobering realities of the fragile state structures and underdeveloped economies they had inherited. With the common European enemy gone, the deep divisions among the various ethnic and religious groups that had been thrown uneasily together in the postcolonial states became more and more apparent and disruptive. The Western-educated leaders soon realized how a few people had genuinely committed themselves to the nationalist identity and goals that had formed the

---

1970s Peak period for the OPEC cartel

1972 Bangladesh becomes an independent nation

1973 Third Arab-Israeli War

1971 Bangladesh revolt against West Pakistan; Indo-Pakistani War

1980s AIDs reaches epidemic proportions in parts of central and eastern Africa

1980–1988 Iran-Iraq War

1979 Shah of Iran overthrown; Khomaini-led Islamic republic declared

1989 De Klerk charts a path of peaceful reform in South Africa

1991 First Gulf War

1992–1993 Political collapse and famine in Somalia; U.S./U.N. intervention in Somalia

1990 Nelson Mandela released from prison; Iraqi invasion of Kuwait

1991 Naguib Mahfouz wins the Nobel Prize for literature

1993 U.N. sponsored elections in Cambodia

backbone of the drives for independence. They were often startled by how shallow loyalty to a common nation was, even among the Westernized elite classes that had led the decolonization struggle.

The leaders of the new nations found their efforts to spur economic growth constricted by concessions made to the departing colonizers and the very nature of the international economy, in which the terms of investment and trade heavily favored the industrialized nations. They saw their ambitious schemes to improve living standards among formerly colonized peoples frustrated by a shortage of expertise and resources and by population growth rates that quickly ate up whatever modest advances could be made. Many of the nationalist leaders despaired as hungry peasants flocked to the rapidly growing cities, where little employment was available, and bad weather and market reverses resulted in famines and mounting debts that left their nations even more at the mercy of the industrialized world. The leaders of the new nations lamented the continuing intellectual and cultural dependence of their societies on the United States and Western Europe. This dependence was reflected in all manner of things, from the architecture of African and Asian cities and the literary output of their novelists, playwrights, and movie directors to university curricula and the pop music and blue jeans the children of the elite classes consumed as avidly as their counterparts in the West.

Increasing poverty, official corruption, and a growing concern for the breakdown of traditional culture and social values produced widespread social unrest and often violence among various religious and ethnic groups. Dissent and civil disturbances called into question the leadership abilities of nationalist politicians who had won independence but floundered as heads of new nations. Challenges to the existing order came from both Communist parties on the left and religious revivalist movements on the right. In order to remain in power and to ensure that they would be able to realize their visions of economic and social development in the postcolonial era, Western-educated nationalist leaders adopted various strategies to beat back these threats. These strategies ranged from attempts by leaders, such as Sukarno of Indonesia and Nkrumah of Ghana to establish themselves as charismatic strongmen at the head of unopposed populist movements to the state-directed reform and development programs nurtured by Nehru in India, where civil rights and democracy were preserved. As we shall see, these strategies met with widely varying degrees of success. The price for failure was often a fall from power

and at times the execution of former nationalist heroes. In many instances they were replaced by military commanders who assumed dictatorial powers, forcibly silenced dissent, and suppressed interethnic and religious rivalries. In a limited number of cases the champions of religious revival and resistance to Western influences, most notably those in Iran, swept moderate reformers and dictators from power.

The many nations carved out of the colonial empires were invariably lumped together as members of the Third World. This grouping of what were very diverse societies and political systems reflected the common dilemmas these nations had to face. The new nations became contested ground between the wealthy First World of the West and Japan and the militant and aspiring states of the Second World, the Communist bloc, which was united in the years right after the war behind the Soviet Union and the People's Republic of China. The newly independent states of Africa and Asia also shared a common experience of colonization and the struggle for freedom, and they came to independence with underdeveloped economies and consequently high levels of poverty, illiteracy, and population growth.

Though most of the Latin American countries have often been included in the Third World category, they had won their political independence much earlier. Because their struggles for development and social justice are discussed in some depth in other chapters, this chapter focuses on responses to these challenges in the newly independent states of Asia and Africa. In some cases similar social and economic problems have produced comparable responses, but it is important to keep in mind the great diversity of Third World societies—a diversity grounded in the widely varying precolonial histories and colonial experiences of the African and Asian peoples. For that reason, after first surveying the common challenges that faced Third World societies in the early independence era, we will then consider the varying solutions leaders of African and Asian nations devised to deal with the urgent and complex problems they faced.

❀ THE CHALLENGES OF INDEPENDENCE

The nationalist movements that won independence for most of the peoples of Africa and Asia usually involved some degree of mass mobilization. Peasants and working-class townspeople, who hitherto had little voice in politics beyond their village boundaries or local labor associations, were drawn into political contests that toppled empires and established new nations. To win the support of these groups, nationalist leaders promised them jobs, civil rights, and equality once independence was won. The leaders of many nationalist movements nurtured visions of postindependence utopias in the minds of their followers. They were told that once the Europeans, who monopolized the best jobs, were driven away and their exploitive hold on the economies of colonized peoples ended, there would be enough to give everyone a good life.

Unfortunately, the realities of the postindependence situation in virtually all new African and Asian nations made it impossible for nationalist leaders to fulfill the expectations they had aroused among their followers and in varying degrees the colonized populace at large. Even with the Europeans gone and terms of economic exchange with more developed countries somewhat improved, there was simply not enough to go around. Thus the socialist-inspired ideologies that had often been embraced by nationalist leaders and propagated to their followers proved misleading. The problem was not just that goods and services were unequally distributed, leaving

some people rich and the majority poor. Rather, there were not sufficient resources to take care of everybody, even if it had been possible to distribute them equitably.

When utopia failed to materialize, personal rivalries and long-standing divisions among classes and ethnic groups, which had been more or less successfully muted by the common struggle against the alien colonizers, resurfaced or intensified. In almost all the new states these rivalries and differences became dominant features of political life. They produced political instability and often threatened the viability of Third World nations. They also consumed resources that might otherwise have been devoted to economic development and blocked—in the name of the defense of subnational interests—measures designed to build more viable and prosperous states. Absorbed by the task of just holding their new nations together, African and Asian politicians neglected problems, such as soaring population increases, uncontrolled urban growth, rural landlessness, and ecological deterioration, that soon loomed as just as great a threat as political instability to their young nations.

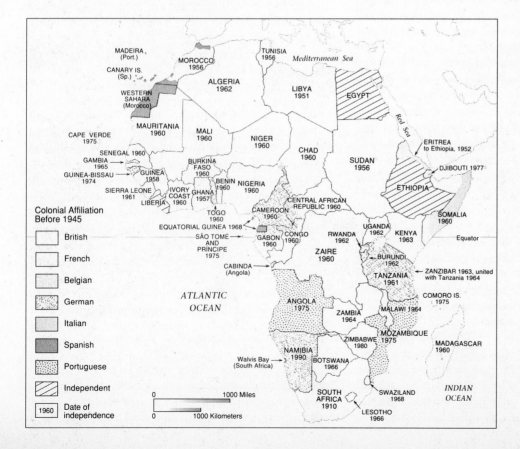

Colonial Division of Africa and the Emergence of New Nations

BUILDING NATIONS AND NATIONAL IDENTITIES

A pernicious precedent was set at the very beginning of the decolonization process. Jinnah's resolve to form a separate Muslim nation could not be broken by Gandhi, the British, or the compromises offered by Congress Party politicians; in 1947 India became two hostile nations rather than a unified state in which Hindus, Muslims, Sikhs, and other religious groups could live together in peace. The communal rivalries and centuries-old hatred and mistrust that surfaced in the era of decolonization in India could be found in equal or even greater measure in virtually all the colonies that made up the European overseas empires. The way the empires had been built and their boundaries demarcated made this inevitable. European generals conquered and European explorers staked out claims to territories in ways that rarely, if ever, took into account the interests or history of the peoples who occupied these lands. In most colonies the pattern that had been set in India prevailed. Peoples who had traditionally lived in separate states and developed very different cultures were thrown together under the same colonial regime. India at least was bound by common institutions, such as the caste system, and Hindus and Muslims had lived together there for centuries before the British came.

In Africa, which was grabbed by the rival European powers in much greater haste, peoples who had little in common except wars over slaves and territory found themselves thrown together as subjects of alien colonizers. As Lord Salisbury, one of the most prominent late-19th-century champions of imperialist expansion, confessed in the 1890s, the conquerors knew next to nothing about the lands they divided up around the green-felt tables at conferences in Berlin, Paris, and other European capitals:

> We have been engaged in drawing lines upon maps where no white man's foot ever trod; we have been giving away mountains and rivers and lakes to each other [Europeans] only hindered by the small impediment that we never knew exactly where the mountains and rivers and lakes were. . . .

If they could not locate the mountains and rivers, European diplomats could hardly have been expected to know much about the peoples who lived on or along them. As a consequence the division of Africa was completely arbitrary. Colonial boundaries cut the Yoruba of

West Africa and the Somalis of the horn of East Africa apart, and they tossed together tens, sometimes hundreds, of very different—often hostile—African peoples. The roads and railways the colonizers built, the marketing systems they established, and the educational policies they pursued all hardened the unnatural boundaries and divisions established in the decades of the late 19th century. It was these artificial units, these motley combinations of peoples that defied the logic of history and cultural affinity, that African nationalist leaders had to try to meld into nations in the decades after World War II.

In virtually all the new states that have emerged from the European colonial empires, ethnic rivalries and communal violence have been endemic. In some cases the unnatural creations of the colonizers did not long survive the transfer of power to indigenous leaders. The most spectacular collapse of a new state came in Pakistan, the unwieldy patchwork of a nation the British had thrown together at the last minute in 1947 to satisfy Jinnah's demands for majority rule in Muslim areas of the Indian subcontinent. A glance at the map revealed the vulnerability of Pakistan; split into two parts, West and East Pakistan were separated by more than 1000 miles of hostile Indian territory. Some attention to the history of the two halves that made up Pakistan would have made clear the problems in store.

Bengal in the east was a region shaped by the tropical monsoons. Its language was akin to Hindi, one of the official languages of India; it was written in a script derived from ancient Sanskrit, the sacred language of the Hindus. The Muslim Bengalis in East Pakistan followed a less fundamentalist, much more Hindu-influenced variant of the Islamic faith than the Muslim peoples of the other half of Pakistan far to the west. The Bengalis were physically closer to the peoples of south India and parts of Southeast Asia than the lighter-skinned, taller peoples of West Pakistan. The latter, molded by the hard, dry climate of the regions they inhabited, were very different from the Bengalis. Their main language was Urdu, written in a script derived from Persian; they were more likely to embrace Islamic fundamentalism, more resistant to Hindu influences. Many traced their descent from the Muslim peoples who had invaded the Indian subcontinent a millennium earlier. This heritage contrasted sharply with that of the Bengalis, most of whom descended from Hindu and Buddhist peoples who had converted to Islam during the early centuries after the Muslims' arrival. Thus even the Islamic religion that the people of the two halves of Pakistan shared and that had been responsible for their being combined in

The contrasting lush tropical and arid semidesert environments of East and West Pakistan underscore the great differences between the two areas—differences that eventually led to the violent breakaway of East Pakistan and the creation of the nation of Bangladesh.

the same country in the first place differed significantly from west to east.

Though efforts had been made to bridge differences between the two Pakistans and especially to ensure that political power was shared equally between two regions, the politicians and military leaders of the West soon gained the upper hand. Though the export of jute and other crops from the East brought in most of the foreign currency Pakistan earned, the West absorbed a lion's share of state revenues, especially those spent on economic development schemes. West Pakistanis held a far greater portion of positions at the upper levels of the national bureaucracy and in the military forces than they warranted in view of the larger population in East Pakistan. Under a succession of military leaders in the 1960s, West Pakistanis sought to limit civil liberties in and further curtail the political influence of East Pakistanis. By the 1970s the heavy-handed, often outright arrogant policy of the West Pakistanis had generated resistance movements in East Pakistan. A brutal attempt in 1971 by the military strongman Yahya Khan to crush

this resistance triggered an all-out revolt in East Pakistan against West Pakistani dominance. Backed by the Indians, always eager to weaken their Pakistani rivals, the East Pakistanis won a war of secession that led to the establishment of the independent nation of Bangladesh in 1972.

At various points in their history, most of the new nations of Africa and Southeast Asia have been threatened by similar secessionist movements. In fact, India, which relished the chance to contribute to the breakup of Pakistan, has itself been repeatedly threatened by civil strife among various linguistic, religious, and ethnic groups. At the present time Sikh guerrillas carry on a violent campaign for separation in the north, and the Indian government has been forced to intervene militarily in the violent struggle among ethnic and religious groups in Sri Lanka (Ceylon), its neighbor to the south.

In Africa, where there was often even less of a common historical and cultural basis on which to build nationalism than in South or Southeast Asia, separatist movements have been a prominent feature of the

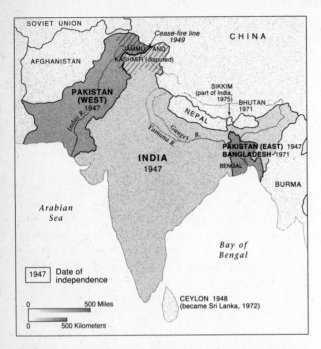

The Partition of South Asia: The Formation of India, Pakistan, Bangladesh, and Sri Lanka

political life of new states. Secessionist movements currently rage from Morocco in the northwest to Ethiopia in the east and Angola in the south. Civil wars, such as the current struggle of the non-Muslim peoples of the southern Sudan against the Muslim rulers from the northern parts of that country, have also abounded. Thus far none of the secessionist movements has succeeded, though that of the Ibo peoples of eastern Nigeria, who proclaimed an independent state of Biafra in 1967, led to three years of bloody warfare in Africa's most populous nation.

Though African leaders have been acutely aware of the injustices and persecutions of minority groups that have often precipitated these conflicts, none has seriously suggested altering the unnatural boundaries established in the colonial era. The reverse, in fact, is the case. These divisions have become sacrosanct, because each African leader fears that a successful secession movement in another country or a redrawing of boundaries elsewhere could provide precedents for dissident minorities in their own country or for neighboring leaders to claim boundary adjustments that would work to their disadvantage.

In all cases the artificial nature of the new nations of the Third World has proved costly. In addition to inter-

nal divisions, boundary disputes between newly independent nations have often led to border clashes and on a number of occasions to open warfare. India and Pakistan have fought three such wars since 1947. Iraq's Saddam Hussein justified his 1990 annexation of Kuwait with the argument that the tiny, oil-rich Arab "sheikhdom" was an artificial creation of the British colonizers, who had carved out land that had historically been part of Iraq. These disputes have done much to confirm the West's view of the Third World as a region of unrest and instability. But it is important to remember that "developed" countries, such as the United States, took decades and numerous boundary disputes (with, for example, the British over Canada) and outright wars, such as that with Mexico, to reach their current size and contours.

Democracy has often been one of the main victims of the tensions among rival ethnic groups in African and

In the late 1960s, posters and photos, such as this one graphically depicting the ravages of the Nigerian civil war, served as reminders of the artificiality and instability of the new states that had been hastily carved out of the European colonial empires.

Asian nations and threats from external neighbors. Politicians in virtually all the new states have been quick to play on ethnic and religious loyalties as well as fears to win votes. The result has been that freely elected legislatures have often been dominated by parties representing these special interests. Suspicions that those in power were favoring their own or allied groups led to endless bickering and stalemated national legislatures, which became tempting targets for the coup attempts of military strongmen. One of the more persuasive reasons these usurpers have given for dictatorial rule was the need to contain communal conflict, which had only been whipped up by democratic election campaigns. Ironically, this was one of the key rationales given by the European colonizers to justify the continuation of colonial rule. The threats from rival ethnic and religious groups felt by those in power have also contributed to exorbitant military spending by Asian and African leaders—spending that their impoverished societies can rarely afford. In countries where civil wars have occurred, such as Ethiopia, Mozambique, and Angola, economic development has ground to a virtual standstill, and disease and famine have reduced their peoples to levels of misery and despair that even the most well-funded international agencies often can do little to alleviate.

THE POPULATION BOMB

The nationalist leaders who led the Third World peoples to independence had firmly committed themselves to promoting rapid economic development once colonial restraints were removed. In keeping with their Western-educated backgrounds, most of these leaders envisioned their nations following the path of industrialization that had brought national prosperity and international power to much of western Europe and the United States. This course of development was also fostered by representatives of the Soviet bloc, who had emphasized heavy industry in their state-directed drives to "modernize" their backward economies and societies. Of the many barriers to the rapid economic breakthroughs Third World leaders hoped for, the most formidable and persistent were the spiraling increases of population that often overwhelmed whatever economic advances the peoples of the new nations managed to make.

Factors facilitating sustained population increases in already quite densely populated areas of Asia and Africa had begun to take effect even before the era of high colonialism. Food crops, mostly from the New World,

had contributed to dramatic population growth in China and India as early as the 17th century. They also helped sustain high levels of population in the Niger delta in West Africa, despite heavy losses of both males and females as a result of the slave trade. The coming of colonial rule reinforced these upward trends in a number of ways. It ended local warfare that had caused population losses and, perhaps more significantly, had indirectly promoted the spread of epidemic diseases and famine. The new railroad and steamship links the colonizers established in order to foster the spread of the market economy also cut down on regional famines that had been a major check against sustained population increase since ancient times. Large amounts of food could now be shipped from areas where harvests were good to those where drought or floods threatened the local inhabitants with starvation.

With war and famine—two of the main checks that Malthus and others had identified as major barriers to population increase—much reduced, growth began to speed up, particularly in areas, such as India and Java, that had been under European control for decades. The death rate declined, but the birthrate remained much the same, leaving more and more sizable net increases. Improved hygiene and medical treatment played little part in this rise until the first decades of the 20th century. From that time efforts to eradicate tropical diseases and global scourges, such as smallpox, and to improve sewage systems and purify drinking water have given further impetus to sharp upswings in population, particularly in sub-Saharan Africa.

Virtually all the leaders of the emerging Third World nations headed states in which the population was increasing at unprecedented levels. This increase continued in the early years of independence. In much of Asia it has begun to level off in recent decades. But in most African populations growth continues at very high rates. In some cases, most notably South Asia, rather moderate growth rates have produced prodigious total populations because they were adding to an already large base. As a result, in the 1970s population experts predicted that if current rates continued, South Asia's population of more than 600 million would more than double by the year 2000. With more than one billion people by the late 1980s, the prophecy appears well on the way to fulfillment.

In Africa, by contrast, which began with relatively low population levels, given its large land area, very high birthrates and diminished mortality rates have resulted in population increases of alarming proportions in recent decades. The magnitude of this increase can be envisioned if one considers the predictions of some population experts that, if present growth rates continue, by the middle of the next century Nigeria will have a population equal to that of present-day China, and Kenya will have a population double that of the United States in the mid-1980s. Some indication of the size of the human calamities that are likely to result is suggested by the fact that the 400 million people of Africa are supported by a continental economy with a productive capacity equal to just six percent of the present U.S. economy, or roughly equal to that of the state of Illinois.

On the face of it the conquest of the Malthusian checks to sustained population growth throughout much of human history—war, disease, and famine—was one of the great achievements of European colonial regimes. It was certainly an accomplishment that colonial officials never tired of citing in defense of the perpetuation of European dominance. But another side of the colonial legacy rendered this increase a trap in which most of the Third World nations were soon to find themselves caught. The European policy of limiting industrialization in their colonial dependencies meant that one of the key ways by which Europe had met its own population boom in the 19th and early 20th centuries was not available to the new nations of the Third World. They lacked the factories to employ the exploding population that moved to the cities from the rural areas, as well as the technology to produce the necessities of life for more and more people. Unlike their European and U.S. counterparts, the Third World nations found it difficult to draw food and mineral resources from the rest of the world to feed their proliferating populations. In fact, these were the very things the colonized peoples had been set up to sell to the industrialized countries. Even in India, where impressive advances in industrialization were made in the postcolonial era, gains in productivity were rapidly swallowed up by the population explosion.

In most Third World countries there has been considerable resistance to birth control efforts aimed at bringing runaway population growth in check. Some of this resistance is linked to deeply entrenched social patterns and religious beliefs. In many Third World societies procreation is seen as a key marker of male virility, and the capacity to bear children, preferably male children, continues to be critical to the social standing of adult women. In some cases resistance to birth control is linked to specific cultural norms. Hindus, for example, believe that a deceased man's soul cannot begin the cycle of rebirth until his eldest son has performed special ceremonies over his

funeral pyre. This belief both increases the already considerable pressure on Indian women to have children and encourages families to have several sons in order to ensure that at least one survives the father.

In Africa children are seen as indispensable additions to the lineage—the extended network of relatives (and deceased ancestors) that, much more than the nuclear family, makes up the core social group over much of the subcontinent. As in India, sons are essential for, among other things, the continuation of the patrilineal family line and the performance of burial and ancestral rites. Their key roles in agricultural production and marketing make female offspring more highly valued in Africa than in many Asian societies, where high dowries and occupational restrictions limit their contribution to family welfare.

Before the 20th century the high incidence of stillbirths and high rates of infant mortality more generally meant that mothers could expect to lose many of the children to whom they gave birth—10 or 12 deaths of 15 or 16 children conceived was not unheard of. Beyond the obvious psychological scars left by these high death rates, they also fostered the conviction that it was necessary to have many children to ensure that some would outlive the parents. In societies where welfare systems and old-age pensions were meager or unknown, surviving children took on special urgency because they were the only ones who would care for their parents once they could no longer work for themselves. The persistence of these attitudes in recent decades, when medical advances have greatly reduced infant mortality, has been a major factor contributing to soaring population growth.

In the early decades after independence many Third World leaders were deeply opposed to state measures to promote family planning and birth control. Some saw these as Western attempts to meddle in their internal affairs; others proudly declared that the socialist societies they were building would be able to take care of the additional population. As it has become increasingly clear that excessive population increase renders significant economic advances impossible, many Third World leaders have begun to reassess their earlier attitudes toward birth control. A particular cause for alarm is the fact that in many Third World countries a high percentage of the population is under the age of 15 (as high as 40 percent in some countries) and thus dependent on others for support. But even for those who now wish to actively promote family planning, the obstacles are staggering. In addition to cultural and social factors fostering resistance, Third World leaders often find that they lack sufficient resources and the educated personnel required to make these programs effective. High rates of illiteracy, particularly among women, need to be overcome, but education is expensive. Perhaps no form of financial and technical assistance from the industrialized to the developing world will be as critical in the coming decades as that devoted to family planning to defuse the global population bomb.

PARASITIC CITIES AND ENDANGERED ECOSYSTEMS

As population increase in the rural areas of Third World countries outstripped the land and employment opportunities available to the peasantry, mass migrations to urban areas ensued. The massive movement of population from overcrowded villages to the cities was one of the most dramatic developments in the postcolonial history of most Third World nations. Ambitious youths and the rural poor crowded into port centers and capital cities in search of jobs and a chance to win the "good life" that the big hotels and restaurants and the neon lights of the city center appeared to offer to all comers. But because Third World cities lacked the rapidly expanding industrial sectors that had made possible the absorption (with considerable difficulty) of a similar migrant influx earlier in the West, they were often dead ends for migrants from the rural areas. There were few jobs, and heavy competition for these ensured that wages would remain low for most workers. The growing numbers of underemployed or unemployed turned to street vending, scavenging, huckstering, begging, or petty crime to survive. The idleness and despair of the urban underclass has been a prominent theme in the novels and plays of Third World writers, such as Mochtar Lubis of Indonesia, Cyprian Ekwensi of Nigeria, and V. S. Naipaul, who was born of Indian parents in the Caribbean and has written about many Third World countries.

In the independence era the urban poor have become a volatile factor in the political struggles of the elite, willing for a price to cheer on one contender or jeer down another, ready to riot and loot in times of government crisis. In deeply divided societies the poor working-class or idle youths of the urban areas have often formed the shock troops in communal clashes among rival ethnic and religious groups. Fear of outbursts by urban "mobs" has also forced Third World regimes to expend considerable portions of their scarce resources to subsidize and thus keep low the price of staple foods, such as bread, and other necessities.

The great and sudden influx of population from the rural areas to cities without the jobs or infrastructure to support them has greatly skewed urban growth in the Third World. Within decades Asian cities have become some of the largest in the world, and African urban areas have sprawled far beyond their modest limits of colonial times. The wealth of the glitzy hotel and high-rise-dominated enclaves of the upper- and middle-class minorities in Third World societies contrasts disturbingly with the poverty of the vast slums that stretch in all directions from the city centers. Little or no planning was possible for the slum quarters that expanded as squatters erected makeshift shelters wherever open land or decrepit buildings could be found. Originally, most of the slum areas lacked electricity, running water, or even the most elementary sewage facilities. As shanties were gradually converted into ramshackle dwellings, many Third World governments scrapped plans to level slum settlements and sought instead to provide them with some semblance of electrical and sanitary systems. As an increasing number of development specialists have reluctantly concluded, slums often provide the only housing urban dwellers are likely to find for some time to come. Only substantially higher levels of economic growth will give most Third World nations the resources to replace them with planned housing at some future date.

These conditions have burdened most Third World societies with parasitic cities heavily dependent for survival on food and resources drawn from their own countryside or from abroad. In contrast to the cities of western Europe and North America—even during the decades of rapid urban expansion in the 19th century—few Third World cities have had the manufacturing base required to generate growth in their surrounding regions or the nation as a whole. They take from the already impoverished countryside but are able to give little in return, though in the more industrialized societies of the Third World, such as India, cement and steel for dam and road construction and farm implements have made some contribution to rural development. Urban dependence on the countryside further stretches the already overextended resources of the rural areas.

Rural overpopulation in the decades after independence has led to the depletion of soils in many areas that have been worked for centuries or millennia. It has also resulted in an alarming rate of deforestation throughout the Third World, as peasant villagers cut trees for fuel or to clear land for farming and for their flocks. Deforestation and overgrazing not only pose major threats to the wild animal life, such as tigers and elephants, but also

In the urbanized areas of the Third World the contrast between the wealth of the few and the poverty of the majority is starkly revealed by the juxtaposition of the high-rise apartments of the affluent middle classes and the ramshackle shantytowns of the urban poor.

upset the balance in fragile tropical ecosystems, producing further soil depletion and erosion and encouraging desertification. This environmental degradation is intensified by industrial pollution, both from developed countries and Third World nations. Though the industrial sectors in the latter are generally small, pollution tends to be proportionally greater than in the developed world because Third World nations rarely have the means to afford the antipollution technology introduced in Western Europe, Japan, and North America.

ANALYSIS
WOMEN AND THE STRUGGLE TO BUILD NEW SOCIETIES IN THE THIRD WORLD

The example of both the Western democracies and the Communist republics of Eastern Europe, where women had won the right to vote in the middle decades of the 20th century, encouraged the founders of the nations of the Third World to write female suffrage into their constitutions. The very active part women played in many nationalist struggles was perhaps even more critical to their gaining the right to vote and run for political office. Female activism also produced some semblance of equality in terms of legal rights, education, and occupational opportunities under the laws of many new nations.

The equality that was proclaimed on paper, however, often bore little resemblance to the rights that the great majority of African and Asian women could exercise or had little bearing on the conditions under which they lived their daily lives. Despite the media attention given to Third World women who have emerged as national leaders, such as Indira Gandhi, Corazon Aquino, and Benazir Bhutto, political life in most African and Asian countries continues to be dominated by males. The overwhelming majority of elected officials and government administrators, particularly at the upper levels of state bureaucracies, are males. Because they are usually less well educated than their husbands, women in societies where genuine elections are held often do not exercise their right to vote, or they simply vote for the party and candidates favored by their spouses. In many Third World societies in which coups or one-party dominance have put an end to democratic politics, female suffrage is meaningless.

Even the rise to power of such women as Indira Gandhi, who proved to be one of the most resolute and powerful of all Third World leaders, is deceptive. In every case female heads of state in the Third World entered politics and initially won political support because they were connected to powerful males. Indira Gandhi was the daughter of Jawaharlal Nehru, India's first prime minister; Corazon Aquino's husband was the martyred leader of the Filipino opposition to Ferdinand Marcos; and Benazir Bhutto's father was a domineering Pakistani prime minister who had been toppled by a military coup and executed in the late 1970s. Lacking these sorts of connections, the vast majority of Third World women have been at best relegated to peripheral political positions; at worst they are allowed no participation in the political process whatsoever.

The limited real gains made by Third World women in the political sphere are paralleled by the second-class position to which most are consigned in many societies. In some respects their handicaps are comparable to those that constrict women in the industrialized democracies and Communist nations. But the obstacles to female self-fulfillment, and in many cases just survival, in Third World societies are usually much more blatant and fundamental than the child-rearing patterns, educational and job discrimination, and other sexist restrictions women have to contend with in developed societies. The fact that early marriage ages for women and large families are still the norm in most Third World societies means that women spend their youthful and middle-age years having children. There is little time to think of higher education or a career.

In many Third World societies large numbers of women are still confined to the home, a trend that has been reinforced by the spread of religious fundamentalism in recent decades. Even in India, which is officially a secular state, it was estimated that decades after independence in 1947, up to 20 percent of all women were still in *purdah,* or domestic seclusion. In Islamic lands the proportion of women confined to the home is often a good deal higher. This trend has not been followed in most of sub-Saharan Africa, where women were traditionally more independent and free to follow occupations outside the home. It has also been resisted by women of the middle and elite classes in many Third World countries, who have had the resources to pursue higher education and professional careers. As the experience of the Iranian revolution suggests, "liberated" women from these classes are likely to lose these outlets in areas where religious fundamentalism takes hold.

Because of the low level of sanitation in many Third World communities and food scarcity, all but upper-class women experience endemic anxiety regarding such basic issues as sufficient and nutritional meals for their hungry children and their susceptibility to disease. The persistence of male-centric customs directly affects the health and life expectancy of women themselves. The Indian tradition, for example, that dictates that women first serve their husbands' and sons' meals and then eat what is left has obvious disadvantages. The quantity and nutritional content of the leftovers is likely to be lower than of the original meals, and in tropical environments flies and other disease-bearing insects are more likely to have fouled the food.

The consequences of these social patterns can be quite injurious for women. In the 1970s, for example, it was estimated that perhaps 20 percent of the female population of India was malnourished and that another 30 percent had a diet that was well below accepted UN levels. In sharp contrast to the industrial societies of Japan, North America, and Europe, where women outnumber (because on the average they outlive) men, in India there are only 930 females for every 1000 males.

In most Third World societies the disadvantages women traditionally faced within the household and in terms of career opportunities were compounded by the prejudices and policies of colonial officials. Whatever education, particularly higher and technical education, that was provided was geared to males. Colonial development schemes and links to the global markets also favored males. Thus in the societies of West Africa and Southeast Asia, where women had traditionally played significant roles in farming and marketing, their position declined in the colonial era.

Traditional religious restrictions on women often remained after independence, and they lagged far behind men in the degree to which they were able to take advantage of what might have been countervailing educational and occupational opportunities. As late as 1975, for example, there were only 300,000 women in India with bachelors degrees in a total population of some 600 million. Though the highly secular property and divorce laws many new states promulgated after independence gave women much greater rights, many of these have been ignored in practice, and very often Third World women have neither the education nor the resources to exercise their legal rights. The spread of religious fundamentalism has in many cases further eroded these rights, most notably in Islamic areas, though advocates of a return to tradition often argue that such practices as veiling and the stoning of women (but not men) caught in adultery enhance the dignity and status of women. Wherever one comes down in these disputes, there is little doubt that most Third World women continue to be dominated by male family members, are much more constricted than males in terms of career opportunities, and are likely to be less well fed, educated, and healthy than males at a comparable social level.

Questions: In what ways would the persistence of some of the traditional religious beliefs of African and Asian societies, which we have discussed in earlier chapters, contribute to the limitation of women's rights and career opportunities in the Third World? Are there comparable obstacles in the religious and secular belief systems of the West? What sorts of programs and measures could be undertaken by international agencies, such as the United Nations, and Third World governments to speed the liberation of African and Asian women?   ✦

"NEOCOLONIALISM," COLD WAR RIVALRIES, AND UNDERDEVELOPMENT

Nationalist leaders' schemes to build an industrial base that would provide adequate support for the rapidly increasing populations of their new nations soon floundered amid the economic realities of the postcolonial world. Most of the nations that emerged from colonialism had little in the way of an industrial base, and their means of obtaining one were depressingly meager. In order to buy the machines and hire or train the technical experts they needed to get industrialization going, Third World countries needed to earn capital they could invest for these ends. Some funds could be accumulated by saving a portion of the state revenues collected from the peasantry. In most cases, however, there was precious little left once bureaucrats had been given their salaries, essential public works and the extension of education had been funded, and other state expenses had been met. Thus most Third World countries have relied on the sale of cash crops and minerals to earn the foreign exchange they need to finance industrialization. As their leaders soon discovered, the structure of the world market was heavily loaded against them.

The pattern of exchange promoted in the colonial era left most Third World countries dependent on the export production of two or three food or industrial crops—such as cocoa, palm oil, coffee, or jute and hemp—or minerals—such as copper, bauxite, and oil—for which there was a high demand in the industrialized economies of Europe, North America, and increasingly Japan. Since the Second World War, the prices of this sort of export—which economists call primary products—have not only fluctuated widely but also steadily declined when compared to the prices of most of the manufactured goods Third World countries usually buy from the industrialized nations. Price fluctuations have created nightmares for planners in the Third World. Revenue estimates from the sale of coffee or copper in years when the price is high are used to plan government projects for the construction of roads, factories, and dams. Market slumps can wipe out these critical funds—thereby retarding economic growth—and throw Third World countries deeply into debt. These setbacks are doubly frustrating because in order to begin industrialization, Third World countries are often forced to export precious and finite mineral resources that they themselves will require if they succeed in industrializing.

Except with oil, the leaders and planners of Third World countries have had little success in improving the terms under which they participate in the global market economy. Even the gains made by the oil cartel have tended to be confined to a select few Third World nations and to be temporary. They were also soon rolled back to a large degree by divisions among the oil-producing states. These differences, including those partly responsible for Iraq's invasion of Kuwait in 1990, have made it difficult to maintain the production quotas that were essential to the great rise in the price of oil in the mid-1970s. Third World leaders have been quite ready to blame the legacy of colonialism and what they have termed the "neocolonial" structure of the global economy for the limited returns yielded thus far by their development schemes. Though there is much truth to these accusations, they do not tell the whole story. Third World leaders and elites must also share the responsibility for the slow pace of economic development in much of the Third World. Few leaders of the new nations had the technical or scientific training to tackle the mundane but complex tasks involved in development. To some extent their deficiencies can be blamed on the low level of technical education available in most colonies. But even where it was available, as in India, the rising Western-educated classes rarely pursued it, preferring instead the training in Western languages and the humanities that opened to them well-paying careers in government, law, and business.

In addition, members of the educated classes that came to dominate the political and business life of newly independent nations often used their positions to enrich themselves and their relatives at the expense of their so-cieties as a whole. Corruption has been notoriously widespread in most of the new nations. Government controls on the import of automobiles, television sets, and stereos, which are luxury items for most of the peo-ple, have often been lax. As a result, tax revenues and ex-port earnings that could have fueled development have often gone to provide "the good life" for small minorities within Third World societies. The inability or refusal of many Third World regimes to carry out key social re-forms, such as land redistribution, which would spread the limited resources available more equitably over the whole population, has contributed significantly to the persistence of these patterns. Leaders who have defied the interests of the elite classes from which they came and pushed for sweeping reforms have often fallen vic-tim to coups and even assassination plots.

Badly strapped for investment funds and essential technology, Third World nations have often turned to international organizations, such as the World Bank and the International Monetary Fund, and the rival Great Powers for assistance. Though considerable resources for development have been generated in this way, the price for international assistance has often been high. Both the United States and the Soviet Union, as well as their allies, have normally extracted major concessions in re-turn for their aid. These have ranged from commit-ments to buy the products of and favor investors from the lending countries to entering into alliances and per-mitting military bases on the territory of the client state. Loans from international lending agencies have almost invariably been granted only after the needy nation agreed to what are called "conditionalities." These are regulations that determine how the money is to be in-vested and repaid, and they usually involve promises to undertake major "reforms" in the economy of the bor-rowing nation.

In recent years these promises have often included a commitment to remove or reduce state subsidies on food and other essential consumer items. State subsidies were designed to keep prices for staple goods at a level that the urban and rural poor—the great majority of the peo-ple in virtually all Third World countries—could afford. When carried through, subsidy reductions have fre-quently led to widespread social unrest, violent riots, and the collapse or near collapse of Third World regimes. These violent outbursts have served as dramatic re-minders both of just how precarious social stability is in much of the Third World and of how limited and per-ilous solutions to the problems facing the new states spawned by decolonization have proved.

PATHS TO DEVELOPMENT

However much the leaders of the new Third World countries might have blamed their nations' woes on the recently departed colonizers, they soon felt the need to deliver on the promises of social reform and economic well-being that had done so much to rally support to the nationalist cause. Different leaders adopted different ap-proaches, and some tried one strategy after another. De-pending on their own skills, the talents of their advisors and lieutenants, and the resources at their disposal, Third World leaders tackled the awesome task of devel-opment with varying degrees of success. Though it is obviously impossible to deal with all of these efforts at nation building and economic development in depth, we will consider the basic elements of several distinctive strategies. Discussion of each strategy will focus on a single, prominent case example, and some attempt will be made to assess the merits and drawbacks of each ap-proach. As this overview clearly reveals, though some countries have done a good deal better than others, suc-cessful overall strategies to deal with the challenges fac-ing the nations of the Third World have yet to be de-vised.

Solutions to specific problems, such as the Green Revolution in agriculture that many development ex-perts credit with averting global famine in the last two decades, have often given rise to new problems. Ways have been found to raise the living standards of some of the population of Third World nations, but these have rarely benefited the majority. Revolutionary movements aimed at genuine redistribution and the benefit of all have thus far floundered due to planning errors and in-sufficient resources. It may be too early to judge the out-comes of many development schemes, but thus far none has proved a path to the social justice and general eco-nomic development that nationalist leaders envisioned as the ultimate outcome of struggles for decolonization.

CHARISMATIC POPULISTS AND
ONE-PARTY RULE

One of the least successful responses on the part of Third World leaders who found their dreams for nation-al renewal frustrated was a retreat into authoritarian rule, which was disguised by calculated, charismatic appeals for support from the disenfranchised masses. Perhaps the career of Kwame Nkrumah, the leader of Ghana's independence movement, illustrates this pattern as well as that of any Third World politician. There can be little question that Nkrumah was genuinely committed to social reform and economic uplift for the Ghanian people during the years of his rise to the position of the first prime minister of Ghana in 1957. After assuming power, he moved vigorously to initiate programs that would translate his high aspirations for his people into reality. But his ambitious schemes for everything from universal education to industrial development soon ran into trouble. Rival political parties, some of them representing regional interests and ethnic groups long hostile to Nkrumah, repeatedly challenged his initiatives and sought to block efforts to carry out his schemes. His leftist leanings won support from the Soviet bloc but frightened away Western investors who had a good deal more capital to plow into his economy. They also led to growing hostility on the part of the United States, Great Britain, and other influential non-Communist countries. Most devastatingly, soon after independence the price of cocoa, by far Ghana's largest export crop, began to fall sharply. Tens of thousands of Ghanaian cocoa farmers were hard hit, and the resources for Nkrumah's development schemes suddenly dried up.

Nkrumah's response to these growing problems was increasingly dictatorial. He refused to give up or cut back on his development plans. As a result most failed miserably due to lack of key supplies and to official mismanagement. In the early 1960s he forcibly crushed all political opposition by banning rival parties and jailing other political leaders. He assumed dictatorial powers and ruled through functionaries in his own Convention Peoples Party.

Nkrumah also sought to hold on to the loyalty of the masses and mobilize their energies by highly stage-managed "events" and the manipulation of largely invented symbols and traditions that were said to be derived from Ghana's past history. Thus he sought to justify his policies and leadership style with references to a uniquely African brand of socialism and the need to revive African traditions and African civilization. Even before independence he had taken to wearing the traditional garb of the Ghanaian elite. The very name of Ghana, which Nkrumah himself had proposed for the new nation that emerged from the former Gold Coast colony, had been taken from an ancient African kingdom that had been centered much farther to the north and had little to do with the peoples of the Gold Coast.

Many monumental statues of Kwame Nkrumah rose in the towns and villages of Ghana as he attempted to cover the failure of his socialist-inspired development programs with dictatorial rule and self-glorification.

Nkrumah went about the country giving fiery speeches, dedicating monuments to the "revolution," which often consisted of giant statues of himself, and taking a prominent role in the nonaligned movement that was then sweeping the Third World. As the French journalist Jean Lacouture reported in the mid-1960s, Nkrumah's posturing had become a substitute for his failed development schemes. His followers' adulation knew no bounds. Members of his captive parliament compared him to Confucius, Muhammad, Shakespeare, and Napoleon and predicted that his birthplace would serve as a "Mecca" for all of Africa's statesmen. But his suppression of all opposition and his growing ties to the Communist party, coupled with the rapid deterioration of the Ghanaian economy, increased his enemies, who laid low and waited for a chance to strike. That chance came early in 1966 when Nkrumah went off on one of his many trips, this time a peace mission to Vietnam. In his absence he was deposed by a military coup. Nkrumah died in exile in 1972, and Ghana moved in a very different direction under its new military rulers.

MILITARY RESPONSES: DICTATORSHIPS AND REVOLUTIONS

Nkrumah is just one of many civilian leaders in the Third World who have fallen victim to military coups. In fact, it is far more difficult to find African and Asian (or Latin American) countries that have remained under civilian regimes since independence than those that have experienced military takeovers of varying durations. India, the Ivory Coast, Kenya, Zambia, and Zimbabwe are some of the more notable of the former; much of South and Southeast Asia and the rest of Africa have been or are now governed by military regimes. Given the difficulties confronted after independence by leaders such as Nkrumah and a number of advantages the military have in crisis situations, the proliferation of coups in the Third World is not all that surprising.

The armed forces in Third World countries have at times been divided by the religious and ethnic rivalries that have proved such a disruptive force in new nations. But the regimentation and emphasis on discipline and in-group solidarity in military training have often rendered soldiers more resistant to these forces than other social groups. In conditions of political breakdown and social conflict, the military possesses the monopoly—or near monopoly—of force that is often essential for restoring order. Their occupational conditioning makes soldiers not only more ready than civilian leaders to use the force at their disposal but also less concerned with its destructive consequences. Military personnel also tend to possess some degree of technical training, which was usually lacking in the humanities-oriented education of civilian nationalist leaders. Because most military leaders have been staunchly anti-Communist, they have often attracted covert technical and financial assistance from Western governments.

Once in control, military leaders have banned civilian political parties and imposed military regimes of varying degrees of repression and authoritarian control. Yet the ends to which these regimes have put their dictatorial powers have differed considerably. At their worst, military regimes—such as those in Uganda, Burma (now Myanmar), and Zaire—have quashed civil liberties and made little attempt to reduce social inequities or improve living standards. These regimes have existed mainly to enrich the military strongmen, as well as their cronies and lackeys, who control them. Regimes of this sort have been notorious for official corruption and the imprisonment and brutal torture or outright elimination of political dissidents. Understandably uneasy about being overthrown, they have diverted a high proportion of their nations' meager resources that might have gone for economic development into expenditures on expensive military hardware, which the Western democracies and the countries of the Soviet bloc have been only too eager to sell to them. Military leaders of this type have also been ready to use quarrels and sometimes military conflicts with neighboring regimes to divert attention from the bankruptcy of their domestic policies.

In a few cases military leaders have proved quite radical with regard to economic and social reform. Perhaps none was more so than Gamal Abdul Nasser, who took power in Egypt following a military coup in 1952. As we have seen, the Egyptians had won their independence, except for the lingering British presence in the Suez Canal zone, in the mid-1930s. But self-centered civilian politicians and the corrupt khedival regime had done little to improve the standard of living of the mass of the Egyptian people. As conditions worsened and Egypt's governing parties did little but rake in wealth for their limited, largely elitist memberships, two revolutionary forces emerged in Egyptian society.

The first was the Muslim Brotherhood, a party founded by Hasan al-Banna in 1928. Though committed to a fundamentalist approach to Islam, al-Banna's organization was also devoted to social uplift and sweeping reform. The Muslim Brotherhood became involved in a wide range of activities, from promoting trade unions and building medical clinics to educating women and pushing for land reform. By the late 1930s, the Brotherhood's social service had become highly politicized. Al-Banna's followers fomented strikes and urban riots and set up militant youth organizations and paramilitary assassination squads. Though stunned by the murder of al-Banna by the khedive Farouk's hit men in 1949, the members of the Brotherhood continued to expand its influence among both middle-class youth and the impoverished masses into the early 1950s. Its ultimate goal of seizing power, however, was thwarted by the second revolutionary force that emerged in this period.

The Free Officers movement, which evolved from a secret organization established by officers in the Egyptian army in the 1930s, was for many decades loosely allied to the Muslim Brotherhood. Founded by idealistic young officers of Egyptian, rather than Turco-Egyptian, descent, the secret Revolutionary Command Council studied conditions in the country and prepared to seize power in the name of a genuine revolution. Following Egypt's humiliating defeats in the first Arab-Israeli War in 1948 and in a clash with the British over the latter's continuing occupation of the Suez Canal zone in 1952, mass anger with a discredited khedival and parliamentary regime gave the officers their chance. In July 1952 an almost bloodless military coup toppled the corrupt and "well-padded" khedive Farouk from his jewel-encrusted throne.

The revolution had begun. The monarchy was ended, and the Egyptians ruled themselves for the first time since the 6th century B.C. By 1954 all political parties had been disbanded—including the Muslim Brotherhood, which had clashed with its former allies in the military—and had been suppressed after an attempt on the life of Nasser. Nasser was only one of several officers at the head of the Free Officers movement, and by no means was he initially the most charismatic. After months of internal power struggles in the officer corps, however, he emerged as the head of a military government that was deeply committed to revolution.

Nasser and his fellow officers used the dictatorial powers they had won in the coup in an attempt to uplift

The growing Egyptian resistance to the continuing British occupation of the Suez Canal zone was dramatically expressed in this effigy of a British soldier that was strung up on a Cairo street corner in January 1952. Within months mass demonstrations and a military coup freed Egypt from the British occupation and the repressive khedival regime.

the long-oppressed Egyptian masses. They believed that only the state possessed the power to carry out essential social and economic reforms, and thus they began to intervene in all aspects of Egyptian life. Land-reform measures were enacted; limits were placed on how much land an individual could own, and excess lands were seized and redistributed to landless peasants. State-financed education was made available to Egyptians through the college level. The government became Egypt's main employer—by 1980 over 30 percent of Egypt's work force was on the state payroll. State subsidies were used to lower the price of basic food staples, such as wheat and cooking oil. State-controlled development schemes were introduced that emphasized industrial growth, just like the Five-Year Plans of the Soviet Union. In order to establish Egypt's economic independence, stiff restrictions were placed on foreign investment, and in some cases foreign properties were seized and redistributed to Egyptian investors. Nasser also embarked on an interventionist foreign policy that stressed the continuing struggle to destroy the newly established Israeli state, forge Arab unity, and foment socialist revolutions in neighboring lands. His greatest foreign policy coup came in 1956, when he rallied international opinion to finally oust the British (and their French allies) from the Suez Canal zone. Despite the setbacks suffered by Egyptian military forces, Nasser made good use of the rare combined backing of the United States and the Soviet Union to achieve his aims in the crisis.

However well intentioned, many of Nasser's initiatives misfired. Land-reform efforts were frustrated by bureaucratic corruption and the clever stratagems devised by the landlord class to hold on to their estates. State development schemes often lacked proper funding and failed due to mismanagement and miscalculations. Even the Aswân Dam project, the cornerstone of Nasser's development drive, was something of a fiasco. Egypt's continuing population boom quickly canceled out the additional cultivable lands the dam produced. The dam's interference with the flow of the Nile resulted in an increase in parasites that spread blindness, as well as in a decline in the fertility of farmlands in the Lower Nile delta that were deprived of the rich silt annually washed down by the river. Foreign investment funds from the West, which Egypt desperately needed, soon dried up. Aid from the much poorer Soviet bloc could not begin to match what was lost, and much of this assistance was military. In the absence of sufficient foreign investment and with Egypt's uncontrolled population rising at an alarming rate, the state simply could not afford all the ambitious schemes to which Nasser and the revolutionary officers had committed it. The gap between aspirations and means was increased in the later years of Nasser's reign (in the 1960s) by the heavy costs of his mostly failed foreign adventures, including the disastrous Six-Day War with Israel that Egypt was drawn into in 1967.

Though he had to move slowly at first, Nasser's successor, Anwar Sadat, had little choice but to dismantle the massive state apparatus that had been created. He favored private rather than state initiatives, and during his tenure in office the middle class, which had been greatly restricted by Nasser, emerged again as a powerful force. After fighting the Israelis to a stalemate in 1973, Sadat also moved to end the costly confrontation with Israel and Egypt's support for revolutionary movements in the Arab world. Sadat expelled the Soviets and opened Egypt to aid and investment from the United States and western Europe.

Sadat's shift in direction has been continued by his successor and the present leader of Egypt, Hosni Mubarak. But neither the attempt at genuine revolution led by Nasser nor the retreat to capitalism and more pro-West positions under his successors has done much to check Egypt's alarming population increases and the corruption of its bloated bureaucracy. Neither path to development has had much effect on the glaring gap between the living conditions of Egypt's rich minority and its impoverished masses.

THE INDIAN ALTERNATIVE: DEVELOPMENT FOR SOME OF THE PEOPLE

Although the approach to nation building and economic development followed by the leaders of independent India has shared the Nasserite emphasis on socialism and state intervention, India's experience has diverged from Egypt's in a number of significant respects. The Indians have managed to preserve civilian rule throughout the four decades since they won their independence from Great Britain. In fact, in India the military has consistently defended secular democracy against religious extremism and other would-be authoritarian trends. In addition, though India, like Egypt, has been saddled with a crushing burden of overpopulation, it came to independence with a larger industrial and scientific sector, a better communications system and bureaucratic grid, and a larger and more skilled middle class in proportion to its total population than any other Third World country.

During the first decades of its freedom, India had the good fortune to be governed by leaders, such as Jawaharlal Nehru and his allies in the Congress party, who were deeply committed to social reform and economic development as well as the preservation of civil rights and democracy. India's success at the latter has been nothing short of remarkable. Despite continuous threats of secession by religious and linguistic minorities, as well as massive poverty, unemployment, and recurring natural disasters, India remains the world's largest functioning democracy. Except for brief periods of rule by coalitions of opposition parties, the Congress party has ruled at the center for most of the independence era. But opposition parties have controlled many state and local governments, and they remain vocal and active in the national Parliament. Civil liberties, exemplified by an outspoken press and free elections, have been upheld to an extent that sets India apart from much of the rest of the Third World. Their staying power was perhaps most emphatically demonstrated by the heavy political price that Indira Gandhi, Nehru's daughter and more dictatorially oriented successor, paid for attempting to curtail press and political freedoms in the mid-1970s, an attempt that led to one of the rare national election defeats the Congress party has suffered thus far.

Nehru's less dictatorial approach to government and development also differed from Nasser's in his more moderate mix of state and private initiatives. Nehru and his successors pushed state intervention in some sectors but also encouraged foreign investment from countries in both of the rival blocs in the cold war. As a consequence India has been able to build on its initial advantages in industrial infrastructure and its skilled managerial and labor endowment. Its significant capitalist sector has encouraged ambitious farmers, such as those in the Punjab in the northwest, to invest heavily in the improved seed strains, fertilizers, and irrigation that are at the heart of the Green Revolution. The new techniques associated with the Green Revolution have produced much higher yields in such key crops as rice, wheat, and corn throughout much of the Third World in recent decades. Considerable growth in both the industrial and agrarian sectors has generated the revenue for the Indian government to promote literacy and village development schemes, as well as family planning, village electrification, and other improvement projects in recent decades.

Despite its very considerable successes, India has suffered from the same gap between needs and resources that all Third World nations have had to face. Whatever the government's intentions—and India has been hit by corruption and self-serving like most polities—there have simply not been the resources to raise the living standards of even a majority of its huge population. The middle class has grown, perhaps as rapidly as that of any Third World nation. Its presence is striking in the affluent neighborhoods of Bombay and Delhi and proclaimed by the Indian film industry, the world's largest, in innumerable sitcoms and dramas about the woes in the lives of yuppies, Indian-style. But perhaps 60 percent of India's people have gained little or nothing from the development schemes and economic growth that have occurred since independence.

In part the reason is that population growth has wiped out economic gains. But social reform has been slow in most areas, both rural and urban. Groups such as the wealthy landlords, who supported the nationalist drive for independence, have continued to dominate the great mass of tenants and landless laborers, just as they did in the precolonial and colonial eras. Some development measures, most notably those associated with the Green Revolution, have greatly favored those cultivators with the resources to invest in new seeds and fertilizer. They have increased the gap between well-off and poor people over much of rural India. India's literacy rate remains well below that of China (the only rival with which it can be reasonably compared given the size of each and the magnitude of the problems they face), and a far larger proportion of India's population remains chronically malnourished. Thus the poor have paid and will continue to pay the price for Indian gradualism, and those favoring more revolutionary solutions to India's continuing social inequities and mass poverty have plenty of ammunition with which to attack the ruling parties.

DOCUMENT

CULTURAL CREATIVITY IN THE THIRD WORLD: SOME LITERARY SAMPLES

Despite, or perhaps because of, political instability and chronic economic difficulties, Third World societies have generated a high level of artistic creativity over the past decades. Nowhere has this creativity been more prominent and brilliant than in literary productivity, for which Third World writers have earned Nobel Prizes and deservedly won a wide readership far beyond their own nations. The selections that follow provide only a small sample of the vast and varied talent Third World writers have displayed, from poetry and drama to novels and short stories.

Much of the literature of Third World writers focuses on the predicament of the Western-educated African and Asian elites who dominate the new nations that emerged from the European colonial empires. In the following stanza from the poem "I Run Around with Them," the Indonesian poet Chairil Anwar reflects on the lack of purpose and the malaise he believed to be widespread among the children of these elite groups.

> I run around with them, what else can I do, now—
> Changing my face at the edge of the street, I use
> their eyes

> And tag along to visit the fun house:
> These are the facts as I know them
> (A new American flic at the Capitol,
> The new songs they dance to).
> We go home: there's nothing doing
> Though this kind of Death is our neighbor, our
> friend, now.
> Hanging around at the corner, we wait for the city
> bus
> That glows night to day like a gold tooth;
> Lame, deformed, negative, we
> Lean our bony asses against lamp poles
> And jaw away the years.

In the next quotation, from the novel *No Longer at Ease*, the widely read Nigerian author Chinua Achebe identifies another dilemma, the pull between Western culture and the ancient civilization of one's own land.

Nothing gave him greater pleasure than to find another Ibo-speaking student in a London bus. But when he had to speak in English with a Nigerian student from another tribe he lowered his voice. It was humiliating to have to speak to one's countryman in a foreign language, especially in the presence of the proud owners of that language. They would naturally assume that one had no language of one's own. He wished they were here today to see. Let them come to Umuofia [the protagonist's home village] now and listen to the talk of men who made a great art of conversation. Let them come and see men and women and children who knew how to live, whose joy of life had not yet been killed by those who claimed to teach other nations how to live.

Like a number of the more famous Third World novelists, V. S. Naipaul is an ex-patriot who was born in the Caribbean and now lives in rural England. In *An Area of Darkness,* his moving account of his return to his Indian ancestral home, Naipaul confronts the problem of massive poverty and the responses of foreigners and the Indian elite to it.

. . . to see [India's] poverty is to make an observation of no value; a thousand newcomers to the country before you have seen and said as you. And not only newcomers. Our own sons and daughters, when they return from Europe and America, have spoken in your very words. Do not think that your anger and contempt are marks of your sensitivity. You might have seen more: the smiles on the faces of the begging children, that domestic group among the pavement sleepers waking in the cool Bombay morning, father, mother and baby in a trinity of love, so self-contained that they are as private as if walls had separated them from you; it is your gaze that violates them, your sense of outrage that outrages them. . . . It is your surprise, your anger that denies [them] humanity.

Questions: Can you think of parallels in U.S. history or contemporary society for the situations and responses conveyed in these passages from recent African and Asian writings? Do they suggest that it is possible to communicate even intimate feelings across cultures, or do you find them alien, different?

IRAN: RELIGIOUS REVIVALISM AND THE REJECTION OF THE WEST

No path of development adopted by a Third World society has provided more fundamental challenges to the existing world order than revolutionary Iran under the direction of Ayatollah Khomaini. In many respects the Khomaini revolution of 1979 was a throwback to the religious fervor of such anticolonial resistance movements as that led by the Mahdi of the Sudan in the 1880s. The emphasis on religious purification and the rejoining of religion and politics that leaders such as the Mahdi and Khomaini regarded as central to the Islamic tradition provided the core motivations for the followers of both movements. The call for a return to the kind of society believed to have existed in the past "golden age" of the prophet Muhammad was central to the policies pursued by both the Mahdist and Iranian regimes once they had gained power. Both movements were aimed at Western-backed governments: the Mahdist at the Anglo-Egyptian presence in the Sudan, Khomaini's against the autocratic Iranian shah and the Pahlavi dynasty, which were pictured as advocates of secularization and unchecked Westernization as well as puppets of the United States.

Though from the Sunni and Shi'ite religious traditions, respectively, both the Mahdi and Khomaini claimed to be divinely inspired deliverers who would rescue the Islamic faithful from imperialist Westerners and corrupt and heretical leaders within the Muslim world. Both leaders promised their followers magical protection and instant paradise should they fall waging the holy war against the heretics and infidels. Each movement sought to build a lasting state and social order on the basis of what were believed to be Islamic precedents. Thus each movement aimed at the defense and restoration of what its leaders believed to be the true beliefs, traditions, and institutions of Islamic civilization. The leaders of both movements sought to spread their revolutions to surrounding areas, both Muslim and infidel, and each believed he was setting in motion forces that would eventually sweep the entire globe.

Though proclaimed as an alternative path for development that could be followed by the rest of the Third World, Khomaini's revolution owed its initial success in seizing power to a number of circumstances that were more or less unique to Iran. Like China, Iran had not been formally colonized by the European powers but rather reduced to a sphere of informal influence, divided between Great Britain and Russia. As a result, neither the bureaucratic nor the communications infrastructures that accompanied colonial takeovers were highly developed there. Nor did a substantial Western-educated middle class emerge. Thus the impetus for "modernization" came suddenly and was imposed from above by the Pahlavi shahs. The initiatives taken by the second shah in particular, which were supported by Iran's considerable oil wealth, wrenched Iran out of the isolation and backwardness in which most of the nation lived until the mid-20th century. The shah sought to impose economic development and social change by government directives. Though advances occurred, the regime managed to alienate the great mass of the Iranian people in the process.

The shah's dictatorial and repressive regime deeply offended the people of the emerging middle class, whom he considered his strongest potential supporters. His flouting of Islamic conventions and neglect of Islamic worship and religious institutions enraged the ayatollahs, or religious experts, and mullahs, or local prayer leaders and mosque attendants, who guided the religious and personal lives of the great majority of the Iranian population. The favoritism he showed foreign investors and a handful of big Iranian entrepreneurs, who had personal connections to highly placed officials, angered the smaller bazaar merchants, who had long maintained close links with the mullahs and other religious leaders. The shah's halfhearted land-reform schemes alienated the landowning classes without really doing much to improve the condition of the rural poor. Even the urban workers, who benefited most from the boom in construction and light industrialization the shah's development efforts had stimulated, were disaffected in the years before the 1979 revolution by a fall in oil prices that had led to an economic slump and widespread unemployment.

Though he had treated his officers well, the shah had badly neglected the military rank and file, especially in the army. So when the crisis came in 1978, the shah found that few of his subjects were prepared to defend his regime. His armies refused to fire on the growing crowds that demonstrated for his removal and the return of Khomaini, then in exile in Paris. Dying of cancer and disheartened by what he viewed as betrayal by his people and allies, such as the United States, the shah fled without much of a fight. Khomaini's revolution triumphed over a regime that looked powerful but in fact proved to be exceptionally vulnerable.

After coming to power, Khomaini, defying the predictions of most Western "experts" on Iranian affairs, followed through on his promises of radical change. Constitutional and leftist parties allied to the revolutionary movement were brutally repressed. Moderate leaders were quickly replaced by radical religious figures eager to obey Khomaini's every command. The "satanic" influences of the United States and Western Europe were purged; at the same time Iran also distanced itself from the atheistic Communist world. Secular influences in law and government were supplanted by strict Islamic legal codes, which included such punishments as the amputation of limbs for theft and stoning for women caught in adultery, as well as rule by the mullahs and ayatollahs. Veiling became obligatory for all females, and the career prospects for women of the educated middle classes, who had been among the most favored by the shah's reforms, were suddenly greatly constricted.

Khomaini's planners also drew up grand schemes for land reform, religious education, and economic development that accorded with the dictates of Islam. Most of these measures came to little because soon after the revolution, Saddam Hussein, the military leader of neighboring Iraq, sought to take advantage of the turmoil in Iran by annexing its western, oil-rich provinces. The war that resulted swallowed up Iranian energies and resources for virtually the entire decade after Khomaini came to power. Though clearly initially the fault of the invading Iraqis, the struggle became a highly personal vendetta for Khomaini, who was determined to destroy Hussein and punish the Iraqis. His refusal to negotiate peace caused heavy losses and untold suffering to the Iranian people. This suffering continued long after it was clear that the Iranians' aging military equipment and handful of allies were no match for Hussein's more advanced military hardware and an Iraqi war machine bankrolled by its oil-rich Arab neighbors, who were fearful that Khomaini's revolution might spread to their own countries.

As the support of the Western powers, including the United States (despite protestations of neutrality), for the Iraqis increased, the position of the isolated Iranians became increasingly intolerable. Hundreds of thousands of poorly armed and half-trained Iranian conscripts, including tens of thousands of untrained and virtually weaponless boys, died before Khomaini finally agreed to a humiliating armistice in 1988. Peace found revolutionary Iran in shambles. Few of its development initiatives had been pursued, and shortages in food, fuel, and the other necessities of life were widespread.

Iran's decade-long absorption in the war makes it impossible to assess the potential of the religious revivalist,

Women played a vital role in the mass demonstrations that toppled the shah and brought Ayatollah Khomaini to power. The fundamentalist version of Islam Khomaini and his allies pursued—expressed, for example, by the return to veiling for women shown here—divided many of the highly Westernized women of the new Iranian middle classes from those of the urban working and merchant classes as well as the peasant class.

anti-Western option for Third World nations. What had seemed at first to be a viable path to genuinely independent development for African and Asian peoples became mired in brutal internal repression and littered with the wreckage of a losing war.

SOUTH AFRICA: DEFENDING AND CHALLENGING THE GARRISON STATE

South Africa was by no means the only area still under some form of colonial dominance decades after

India became the first of the former European colonies to gain its independence in 1947. Portugal, the oldest and long considered the weakest of the European colonizers, held onto Angola, Mozambique, and its other African possessions until the mid-1970s. Zimbabwe (formerly Southern Rhodesia) was run by white settlers, who had unilaterally declared their independence from Great Britain, until 1980. Southwest Africa became fully free of South African control only in 1989, and some of the smaller islands in the West Indies and the Pacific remain under European or U.S. rule to the present day.

By the 1970s, however, South Africa was by far the largest, most populous, richest, and most strategic area where the great majority of the population had yet to be liberated from colonial domination. Since the 1940s, the white settlers, particularly the Dutch-descended Afrikaners, have solidified their internal control of the country under the leadership of the Nationalist party. In stages and through a series of elections in which the blacks, who made up the great majority of South Africans, were not allowed to vote, the Nationalists won complete independence from Great Britain in 1960. From 1948, when the Nationalist party first came to power, the Afrikaners moved to institutionalize white supremacy and white minority rule by the passage of thousands of laws that composed the system of apartheid.

The system of apartheid was designed not only to ensure a monopoly of political power and economic dominance for the white minority, both British and Dutch descended, but also to impose a system of extreme segregation on all races of South Africa, in all aspects of their lives. Separate and patently unequal facilities were established for various racial groups for recreation, education, housing, work, and medical care. Dating or sexual intercourse across racial lines was strictly prohibited. Skilled and high-paying jobs were reserved for white workers. Nonwhites were required to carry passes that listed the parts of South Africa where they were allowed to work and reside. If caught by the police without their passes or in areas where they were not permitted to travel, nonwhite South Africans were routinely given stiff jail sentences.

Spacial separation was also organized on a grander scale by the creation of numerous homelands within South Africa, each designated for the main ethnolinguistic or "tribal" groups within the black African population. Though touted by the Afrikaners as the ultimate solution to the racial "problem," the homelands scheme would leave the black African majority with a small percentage of some of the poorest land in South Africa. Because the homelands were overpopulated and poverty stricken, the white minority was guaranteed a ready supply of cheap black labor to work in their factories and mines and on their farms. Denied citizenship in South Africa proper, these laborers were forced eventually to return to the homelands, because they had left their wives and children there while emigrating in search of work.

To maintain the blatantly racist and inequitable system of apartheid, the white minority had to build a police state and expend a large portion of the federal budget on a sophisticated and well-trained military establishment. Because of the land's great mineral wealth, the Afrikaner nationalists were able to find the resources to fund their garrison state. Until the late 1980s, the government prohibited all forms of black protest and

The blatant segregation of public facilities was a key feature of the apartheid regime in South Africa. The police stood ready to enforce the multitude of laws that confined the blacks to designated areas and a very limited range of low-paying occupational roles.

brutally repressed even nonviolent resistance. Black organizations, such as the African National Congress, were declared illegal, and African leaders, such as Walter Sisulu and Nelson Mandela, were shipped off to maximum-security prisons for life. Other leaders, such as Steve Biko, one of the young organizers of the Black Consciousness movement, died under very suspicious circumstances while in police custody.

Through spies and police informers, the regime sought to capitalize on personal and ethnic divisions within the black majority community. Favoritism was shown to some leaders and groups to keep them from uniting with others in all-out opposition to apartheid. With all avenues of constitutional negotiation and peaceful protest closed, many advocates of black majority rule in a multiracial society turned to guerrilla resistance. The South African government responded in the 1980s with a state of emergency, which simply intensified the restrictions already in place in the garrison state. The government repeatedly justified its draconian repression by labeling virtually all black protest as Communist inspired and by playing on the racial fears of the white minority.

Through most of the 1970s and early 1980s, it appeared that the hardening hostility between the unyielding white minority and the frustrated black majority was building to a major and violent upheaval. This may still prove the end result of apartheid and the Afrikaners' garrison state. In recent years, however, there have been signs that some Afrikaner leaders are beginning to realize that these solutions are dead ends. Reforms that would have been unthinkable even a decade ago, such as the abolition of the pass laws and the antimiscegenation acts, have begun the process of dismantling the system of apartheid. The release of key black political prisoners, such as the dramatic freeing of Nelson Mandela in 1990, and permission for peaceful mass demonstrations are signs that those in power, most notably the Afrikaner-descended president F. W. de Klerk, may finally be willing to listen to and negotiate a settlement with black leaders. A multiracial conference is presently writing a new constitution and preparing the country for elections that will allow black Africans, coloreds and Indians to vote and be elected to parliament for the first time.

Black African leaders are understandably wary after so many years of oppression and repression, but so far most have been willing to wait and explore peaceful ways to put pressure on the regime. The differences between the two sides remain colossal, and more radical and violence-prone alternatives threaten both those in power and the more moderate leaders of the black majority. Bitter interethnic rivalries within the black majority community, which have frequently flared into bloody battles between Zulus and Xhosas, also threaten to be a major obstacle to a peaceful settlement. It is still possible for stalemate to develop and a massive civil war to erupt. Yet for the first time since the white majority won their independence in the 1940s and 1950s, there are clear signs that the internal colonization that has continued for the great majority of the peoples of South Africa under apartheid is breaking down. Its demise may well pave the way to the peaceful creation of a truly free, multiracial society in South Africa.

CONCLUSION:

THE THIRD WORLD EXPERIENCE IN HISTORICAL PERSPECTIVE

Although the years of independence for the nations that have emerged from the colonial empires have been filled with political and economic crises and social turmoil, it is important to put recent Third World history in a larger perspective. Most of these new nations have been in existence only a few decades, and they came to independence with severe handicaps, many of which were a direct legacy of their colonial experiences. Some observers have been tempted to question whether Africans and Asians are able to govern themselves, given the widespread occurrence of communal violence, civil strife, and military takeovers in the new states. But if we consider that the far smaller, resource-rich, and relatively homogenous population of the young American republic in the late 18th century remained so deeply divided for nearly 100 years that only a massive civil war in the 1860s could salvage the union, the political tensions in Third World nations do not seem so exceptional. If one takes into account the artificial nature of these states, most have held together rather well. This is especially striking if they are compared to European nations, such as the former Yugoslavia, that have disintegrated due to regional and religious clashes, despite the fact that the peoples who make them up have a lot more in common historically and culturally than the populations of most Third World countries.

India's success is particularly striking here. In size—both population and ethnic—as well as in linguistic and religious diversity, India is a continent comparable to western Europe. Yet few see Europe's long centuries of national rivalries, quarrels, and wars as a sign that the Europeans are incapable of governing themselves. India's continuing unity contrasts sharply with Europe's disunity, but India's very considerable political achievements are passed over in favor of sensationalist accounts of religious and regional strife in the subcontinent.

What is true in politics is true of all other aspects of the Third World experience. With much lower populations and far fewer or no industrial competitors, as well as drawing on the resources of much of the rest of the world, European and North American nations had to struggle to industrialize and thereby achieve a reasonable standard of living for most of their people. Even with their advantages, the human cost in terms of horrific working conditions and urban squalor was enormous, and we are still paying the high ecological price. Third World countries have had few or none of the West's advantages. They have begun the "great ascent" to development burdened by excessive and rapidly increasing populations that overwhelm their limited resources, which must be exported to earn the capital to buy food and machines. They struggle to establish a place in the world market system that is heavily loaded in favor of the established industrial powers in terms of pricing and investment. Their efforts to build modest industrial sectors are frustrated by competition from the many nations that have industrialized ahead of them.

Despite the cultural dominance of the West, which was one of the great legacies or burdens of the colonial era, Third World thinkers and artists have achieved a great deal. If much of this—such as African and Asian political organizations and economic planning—has been dependent on Western models, one should not be surprised given the educational backgrounds and personal experiences of the first generations of African and Asian leaders.

The challenge for the coming generations will be to find genuinely Third World solutions to the problems that have stunted political and economic development and to the dependence on the West that once had checked intellectual originality. If the promise Iran once seemed to offer in this respect has faded after a decade of brutal internal repression, economic retreat, and war, the conviction among Third World leaders and thinkers that other options must emerge is growing. The solutions reached are likely to vary a great deal, given the diversity of the nations and societies of the Third World. They are also more likely to be forged from a combination of Western and indigenous influences than from the Iranian revolution, whose leaders have been so determined to ban and destroy all Western influences, even those that might be critical to building viable and prosperous nations. They are also likely to draw heavily on the ancient and distinguished traditions of civilized life that have been nurtured by African and Asian peoples for millennia.

FURTHER READINGS

Much of the extensive literature on political and economic development in the Third World is focused on individual nations, and it is more helpful to know several cases in some depth rather than try to master them all. Robert Heilbroner's writings, starting with his *The Great Ascent* (1961), still provide the most sensible introduction to challenges to the new states in the early decades of independence. Peter Worsley's *The Third World* (1964) provides a provocative, if somewhat disjointed, supplement to Heilbroner's many works. Though focused mainly on South and Southeast Asia, Gunnar Myrdal's *Asian Drama* (3 vols., 1968) is the best exploration in a single cultural area of the complexities of the challenges to development. A good overview of developments in India can be found in W. N. Brown's *The United States and India, Pakistan, and Bangladesh* (1984 ed.),

despite its misleadingly Western-centric title. Michael Brecher's *Nehru: A Political Biography* (1969) is a very readable account of Indian history in the Nehru years after independence. Ali Mazrui and Michael Tidy's *Nationalism and New States in Africa* (1984) gives a good overview of developments throughout Africa. Also useful are S. A. Akintoye's *Emergent African States* (1976) and H. Bretton's *Power and Politics in Africa* (1973). For the Middle East, John Waterbury's *The Egypt of Nasser and Sadat* (1983) provides a detailed account of the politics of development, and Peter Mansfield's *The Arabs* (1978) supplies a decent (if now a bit dated) overview.

On military coups, see Ruth First's *The Barrel of a Gun* (1971) and S. Decalo's *Coups and Army Rule in Africa* (1976). Shaul Bakash's *The Reign of the Ayatollahs* (1984) is perhaps the most insightful of several books that have appeared on Iran since the revolution. Brian Bunting's *The Rise of the South African Reich* (1964) traces the rise of the apartheid regime in great (and polemical) detail; Gail Gerhart's *Black Power in South Africa* (1978) is one of the better studies devoted to efforts to tear that system down. Among the many fine Third World authors whose works are available in English, some of the best include (for Africa) Chinua Achebe, Wole Soyinka, and Ousmane Sembene; (for India) A. K. Narayan and V. K. Naipaul; (for Egypt) Nawal el Saadawi and Neguib Mahfouz; and (for Indonesia) Mochtar Lubis and P. A. Toer. For white perspectives on the South African situation, the works of Nadine Gordimer and J. M. Coetzee are superb.

1950–1953 Korean War

1958–1960 "Great Leap Forward" in China

1959 Revolution brings Castro to power in Cuba

mid–1950s Build-up of U.S. advisors in South Vietnam

1957 "Let a Thousand Flowers Bloom" campaign in China

1950–1951 Purge of the landlord class in China

1961 Failed Bay of Pigs invasion in Cuba

1949 Victory of the Communists in China;
People's Republic of China established

1966–1969 Era of the Cultural Revolution in China

1963 Beginning of state family planning in China

1953 Beginning of China's first Five-Year Plan
1954 French defeated at Dien Bien Phu;
Geneva accords, French withdrawal from
Vietnam; beginning of the Sino-Soviet split

1965–1973 Direct U.S. military
intervention in Vietnam

1945 Ho Chi Minh proclaims
the Republic of Vietnam

1968 Tet offensive in
Vietnam

13

Cold War Confrontations and the Resurgence of Revolution in the "Third World"

INTRODUCTION. The revolutionary surge that had erupted in the years on either side of the First World War was stifled or thrown back throughout much of the world by the rise of powerful Fascist and military regimes in the 1930s. But the dislocations of a second and even more devastating round of global war in the 1940s gave new life to continuing revolutionary struggles in China and Vietnam. The Soviet Union's emergence from the war as one of the two global superpowers gave new impetus to these revolutionary movements and supplied inspiration (and at times material support) for leftist revolutionaries throughout Latin America. The Soviet Union and its Communist allies also provided encouragement and often direct support for anticolonial movements throughout Africa and Asia. The bourgeois elites who led these movements were often quite willing to accept Soviet backing. But as we have seen in Chapter 12, they usually worked toward peaceful and basically nonrevolutionary transfers of power. They also favored more democratic political institutions and a larger role for market forces in their newly independent societies than was possible under Soviet-style, Communist command economies.

The assistance that the Soviet Union and other nations in the Communist bloc provided for leftist revolutionaries throughout the Third World, as well as in Europe, was almost invariably counterbalanced by the often formidable aid provided by the United States and its allies for the bourgeois and elite opponents of the revolutionaries. For much of the last third of the 20th century, much of the Third World—which was made up mainly by the nations of Latin America, Africa, and Asia—became contested terrain in the global struggle between

1975 Communist victory in Vietnam; collapse of the Republic of South Vietnam

1980s Era of economic liberalization in China

1989 Tiananmen Square massacre in Beijing; Pro-democracy movement is crushed

1976 Death of Zhou Enlai and Mao Zedong; purge of the Gang of Four

1993 Castro runs for president for first time and is victorious

the capitalist and Communist camps—or the First and Second Worlds, respectively. The struggle was in part ideological, with the proponents of communism and capitalism vying to convince the peoples of the Third World that they, not their rivals, could provide the best path to economic development and social stability. But it was also a contest for control of the considerable natural resources, market outlets, and strategic locales of Latin America and the formerly colonized areas of Africa and Asia. Ironically, both the Communist and capitalist blocs offered the peoples of the Third World surprisingly similar models for development. Most critically, both emphasized large-scale projects and heavy fossil-fuel consumption that had their origins in the process of industrialization as it had occurred in western Europe and the United States. The Communists stressed state control, whereas the capitalists touted the advantages of market mechanisms, but both gave priority to high tech and industrialization, and both approaches to development have had devastating effects on the fragile tropical environments of much of the Third World.

At times the small and underdeveloped nations of the Third World were little more than pawns in these ongoing contests. But often the larger and more advanced nations, such as Egypt and India, could take advantage of superpower conflicts by playing off one camp against the other to win economic aid and military hardware. In the long term these stratagems often backfired against the peoples of Third World countries. Aid usually proved to have strings attached that stunted overall growth or, by favoring established elite groups, further skewed social and economic imbalances in Third World societies. The armaments that the superpowers funneled—often at great profit to themselves—into Latin America, Africa, and Asia both drained resources from productive investments and took a heavy toll in the wars and civil strife that have been so pervasive in Latin America and newly independent regions since 1945. In areas where revolutionary movements (which were usually labeled Communist whatever the predilections of those waging them) were an important force, military intervention by the United States or its surrogates became a familiar occurrence in the last decades of the 20th century. Beyond the human casualties that resulted, U.S. intervention often meant significant shifts in the recent history of many Third World societies.

Although cold war confrontations between the Soviet bloc and the capitalist West influenced the outcomes of civil wars and revolutionary insurgencies throughout the Third World, the forces that created social conflict and revolutionary movements were overwhelmingly indigenous to the societies where these struggles occurred. As we shall see in the case examples of both failed and successful revolutions in China, Vietnam, and Latin America, perceived exploitation by foreign powers contributed to the conditions that produced social unrest and dissident movements. But internal dislocations—natural calamities, the breakdown of bureaucratic systems, rampant social injustice, and economic inequities—were the central factors behind the risings of the peasantry and the working poor of Third World societies convulsed by revolutionary movements. With the exception of small and excessively vulnerable nations, such as those of Central America, interventions by one or the other of the superpowers or their proxies could prolong the life of repressive regimes and thus delay the seizure of power by revolutionary forces. But as the cases of China, Cuba, and especially Vietnam illustrate so tellingly, even the military might of the United States colossus could not turn back the revolutionary tide if insurgent movements had won the support of large numbers of the indigenous population and, conversely, the regimes in power were corrupt and inept.

As we see in this chapter, the victory of the revolutionaries did not guarantee utopia for the societies in which leftist parties came to power. In fact, China, Vietnam, and Cuba were often isolated from all but a few sympathetic, but themselves impoverished, Communist nations and as a consequence deprived of critical economic assistance. In addition, once in power, successful revolutionaries have often proved unwilling to tolerate opposition parties and willing to sacrifice some human rights—free speech and elections, for example—for others, such as universal employment, education, and health care. Leftist leaders have tended to direct state resources toward centrally controlled, large-scale industrial development and mechanized, communal farming, both of which have proved much less productive and usually much more damaging to the environment than their capitalist counterparts. As a result, the same malaise and societywide crisis that overtook Communist societies in the Soviet Union and Eastern Europe have also affected Vietnam, Cuba, and to a lesser extent China in recent years.

In order to understand the long-term effects of revolutionary upheaval in the 20th century, it is necessary to examine these recent developments. But this chapter begins with a survey of the final stages of the civil war in China between the militarily dominated Guomindang and the revolutionary Communist party. After tracing the history of the victorious Communist regime into the early 1990s, we turn to the successive revolutionary struggles of the Vietnamese Communists: first against the French, then against the puppet regimes installed in the south, and finally in the David-and-Goliath contest against the United States and its South Vietnamese allies. The final sections of the chapter explore revolutionary and repressive impulses in Latin America, with emphasis on Cuba, where the most dynamic and influential Communist regime in the Western Hemisphere has held power since the late 1950s.

MAO'S CHINA AND BEYOND

As we have seen in Chapter 7 the guerrilla warfare that the Chinese Communists waged against the Japanese armies proved much more effective than Chiang Kai-shek's attempts to defeat the invaders with set-piece battles and convential warfare. With the Nationalist extermination campaigns against the Communists suspended, the Red army used its anti-Japanese campaigns to extend Communist control over large areas of north China. By the end of World War II Nationalist control in the strategically vital northern plains was confined mainly to the cities. These urban centers had become (as Mao prescribed in his political writings) islands surrounded by a sea of revolutionary peasants. The Communists' successes and determination to fight the Japanese, while Chiang and his advisors vacillated, had won them the support of most of China's intellectuals and many of the students who had earlier looked to the Nationalists for China's salvation. By 1945 the balance of

power within China was clearly shifting in the Communists' favor. In the four-year civil war that followed, Communist soldiers, who were led by superior commanders, well treated, and fighting for a cause, consistently routed the much abused and poorly led Nationalist soldiers. By the last years of the civil war, Nationalist soldiers were defecting in droves to the Communist side.

Massive arms shipments to the Nationalists from the United States, whose postwar leaders were anxious to prevent the loss of China to the Communist camp, delayed but could not prevent the rout of Chiang and his allies. By 1949 it was over. Chiang and what was left of his Nationalist supporters fled to the island of Formosa (renamed Taiwan) off the China coast, and Mao proclaimed the establishment of the People's Republic of China in Beijing.

In assuming power in 1949 the Communists faced the formidable task of governing a vast nation in ruins. Over a century of foreign invasions, civil warfare, and natural calamities had ravaged China's cities and villages, destroyed much of its economic infrastructure, and left its population physically exhausted and deeply demoralized. The confidence of Mao and the Communist leaders that they could build a better future did much to lift spirits and rally popular support for the ambitious projects of the new regime.

The Communists could also draw on the enthusiastic support of those peasants, students, and soldiers who had already been liberated by the experience of living in Communist-controlled areas during the mid-1930s and the years of Japanese occupation. In these zones land

By the end of World War II the Communists under Mao Zedong had built a conventional army that could hold its own against the larger forces of the Guomindang. Here Communist machine gunners cover an infantry assault on Guomindang entrenchments.

reforms had already been put into effect, mass literacy campaigns had been mounted, and young men and women had enjoyed opportunities to rise in the party ranks on the basis of hard work and personal talents. Thus in contrast to the Bolsheviks, who seized power in 1917 in Russia quite easily but then had to face years of civil war and foreign aggression, the Communists in China claimed a unified nation from which foreign aggressors had been expelled. Unlike the Bolsheviks, the Chinese Communist leadership could move directly to the tasks of social reform and economic development that China so desperately needed, and they could build on the base they had established in the "liberated" zones during their long struggle for power.

POLITICS AND SOCIAL REVOLUTION

Although deep social divisions remained, the Chinese faced much less serious splits among religious and ethnic groups than did most other new nations of Africa and Asia. Millennia of common history and common cultural development had given the peoples of China a sense of identity and a tradition of political unity. The long struggle against foreign aggressors had strengthened these bonds and impressed on the Chinese the importance of maintaining a united front against outsiders if they were to avoid future humiliations and exploitation. The Communists' "long march" to power had left the party with a strong political and military organization that was rooted in the party cadres and the People's Liberation Army. The continuing importance of the army was indicated by the fact that most of China was administered by military officials for five years after the Communists came to power. But the army remained clearly subordinate to the Party, with cadre advisors attached to military contingents at all levels and the central committees of the Party dominated by nonmilitary personnel.

With this strong political framework in place, the Communists moved quickly to assert China's traditional preeminence in East and much of Southeast Asia. Potential secessionist movements were forcibly repressed in Inner Mongolia and Tibet, though resistance in the latter has erupted periodically and continues to the present day. In the early 1950s the Chinese intervened militarily in the conflict between North and South Korea, an intervention that was critical in forcing the United States to settle for a stalemate and a lasting division of the peninsula. Refusing to accept a similar but far more lopsided, two-nation outcome of the struggle in China, the Communist leadership has periodically threatened to in-

vade the Nationalists' refuge on Taiwan, in a number of cases touching off international incidents in the process. China also played an increasingly important role in the liberation struggle of the Vietnamese to the south, though that would not peak until the height of U.S. involvement in the conflict in the 1960s.

By the late 1950s the close collaboration between the Soviet Union and China that marked the early years of Mao's rule had broken down. Border disputes, focusing on territories the Russians had seized during the period of Manchu decline, and the Chinese refusal to play second fiddle to the Soviet Union, especially after Stalin was succeeded by the less imposing Khrushchev, were key causes of the split. Together, these causes of the breakdown greatly exacerbated differences resulting both from the disappointingly meager economic assistance provided by the Soviet "comrades" and from Mao's very Chinese sense that with the passing of Stalin, he was the number-one theoretician and leader of the Communist world. In the early 1960s the Chinese flexed their very considerable military and technological muscle by thrashing India in a brief war that resulted from a border dispute and more startlingly by exploding the first nuclear device developed by a nonindustrial nation.

On the domestic front the new leaders of China moved with equal vigor, though with a good deal less success. Their first priority was to complete the social revolution in the rural areas that had been, to some extent, carried through in Communist-controlled areas during the wars against the Japanese and Guomindang. Between 1950 and 1952 the landlord class and the large landholders, most of whom had been spared in earlier stages of the revolution, were dispossessed and purged. Village tribunals, overseen by Party cadre members, gave tenants and laborers a chance to get even for decades of oppression. Perhaps as many as three million people who were denounced as members of the exploitive landlord class were executed. At the same time, the land taken from the landowning classes was distributed to peasants who had none or little. For a brief time, at least, one of the central pledges of the Communist revolutionaries was fulfilled: China became a land of peasant smallholders.

Communist planners, however, saw rapid industrialization, not peasant farmers, as the key to successful development. With the introduction of the first Stalinist-style Five-Year Plan in 1953, the Communist leadership turned away from the peasantry, which had brought them to power, to the urban workers as the hope for a new China. With little foreign assistance from either the West or the Soviet bloc, the state resorted to stringent measures to draw resources from the countryside to finance industrial growth. Though some advances were made in industrialization, particularly in heavy industries, such as steel, the shift in direction had consequences that were increasingly unacceptable to Mao and his more radical supporters in the party. State planning and centralization were stressed, party bureaucrats greatly increased their power and influence, and an urban-based privileged class of technocrats began to develop. These changes and the external threat to China posed by the U.S. intervention in Korea and continuing U.S.-China friction led Mao and his followers to force a change of strategies in the mid-1950s.

Mao had long nurtured a deep hostility toward elitism, which he associated with the discredited Confucian system. He had little use for Lenin's vision of revolution from above, led by a disciplined cadre of professional political activists. He distrusted intellectuals, disliked specialization, and clung to his faith in the peasants rather than the workers as the repository of basic virtue and the driving force of the revolution. Acting to stem the trend toward an elitist, urban-industrial focus, Mao and his supporters introduced the Mass Line approach, beginning with the formation of agricultural cooperatives in 1955. In the following year cooperatives became farming collectives that soon accounted for over 90 percent of China's peasant population. The peasants had enjoyed their own holdings for less than three years. As had occurred earlier in the Soviet Union, the revolutionary leaders who had originally won the land for the mass of the peasants later took it away from them through collectivization.

In 1957 Mao struck at the intellectuals through what may have been a miscalculation or perhaps a clever ruse. Announcing that he wished to "let a thousand flowers bloom," Mao encouraged professors, artists, and other intellectuals to speak out on the course of development under Communist rule. His request stirred up a storm of angry protest and criticism of Communist schemes. Having flushed the critics into the open, if the campaign was indeed a ruse, or having been shocked by the vehemence of the response, the Party struck with demotions, prison sentences, and banishment to hard labor on the collectives. The flowers rapidly wilted in the face of this betrayal.

THE GREAT LEAP BACKWARD

With political opposition within the party and army apparently in check (or in prison), Mao and his support-

ers launched the Great Leap Forward in 1958. The programs of the Great Leap represented a further effort to revitalize the flagging revolution by restoring its mass, rural base. Rather than huge plants located in the cities, industrialization would be pushed through small-scale projects integrated into the peasant communes. Instead of siphoning off the communes' surplus to build steel mills, industrial development would be aimed at producing tractors, cement for irrigation projects, and other manufactures needed by the peasantry. Enormous publicity was given to efforts to produce steel in "backyard" furnaces, relying on labor rather than on machine-intensive techniques. Mao preached the benefits of backwardness and the joys of mass involvement and looked forward to the withering away of the meddling bureaucracy. Emphasis was placed on self-reliance within the peasant communes, and all aspects of the lives of their members were regulated and regimented by the commune leaders and the heads of the local labor brigades.

Within months after it was launched, all indicators suggested that the Great Leap Forward and rapid collectivization were leading to economic disaster. Peasant resistance to collectivization, the abuses of commune leaders, and the dismal output of the backyard factories combined with the failure of the rains to turn the Great Leap into a giant step backward. The worst famine of the Communist era spread across virtually all of China. For the first time since 1949 China had to import large amounts of grain to feed its people. And the numbers of Chinese to feed continued to grow at an alarming rate. Defiantly rejecting Western and UN proposals for family planning, Mao and like-thinking radicals charged that socialist China could care for its people, no matter how many they were. Birth control was viewed as a symptom of capitalist selfishness and inability to provide a decent living for all the people.

Like those of India, China's birthrates were actually a good deal lower than those in many Third World nations. Also like India, however, the Chinese were adding people to a massive population base. At the time of the Communist rise to power China had approximately 550 million people. By 1965 this number had risen to approximately 750 million. If that rate of growth had continued, some experts predicted that China would have 1.8 billion people by the year 2000.

In the face of the environmental degradation and overcrowding that this leap in population inevitably produced, even the Party ideologues came around to the view that something must be done to curb the birthrate. Beginning in the mid-1960s the government launched a

The famous backyard steel furnaces became a central symbol of China's failed drive for self-sufficiency during the "Great Leap Forward" in the late 1950s.

nationwide family-planning campaign designed to limit urban couples to two children and those in rural areas to one. In the early 1970s, these targets had been scaled back to two children for either urban or rural couples. But by the 1980s just one child per family was allowed. Though there is considerable evidence of official excesses—undue pressure for women to have abortions, for example—these programs have greatly reduced the birthrate and have begun to slow China's overall population increase. But again, the base to which new births are added is already so large that China's population will not stabilize until well into the next century, when there will be far more people than even now to educate, feed, house, and provide with productive work.

Advances made in the first decade of the new regime were lost through amateurish blunders, excesses of overzealous cadre leaders, and students' meddling. China's national productivity fell by as much as 25 percent. Population increase soon overwhelmed the stagnating productivity of both the agricultural and industrial sectors. By 1960 it was clear that the Great Leap must be ended and a new course of development adopted. Mao lost his position as State Chairman (though he remained the head of the Party's Central Committee). The "pragmatists," including Mao's old ally Zhou Enlai,

along with Liu Shaoqui and Deng Xiaoping, came to power determined to restore state direction and market incentives at the local level.

"WOMEN HOLD UP HALF OF THE HEAVENS"

In Mao's struggles to renew the revolutionary fervor of the Chinese people, his wife, Jiang Qing, played an increasingly prominent role. Mao's reliance on her, which had become dependence by the time of his death in 1976, was quite consistent with the commitment to the liberation of Chinese women he had acted on throughout his political career. As a young man he had been deeply moved by a newspaper story about a young girl who had committed suicide rather than be forced by her family to submit to the marriage they had arranged for her with a rich but very elderly man. From that point onward, women's issues and the support of women for the Communist movement became important parts of Mao's revolutionary strategy. Here he was drawing on a well-established revolutionary tradition, for women had been very active in the Taiping Rebellion of the mid-19th century, the Boxer revolt in 1900, and the 1911 revolution that had toppled the Manchu regime. One of the key causes taken up by the May Fourth intellectuals, who had a great impact on the youthful Mao Zedong, was women's rights. Their efforts put an end to foot-binding and did much to advance campaigns to end female seclusion, win legal rights for women, and open educational and career opportunities to them.

The Nationalists' attempts in the late 1920s and 1930s to reverse many of the gains made by women in the early revolution brought many women into the Communist camp. Led by Chiang's wife, Madam Chiang Kai-shek, the Nationalist counteroffensive (like comparable movements in the Fascist countries of Europe at the time) sought to return Chinese women to the home and hearth. Madam Chiang proclaimed a special Good Mother's Day and declared that "virtue was more important [for women] than learning." She taught that it was immoral for a wife to criticize her husband (an ethical precept she herself apparently ignored).

The Nationalist campaign to restore Chinese women to their traditional domestic roles and dependence on males contrasted sharply with the Communists' extensive employment of women to advance the revolutionary cause. Women served as teachers, nurses, spies, truck drivers, and laborers on projects ranging from growing food to building machine-gun bunkers. Though the Party preferred to use them in these support roles, in moments of extreme crisis women became soldiers on the front lines, where many won distinction for their bravery under fire. Some rose to become cadre leaders, and many were prominent in the antilandlord campaigns and agrarian reform. Their contribution to the victory of the revolutionary cause truly bore out Mao's early dictum that the energies and talents of women had to be harnessed to the national cause because, after all, "women hold up half of the heavens."

As was the case in many other African and Asian countries, the victory of the revolution brought women legal equality with men—in itself a revolutionary development in a society like China. Women were expected to choose their marriage partners without familial interference. But arranged marriages persist today, especially in rural areas, and the need to have Party approval for all marriages represents a new form of control beyond the choice of the couple involved.

Women were also expected to work outside the home. Their opportunities for education and professional careers have greatly improved. As in other socialist states, however, openings for employment outside the home have proved something of a burden for Chinese women. Until the late 1970s traditional attitudes toward child rearing and home care prevailed. As a result women were required not only to hold down a regular job but also to raise a family, cook meals, clean, and shop—and all without the benefit of the modern appliances available in Western societies. Though considerable numbers of women held cadre posts at the middle and lower levels of the Party and bureaucracy, the upper echelons of both were overwhelmingly controlled by males.

As in other developing societies the rather brief but very considerable power amassed by Mao's wife, Jiang Qing, in the early 1970s runs counter to the overall dominance of males in politics and the military. In any case, like her counterparts elsewhere, Jiang Qing got to the top because she was married to Mao. She exercised power mainly in his name and was toppled soon after his death when she tried to rule in her own right. Women have come far in China, but, as is the case in most other societies in both the "developed" and "developing" worlds, they have by no means attained full equality with males in career opportunities, social status, or political power.

MAO'S LAST CAMPAIGN AND THE FALL OF THE "GANG OF FOUR"

Having lost his position as head of state but still powerful in the Communist party and by far the most charismatic and popular of the Communist leaders, Mao worked throughout the early 1960s to establish grass roots support for another renewal of the revolutionary struggle. He fiercely opposed the efforts of Deng Xiaoping and his pragmatist allies to scale back the communes, encourage peasant production on what were in effect private plots, and promote economic growth over political orthodoxy. By late 1965 Mao was convinced that his support among the students, peasants, and military was strong enough to launch what would turn out to be his last campaign, the Cultural Revolution. With mass student demonstrations paving the way, he launched an all-out assault on the "capitalist-roaders" in the Party.

Waving the little red books of Mao's pronouncements on all manner of issues, the infamous Red Guard student brigades publicly ridiculed and abused Mao's political rivals. Liu Shaoqui was killed, Deng Xiaoping was imprisoned, and Zhou Enlai was driven into seclusion. The aroused students and the rank and file of the People's Liberation Army were used to pull down the bureaucrats from their positions of power and privilege. College professors, plant managers, and the children of the bureaucratic elite were berated and forced to confess publicly their many crimes against the people. Those who were not imprisoned or, more rarely, killed were forced to do manual labor on rural communes to enable them to understand the hardships endured by China's peasantry. In Shanghai the workers seized control of the factories and local bureaucracy. As Mao had hoped, the centralized state and technocratic elites that had grown steadily since the first revolution won power in 1949 were being torn apart by the rage of the people.

However satisfying for an advocate of continuing revolution like Mao and supporters like his wife, Jiang Qing, who saw her power grow by leaps and bounds as Mao's former compatriots were purged, it was soon clear that the Cultural Revolution threatened to return China to the chaos and vulnerability of the prerevolutionary era. The rank-and-file threat to the leaders of the People's Liberation Army proved in the end decisive in prompting countermeasures that forced Mao to call off the campaign by late 1968. The heads of the armed forces moved to bring the rank and file back into line; the student and worker movements were disbanded and in some cases forcibly repressed. By the early 1970s Mao's old rivals had begun to surface again, and until the mid-1970s a hard-fought struggle was waged at the upper levels of the Party and the army for control of the government. The reconciliation between China and the United States negotiated in the early 1970s suggested that, at least in foreign policy, the pragmatists were gaining the upper hand over the ideologues. Deng's growing role in policy formation from 1973 onward also represented a major setback for Jiang Qing and her three allies, who made up the notorious Gang of Four that increasingly contested power on behalf of the aging Mao.

The death in early 1976 of Zhou Enlai, who was second only to Mao in stature as a revolutionary hero and who had consistently backed the pragmatists, appeared to be a major blow to those whom the Gang of Four had marked out as "capitalist-roaders" and betrayers of the revolution. But Mao's death later in the same year cleared the way for an open clash between the rival factions. While the Gang of Four plotted to seize control of the government, the pragmatists acted in alliance with some of the more influential military leaders. The members of the Gang of Four were arrested, and their supporters' attempts to foment popular insurrections were easily foiled. Later tried for their crimes against the people, Jiang Qing and the members of her clique were purged from the Party and imprisoned for life, after having death sentences commuted.

In the past decade the pragmatists have been ascendant, and leaders such as Deng Xiaoping have opened China to Western influences and considerable capitalist development, if not yet democratic reform. Under Deng and his allies the farming communes have been discontinued and private peasant production for the market encouraged. Private enterprise has also been encouraged in the industrial sector, and experiments have been made with such archcapitalist institutions as a stock exchange and foreign hotel chains.

Unfortunately, economic reforms have not been reinforced by political liberalization. This fact was brutally demonstrated by the government's violent repression of students and workers participating in prodemocracy demonstrations in Tiananmen Square in Beijing and other Chinese cities in June 1989. The harsh prison sentences and summary executions meted out to prodemocracy advocates since the Tiananmen massacres suggest the continuing refusal of China's aging leadership to allow for greater freedom of expression or for fuller participation by the people of China in the political process. The feebleness of the international response to the persecution of dissidents in the People's Republic abets an increasingly dangerous disjuncture between economic change and political repression. The new climate of free enterprise and market competition clashes strongly with the state's ossified Marxist-Leninist ideologies and the corrupt and bloated bureaucracy of an overcentralized political system. As the leaders who made the Maoist revolution and have ruled China for over 40 years die off, the deep contradictions that have developed in Chinese society could lead to renewed social unrest and perhaps widespread civil strife in the coming decades.

Though it has become fashionable to dismiss the development schemes of the Communist states as misguided failures, the achievements of the Communist regime in China over the past four decades have been considerable. Despite severe economic setbacks, political turmoil, and a low level of foreign assistance, the Communists have managed a truly revolutionary redistribution of the wealth of the country. China's very large population remains poor, but in education, health care, housing, working conditions, and the availability of food, most Chinese are far better off than they were in the prerevolutionary era. The Chinese have managed to provide a decent standard of living for a higher proportion of their people than perhaps any other large developing country. They have also achieved higher rates of industrial and agricultural growth than neighboring India, with its mixed state-capitalist economy and

Crack regiments and heavy tanks crush bicycle-wielding student demonstrators in Tiananmen Square, Beijing, in early June 1989.

democratic polity. And the Chinese have done all of this without leaving up to half their people in misery and with much less foreign assistance than most Third World nations. If the pragmatists remain in power and the champions of the market economy are right, China's growth in the coming decades should be even more impressive. But the central challenge for China's leaders will be how to nurture that growth as well as improved living standards without a recurrence of the economic inequities and social injustice that fostered the revolution in the first place.

❦ THE VIETNAM WARS FOR DECOLONIZATION AND NATIONAL LIBERATION

The crumbling of the Confucian order and the nature of French rule in Vietnam made it essential for those who sought to mobilize opposition to the French to promise far-reaching social and economic transformations. As in China and Korea, the failure of the Confucian elite in Vietnam to ward off the intrusions of the West led to the rejection of Confucian civilization as a whole. As a result and in contrast to the peoples of most of the rest of the Afro-Asian world, the Vietnamese were left without a tradition to defend and to revive as an alternative to European colonialism. Unlike Islam, Hinduism, and Buddhism elsewhere, the depoliticized, eclectic, and rather amorphous variant of Buddhism in Vietnam was not seen by the emerging nationalists of the country as a viable base on which to build a postcolonial order. The fact that the breakdown of the Confucian system was paralleled by the worsening condition of the peasantry resulting from French exploitive policies rendered mere political responses insufficient. The substitution of French-educated, middle-class Vietnamese politicians for French colonial officials would do little to alleviate the misery of the peasant farmers of the north or the plantation workers in the south.

In any case the middle class could make little headway even in the political sphere against determined repression by the French. In contrast to the policies followed in most other nonsettler colonies, the French prohibited all but the most innocuous political organizations. The Vietnamese press was tightly controlled; even moderate political parties were smashed, and mass demonstrations of any kind were strictly prohibited. The French doggedly refused to negotiate seriously with, much less make any significant constitutional concessions to, the bourgeois nationalists, whose collaboration was a major prop of their continued domination in Indochina. Under these circumstances the gradual transfer of power from the colonizers to the nationalists, which had been a key factor in peaceful decolonization in other areas, was out of the question. As a consequence underground terrorist and guerrilla organizations, such as the VNQDD and the Communist party, dominated the struggle for independence by the 1920s.

Even the Japanese takeover in the 1940s, which proved so crucial to the strengthening of moderate, constitutional nationalist organizations in Burma, Indonesia, the Philippines, and other areas they occupied, had the reverse effect in Indochina. For most of the period of occupation the Japanese were content to let French collaborators, linked to the Nazi-puppet Vichy regime then in power in France, continue to run the colony under their supervision. As a result the policy of repressing nationalist organizations continued. Thus any hopes for building a nonviolent, moderate party that could rival the Communists were again crushed. The violent struggle against the Japanese, the French, and later the Americans only reinforced the revolutionary orientation of the Vietnamese Communist party.

THE WAR OF LIBERATION AGAINST THE FRENCH

Operating out of bases in south China during World War II, the Communist-dominated nationalist movement, known as the Viet Minh, established liberated areas throughout the northern Red River delta. As in Korea the abrupt end of Japanese rule left a vacuum in Vietnam, which only the Viet Minh was prepared to fill. Its programs for land reform and mass education had wide appeal among the hard-pressed peasants of the north, where they had been propagated during the 1930s and especially the war years. The fact that the Viet Minh put their reform and community-building programs into effect in the areas they controlled won them very solid support among much of the rural population. The Viet Minh's efforts to provide assistance to the peasants during the terrible famine of 1944 and 1945 also convinced the much abused Vietnamese people that here at last was a political organization that was genuinely committed to improving their lot.

Under the leadership of General Giap the Viet Minh skillfully employed guerrilla tactics similar to those devised by Mao in China. These offset the advantages that first the French and then the Japanese enjoyed in conventional firepower. With a strong base of support in much of the rural north and the hill regions, where they had won the support of key non-Vietnamese "tribal"

peoples, the Viet Minh forces advanced triumphantly into the Red River delta as the Japanese withdrew. By August 1945 the Viet Minh were in control of Hanoi, where Ho Chi Minh proclaimed the establishment of the independent nation of Vietnam.

Though the Viet Minh had liberated much of the north, they had very little control in the south, where a variety of Communist and bourgeois nationalist parties jostled for power. The French, eager to reclaim their colonial empire and put behind them their humiliations at the hands of the Nazis, were quick to exploit this turmoil. With British assistance, the French reoccupied Saigon and much of south and central Vietnam. In March 1946 they denounced the August declaration of Vietnamese independence and moved to reassert their colonial control over the whole of Vietnam and the rest of Indochina. An unsteady truce between the French and the Viet Minh quickly broke down, and Vietnam was soon consumed by a renewal of the Viet Minh's guerrilla war for liberation, as well as bloody in-fighting between the various factions of the Vietnamese. After nearly a decade of indecisive struggle, the Viet Minh had gained control of much of the Vietnamese countryside, while the French, with increasing U.S. financial and military aid, clung to the fortified towns. In 1954 the Viet Minh decisively defeated the French at Dien Bien Phu in the mountain highlands near the Laotian border. The victory won the Viet Minh control of the northern portions of Vietnam as a result of an international conference at Geneva in the same year. At Geneva elections throughout Vietnam were promised within two years to decide who should govern a reunited north and the still politically fragmented south.

THE WAR OF LIBERATION AGAINST THE UNITED STATES

The promise at Geneva that free elections would be held to determine who should govern a united Vietnam was never kept. Like the rest of East Asia, Vietnam had become entangled in the cold war maneuvers of the United States and the Soviet Union. Despite very amicable cooperation between the Viet Minh and U.S. armed forces during the war against Japan, U.S. support for the French in the First Indochina War and the growing fame of Ho Chi Minh as a Communist leader drove the two farther and farther apart. The anti-Communist hysteria in the United States in the early 1950s fed the perception of influential U.S. leaders that, like South Korea, South Vietnam must be protected from Communist takeover.

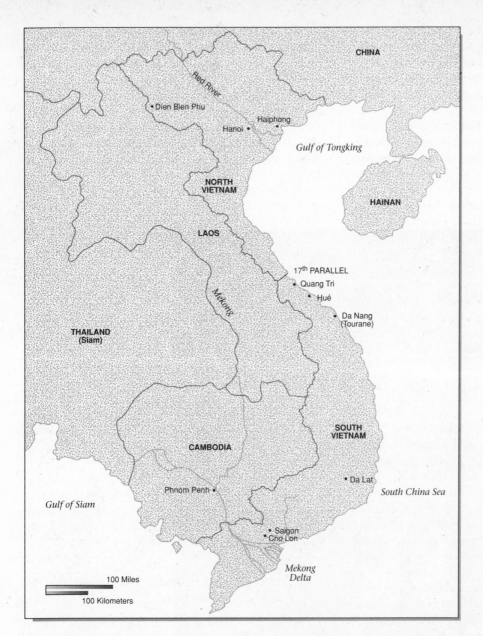

Vietnam After Division into North and South in 1954

The search for a leader to build a government in the south that the United States could prop up with economic and military assistance led to Ngo Dinh Diem. Diem appeared to have impeccable nationalist credentials. In fact, he had gone into exile rather than give up the struggle against the French. His sojourn in the United States in the 1940s and the fact that he was a Catholic also recommended him to U.S. political and church leaders. Unfortunately, these same aspects of his personal history would alienate him from the great majority of the Vietnamese people.

With U.S. backing, Diem was installed as the president of Vietnam, a status he tried to legitimatize in the late 1950s by holding rigged elections in the south, in which the Communists were not permitted to run. Diem also mounted a series of campaigns to eliminate by force all possible political rivals in the south. Because the Communists posed the biggest threat (and were of the greatest concern to Diem's U.S. backers), the suppression campaign increasingly focused on the Communist cadres remaining in the south after Vietnam had been divided at Geneva. By the mid-1950s the Viet

Cong (as the Diem regime dubbed the Communist resistance) were threatened with extermination. In response to this threat the Communist regime in the north
began to supply weapons, advisors, and other resources
to the southern cadres, which were reorganized as the
National Liberation Front in 1958.

As guerrilla warfare spread and Diem's military responses expanded, both the United States and North
Vietnam escalated their support for the warring parties.

When Diem proved unable to stem the Communist tide
in the countryside, the United States gave the go-ahead
for the military to overthrow him and take direct charge
of the war. When the Vietnamese military could make
little headway, the United States stepped up its direct
military intervention.

The U.S. commitment rose from thousands of special
advisors in the early 1950s to nearly 500,000 men and
women, who made up a massive force of occupation, by

After decades of struggle
against foreign invaders,
Vietnamese guerrillas
marched with the regular
forces of the North
Vietnamese army into
Saigon in May 1975. The
capture of the city marked
the end of the long wars to
free a unified Vietnam.

1968. But despite the loss of nearly 60,000 U.S. lives and hundreds of thousands of casualties, the Americans could not defeat the Communist movement. In part their failure resulted from their very presence, which made it possible for the Communists to convince the great majority of the Vietnamese people that they were fighting for their independence from yet another imperialist aggressor.

Though more explosives were dropped on both North and South Vietnam than in all the theaters of the Second World War and the United States resorted to chemical warfare against the environment of the South Vietnamese they claimed to be trying to save, the Communists would not yield. The indomitable Vietnamese emerged as the victors of the Second Indochina War. In the early 1970s U.S. diplomats negotiated an end to direct U.S. involvement in the conflict. Without that support the unpopular military regime in the south fell apart by 1975. The Communists united Vietnam under a single government for the first time since the late 1850s. But the nation they governed was shattered and impoverished by decades of civil war, revolution, and armed conflict with two major colonial powers and the most powerful nation of the second half of the 20th century.

AFTER VICTORY—THE STRUGGLE TO REBUILD VIETNAM

In the years since 1975 and the end of what was for the Vietnamese decades of wars for liberation, Communist efforts to complete the revolution by rebuilding Vietnamese society have floundered. In part this failure can be linked to Vietnam's isolation from much of the rest of the international community. This isolation resulted both from pressures applied by a vengeful United States against relief from international agencies and from border clashes with China that were linked to ancient rivalries between the two countries. Deprived of substantial assistance from abroad and faced with a shattered economy and a devastated environment at home, Vietnam's aging revolutionary leaders pushed hard-line Marxist-Leninist (and even Stalinist) political and economic agendas. Like their Chinese counterparts, they devoted considerable energies to persecuting old enemies (thus setting off mass migrations from what had been South Vietnam) and imposed a dictatorial regime that left little room for popular responses to government initiatives. In contrast to the Chinese in the past decade, however, the Vietnamese leadership also sought to maintain a highly centralized, command economy that

stifled growth and, if anything, left the Vietnamese people almost as impoverished as they had been after a century of colonialism and decades of civil war.

By the late 1980s the obvious failure of these approaches and the collapse of Communist regimes throughout Eastern Europe prompted measures aimed at liberalizing and expanding the market sector within the Vietnamese economy. The encouraging responses of Japanese and European corporations, eager to open up Vietnamese markets, have done much to begin the revival of the Vietnamese economy. Growing investments by their industrial rivals have placed increasing pressure on U.S. firms to move into the Vietnamese market. Combined with a genuine willingness shown by the Vietnamese leadership in the past few years to work with U.S. officials to resolve questions about POWs and MIAs from the Vietnam War, these economic incentives give promise of a new and much more constructive era in Vietnamese-U.S. relations in the 21st century.

REVOLUTIONS AND SUPERPOWER INTERVENTIONS IN LATIN AMERICA

By the 1940s frustration had built up considerable pressure for change throughout much of Latin America. Across the political spectrum there was a desire to improve the social and economic conditions throughout the region and a general agreement that development and economic strength were the keys to a better future. How to achieve those goals, however, remained in question. One-party rule continued in Mexico, and the "Revolution" became increasingly conservative and interested in economic growth rather than social justice. In Venezuela and Costa Rica reform-minded democratic parties were able to win elections in an open political system. In other places such a solution was less likely or less attractive to those who wished to bring about reform. Unlike the Mexican revolutionaries of 1910 through 1920, those seeking change in the post–World War II period could turn to the well-developed political philosophy of Marxian socialism as a guide. Such models, however, were fraught with dangers because of the context of the cold war and the ideological struggle between Western Europe and the Soviet bloc.

Throughout Latin America the failures of political democratization, economic development, and social reforms led to the consideration of radical and revolutionary solutions to national problems. During the 1950s three major attempts at radical change were made in Latin America with very different results.

GUATEMALA: REFORM AND
U.S. INTERVENTION

The first place where more radical solutions were tried was Guatemala. This predominantly Indian nation suffered from some of the worst features of the region's problems. Its population was mostly illiterate and suffered poor health conditions and high mortality rates. Land and wealth were very unequally distributed, and the whole economy depended on the highly volatile prices for its main exports, coffee and bananas. In 1944 a middle-class and labor coalition elected a reformer, Juan José Arevalo as president. With a new constitution he began a series of programs within the context of "spiritual socialism" that included land reform and an improvement in the rights and conditions of rural and industrial workers. An income tax, the first in the nation's history, was projected, and educational reforms were planned. These programs and his sponsorship of an intense nationalism brought the Arevalo government into direct conflict with foreign interests operating in Guatemala, especially the United Fruit Company, the largest and most important foreign concern there. That company had operated in Guatemala from the turn of the century, had acquired extensive properties, and also controlled transportation and shipping facilities. Its workers were often better paid than the average, and its health and other benefits were more extensive; but because it was a foreign company with such a powerful role in Guatemala, United Fruit was the target of nationalistic anger.

After a free election in 1951 the presidency passed to Colonel Jacobo Arbenz, whose nationalist program was more radical and whose public statements against foreign economic interests and the landholding oligarchy were more extreme than under Arevalo. Arbenz announced a number of programs to improve or to nationalize the transportation network, the hydroelectric system, and other areas of the economy. A move to expropriate unused lands on large estates in 1953 provoked opposition from the landed oligarchy and from United Fruit, which was eventually threatened with the loss of almost half a million acres of "reserve" land. The U.S. government, fearing "Communist" penetration of the Arbenz government and under considerable pressure from United Fruit Company, denounced the changes and began to impose economic and diplomatic restrictions on Guatemala. At the same time, the level of nationalist rhetoric intensified, and the government increasingly received the support of the political left in Latin America and in the socialist bloc.

In 1954, with the help of the Central Intelligence Agency, a dissident military force was organized and invaded Guatemala. The Arbenz government fell, and the pro-U.S. regime that replaced it then turned back the land reform and negotiated a settlement favorable for United Fruit. The reform experiment was thus brought to a halt. In retrospect, by the standards of the 1960s, the programs of Arevalo and Arbenz seemed rather mild, although undoubtedly Arbenz's statements and his acceptance of arms from Eastern Europe had contributed to U.S. intervention. The reforms promised by the U.S. supported governments were minimal. Guatemala continued to be characterized by a low standard of living, especially for its Indian population. The series of military governments following the coup failed to address the nation's social and economic problems. That failure led to continual violence and political instability. A coalition of coffee planters, foreign companies, and the military controlled political life. A guerrilla movement grew and provoked brutal military repression, which once again fell particularly hard on the rural Indian population. Guatemala's attempt at radical change, which began with an eye toward improving the conditions of the people, failed because of external intervention.

THE BOLIVIAN REVOLUTION: A LOSS
OF DIRECTION

Another predominantly Indian nation, Bolivia, was the scene of a similar movement for revolutionary change, but its outcome differed. Long characterized by political instability and with an economy considerably weakened after the loss of territory and access to the sea in the War of the Pacific against neighboring Chile (1879–1883), Bolivia experienced a period of expansion in the 1920s as demands for its major products, silver and tin, increased. Foreign companies, such as Standard Oil of New Jersey, secured concessions to exploit its major resources, and the government took large loans from U.S. banks to finance various projects. With the world financial crisis of 1929 and a drop in the price of tin, the Bolivian economy was thrown into crisis. To make matters worse, a war broke out with neighboring Paraguay over the disputed region of the Chaco, which blocked Bolivia's access to the rivers leading to the Atlantic and which was thought to contain rich petroleum deposits. The Chaco War (1932–1935) led to high casualties on both sides and more political instability in Bolivia, as defeat by Paraguay led to disillusionment.

U.S. fears of Soviet influence in Guatemala and sweeping land reforms that threatened U.S. interests led to the coup of 1954. Members of the U.S.-supported "Liberation Army" train their guns on an effigy of the overthrown leftist president, Arbenz. The sign on the effigy says, "I am going back to Russia with Arevalo."

Despite rhetoric to the contrary, little was done through the 1920s and 1930s to lessen the great social gap between the mass of the Indian population and the urban elites or to improve the conditions of the miners, the backbone of the nation's work force. As late as 1950 more than 90 percent of the land was owned by 6 percent of the population, and Indians were often treated like serfs. Conditions in the mines were abysmal, and to a large extent three foreign-owned or controlled mining companies regulated that sector of the economy. Little could be done to change this situation. Because of literacy requirements and gender exclusion for voting, less than 7 percent of the population was entitled to cast ballots.

After an army coup to forestall the electoral victory of a reformist and nationalist political coalition called the National Revolutionary Movement (MNR), a revolt erupted in 1952. Although initially an urban political movement, it soon became a real revolution as Indian peasants and mining workers joined in, taking up arms and seizing lands and mines. This was a violent social movement in which armed workers and peasants joined with students and radical middle-class interests against the army, the mine owners, and the landed elite. Winning the government, the MNR initiated a series of reforms, including universal suffrage, nationalization of the mines, land expropriation and redistribution, and the movement of population from the Andes to unused lands in the nation's eastern lowlands. The mines, long controlled by three great companies, were nationalized, and the government raised wages and benefits. Land redistribution was extensive. With militant and armed worker and peasant organizations, the government cut back on support for the military, whose power was greatly reduced for a while. The United States, faced with these revolutionary changes, acted cautiously, but since the level of socialist rhetoric was relatively muted and there seemed to be no direct "external" involvement, the United States recognized the revolutionary government and offered financial assistance, sometimes in large amounts.

The momentum of revolutionary change could not be maintained, however. The mining and agricultural sectors were disrupted by the changes and by poor world prices in the 1960s for tin and other Bolivian minerals. Fearing the radical unions, the government allowed the military to regain some of its power, and then the MNR began to maneuver to ensure its continuance in power. By 1964 the military stepped in again. Since then a series of military governments has ruled for most of the time. Although a few of the governments have promised reforms and continuation of the principles of the 1952 revolution, most have been more interested in the maintenance of order. By the 1980s little was left of the revolutionary program, and new cartels of cocaine producers linked to the government and the military emerged. The Bolivian Revolution failed not because of outside intervention as much as from the mistakes of its leadership, the weight of the nation's past, and its problems that continue to the present day.

THE CUBAN REVOLUTION: SOCIALISM IN THE CARIBBEAN

The differences between Cuba and Bolivia or Guatemala underline the diversity of Latin America. The island nation had a population of about six million, most of whom were the descendants of Spaniards and the African slaves who had been imported to produce the sugar, tobacco, and hides that were the colony's mainstays. Cuba had a relatively large middle class, and levels of literacy and health care were better than in most of the rest of the region. Rural areas lagged behind in these matters, however, and there the working and living conditions were poor, especially for the workers on the large sugar estates. Always in the shadow of the United States, Cuban politics and economy were rarely free of U.S. interests. By the 1950s about three-fourths of Cuba's imports came from the United States; U.S. investments in the island were heavy during the 1940s and 1950s. Although the island experienced periods of prosperity, fluctuations in the world market for Cuba's main product, sugar, revealed the tenuous basis of its economy. Moreover, the disparity between the countryside and the growing middle class in Havana underlined the nation's continuing problems.

From 1934 to 1944 Cuba had been ruled by Fulgencio Batista, a strong-willed, authoritarian reformer who had risen from the lower ranks of the army. Among his reforms were a democratic constitution of 1940 that promised major changes, nationalization of natural re-

sources, full employment, and land reform. Batista's programs of reform, however, began to founder on the shoals of graft and corruption, and when in 1952 he returned to the presidency, there was little left of the reformer but a great deal of the dictator. Opposition developed in various sectors of society. Among the regime's opponents was Fidel Castro, a young lawyer experienced in leftist university politics and an ardent critic of the Batista government and the ills of Cuban society. On July 26, 1953, Castro and a few followers launched an unsuccessful attack on some military barracks. Captured, Castro faced a trial, an occasion he used to expound his revolutionary ideals, which were mostly aimed at a return to democracy, social justice, and the establishment of a less dependent economy.

Released from prison, Castro fled to exile in Mexico, where, with the aid of Ernesto "Che" Guevara, a militant Argentine revolutionary, a small military force was gathered. They landed in Cuba in 1956 and slowly began to gather strength in the mountains. By 1958 the

Fidel Castro and his guerrilla army finally brought the downfall of the Batista government in January 1959, to the wild acclaim of many Cubans. Castro began to initiate sweeping reforms in Cuba that eventually led to the creation of a socialist regime and the hostility of the United States.

"26th of July Movement" had found support from students, some labor organizations, and rural workers and was able to conduct operations against Batista's army. The bearded rebels, or *barbudos,* won a series of victories. The dictator, under siege and isolated by the United States (which refused to support him any longer), was driven from power, and the rebels took Havana amid wild scenes of genuine joy and relief.

What happened next is highly debatable, and Castro himself has offered varying interpretations at different times. Whether Castro was already a Marxist-Leninist and had always intended to introduce a socialist regime (as he now claims) or whether the development of this program was the result of a series of pragmatic decisions is in question. Rather than simply returning to the constitution of 1940 and enacting moderate reforms, Castro launched a program of sweeping change that altered the nature of Cuba. Foreign properties were expropriated, farms were collectivized, and a centralized socialist economy was put in place. Most of these changes were accompanied by a nationalist and antiimperialist foreign policy. Relations with the United States were broken off in 1961, and Cuba increasingly depended on the financial support and arms of the Soviet Union to maintain its revolution. With that support in place, Castro was able to survive the increasingly hostile reaction of the United States. That reaction included a disastrous U.S.-sponsored invasion by Cuban exiles in 1961 and an embargo on trade with Cuba. Dependence on the Soviet Union led to a crisis in 1962, when Soviet nuclear missiles were discovered in Cuba and a confrontation between the superpowers ensued. Despite these problems, to a large extent the Cuban Revolution survived because the politics of the cold war provided Cuba with a protector and a benefactor.

The results of the revolution have been mixed. The social programs were extensive. Education, health, and housing have greatly improved, especially in the long neglected rural areas, and rank Cuba among the world's leaders—quite unlike most other nations of the region. A wide variety of social and educational programs has mobilized all sectors of the population. To some extent the achievements have been accompanied by severe restrictions of basic freedoms.

Attempts to diversify and strengthen the economy have been less successful. An effort to industrialize in the 1960s failed, and Cuba turned again to its ability to produce sugar. The world's falling sugar and rising petroleum prices led to a disastrous situation. Only a subsidy for Cuban sugar and the supply of petroleum below the world price enabled the Soviet Union to maintain the Cuban economy, which has become increasingly dependent on the Soviet Union and the nations of Eastern Europe. Despite these problems the Cuban Revolution has offered an example that has proved attractive to those seeking the transformation of Latin American societies. Early direct attempts to spread the model of the Cuban Revolution, such as Che Guevara's guerrilla

---

DOCUMENT
THE PEOPLE SPEAK

Scholarly analysis of general trends often cannot convey the way in which historical events and patterns affect the lives of people or the fact that history is made up of the collective experience of individuals. It is often very difficult to know about the lives of common people in the past or to learn about their perceptions of their lives. In recent years in Latin America, however, a growing literature of autobiographies, interpreted autobiographies (when another writer puts the story down and edits it), and collections of interviews have provided a vision of the lives of common people. These statements, like any historical document, must always be used carefully because their authors or editors sometimes have political purposes, because they reflect individual opinions, or because the events they report may be atypical. Nevertheless, these personal statements do put flesh and blood on the bones of history and provide an important perspective from those whose voice in history is often lost.

A BOLIVIAN WOMAN DESCRIBES HER LIFE

Domitilia Barrios de Chungara, a miner's wife, became politically active in the mine workers' political movement. Her presence at the UN-sponsored

International Woman's Year Tribunal in 1975 moved a Brazilian journalist to organize her statements into a book about her life. This excerpt provides a picture of the everyday struggle for life.

My day begins at four in the morning, especially when my compañero is on the first shift. I prepare his breakfast. Then I have to prepare *salteñas* [small meat pastries] because I make about one hundred salteñas every day and I sell them on the street. I do this in order to make up for what my husband's wage doesn't cover in terms of our necessities. The night before, we prepare the dough and at four in the morning I make the *salteñas* while I feed the kids. The kids help me.

Then the ones that go to school in the morning have to get ready, while I wash the clothes left soaking over night.

At eight I go out to sell. The kids that go to school in the afternoon help me. We have to go to the company store and bring home the staples. And in the store there are immensely long lines and you have to wait there until eleven in order to stock up. You have to line up for meat, for vegetables, for oil. So it's just one line after another. Since everything is in a different place, that's how it has to be.

From what we earn between my husband and me, we can eat and dress. Food is very expensive: 28 pesos for a kilo of meat, 4 pesos for carrots, 6 pesos for onions. . . . Considering that my compañero earns 28 pesos a day, that's hardly enough is it?

We don't ever buy ready made clothes. We buy wool and knit. At the beginning of each year, I also spend about 2,000 pesos on cloth and a pair of shoes for each of us. And the company discounts some of that each month from my husband's wage. On the pay slips that's referred to as the "bundle." And what happens is that before we finish paying the "bundle" our shoes are worn out. That's how it is.

Well, from eight to eleven in the morning I sell *salteñas*. I do the shopping in the grocery store, and I also work at the Housewives Committee, talking with the sisters who go there for advice.

At noon, lunch has to be ready because the rest of the kids have to go to school.

In the afternoon I have to wash clothes. There are no laundries. We use troughs and have to get the water from a pump.

I've got to correct the kids' homework and prepare everything I'll need to make the next day's *salteñas*.

FROM PEASANT TO REVOLUTIONARY

Rigoberta Menchú, a Quiché Indian from the Guatemalan highlands, came from a peasant family that had been drawn into politics during the repression of Indian communities and human rights in the 1970s. In these excerpts she reveals her disillusionment with the government and her realization of the ethnic division between Indians and *ladinos*, or mestizos, that complicates political action in Guatemala.

The CUC [Peasant Union] started growing; it spread like wildfire among the peasants in Guatemala. We began to understand that the root of all our problems was exploitation. That there were rich and poor and that the rich exploited the poor— our sweat, our labor. That's how the rich got richer and richer. The fact that we were always waiting in offices, always bowing to the authorities was part of the discrimination that we Indians suffered.

The situation got worse when the murderous generals came to power although I did not actually know who was the president at the time. I began to know them from 1974 when General Kjell Langerud came to power. He came to our region and said: "We're going to solve the land problem. The land belongs to you. You cultivate the land and I will share it out among you." We trusted him. I was at the meeting when [he] spoke. And what did he give us? My father tortured and imprisoned.

Later I had the opportunity of meeting other Indians. Achi Indians, the group that lives closest to us. And I got to know some Mam Indians too. They all told me: "The rich are bad. But not all *ladinos* are bad." And I started wondering: "Could it be that not all *ladinos* are bad? . . ." There were poor *ladinos* as well as rich *ladinos*, and they were exploited as well. That's when I began recognizing exploitation. I kept on going to the *finca* [large farm] but now I really wanted to find out, to prove if that was true and learn the details. There were poor *ladinos* on the *finca*. They worked the same, and their children's bellies were swollen like my little brother's. . . . I was just beginning to speak a little Spanish in those days and I began to talk to them. I said to one poor *ladino:* "You are a poor *ladino,* aren't you?" And he nearly hit me. He said: "What do you know about it, Indian?" I wondered: "Why is that when I say poor *ladinos* are like us, I'm spurned?" I didn't know then that the same system which tries to isolate us Indians also puts barriers between Indians and *ladinos.* . . . Soon afterwards, I was with the nuns and we went to a village in Uspantán where mostly *ladinos* live. The nun asked a little boy if they were poor and he said: "Yes, we're poor but we're not Indians." That stayed with me. The nun didn't notice, she went on talking.

She was foreign, she wasn't Guatemalan. She asked someone else the same question and he said: "Yes, we're poor but we're not Indians." It was very painful for me to accept that an Indian was inferior to a *ladino.* I kept on worrying about it. It's a big barrier they've sown between us, between Indian and *ladino.* I didn't understand it.

Questions: What was distinctive about lower-class life and outlook in late-20th-century Latin America? How had life of the lower class changed from the 19th century?

operation in Bolivia, where he lost his life in 1967, were failures, but the Cuban model and the island's ability to resist the pressure of a hostile United States proved attractive to other nations in the Caribbean and Central America, such as Grenada and Nicaragua, that have also sought the revolutionary option.

THE SEARCH FOR REFORM AND THE MILITARY OPTION

The revolutionary attempts of the 1950s, the durability of the Cuban Revolution, and the general appeal of Marxist doctrines in the Third World underlined Latin America's proclivity for revolutionary change, so long as real reforms in its economic and social structures remained unrealized. How could the traditional patterns of inequality and international dependency be overcome? What was the best path to the future?

For some, the answer was political stability, imposed if necessary, in order to ensure conditions for capitalist economic growth. The one-party system of Mexico demonstrated its capacity for repression when student dissidents were brutally killed during disturbances in 1968. Mexico enjoyed some prosperity from its petroleum resources in the 1970s, but poor financial planning, corruption, and foreign debt had again caused problems by the 1980s, and the PRI seemed to be losing its ability to maintain control of Mexican politics.

For others the Church, long a power in Latin America, provided a guide. Christian Democratic parties formed in Chile and Venezuela in the 1950s, hoping to bring reforms through popularly based mass parties that would preempt the radical left. The Church, in fact, was

often divided politically, but the clergy took an increasingly "engaged" position, arguing for social justice and human rights, often in support of government opponents. A few, such as Father Camilo Torres in Colombia, joined armed revolutionary groups in the 1960s.

More common was the emergence within the Church hierarchy of an increased concern for social justice. By the 1970s a "liberation theology" combined Catholic theology and socialist principles in an effort to bring about improved conditions for the poor. When criticized for promoting communism in his native Brazil, Dom Helder da Camara, archbishop of Pernambuco, remarked: "The trouble with Brazil is not an excess of Communist doctrine, but a lack of Christian justice." The position of the Church in Latin American societies was changing, but there was no single program for this new stance or even agreement among the clergy about its validity. Still, this activist position provoked attacks against such clergymen as the courageous Archbishop Oscar Romero of El Salvador, who was assassinated in 1980. The Church also played an important role in the fall of the Paraguayan dictatorship in 1988.

OUT OF THE BARRACKS: SOLDIERS TAKE POWER

The success of the Cuban Revolution also impressed and worried those who feared revolutionary change within a Communist political system. The military forces in Latin America had been involved in politics since the days of the caudillos in the 19th century, and in a number of nations military interventions had been relatively common. As the Latin American military became more professionalized, however, a new philosophy underlay the military's involvement in politics. The soldiers began to see themselves as above the selfish interests of political parties and as the "true" representatives of the nation. With considerable technical training and organizational skills, military officers by the 1920s and 1930s believed that they were best equipped to solve their nations' problems, even if that meant sacrificing the democratic processes and imposing martial law.

In the 1960s the Latin American military establishments, made nervous by the Cuban success and the swing to leftist or populist regimes, began to intervene directly in the political process, not simply to clean out a disliked president or party, as they had done in the past, but to take over government itself. In 1964 the Brazilian military (with the compliance of the United States and supported by the middle class) overthrew the elected president after he threatened a number of sweeping social reforms. In Argentina growing polarization between the Peronists and the middle class led to a military intervention in 1966. In Chile President Salvador Allende's Socialist government was overthrown in 1973 by the Chilean military, which until then had remained for the most part out of politics. Allende had nationalized industries and banks and had sponsored peasant and worker expropriations of lands and factories. His government was caught in an increasing polarization between groups trying to halt these changes and those pushing for faster and more radical reforms. By 1973 the economy was in serious difficulty, undermined by resistence in Chile and by U.S. policies designed to isolate the country. Allende was killed during the military coup against him, and throughout Latin America there were demonstrations against the military and U.S. involvement. But Chile was not alone. Similar coups took place in Peru in 1968 and in Uruguay in 1973.

The soldiers in power imposed a new type of "bureaucratic authoritarian regime." Their governments were supposed to stand above competing demands of various sectors and establish economic stability. Now, as arbiters of politics, the soldiers would place the national interest above "selfish interests" by imposing dictatorships. Government was essentially a presidency controlled by the military in which policies were formulated and applied by a bureaucracy organized like a military chain of command. Political repression and torture were used to silence critics, and stringent measures were imposed in order to control inflation and strengthen the economies. Laws limited political freedoms, and repression often was brutal and illegal. In Argentina violent

opposition to military rule led to a counteroffensive and a "dirty war" in which thousands of people were "disappeared" [kidnapped] and brutally tortured or killed by government security forces.

Government economic policies fell heaviest on labor and the working class. The goal of the military in Brazil and Argentina was "development" and to some extent, in Brazil at least, considerable economic improvements took place, although income distribution became even more unequal than it had been. Inflation was reduced, industrialization increased, and gains were made in literacy and health, but basic structural problems, such as land ownership and social conditions for the poorest members of society, remained unchanged.

There were variations within these military regimes. All were nationalistic. The Peruvian military tried to create a mass base for its programs and sought to mobilize popular support among the peasantry. It had a real social program, including extensive land reform, and was not simply a surrogate for the conservatives in Peruvian society. In Chile and Uruguay the military was fiercely anti-Communist. In Argentina nationalism and a desire to gain popular support in the face of a worsening economy led to a confrontation with Great Britain over the Falkland Islands (Islas Malvinas), which both nations claimed. A short war in 1982 resulted in an Argentine defeat and a loss in the military's credibility that contributed to its loss of authority.

THE NEW DEMOCRATIC TREND

By the mid-1980s the military had begun to return government to civilian politicians in Argentina and elsewhere in South America. Continuing economic problems and the pressures of containing opponents wore heavily on the military leaders, who began to realize that their solutions were no more destined to success than those of civilian governments. Moreover, the populist parties, such as the Peronists and Apristas, seemed less of a threat, and the fear of Cuban-style communism had diminished. In Argentina elections were held in 1983. Brazil began a process to restore democratic government after 1985 and in 1989 chose its first popularly elected president since the military takeover. The South American military bureaucrats and modernizers were returning to their barracks.

The process of redemocratization was neither easy nor universal. In Peru "Sendero Luminoso (Shining Path)," a long-sustained leftist guerrilla movement, controlled areas of the countryside and tried to disrupt national elections in 1990. The organization was considerably weakened however in 1992 by the capture and imprisonment of its leader "Chairman Gonzalo" (Abimael Guzmán). In Central America the military cast a long shadow over the government in El Salvador. After the elections of 1990, which removed the Sandinistas from control in Nicaragua, an uneasy truce continued between them and the centralist government of Violeta Chamorro, the newly elected president. The United States demonstrated its continuing power in the region in its invasion of Panama and the arrest of its strongman leader Manuel Noriega.

Latin American governments in the 1980s faced tremendous problems. Large foreign loans taken in the 1970s for the purposes of development, sometimes for unnecessary projects, had created a tremendous level of debt that threatened the economic stability of Brazil, Peru, and Mexico. High rates of inflation provoked social instability as real wages fell. Pressure from the international banking community to curb inflation by cutting government spending and reducing wages often ignored the social and political consequences of such actions. Programs to control inflation, such as that introduced by Brazilian president Fernando Collor de Mello, were shock treatments that often disrupted the economy as a whole.

By the late 1980s an international commerce in drugs, which produced tremendous profits, stimulated criminal activity and created powerful international cartels that could even threaten national sovereignty, as they did in Colombia. In countries as diverse as Cuba, Panama, and Bolivia the narcotics trade penetrated the highest government circles.

THE UNITED STATES AND LATIN AMERICA

As a backdrop to the political and economic story we have traced thus far stands the continuing presence of the United States. After World War I the United States had emerged as the predominant power in the hemisphere, a position it had already begun to assume at the close of the 19th century with the Cuban-Spanish-American War and the building of the Panama Canal. European nations were displaced as the leading investors in Latin America by the United States. In South America private investments by U.S. companies and entrepreneurs, as well as loans from the U.S. government, were the chief means of U.S. influence. U.S. investments rose to over $5 billion by 1929, or more than one-third of all U.S. investments abroad.

In Cuba and Puerto Rico, of course, there was direct U.S. involvement and almost a protectorate status. But in the Caribbean and Central America the face of U.S. power, economic interest, and disregard for the sovereignty of weaker neighbors was most apparent. Military interventions to protect U.S.-owned properties and investments became common. There were over 30 prior to 1933. Haiti, Nicaragua, the Dominican Republic, Mexico, and Cuba all witnessed one or more direct interventions by U.S. troops. Central America was a peculiar case because the level of U.S. private investments of companies such as United Fruit was very high, and the economies of these countries were so closely tied to the United States. Those who resisted the U.S. presence were treated as "bandits" by expeditionary forces. In Nicaragua Augusto Sandino led a resistance movement against occupying troops until his assassination by the U.S.-trained Nicaraguan National Guard in 1934. His struggle against U.S. intervention made him a hero and the figurehead of the Sandinista party, which carried out a socialist revolution in Nicaragua in the 1980s.

The grounds for these interventions were economic, political, strategic, and ideological. The direct interventions were usually followed by the creation or support of conservative governments, often dictatorships that would be "friendly" to the United States. These became "Banana Republics," a reference to not only their dependence on the export of tropical products but also their often subservient and corrupt governments.

Foreign interventions contributed to a growing nationalist reaction. Central America with its continuing political problems became a symbol of Latin America's weakness in the face of foreign, especially U.S., influence and interference. The Nobel Prize–winning Chilean Communist poet Pablo Neruda, in his poem "The United Fruit Co." (1950), spoke of the dictators of Central America as "circus flies, wise flies, learned in tyranny" who buzzed over the graves of the people. He wrote the following eight lines with passion:

> *When the trumpet sounded, all was prepared*
> * in the land,*
> *and Jehovah divided the world between*
> * Coca Cola Inc.,*
> *Anaconda, Ford Motors, and other companies:*
> *United Fruit Co. reserved for itself the juiciest part,*
> *the central coast of my land,*
> *the sweet waist of America*
> *and baptized again its lands*
> *as Banana Republics. . . .*

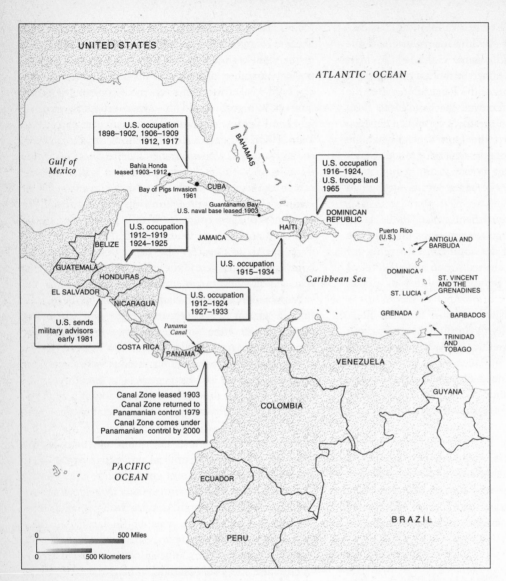

Intervention in Central America and the Caribbean, 1898–1981

The actions of the United States changed considerably after 1933, when President Roosevelt introduced the Good Neighbor Policy, which promised to deal more fairly with Latin America and to stop direct interventions. After World War II, however, the U.S. preoccupation with containment of the Soviet Union and communism as an ideology led to new strategies in Latin America. These included participation in regional organizations, the support of governments that at least expressed democratic or anti-Communist principles, the covert undermining of governments considered unfriendly to U.S. interests, and, when necessary, direct intervention. Underlying much of this policy was also a firm belief that economic development would eliminate the conditions that contributed to radical political solutions. Thus U.S. programs such as the Alliance for Progress, begun in 1961, aimed at the development of the region as an alternative to those solutions. The alliance had only limited success despite good intentions and more than $10 billion of aid. Because of its record, Latin Americans and North Americans both began to question the assumption that "development" was basically a problem of capital and resources and that appropriate strategies would lead to social and economic improvement, which in turn would forestall revolution.

During the 1970s and 1980s U.S. policy was often "pragmatic," accepting Latin America "as it was," which meant dealing on friendly terms with the military dictatorships. President Jimmy Carter (1976–1980) made a new initiative to deal with Latin America and to influence governments there to observe civil liberties. Most significantly, a treaty was signed with Panama ceding to that nation eventual control of the Panama Canal.

Increasing violence in Central America in the 1980s and the more conservative presidencies of Ronald Reagan and George Bush led the United States back to policies based on strategic, economic, and defense considerations in which direct intervention or support of counterrevolutionary forces played a part. Thus in 1989 and 1990 the United States toppled a government in Panama—authoritarian but defiant of U.S. policies, including control of drug smuggling—replacing it with a cooperative regime backed by U.S. troops.

ANALYSIS

HUMAN RIGHTS IN THE 20TH CENTURY

In Latin America the question of human rights became a burning issue in the decade of the 1960s and continued thereafter. The use of torture by repressive governments, the mobilization of death squads and other vigilante groups with government acquiescence, and the use of terrorism against political opponents by the state and by groups opposed to the state became all too common in the region. Latin America's record on violation of human rights was no worse than that of some other areas of the world. However, the demonstrations by the Argentine "Mothers of the Plaza del Mayo" to focus attention on their "disappeared" children; the publication of prison memoirs recounting human rights violations in Brazil, Cuba, and Argentina; and films dramatizing such events as the assassination of Archbishop Oscar Romero in El Salvador have all focused attention on the problem in Latin America. Moreover, because Latin America shares in the cultural heritage of Western societies it is difficult to make an argument that human rights there have a different meaning or importance than in Europe or North America.

The concept of "human rights," that is, certain universal rights enjoyed by all people because these are justified by a moral standard that stands above the laws of any individual nation, may go back to ancient Greece. The concept of "natural law" and the protection of religious or ethnic minorities also moved nations in the 19th century toward a defense of human rights. To some

extent the international movement to abolish the slave trade was an early human rights movement. In modern times, however, the concept of human rights has been strongly attached to the foundation of the United Nations. In 1948 that body, with the experience of World War II in mind, issued the Universal Declaration of Human Rights and created a commission to oversee the human rights situation. The Universal Declaration, which guaranteed basic liberties and freedoms regardless of color, sex, or religion, proclaimed that it should be the "common standard for all peoples and nations." One critic has stated, however, that of the 160 nations in the United Nations, only about 30 have a consistently good record on the matter of human rights.

A major problem for the international community has been enforcement. The UN commission did not have any specific powers of enforcement, and much debate subsequently has taken place on the power of the United Nations to intervene in the internal affairs of any nation. More recently, various regional organizations have tried to establish the norms that should govern human rights and to create institutions to enforce these norms. In the 1950s the European community established a body to deal with human rights. Since 1969, under the auspices of the Organization of American States, the American Convention on Human Rights has been active in the Americas. More recently, in the 1980s, the Organization of African Unity created a similar body. In addition, there are private groups, such as Amnesty International, which seek to investigate and reveal abuses. Throughout much of the world there is a growing feeling that the issue of human rights transcends national boundaries.

One specialist has claimed that "human rights is the world's first universal ideology." The defense of human rights would seem to be a cause that most people and governments would be able to accept without hesitation, but the question is, in fact, a complex one. Although the rights to life, liberty, security, and to be free from torture or degrading punishment are generally accepted in principle by all nations, other "rights" remain open to question. What is a "right," and to what extent are definitions of "rights" determined by culture?

The question of universality versus relativism quickly emerged in the debate over human rights. What seemed to be obvious human rights in Western societies were less obvious in other parts of the world, where other priorities were held. Laws prohibiting child labor, for example, were enforced by most Western societies, but throughout the world perhaps 150 million children worked, often in unhealthy and exploitive conditions. They worked often because of economic necessity, but in some societies they also worked because such labor was considered moral and proper. Such cultural differences have led to a position of relativism, which recognizes that there are profound cultural variations in what is considered moral and just. Critics of the original Universal Declaration, for example, have contended that its advocacy of the right to own property and the right to vote imposed Western political and economic values as universals, which in fact they were not. Cultural relativism had the advantage of recognizing the variety of cultures and standards in the world, but it has at times also been used as a shield to deflect criticism and to continue to violate human rights.

The definition of human rights is also political. The West has placed considerable emphasis on civil and political rights of the individual. The socialist nations have placed social and economic justice above individual rights, although by the 1990s movements in Eastern Europe and China indicated that there was considerable pressure to modify this approach. In the Third World an argument for "peoples' rights" has emerged in which the "right to development," which calls for a major structural redistribution of the world's resources and economic opportunities, is a central concept. As Leopold Senghor of Senegal put it: "Human rights begin with breakfast"; or as a report on Ghana stated: "'One man, one vote,' is meaningless unless accompanied by the principle of 'one man, one bread.'" Needless to say, although the "right to development" is seen as a human right in the Third World, it is viewed instead as a political and economic demand in wealthier nations of the West.

Another dimension of human rights is the extent to which it influences national foreign policies. Governments may make statements pledging respect for human rights in their foreign policy, but often considerations of national defense, sovereignty, or such goals as the maintenance of peace may move human rights concerns into a secondary position. Sometimes disputes over the role of human rights in foreign policy have been posed as a conflict between "moralistic utopians" who see the world as it should be and "pragmatists" who see the world as it is. Neither approach necessarily denies the importance of human rights, but there are differences in priority and strategy. Pragmatists might argue that it is better to maintain relations with a nation violating human rights in order to be able to exercise some influence over it in the future or that other policy considerations must be weighed along with those of human rights in establishing foreign policy. Moralists would hope to bring pressure by isolating and condemning a nation that violates international standards.

These varying approaches have been reflected in U.S. policy shifts toward Latin America. In the 1950s human rights considerations were secondary to opposing the spread of communism in the hemisphere, and the United States was willing to support governments that violated human rights so long as they were staunch anti-Communist allies. During the 1960s this policy continued, but increasing and systematic abuses by military regimes in Brazil, Uruguay, Chile, Nicaragua, and elsewhere in Latin America began to elicit some changes. In 1977 President Carter initiated a new policy in which human rights considerations were given high priority in U.S. foreign policy. U.S. refusal to support or aid governments that violated human rights contributed to the weakening of some regimes and stimulated resistance to human rights violations in Latin America, but by the 1980s a more pragmatic approach had returned to U.S. policy. Criticism of human rights violations was sometimes made selectively, dismissing abuses in "friendly" governments. The extent to which human rights concerns must be balanced against such issues as security, the maintenance of peace, and nonintervention continues to preoccupy policymakers.

During the 1990s attention to human rights will play an increasingly important role in international affairs. Problems of definition still remain, and there is no universal agreement on the exact nature of human rights. Controversy on the relative weight of political and civil rights and social, cultural, and economic ones continues to divide richer and poorer nations. Still, the United Nations Declaration of Human Rights, to which 160 nations are signatories, provides a basic guideline and an outline for the future.

Questions: Why might various regimes oppose human rights, and on what basis? Is the human rights movement a Western replacement for imperialism as a means of international political influence? Have international human rights movements produced political change? ❧

SOCIETIES IN SEARCH OF CHANGE

Despite the structural, political, and international conditions that have frustrated Latin American attempts at profound reform, there have been considerable changes during the 20th century. Problems of ethnicity, gender, and class continue to influence many of these societies. The movement of populations and their settlement has also been a major feature of the century. These two aspects of social life represent just two of the continuing historical processes of Latin America.

Social and gender relations have changed during the century. We have already seen how Mexico, Peru, and Bolivia sought to enfranchise their Indian populations during this century in different ways and with varying degrees of success. National ideologies and actual practice are often not the same, and discrimination on the basis of ethnicity continues in many places. To be called "Indian" is still an insult in many places in Latin America. Although ethnic and cultural mixture characterizes many Latin American populations and makes Indian and African elements important features of national identity, relations with Indian populations often continue to be marked by exploitation and discrimination in nations as diverse as Brazil, Nicaragua, and Guatemala.

WOMEN'S ROLES

The role of women has changed considerably but relatively slowly. In the years following World War I women in Latin America continued to live under disabilities in the work place and in politics. Women were denied the right to vote anywhere in Latin America until Ecuador enfranchised women in 1929 and Brazil and Cuba did the same in 1932, but throughout most of the region those examples were not followed until the decades of the 1940s and 1950s. In some nations the traditional associations of women with religion and the Catholic church in Hispanic life made reformers and revolutionaries fear that women would become a conservative force in national politics. This attitude, combined with traditional male attitudes that women should be concerned only with home and family, led to a continued exclusion of women from political life. In response, women formed various associations and clubs and began to push for the vote and other issues of particular interest to them.

Feminist organizations, suffrage movements, and international pressures eventually combined to bring about change. In Argentina 15 bills for female suffrage were introduced into the senate before the vote was won in 1945. Sometimes the victory was a matter of political expediency for those in power. In a number of places, such as the Dominican Republic, enfranchisement of women was a strategy used by conservative groups to add more conservative voters to the electorate in an effort to hold off political change. In Argentina recently enfranchised women became a major pillar of the Peronist regime, although that regime was not averse to suppressing female political opponents, such as Victoria Ocampo, editor of the important literary magazine *Sur.*

Women eventually discovered that the ability to vote did not by itself guarantee political rights or the ability to have their specific issues heard. After achieving the vote, women tended to join the national political parties, in which traditional prejudices against women in public life limited their ability to influence political programs. In Argentina, Brazil, Colombia, and Chile, for example, the integration of women into national political programs has been slow, and women have not participated in proportion to their numbers. In a few cases, however, such as in the election of Perón in Argentina in 1946 and Eduardo Frei in Chile in 1964, or in the popular opposition to Salvador Allende in 1973, women played a crucial role.

Some of the earliest examples of mobilization of women and their integration into the national labor force of various Latin American nations came in the period just before the First World War and continued thereafter. The classic roles of women as homemakers, mothers, and part of the agricultural work force were increasingly expanded as women entered the industrial labor force in growing numbers. By 1911 in Argentina, for example, women made up almost 80 percent of the textile and clothing industry's workers. But women found that their salaries were often below those of comparable male workers and that their jobs, no matter the skill levels demanded, were considered "unskilled" and thus less well paid. Under these conditions women, like other workers, joined the anarchist, socialist, and other labor unions and organizations.

Labor organizations are only a small part of the story of women in the labor force. In Peru, Bolivia, and Ecuador market women control much small-scale commerce and have become increasingly active politically. In the growing service sectors women have also become an important part of the labor force. Shifts in attitudes about women's roles have come more slowly than political and economic changes. Even in revolutionary Cuba, where the Law of the Family guarantees equal rights and responsibilities within the home, enforcement has been difficult.

By the mid-1980s the position of women in Latin America stood closer to the status of women in western Europe and North America than it did to the other areas of the world. Women made up 9 percent of the legislators in Latin America, a percentage higher than in any other region of the world. They also held 9 percent of the cabinet posts, a figure behind only North America (12 percent). In terms of demographic patterns, health,

One of the more troubling trends in the economies of the developing world has been the great proliferation of sweatshops, like the one shown here, usually employing women, for the mass production of consumer goods intended for markets in the industrial world.

education, and place in the work force, the comparative position of women reinforced Latin America's intermediate position between the developed nations and the Third World.

THE MOVEMENT OF PEOPLE

In 1950 the populations of North America (United States and Canada) and Latin America were both about 165 million, but by 1985 Latin America's population had grown to over 400 million, compared to 265 million for North America. Declining mortality and continuing high fertility were responsible for this situation.

Although at the beginning of the 20th century the major trend of population movement was emigration to Latin America, the region has long experienced internal migration and the movement of people within the hemisphere. By the 1980s this movement had reached significant levels, fed by the flow of workers seeking jobs, the demands of capital for cheap labor, and the flight of political refugees seeking basic freedoms. Large numbers of West Indians from Jamaica, Barbados, and other islands have migrated to Great Britain or the United States. In the 1920s Mexican workers crossed the border to the United States in large numbers at the same time that Guatemalans crossed the border to Mexico to work on coffee estates. During World War II government programs to supply laborers were set up between the United States and Mexico, but these were always accompanied

by a considerable amount of extralegal migration, which fluctuated with the economy. Conditions for migrant laborers were often deplorable, although the extension of social welfare to them in the 1960s began to address some of the problems. By the 1970s more than 750,000 illegal Mexican migrants a year were crossing the border—some more than once—as the United States continued to attract migrants.

This internationalization of the labor market was comparable in many ways to the movement of workers from poorer countries, such as Turkey, Morocco, Portugal, and Spain, to the stronger economies of West Germany and France. In Latin America it also reflected the fact that industrialization in the 20th century depended on highly mechanized industry that did not create enough new jobs to meet the needs of the growing population. Much of the migration has been to the United States, but there has also been considerable movement across Latin American frontiers, as Haitians migrate to work in the Dominican Republic or Colombians illegally migrate to Venezuela. By the 1970s about five million people a year were migrating in Latin America and the Caribbean.

Politics has also been a major impulse for migration. Haitians fleeing political repression and abysmal conditions have risked great dangers in small open boats to reach the United States. One of the great political migrations of the century has been caused by the Cuban Revolution. Beginning in 1959 with the middle class fleeing socialism and continuing into the 1980s with the flight of Cuban workers, close to one million Cubans have left the island. The revolutionary upheaval in Nicaragua and political violence in Central America have contributed to the flight of refugees. Often it is difficult to separate political and economic factors in the movement of people from their homelands.

International migration is only part of the story. During the century there has been a marked movement in Latin America from rural to urban areas. Although in the 19th century Latin America had been an agrarian region, by the 1980s about one-half of the population lived in cities of over 20,000, and over 25 of these cities had populations of over one million. Some of these cities had reached enormous size; in 1988 Mexico City had more than 16 million inhabitants, São Paulo had 10 million, and Buenos Aires had 8 million. Latin America was by far the most urbanized area of the developing world and only slightly less urbanized than Western Europe.

The problem is not one simply of size but of the rate of growth as well. The urban populations have grown at a rate about three times that of the population as a whole, which itself was growing rapidly. Urban economies have not been able to create enough jobs for the rapidly increasing population. Often recent migrants lived in marginal neighborhoods or in shantytowns, which have become characteristic of the rapid urban growth of Latin America. These *favelas,* to give the Brazilian term for them, have created awful living conditions, but over time some have become poorer neighborhoods within the cities in which community cooperation and action have taken place to secure basic urban services.

In socialist Cuba, a concerted effort to deemphasize Havana and other large cities and reverse the rural-urban migration pattern was made, but in most of the region urbanization has continued as growing populations seek better opportunities. In part this movement is explained by a general population growth rate of more than 2.5 percent a year since the 1960s.

Although Latin American urbanization has increased rapidly since 1940 (see Table 13–1), the percentage of its people living in cities is still less than in western Europe but more than in Asia and Africa. Unlike the 19th-century European experience, Latin American urban unemployment has kept rural migrants from becoming part of a laboring class with a strong identification with fellow workers. Those who do succeed in securing industrial jobs often join paternalistic labor organizations that are linked to the government. Thus there is a separation between the chronically underemployed urban lower class and the industrial labor force. Whereas industrialization

TABLE 13–1

Population of Capital Cities as a Percentage of Total Population in Ten Latin American Nations

Nation	Capital	1880	1905	1930	1960	1983
1. Brazil	Rio	3	4	4	7	(4)
2. Mexico	Mexico City	3	3	5	15	20
3. Argentina	Buenos Aires	12	20	20	32	34
4. Colombia	Bogotá	1	2	2	8	11
5. Peru	Lima	3	3	5	19	27
6. Chile	Santiago	6	10	13	22	37
7. Uruguay	Montevideo	12	30	28	31	40
8. Venezuela	Caracas	3	4	7	20	18
9. Cuba	Havana	13	15	15	18	20
10. Panama	Panama City	7	14	16	25	20

( ) = no longer capital city

Source: From J. P. Cole, *Latin America: An Economic and Social Geography* (1965), 417.

and urbanization promoted a strong class solidarity in 19th-century Europe that led to the gains of organized labor, in contemporary Latin America nationalist and populist politics have weakened the ability of the working class to operate effectively in politics.

CULTURAL REFLECTIONS OF DESPAIR AND HOPE

Latin America remains an amalgamation of cultures and peoples seeking to adjust to changing world realities. Protestant denominations have made some inroads, but the vast majority of Latin Americans are still nominally Roman Catholics. Hispanic traditions of family, gender relations, business, and social interaction influence everyday life and help to determine responses to the modern world.

Latin American popular culture remains vibrant. It draws on African and Indian traditional crafts, images, and techniques but arranges them in new ways. Also part of popular culture are various forms of Latin American music. The Argentine tango of the turn of the century developed from the music halls of lower-class working districts of Buenos Aires into an international craze. The African-influenced Brazilian *samba* and the Caribbean *salsa* have been widely diffused, a Latin American contribution to world civilization.

The struggle for social justice, economic security, and political formulas in keeping with the cultural and social realities of their nations has provided a dynamic tension that has produced tremendous artistic achievements. Latin American poets and novelists have gained worldwide recognition. We have already noted the artistic accomplishments of the Mexican Revolution. In 1922 Brazilian artists, composers, and authors staged a Modern Art Week in São Paulo, which emphasized a search for a national artistic expression that reflected Brazilian realities.

That theme also preoccupied authors elsewhere in Latin America. The social criticism of the 1930s produced powerful realist novels that revealed the exploitation of the poor, the peasantry, and the Indians. Whether in the heights of the Andes or in the dark streets of the growing urban slums, the plight of the common folk provided a generation of authors with themes worthy of their effort. Social and political criticism has remained a central feature of Latin American literature and art and has played an important role in the development of newer art forms, such as filmmaking.

Latin American artists, such as Colombian Fernando Botero (b. 1932), have used surrealism and irony to depict Latin American realities. The dominance of military regimes in the 1970s called forth the imaginative parody of the soldiers reflected in this painting.

The inability to bring about social justice or to influence politics has also sometimes led Latin American artists and intellectuals to follow other paths. In the 1960s a "boom" of literature took place in which novels that mixed the political, the historical, the erotic, and the fantastic were produced by a generation of authors who found the reality of Latin America too absurd to be described by the traditional forms or logic. Writers such as the Argentine Jorge Luis Borges (b. 1899) and the Colombian Gabriel García Marquez (b. 1928) won acclaim throughout the world for their literary ability. García Marquez's *One Hundred Years of Solitude* (1967) used the history of a family in a mythical town called Macondo as an allegory of Latin America and traced the evils that befell the family and the community as they moved from naive isolation to a maturity that included oppression, exploitation, war, revolution, and natural disaster but that never subdued the spirit of its people. In that way his book outlined the trajectory of Latin America in the 20th century.

CONCLUSION

MIXED RETURNS FROM REVOLUTION IN THE 20TH CENTURY

Many more revolutions have occurred in the 20th century than in any comparable time span in human history. Between the Mexican peasant risings in the first decade of the century and the Iranian upheavals of the late 1970s, tens of revolutionary movements have threatened or toppled seemingly powerful regimes in virtually all regions of the globe. Without question, revolutions have been one of the most powerful forces shaping global history in the 20th century. But as the tide of revolution has apparently receded in the past decade or so and the revolutionary regimes of Eastern Europe and elsewhere have collapsed or fallen on hard times, there has been a tendency to disparage the accomplishments and stress the high costs of violent revolutionary upheavals. Gradualist reforms and the peaceful workings of the marketplace are currently widely seen as the best antidotes to pervasive poverty, corrupt governments, and state oppression.

It would be absurd to ignore the appalling costs in human lives and material destruction caused by revolutionary struggles and the civil wars and external aggressions often associated with them. But it is equally distorting to ignore or minimize the quite considerable accomplishments of successful revolutions. As the histories of the many revolutions we have considered reveal, the returns from these upheavals in the 20th century have been mixed and have varied widely. Though revolutionary regimes have not managed to create the utopian societies that radical 18th- and 19th-century political theorists, such as Saint-Simon and Marx imagined, each has brought some clear improvements in the lives of many of the ordinary citizens for whom they ostensibly seized power in the first place.

On the political side the revolutionary balance sheet has shown only meager gains and at times substantial losses. Inept despotisms, such as that of Qing China or tsarist Russia, and corrupt dictatorships, like Batista's in Cuba or Díaz's in Mexico, have been toppled. But very often they have been replaced by even more highly centralized bureaucratic machines, with a greatly increased capacity to intervene in the everyday lives of those whom they govern. In some instances, such as in the Soviet Union under Stalin or in China in the period of the Cultural Revolution, state repression has vastly exceeded anything that prerevolutionary despots could imagine. Revolutions have also often brought about the substitution of a class of rapacious and self-serving state functionaries for the extravagant and aloof aristocrats or self-styled patricians who dominated prerevolutionary societies. These new elites of revolutionary functionaries, whom Milovan Djilas dubbed the "new class" in the 1950s, have often stunted reform and innovation by monopolizing political power, stifling all criticism, and siphoning off for their own purposes resources that might have been invested in broader social improvements. Often in response to perceived external threats, revolutionary elites have militarized their societies to an extent far exceeding that achieved by prerevolutionary regimes. They have also expended scarce resources in foreign wars and efforts to spread their revolutions to other countries.

Revolutionary regimes have rarely tolerated meaningful political opposition or championed those human rights so prized in Western democracies—the freedoms of speech, the press, and genuine elections. But some of their greatest accomplishments have involved developing social programs aimed at providing all of their citizen-subjects with other sorts of human amenities that have been denied to large and increasing minorities in the industrial West and to the majority of the populations of most nonrevolutionary developing nations. Communist

regimes in particular, like those in the Soviet Union, the People's Republic of China, and Cuba, have transformed the lives of once poverty- and disease-ridden workers and peasants through the provision of universal health care, schooling and recreation facilities, and state-built housing. In Communist societies women at all income levels have enjoyed opportunities for advanced education and work outside the home that are made possible by state-financed child care services. In most Communist societies women have played major roles in medicine and education, though these pursuits often do not earn them the prestige or salaries attained by doctors or university professors in the West. A lower level of consumer production, especially in household appliances, has meant that working women in postrevolutionary societies, Communist as well as Islamic, have had to perform traditional chores in the home after long hours on the job. Persisting macho notions of appropriate male activities have done much to discourage men from reducing the burden of women's dual roles.

In the economic sphere the gains under postrevolutionary regimes were once thought to be impressive. Within decades the Soviet Union joined the ranks of the industrial giants, and the countries of Eastern Europe greatly expanded their industrial sectors. Cuba's drive for industrialization in the 1960s failed, and Iranian aspirations to build on the start made under the shah were frustrated by the long war with Iraq in the 1980s. But China, however, has built an impressive industrial sector with very little foreign assistance; and as Vietnam breaks out of the isolation imposed largely by U.S. hostility, it shows considerable potential for healthy growth. Industrialization has brought impressive military power to many postrevolutionary nations—power that, for example, allowed the Soviet people to withstand the fierce Nazi onslaught and China to support successfully small neighbors such as North Korea and Vietnam in their wars against the U.S. colossus.

Nonetheless, the collapse of the Soviet Union and its satellites has revealed the waste and inefficiency that have stunted growth in the highly centralized, command economies of the Communist bloc. In trying to catch up with the industrialized West and Japan, Communist regimes sacrificed sophistication to sheer scale and volume and ravaged the rich environments of a substantial portion of the globe. Most critically, the burden of the prolonged arms race between the Soviet and U.S. superpowers had much to do with the collapse of the Soviet economy, just as it helps to account for the erosion of the U.S. stature as the leading industrial nation.

State controls over intellectual expression and artistic creativity, which have been characteristic of postrevolutionary regimes, have greatly constricted cultural productivity. When contrasted with prerevolutionary painting, music, and architecture, the massive and pedestrian buildings, murals, and statues of the Social Realist and functionalist schools underscore the heavy cultural costs of revolutionary dogmatism. These have been somewhat counterbalanced by considerable achievements in the sciences and engineering of Communist regimes, particularly in the Soviet Union and China. At another level, Communist regimes from China to Cuba have developed athletic programs that despite their grueling training routines were the envy of the West for decades. In addition, despite state controls, writers and artists in postrevolutionary societies have produced a surprisingly large corpus of significant work, from Boris Pasternak's poetry to the plays of Vaclav Havel.

As the foregoing discussion suggests, evaluating the impact of 20th century revolutions is not a simple matter. They have not produced utopian societies, but they have resulted in real improvements in the conditions under which once oppressed groups, such as peasants and workers, live their lives and raise their children. In any case, in most of the societies where successful revolutions have occurred, prerevolutionary conditions for the great majority of the people were so desperate that there was little inclination to speculate about revolutionary outcomes. Meaningful reforms were blocked by the regimes struggling to hold power, and they were in any case seen by revolutionary leaders and those who supported them as inappropriate for societies where human misery was too acute and pervasive to allow for gradualist solutions. Though Communist solutions are presently in disrepute, the persisting poverty and state oppression of a sizable portion of the world's population provide ample grounds for further revolutionary upheavals. The spreading appeal of Islamic fundamentalism and Christian liberation theology suggests that new revolutionary alternatives may prove a major force in shaping global history in the 21st century.

FURTHER READINGS

A good summary of the final stages of the civil war in China is provided in Lucien Bianco's *Origins of the Chinese Revolution* (1971). Perhaps the best overview of modern Chinese history from the Qing dynasty era through the Tiananmen Square massacres can be found in Jonathan D. Spence's *The Search for Modern China* (1990). Other useful accounts of the post-1949 era include Maurice Meisner's *Mao's China* (1977), Michael Gasster's *China's Struggle to Modernize* (1987 ed.), and Immanuel C. Y. Hsu's *China Without Mao* (1983). On the pivotal period of the Cultural Revolution, see Rodney MacFarquhar's *Origins of the Cultural Revolution* (two vols., 1974, 1983) and Lowell Dittmer's *Liu Shao-ch'i and the Chinese Cultural Revolution* (1974). For a highly critical assessment of the Maoist era, it is difficult to surpass Simon Leys's *Chinese Shadows* (1977). On cultural life in the postrevolutionary era, see the essays in R. MacFarquhar, ed., *The Hundred Flowers Campaign and the Chinese Intellectuals* (1960) and Lois Wheeler Snow's *China on Stage* (1972). Elizabeth Croll's *Feminism and Socialism in China* (1978) remains by far the best single work on the position of women in revolutionary and Maoist China.

The first war of liberation in Vietnam is covered in Ellen J. Hammer's *The Struggle for Indochina 1940–1955* (1966 ed). The best of many surveys of the second is Marilyn Young's *The Vietnam Wars* (1989). Of a number of fine studies on the origins of U.S. intervention in the area, two of the best are Archimedes Patti's *Why Vietnam?* (1980) and Lloyd Gardner's *Approaching Vietnam* (1988). A fine assessment of the roots of the failure of U.S. intervention and the course of the second war of liberation is provided in Jeffrey Race's *The War Comes to Long An* (1972). Powerful first-hand accounts of the guerilla war and U.S. combat include Mark Baker's *Nam* (1981), Philip Caputo's *A Rumor of War* (1977), and Troung Nhu Tang's *A Viet Cong Memoir* (1985).

The post-1945 period in Latin American history is ably covered in Thomas Skidmore and Peter Smith's survey *Modern Latin America* (1989); cultural trends are covered in Jean Franco's *The Modern Culture of Latin America* (2nd. ed., 1970). A large literature has developed over the past decades on the Cuban revolution. Louis Perez's *Cuba: Between Reform and Revolution* (1988) contains the most up-to-date and reliable account. Varying perspectives can be found in Hugh Thomas's *Cuba: The Pursuit of Freedom* (1971), Tad Schultz's *Fidel: A Critical Portrait* (1968), and Lee Lockwood's *Castro's Cuba; Cuba's Fidel* (1969).

Epilogue
Toward the 21st Century:
Global History Yet to Come

INTRODUCTION. Since the formation of civilizations the history of the world has involved relatively rapid change—sometimes in directions already set, sometimes in new trajectories. This pattern obviously continues as we near the 21st century. Indeed, some people would argue that the pace of change has accelerated as new discoveries and new technologies press against older ideas and habits. World history, in other words, offers no convenient stopping point at which one can lean back and say, "This is what it all means." Contemporary world history provides no magic vantage point, either, on what is to come. The only thing we know for sure about the future is that we do not know what it will bring.

People in various civilizations have attempted to devise schemes to look beyond their present. From the time of the ancient river-valley civilizations to the 20th century, some people have used astrology or other divinations to predict the future. More systematically some scholars have assumed that time moves in cycles, so that one could count on repetition of basic patterns. This was a common assumption in Chinese historical thought and also among Muslim historians in the postclassical period. Others, including Christian thinkers and advocates of more secular faiths, such as Marxism, have looked toward some great change in the future: the Last Judgment, for example, or the classless society to which history is steadily working. The idea of some master plan guiding history, moving it in a steady direction and toward a purpose, runs deep in the thought of several cultures, including our own. Whatever the approach, the human impulse to know what we cannot definitely know seems inescapable.

Yet all the evidence suggests that our vision of the future remains cloudy at best. It has been calculated that well over 60 percent of all predictions or forecasts offered by serious social scientists in the United States since 1945—called on to sketch future business cycles, family trends, or political currents, for instance—have been wrong. How many observers just 50 years ago could have predicted such basic recent transformations as decolonization; the rise of new kinds of authoritarianism; fundamental revolutions in China, Iran, and Cuba; the challenge to Communist rule in the Soviet Union; the invention of computer and genetic engineering technologies; or the industrial breakthroughs of many Pacific coast regions of Asia? A few of these events could be discerned in advance, to be sure, but many were great surprises. And other developments that were confidently predicted have not come to pass: people are not normally riding about in helicopters rather than automobiles (a U.S. image of the 1940s), and families have not been replaced by promiscuous communes (a forecast of the 1960s).

Even though we cannot know the future, we can use history to develop a framework for evaluating it and partially anticipating it as it unfolds. We can know what factors to monitor. Recent patterns and their relationship to older themes in world history allow an orientation toward what is to come. This final chapter suggests several vantage points from which to relate past to present to future. We deal with issues of progress and deterioration, with the ongoing tensions between separate civilizations and forces that impact throughout the world, and with trends in the basic political, cultural, economic, and social functions of human society.

This chapter presents several methods of approaching the future, all of which require knowledge of history and analytical skills in assessment. No method offers certainty, which is why some historians refuse to deal with forecasting in any form, lest it corrupt their true craft. All the approaches, however, promote further thinking, not only about the future but also about the various kinds of historical trends that are shaping it.

We begin with the easiest relationship—extrapolating from recent trends. We then turn to two more dramatic forms: the moral evaluation based on judgments of whether world society is getting better or worse and the dramatic forecast based on a revolutionary factor that will provoke a major disruption between future and past. Finally, we look at the future in terms of a set of issues fundamental to world history for many centuries, though taking new form in our own era.

PERIODIZATION: NEW EVENTS AND UNCERTAINTY

What we know about 20th-century history both helps and hinders use of the recent past to organize some sense of the future. It seems clear that in the 1920s and 1930s a new phase in world history began to take shape by the usual periodization criteria: parallel developments in major civilizations; reshuffling of geographical boundaries, including changes in the roster of particularly influential civilizations; and intensification of

international contacts. More extensive trade, unprecedented worldwide alliance systems, and the new variety of cultural exchanges readily illustrate the international intensification theme. Geographical changes include the loosening of Western domination through the decolonization movement and the new sources of industrial competition; they also include realignments in the societies of East and Southeast Asia and new configurations of the Middle East and the Indian subcontinent. Developments that cut across diverse societies include shared technologies (despite continuing gaps in overall technological levels), new political forms, and a tendency toward cultural secularization. The patterns add up, as we have seen, to a break in world history at least as great as the one that occurred in the 15th century, as Arab dominance yielded and new empires and trade patterns emerged.

The fact of a recent major break in world history means that many patterns familiar from the 19th century will almost surely continue to recede—we need not expect a revival of Western colonial dominance, for example. More positively, it is reasonable to expect continuing intensification of many world contacts—the necessary technology is increasingly available with international computer linkages and air-delivery systems, and the increase in contacts has formed a fairly steady trend in world history for at least 1000 years. Societies in the 20th century that have tried to isolate themselves from larger world currents—the Soviet Union in the 1930s to an extent, as well as China under Mao, for example—have usually found it necessary to open somewhat more fully, lest they lose the technological and economic benefits of contact.

The fact that the 20th century launches a major new period, however, automatically limits more precise prediction. We may know that the West's relative dominance has declined, but we do not know whether it will continue to do so. Events in the early 1990s, including the reunification of Germany, hopes for firmer Western European unity, and Westernized leadership for many of the newly independent Eastern European nations, point to a European revival—not back to 19th-century imperialist levels but well beyond what could have been foreseen just two decades ago. By 1993, however, widespread disunity in Europe, including bitter warfare in Yugoslavia, racial tensions in Germany, and bickering within the Common Market, showed the difficulty of making predictions about even Europe's future. There may in fact be no single center of dominance—of the sort that Arab and then Western civilization represented in past eras—in the 21st century. The world of the future may continue the present pattern of several major centers of power and influence.

Other forecasts, based on recent trends, are also uncertain. The century has seen growing secularization of belief in otherwise varied societies. Trends are not uniform, given Muslim and Christian missionary activity in Africa and the Islamic resurgence elsewhere, but the general point—describing the spread of communism, consumer materialism, and nationalism—has been clear. Yet the idea of a world without dominant religions is so strange to some observers that they predict a major religious revival—perhaps under some new doctrine—for the coming century. Who is to say they are wrong? The revival of religion in Eastern Europe and new conversions to Protestantism in Latin America or Islam in Africa certainly contradict any worldwide secular trend.

Biology added another uncertainty for the future. The spread of AIDs in several areas, particularly East Africa, reached serious proportions by the 1990s, affecting not only general health but also the economic performance of the adult population. The AIDs epidemic spread, threatening other regions such as Brazil; and most parts of the world were affected to some degree. How extensive the human suffering and economic cost would be, in this latest international disease wave, were important, if not clearly calculable, questions for the future.

Obviously, the new ingredients in the world's future were extremely diverse, from power relationships to cultural innovations to new forms of illness. The additional point is that a new period in world history inevitably produces doubts about the directions of the future precisely because old patterns are shaken up and emerging trends are difficult to gauge.

MAKING SENSE OF RECENT DEVELOPMENTS

Events themselves establish uncertain directions. The biggest political development of the late 1980s involved the explosions in the Communist world. China experimented through the entire decade with a range of interactions with the capitalist world and with the introduction of more market devices into its own economy. Consumer interest grew in Chinese cities, and a number of peasant entrepreneurs amassed considerable earnings by catering to market demand in their agricultural production. Gorbachev's ascent to leadership in the Soviet Union in 1985 triggered sharper change. Reforms and protest vied within the Soviet Union, and the smaller Eastern European states burst from Soviet Europe.

This was almost unprecedented ferment. Most observers, including seasoned intelligence experts, were astounded at the events throughout the Communist system, precisely because they overturned settled assumptions about Soviet power and the hold of what had been effective police states. Although it was essential to recast these assumptions, it was not clear how to predict subsequent patterns. Would Boris Yeltsin, Gorbachev's successor, manage to reform Soviet politics by firming up democracy and coping with his country's admitted economic doldrums and massive environmental problems? Would the clashes among former minority nationalities in what had been the Soviet Union continue to hamstring economic recovery and to threaten continuing civil strife? Here was a reminder of continuities of cultural identity and political interest, even amid apparent change. Indeed, the demands of regional nationalities in Eastern Europe by 1993 recalled tensions in the area before World War I; not only Soviet groups but also Bulgarians, Turks, Hungarians, Serbs, Croats, and Romanians began to raise intense and conflicting territorial demands. It was possible that the collapse of the Soviet empire would bring new diplomatic and even military turmoil to key parts of the world.

Within Russia, it was not clear that Yeltsin could survive widespread discontent, and many predicted that a more authoritarian regime, bent on restoring the old Soviet empire, would replace him. Further, there were doubts regarding the capacity of Russia and the other Eastern European economies to break out of their old industrial frameworks, adopt the newer technologies, and achieve the affluence of the advanced industrial societies of the West and the Pacific Rim.

In China, meanwhile, a massive student demonstration in 1989 in favor of greater democracy had been brutally repressed. Would China remain an exception to trends in European communism, or had a seed of liberalization been planted that must someday flower more fully?

Historical understanding aids in sorting out possibilities but only to a point, simply because the future does not cleanly reproduce the past, and the past itself offers various models. Some experts emphasized Russia's long authoritarian tradition and the more specific antecedents of Stalinist communism: Yeltsin's reformism must fail, in this view, because it countered Russian officialdom's commitment to a strong state and a controlled social order. Others, however, argued that Yeltsin was reviving an important Russian tradition of looking to partial Western models and experimenting on this base, an

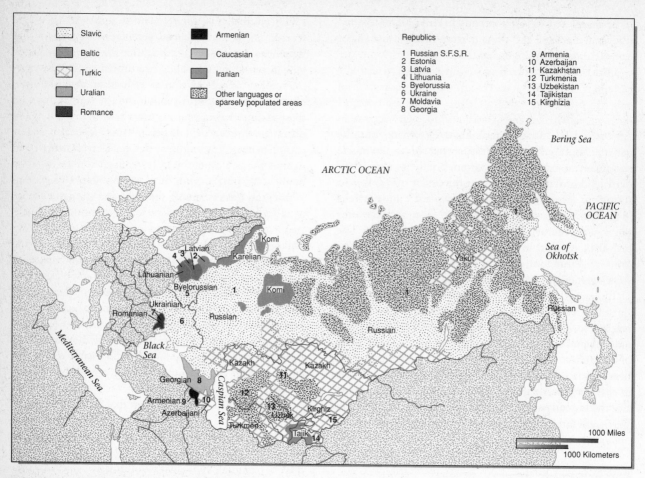

New Political Divisions of the Soviet Union

impulse visible not only in pre-Soviet experience but also during the 1920s. Here was a more optimistic rendering that could be supplemented by the possibility that new factors, including the nation's productivity problems, could wipe away some historical precedents. The failure of the 1991 coup, amid democratic resistance to revived authoritarianism, emphasized the extent of real change in Russian political culture. Prognostication about China was no easier. It was nice to believe that democratic agitation, once launched, could not be permanently repressed, particularly if China continued a policy of economic reforms and contacts with the wider world economy. On the other hand, China's traditions of control and the specific precedents of Maoism might support a long period of suppression. It was also worth noting that student protest movements in 1989 had not precisely called for Western-style politics anyway, for they were directed in part toward smoother and less cor-

rupt bureaucratic procedures, evoking Confucianism as much as Western liberalism.

Upheavals in Eastern Europe and potentially in China raised questions about the future of communism and the world balance of power. The rise of the Soviet Union and the United States had followed on the decline of Western Europe by the late 1940s. However, by the 1990s the Soviet Union was in eclipse, and the United States, burdened by heavy international debt, found its international activities somewhat constrained. With the cold war and its leading practitioners receding, what global pattern would follow? Analogy could be suggestive. The first initiative that briefly replaced Arab dominance in the 15th century—the Chinese surge in international trade—proved to be a false start. Perhaps the cold war, with the U.S. and Soviet international rivalry, would be a similar episode, revealing the decline of the older Western European dominance but not providing more than a temporary alternative. This possibility does not, however, predict what patterns may prove more durable; nor does it forecast the extent of Russian decline or U.S. constraint.

THE TRIUMPH OF THE WEST?

A few popularizers, to be sure, tried to make sense of complex trends as the 20th century neared its close. One writer from the State Department, briefly popular in official U.S. government circles, projected an "end to history." He argued that the cold war had ended with a Western victory; all parts of the world were bent on imitating Western institutions. With this development, history with its massive conflicts and ideological competitions had ended. Peace would prevail through a somewhat boring eternity, sparked mainly by marketplace competitions in a thoroughly capitalist world. Such a prospect might be comforting, particularly as it seemed to glorify Western values. Yet the attempt to judge the future on the basis of recent events, while simplifying those events in turn, might also be judged foolhardy. Various Western historians have periodically attempted to postulate an end to the normal ups and downs of history. Middle-class liberals—the British Whig school—argued over a century ago that bourgeois

values of education, social mobility, and political rights would lead to such general justice or satisfaction that there would be no reason for further change; all of history had been pointing to this moment of supreme enlightenment. Marx, of course, anticipated an end to historical process through communism's victory, though he did not claim to be quite so clear about the details of the future order. Hopes for a simpler future based on real or imagined recent trends thus has a pedigree; whether it greatly aids understanding or intelligently uses what we know of the past to predict the future is doubtful.

Indeed, the decline of the cold war clearly encouraged realignments in troubled regions, now that superpower rivalry no longer served as constraint. German reunification in 1990, resulting from the expulsion of the Communist regime from East Germany and creating a powerful state in Europe's center, raised some questions about European tensions, though plans for full economic unity in the Common Market proceeded. Iraq's ambitious leader, Saddam Hussein, judged the moment opportune for a more daring realignment in the Middle East. He invaded the small, oil-rich nation of Kuwait and may have hoped to use invasion to spearhead Muslim unity in the whole region, in the tradition of such earlier conquerors as the caliphs or the Ottomans. A U.S.-led coalition defeated Hussein, changing the

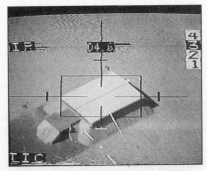
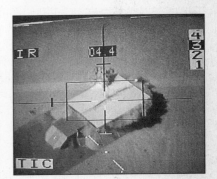
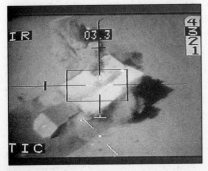
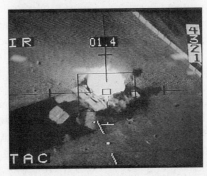

One of the more disturbing aspects of the recent Gulf War was the video-game quality of television coverage of this high-tech conflict. This famous sequence shows the destruction of a munitions depot by a so-called smart weapon. It is easy to forget that human beings were inside the targeted position.

balance of power in the area but again making future arrangements extremely unpredictable. The victorious U.S. president called for a "new world order" of stability, but the prospects for regional disruptions in the Middle East and elsewhere may have become more likely rather than less, as various leaders probed the decline of super-power rivalry.

✳ TRENDS IN WORLD SOCIETIES

Prediction based on dramatic recent events is both essential and frustrating; the complication of the larger issues of 20th-century periodization recurs continually. One forecasting mode, however, seeks to cut through some of the problems by focusing on processes rather than events and by identifying strong current trends in order to gain some sense of the future's shape or at least of the questions that might be sensibly asked about it.

Trend extrapolation can be quite precise. Within a particular society, such as the West or Japan, for example, it is easy to predict an expansion of problems associated with retirement and old-age costs in the near future, based on current patterns and the almost certain further results of low birthrates and growing longevity. The problems are present already, and they will increase. Only unforeseen changes, such as a spurt in the birthrate or new policies that deny medical care for older adults and so reduce longevity gains, can throw such short-term projections off.

Extrapolating vaguer trends, as well as adding an international basis, is obviously riskier. Nevertheless, several common questions or issues emerging in the later 20th century provide a valid framework for anticipating ongoing opportunities or problems.

POLITICAL ISSUES

In the political sphere the changing balance between democracy and other 20th-century government forms, notably communism and authoritarianism, provided the most obvious link between recent trends and future prospects.

Democratic parliamentarianism is now a well-established tradition in much of the West. Extremist movements still challenge it in some countries, and the fact that democratic trends were dislodged by nazism in Germany scarcely one-half century ago reminds us not to be too complacent. Major economic setbacks might again call the regimes into doubt. But despite many problems with Western politics, the regimes do seem firmly rooted. They have withstood massive shocks, such as loss of colonies. Indian and Japanese democracies are more recent and possibly less rooted in prior political forms. Japanese democracy still combines somewhat uneasily with the tradition of upper-class dominance, whereas Indian democracy seeks to accommodate the old tendency toward regional fragmentation with new class and religious tensions. Here too, however, comparative stability has by now described a span of several decades.

More generally, there is no question about the democratic impulse spreading in the world by the late 1980s, as it had in the first flush of decolonization in the 1940s and 1950s. New currents in the Communist world suggested a clear link between democracy and economic reform, which resulted in widespread popular aspiration toward a democratic system.

The authoritarian form of government also showed new weaknesses. Authoritarian forms in the 20th century had resulted from the tensions experienced by many new nations after the destruction of earlier political institutions and from sources of available leadership, such as the military. Authoritarianism has a strong base in Latin American tradition, where it goes back to the 19th century and where it has proved capable of both change and popularity. By the 1980s, however, democratic institutions had effaced authoritarianism in all but a few cases in Latin America. Again in the 1980s attacks on authoritarianism in the Philippines, Korea, and Pakistan raised new doubts about the system's future, though particularly in Korea authoritarian overtones remained even under an elected president. Early in the 1990s new democratic movements challenged authoritarianism in many African states.

Buoyed by the trends, some observers argued that a form of liberal democracy would prove to be the only viable political style for modern nations, because of the prestige it carried and because of the flexibility it allowed in responding to rapid social and economic change. Arguments of this sort were not new, but they gained increasing credibility with the overturning of authoritarian regimes in Latin America during the 1970s and then the upheaval of the Communist world. Certainly a worldwide turn to democracy would have simplified political analysis, yet doubts about the forecast remained because of the distinctiveness—both traditional and recent—of Chinese political systems, for example, or the stubborn persistence of authoritarian regimes in the Middle East.

CULTURAL ISSUES

The idea of a set of cultural issues affecting the world's future is hardly commonplace. We are instead accustomed to thinking about political and military scenarios or the tensions of economic development. Furthermore, many cultural patterns apply primarily to individual civilizations, which are defined more clearly by cultural styles than by any other characteristic.

A few cultural themes cut across civilizations, however, raising questions about what is to come. Many people have periodically wondered or worried about the results of pressures for homogeneity, as the trappings of consumer culture, the popularity of Western fads, and the impact of the leading international artistic and architectural styles continue to spread. One can travel to most of the world's cities today and stay in hotels, eat in restaurants, and buy goods that would scarcely differentiate downtown Chicago from downtown Istanbul. The dissemination of English as a world-currency language for travel, business, and science adds to the impression of growing homogeneity. The popularity of Western-dominated cultural styles has raised issues for Japan, has added to the confusions of growing up in modern African cities, and has helped divide Islamic societies. So the issue of balancing international modes and distinctive traditions has wide applicability. To date, most

civilizations have maintained their own tone, even as they selectively use international fads and products. But the further spread of global customs will probably intensify the friction between tradition and modernity, while possibly undermining diversity around the world. Further internationalization might also, at the same time, promote greater understanding. Already, at their best, the modern Olympic Games, based on an internationalization of key sports, have bridged some gaps that political leaders cannot close.

A more subtle issue involves the role of such expressions as art or music in human life. Industrialization forces such concentration on economic and technical needs and involves such uprooting of established habits through emphasis on technical training that the arts may be pushed to the periphery. This concern, of course, is phrased in various ways, depending on the civilization. Westerners worry that a rich popular cultural tradition has been replaced by commercialized, shallow entertainments designed to sell goods. The most creative artists may have become unusually remote from public taste. Non-Western intellectuals worry that their cultural traditions are being displaced by urban squalor or Westernization or that government controls bend culture to purposes of political obedience. Japanese intellectuals sometimes lament the materialism of their own culture, where traditional art survives but, again, may play a less

This photo of downtown Lagos, Nigeria, shows the Western influence on international urban architecture.

central role than in the past. Some dissident intellectuals in the former Soviet Union have expressed the same concern about their industrial society; Africans worry that traditional art degenerates into mass-produced trinkets for tourists.

The problem of integrating science with more traditional religious and artistic endeavors constitutes a related theme. Science has long been part of the intellectual arsenal of most civilizations, but it played a role subordinate to religious and esthetic interpretations of nature and human nature. Starting with the West, modern intellectual history has involved a steady upgrading of science, which became linked to the broader process of technical and industrial development. Yet even in the West, science has not satisfied all human needs and has not provided as encompassing a framework as traditional religion once did for relating separate portions of the human cultural experience. The result in the West, during the past two centuries, has been enduring tension, dividing science from the arts or humanistic disciplines. Several non-Western societies have lagged in developing scientific research to match better-established interests in arts, religion, and literature, or, as with Islamic fundamentalism, they have insisted on the primacy of a religious view. Tensions between science and nonscience may be healthy—and seem inevitable—but in various ways in various major cultures, they raise important issues about the integration of intellectual outlook for the future.

World culture in the future must also deal with technological change. The omnipresence of the radio is already an accomplished fact; most villages, not to mention urban families, have their own transistors. Television too is becoming a global medium, as more than half the world's population has relatively ready access to a TV set. The potential spread of computer-based information systems raises an additional prospect for the future. Most people today are contending with standardized sources of information and with increased amounts of information. The question of the ongoing impact of new transmission technologies on popular culture, as well as on creativity in the sciences and nonsciences alike, forms a final open-ended issue for the world's cultural evolution at the end of the 20th century and beyond.

ECONOMIC ISSUES

Economic problems and prospects form the most familiar framework for discussing the future. Will the agricultural civilizations, as in Africa or Latin America, manage to industrialize? Can the environment withstand mounting industrialization? How will the growing parity between the West and East Asia in industrial development work out—will the West decline, or can it live with a new balance? Has Eastern European development, so vigorous earlier in the century, reached a plateau, and if so, what will the results be in terms of Russian politics and diplomacy?

The gap that opened between early industrializing societies—including those initial latecomers, Russia and Japan—and those that are still industrializing remains stubbornly wide. Several major civilizations besides the industrial pioneers—most notably India, China, and Southeast Asia—have been generating economic growth above population increase in recent decades. They have invested substantially in agriculture and in manufacturing. The industrial world continues to undergo change as well, as the advent of postindustrial technologies and labor-force structures attests.

The economic divisions of the contemporary world are more subtle than the convenient dichotomy between industrial and developing nations suggests. Gaps have opened among industrial nations, depending on use of the newest technology; thus Eastern Europe again lags, as in the 18th and 19th centuries, which is an important source of the recent turmoil. Important differences divide nations struggling for agricultural subsistence from those involved in rapid economic transformation. A few smaller nations, particularly on Asia's Pacific Rim, have joined the ranks of industrialized states, whereas other nations, such as Brazil and India, have developed strong industrial sectors amid many severe economic problems. Economic inequalities are complex and remain a concern. In an increasingly interconnected world the political and military tensions resulting from economic differences can be acute. Unequal levels of wealth among major civilizations are no novelty in history, but disparities in levels of development in such a tightly linked global economy constitute a novel combination. The stresses of playing catch-up in the economic development game and the resentments that can result on all sides—including those in wealthy nations seeking to preserve their lead—are an important if incalculable ingredient in the world's future.

Economic imbalances also helped explain other important developments in the later 20th century for which no clear end was in sight. The international drug trade picked up steam from the 1920s onward. Supplies came largely from countries with poor peasantries, desperate need for foreign exchange, and in some cases weak governments. Between the world wars, Turkey and

China served as key suppliers; after World War II, as these countries moved toward greater economic development, northwestern Latin America moved toward center stage. Demand for the drugs resulted from tensions in several industrial societies, as the burgeoning trade served as a perverse link among quite different kinds of economies in the interconnected world market.

The world's economic imbalances, as well as different rates of population growth, also generated new pressures for immigration. Arabs and South Asians moved toward the oil-rich states of the Middle East. Growing minorities from Africa, Latin America, and Asia gravitated toward the United States and western Europe. Japan, though leery of immigrants, admitted laborers and also prearranged brides from various Asian countries. The result of these movements has been a cross-civilization mixture of peoples unusual in world history and often associated with considerable tension and confusion. Continued relocation pressures form vital issues for many societies, including those that depend on sending excess labor elsewhere.

SOCIAL ISSUES

Diverse civilizations and unequal levels of industrial and urban development produce radically different social forms. Concern about family stability in the West and Africa contrasts with substantial family stability (and undue traditionalism?) in India and Latin America. Pressures of economic development have called some traditional social forms into question; most societies now attempt to encourage some social mobility as part of an effort to recruit talented leadership, spread education, and promote social justice. But specific social issues continue to vary greatly; India faces persistent, if now informal, gaps among castes, Communist societies uneasily accommodate a managerial or bureaucratic middle class, peasant unrest continues in parts of Latin America, and the West worries about racial tensions surrounding new or traditional minorities. Even relations among the generations vary, with most industrial societies gradually coming to terms with a growing old-age segment, and most agricultural civilizations still focusing on problems of nurturing and educating the young.

A few fundamental questions do apply to all societies. Industrialization has involved city growth, and in many cases urbanization now races ahead of other economic changes. City life, in turn, poses some basic challenges, such as dealing with crowding, providing appropriate entertainment, and dealing with psychological stress stemming from the excitement and tension of city life. At times, though not invariably, urbanization brings heightened crime. It certainly reduces traditional community control over behavior, so that other devices, including formal policing, must be extended. The impact of urbanization, both its promise and its difficulties, thus raises global questions for the present and future alike. Urbanization also creates new divisions between rural and urban people, a source of heightened misunderstanding, and, in many societies a neglect of farming populations and even of agriculture.

Economic change and the spread of mass education also affect the family, including conditions for women and the position of other groups. Young people are subjected to examples other than those of their immediate relatives. Children who are better educated than their parents or who work outside the home often develop a taste for independence—a theme that, in the contemporary world, runs from Hong Kong to Nairobi to St. Louis. Although the West, as the first industrializer, faced the changing role of children somewhat earlier than did other societies, it has hardly resolved the resulting issues, and some common concerns about youth unrest and family solidarity have cut across a number of cultures, including that of Russia and Eastern Europe in recent decades.

Another trend to monitor involves social structure. Control of the land becomes steadily less important as the basis for social position. Aristocracies and landlord classes loom less large in late-20th-century world history than at any time since the dawn of civilization. Urbanized societies tend to emphasize wealth, knowledge, and managerial control as the basis of social prestige. This has been the clear pattern in the West and in Eastern Europe even under communism; the pattern seems to be emerging in Africa and Asia as well. Division between wealthy managerial classes and laboring groups with little or no property and inferior education forms a set of tensions that cuts across several different civilizations. Educational access and attainment, for example, become everywhere more important as a basis for upward mobility, though this is a less novel phenomenon in Chinese tradition than, say, in Latin American tradition.

In sum: What we know about industrialization patterns and the impact of efforts to industrialize in various parts of the world suggests some ongoing questions about social and family structure that apply to a number of societies despite vastly different specific patterns. The social structures of the world range from remnants of India's caste system to the managerial bureaucracies of

China and the former Soviet Union and from highly urbanized Japan to societies where urban elites struggle to control rural majorities. Quite generally, however, tension between expectations of opportunity and ongoing social hierarchies raises another set of leading questions for the future.

THE WORLD'S FUTURE AS PROMISE OR THREAT

Talking about future issues on the basis of recent trends provides a vital connection between what we know about the late 20th century and the issues we can anticipate in the 21st century. The strategy can be applied to a vast range of specific issues and specific societies, beyond the general points raised in the previous section. The approach lacks flair, however, and many observers prefer a different and more dramatic means of linking society past and society to come.

One mode is to offer glowing words of hope about the achievements and bright prospects of humankind. Moral judgments here substitute for precise forecasts. Contemporary Western culture continues to value optimism and to believe that students, especially, should be inspired to think well of the society around them, hopeful as they face their own future. Yet the message of history, including contemporary history, is decidedly ambiguous on the question of hopefulness.

THE BRIGHT SIDE

World history is without question a record of impressive, even inspiring, human achievement. Through art, music, and literature people have created moments of great beauty. Through religion and science people have gained new understanding of the world they live in; the daily environment is surely a less fearful and more intelligible habitat for us than it was for our hunting-and-gathering ancestors. Political institutions have been generated that at certain times, at least, brought impressive stability and mechanisms of justice to many people. Technological mastery of nature has increased fairly steadily in human history. Certainly our species has learned how to support ever greater numbers of people, as agricultural techniques and then industrialization provided more reliable means of subsistence. Humankind, at first a rather frail competitor for survival, now easily outnumbers any of the other complex mammalian species and thus has to date handily passed this basic biological test of success.

The 20th century has contributed at least its share to the record of progress. Advances in industry and agriculture have permitted the birth and survival of more people in our century than in all previous centuries combined. Life expectancy has risen notably in all societies, not just those with a sophisticated industrial apparatus. New seeds and fertilizers in the agricultural "Green Revolution" have greatly improved food supplies in otherwise "poor" societies, such as India and Mexico. Scientific discoveries add greatly to our knowledge as well as to our technology, though some civilizations continue to value nonscientific ways of viewing the world. Experts in virtually every nation know more about the functioning of the human body, about weather and climate patterns, about astronomy, and indeed about human history than any society has ever known before. The capacity to organize large groups of people has also improved, at least in certain respects. Most societies today can operate larger businesses or school systems or census-taking operations than ever before. Along with this bureaucratic achievement come some probable improvements in certain aspects of social relationships. Slavery has been almost totally eradicated. Although great variety persists, women have won new opportunities in many parts of the world in terms of political rights and less complete confinement to domestic functions. No one would argue that injustice has been eliminated, but there may be some measurable gains. The spread of education, another general development in the 20th century, also provides a basis for claiming a genuine increase in human knowledge, not just at the level of advanced research but also among peasants and workers.

Many of these developments provide additional hope for the future. Better medical care and nutrition may broaden the human potential. Mass schooling, still a relative novelty in many societies, may join with electronic technologies, such as radio and television, to bring formal education even to remote regions that remain largely agricultural. Additional research gains seem virtually assured, as physicists, for example, make almost daily discoveries about the nature of the universe. Unquestionably, the human potential remains vast. It seems likely, though not certain, that women in most societies will continue to gain new rights and functions, based on worldwide trends of rising educational levels, falling birthrates, and greater legal and suffrage equality. Women's conditions may vary considerably according to the particular standards of each civilization, but there are some general trends away from traditional patriarchy—in Africa, China, and parts of the Middle East, as well as in industrial societies.

THE DOWN SIDE

Yet history is also, unquestionably, the record of humankind's inhumanity to its own members. The historical record is peppered with acts of massive cruelty and bitter hatreds that have divided nations and races. Although certain civilizations may claim to have tamed some destructive impulses and certain cruelties, such as deliberate human sacrifice have ended, it is difficult to argue that the overall record of world history reveals measurable improvements in human relationships.

The 20th century has generated particularly troubling questions about human impulses wedded to awesome technologies and wider contacts among peoples. The century has produced the bloodiest wars on record; 60 million people were killed in World War II alone. Even small wars have produced great carnage, such as the more than 100,000 Iraqis killed by Western bombing in the 1991 Persian Gulf conflict. The introduction of sophisticated weaponry, combined with ongoing political tensions, has resulted in massive slaughter even aside from formal wars: the deaths of hundreds of thousands as part of revolution in Russia and China, Hitler's insane efforts to exterminate the Jews, and the execution of additional hundreds of thousands stemming from racial or religious conflict in Uganda, Cambodia, and on the Indian subcontinent, for example. Less massive but surely menacing has been the rise of new kinds of terrorism in the West, the Middle East, and parts of Asia, as political fanatics attack civilian populations to dramatize their desire for social revolution or the redress of nationalist grievances. The 20th century has been a violent period, surpassing even the most ravaged periods of the past in the sheer volume of slaughter if only because of the availability of technologies for mass killing. As a result of revolutionary or other tensions, a number of societies developed new nonchalance about killing during key periods of tension. Even India, long a tolerant civilization and known in the 20th century for its emphasis on nonviolence, exhibited unusual levels of internal religious warfare, intolerant hatreds, and attendant killing.

Our violent century has also generated a nuclear capability that makes the prospect of future war a new shadow on world history. Humankind may now have the weaponry necessary to destroy itself as a species and to destroy its habitat, the planet Earth, as well. The atomic bomb has been used only twice by the United States, and it is possible to hope that the fearsomeness of the nuclear arsenal will teach world leaders to avoid all-out war in the future. But the peace that many regions of the world have enjoyed since 1945 rests on a balance of terror more than on demonstrable enlightenment, and most efforts to negotiate serious nuclear disarmament have at best slowed rates of arsenal expansion, not reversed the trend of growing weapons sophistication.

We can hope that further escalation of human violence will not occur. Amid the new economic problems in Russia and budget pressures in the United States, greater willingness to reduce some weapons stocks emerged at the end of the 1980s, though both superpowers continued research into lasers and space shields. Although almost one-half century without direct major-power warfare was encouraging, it hardly offered guarantees for the future. Further, the spreading capacity for nuclear and chemical warfare in other nations, such as Iran, Iraq, and South Africa, heightened anxieties about escalating tensions in some future regional conflict. The dependence of the United States and France on export sales of advanced weaponry added to a host of area arms races. Although most people have learned to carry on their lives without anxieties about nuclear disaster, no one can believe that the world is secure.

The pattern of 20th-century war, terror, and weaponry forms the clearest blot on any idea of overall progress, but there are other nightmares. In the first place, the technologies that allow more people to survive in our world have also generated frightening levels of pollution and created potential imbalances in the natural environment. The daily elimination of acres of natural vegetation in expanding societies, such as those of Latin America and Africa, hinders the natural production of oxygen through photosynthesis; in other regions industrial plants lower air and water quality, and the increased output of human wastes produces still other environmental problems. Our ability to sustain growing populations, though unquestionable in recent history despite warfare, may be jeopardized in the future, or at least the amenities to which many people have become accustomed may be reduced.

Major environmental accidents during the 1980s pointed up the severity of the problems. Many societies were involved in the generation of these accidents. A Soviet nuclear reactor at Chernobyl in the Ukraine experienced partial meltdown, devastating the immediate regions with radiation and increasing radioactive levels in a wide area of Europe. A U.S.-owned chemical plant in Bhopal, India, suffered a massive leak of toxic gas, killing hundreds of people and maiming even more. In 1989 a series of oceanic oil spills around the United States, including a particularly extensive accident in

The first true thermonuclear explosion in 1945 introduced the nuclear age.

Alaska, severely damaged shorelines and marine life; another major spill occurred off the coast of Spain in 1992. The 1991 Persian Gulf War resulted in massive oil spills and oil fires. More general findings about penetration of the ozone layer because of chemical pollution and about widely anticipated global warming because of the growing use of hydrocarbons demonstrated the international scope of environmental issues and the lag between policy controls and the acceleration of problems.

Other areas of concern more directly involve human relations. Improvements in bureaucratic capacity have brought new means of police control over many people around the world, most obviously in some authoritarian and Communist nations but also in places such as the United States, which maintains an unusually large prison population. Human freedom is difficult to mea-

sure over time, but it would certainly be difficult to assert that it has steadily increased in recent decades. The 20th century also stands open to some attack for its relative neglect of spiritual and esthetic expressions, though here, of course, evaluation is particularly subjective. Crowding, war, and the sheer concentration on economic development may have tended to shunt artistic and religious creativity to the side, reducing the beauty available in many human lives. Critics who worry about the undermining of African cultural traditions and those who bemoan the mindless mass entertainments of the contemporary West may be identifying an important common problem in our own time and in our future.

New formulations of social and economic inequalities also support a pessimistic rendition of recent history.

The greatest nuclear disaster to date occurred at Chernobyl, in the Soviet Union, in 1986. The nuclear plant was in ruins after the reactor's explosion.

Slavery and caste systems have officially gone, to be sure. But the deteriorating position of unskilled wage labor, including much immigrant labor, within individual nations, such as the United States, and the growing worldwide gaps between labor standards of the industrial and the less developed nations posed troubling new trends. Freedom from want is not uniformly increasing.

A review of both optimistic and pessimistic cases provides useful ways of summing up historical patterns and deciding what one's own standards of evaluation are.

The rain forest is threatened by each new road through the Amazon. Economic development versus world ecological balance is a major problem of the region.

But it seems fatuous to pretend that either an optimistic or a pessimistic approach is so clear-cut as to define the meaning of recent world history or the world's probable future. Some of humankind's most hopeful recent endeavors have not worked out particularly well. The UN organization, for example, has not produced serious mechanisms for conflict resolution, though it has usefully facilitated discussion and has been able to increase its policing activities in the aftermath of the cold war. On the other hand, some of humankind's most dire recent fears have not come to pass. World population has not yet overwhelmed the available food supply, the United States and the former Soviet Union have not as yet yielded to some inevitable cataclysm, and Nazi-style racism and brutality have not gained ground in the world's repertoire of political movements.

PROBLEMATIC PREDICTIONS

Another common approach to the future, sometimes related to optimism or pessimism, involves identification of an overwhelming causal factor that will fundamentally alter the framework in which the societies of the world operate. Just as some historians have long sought a basic factor to explain historical change—through technology, trade levels, or cultural values—so the most dramatic breed of forecasters points to the single emerging revolutionary factor that will make almost everything different. The resultant dramatic forecast differs from general extrapolation from trends by seizing on one decisive ingredient and by anticipating massive contrasts between future and present.

THE OVERCROWDING SCENARIO

In the 1960s and early 1970s gloomy "population bomb" predictions received a considerable audience. Experts correctly noted the unprecedented size and growth rates of world population and argued that, unchecked, the sheer number of people would outstrip available resources, produce unmanageable environmental degradation, and create rivalries for space that could usher in a series of bitter wars. Concern about world population trends had lessened somewhat by 1990, in part because growth rates had slowed in critical areas, such as China and Latin America, but by no means everywhere. Some experts claimed that resources could expand with population growth and noted that historically population expansion had often been a major source of innovation and creativity. Some also claimed a racist element in population-bomb forecasts, insofar as these involved Western pundits urging people of color to have fewer babies. Such forecasts have not been discounted entirely, and environmentalists have picked up some of their con-

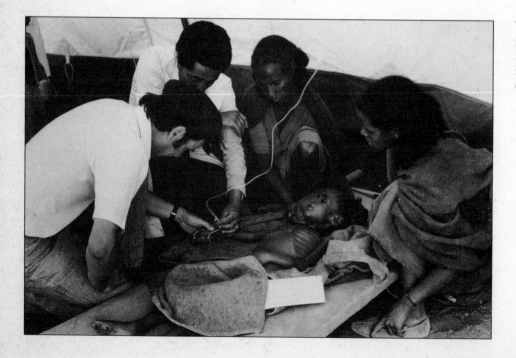

World hunger and international aid. Ethiopian famine victims receive aid at a Red Cross center in 1984.

cerns. As a tool for gauging the future, however, the "bomb" approach is yesterday's fad, though in 1990 it remained true that world population continued to grow at a rate of 250,000 new people every day.

A variant on the population-bomb approach, though less widely publicized, played up the exhaustion of frontiers. Only by the later 20th century, some world historians argued, had human societies fully run out of room to expand—pending as yet unrealized space travel. Each previous period of world history had featured expansions into relatively empty spaces; thus the postclassical period saw movements into Eastern Europe and western China and Bantu migrations southward in Africa, whereas the 19th century had climaxed the history of human frontiers with the fuller peopling of the Americas and Australia and Russian settlement in Siberia. With frontiers gone by the late 20th century, organized societies bumped against one another far more than ever before, whereas immigration inevitably meant movement not into relatively unsettled terrain but rather into highly populous, often suspicious host societies. The implications for potential conflict, environmental exhaustion, and efforts to impede human movement were considerable, if this major factor is viewed as a basic distinction between society future and society past.

A POSTINDUSTRIAL WORLD

Another effort to identify deterministic causation highlights a revolutionary wave of technological change associated with computers, genetic engineering, robotics, and new devices for transmitting energy. According to some popular forecasters, late-20th-century society entered a postindustrial revolution fully as dramatic as the Industrial Revolution two centuries ago—with exactly the same potential for altering the whole framework of human existence. As technology continues to take over production, postindustrial society will feature service occupations dealing with people and information exchange, as not only agriculture but also industrial production is handled largely by machines. Social status will depend on technical knowledge, not money or landed property. Cities will change, becoming centers for meetings and recreation, not basic points of exchange and production. This picture is dramatic, and some observers have claimed to find ample evidence of its accuracy in existing trends. The postindustrial vision is also usually optimistic in assuming that key industrial problems will be resolved in the new order. Routine, repetitive work, for example, will be eliminated by automation, and computers will allow labor to become more varied and individualized.

Critics of the postindustrial vision raise several objections. They are not sure that the transformation discernible in the United States or Western Europe, for example, is as fundamental as the analogies to the Industrial Revolution suggest. Change is occurring, to be sure, but it preserves management and labor structures similar to the patterns of industrial society. There is no relocation of people as massive as industrial-based urbanization had involved and no need for such fundamental shifts in habits of thought. Computers can make work more routine, not less, as rigorous supervision becomes automated. Corporate and government bureaucracies continue to expand. New technology, in other words, does not necessarily change most basic trends, and technological determinism should not be pressed too far. Further, if distinctive postindustrial societies are developing, they concentrate in the West and Japan; postindustrialization mainly exacerbates the economic inequalities among major areas that had already arisen as part of the world economy. How useful, then, is the concept for forecasting overall world history?

Dramatic forecasting of this sort—whether imbued with postindustrial optimism or population-bomb gloom, relies heavily on a single basic causal factor—technology or population determines all, and everything falls into place once this factor is established. Yet most historians reject this kind of determinism. The analysis of the past shows the power of continuity rather than a single-minded transformation. Major changes do occur, but they result from the confluence of several factors, not a single cause. Though some cataclysm is always possible, most historians assume that complexity will continue. Eye-catching forecasts can help organize thinking about what makes history tick and how present relates to past, but there are other orientations toward the future as well.

REGIONS, CIVILIZATIONS, AND WORLD FORCES

A final set of issues for the future returns us to more complex prospects, different from the stark drama of all-or-nothing forecasts and their reliance on one primary source of causation. These final issues really involve another assessment based on current trends but of a special sort that reaches into developments of the late 20th century, as well as back into world history and its fundamental dynamics.

Since the classical period, world history has involved a tension between the operations of individual civilizations and wider international forces that shape the way people think and behave across civilizational boundaries and sometimes almost through the entire world. As a new period in world history, the 20th century raises important new questions about this tension. As usual when large but inherently uncertain interpretive problems are at stake, some polar positions are available. It is possible to predict a new splintering among civilizations, even a new selfish regionalism, with each area emphasizing its own flavor now that the hothouse period of Western dominance is cooling down. There are also new centripetal forces, however, that may reduce the scope for individual cultures in favor of more literally international trends.

THE QUEST FOR SEPARATE IDENTITIES

Because the history of civilization began against a backdrop of widely separated communities, whether agricultural villages or hunting-and-gathering bands, patterns of aggregation and of building larger units form an underlying theme in the larger world-historical process. Yet aggregation into regions or whole civilizations has never been a constant. Empires and even cultural units fragment. The great multinational empires of the early modern period—the Mughal, Ottoman, and now Russian, for example—all split apart. Events in the 1980s raised the prospect of new fragmentations to a surprising level. Peoples in relatively small regions showed the fierce persistence of old loyalties. Thus Slavic groups in Eastern Europe, even in a single small nation such as Yugoslavia, turned on one another with demands for separation or at least autonomy. French descendants in Quebec, seeking greater independence, encountered hostility from their English-descended neighbors elsewhere in Canada. A host of established units, including the successor states of the former Soviet Union, were newly vulnerable to regional ethnic, linguistic, and religious loyalties.

Amid the welter of new or newly recognized issues in the 20th century, it was easy to forget the persistence of many separate traditions. Various societies were grouped under common headings—nonindustrial, overpopulated, authoritarian—and these labels had real meaning.

Nevertheless, regional patterns still counted and in some cases were supplemented by distinctive recent experiences—such as India's interaction with Britain in the 19th and early 20th centuries, compared to China's more complex contacts with the West. Areas where traditional religion remained intense, as in the Middle East and India, might share some results in the relatively low status of women, but they also divided depending on what the religion was. Islam's role in the Middle East thus helped differentiate this region from Hindu-majority India. Artistic styles picked up other long-standing distinctions, as did commitment to political centralization versus emphasis on greater regional autonomy. Even revolutionary China showed the hand of its particular past, despite great changes, in the continued emphasis on an embracing central state and the extensive reliance—interrupted only during Mao's Cultural Revolution—on elders in political leadership.

Developments after 1950 continued to reflect civilization boundaries. Thus both China and India newly struggled against high birthrates. The Indian government, however, proved relatively ineffective, given traditional resistance to state involvement, whereas Chinese efforts, though far from completely successful against older family habits, could build on earlier patterns of state intervention. Japan's reliance on honor and group loyalty rather than on lawyers reflected inherited values different from those of the more contract-minded West.

Regions and civilizations have not remained changeless, but they combine distinctive traditions, distinctive recent experiences, and a distinctive filter by which even common experiences are modified. This pattern survives in the later 20th century. Thus the Indian interpretation of the problem of economic development differs from that of the Chinese, whereas the Chinese interpretation of what a Communist society involves turns out to differ from that of Russia. Moreover, despite important common themes, including nationalism, mass education, and attempts to improve agricultural and industrial technology, no overriding pattern of modernization has yet obliterated key boundaries among the major civilizations.

A basic theme of 20th-century history, almost certain to extend into the 21st century, thus involves an understanding of how each major civilization will interpret the forces of modern politics and industrialization to create its own amalgam. We can begin to see that this process may well resemble the earlier interplay between the spread of agriculture and local cultures, when a similar force of economic change—in this case, from hunting and gathering to farming—generated a variety of political, religious, and family institutions, all of which differed from the hunting past. Correspondingly, any common international process—for example, the forces that work toward modification of a patriarchal structure for women—must be evaluated specifically for each civilization. Generalization about the whole world could easily misfire in light of separate traditions (such as the specific forms of patriarchy) and distinctive recent experience.

A key result of decolonization and the growing challenge to Western dominance was, in fact, a reassertion of the cultural independence of several civilizations. The end of the cold war enhanced the prospects for new regional separations. This was a strong ingredient both of the Iranian revolution, bent on guiding a reinvigoration of Islam more generally, and of Chinese Communist reactions to the protest currents at the end of the 1980s, when renewed claims to China's separate and superior path surfaced quickly.

The quest for cultural autonomy in several major societies is particularly marked in contrast to the homogenizing impulses of modern mass culture. Indian films reproduce the themes and spirit of the great Hindu sagas in the world's largest movie industry. Islamic societies, quite like other Third World areas in many respects, maintain particularly vigorous religious strains, expressed also in distinctive birthrates and family patterns. Latin American intellectuals deal with problems of identity and loneliness that derive from this civilization's particular past. Japan uses habits of group loyalty to generate modes of industrial governance different from those of the West, within an equally successful economic framework.

One key theme for the future, then, involves identifying separate paths for major civilizations and regions, including new ingredients and new vitalities as well as outright continuities from the past—as has long been the pattern in world history. It is certainly not possible to predict an international spread of a Western-type women's rights movement, though it is valid to note that

The surge of feminism led to this women's rights rally in the United States in the 1970s.

conditions for women are changing everywhere. Formal feminism may depend heavily on prior political and cultural traditions, and though Western feminism has had some international echoes, it may not emerge as a strong popular force in Japan or Egypt. Again, each specific civilizational context balances larger world trends.

Yet the emphasis on distinctive civilizations, increasingly conscious of their unique qualities, is not the only focus of world history as we approach the future. In the first place, there is little assurance that the civilization areas identifiable in the late 20th century will remain constant. Societies do collapse and merge, and they may split apart. The differences between China and Japan in recent centuries prevent ongoing reference to a single pattern in eastern Asia, and the emergence of the Pacific Rim adds further complexities. In another case, Turkey at the end of the 1980s applied for admission to the European Common Market. Without renouncing Islam but building on the special relationship Turks have long maintained with the West, Turkey asked essentially to become part of the West. The application roused great anxieties in Western Europe, concerned about not only Turkey's backwardness despite considerable recent industrial advance but also its strangeness. Possibly, however, the map of the Middle East was about to be redrawn once again, in terms of a division among separate identities.

The most important question for the future, however, involves the civilizational framework itself, as it has been elaborated over a 5000-year span, and whether it will persist. Civilizations, long functioning as forms that integrated more disparate and smaller regions to some degree, now may see a similar process pulling them into closer synchronism on a global basis.

THE FORCES OF INTERNATIONAL INTEGRATION

Previous crosscutting forces in world history, from agricultural technologies to the great world religions to new foodstuffs or inventions, such as the printing press, all promoted transformation *within* the separate civilizations. Even the rise of Western-dominated world trade did not fuse the civilizations into a single basic pattern. Arab or Western dominance reduced the autonomy of most civilizations only modestly, save in special cases such as Latin America, where a prior civilization was substantially destroyed. Even in Latin America international contact brought massive change but not full merger into Western cultural, political, or economic forms.

This balance, between separate regional and civilizational identities and international pressure, may now be changing decisively. The crosscutting forces of the past century or so have unquestionably stepped up the impact of international forces. One sign of this is the difficulty major societies have in trying to isolate themselves for whatever ideological reason. Although the distinct features of individual civilizations can readily be discerned even in the way apparently common ideas, such as feminism, are handled, this may not always be the case. International movements of women, computer hackers, or soccer fans clearly override civilization boundaries, and they may gradually make those boundaries less distinct.

The internationalization of the world embraces a number of familiar ingredients. The speed of modern transportation and communication brings societies closer together, as does the rising volume of world trade. International artistic styles, particularly in urban architecture, have more vitality than ever before. The popularity of Western fads and fashions, from clothes to television to sports, leads to cultural contact among ordinary people in daily activities. In this sense the rise of the West continues to reverberate even as its relative dominance recedes. Diverse international alliances and alignments touch virtually every regional conflict in ways that no single international pattern ever did before. At the elite level, if not at the level of mass culture, the spread of scientific training cuts across cultural boundaries as no world religion ever did.

The fact of growing world contacts and a spreading array of global forces produced the understandable but erroneous attempt a generation ago to simplify recent world history into a study of how rapidly each society yielded to the inevitable impulse to become essentially Western. Thus serious scholars assumed that the Western version of modernization, including industrialization, mass education, democratic parliamentary politics, low birthrate, a consumer society, and greater equality for women, would take hold around the world. Each civilization could thus be measured by the speed at which it generated the standard modern (meaning Western) features. This analytical approach confused some undeniably common impulses, including the desire to alter traditional patterns in the name of nationalism and economic development with homogeneity. And it did not, moreover, allow for the revived force of traditional values in societies such as Islam.

Still, if the simplest modernization model has proved clearly inaccurate, as the world's civilizations continue to handle certain common impulses distinctively, the sense

The computer age comes to life at an office of the International Business Machines corporation.

that a new simplifying framework may be right around the corner persists. Will one of the new technologies taking hold, for example, do the trick? This is a crucial aspect of any postindustrial argument applied at a world level. The spread of computer networks is sometimes held to foreshadow new, common patterns of organization, research, and thinking, bringing far greater similarities to the societies involved than the rhythms of the factory or the farm ever did. Some advocates even believe that agricultural societies can shift to a computer system for production and communication without going through a classic industrial phase. The idea of a computer-generated system of organization providing new common ground among civilizations applies most readily to the West and Japan, where structural changes have already brought similarity without obliterating vital diversities. But technologies have cut across cultural divides before, and possibly the power and speed of the computer revolution will have even more sweeping impacts.

Common cultures generate other forces through which specific international communities are obliterating civilizational distinctions. Scientists and social scientists from almost every society can now meet and discuss common methods and common basic assumptions. Political or other divisions may complicate this harmony, but a fundamental international community exists with a shared frame of reference. At another level, soccer football and a few other sports elicit very similar enthusiasms around much of the world, even though they also express competition among the societies fielding the teams.

International business constitutes another integrating force. As Japanese and Korean firms join with North American and European businesses in setting up branches of production in almost every regional market and as business leaders strive to imitate each other's organizational forms and labor policies, civilizational boundaries retreat considerably.

On several different fronts, then, the intensification of international networks, itself part of a long and varied process in world history, has proceeded to the point that various scholars could seriously see in the late 20th century the beginning of the end for the civilizational form. World diversities and inequalities will obviously persist amid new international communities, but coherent regional civilizations may gradually pull apart at the seams.

For the moment, separate civilizations are still very much alive. An equilibrium between distinct civilizations and unifying developments provides the most obvious interpretive basis for asking questions about the future. Increasingly rapid and intense contacts around the world have not created a single framework for world history. The pull of regional as well as civilizational loyalties remains strong. The revival of divisive allegiances in many parts of the world in the early 1990s surely reflects a human need to find a way to counterbalance the large, impersonal forces stemming from international developments. The world, in some ways growing smaller, is becoming no less complex. Distinctive traditions continue to modify, sometimes to reverse, seemingly powerful unifying forces, though these forces persist as well.

CONCLUSION

ASKING QUESTIONS

Whatever the vantage point, questions easily outweigh answers in contemplating the future. The power of particular models—such as Western democracy or mass culture—and the international power of industrial business and technology pose new challenges to particular civilizations. This is not a mere replay of earlier tensions between world currents and separate civilizational traditions. Yet continuities from the past—the surge of religious sentiment in Eastern Europe, for example—and possibly new needs for smaller-scale identities make predictions of an imminent triumph of a single world framework sheer folly. We know that tensions between international forces and needs, as well as the distinct reactions of individual societies, will shape the future and that the tensions have some ingredients in this newest period of world history different from those in earlier periods. We know that the resultant interplay will be an important part of the future, along with new technologies and crucial environmental issues—for such interplay between contacts and divisiveness has shaped world history for many centuries. We do not know, however, what the precise results will be.

History contributes more than an understanding of the traditions and patterns that will continue to play some role in the future. Through analogies to past situa-

tions—such as earlier interactions between individual societies and a world economy—and through an understanding of changing trends, history improves our ability to ask good questions about the future and to evaluate the major types of forecasting available. We can count on the emerging world future to challenge our understanding, but we can also learn to use a grasp of the world past as a partial guide.

FURTHER READINGS

Several serious books (as well as many more simplistic popularized efforts) attempt to sketch the future of the world or the West. On the concept of the postindustrial society, see Daniel Bell's *The Coming of Post-Industrial Society* (1974). For other projections, consult R. L. Heilbroner's *An Inquiry into the Human Prospect* (1974) and L. Stavrianos's *The Promise of the Coming Dark Age* (1976).

On environment and resource issues, D. H. Meadows and D. L. Meadows's *The Limits of Growth* (1974), Al Gore's *The Earth in the Balance* (1992), and L. Herbert's *Our Synthetic Environment* (1962) are worthwhile. M. ul Haq's *The Poverty Curtain: Choices for the Third World* (1976) and L. Solomon's *Multinational Corporations and the Emerging World Order* (1978) cover economic issues, in part from a non-Western perspective.

On military and diplomatic issues, A. Sakharov's *Progress Coexistence and Intellectual Freedom*, rev. ed. (1970), is an important statement by a Russian dissident; other useful texts include S. Hoffman's *Primacy or World Order: American Foreign Policy Since the Cold War* (1978), S. Melman's *The Peace Race* (1961), and W. Epstein's *The Last Chance: Nuclear Proliferation and Arms Control* (1976).

On a leading social issue, see P. Hudson's *Third World Women Speak Out* (1979). A major interpretation of the 20th-century world is Theodore von Laue's *The World Revolution of Westernization* (1989).

Credits

LITERARY CREDITS

CHAPTER 3

Gifford, P. et al. (eds.), *Britain and Germany in Africa*, p. 670. Copyright © 1967 Yale University Press.

René Maran, *Bataoula: A True Black Novel*, translated by Barbara Beck and Alexandre Mboukou. Copyright © 1972 Black Orpheus Press. All rights reserved.

CHAPTER 4

Liang Qichao, *A People Made New* (1902–1905), translated in W. T. de Bary *Sources of Chinese Tradition*. Copyright © 1960 by Columbia University Press. Reprinted with the permission of the publisher.

CHAPTER 6

Hisako Yoshizawa, *Showa sensoo bungaku zenshuu; shimin no nikki (War Literature of Showa; Diaries of Citizens)*. All rights reserved.

CHAPTER 7

Ba Jin (Pa Chin), *Family*, p. 258. Copyright © 1972 by Doubleday & Company.

Arlene Eisen, *Women and Revolution in Viet Nam*. 1984. Copyright © 1984 Arlene Eisen. Reprinted by permission of Zed Books Ltd.

CHAPTER 8

Margery Perham, *Lugard: The Years of Authority 1898–1945*. London: Collins Publishers. All rights reserved.

Aimé Cesaire, *Return to My Native Land*, translated by John Berger and Anna Bostock. Reprinted by permission of Presence Africaine.

Léopold Sédar Senghor, "Snow Upon Paris" from *Selected Poems*, translated and introduction by John Reed and Clive Wake. Copyright © 1964 by Oxford University Press. Reprinted by permission of Georges Borchardt, Inc. for the author.

CHAPTER 9

Steven M. Tipton, *Getting Saved in the Sixties: Moral Meaning in Conversion and Cultural Change*. Copyright © 1981 The Regents of the University of California. Reprinted by permission of University of California Press.

Table adapted from "What They Believe: A Fortune/Yankelovich Survey," *Fortune*, January 1969. Copyright Time Inc.

Table adapted from Melvin Zelnik, John F. Kantner, Kathleen Ford, *Sex and Adolescence*. Beverly Hills: Sage, 1981, p. 65.

Table adapted from *The Europa Year Book 1959* (London: Europa Publications, 1959) and *The Europa Year Book 1967*, Vol. I (London: Europa Publications, 1967). Reprinted by permission.

CHAPTER 10

From *The Crimes of the Stalin Era*, annotated by Boris I. Nicolaevsky, in *The New Leader*, New York, 1956, S12–15, S19–20, S32, S36, S38, S41, S45, S48, S54, S64–65. Reprinted by permission of *The New Leader*.

CHAPTER 11

Yukio Mishima, *Runaway Horses*, p. 128. Reproduced by permission of Alfred A. Knopf, Inc.

Kenzaburo Oë, *A Personal Matter*. Copyright © 1968 by Grove Press. Used with the permission of Grove/Atlantic Monthly Press and Weidenfeld & Nicholson, Publishers.

CHAPTER 12

V. S. Naipaul, from *An Area of Darkness*. Copyright © 1964 by V. S. Naipaul. Reprinted by permission of Aitken, Stone, & Wylie, Ltd.

Chairil Anwar, "I Run Around with Them," from *The Voice of the Night: Complete Poetry and Prose by Chairil Anwar*. Translated by Burton Raffel. Copyright © 1962 Burton Raffel. Copyright © 1993 by the Center for International Studies Ohio University. Reprinted by permission of Burton Raffel.

Chinua Achebe, *No Longer at Ease*. Copyright © 1960 Chinua Achebe. Reprinted by permission of Heinemann International. All rights reserved.

CHAPTER 13

Domitilia Barrios de Chungara with Moema Viezzer, *Let Me Speak: Testimony of Domitilia, a Woman of the Bolivian Mines*, pp. 32–33. Translated by Victoria Ortiz. Copyright © 1978 by Monthy Review Press. All rights reserved. Reprinted by permission of Monthly Review Foundation.

Rigoberta Menchu, *Rigoberta Menchu: An Indian Woman in Guatemala*. Introduction by Elizabeth Burgas-Debray. Translated by Anne Wright. Reprinted by permission of Verso, London, New York. All rights reserved.

Pablo Neruda, "United Fruit Co." from *Selected Poems of Pablo Neruda*, pp. 148–159. Copyright © 1961 by Grove Press, translation copyright © 1989 by Ben Belitt. Used with the permission of Grove/Atlantic Monthly Press and Agencia Literaria Carmen Balcells.

J. P. Cole, table "Population of Capital Cities as a Percentage of Total Population in Ten Latin-American Nations" from *Latin America: An Economic and Social Geography* 1/e, p. 417. 1965. © Butterworth and Company (Publishers) Ltd. 1975. First published 1965.

PHOTO CREDITS

PART I

8 The Bettmann Archive; 11 The Bettmann Archive; 14 Library of Congress

CHAPTER 1

18 Library of Congress; 21 The Bettmann Archive; 26 The Granger Collection, New York; 28 Courtesy of the Board of Trustees of the Victoria & Albert Museum; 32 Hulton-Deutsch Collection/The Hulton Picture Company; 34 Potter Palmer Collection/The Art Institute of Chicago. All Rights Reserved; 39 Culver Pictures; 41 The Bettmann Archive; 43 (T) From A PICTOGRAPHIC HISTORY OF OGLALA SIOUX by Amos Bad Heart Bull, text by Helen Blish. Published by the University of Nebraska Press; 43 (B) The Bettmann Archive, 45 Hulton-Deutsch Collection/The Hulton Picture Company

CHAPTER 2

48 Novosti Press Agency; 51 California Museum of Photography of California, Riverside; 55 Novosti Press Agency; 59 The Metropolitan Museum of Art, Gift of Lincoln Kirstein, 1959; 61 The Granger Collection, New York

CHAPTER 3

64 APA Photo Agency; 70 Mary Evans Picture Library; 71 National Army Museum; 73 Hulton-Deutsch Collection/The Hulton Picture Company; 79 Culver Pictures; 80 The Granger Collection, New York; 83 The Bettmann Archive

CHAPTER 4

86 Culver Pictures; 93 The Granger Collection, New York; 98 Historical Pictures/Stock Montage, Inc.; 102 Mary Evans Picture Library; 103 Mary Evans Picture Library; 105 Mary Evans Picture Library; 106 Woodfin Camp & Associates; 114 The Von Harringa Collection

PART II

118 Ella Gallup Summer and Mary Catlin Summer Collection/Wadsworth Atheneum, Hartford Ct.; 126 The Bettmann Archive; 127 AP/Wide World

CHAPTER 5

128 Trustees of The Imperial War Museum, London; 134 Trustees of The Imperial War Museum, London; 138 The Bettmann Archive; 141 Dorothea Lange Collection/Library of Congress; 145 UPI/Bettmann; 147 AP/Wide World; 149 AP/Wide World; 150 Trustees of The Imperial War Museum, London

CHAPTER 6

156 AP/Wide World; 160 John Held, Jr./Life Magazine/Time Warner Inc.; 162 Pix Publishing; 166 Louis and Walter Arensberg Collection/Philadelphia Museum of Art Collection; 169 AP/Wide World; 171 The Bettmann Archive; 173 Culver Pictures; 175 The Bettmann Archive; 180 Hulton/UPI/Bettmann

CHAPTER 7

184 Culver Pictures; 188 FPG; 191 Laurie Platt Winfrey/Carousel, Inc., N.Y.; 195 UPI/Bettmann; 197 Bildarchiv Preussischer Kulturbesitz; 201 SOVFOTO; 203 SOVFOTO; 207 Eastfoto/SOVFOTO; 210 AP/Wide World; 213 Hoover Institution Archives/Jay Calvin Huston Collection; 217 Maurice Durand Collection of Vietnamese Art/Copyright Yale University Art Gallery

CHAPTER 8

220 Margaret Bourke-White/Life Magazine/Time Warner Inc.; 224 The Bettmann Archive; 225 The Bettmann Archive; 228 The Granger Collection, New York; 231 ACME/UPI/Bettmann; 236 Camera Press/Globe Photos, Inc.; 241 UPI/Bettmann; 243 AP/Wide World

PART III

246(L) UPI/Bettmann; 246(R) Reuters/Bettmann; 250 UPI/Bettmann; 252 Jean-Pierre Laffont/Sygma

CHAPTER 9

256 Charles Kennard/Stock Boston; 260 UPI/Bettmann; 263 AP/Wide World; 267 The Bettmann Archive; 272 UPI/Bettmann; 275 Robert George Gaylord; 279 Hedrich Blessing; 281 The Granger Collection, New York

CHAPTER 10

284 SOVFOTO; 288 UPI/Bettmann; 292 SOVFOTO; 293 Reuters/Bettmann; 296 Tass/SOVFOTO; 300 Alain Nogues/Sygma; 302 Leh/Saukkomaa/Woodfin Camp & Associates

CHAPTER 11

306 Nathan Benn/Woodfin Camp & Associates; 310 Official U.S. Navy Photograph; 313 Palmer Pictures; 317 Mike Yamashita/Woodfin Camp & Associates; 321 AP/Wide World

CHAPTER 12

326 Keller/Sygma; 331(L) UPI/Bettmann; 331(R) Abbas/Magnum Photos; 332 UPI/Bettmann; 336 Sygma; 340 UPI/Bettmann; 342 UPI/Bettmann; 347 AP/Wide World; 348 William Campbell/Sygma

CHAPTER 13

352 AP/Wide World; 355 SOVFOTO; 358 Eastfoto/SOVFOTO; 361 Jacques Langevin/Sygma; 364 Yves Billy/Sygma; 367 UPI/Bettmann; 368 UPI/Bettmann; 378 Susan Meiselas/Magnum Photos; 380 Private Collection/Courtesy Marlborough Gallery, New York

EPILOGUE

384 Jacques Pavlovsky/Sygma; 389 Orban/Sygma; 391 AP/Wide World; 396 Los Alamos National Laboratory; 397T Sygma; 397(B) Loren McIntyre; 398 William Campbell/Sygma; 401 Los Angeles Times Photo; 403 Courtesy of IBM

Index